THE THISTLE
AND THE DRONE

Praise for *The Thistle and the Drone*

"In the end, like the Kurdish observers of Noor in Sulaimani in the book, I was close to tears. *Lagrimas caudales* or "flowing tears," to use the apposite phrase of Blas de Otero, seems to be what the book's conclusions lead to. This is particularly true if, like me, you have been very, very close to the center of decisionmaking in the U.S. and you know how incapable it is of embracing such sophisticated reasoning, let alone developing and applying strategies in accordance with such reasoning. Thus *lagrimas* for the tribes, for the soldiers, and for the United States. If one extrapolates from Professor Ahmed's findings and from the history of torture as well, 'bug splat', as the victims of drone strikes are called, and torture live in the same house. Ahmed makes clear that, like torture, the creation of such profound fear wounds the creators as well—destroying their liberties, polluting their democracy, and devouring their souls. Professor Ahmed gives us the only way out of this dangerous dilemma, a way to coexist with the thistle without the drone."—COLONEL LAWRENCE WILKERSON, *former chief of staff to Secretary of State Colin Powell and Professor of Government and Public Policy at the College of William and Mary*

"Riveting in its original description of events we thought we knew and revealing in its trenchant analysis of their contexts, Akbar Ahmed shows us how vital are the world's tribes to our understanding of and interactions with the Muslim world. This highly original combination of firsthand experience and insightful synthesis is an indispensable guide to policymakers and concerned readers who want to comprehend just how astonishing is the world when seen through the eyes of a brilliant and dedicated guide." —LAWRENCE ROSEN, *William Nelson Cromwell Professor of Anthropology, Princeton University*

"This book is the culmination of a lifetime's work. The contribution of Professor Akbar Ahmed to peace and harmony and broader understanding among the human race is beyond any imagination. I believe he is the most humble, inspirational and highly respected scholar amongst all faiths and communities today. I support wholeheartedly what he has done in this book—pleading for compassion and rejecting violence of any kind against fellow humans. May God help and support his Mission!"— DR. JAMES SHERA, *MBE, Sitara-e-Pakistan (Star of Pakistan), former mayor of Rugby and prominent Christian Pakistani leader in the UK*

"Akbar Ahmed is one of the few scholars intimately familiar with East and West as well as Judaism, Christianity, and especially Islam. He provides the reader with a treasure trove of wisdom and knowledge. By applying different fields of learning, notably anthropology, to explore cross-cultural and even cross-civilizational encounters, Ahmed has produced a profound and significant book. The 20th century witnessed mass destruction and genocide. The 21st century is going the same way, and *The Thistle and the Drone* is a wake-up call to all of us before it is too late. This is a must-read book."
—DR. EDWARD KESSLER, *MBE, Founder and Director, The Woolf Institute, and Fellow of St. Edmunds College, University of Cambridge, UK*

"In this groundbreaking and startling book, Akbar Ahmed bravely uncovers an inconvenient truth, a fearful reality which endangers us all and in which we are all implicated. It should be required reading for those working in the media, policymaking, and education—and, indeed, for anybody who wishes to understand our tragically polarized world."—KAREN ARMSTRONG, *Author of* A History of God *and creator of the Charter for Compassion*

"Yet another brilliantly written masterpiece, a must-read for all, particularly Muslims who have an interest in understanding the roots of the conflicts that go back in history but have become accentuated since 9/11. Only Akbar Ahmed can give us these insights into the post-modern era we live in and the conflicts that bedevil our times through this highly readable and deeply engaging narrative."—DR. JAFER QURESHI, *Fellow of the Royal College of Psychiatry, Trustee of Muslim Aid, and co-convenor of the UK Action Committee on Islamic Affairs*

"The author has examined drone operations in the Tribal Areas of Pakistan and elsewhere in Muslim tribal societies from a rare combina-tion of perspectives. Firstly those of a political agent managing tribes in Pakistan's lawless Tribal Areas, then as a top notch anthropologist, and finally as a diplomat and a teacher of comparative religion. It is a wonder how one could encompass so many diverse careers in one lifetime. Policymakers need to pay heed to Akbar Ahmed's message. This writing is a *tour de force* on the subject and replete with practical wisdom."—KHALID AZIZ, *former political agent, North Waziristan Agency and Chief Secretary, North-West Frontier Province, Pakistan, and Chairman, Regional Institute of Policy Research and Training, Peshawar, Pakistan*

"*The Thistle and the Drone* provides a trenchant and original critique of the conduct of the U.S. government's declared war on global terrorism. Ambassador Akbar Ahmed brilliantly illuminates the complex and little understood world of Islamic tribal societies. Policymakers should take heed."
—THOMAS BANCHOFF, *Professor of Government, and Director, Berkley Center for Religion, Peace, and World Affairs, Georgetown University, Washington D.C.*

"While being faithful to Islam, Akbar Ahmed is also a true humanist, looking for the best in other religions, in Euro-American traditions of human rights, and in cultural anthropology. Yet he also has an unsentimental grasp of geopolitical realities and dangers. He deserves a wide readership for his new analysis of center-periphery relations in the Muslim world, which is reminiscent of past masters of social science such as Ibn Khaldun and Ernest Gellner but also brings to bear his unique practical experience as a former government administrator in the Tribal Areas of Pakistan."—JONATHAN BENTHALL, *former director of the Royal Anthropological Institute and Founding Editor of* Anthropology Today

"While our technology is advancing at such an unprecedented pace, our cultural and human intelligence seems not only not to have kept pace but is increasingly being marginalized where fast but far-reaching decisions are being made every day. Professor Ahmed's excellent book is a must-read for policymakers and students of international affairs as it opens our eyes to the complexities faced by governments and societies around the world. It is also a timely book that brings to our attention vast areas of human suffering from which we have become detached."— HIS IMPERIAL HIGHNESS ERMIAS SAHLE SELASSIE OF ETHIOPIA

"Akbar Ahmed's latest literary journey—*The Thistle and the Drone*—is a compelling and insightful study of the suffering, the dilemmas, the dangers and the challenges facing our world. It is the first-ever comprehensive study dealing with tribal societies forming the interstices between states and borders. Through over forty case studies he addresses the difficult issues of identity and power with respect and reverence, honesty and humility. In this profound study, Ahmed draws on non-Abrahamic and Abrahamic societies to offer a perfectly balanced approach, a panacea, for the deeply embedded problems between center and periphery. Sharing a common South Asian culture and history with the author, I am awestruck and spellbound by the compelling narrative, the poetic analysis, and the sheer scope of the work. A must-read for all—the academic, the student, the policymaker, and the concerned citizen of the world—this is a work of epic stature imbued with the lofty spirit of humanity captured in the Sufi motto *sulh-i-kul*—Peace with All."
— MANJULA KUMAR, *Project Director of the Smithsonian Center for Education and Museum Studies, Smithsonian Institution, Washington, D.C.*

THE THISTLE
AND THE DRONE

How America's War
on Terror Became
a Global War
on Tribal Islam

AKBAR AHMED

BROOKINGS INSTITUTION PRESS
Washington, D.C.

Library of Congress Cataloging-in-Publication data
Ahmed, Akbar S., author.
  The thistle and the drone : how America's War on Terror became a global war on tribal Islam / Akbar Ahmed.
      pages ; cm
  Includes bibliographical references and index.
  Summary: "Analyzes the war on terror from an anthropological viewpoint, focusing on the tribal nature of societies that are increasingly the focus of military incursions by the United States, especially through the use of drones, and how the West's anti-terror efforts are decimating tribal communities about which there is little understanding"—Provided by publisher.
  ISBN 978-0-8157-2378-3 (hardcover : alkaline paper)
  1. Islamic countries—Relations—United States. 2. United States—Relations—Islamic countries. 3. War on Terrorism, 2001-2009. 4. Afghan War, 2001–5. Tribes—Islamic countries. 6. Islamic sociology. 7. Islamic countries—Politics and government. I. Title.
  DS35.74.U6A37 2013
  909.83'1—dc23   2013003952

9 8 7 6 5 4 3 2 1

Printed on acid-free paper

Typeset in Minion

Composition by Cynthia Stock
Silver Spring, Maryland

Printed by R. R. Donnelley
Harrisonburg, Virginia

For

ALEXANDER AKBAR AHMED

with love

CONTENTS

1

The Thistle and the Drone

"The Jonas Brothers are here. They're out there somewhere," a smiling and confident President Barack Obama told the expectant and glittering audience attending the White House Correspondents' Dinner in Washington on May 1, 2010. "Sasha and Malia are huge fans, but boys, don't get any ideas. I have two words for you: 'predator drones.' You will never see it coming. You think I'm joking?"

Obama's banter may have seemed tasteless, given that he had just been awarded the Nobel Peace Prize, but this was not a Freudian slip. The president was indicating he possessed Zeus-like power to hurl thunderbolts from the sky and obliterate anyone with impunity, even an American pop group. One report said he had a "love" of drones, noting that by 2011 their use had accelerated exponentially.[1] It was also revealed that Obama had a secret "kill list."[2] Having read Saint Augustine and Saint Thomas Aquinas, and their ideas of the "just war" and "natural law," which promote doing good and avoiding evil, did not deter Obama from a routine of going down the list to select names and "nominate" them, to use the official euphemism, for assassination.[3] I wondered whether the learned selectors of the Nobel Peace Prize had begun to have second thoughts.

As its use increased, the drone became a symbol of America's war on terror. Its main targets appeared to be Muslim tribal groups living in Afghanistan, Pakistan, Yemen, and Somalia. Incessant and concentrated strikes were directed at what was considered the "ground zero" of the war on terror, Waziristan, in the Tribal Areas of Pakistan. There were also reports, however, of U.S. drones being used against other Muslim tribal groups like the Kurds in Turkey and the Tausug in the Philippines, and also by the United Kingdom against the Pukhtun tribes of Afghanistan, by France in northern Mali against the Tuareg, and even by Israel in Gaza. These communities—some of the most impoverished and isolated in the world, with identities that are centuries-old—had become the targets of the twenty-first century's most advanced kill technology.

The drone embodied the weaponry of globalization: high-tech in performance, sleek in appearance, and global in reach. It was mysterious, distant, deadly, and notoriously devoid of human presence. Its message of destruction resounded in its names: Predator and Reaper. For its Muslim targets, the UAV, or unmanned aerial vehicle, its official title, had an alliterative quality—it meant death, destruction, disinformation, deceit, and despair. Flying at 50,000 feet above ground, and therefore out of sight of its intended victims, the drone could hover overhead unblinkingly for twenty-four hours, with little escaping its scrutiny before it struck. For a Muslim tribesman, this manner of combat not only was dishonorable but also smacked of sacrilege. By appropriating the powers of God through the drone, in its capacity to see and not be seen and deliver death without warning, trial, or judgment, Americans were by definition blasphemous.

In the United States, however, the drone was increasingly viewed as an absolutely vital weapon in fighting terrorism and keeping America safe. Support for it demonstrated patriotism, and opposition exposed one's anti-Americanism. Thus the debate surrounding the drone rested on its merits as a precisely effective killing machine rather than the human or emotional costs it inflicted. Drone strikes meant mass terror in entire societies across the world, yet little effort was made on the part of the perpetrators to calculate the political and psychological fallout, let alone assess the morality of public assassinations or the killing of innocent men, women, and children. Even those who rushed to rescue drone victims were considered legitimate targets of a follow-up strike. Nor did Americans seem concerned that they were creating dangerous precedents for other countries.

Instead, boasting with the pride of a football coach, CIA director, and later secretary of defense, Leon Panetta referred to the drones as "the only game in town."[4] Fifty-five members of Congress organized what was popularly known as the Drone Caucus and received extensive funds for their campaigns from drone manufacturers such as General Atomics and Lockheed Martin. The drones' enthusiastic public advocates even included "liberal" academics and self-avowed "hippies" such as philosophy professor Bradley Strawser of Monterey, California.[5] Americans exulted in the fact that the drone freed Americans of any risk. It could be operated safely and neatly from newly constructed high-tech, air-conditioned offices. Like any office worker in suit and tie, the "pilot" could complete work in his office and then go home to take his family bowling or join them for a barbecue in the backyard. The drone was fast becoming as American as apple pie.

Typical of its propensity for excess in matters of security, by 2012 America had commissioned just under 20,000 drones, about half of which were in use. They were proliferating at an alarming rate, with police departments, internal security agencies, and foreign governments placing orders. In September 2012 Iran unveiled its own reconnaissance and attack drone with a range of over 2,000 kilometers. The following month, France announced it was sending surveillance drones to Mali to assist the government in fighting the Tuareg rebels in the north. In October 2012 the United Kingdom doubled its number of armed drones in Afghanistan with the purchase of five Reaper drones from the United States, to be operated from a facility in the United Kingdom. It was estimated that by the end of the decade, some 30,000 U.S. drones would be patrolling American skies alone. There was talk in the press of new and deadly varieties, including the next generation of "nuclear-powered" drones. Despite public interest, drone operations were deliberately obscured.

Ignoring the moral debate, drone operators are equally infatuated with the weapon and the sense of power it gives them. It leaves them "electrified" and "adrenalized"—flying a drone is said to be "almost like playing the computer game *Civilization*," a "sci-fi" experience.[6] A U.S. drone operator in New Mexico revealed the extent to which individuals across the world can be observed in their most private moments. "We watch people for months," he said. "We see them playing with their dogs or doing their laundry. We know their patterns like we know our neighbors' patterns. We even go to their funerals." Another drone operator spoke of watching people having sex at night through infrared cameras.[7] The last statement, in particular, has to be read keeping in mind the importance Muslim tribal peoples give to notions of modesty and privacy.

The victims are treated like insects: the military slang for a successful strike, when the victim is blown apart on the screen in a display of blood and gore, is "bug splat." Muslim tribesmen were reduced to bugs or, in a *Washington Post* editorial by David Ignatius, cobras to be killed at will. Any compromise with the Taliban in the Tribal Areas of Pakistan, officially designated as the Federally Administered Tribal Areas (FATA), is "like playing with a cobra," he wrote.[8] And do we "compromise" with cobras? Ignatius asked. "No, you kill a cobra." Bugs, snakes, cockroaches, rats—such denigration of minorities has been heard before, and as recent history teaches, it never ends well for the abused people.

It is these tribal societies that form the subject of this book. Each is to be understood within its own cultural and historical context, with the main focus on four major groups: the Pukhtun, Yemenis, Somalis, and Kurds. Like their ancestors before them, these communities lived by an ancient code of honor embodied in the behavior of elders and, over the centuries, orally transmitted from generation to generation. According to anthropologists, these societies are organized along the principles of the segmentary lineage system, in which societies are defined by clans linked by common descent. All four societies have become embroiled in different ways in America's war on terror. The Pukhtun, Yemenis, and Somalis have been the main targets of American drone attacks, and there are reports of similar strikes against the Kurds. These various populations have been traumatized not only by American missiles but also by national army attacks, suicide bombers, and tribal warfare, forcing millions to flee their homes to seek shelter elsewhere and live in destitute conditions as hapless refugees. "Every day," say Muslim tribesmen, "is like 9/11 for us."

These societies live in areas administered by central governments whose ability to bomb, kidnap, humiliate, and rape tribal members at will has been enhanced by U.S. financial and military backing in the war on terror. For the tribes, this has been the worst of fates, leaving them emasculated and helpless, with every moral boundary crossed, every social structure attacked. The wholesale breakdown of their tribal system is not unlike the implosion of a galaxy, with fragments shooting off in unpredictable directions.

With their ancient practices, these tribal communities represent the very foundations of human history. In the most profound sense, they allow all societies a glimpse of their origins. The disruption of these fragile societies is a high-stakes gamble for civilization. Unless urgent and radical steps are taken to prevent this process and ensure a modicum of stability, the future for these communities looks grim; their codes of honor and revenge will lead to escalating global violence that, in the end, may well bring about the destruction of one of the oldest forms of human society.

THE THISTLE AND THE DRONE

Just as the drone is an appropriate metaphor for the current age of globalization, the thistle captures the essence of tribal societies. It was aptly introduced by Leo Tolstoy in *Hadji Murad,* a fictionalized account of a Muslim tribal leader's struggles under the yoke of Imperial Russia. Tolstoy himself had witnessed the army's attempts to subjugate the independent Muslim tribes of the Caucasus in the nineteenth century and likened their courage, pride, and sense of egalitarianism to the prickly thistle. On a walk, while collecting a bouquet, the narrator of *Hadji Murad* leaned down "to pluck the flower. But this proved a very difficult task. Not only did the stalk prick on every side—even through the handkerchief I wrapped round my hand—but it was so tough that I had to struggle with it for nearly five minutes, breaking the fibres one by one; and when I had at last plucked it, the stalk was all frayed, and the flower itself no longer seemed so fresh and beautiful." At the end of his musing about the thistle, the narrator concludes: "But what energy and tenacity! With what determination it defended itself, and how dearly it sold its life! . . . 'What energy!' I thought. 'Man has conquered everything, and destroyed millions of plants, yet this one won't submit.'"[9]

One of the hardiest, most self-reliant of flowers, the thistle has a beauty all its own, despite its lack of sparklingly bright colors, soft petals, or fragrance. Some find its cactus-like air of defiance, clearly a warning to passersby, rather appealing. The tribal Scots were impressed enough to make it their national symbol. In it they saw something of their own character as a proud, hardy, and martial people ready to protect their independence with grit and determination.

Indeed, the Scottish clans are frequently compared with other thistle-like tribes such as the Pukhtun, Somali, Kurd, and Bedouin. Sir Walter Scott in the early nineteenth century, for one, was "forcibly struck with the curious points of parallelism between the manners of the Afghan tribes and those of the ancient Highland clans. They resembled these Oriental mountaineers in their feuds, in their adoption of auxiliary tribes, in their laws, in their modes of conducting war, in their arms, and, in some respects, even in their dress."[10] The British administrator-scholar and former governor of the North-West Frontier Province of India, Sir Olaf Caroe, who knew the Pukhtuns well, also compared them to the Scots in his classic book *The Pathans*.[11] More recently, Kurds holding training exercises in the hills and caves of Qandil in northern Iraq have tried to inspire recruits with showings of Mel Gibson's *Braveheart*, a film about William Wallace, the legendary Scottish freedom fighter.[12] In the film's final scene, Wallace is tortured to death but refuses to compromise, instead shouting with his last breath the one word tribesmen everywhere find closest to their hearts—"Freedom!"

Love of freedom, egalitarianism, a tribal lineage system defined by common ancestors and clans, a martial tradition, and a highly developed code of honor and revenge—these are the thistle-like characteristics of the tribal societies under discussion here. Moreover, as with the thistle, there is a clear correlation between their prickliness, or toughness, and the level of force used by those who wish to subdue these societies, as the Americans discovered after 9/11.

For all that these thistle-like tribes knew, the Americans who arrived in their midst could have been from Mars, a reaction not unlike that captured by the 2011 Hollywood film *Cowboys and Aliens,* set in the Old West of the nineteenth century. In the opening scene, some Americans are attacked without provocation by aliens who use unknown technology to capture humans and fly them away for torture and interrogation. To the tribesmen, the Americans who came from nowhere in flying machines no one had seen before and abruptly disappeared with their catch were seen as aliens, with their abnormally large frames covered in strange padding, protruding wires, protective helmets, and peculiar weapons. These invaders could see at night through their glasses, speak into those wires, and command deadly airstrikes while resting on the ground. They appeared to have few social skills and neither offered nor received hospitality. Americans were loud, rude, and violent and expressed no interest in the land or its people. The tribes thought the reasons the Americans gave for invading their regions were incomprehensible: for example, 92 percent of the people surveyed in the Pukhtun-dominated areas of Kandahar and Helmand a decade after the war began in Afghanistan had never heard of 9/11 and therefore had no idea of its significance for Americans.[13]

The Americans, even the few who stopped to remember their own Native American tribes, considered the Muslim tribes they encountered after 9/11 a remnant of the past and did not quite know what to make of them. In their dusty settlements—outside Kandahar, for instance—the Americans saw them as primitive characters living in God-forsaken regions, some families still inhabiting caves or mud huts. Their unsmiling men wore turbans and had long beards, the women were covered from head to toe and restricted to domestic chores, donkeys and camels were the main means of transport, and their code of behavior demanded savage forms of revenge. Stories circulating of the brutal slaughter of enemies or "honor killings" of women weighed heavy on many American minds. Most worrying of all, every one of these tribesmen was a potential al Qaeda sympathizer and therefore a terror suspect. In other words, the Muslim tribesman was at best a relic from another time and at worst an enemy to be eliminated.

These perceptions of each other are not mere cinematic or literary conjecture. They are confirmed by an authoritative American survey of Afghan and American soldiers in uniform that indicates a large chasm exists between the two and explains the alarming increase in the number of Afghan soldiers attacking American and NATO forces. These incidents are described as "green on blue"—color codes that are accepted by modern Western armies to denote neutral forces (green) and friendly forces (blue). By August 2012 these attacks had become the foremost cause of death of NATO troops.[14] The frequency, unpredictable nature, and implications of these attacks have had a devastating impact on the morale of international forces. "Green on blue" attacks can only be understood in the context of how Afghans and Americans view each other. Afghans thought this of Americans:

They always shout and yell "Mother Fucker!" They are crazy.

U.S. soldiers swear at us constantly, saying "Fuck You!"

Their arrogance sickens us.

We [the Afghan National Army, ANA] once loaded and charged our weapons because we got tired of the U.S. Soldiers calling us "Mother Fuckers."

We have been ordered not to react to their insults; but we very much want to.

For years U.S. military convoys sped through the streets of villages, running over small children, while shouting profanities and throwing water bottles at people.

U.S. soldiers kill many innocent civilians if attacked. They kill everyone around.

They don't care about civilian casualties.

They take photos of women even when we tell them not to.

They tried to search a woman. We aimed our guns at them to stop it.

They pee all over, right in front of civilians, including females.

They pee in the water, polluting it. We told them to stop but they wouldn't listen.

Two U.S. Soldiers even defecated within public view.

[U.S. troops] constantly pass gas in front of ANSF [Afghan National Security Forces], in public, in front of elders.

They obviously were not raised right. What can we do with people like that? They are disgusting. They are a very low class of people.

They don't meet with the elders very often.

Often the U.S. lets itself get involved in personal feuds by believing an unreliable source. These people use the U.S. to destroy their personal enemies, not the insurgents.

Many ANSF respondents, the study found, "denigrated the personal integrity of U.S. Soldiers, and declared them to be cowards hiding behind their MRAPs [mine-resistant ambush protected vehicles], their close air support and overwhelming fire power."[15] The Afghans thought that "U.S. Soldiers would not be brave if they had to fight under the same operational conditions as the ANSF did, without body armor, with older weapons, light-skinned vehicles, poor logistical support, and no dedicated air cover."[16]

American soldiers were equally disenchanted with the Afghan forces representing, ironically, a so-called major non-NATO ally:

They are turds. We are better off without them.

The ANP [Afghan National Police] are locals. I don't trust locals. They can be sleepers.

I would never like to admit that Iraqis are smarter, but they are Einsteins compared to Afghans.

These guys only seem to care about their own tribes or families.

There is a great deal of favoritism and tribalism in appointments. An officer is not promoted for meritorious work but due to tribal affiliations and depth of pockets.

How they treat their women and children is disgusting; they are just chattel to them.

They are fucking thieves.

They seem to act on emotion rather than common sense.

We do everything for them. It's like a kid you have to spoon feed.

They fucking stink.

They simply don't wash themselves.

They are as high as fuck (on hash).

They are stoned all the time; some even while on patrol with us.

The people don't want us here, and we don't like them.

Each protagonist saw the other through the prism of his own culture. The Americans with their technology and ideas of progress and the tribesmen with their notions of honor, revenge, and tribal loyalty confronted each other with ignorance as much as contempt. One represented a society that had been to the moon and landed a vehicle on Mars; the other a people who spoke of past invaders they had resisted successfully—Alexander the Great, Genghis Khan, the Mughal emperor Aurangzeb, and British and Soviet troops—as if it were yesterday.

The Clash of Civilizations and the Triangle of Terror

American troops were in Afghanistan as a consequence of the events on 9/11, which many believed to represent the larger concept of the "clash of civilizations." While Bernard Lewis was the author of this phrase and deployed his material as a historian to expand on it, Samuel Huntington popularized the term. Most people hearing of it took it on face value to mean an ongoing confrontation between two inherently opposed civilizations—the West and the world of Islam. The war on terror may thus be seen as an extension of the "clash." While the phrase is a gross reduction of an already simplistic frame for the understanding of history, it became hugely influential after 9/11. The attacks on that day by Muslims seemed to confirm the core idea of the clash of civilizations and offered a plausible explanation of contemporary events. Lewis was instantly elevated to the role of public prophet. Dick Cheney, the American vice president, consulted him frequently and cited his ideas on television when justifying the war on Iraq.

Cast as the irredeemably villainous enemy of the West, Islam was widely vilified and studied with the purpose of establishing its evil credentials. Commentators warned that the Quran ordered Muslims to kill innocent Jews and Christians and as a reward promised seventy-two virgins in heaven. This was both malicious and incorrect, but it was another powerful argument among the public, along with the deaths on 9/11, to justify the war on terror.

The clash of civilizations, expressed through the war on terror, was now the dominant metanarrative in world affairs. Because globalization had already created international networks in the last few years, the U.S.-led war effort was smoothly integrated into global information, economic, transport, financial, and military systems. In the aftermath of 9/11, the American philosophy of globalization, reduced to the catchy phrase "the world is flat" (popularized by American commentators like Thomas Friedman who equate globalization with "Americanization"), thus became intertwined with the war on terror.[17] The war also provided the groundwork for the arguments to torture prisoners, suspend human rights, and support autocratic and blood-thirsty rulers abroad, while turning a blind eye to the desperate suffering of people on their peripheries. Considering the gravity of a war that was global in scope, hastily formulated laws and regulations were passed that blocked, distorted, and obfuscated information. A miasmic fog descended on the war on terror and soon spread across the planet.

Because the war on terror was the first truly worldwide conflict in the age of globalization, Western nations and their allies swiftly and efficiently mobilized every aspect of society in its support. The global armada thus assembled set forth with great élan for Afghanistan. Fifty nations deployed troops. The objectives were vague and many—from introducing democracy, development, and human rights, and "freeing" women to destroying al Qaeda, the Taliban, and Osama bin Laden. Much of the armada then inexplicably changed course and headed for Iraq with a quite different objective: to locate the elusive and illusory "weapons of mass destruction." As the force ploughed deeper and deeper into the two wars, it became clear that no resounding victory was remotely in sight. As if these two wars were not messy enough, new fronts, however limited and temporary, were opened elsewhere—in the Tribal Areas of Pakistan, Yemen, Somalia, the Philippines, and the Sahel in West Africa. Of course, the United States and central governments of these various regions also implemented educational, developmental, and other schemes to benefit the periphery. But their effect was diluted by the outsiders' ignorance of the local culture and the periphery's problems with the central government, not to mention acts of violence by both center and periphery, especially those in which ordinary civilians were killed.

As the conflicts escalated, the U.S. State Department began including on its terrorist list Muslim groups suspected of any possible links to al Qaeda—such as the East Turkestan Islamic Movement (ETIM) based in China's Xinjiang Province inhabited by the Uyghurs. This action immediately cast suspicion on entire communities as potential terrorists. Already persecuted minority groups now found themselves even more oppressed. Even the hapless and docile Rohingya of Burma (now called Myanmar), who were prohibited from traveling outside their villages and were generally too poor to afford a bicycle, let alone an improvised explosive device (IED), were suspected of al Qaeda links owing to one Western journalist's articles, as explained in a later chapter. Central governments cynically and ruthlessly exploited the war on terror to pursue their own agenda against the periphery. Meanwhile the periphery was unable to come to terms with this new era of globalization that had made it an easy and fatal target; indeed, the prickliest of the tribes are the ones now suffering the most.

In fact, as this study sets out to establish, if there is a clash it is not between civilizations based on religion; rather, it is between central governments and the tribal communities on the periphery. The war on terror has been conceptualized as a triangle formed by three points—the United States, the modern state within which the tribes live, and al Qaeda. The arguments presented below indicate that the third point, however, is actually not al Qaeda, which at its height had perhaps no more than a few thousand members, if that, and is now reduced to one or two dozen. It is the tribal societies that have directly or indirectly provided a base for al Qaeda and other groups advocating violence. Many of these peripheral groups had been clamoring, or even fighting, for their rights from central governments for decades. A small number of al Qaeda operatives, in Afghanistan and elsewhere, found these tribes to be receptive hosts.

The United States, however, has failed to understand not only the nature of tribal society but also the dimensions of this simmering conflict between the center and the periphery. As a result, Americans have never been clear as to where al Qaeda ends and where the tribe begins and why they resort to violence. Instead they have viewed central governments as the only legitimate source of authority and force, while ignoring all reports of the loutish and sadistic behavior of the center's soldiers, preferring to deal with Hosni Mubarak as representing all of Egypt and Pervez Musharraf all of Pakistan. Anyone opposed to these leaders was automatically seen as a foe of the United States.

The United States and central governments around the world found it mutually beneficial to forge alliances and make agreements within the ideological frame of the war on terror. For the United States and its allied central governments, the tribes across the Muslim world effectively became public enemy number one because they were outside globalization, resistant to it, and seen as the natural allies of al Qaeda. Opposition to either the war on terror or globalization was thus seen as one and the same thing, thereby risking the wrath of the United States and casting those opposed as potential "terrorist sympathizers."

The problem was that many such tribes and communities wished to benefit from globalization but not to compromise their thistle-like identity. They also had to contend with central governments more interested in monopolizing globalization's many benefits—developments in information technology, transport and communications, medicine, trade, and commerce—and in the central government's policy of promoting the politics, language, and culture of the dominant group at the center. Little more than crumbs—a cell phone here, a job in a security firm there—fell to the periphery.

Under the rubric of the war on terror, different combatants were conducting different wars for different objectives within the triangle of terror. Some were big powers fishing in troubled waters. Others were nationalist entities wanting to assert central authority. Still others were tribesmen battling to maintain their ethnic and cultural boundaries, some also unabashedly seeking to discomfit their tribal rivals. Lurking somewhere in the background were the ever-thinning numbers of individuals associated with or accused of being al Qaeda. Shifting alliances, general distrust, betrayals, paranoia, and fear marked the war on terror.

It is in the interest of the United States to understand, in all the tribal societies with which it is engaged, the people, their leadership, history, culture, their relationship with the center, their social structures, and the role Islam plays in their lives. These issues are, in fact, the subject matter of anthropology, and those commenting on or involved with the war on terror, therefore, need to become better informed about the anthropology of tribal societies. Without this understanding, the war on terror will not end in any kind of recognizable victory as current military actions and policies are only exacerbating the conflict.

State and Tribe, Center and Periphery

The relationship between state and tribe, center and periphery, ruler and those living on the boundaries of the realm has interested scholars, commentators, and politicians throughout recorded history. Those drawn to the subject range from the likes of Herodotus, Plutarch, Julius Caesar, and the Indian Kautilya of long ago to the Arab Ibn Khaldun of medieval times and Bernard Lewis and Albert Hourani of the modern era. In recent decades, anthropologists have made a rich ethnographic contribution to the discussion.[18] In addition, many anthropologists have sounded the alarm about the current plight of tribal societies and connected the dots between their predicament and the role of the modern state.[19]

Anthropologists have traditionally found two distinct social and political structures in tribal societies: a segmentary lineage system existing outside the state, as exemplified by the animist Nuer tribes of East Africa, and a centralized kingdom with standing armies and a functioning bureaucracy, like the Zulu kingdoms of South Africa.[20] One category of centralized kingdoms even bigger and more complex than that of the Zulus consists of vast, highly centralized, hierarchical, densely populated, dynastic political and social entities deriving their economic and political wealth from agricultural lands with complex irrigation systems. Karl Wittfogel calls this category "hydraulic society" or "Oriental Despotism."[21] As Wittfogel points out, the central authorities of such societies had massive military resources at their disposal to subjugate and terrorize their populations. Xerxes of Persia had an army of 360,000 soldiers. Chandragupta of India had a standing army of 690,000 not counting his cavalry. Harun al-Rashid, the Arab caliph, gathered 135,000 regular soldiers for a summer campaign. The Mughal emperor Akbar boasted a contingent of 50,000 armor-plated elephants, which functioned much like modern tank divisions, and his grandson, Emperor Shah Jehan, had an elite cavalry corps of 200,000 horsemen. The Chou dynasty of China could mobilize 3.5 million foot soldiers and 30,000 horsemen.[22] "Oriental despotism," writes Wittfogel, confers "total power" on those at the center—as it did on Chinese, Indian, and Middle Eastern emperors and more recently on Stalin and Hitler—and unleashes "total terror, total submission, and total loneliness."[23] Oriental despotism is the exact opposite of the political, social, and economic structure of the tribal communities examined in this study.

Rulers and administrators representing a strong center tended to view the periphery as an unattractive or less than admirable segment of society. The periphery, in turn, saw the center as predatory, corrupt, and dishonorable, an entity to be kept at arm's length. From the time of the Mughals to that of the British, for example, the Indian center referred to the Pukhtun areas as *yaghistan,* or a "land of rebellion," and *ghair ilaqa,* which means alien, strange, or foreign (as opposed to *ilaqa,* which means area under central government control). Central

Family of Bugti tribesmen in Baluchistan, Pakistan, in the 1980s (author's collection).

governments in North Africa have also described tribes in their mountain fast-
ness as living in *bled es siba,* the land of rebellion, as opposed to *bled el makhzen,*
the land of government. In time the sense of remoteness entered into the names
of the tribes and their areas: the Tuareg in West Africa, for example, meant
"abandoned by God," the Hadhramaut region in Yemen "death has come," and
Asir in Saudi Arabia "inaccessible." Central governments created new names for
the people at the periphery regardless of their deep attachment to traditional
names: the Pukhtun peoples, for example, were renamed Pathans, the Amazigh
people Berbers, Nokhcha people Chechen, and the Tausug and other Muslim
groups in the Philippines Moro. Many of the new names were of a derogatory
nature, as in the case of *shiptar,* a racial slur applied to Albanians, *shifta* (bandit)
used for the Somalis, *galla* (lowly outsiders) for the Oromo of Ethiopia, and *niak*
(forest people or savages) for the Jola of Senegal.

Despite their views of each other and continued wariness, over time the center
and periphery developed a modus vivendi, even a level of accommodation and
understanding, described as a "delicate balance" and "uneasy truce between center and perimeter" by noted anthropologist Clifford Geertz.[24] For Carleton Coon,
an anthropologist of an earlier generation, the relationship between the center
and periphery was "a loose system of give and take" whereby "mountaineers
and nomads come to town freely, their fastnesses are left alone, and they let the
caravans of travelers, traders, and pilgrims cross the 'Land of Insolence' without
hindrance or inconvenience over and above the normal rigors of travel."[25]

Kurdish children, some without shoes, in Turkey (photo by Durzan Cirano).

History shows a direct correlation between waning power at the center and increasing independence at the periphery. When strong, the center attempted to create pliable leadership and eliminate those elements on the periphery that resisted it. When weak, it withdrew to attend to its own affairs, leaving the communities on the periphery to their own devices.

In the modern age, beginning with colonization, that balance was severely threatened, only to be completely upset in the postindependence era after World War II. A common feature of the tribal groups examined here, apart from their Islamic faith, is that they found themselves, without their permission and in many cases against their choice or will, part of a newly formed modern nation-state. Clans and communities that had lived together for centuries were overnight sliced into two—and some more than two—by international boundaries. Many tribes were now at the mercy of those they had traditionally opposed or fought against. Some new states had a Muslim majority and some were non-Muslim with only a small Muslim population.

A puzzling feature of today's world is that tiny nations like Nauru (with a population of 9,300), Tuvalu (10,000), and Kiribati (barely 100,000) have independent status with full membership in the United Nations, whereas much larger ethnic groups that not long ago lived as independent or semi-independent societies find themselves divided among different nations and subjected to increasingly repressive policies in their own land. An estimated 50 million Pukhtuns have been split mainly between Afghanistan and Pakistan (Afghan, Pukhtun,

Pashtun, and Pathan all refer to the same ethnic group, and in order to avoid confusion I will use Pukhtun because that is what is used by major Pukhtun tribes like the Yusufzai, who are the proud carriers of the literary traditions of the Pukhtu language); some 30 million Kurds between Turkey, Syria, Iran, and Iraq; about 30 million Oromo between Ethiopia (which has the largest share) and Kenya; about 15 million Fulani among Nigeria, Cameroon, Ghana, Senegal, and across West Africa; and 6 million Tuareg among half a dozen countries in Africa—Mali, Niger, Algeria, Libya, Burkina Faso, and Nigeria.

Once the masters of their universe, these communities have been reduced to third-class citizenship in their own homes. Ironically, those responsible for this shift were not even European imperialists; in most countries, they were either fellow Muslims or non-Muslim neighbors. In many of the regions, the discovery of oil and minerals in the twentieth century compounded tribal problems with the center, which relentlessly pursued the potential wealth for its own gains. As a result, the disparity in economic and political power between center and periphery, already wide, grew wider. Little was done for the people on the fringe—as is obvious from a cursory glance at the Baluch in Pakistan, Kurds in Turkey, and the Uyghur in China.

Now reduced to impotency, tribal peoples saw the state encroach on their lands, forcing them to settle elsewhere while flooding their areas with settlers of different ethnicities linked to the center. Government officials mocked their customs and language and denied them employment. These minority communities were demonized by the majority. Children at school and even the press and government officials often referred to them as "monkeys without tails," "reptiles," or "animals."

The sheer desperation of these communities and the brutality they faced from the center are highlighted in films like *Turtles Can Fly* (2004). In it, a small group of Kurdish orphans, many of them limbless because of land mines, live between the border of Turkey and Iraq and face systematic persecution by the state. Their struggle merely to keep hope alive in a world that has shattered around them and is full of cruel adults reflects the grim realities of Muslims living on the periphery. An entire generation of young people on the periphery is growing up in a climate of fear and violence. Both Muslim and non-Muslim leaders who deal with Muslim populations need to keep this demographic reality in mind.

The assault on tribal peoples caused traditional tribal and Islamic behavior to mutate, as witnessed in the bloody and frenzied suicide bombings by young Muslim males and females of schools, bazaars, mosques, and symbols of central authority. Such incidents occur at random almost daily across regions in which tribal communities live. On August 19, 2011, for example, the Pakistani press reported that a suicide bomber blew himself up in a mosque on a Friday in the Khyber Agency, killing 56 people and wounding over 120. A Muslim killing fellow Muslims in a mosque during holy day prayer in the month of Ramadan in the Tribal Areas is the most serious violation of tribal and Islamic tradition.

Though some violent groups like the Tehrik-e-Taliban Pakistan (TTP) claim their motives are to impose *sharia,* or Islamic law, their actions reflect primeval notions of revenge. Their own larger communities are baffled by their emergence, and rumors abound that they are part of a "conspiracy" against the state of Pakistan, perhaps concocted by elements in the central government itself or "foreign" powers. No arguments about injustice or loss can be sustained amid the random and widespread violence now being inflicted by these Muslims, most often against other Muslims. While explanations of the violence are provided in this book, they cannot justify or rationalize it in any way.

The center and the periphery are engaged in a mutually destructive civil war across the globe that has been intensified by the war on terror. A clear principle of cause and effect shapes the relationship between the attacking central authority and the resisting tribes. The draconian and often indiscriminate measures enacted by the center's security agencies and the military provoke the unrestrained retaliation of the desperate periphery. Indeed, the greater the brutalization of peripheral communities, the harsher their retaliatory violence. Neither side is prepared to give any quarter. Neither side appears to understand the interplay of cause and effect. The best place to begin seeking the causes of the breakdown between center and periphery is in the segmentary lineage system.

THE SEGMENTARY LINEAGE SYSTEM

No ancient society—the Greek city-states, the Roman Empire, the Indian kingdoms—survives today, with one exception: tribes that are organized along the segmentary lineage system. Such tribal groups have proved resilient and long lasting. Anthropologists categorize these tribes as acephalous, or without leaders—ones in which each man guards his status and independence jealously. "Every man is a Malik [elder]" is a common saying among the Pukhtun, and "every man his own sultan" among the Somalis. The same sentiment is reflected in a Mahsud elder's suggestion to Sir Evelyn Howell, a British administrator in Waziristan in the early twentieth century: either "blow us all up with cannon, or make all eighteen thousand of us Nawabs [chiefs]."[26]

Most authoritative accounts of Muslim tribesmen by Western scholars and administrators cite parallels with the ancient Greeks in their independent character and democratic social organization. Perhaps they thought there was no greater compliment than to acknowledge similarities with the very fountainhead of Western civilization. The nineteenth-century English scholar, explorer, and administrator Sir Richard Burton found Somali tribes to be "a fierce and turbulent race of republicans. . . . Every free-born man holds himself equal to his ruler, and allows

ALEXANDER THE GREAT   A PATHAN MILITIAMAN IN KURRAM
A LIKENESS

Profiles of Alexander the Great and of a Pukhtun tribesman (used with permission of Oxford University Press).

no royalties or prerogatives to abridge his birthright of liberty."[27] Howell used the very term "Athenian" to describe the egalitarian spirit of the Waziristan tribes.[28] In *The Pathans,* Caroe, in keeping with the intellectual trends of his time, supports the comparison between the ancient Greeks and Pukhtuns by providing a striking pictorial juxtaposition of Alexander the Great and a Pukhtun tribesman in profile.

The Study of Segmentary Lineage Systems

Tribal societies with segmentary lineage systems had pride of place in British social anthropology when I began my studies in the United Kingdom in the 1970s. While the stock-in-trade of the discipline was to focus on the rites of passage of the peasant struggling with caste rules in an Indian village or the dance rituals of the witch doctor in an African settlement, those wanting to make a name in the discipline went to the deserts and mountains in search of tribes. These groups, with their small, scattered populations, lived in border areas of various countries and were known for their codes of honor and revenge, their feuds, and fighting. Conducting fieldwork among them carried a whiff of danger. Here was where the anthropologist became Indiana Jones.

Some notable work regarding tribes dates back six centuries, however. Renowned Arab philosopher and historian Ibn Khaldun put forth a cyclical theory of tribal society that drew on the relationship between tribal groups living in remote areas and settled groups in towns and cities in his seminal *Muqaddimah.*[29]

Khaldun's theory stemmed from the character differences between the two groups and impact of contact between them: tribal "nomadic" peoples in remote areas lived by a code of honor rooted in notions of being equal and united by what he called *asabiyah,* or social cohesion, whereas populations in urban areas lacked these traits. As nomads raided towns or settled in them, they, in turn, began to assimilate, losing their sense of asabiyah; in three generations they, too, became vulnerable to domination by fresher nomads from the mountains. This was, and remains, a strong and neat depiction of a certain kind of society and gathered a large network of scholarly admirers, including prominent Western anthropologists.

But it was left to British anthropologists, E. E. Evans-Pritchard foremost among them, to articulate the discussion of tribal groups organized on the basis of the segmentary lineage system. Such tribes lived *outside* state systems and possessed their own territory, language, and particular customs and traditions that provided a blueprint for perpetuating their specific identity through succeeding generations. These societies had an organized mechanism for resolving conflict and maintaining order that was centered on the role and mediation of elders. Segmentary lineage tribal societies contained fully formed and functioning social systems; they were not one rung on an evolutionary ladder waiting to evolve in due time to a higher more "advanced" one.

As a Muslim administrating similar tribes in some of the most inaccessible areas of the world, I was particularly interested in the authoritative studies of Muslim segmentary lineage tribal groups, such as the Sanusi tribes of Cyrenaica by Evans-Pritchard, the Berbers in the Atlas mountains of Morocco by Ernest Gellner, and the Somalis in the Horn of Africa by I. M. Lewis. The British concept of the segmentary lineage system was taken up by other anthropologists of note, such as the Norwegian Fredrik Barth, who studied the Pukhtun in Swat, the Kurds in Iraq, and the Basseri nomads of southern Iran.[30] It should be noted, however, that not all segmentary lineage systems are Muslim. Those that are Christian, besides the Scots, include the Tiv of Nigeria, the Acholi of Uganda, the Timorese of Timor-Leste, and the Basques of Spain.

Although American anthropologists worked extensively among tribes, their views of British theories about the segmentary lineage system were mixed. Among enthusiasts were Laura and Paul Bohannan, who adopted British ideas about the segmentary lineage system in their work on the Tiv. In contrast, Clifford Geertz and Lawrence Rosen, working in Morocco, argued that the limitations of the segmentary lineage system were painfully apparent. Geertz and Rosen emphasized culture and the symbols that represent its various aspects, the capacity of the individual to manipulate networks regardless of clan and tribe, and the transformative influence of interaction outside the community. Amid the dazzling asides, devastating broadsides, cross-continental cultural comparisons, and interdisciplinary insights that Geertz deploys in *The Interpretation of*

Cultures (1973) and *Islam Observed* (1968), together forming arguably his most magisterial overview of the subject, the reader will look in vain for musings on the segmentary lineage system.[31] It does not even merit a mention in Geertz's index; rather, the focus is on the concept of symbol systems. Some anthropologists took the middle ground, adopting points best suited to their own material, as in the case of Steven Caton's recognition of lineage blocs, alliances, ancestors, and honor in his studies of Yemen.

There are tribal peoples, however, that share many of the fundamental characteristics of the segmentary lineage system and are yet completely different in their own right. The Tausug of the southern Philippines are an example.[32] They are acephalous, identified on the basis of their clan segments, and have a developed code of honor, hospitality, and revenge evidenced by their blood feuds, which can last for decades. The proverbs of the Tausug echo those of the segmentary lineage tribes, "It is better to die than be dishonored."[33] The Tausug, however, are not organized along the lines of the segmentary lineage system and do not feel the need to possess long genealogical lines of ascent to common ancestors. The Tausug may be seen as segmented tribal groups rather than segmentary lineage ones.

Controversy has also long surrounded the definition of "tribe" itself—quite understandably. Early anthropologists used the word "savage" freely to describe tribal communities. Fresher generations have challenged the very term "tribe," with its connotation of being "backward" and "primitive." Many such peoples, once the subject of Western anthropologists, are now producing their own first-class material on their communities.

One conundrum for me in this regard—while appreciating the sensitivity to political correctness and acknowledging the historical background of the controversy—is that the people under study themselves use words that are the exact equivalent of "tribe" or "clan," such as *qam, khel, teip, fis, qabila,* or *qabail.* Without getting entangled in the nuances of definition (the meaning of "tribe" will remain a source of debate as long as people ponder societies and communities), I will use "tribe" to refer to a unit of ethnic, social, and political organization in which kinship is the defining principle of social organization and interaction. While I am aware of the term's shortcomings and with all the cautions and caveats in mind, this is still perhaps the most useful way to understand a certain kind of peoples that I encountered on the borders of Afghanistan and Pakistan.

The Structure of the System

The segmentary lineage system is a closed world, bounded by the genealogical charter and its concomitant code; those not included in the charter simply belong to another world. For the purposes of this study, I define segmentary lineage systems in the ideal as characterized by (a) highly egalitarian segments of a genealogical charter, and within them smaller and smaller segments, all claiming descent

Yemeni tribesman with traditional dagger in vertical position signifying a warrior identity (photo by Bernard Gagnon).

from a common, often eponymous, ancestor; (b) male cousin rivalry and a council of elders to mediate conflict; (c) recognition of rights to territory corresponding to segments, as acknowledged by tradition; and (d) a normatively acknowledged set of customs that includes a code of honor and a distinctive language.

The system is largely based on patrimonial descent and exhibits the nesting attributes of pyramid-like structures of clans and subclans on the genealogical charter. The operative level is the subsection, consisting of several extended families, which is part of a larger section, which, in turn, is part of an even larger clan. It is at this level of society that communities not only choose to lead their lives but also conceive them. Smaller units come together to oppose larger ones, as reflected in the Bedouin saying "Me and my brothers against my cousins, me and my cousins against the world."

The tribes examined here can trace connections back through many generations to their common ancestor, whose name has often been applied to the tribe itself. For example, the Wazir along the border between Afghanistan and

Pakistan are named after their eponymous ancestor Wazir, and the Yusufzai on the Pakistani side of the border after theirs, Yusuf (*zai* means "sons of"). The Oromo in Ethiopia and Kenya are descended from their ancestor named Orma, and the Somalis from Samale. Reputed to be fiercely independent people, living in generally dry, unirrigated, low-production, and, for the most part, inaccessible areas that could not support large populations, they were isolated and avoided by outsiders. These tribes are commonly nomadic or semi-nomadic with animal herds of sheep, goats, cows, or camels. They typically live on small plots of land, which they own as members of a tribe or clan.

A tribal unit is traditionally defined by territory and usually lives in an area named after the tribe itself. Thus, the two Waziristan Agencies (administrative districts in the Tribal Areas of Pakistan) are named after the Wazir tribe, the Orakzai Agency after the Orakzai tribe, and the Mohmand Agency after the Mohmand tribe. Entire provinces and countries are also named after tribes: Baluchistan after the Baluch tribe, Afghanistan after the Afghan or Pukhtun tribes, and Saudi Arabia after the Saud tribe. Although these administrative and political units bear the name of a particular tribe, other tribes having their own genealogical charter and leadership may also live there. At least a dozen tribes, for example, the Burkis and the Bhittani, inhabit the two Waziristan Agencies. Each of these tribes is a world unto itself, and though each shares many characteristics with the others, and some even a common ancestor, each sees itself as a distinct social entity.

The competitiveness for political, economic, and social gain plays out in what anthropologists call "agnatic rivalry" between father's brother's sons. This rivalry is captured in the Pukhtun saying, "God knows that the uncle is an infidel."[34] Agnatic rivalry engenders long-standing feuds and vendettas that often end in the destruction of entire families. Viewing the constant conflict within the tribal structure, British anthropologists described these societies as "ordered anarchy."

The authority to make decisions—including declarations of war, agreements for peace, or the mediation of disputes and blood feuds according to the tribal code of honor that encompasses all areas of tribal life—rests in the hands of a council of elders. Since their sense of egalitarianism and independence precludes the establishment of a central authority in many of these tribes, the elders rely on personal charisma, wisdom, bravery, knowledge of the code, and other personal characteristics to lay claim to that authority. Ultimately, though, their legitimacy derives from the lineage charter of the tribe. The terms for the bearers of this authority vary from tribe to tribe: among the Pukhtuns, the council of elders, or *jirga,* is composed of the *mashar,* meaning elder; decisions among the Somalis are made by the *shir,* composed of every adult male in the clan, all of whom are considered elders; and for the Kurds, it is the *ri spi,* literally "the white beards." What remains fundamentally the same among all the tribes is the central role of the elder and the council to which he belongs.

It is a man's world, and the male carries the weight of tribal honor. The most tangible expression of this code of honor is the weapon that tribesmen in our case studies all carry, traditionally a dagger or sword, but more recently the Kalashnikov assault rifle. The mandatory weapon has long symbolized the status of a man in tribal society, signifying that he is the protector of his community. "A man's gun is his jewelry" is a popular proverb among Pukhtuns. In the ideal, a man must combine courage and honor. He must know who he is in the lineage of his tribe and be prepared to uphold its code. This outlook has given tribal men a certain air of confidence. British writers captured the essence of the Pukhtun tribesmen in their swagger and gait. As one wrote of the Tuareg in the 1920s, "The men are born to walk and move as kings, they stride along swiftly and easily, like Princes of the Earth, fearing no man, cringing before none, and consciously superior to other people."[35]

A man's and a woman's place in their tribal genealogical charter is known in the community and allocates various responsibilities that carry social prestige— membership in the jirga for men and the organization of the rites of passage, such as marriage rituals, for women. However, certain groups are not included in the charter, yet play an equally important role—most notably *mullahs* or religious leaders, blacksmiths, musicians, barbers, and small shopkeepers. Although these groups provide services necessary for the business of everyday life, the tribesman's ideas of descent and accompanying notions of honor prevent him from performing such activities himself. Over time, these social divisions may assume an almost caste-like sanctity in certain tribal societies.

Small groups of non-Muslims have also become affiliated with some of the main tribes, as in the case of a Hindu community living among the Bugti in Baluchistan. During my time in Baluchistan in the 1980s, Arjun Das Bugti, who represented the Bugti Agency as a member of the provincial assembly, proudly carried both his Hindu name and that of his affiliated tribe, the Bugti. Yemen and the North Caucasus provide examples of Jews connected with Muslim tribes, and the Kurds with Christian groups. In the ideal, the tribal code encompasses all groups living within the purview of the tribe, which means these groups are protected; their honor has become a matter of honor for the main tribe.

Tribal Identity and the Code of Honor

Wali Khan, a Pukhtun leader in Pakistan and the son of the famed "Frontier Gandhi," Abdul Ghaffar Khan, was once asked about the "first allegiance" of his identity. It was 1972, a time of great ethnic tension in Pakistan, when East Pakistan had just broken away on the basis of Bengali ethnicity. A traumatic Pakistani nation wondered whether the state would survive, its people apprehensive about other communities and their ethnic loyalties. Wali Khan, who had clearly been thinking about the issue, replied, "I have been a Pashtun for six thousand years, a Muslim for thirteen hundred years, and a Pakistani for twenty-five."[36] In short, by explicitly relegating the position of nationalism and religion below that of tribal identity, Wali Khan was highlighting the primordial basis of his sense of self. He could have been speaking on behalf of any of the Muslim tribal groups discussed in this volume—the Kurds, Somalis, Yemenis, Bedouin, and so on.

For the segmentary lineage tribes on the periphery, tribal lineage and the code of honor are the basis of identity as much as Islam is, sometimes more so. Some of these codes have specific names directly related to their tribal identity—*Pukhtunwali* means "the way of the Pukhtun," *Baluchiat,* "the way of the Baluch"; the Fulani code is known as *Pulaaku,* the "Fulani way"; the Yemeni code, *Gabyilah,* derives from the Arabic word for tribe; and the Chechen code, *Nokhchalla,* is named after Nokhcho, their mythological ancestor. The Tuareg have named their code *asshak,* meaning "honor" itself, and the Albanians *besa,* meaning "word of honor," while the Somalis speak of *xeer,* or "tribal law." The Bedouin of Sinai and Negev use *orf* or *urfi,* meaning "traditional law," while the Tausug and Avars use *adat,* which is Arabic for "custom."

The code's paramount principle is the law of hospitality pertaining to the welcoming and protection of guests, which is said to reflect the honor of the host. Even a stranger seeking refuge, whatever his background, will find shelter among those adhering to the code. A dramatic example is provided by Mullah Omar, the Taliban leader in Kandahar, refusing to hand over his guest, Osama bin Laden, to the Americans or even to fellow Muslims, the Saudis and Pakistanis. When Muslim officials argued that under Islamic principles bin Laden should be apprehended and handed over for trial, Mullah Omar countered that the tribal code of honor took precedence. Although Mullah Omar was aware that his refusal would cost him and his people a heavy price, he was still unwilling to compromise on the code. To tribal peoples, tradition and custom need to be enacted, preserved, and guarded. While political and economic prosperity matter, and may indeed challenge traditional ways of doing things, they are disguised or couched in tribal terms.

The Bedouin refer to this characteristic hospitality as the Law of the Tent, as it gives individuals in distress the right to enter another's tent and demand assistance, knowing that they will receive it. Hospitality entails not only protecting visitors but also representing their interests in mediations of conflict. Hospitality extends even to viewing hostages kidnapped by tribesmen as guests to be treated with respect (kidnapping is a tactic often used to highlight some complaint). In 1904, for example, Mulai Ahmed el Raisuli, a Berber chief in the Rif region of northern Morocco, kidnapped an American expatriate, Ion Perdicaris, and his son for a ransom and control of two government districts from the Moroccan sultan. This incident was portrayed in the 1975 film *The Wind and the Lion* with

Bugti elder in Baluchistan, Pakistan, during the 1980s (author's collection).

Sean Connery depicting Raisuli's notions of honor and hospitality with empathy, perhaps because of his own Scottish background. In the film, a female character played by the glamorous Candice Bergen stood in for Perdicaris to lend a romantic element to the story. Perdicaris would later write of el Raisuli, "I go so far as to say that I do not regret having been his prisoner for some time. I think that, had I been in his place, I should have acted in the same way. He is not a bandit, nor a murderer, but a patriot forced into acts of brigandage to save his native soil and his people from the yoke of tyranny."[37]

The concept of hospitality is held in such high regard that it often trumps tribal requirements for revenge, as seen in the chivalrous offering of food and provisions even to enemies. During the Crusades, the famous Saladin, a Kurd, was known to infuriate his generals by giving shelter and safe passage to Christian soldiers who would then later go on to fight against Saladin's forces, while the Tuareg, as a British author wrote in the 1920s, "will give water in the desert to their worst enemy."[38]

Tribal hospitality on the battlefield was also evident in late 1920 when Bolshevik forces launched an offensive to subdue an Avar rebellion in the north Caucasus and reopen a major road the Avars had blocked. As the Bolsheviks captured towns, including the old Avar capital Khunzakh, and committed indiscriminate atrocities against local civilians, the Avar clans withdrew into the countryside. They then returned to besiege the towns, cutting off all supply routes and leaving the Bolsheviks to face mass starvation in the depth of winter. Their leader, Najmuddin Samurskii, saved the Bolsheviks by appealing to the Avar code of honor: "If you have honour, if you are indeed the sons of Shamil as you claim, if you want to show yourselves to be eagles of the mountain, send us some food and then we will see who will win."[39] The next night, the Avars approached the Russian garrison in the darkness and left sacks of food, all the while under fire from the Bolshevik troops.

The obligation for hospitality and honor can last for decades, as the following example, also from the Caucasus, shows. After the breakup of the Soviet Union and the splitting up of Soviet agricultural collectivization, an Avar descendant of Hadji Murad, who lived in Moscow, received an unexpectedly large sum of money in the mail. She realized that after the Soviet collapse a plot of land that had belonged to her clan had been given to a young family in the village of Tlokh in Dagestan. Tlokh elders had advised the family to send the woman the money, which they considered the honorable thing to do.[40]

As already mentioned, the obligation to take revenge is also an integral part of the tribal code. For societies traditionally lacking the organs of civil government, such as police, courts of law, and a prison system, the collective demands for revenge help regulate behavior. An individual knows full well that any transgression against another's honor calls for revenge against the transgressor and his family, subclan, or clan by the victim's family, subclan, or clan. It is therefore in the interest of the clan to ensure that none of its own members exceed the normative boundaries of revenge. When serious wrongs do occur—such as murder, theft, or rape—revenge is taken to correct the wrong and restore honor and face. However, these acts often precipitate a cycle of revenge and counter-revenge between families and clans that can last for generations, as reflected in the saying "The Pukhtoon who took revenge after a hundred years said, I took it quickly."[41]

This emphasis on revenge accounts for the vital role that elders play in tribal society: they must attempt to mediate between rival parties and settle matters peacefully through methods such as blood compensation, which is paid by members of the family, subclan, or clan of the accused or through arranged marriages between rivals, often cousins, so as to turn them into allies. According to elder tribesmen, the aim of revenge in traditional society is to provide a measured response aimed at correcting an injustice and ensuring stability.

Tribesmen are obliged to seek revenge even when a modern court system is available to them. I was struck by this reality during an interview in Washington, D.C., with Agri Verrija, an urbane Albanian with a tribal background. He recounted a recent case in Albania in which a man, tried and imprisoned for murdering a rival, was released after nine years, whereupon he returned to his village and was elected its head. In the meantime, the victim's sons had left the country and become U.S. citizens, but when they heard their father's murderer had been released from what they believed a corrupt state system, they flew back to Albania and avenged their father's death by killing him. As Agri explained, "The sons did not feel the accused was punished according to *kanun,* or tribal law."

The most sensitive subject pertaining to tribal honor is the behavior of and transgression against women as it directly relates to the honor of men in the family and clan. Because women play such an important role in tribal society, the violation of their honor is one of the greatest threats to a tribe's honor and therefore provokes the most intense blood feuds. As one anthropologist observed while studying typical marriage practices between Kurd cousins in eastern Turkey, "On a visit to a [father's brother's daughter's] family, to ask formally for her hand, the main speaker of the [wife-taking brother's] party used the following metaphor: that the *mal* (here, lineage) is like a 'house' and the daughter of a *mal* is like its 'door.' One should not open one's door to strangers (*biyani* in Kurdish), but only to one's brother."[42] To maintain their status and safeguard their reputation, women are by and large responsible for conducting household tasks and raising children and do not participate in the male sphere of tribal activity such as the council of elders or acts of revenge. In addition, women play a crucial role in the making and breaking of social and political alliances through the rites of passage such as funerals and marriage ceremonies known as *gham khadi* (sorrow and joy) among the Pukhtun.[43] At the same time, women can be treated abominably, or even put to death, if suspected of compromising their honor in dress and behavior, particularly if they have contact with other men, especially outside the home.

Traditional Muslim tribes and their values are alien to modern populations in this age of globalization. Tribal emphasis on a genealogical charter that promotes ethnic exclusivity, the unacceptable and brutal treatment of women, and a complex code of revenge is neither Islamic in nature nor in keeping with the spirit of the present age. However, there is much to be applauded and in some instances emulated in tribal values—most notably the community's genuine and deep egalitarian spirit. In addition, law and order maintained through the council of elders provides swift and sure justice. The steady rhythm of life over the generations makes for a stable society and provides security for the individual. Furthermore, unlike citizens who are part of and defined by globalization with their ambiguous and competing identities, most tribesmen know exactly who they are.

"Honor Ate Up the Mountains, Taxes the Plains"

The tribes discussed in this volume are not monolithic. Over the centuries, some of their members came down from the mountains and settled by rivers or on cultivated lands with ample rainfall. Others drifted to towns in search of better prospects. In time, the tribesmen who prospered were wearing silks and satins and eating spices and delicacies. As a result, their original tribal identity eventually became diluted and reinterpreted in different ways. Agnatic rivalry, for example, found new form in the competition for government employment or in becoming successful shopkeepers. Lineage as such became less important in defining identity, and marriages outside the community and even ethnic group for the sake of economic and political alliances became common.

Those in the hills and mountains continued to live on smallholdings as had their forefathers, with their herds of goats and camels. Clinging to tribal identity also meant doing without the facilities available to those in the towns and cities, whether hospitals, universities, or large markets. Life was simple, and no one starved because of the tribal nature of the extended family, but no one was particularly well off either. Priding themselves on their independence, the tribes in the hills, deserts, and jungles developed an uneasy relationship with those who settled in more urban areas. Despite having the same origins, over time the two developed distinct, and even antithetical, social and political ways of organizing their lives.

Tribesmen are keenly aware of the differences between these societies and their respective obligations. The dilemma for mountain tribes living by the code of honor is that it requires hospitality and revenge even at great cost to themselves. Yet those in the settled areas may not be much better off as they must deal with rapacious revenue officials and tax collectors who drain their meager earnings in the form of taxes and rents. Life is hard in either case. As the Pukhtu proverb says, "Honor [*nang*] ate up the mountains, taxes and rents [*qalang*] ate up the plains."

During fieldwork among the border tribes of Afghanistan and Pakistan, it seemed appropriate to divide tribal peoples according to whether they defined themselves on the basis of nang or qalang.[44] More closely adhering to the segmentary lineage structure, nang populations are small and dispersed, whereas the qalang societies are typically large, concentrated, and hierarchical. The nang group I studied clearly corresponded with Ibn Khaldun's nomadic category and the qalang with his sedentary category. Furthermore, Pukhtunwali appears equivalent to Ibn Khaldun's asabiyah. Because the tribes of Waziristan—like those of the Tribal Areas—have been able to preserve Pukhtunwali, with its emphasis on nang, they have maintained the tribal spirit and its thistle-like nature.

Beyond the Pukhtun tribes, the other examples of core segmentary lineage systems that my team and I investigated can all be divided along similar societal lines between the local equivalent of nang and qalang. Somalia is split between egalitarian nomadic clans known as Samale after their common ancestor, with a strong adherence to their code of honor, and more hierarchically structured agricultural clans known as Sab. The division is stark, with the two groups even speaking different dialects of Somali as distinct as Spanish and Portuguese. Similarly, the Kurds divide themselves into "tribal" and "nontribal" populations. On the whole, the segmentary lineage system has remained "purest" among the Kurds in the most mountainous and isolated areas of the Middle East. The further the Kurdish communities are from the mountains, the less tribal and more peasant-like they are in their organization and behavior.[45] Not surprisingly, then, honor feuds are prevalent in the mountains but much less common in the plains, where the nontribal Kurds are more answerable to the interests of powerful landlords.[46] While tribesmen do not work for others in their own area, the nontribal Kurds are deemed unsuitable for fighting. Upper Yemen, too, has a strong tribal, egalitarian ethos. Large areas of Lower Yemen, on the other hand, have a hierarchical system of authority based on sharecropping and taxes, with settled peasants making up the majority of the population. For the settled people, the "land of the tribes" has come to be seen as an alien, primitive, and even threatening place.

DEFINING TRIBAL ISLAM

The tribesman defines himself by his Islamic faith as much as by blood, clan, and loyalty to the code. Covering his head with a turban or cloth, wearing loose flowing garments, dying a white beard with red henna, consciously invoking God before meals or important journeys, punctiliously praying five times a day, and fasting during the month of Ramadan—all these practices signal his religious affiliation with the Prophet, from whom he self-consciously derives all these actions. Similarly, Muslim tribal women are inspired by the example of the Prophet and that of the women in his household. These tribal communities approach God through oral folk traditions and emulation of the Prophet.

The Prophet as Tribal Chief Par Excellence

Tribesmen view the Prophet of Islam in a special way. They argue that no figure in human history—neither the Sanskritic sages, Buddha, Socrates, Aristotle, the biblical prophets, nor the Chinese emperors—managed to introduce a world religion, lead armies in war and congregations in prayer, preside over councils of peace, create a new state, yet remain austere and pious in personal life, deliver a message of compassion and mercy and demonstrate its practical applicability in the running of government machinery while acting as a loving parent, spouse, and friend. The exception is the Prophet of Islam. For the tribesmen, the Prophet became—and remains—a kind of tribal chief par excellence.

The Prophet himself had emerged from a tribal society, being a member of the Quraysh tribe of Mecca, with its emphasis on clans, codes, and notions of hospitality, courage, and revenge. However, the Prophet placed the universal laws of Islam over those of tribal custom, whereas Muslim tribesmen proclaimed their faithfulness to the former yet adhered to the latter. Aware of the pulls of tribalism, the Prophet decried tribal loyalties and identity, as in his saying "There is no Bedouinism in Islam."

All the same, tribesmen believed the Prophet made perfect sense in their tribal context and remained loyal to him throughout the vicissitudes of history. They created various genealogical links to the Prophet, placing him on their tribal charter, thereby reinforcing their relationship to him and enhancing their own prestige. Many of the tribes in this study can produce such links as proof of their Islamic credentials in terms of lineage, whether claiming their ancestors descended directly from him or had been converted by him. Anthropologists call links of this kind, meant to enhance social prestige but built on dubious evidence, fictitious genealogy.

Descent from, and association with, the Prophet is crucial to the discussion of tribal Islam. Claims that a tribe's ancestors were converted by the Prophet establish a legitimacy in denoting the "purest" of Muslims. "Who could be a better Muslim than us?" "We carry his blood in our veins" or "We were converted to Islam by the Prophet himself," they will say with pride. Thus, tribesmen say that on judgment day, when their fate will be decided, the Prophet will vouch for them and overlook their shortcomings as they will receive the infinite blessings of the greatest of God's messengers. These links to the Prophet provide "a kind of cover for impurity" for groups largely ignorant of orthodox Islamic theology and practices.[47] Despite its fiction, the link with the Prophet enables tribesmen to brush aside any criticism of their unorthodox practices. To the tribesman, his tribal identity and his Islamic identity are fused, they are one and the same thing.

The notion of lineage affiliation with the Prophet makes Muslim tribal peoples even more loyal to him than are other Muslims. Any perceived attacks on the Prophet are likely to incite a defense of his honor, a reaction that stems from the combination of religious fervor and the tribal code, with its emphasis on revenge. Such was the response to Salman Rushdie's novel *The Satanic Verses*,[48] Danish cartoons depicting the Prophet, and the poorly produced and conceived American film attacking the Prophet, which caused riots in the Muslim world amid which occurred the distressing deaths of the U.S. ambassador to Libya and his colleagues in Benghazi in September 2012.

Among the claimed affiliations, the Pukhtuns believe their common ancestor, Qais Abdur Rashid, was converted by the Prophet himself. The Yemeni tribes, well known during the time of the Prophet, were also converted by him and mentioned favorably in many of his sayings, the *hadiths* (for details of these links, see chapter 3). Samale, the ancestor of the Somali tribes, is supposed to have come from Yemen in the ninth century and is said to be descended from Aqil Abu Talib of the Quraysh, the son of Abu Talib who was a cousin of the Prophet and brother of Ali. Farther afield, the Tausug of Jolo in the southern Philippines mention with pride that Salip Muda, also a cousin of the Prophet, was a Tausug.[49] The Berbers, too, believe that their ancestors were converted to Islam by the Prophet and that the Prophet's ability to speak the Berber language gave them special dispensation within the faith. Kurds commonly believe that Abraham's wife Sara was a Kurd and that this connection to the Abrahamic line links them to the Prophet. The Uyghur, too, claim ties with the Prophet through their putative descent from Noah and Abraham.

Few such links are as interesting and inventive as that of the Tera clan of the Kanuri in northeastern Nigeria. The Tera claim to be descended from a barber who shaved the head of the Prophet. It seems that one day this barber nicked the Prophet's scalp and it began to bleed. The barber quickly tasted the blood and claimed it imbued him with special powers that were passed on to his descendants. The Tera were thus recognized as *sherif,* a title reserved for those of noble birth and descendants of the Prophet.[50]

Those directly descended from the Prophet through his daughter Fatima are called *sayyeds* and can substantiate their links to him through genealogical charters enumerating ascendants. They are especially revered among tribal societies as men of peace and learning who are often asked to mediate between warring clans. Sayyeds who have lived extraordinary lives of wisdom, piety, or grace are considered "saints." Apart from religious leadership, sayyeds provide a sociological connection to the person of the Prophet. Sayyeds more than any other group were frequently invited to become leaders and even rulers during the emirate period of Muslim history, which lasted more than a thousand years from the coming of Islam to the modern era.

Along with others who have displayed leadership and moral characteristics, the sayyeds formed the focus of saintly worship in their lifetimes, and their shrines continue to inspire their followers after their deaths. Sufis in particular are associated with saint and shrine worship. Tribesmen believe their saint, often a Sufi, whether alive or dead, will intercede with God on their behalf. Given their high levels of illiteracy, the line between appealing to spiritual figures for intercession and actually praying to them is often blurred. To orthodox Muslims, however, the Sufi reverence for shrines smacks suspiciously of praying to a pile of stones at the grave of a saint and is tantamount to heresy.

While the strength of their loyalty to the Prophet allowed ordinary tribesmen to claim Muslimness, their tribal or informal Islam did not comport with formal orthodox Islam, which is based in holy text and relies on learned scholars with a capacity for research and debate to interpret its fine points. Muslim scholars spend a great deal of time getting it exactly right. Debates about the exact length of trousers over the ankles while saying prayers or the proper shape of the beard, for example, can therefore be heated. Formal Islam is rooted in the learning at the great centers of Islam such as those in Mecca, Medina, Al Azhar, and elsewhere.

For the purposes of this study, I cannot emphasize enough that tribal Islam practiced by largely illiterate tribesmen is antithetical in every way—sociological, ideological, and theological—to fundamentalist or literalist versions of Islam, especially the Salafi or Wahhabi Islam promoted by Saudi Arabia. The tribesmen approach God through the heart, the orthodox through the head. The dichotomy between these two interpretations of Islam has never been resolved for the large tribal groups that embraced it at its very birth. As a result, tribal attitudes to the community, elders, women, and Muslim customs and traditions differ from those of the literalists. As already mentioned, the tribesman equates tribal custom with Islamic faith, which together form his identity. By contrast, the literalist finds tribal custom un-Islamic and thinks it should be removed from Islam's pristine message and practice. Furthermore, the two even view God and the Prophet in a different light. To the tribesman, God is a benign if distant presence in his life. He knows God largely through loyalty to the Prophet. To the literalist, on the other hand, God is transcendental spirituality best approached through study of the sacred texts and prayer in the orthodox tradition. The Prophet is little more than one of the many messengers bringing the word of God to humanity. Admittedly, he is the last of the Prophets and therefore his position is singular, but any displays of excessive loyalty or devotion to the Prophet smack of idolatry and must be discouraged. Yet the aim of both approaches is to move toward God. Although the two overlap to some extent in that they are both Muslim groups, many in each camp see the other as the exact opposite of Islam and believe the two versions cannot coexist comfortably.

Pre-Islamic and Non-Islamic Tribal Customs

Another characteristic of tribal Islam, one that infuriates the literalists, is its pre-Islamic and non-Islamic tribal customs. Not sanctioned by Islam, but widely perceived to be Islamic, are syncretic practices such as honor killings and female circumcision, which are a holdover from pre-Islamic tribal traditions and are prevalent among many tribal societies. Similarly, many such societies deny the fundamental rights given to women in Islam, including the right to inherit property, initiate divorce proceedings, and give their permission before marriage. Tribal Islam is embedded in a traditional world of spirits, magic, and spells wherein tribesmen conduct rain ceremonies in the dry Saharan sands in the name of Allah, the Asir tribesmen in Saudi Arabia pray facing the sun and with their backs to Mecca, and a Tausug imam in the Philippines can ritually become the Prophet by reading an Arabic incantation while holding a dagger and spear.[51]

The syncretic nature of tribal Islam and the durability of pre-Islamic customs are perhaps best demonstrated by "trial by ordeal," known in the West from the witch hunts of medieval Europe. This custom, fused with the trappings of Islam, incorporates the elements of a physical ordeal to prove criminal guilt or innocence. I first came across this practice as the commissioner of Sibi Division in Baluchistan in the mid-1980s when I found the Bugti tribe in my charge.[52] Faced with serious offenses such as murder, rape, or kidnapping, for example, the Bugti tribe resorted to trial by fire, locally known as *asa janti,* "to put in fire." The entire proceedings were given an Islamic sheen, with a religious figure usually conducting the ritual. This person would walk around the fire seven times while holding up the Quran and then address the holy book seven times, the number seven having significance in Islamic mythology and sanctioned as special in the Quran, and in a loud voice pronounce: "The power of truth rests in you. If this person is guilty, he should burn; if innocent, he should not." Turning to the fire, he would mention the name of the accused and the alleged crime and say, "If he is guilty he should burn; if not, Oh fire, be cold in the name of God Almighty and the Holy Quran." The accused would then take seven steps while barefoot through the fire. Once finished, he would have his feet washed and placed in a bowl of fresh blood from goats he had purchased. The figure conducting the ceremony and others present would then examine the feet for marks of burning. If there were none, the accused would be declared innocent, and if signs of burning were present, the verdict would be guilty.

The fire ritual clearly originated in a pre-Islamic past. Both the Zoroastrian and Hindu religions accorded fire a central role in their rituals. Surya is the sun god, and Agni, the son of Brahma, personifies fire. It is said that "Agni shall purify everything that enters his flames." In one of the most celebrated stories from the ancient Sanskrit epic *Ramayana,* Sita, the ideal wife of Lord Ram, was kidnapped by Ravan and, when eventually returned to her husband, underwent ordeal by fire to prove that she was still "pure." Ignoring the pre-Islamic origins of the ritual, its Muslim supporters will argue it is surely Islamic. For them, it proves *khuda ki shan,* "the glory of God," and establishes the Quran's power. The accused and the plaintiff both preferred this method to the delayed processes of Pakistani courts, which drag cases out for several years. Here, justice was delivered immediately, however crude and unlikely it may have been.

Trial by ordeal is also found in the Middle East and has been observed as recently as the summer of 2006.[53] In grievous criminal cases without witnesses, the Bedouin tribes of the Sinai and Negev practice trial by ordeal using both fire and water in a ritual called *bisha.* Here the accused individual is called on to lick a large spoon heated in a charcoal fire. At the beginning of the ceremony, the *mubasha,* the leader of the ceremony, who is considered an intermediary with God, recites the al-Fatiha, the opening chapter of the Quran. He then announces to the gathered crowd, "They will lick three times and will be left in God's hands." The *mubasha* tells the accused individual, "God is one," and asks, "Will you lick for that which is written?" The response is, "Yes, I will. I put my trust in God. Muhammad, God is one."[54] The accused then licks the heated spoon three times, washes out his or her mouth with water three times, and has the tongue examined by the *mubasha*. If the defendant's tongue is blistered or burned, the verdict is guilty, but if unharmed, it is innocent. There is also evidence of a similar ritual among the Yemeni Asir tribes of southern Saudi Arabia.[55]

The Bedouin ceremony derives from a story of Moses found in Hebrew *midrash,* or teachings. The story recounts that when Moses was three years old, he was brought before the pharaoh, who had been warned that Moses would one day usurp his throne. Setting a gold crown and a burning ember in front of Moses, the pharaoh had him select one. If Moses chose the crown, the pharaoh would send him to his death, but if he chose the ember, this would disprove the prophecy. As he was reaching for the crown, the angel Gabriel appeared before Moses and pushed his hand toward the ember. Gabriel then made Moses pick up the ember and carry it to his mouth to lick it, thereby proving his innocence.

Trial by ordeal not only predates Islam but is rejected by Islamic jurisprudence, which relies on presiding judges who are well versed in Islamic court procedures and precedents, laws of evidence, credible witnesses, and recorded statements. Considered blasphemy by the Islamic scholar, mumbo jumbo and witchcraft by the Muslim modernist, trial by ordeal nonetheless offered many in the tribe a sense of identity and therefore pride.

Muslim Tribes in History

Despite the exotic nature of some of their customs, tribal societies are far from marginal in Muslim history. Most have proud memories of contributing in sophisticated ways to the *ummah,* or global Muslim community. Learning and scholarship are widely respected among them, as is the case with the Cyrenaica Sanusi tribes in North Africa and the Uyghurs in Central Asia. Some tribal societies evolved into kingdoms, notably the Fulani in West Africa, the Yemenis of Asir in the Arabian Peninsula, the Acehnese in Indonesia, and the Tausug in the Philippines. These societies established dynasties whose kings came to rule over more powerful neighboring centers in which the tribes were soon assimilated. Pukhtun tribal dynasties from Afghanistan—for example, the Khiljis, Lodhis, and Suris—became noted kings of Delhi.

Sher Shah Suri, the enlightened Suri king of Delhi, established an administration that would become the envy of other rulers, while the Tuareg of the Sahel founded one of the most celebrated dynasties in West Africa, the Almoravids, whose rule extended to southern Spain. Until recently, some tribes enjoyed semi-independent status in their own states with their own rulers—as did the Orakzai

Pukhtuns represent the largest Muslim tribal population in the world and have contributed to every
sphere of life: Zakir Hussain, former president of
India (used with permission of Narayanaswamy
Ulaganathan and Subhajyoti Banerjee).

Shah Rukh Khan, Bollywood superstar
(bollywoodhungama.com).

Ghaffar Khan, the "Frontier Gandhi," with Mahatma
Gandhi (courtesy of Gandhi Memorial Center).

Imran Khan, who led Pakistan to victory over England in the Cricket World Cup in 1992 (flickr.com).

Pukhtun tribe, granted its own princely state of Bhopal under the Mughal
Empire, the Yusufzai rulers of Rampur in India, the Khan of Kalat in Baluchistan,
and the Wali of Swat in the North-West Frontier Province. Some even achieved
independent rule, as did the Pukhtun royal dynasty that governed Afghanistan.

Some of the most celebrated Muslim figures in history have a tribal background: the historian Ibn Khaldun was descended from Yemeni tribesmen;
Saladin and the Sufi scholar Said Nursi were Kurdish; Usman dan Fodio and his
daughter Asmau, whose voluminous poetry continues to inspire millions today,
belonged to the Fulani people; the religious scholar and leader Imam Shamil,
who fought Czarist Russia, was an Avar; Baybars, the Mamluk sultan, who halted

the Mongol juggernaut in its tracks and thus changed the shape of Middle East history, was Circassian; and Ali Haidar, who won the Victoria Cross, the highest British military decoration, for his outstanding valor against the German army during the Second World War, was a Pukhtun.

In spite of their martial reputation, the Pukhtun have produced celebrated artists, sportsmen, statesmen, Sufi saints, and advocates of nonviolence. Some of the most glittering Bollywood movie stars have a Pukhtun background, among them Muhammed Yusuf Khan, with the screen name Dilip Kumar; Mumtaz Jahan, known as Madhubala; and the current box office stars Saif Ali Khan and Shah Rukh Khan. Pukhtuns—Imran Khan and Mansoor Ali Khan, known as Tiger Pataudi and the father of Saif Ali Khan—have successfully led the cricket teams of Pakistan and India, respectively, and the Khan brothers from Peshawar in Pakistan dominated world squash for decades. Pukhtuns have reached the highest levels of government in modern times: Ayub Khan, a Tarin Pukhtun, became president of Pakistan; Zakir Hussain, an Afridi Pukhtun, president of India; and Salman Khurshid, Zakir Hussain's grandson, was appointed India's external affairs minister in October 2012. They have produced Sufi saints like Pir Baba and the Akhund of Swat and world-renowned leaders who advocated nonviolence like Ghaffar Khan.

METHODOLOGY

This is the third and final part of a trilogy of books in which I examine relations between the United States and the Muslim world. The first of these focused on Muslim societies in the Muslim world and their perceptions of the United States and its allies in the West.[56] The second examined Muslim communities in the United States and American views of Islam.[57] While conducting these studies, I discovered that the numerous and influential Muslim groups with a tribal background that live on borders between states and form the periphery of their nation were often overlooked by many in the discussion about U.S. and Muslim relations. Hence this work is concerned with precisely those interstices between borders where tribal Islam is found.

A good deal of my academic work and professional career has been spent studying and administering tribal communities, the one part of my life feeding the other. At different times, I was the political agent in charge of South Waziristan and Orakzai Agencies. I served as commissioner of three divisions consecutively in Baluchistan. My Ph.D. thesis focused exclusively on the Mohmand tribe in the Tribal Areas of Pakistan, and I coauthored a study that compared tribes across continents and regions.[58] My study of Waziristan, first published in 1983, found a second life after 9/11.[59] Zeenat, my wife, who accompanied me during my fieldwork and postings, and our daughter Amineh, as she grew into a professional anthropologist, supplemented my information with valuable insights on tribal women.

I felt I had contributed as much as I could to this field and moved on in the 1990s to what I felt was the looming challenge on the horizon: a growing clash between Western and Muslim civilizations. I devoted the next decades, an effort accelerated by 9/11, to generate interfaith dialogue and build bridges between different religions. My most recent studies, *Journey into Islam* (2007) and *Journey into America* (2010), were part of the same momentum. The latter of the two won the American Book Award in 2011, and I was able to speak of its themes in the media, including the *Daily Show with Jon Stewart*. In the midst of trying to explain Islam to America, I became concerned about reports filtering through the thick curtain of obfuscation and disinformation hanging over the Tribal Areas of Pakistan. All was not well there. My thoughts drifted to my earlier academic interest—tribal societies. I had left them decades ago, those rather special people, seemingly safe and secure in their remote mountains and valleys. Although a posting in Waziristan was considered one of the most difficult and dangerous of assignments, I often thought of its land and people with nostalgia.

The feeling was not unlike that expressed by Sir Evelyn Howell on looking back on his time in Waziristan from the tranquility of Cambridge in England. Howell had shared his sentiments shortly before he died with his friend Caroe, who wrote to me: "When I met him in Cambridge about four years ago he said so many years had gone by. But he would feel happier in the mountain ranges of Waziristan. It was, he said, precisely because that was the most dangerous period of his life that it had become the period that he loved most. Often in his dreams he found himself in Waziristan, and his heart flying in those precipitous gorges."[60]

That is why, when I first heard that President Pervez Musharraf had launched an ill-thought-out and hastily conceived military invasion of Waziristan in 2004, ostensibly under American pressure, I was distressed. As a political officer once in charge there, I knew these actions would not end well for the United States, Pakistan, or the tribes. I then heard of Musharraf's order to attack the Baluch tribal leader Nawab Akbar Bugti, whom I knew when I was commissioner in Baluchistan. The military action in 2006 inevitably resulted in the Nawab's death. With mounting anxiety, I began making inquiries, only to receive disturbing reports from both Waziristan and Baluchistan that confirmed my fears. It was time, I felt, to pause and reflect on the missing part of the jigsaw puzzle in the trilogy. I hoped my expertise in tribal studies would benefit all concerned—the communities on the periphery and the people at the center, Americans and non-Americans alike.

Reminders of my past life began to arrive in Washington. One came in the form of a letter from a young man called Akbar. He said his father, Iftikhar Ahmed, named him after me as a token of respect and affection—his father had been my personal assistant in Orakzai Agency. Iftikhar then went on to become a political officer himself in North Waziristan Agency, where he was recently assassinated by the Taliban. I recall Iftikhar from my days as political agent as a quiet, gentle, and energetic young man. I was sorry to hear that he had become a target of the violence in Waziristan. I realized quickly that the relationship between the tribes of Waziristan, predominately the Wazir and the Mahsud, and the central government of Pakistan had become complicated after 9/11, and each party was now involved in the war on terror in different ways. The result was widespread chaos in the Tribal Areas. I began to hear of suicide bombers, and by 2010 even more disturbing reports of female suicide bombers, although their activity appeared to be restricted to Peshawar and the northern agencies. I knew that they were violating both tribal and Islamic traditions that categorically reject suicide and indiscriminate murder. I sensed that something terrible was happening among the people I had served.

The images of the people I had once met in the remote villages and settlements now came flooding back to me. These people were invariably poor, but they always impressed me with their dignity, faith, and hospitality. At that time, with all the authority I had vested in me as the representative of the central state, I could assist in so many ways. If I could do nothing for them, they still seemed happy to simply talk with me over a cup of tea. All they wanted in return was to be heard; they were grateful that by being with them I had acknowledged their humanity, and by treating them with respect I had honored them. Now, decades later and thousands of miles away, I felt that in my own limited way, as an academic on campus, I could employ my scholarship to give them a voice.

Many anthropologists, once secure in the safety of their professional lives, tend to return to their fieldwork location. They have many reasons; some have an urge to write their memoirs, others to express plain nostalgia. I, too, returned to the past. My journey had a specific purpose, however. It was to build a model of society based in the time I was there, which would allow comparison with the present. One could thus see what had changed and what remained of the past. I was particularly interested in those social institutions, such as leadership structures and the code of honor, that had helped to define society in my time.

I also had personal reasons for feeling emotionally involved with the Pukhtun. My mother was the daughter of Sir Hashmatullah Khan, whose Barakzai forefathers came from Afghanistan to India. Zeenat, my wife, is the granddaughter of the Wali of Swat, the direct descendant of the Akhund of Swat, and my daughter Amineh is married to Arsallah Khan Hoti, whose Hoti clan is considered the aristocrats among the Yusufzai, the aristocratic tribe of the Pukhtun. I believed I understood the way of the Pukhtuns and admired them. My father was the opposite of tribal in every way. Born in Allahabad, India, deep in the Ganges Valley, descended from holy lineages, he was a senior civil servant with the British Raj, and then, when it was created, in Pakistan, and spent the last part of his career with the United Nations in Bangkok. His gentle, inclusive Sufi Islam gave him the moral compass to interact with the different cultures and religions he encountered over the span of his life contentedly and calmly. I admired him immensely, and in him I saw the Sufi precept *sulh-i-kul* or "peace with all."

Besides, as a father and grandfather myself, I was concerned about the kind of world my children and grandchildren would be living in. If the Pukhtun and Baluch faced such severe challenges, I could only imagine the predicament of other similar tribes like the Somalis, Yemenis, Bedouin, Kurds, Fulani, or Tuareg. I contemplated the fate of these traditional peoples, renowned in history as proud warriors, and worried that they would be vulnerable and adrift in the age of globalization.

Reactions from the Field

As my team and I began putting together the material for this book, interviewing individuals associated with our case studies and publishing articles about the people we were studying, we received positive feedback indicating that we were on the right track. When Al Jazeera offered to publish a series of op-eds, I coauthored them with Frankie Martin and Harrison Akins, my senior research assistants, each one covering a different country and its problematic relationship with its periphery. With this exercise, we hoped to obtain a sense of how people would react to the ideas we were exploring in our study. The responses from the individuals living in the periphery were overwhelmingly positive in that by sharing their innermost thinking, it confirmed for us both the direction of our study and its integrity. After reading the article on his people, a Sinai Bedouin tribesman sent the following message:

> I am Said Khedr, from the Aleghat Bedouin tribe. I would like to thank you for writing the article, "No Arab Spring for the Sinai Bedouin." It is spreading quickly through the community here, and our many friends around the world. I hope that the Egyptian authorities will learn from your example, for they have never taken the time to study us or get to know us as you have. We are finding our feet in the new political system in South Sinai. Articles like this, by people like you, are very welcome support. Thank you again, and if I can ever be of help in the Sinai, please let me know.

After he read our op-ed on the Tausug, Neldy Jolo, a Tausug writer and activist from the Philippines, wrote to Frankie—addressing him as "Sir" out of traditional respect and with no intention, I am sure, of appropriating Queen Elizabeth's prerogative to confer knighthood: "Waalaikumsalam Sir Frankie," he began. "Warm regards from our Tausug comrades. Thank you very much. Your article last time indeed help[ed] and boosted the Tausug cry for peace. It really helps. Your coming book is indeed helpful to any people of the world, especially those of oppressed." An Eritrean reading our op-ed on Eritrea expressed his gratitude: "Thank you so much for writing about this. It's so rare to hear news agencies speak about Eritrean people. . . . [T]hey have become the Forgotten people. We really need more people to speak out!"

Wakar Uddin, a professor at Pennsylvania State University and a leading figure in the Rohingya community, became an ardent supporter of our project: "On behalf of Rohingya people, I would like to express our heartfelt gratitude to you for your persistent support for the oppressed Rohingya people. Again, your article will go a long way in fighting for the cause of Rohingya human rights and political rights. Thank you very much." Iyad Youghar, chairman of the International Circassian Council, was equally enthusiastic about our Al Jazeera op-ed: "This is a great paper on Circassians. It is the best I have read. It is like a statement Circassians will be able to use always to tell about our plight."

Ufuk Gokcen, the Organization of Islamic Cooperation's (OIC's) ambassador to the United Nations, also acknowledged our efforts: "I am following with admiration and appreciation the series of articles that you have been posting one by one on the issues that are part of your new study." The OIC is one of the few Muslim organizations that have made courageous, if not entirely successful, attempts to improve the plight of societies included in our study, such as the Rohingya. The scholarly OIC secretary general, Ekmeleddin Ihsanoglu, appreciated the scope of the project and noted its importance given the lack of "justice and human rights and the humanitarian crisis that exists in many areas."

After I was interviewed for the Pakistani newspaper *Dawn* by Malik Siraj Akbar, a Baluch journalist who had been given political asylum in Washington, D.C., and my article on Baluchistan appeared in Al Jazeera, Malik sent this note: "Your presence among us is a blessing and your voice is one of sanity in the midst of insanity that prevails and dominates Pakistan's power circles. I have heard from many Baluch friends who loved your quotes and advice. They may not have your contact details but they asked me from Baluchistan to convey their gratitude to you for your kind support." The article's comment section included expressions of encouragement like "Dr. Ahmed is an asset to all Muslims. Very intelligent, nice and logical person, wish we had someone of his calibre at the top of Pakistan's ruling class right now."

My team and I also received negative responses from people who felt we were exaggerating the suffering of people on the periphery. Commentators who represented their country's majority views were always more numerous and well organized than those on the periphery. Their views were as fixed about the periphery as those of the periphery about them. We were accused, especially me, of being "American agents," purveyors of "Zionist ideas," and "Muslim fundamentalists," and I was called a "Muslim traitor."

Examining the Interstices

All members of my team were meticulous in attempting to locate information for our case studies. We read as much of the literature as possible—colonial, literary, ethnographic, and the post-9/11 work that is often framed in the context of the war on terror. We interviewed members of both the center and the periphery. We made a special effort to track down those from the periphery in the field and were able to interview them both in face-to-face situations and through the marvels of Skype. We shared ideas and material in the book with the acknowledged experts and scholars at the established universities. However, we need to add a caveat about statistics concerning tribal societies. Due to their remote nature, the displacement of populations, and the reluctance of central governments to acknowledge them, population figures are difficult to ascertain with accuracy.

We also found that invariably all figures relating to instances of mass killing involving the center and the periphery are disputed, as in the case of Armenians under the Ottomans and Bengalis at the hands of the Pakistanis. Our approach has been to consult the most authoritative sources possible. It is important to point out for the record that even in our post-9/11 age of globalization with the unprecedented and free access to information, figures of numbers killed as a result of drone strikes and other military actions, or even confirmation that they ever took place or where they took place, are shrouded in darkness. The American Civil Liberties Union, for example, estimated that some 4,000 people have been killed by drone strikes, but this figure has been questioned by other organizations. There appears to be a deliberate attempt by official agencies in the war on terror to obfuscate and distort.

Although this study is anchored in the field of anthropology, I am acutely aware that other disciplines outside my own need to be consulted in order to fully examine tribal societies. We therefore turned to political scientists to tell us about the political systems in which they operate and the limitations of the state that they must deal with. We needed scholars of religion to inform us whether in fact some of the actions of the Muslim tribes can be traced to Quranic verses and whether their use is sanctioned. Authorities in international law were best suited to comment on matters such as rendition, regime change, and the legality of military actions like drone strikes. Human rights activists dealt with subjects such as torture and violations of the rights of individuals. Experts in international relations and development commented on the role of multinational corporations in our age of globalization and their impact on the periphery. In sum, our methodology has been to rely on a number of disciplines in order to develop as full and as rich an understanding of our subject as possible.

When I discuss "segmentary lineage systems" and "models," readers must not lose sight of the fact that these are abstract terms employed to provide an idea of reality on the basis of surveys and aggregates. So when I place communities into categories, keep in mind that this is little more than an exercise in imagination and merely the basis for further discussion and debate. These categories are not watertight and frequently overlap.

Our findings are presented in the form of forty "case studies" of peripheral societies and their relationship to the central state. These are not typical case studies that are expected to provide detailed ethnographic descriptions of history, culture, and contemporary affairs of one particular community. While we have examined the societies represented by these cases thoroughly, our method is to select the most striking episodes, events, and anecdotes to illustrate the relationship between center and periphery.

In examining distinct ethnic and tribal groups spread over three continents—they span Muslim communities from Morocco to the Philippines—we first had to decide how to classify them. We chose the sociological route by dividing them into four broad social categories. The first category consists of our core case studies of segmentary lineage systems that have a highly developed code of honor and that have been the main targets of drones in America's war on terror. These societies have over time split into nang (honor) and qalang (taxes and rent) populations, the former being the one explored in this book. Our core case studies examine four societies of the nang type: the Pukhtun of Afghanistan and the Tribal Areas of Pakistan; the Somali of the Horn of Africa; the Yemenis of Yemen and the Asir and Najran regions of Saudi Arabia; and the Kurds of Turkey, Iran, Iraq, and Syria.

The second category consists of Muslim societies rooted in the segmentary lineage system in the recent or distant past but not yet widely associated with the U.S. drone war. Our case studies in this category, listed alphabetically, include the Acehnese of Aceh Province in Northern Sumatra, Indonesia; the Ahwazi, Qashqai, and Bakhtiari of southern Iran; the Albanians of Albania, Kosovo, Montenegro, and Macedonia; the Avars and Lezgins of Russian Dagestan and Azerbaijan; the Azeris of Azerbaijan and northern Iran; the Baluch of Pakistan and Iran; the Bedouin tribes split between the Egyptian Sinai, the Negev Desert of Israel, and the Palestinian territories; the Rif and Atlas Berbers of Morocco; the Chechens of Chechnya in Russia; the Circassians of the Republics of Kabardino-Balkaria, Adyghe, and Karachay-Cherkessia in Russia, with their diaspora populations in Turkey, Jordan, Syria, and the West; the Fulani of northern Nigeria, Ghana, Senegal, and many other West African countries; the Ingush of Ingushetia and North Ossetia, Russia; the Jola of southern Senegal and The Gambia; the Kabyle Berbers of northern Algeria; the Kanuri of northeastern Nigeria, Chad, and Niger; the Karakalpaks of western Uzbekistan; the Nuba of southern Sudan along the new border with South Sudan; the Oromo of Ethiopia and Kenya; the Palestinians of Gaza and the West Bank; the Sahrawi of Moroccan-administered Western Sahara, with their large refugee populations in western Algeria; the Talysh of Azerbaijan and Iran; the Tuareg of the Sahel found predominately in Mali, Niger, and Algeria; the Turkmens of Turkmenistan, Iran, and Afghanistan; the Uyghur of Xinjiang Province of western China; and the Uzbeks of Uzbekistan, Afghanistan, and Kyrgyzstan. In addition, we examined holy lineages and tribes that became royal dynasties, including those in Morocco, Jordan, and on the Arabian Peninsula in Saudi Arabia, Kuwait, United Arab Emirates, Bahrain, Oman, and Qatar, along with the stateless workers of the Gulf nations known as the Bidoon.

The third category consists of Muslim societies that do not operate on segmentary lineage principles but are segmented tribal societies organized into clans not based on the lineage charter. These societies nonetheless have a highly developed code of honor and thus exhibit important characteristics of the nang segmentary lineage tribesmen. Segmented tribal case studies cover the Tausug, Maguindanao, and other Muslim groups of the southern Philippines, and the Malays of South Thailand.

Fourth, I provide supplementary case studies of Muslim societies that are not necessarily tribal in the context of our study but do reflect the larger tension between center and periphery. These groups include the Cham of Cambodia and Vietnam; the Kashmiris of Indian and Pakistani Kashmir; the Mandinka people of The Gambia, Ivory Coast, and several other West African countries; and the Rohingya of Arakan State in western Burma/Myanmar, with a large refugee population in eastern Bangladesh and elsewhere in South Asia.

Apart from the forty case studies, additional material is also provided to support the argument that if the center does not accommodate Muslim peoples on the periphery, it will most likely treat non-Muslim minority communities in the same unfair manner. Non-Muslims in Muslim nations—Christians in Egypt, Bahai in Iran, and Hindus and Christians in Pakistan—have long complained about being persecuted. But similarly, non-Muslim peripheries in non-Muslim nations, such as the Tibetans and Mongolians in China and the Nagas, Adivasis, and Sikhs in India, have a long list of grievances against the center. Each case is different, yet each falls within the frame of this study.

In all the cases just mentioned, and there are many more in each category, the center is failing to protect its citizens on the periphery and is not giving them their due rights and privileges according to the principles of modern statehood. The poor relationship between center and periphery is clearly not confined to Muslim groups but reflects a larger problem concerning the way in which the modern state is conceived and administered. Even a cursory glance at the case material makes it clear that wherever the tribes have lived and however fierce their resistance, the intensity and scale of the onslaught from the center has created the same results: massive internal disruption in the periphery that has consequences for the center. But these peripheral communities responded differently. Those of Waziristan, for example, were not prepared to submit without a fight and inflicted damage on their tormentors, while the Rohingya appeared to embrace their fate with baffling passivity. The reasons for these different reactions are explored in the following chapters.

The book is divided into six chapters. As should be clear by now, the first provides an outline of the main arguments. Chapter 2 is a study of Waziristan built on sound information and research, confirming that the Wazir and Mahsud tribes living there closely approximated to the segmentary lineage system. The terrain and nature of Waziristan's tribes have historically ensured the maximum possible isolation. I have written extensively about the region, lived among its people, and come to know its clans, their code, and their customs. I am in touch with them and am aware of their current situation. My information from three decades ago—the standard anthropological period for one generation—is used to construct the "Waziristan model" and to compare the situation then with that of today and thereby determine what changes have taken place over this period.

As a rough and ready construct, the Waziristan model makes it possible to examine similar tribal societies elsewhere in the context of their current relationship with their central governments. Indeed, elements of the Waziristan model can be recognized in the Pukhtun of the Tribal Areas in Pakistan and eastern Afghanistan, the Chechens, the Bedouin, the Kurds, and the tribes of Somalia, Yemen, and eastern Libya. It can also be seen among the Tausug in the Philippines and the Malay in Thailand, with their segmented clans and highly developed codes of honor. The model may also shed light on what contributes to peace and stability in tribal society and what does not. This is especially relevant in the post-9/11 world.

The next three chapters are structurally linked, and the findings in one have bearing on the others. Chapter 3 is about the dilemma an individual in tribal society faces in balancing the compulsions of religion and those of tribal customs. Chapter 4 turns to tribal relations with the center, and the need for it to accommodate the periphery while maintaining the writ of the state. It is the longest chapter because it depicts the historical sweep of the case studies and puts them in the context of the book's conceptual frame; without this background, it is well-nigh impossible to fully understand relations between the center and periphery. Chapter 5 continues the narrative in the context of the United States struggling to balance its security concerns and the imperative to preserve human rights and civil liberties. Together, the three chapters illustrate the tribal, national, and international levels of conflict since 9/11.

Chapter 6 shows why the United States—despite its resolve, resources, and sophisticated techniques in information gathering—has failed to understand the nature of tribal societies and the consequences of this failure. It calls for a realignment of the paradigm propelling the war on terror thus far and presents our findings and concrete recommendations for shifting from a confrontational approach to one aimed at peace and stability. Otherwise, death and destruction will continue their rampage across the world, bringing entire communities to the brink of cultural, economic, and even physical disaster. This volume's journey into tribal societies begins in Waziristan, the epicenter of the war on terror.

2

WAZIRISTAN:

"The Most Dangerous Place in the World"

Three decades before President George W. Bush began his manhunt for Osama bin Laden, the most wanted individual on his terrorist list and hiding among the tribes along the border between Afghanistan and Pakistan, I had faced a similar challenge, but in a different context and on a different scale. As political agent in charge of South Waziristan Agency, I was tasked with bringing in Safar Khan, the most wanted man in my area, an outlaw who was also hiding among the same tribes on the same border as bin Laden.

Just as the job Bush held made him the most powerful man in the world, mine made me the most powerful man in the agency. And just as Bush was determined to keep the United States safe and believed bin Laden needed to be captured in order to do so, I believed Safar Khan needed to be brought to justice for the safety of the agency, although his crimes clearly did not match those of bin Laden.

In the end, it was not Bush but his successor, Barack Obama, who located and killed bin Laden. But it would take a decade of war costing trillions of dollars, with hundreds of thousands of lives lost and millions displaced. Entire nations would be thrown into turmoil and the world put on high alert. I got my man alive without a single shot being fired. The writ of the government was established, justice served, and the guilty man brought to book. The difference was that I worked entirely within the tribal framework and traditional social structure.

Safar Khan (pronounced Sappar Khan), a Mando Khel Pukhtun from Baluchistan, had resorted to an infamous life of crime, raiding, and kidnapping after concluding he had been treated unfairly by the political agent (PA) of his agency following a land dispute with a neighboring clan. I had discovered that breaches of law such as shooting at or even kidnapping government officials were sometimes a desperate attempt to draw attention to an imagined or real grievance. It was the equivalent of presenting a written petition for redress to the administration. Safar Khan was involved in outright criminal acts, however, and had to be dealt with accordingly.

Safar eventually allied himself with the Kharoti Pukhtun outlaw Nemat, a "most wanted man" in both Zhob Agency in Baluchistan and South Waziristan Agency for having killed two officers of the Zhob Militia, a paramilitary force linked to and manned by the Pakistan army. In the 1960s and 1970s, Safar Khan's notoriety grew as the major offenses attributed to him mounted, among them the destruction of railway bridges and the abduction of government officials, both civil and military. Various councils of elders, jirgas, and raiding parties had failed to capture him as he moved adroitly between distinct tribal, agency, provincial, and international boundaries.

Then, in a daring and perfectly executed operation in November 1979, Safar Khan kidnapped Lance-Naik (Lance Corporal) Baramat Khan of the Zhob Militia and escaped with his prey across the border into Afghanistan. The militia's colonel and the inspector general of the Baluchistan Frontier Corps, General Alam Jan Mahsud, were furious about Khan's apparent ability to operate without check. Both officers were Pukhtun themselves—in fact, Alam Jan was from South Waziristan—and felt that their honor was at stake. They threatened to conduct commando raids. The general challenged me, half in earnest: either to "bag Safar Khan" or step aside and let him use his tactics. As civilian head of the agency, I strongly felt that the use of military force to solve a tribal problem implied a failure of the civil administration and would complicate matters further. Advising the general to be patient, I concentrated on the capture of Safar Khan.

Once word got out, I simply had to get my man and do so within a certain time frame. My prestige was on the line. It was a high-risk strategy. If I failed, my administration would have been considered ineffective, and others would have been encouraged to challenge it. The tribes would have said I could not live up to my word, that my threats and promises were hollow. As so often happens on the frontier, I was thrown into a situation not of my choosing in which failure or success would determine my reputation. The question was how to proceed when the effectiveness of a political officer was defined by factors outside his control.

I decided to send messages to Safar Khan in Afghanistan through the Wazir, a tribe whose members lived on both sides of the international border and were harboring him. I had won over the Wazir only a few months earlier when I had made a dramatic and risky visit to the grave of their ancestor, Musa Nikka at Birmal, along the lawless and undemarcated international border, often referred to as the Durand Line. No government official, British or Pakistani, had ever visited this dangerous area before. The tribesmen, alienated by the previous administration, saw the visit as a gesture of respect for their ancestor.[1] At the same time, I contacted the outlaw Nemat through Abdul Maalik, a prominent Mahsud elder of the Shabi Khel clan, who was hostile to the administration until I appealed to his sense of honor and earned his loyalty. After lengthy negotiations, Safar was promised a fair trial by jirga in Baluchistan, where his crimes were committed,

The outlaw Safar Khan seated in front of the author with a tribal *jirga* in 1980 (author's collection).

if he surrendered to me. I assured him that I would also speak with the political agent in Zhob to see that he was treated fairly under tribal custom, but I could only do this if he came to me unconditionally. The exchanges were thick with the words "trust" and "honor." Safar agreed. In January 1980, accompanied by the leading Wazir and Mahsud *malik*s (elders), Safar formally surrendered to me along with Nemat, who swore loyalty to Pakistan.

Safar was brought to the PA's bungalow in Tank and in the photograph taken on the occasion—of him, myself, and the elders—he is crouched sullenly at our feet while the rest of us are standing.[2] The picture illustrates not only the unity between the elders and the political agent regarding Safar but also the reality that like many men with a fearsome reputation, he was rather unimpressive in person.

The jirga traveled to Baluchistan like a victory procession with Safar Khan as their prize. The Zhob Militia there escorted him from the border. Safar's traditional rivals suspended their animosity and held a dinner for the jirga, in keeping with Pukhtunwali, to indicate their desire for peace and a healing of past wounds. The jirga, after concluding its often tense proceedings, announced a settlement of the original land dispute that was largely satisfactory to both parties involved, binding them to sureties worth 200,000 rupees each. More important, the jirga ensured Safar's future good behavior. From my opening moves to reach Safar to the tribal jirga in Baluchistan, the long months were filled with intense negotiations, lengthy meetings, favors called in, theatrical flourishes that conveyed threats and promises, and the determination to persevere with the patience of a saint. The slightest thing, even an imagined insult, could have caused the entire proceedings to unravel. By working within traditional tribal structures based on codes of honor and negotiating with various clans, particularly the fearsome Shabi Khel—from which would later emerge the most notorious of the Taliban mutations, the Tehrik-e-Taliban Pakistan (TTP)—I was able to "bag my man" without bloodshed.

Today all major decisions and initiatives in this area are being made by military officials, whereas the entire operation to get Safar Khan was led by the civil administration in close cooperation with tribal elders and within the region's larger tribal networks that crossed several borders. This fact was acknowledged by none other than the militia's delighted colonel in an official letter to me when his junior officer was returned to him: "I will not hesitate to say that where all possible force failed to achieve desired results your political maneuver was unique for unconditional and prompt recovery of the individual from *Ferari* (outlaw). I must appreciate that this is such a precedence which has never been set by any civil administration, particularly in agency area in the past."[3]

Writing to the governor and martial law administrator of Baluchistan, an equally pleased inspector general pointed out the complicated nature of the case because Safar Khan was "alternately under the tutelage of certain Wazirs along the border and some tribes within Afghanistan," and he highly commended the civil administration for its role: "The surrender of Safar Khan . . . could not have been secured without the resolute and adroit handling of the case by Political Agent South Waziristan Mr. Akbar S. Ahmed. In fact, it will not be amiss to state that but for P.A. South Waziristan's efforts and political acumen, this surrender which has had a healthy effect all over the area, would not have materialized."[4]

The strategy I had adopted was not new. My predecessors in the British Empire, who had set up the administrative structure through which the Pakistan government functioned, had discovered early on the most effective method for dealing with such cases. As Sir Olaf Caroe noted, "The principle seemed simple and sage enough; if you want to get anything done in dealings with tribes, work through the tribal organization; let the tribal leaders produce the goods in their own way. In other words, it was the principle of indirect rule."[5] Caroe gives the example from the late nineteenth century of a British political agent tasked with apprehending five Mahsud tribesmen who had murdered a British Public Works Department officer in Zhob. Working within the tribal structure, the PA was able to secure the surrender of the men by means of prolonged negotiations reinforced by personal relationships with the elders. In the end, the accused submitted to a trial by jirga. The case of Safar Khan thus reflects the traditions of tribal administration on the frontier.

About the time that I was dealing with Safar Khan, Soviet troops were pouring into Afghanistan. Their action triggered a sequence of events that would involve not only Afghans but also, over the next three decades, Pakistanis, Americans,

Federally Administered Tribal Areas and North-West Frontier Province of Pakistan (wikimedia.org).

Indians, Arabs, NATO, and others; it would give rise to the Taliban and the TTP, the drone attacks, and the chaos that erupted in Waziristan.

I did not know it then, but I was standing on the cusp of history, straddling the past and the future in ways that became clear only in retrospect. From the past, I had met the legendary British officers who had dealt with this land and its peoples: Sir Evelyn Howell, Caroe, and M. M. Kaye, the novelist who wrote popular romantic stories about them. A handwritten letter from T. E. Lawrence thanking the South Waziristan Scouts for their hospitality was still displayed in the mess hall in the Wana camp, the headquarters of the political agent, and the basic British administrative, tribal, and political structures were still in place.

The bugle still sounded at sunset to indicate the end of the day and the closing of Wana's gates. Even into the 1970s, electricity and telephone lines were a rarity except for a rather precarious one along the main road.

Decades later, on March 27, 2009, I was in the audience at the White House when the newly elected president Barack Obama outlined his policy for Afghanistan and Pakistan. It would focus in large measure on the Federally Administered Tribal Areas of Pakistan (FATA), declaring it "the most dangerous place in the world." The FATA is a semi-autonomous tribal region in the northwest of present-day Pakistan along the Afghan border and is composed of administrative districts known as agencies. Obama's military advisers had no doubt rightly concluded that Waziristan, which consists of two agencies—North Waziristan and South Waziristan—was the most important part of the Tribal Areas. Although the Afridi, the Mohmand, and other FATA tribes had as fierce a reputation as Waziristan's Wazir and Mahsud, only South Waziristan Agency had an international border to the west and a provincial border to the south, and abutted the settled districts in the east. Its borders were a sieve that provided escape routes to possible fugitives from the law like Safar Khan. It was inevitable that the focus of the American military campaign in Afghanistan would shift to Waziristan.

Within my lifetime, I have observed the old structures of society in Waziristan beginning to crumble. New names like George W. Bush, Dick Cheney, Osama bin Laden, Ayman al-Zawahiri, Pervez Musharraf, Hamid Karzai, and Barack Obama were now, directly or indirectly, intertwined with that of Waziristan. This small area would be the target of one of the most concentrated drone campaigns on earth.

What I could not imagine for a moment as a PA in the 1970s was that one day an event across the world in the United States would bring a series of unprecedented and unwelcome developments to this very area; that it would become the target of a new kind of weapon; that a new breed of Muslim warriors called suicide bombers would blow themselves up slaughtering women, children, passengers, and worshippers in mosques, targeting especially the very elders and officials who had helped me apprehend Safar Khan; that the Pakistan army, whose officers were seconded to Waziristan to protect its people, would indiscriminately launch a series of invasions on its tribes as if they were a foreign enemy; that Pukhtunwali, the code that defined these tribes and was the core of tribal identity, would be shattered; that Waziristan, so famously inaccessible, would one day become the focus of the world's attention in the first truly global war of the twenty-first century as Americans pursued an elusive group called al Qaeda; and that hundreds of thousands of tribal peoples from this area would be driven out as destitute refugees to live on charity outside the agency, waiting for the time they could return home.

The question for all parties involved was how to approach the relationship between the past and the future—that is, how best to apply lessons from the past, if they are apt and suitably adjusted, as guideposts in the future. Problematically, neither the Americans nor the Pakistanis were known for attending to the lessons of history. If they had done so, the Americans would have asked themselves why Afghanistan was called the graveyard of empires and approached it with less arrogance and ignorance; and Pakistanis would not have attempted a military solution in the Tribal Areas and thus put themselves in danger of repeating their catastrophic handling of East Pakistan (see the appendix). Obviously, neither the Americans nor the Pakistanis were aware, as Caroe pointed out in his history of the Pukhtuns, that "no empire of which we have any record has ever succeeded in making subjects of the tribes of Waziristan."[6]

THE WAZIRISTAN MODEL

The case of Safar Khan demonstrates how a common objective can be achieved when different components of a society such as that in Waziristan function together within the local cultural frame: traditional tribal leaders, religious leaders, and the political administration. By approaching Waziristan from an anthropological perspective, I was able to develop a model describing how those components with their various sources of authority functioned and interacted with one another.[7] The Waziristan model, it should be emphasized, is applicable to a great degree to the other thistle-like nang tribes in the Tribal Areas of Pakistan, and in significant ways, as explained shortly, to tribes of a similar nature elsewhere.

The Three Sources of Authority

The Waziristan model posits three distinct, overlapping, and in some ways mutually interdependent, though often in opposition, sources of authority: (1) the tribal elder, or malik; (2) the religious leader, or mullah; and (3) the political agent representing the central government. These are the three pillars of authority in tribal society. Each has a symbiotic relationship with the others while using them as a foil. This three-way relationship is inevitably a changing and dynamic one as each pillar strives for dominance.

The pillar formed by the elders represents lineage-based authority vested in the jirga (council of elders) and expressed through Pukhtunwali (the tribe's code). The elders derive authority from their position in the segmentary lineage system with its genealogical charter, and that authority is understood in terms of the charter or *nikkat*—which literally means grandfather or ancestor. Nikkat confers certain privileges and status while defining responsibilities.

Nikkat was the central principle by which Wazir and Mahsud tribes organized themselves and adjudicated contentious matters. It was codified in the time of the first Afghan king, Ahmad Shah Abdali, in the mid-eighteenth century on the basis of their relative populations and set forth in a formal agreement between the tribes. Henceforth the agreement established the basis for all dealings, privileges, responsibilities, and distribution of lands between the tribes, clans, and subclans. As political agent, I was frequently confronted with the mathematical reality of nikkat in tribal society. The PA's place of residence, for example, was based on nikkat: he spent eight months of the year among the Mahsud in Tank and four in Wana in Wazir territory. The PA's personal escort, or *badragga,* especially when on tour, consisted of thirty tribesmen drawn from clans and subclans according to nikkat. The PA's personal bodyguard unit, which protected him round the clock, consisted of five Mahsud and one Wazir. Any suggestions about reducing the number or utilizing the bodyguard in a more practical or useful way was met by a storm of protest. It would upset the delicate balance of nikkat, tribesmen would argue. Violation of traditional understanding of nikkat frequently led to feuds.

Given the centrality of nikkat, rivalry between male cousins (*tarboor*) is intense. Cousin rivalry, especially in matters of marriage and political or social leadership, operates through a code called *tarboorwali,* normatively seen as important as Pukhtunwali. Agnatic rivalry and a mechanism to contain it characterize the predominant marriage patterns between cousins. In this way, political power and economic wealth are kept within the family and the integrity of the lineage maintained.

The second source of authority is also linked to traditional tribal life as it rests with the mullahs who are usually appointed by elders to tend to the mosque and provide young boys an Islamic education in *madrassahs,* or Islamic schools. Because the mullah is not on the tribal charter, nor part of nikkat, he does not have a place in the jirga and remains essentially an outsider. These mullahs are typically not the learned imams educated at the great centers of Islam but represent the tribal and informal Islam discussed in chapter 1.

Elders have successfully challenged mullahs on the most sensitive of public issues such as education and war. When Mir Badshah, the father of General Alam Jan Mahsud (the same general I encountered during the Safar Khan incident), opened a school in the agency during the time of the British, the local mullah gathered a large armed group along with a drummer to burn it down because it was viewed as a symbol of British imperialism. Mir Badshah resisted, and firing was exchanged. The mullah's horse was shot from under him. Two people died in the shooting. But because Mir Badshah stood up to the mullah, the school survived. In another instance, when Mullah Fazal Din, the son of Mullah Powindah who had gained fame fighting the British, criticized Mir Badshah for his battle tactics in Kashmir in 1947, Mir Badshah reprimanded the mullah and told him to leave matters of war to tribal elders and concentrate on his own job of leading the prayers. The laws of revenge stay in effect, however, until the matter is resolved. Decades later Alam Jan feared that the mullah's supporters were still seeking ways to harm him and his family.

In an interview for this study, Alam Jan did not fail to blame the religious clerics for the chaos in Waziristan today, calling the mullah a *shudra* (low-caste Hindu, implying a man of low social standing). Of course, during times of social upheaval—invariably linked to invasions of Waziristan—the mullah could assume an overarching leadership role in spite of being outside the lineage charter. In such a situation, the fact that the mullah was, by definition, not part of local agnatic rivalry would play to his advantage as he could unite feuding clans.

Because the tribes of Waziristan, like other Pukhtun groups, indeed most other nang tribes, consider themselves unequivocally Sunni Muslim, this association gives the mullah a confirmed position in society as he leads them in prayer and teaches their children the Islamic faith. The leadership role of religious figures can expand and contract, however, depending on the personality and skills of the individuals. In religious matters, they see themselves as the champions of Islam, the final arbiters on matters of faith. They say this loudly and aggressively when their position is unassailable, less loudly in normal times.

Despite its isolation, Waziristan has consistently produced religious leaders who have made a large mark on the history of the region: the Pir-i-Roshan in the sixteenth century; Mullah Powindah, the Fakir of Ipi, and the Shami Pir in the first half of the twentieth century (all three were well known to British political officers in Waziristan); and in the second half, Mullah Shahzada Tajudin, the grandson of Mullah Powindah and a Shabi Khel Mahsud tribesman, and Mullah Noor Muhammad of the Wazir. When I took charge, Shahzada had been urging his followers to attack electric poles and the conductors attached to them along the main road as they represented the genitals of the devil. Shahzada was rejecting modernity, which included development projects such as electricity, because he saw it as an encroachment on traditional life and independence. He was persuaded to desist only after a long, tense, and tortuous series of indirect negotiations, complicated by the fact that he was aware of being out of my reach deep in mountainous Mahsud territory. Mullah Noor Muhammad, who had dominated politics among the Wazir just before I arrived, was in prison outside the agency throughout my tenure.

The third source of authority is the office and person of the political agent, who represents the central government. I discuss the PA in greater detail in the next section and in the context of British administration. Suffice to say, he needed to rely on his wits and considerable resources to keep his foot in the tribal door. The mullah often clashed with the PA, considering his office outdated as it originated with the Christian colonial power. After the creation of Pakistan, the two represented fundamentally opposed interpretations of Islam: the PA a modern, nationalist version and the mullah a more traditionalist and tribal one.

Each source of authority needed to underline its religious legitimacy in a society so self-consciously Muslim. Tribal leaders emphasized the mythological memory of their common ancestor Qais and his conversion to Islam by the Prophet himself. The mullahs reminded their listeners that the Prophet had emphasized a religious identity over a tribal identity. The PA—along with the entire administrative apparatus—was extraneous to tribal society and therefore had to overcompensate in order to successfully engage with it by acting with the utmost neutrality, fairness, and understanding. Unlike their British predecessors, Pakistani PAs had the advantage of being able to share in Muslim ritual activity such as prayer.

Of course, the Waziristan model is merely an ideal construct and a useful way of entering the society under study. Even in my time, there were rumblings of discontent about the pillars of authority. I found tribal elders entrenched in their status and privileges because of their access to the PA, which they were reluctant to share with the rest of the tribe. Furthermore, a younger generation—called the *kashar* (the youth) as opposed to the *mashar* (the elder)—had emerged, demanding a greater voice in the agency. Calling for change, the kashar argued that the mashar were selfish and corrupt, nothing more than stooges of the government who exaggerated the role of the genealogical charter and Pukhtunwali to further their own interests. By challenging nikkat, the kashar were, in fact, challenging the very foundations of Waziristan tribal society. Since Waziristan, like the rest of the Tribal Areas, elected its member of Pakistan's national assembly through votes cast by the recognized tribal maliks, they could manipulate the extraordinary powers this conferred on them for personal gain. The kashar agitated for elections to be held on the basis of one man, one vote as in the rest of the country. Also of great concern was the lack of educational and medical facilities, which were appalling and, compared with the rest of the country, unacceptable. Even roads and electricity barely existed and then only to connect one government post to another.

Nevertheless, and in spite of the dramatic changes that began to take place in the late twentieth century, Waziristan still saw a certain kind of stability and continuity. From the time of its creation in the 1890s to my posting there in the late 1970s, except during the incursions by the British between the world wars, the system worked, and there were established mechanisms able to resolve problems. That was the best any administration, constructed as it was then, could hope for, and it can be attributed to the Waziristan model with Pukhtunwali at its heart.

Pukhtunwali: The Code of the Pukhtun

The code of the Pukhtun, generally referred to as Pukhtunwali, is as pervasive and influential as it is elusive and ambiguous. Some call it Pukhtu (the language of the Pukhtun), others *tarboorwali* (the rivalry between male cousins), or even *nangwali* (the code of honor). The Pukhtun code is a combination of hospitality, revenge, and the constant compulsion to safeguard what is normatively understood as honor. It was this combination that was on display every time I visited a Pukhtun home in the Tribal Areas; regardless of the economic situation of the hosts and my insistence on simplicity, there would invariably be a lavish meal with many guests in attendance. Honoring the guest reflects the honor of the host. Indeed, honor is at the core of the concept. "I despise the man who does not guide his life by honor," wrote Khushal Khan Khattak, the seventeenth-century Puhktu poet. "The very word honor drives me mad."[8]

Khattak was right: honor can drive a man insane, as in a story I heard in the Tribal Areas that involved a woman, the most sensitive subject where a man's honor is concerned. It tells of an elder who gave shelter to a couple escaping from a tribal feud and asked his oldest son to care for them. Before long, the son developed a relationship with the man's wife. The man complained to the elder, who responded by arranging a feast. At the end of it, the elder asked everyone to say a prayer, then pulled out his revolver and shot six bullets into his son. After the forty days of Islamic mourning, the elder called on the man to shoot his wife with the same revolver and uphold his honor. Upon her death, the elder adopted the man as his own son and arranged a marriage between him and his dead son's wife.

A tribesman without honor is much like a Christian without a soul. Honor thus has social as much as spiritual content. Transgressions against honor necessitate revenge, which can often get out of hand. This brings to mind a Pukhtu proverb: "He is not a Pukhtoon who does not give a blow in return for a pinch."[9] Elders are expected to convene the jirga and settle cases before the impulse to revenge mushrooms into lengthy and anarchic blood feuds. In several sayings, Pukhtun tribesmen had warned of the destructive power of pursuing honor to the point of obsession. Pukhtuns themselves recognize this prickliness in their character: "Where does the sharpness of the thorn come from (but from the time the plant is born)."[10]

For all their talk of Pukhtunwali and honor, the Pukhtun have a practical and open-minded approach to the world, as captured in the proverb, "In bad days a man calls even a donkey his uncle."[11] In short, Pukhtunwali is about a man's conduct while balancing honor and the need to live in this world.

Pukhtuns pride themselves on Pukhtunwali and see it as entirely consonant with their Islamic identity. The link to the Prophet through their common ancestor was a cultural master stroke: in effect it sanctified Pukhtunwali and nikkat, which meant that almost every kind of local custom had some religious cover, however tenuous. The segmentary lineage system itself was now blessed, as it were, by Islam's highest authority. As if to confirm this close relationship, the symbols and practice of Islam are visible and respected in society. Thus there is an almost absolute observance of the fast during the month of Ramadan. Most males, especially the elders, say prayers regularly in the settlement or village mosque. Tribal societies take great pride in the title conferred on its members after the pilgrimage to Mecca: *Hajji* for men or *Hajjan* for women.

When custom does not quite square with Islamic law, however, tribesmen may shrug it off, invoking their relationship to the Prophet, and say with a chuckle, "We are the most loyal of God's believers. How can God be angry with us for a minor trespass?" Among such tribal customs, the father of the bride can demand payment from the groom; a woman suspected of sexual indiscretion may be put to death; a family's females can be excluded from inheritance, especially of land; bloody rivalry between male cousins can last for years; interest can be charged on loans; and Pukhtunwali tends to be glorified over all other forms of identity, including Islam itself.

While Pukhtunwali is an ideal, its actual practice often strays from the original intent of upholding honor, being muddled with agnatic rivalry and attitudes toward women, who are then particularly vulnerable under the manner in which the code and custom are interpreted. In a number of cases I recorded in Waziristan, the misguided attempt to uphold the honor of women accused of adultery led to their deaths, which tribal jirgas justified as being consistent with Pukhtunwali.[12] A woman suspected of compromising her reputation—and that of her family—was said to be *tor*, or black, signifying sin. Since the other party in these cases was often the cousin of the husband or wife, that exacerbated an already tense situation because of agnatic rivalry with the tribesmen using the affair as an excuse to settle old scores, resulting in further deaths.

The soaring ambitions and noble urges of Pukhtunwali and the ideals of egalitarianism are easily subverted by selfish or charismatic individuals who are skillful at building alliances, or those who are newcomers to the area prepared to spend money in order to further a personal agenda. Both the code and family relationships are equally disturbed when individuals migrate out of the agency, new development schemes are brought in, or circumstances change for some other reason, often triggering a redefinition of elements of the code. The violent actions of the TTP reflect such a departure from one of the code's normative principles, that of exacting revenge proportionate to the perceived wrong. Many people in Waziristan have come to believe everyone is now selfish, materialistic, corrupt, and bent on pursuing his or her own interests. The maliks and the mashars have gone, they say; the jirga is ineffective, and Pukhtunwali is dead.

The History of Waziristan

Waziristan is central to this study because of its very isolation, which until recently made it possible to preserve the region's tribal customs and code. With its

Waziristan landscape (Northampton Museums Service, flickr.com).

inaccessible terrain, tribes, and location, it has traditionally been a mysterious land beyond the pale, a hostile and forbidding zone best avoided by visitors and soldiers alike. Waziristan is characterized by high mountains (Preghal is the highest peak at 11,500 feet), a varied and often uninviting landscape ranging from thick forests to deserts, and a climate of extremes, with temperatures reaching 120 degrees Fahrenheit in the summer and well below freezing in the winter. The region's names reflect the harsh terrain: Dozakh Tangi, "the gorge of hell," and Giddar Khula, "the mouth of the jackal." It has aptly been described as "a fortress built by nature for herself, guarded by mountains which serve it in the office of a wall."[13]

It is no coincidence that the "fortress" has provided a safe haven for the TTP, causing mayhem in the Tribal Areas and elsewhere in Pakistan. "Security literature" after 9/11 cites Waziristan as a popular training ground for Muslim insurgents from regions as varied as Libya, Xinjiang, and Chechnya. Not surprisingly, rumor had it that bin Laden first fled to Waziristan from Tora Bora. The very name of the house in Abbottabad where bin Laden lived and was killed—Waziristan House—is an acknowledgment of the importance of the region and its tribes.

The main tribes of Waziristan, the Wazir and the Mahsud, are descended from a common ancestor, Wazir. The Utmanzai Wazir, literally the sons of Utman, live in North Waziristan Agency, and the Ahmadzai, the sons of Ahmad, in South Waziristan. The Mahsud, though also descended from Wazir, have in time taken on a distinct identity as a separate tribe and refer to themselves as *mizh,* which means "we" or "ourselves." While the Wazir and Mahsud have a common ancestor, they have developed distinct characteristics as warriors. Sir

Olaf Caroe likened the Wazir to a panther and the Mahsud to a wolf: "Both are splendid creatures; the panther is slier, sleeker and has more grace, the wolf-pack is more purposeful, more united and more dangerous."[14]

Wazir, the ancestor of the Wazir tribes, was in turn descended from Karlanri, the fourth son of Qais Abdur Rashid, the ancestor of all the Pukhtun tribes. Karlanri was the ancestor of most of the nang tribes of the Tribal Areas, but there is some debate about his relationship to his siblings. Pukhtun tribes descended from Karlanri live on either side of the international border and continue to have strong blood, social, and emotional ties with each other. That is why the Haqqani group, which is based in the Zadran tribe related to the Wazir through Kuki, the descendant of Karlanri, finds such strong support in Waziristan.

The tribes of Waziristan live in small scattered settlements on un-irrigated lands that underline the egalitarian nature of their society. During my time in the South Waziristan Agency in the late 1970s, the latest population census, taken in 1972, registered about 250,000 Mahsud and about 60,000 Wazir (figures in the Tribal Areas are estimates at best). The Mahsud population is concentrated in the eastern part of the agency, away from the international border. Today's population of the two tribes is about double the number of the 1972 populations. Estimates for the entire Tribal Areas range from 3 million to 4 million.

The Thistle Rampant

History has followed much the same pattern in Waziristan and the Tribal Areas as in the other main tribal groups under discussion. It may be divided into four distinct phases: more than a thousand years of independence or semi-independence, a century of European colonization, half a century as part of a modern state, and a decade of turmoil in the war on terror. With the increasing pace of recent history, every aspect of life in Waziristan—religious and political leadership, customs, and codes—is in danger of being turned upside down. The particles that formed the kaleidoscope of history and remained stationary for so long have now been shaken about in bewildering patterns, with no telling when and how they will settle into some recognizable forms.

The history of relations between the Indian imperial center and tribal periphery that included Waziristan is little more than a series of attempts by the center to establish its authority over the periphery, usually desultory, often haphazard, and invariably ending in failure. Akbar, the mighty Mughal emperor of the sixteenth century, sent his forces to subjugate the recently settled Yusufzai tribes in the Peshawar valley and in areas approaching Swat to the north. Accompanying his army was the legendary Birbal, his favorite adviser and a Brahmin known for his wisdom. The Yusufzai not only destroyed Akbar's army in 1586, with 8,000 men losing their lives, but also killed Birbal in the process.[15] A distraught emperor withdrew from public sight and was said to be so dismayed that he gave up eating for several days. While Akbar's fury descended on the Yusufzai, he felt Waziristan was too deep in the mountains and the reputation of its tribes too fierce to justify attempts at conquest.

To preserve a lifeline to their province in Kabul, imperial governments in Delhi needed to keep the Khyber Pass open by paying the Afridi tribesmen who controlled the pass a kind of toll. Those who did not did so at their own peril, as emperors in faraway Delhi discovered when they made the mistake of attempting to force passage militarily. In 1672 the Mughal emperor Aurangzeb, Akbar's direct descendant, sent a large army to subdue the Afridis, but it met with a characteristic ambush in the Khyber Pass that left some 10,000 soldiers dead and 20,000 captured (Khushal Khan Khattak claimed that as many as 40,000 Mughal soldiers were slain).[16] Only the emperor's governor, Amin Khan, survived with four others to return to Peshawar. Toward the latter part of Aurangzeb's reign, Mughal authority south of Peshawar barely existed. Waziristan was left free of any imperial control.

In contrast to the remote mountains and their nang tribes, the Swat and Peshawar valleys, with their high rainfall and river channels, supported fine corn and sugarcane crops that in turn gave rise to a hierarchical society of powerful landlords and landless peasants. The landowning and dominant tribe, the Yusufzai, was a good example of the qalang category of tribal society (see chapter 1), while the mountainous Afridi, like the tribes of Waziristan, represented nang. The Yusufzai were considered the aristocrats of the Pukhtun tribes, and their dialect the most cultivated and sophisticated version of Pukhtu, the equivalent of the King's English. In time, the Yusufzai chiefs became allies of the imperial power during both the time of the Mughals and the British, rising to prominence in their civil and military structures.

In one case at least, in Swat, Yusufzai tribal alliances in the nineteenth century, spurred by charismatic figures, eventually led to the formation of a state. As their power grew, the landlords began vying with one another, and arbitration became necessary. Tribal elders repeatedly asked the Akhund, a widely celebrated and respected Sufi saint of the Naqshbandi order, to become their ruler. The Akhund preferred to concentrate on his spiritual life and refused. Early in the twentieth century, however, a direct male descendant of the Akhund was able to forge tribal alliances from which he emerged as the Wali, or ruler, of Swat, a new state duly acknowledged by the British. The Wali administered justice through sharia, but kept tribal customs and traditions in mind. By combining temporal and spiritual authority, the Wali gained legitimacy in controlling the traditionally unruly Pukhtun tribes. The capital of the state, Saidu Sharif, was named after the Akhund, also called Saidu Baba, while Sharif signifies a term of respect. Marriages between the Wali's family and leading Yusufzai khans further reinforced his authority. Swat emerged as a model Pukhtun state. Justice was swift and fair, education was free (both boys and girls were encouraged to attend schools), and the Wali and his officials were accessible. A small but well-organized army ensured that no Yusufzai khan could challenge the ruler's authority. Besides, the British were always on hand to support the Wali and ensure that law and order were preserved.

The Waziristan story is quite different. Even if the imperial armies marched south of Peshawar toward the settled towns of Kohat and Bannu, they avoided Waziristan deep in the mountains. Therefore the area was left largely undisturbed. Even the triumphant Pukhtun warrior from Kandahar, Abdali, who in the eighteenth century united the tribes of Afghanistan into a kingdom that included the lands up to the Indus River, left Waziristan alone. Indeed, his policy remained one of paying allowances to and assuring the freedom of the Pukhtun tribes, especially of the nang category. With the Mughal Empire growing weaker and beginning to disintegrate, Abdali had his eyes on a bigger prize in India—the capital city of Delhi. Waziristan would be little more than a military diversion, yielding nothing that he wanted. It was best to avoid the place altogether.

The British in Waziristan

The relationship between center and periphery changed dramatically in the nineteenth century when the British assumed control over India and Queen Victoria was declared its sovereign. The British were not only determined to extend their borders as far north as possible but, with an eye to the encroaching Russian Imperial Army, wished to build a buffer zone to prevent any incursions from Central Asia. One by one, the great Indian empires and kingdoms had fallen to the British—the Mughal, the Marathas, and the Sikhs. Only the mountain regions to the northwest, beyond which lay Afghanistan and Central Asia, remained outside Britain's control.

It took the better part of a century for the British to recognize that what they called the trans-Indus districts, the lands of the Pukhtun and the Baluch, could not be dealt with in the same way as the rest of India. Two Afghan wars had demonstrated that military might and punitive measures could not sway these peoples. On the contrary, this only seemed to provoke bitterness, anger, and violence. The people in the hills were unlike the supine princes of the Indian states, the oppressed small farmers and peasants in their fields, or the desperately poor laborers looking to feed their families. Thus British policy eventually relied more on "indirect rule" or "masterly inactivity," leaving the tribes their own areas, free to pursue their own customs and traditions.

In 1893 Colonel Algernon Durand, who headed the British Afghan Boundary Commission, was dispatched to demarcate a boundary between British India and Afghanistan. The boundary is commonly called the Durand Line after the colonel, although some sources suggest it refers to his brother, Sir Henry Mortimer

Durand, then foreign secretary of India, who signed the border agreement in Kabul.[17] The boundary effectively divided the tribes of one larger ethnic community into two parts along a border that began at the foothills of the Himalayas and ran south to Baluchistan and the Arabian Sea. The boundary has been a source of controversy and anger between Afghanistan and Pakistan ever since.

In the late 1890s, the British created five special administrative units called agencies (there are now seven), which together constituted the Tribal Areas. To underline the importance of the Khyber Pass, this region was the first to be granted agency status. Next was the Kurram valley south of Peshawar, and shortly thereafter, the two Waziristan agencies (North and South), and Malakand, which gave access to the Swat valley in the north. North Waziristan was dominated by the Wazir tribe, while South Waziristan was home to both the Wazir and their cousins, the Mahsud. The Mahsud were thus confined entirely to the south, surrounded almost on all sides of the agency by their agnatic rivals, the Wazir. Although Waziristan was divided into two agencies for purposes of administration, the entire area was referred to as Waziristan.

During the period of British supremacy, which came to be known as Pax Britannica, Britain's authority in the Tribal Areas extended only to the main road in the agency and a hundred yards on either side of it as a reflection of the policy of indirect rule. Beyond that lay the world of *riwaj,* tribal customs and traditions. Unlike settled districts, agencies had no civil and criminal codes, taxes, rents, police, or judicial or revenue officials.

Until the departure of the British in 1947, Waziristan remained a constant source of anxiety for the central government in Delhi. So great was its concern that at one point Lord Curzon, the viceroy of India, in an unprecedented move, took charge of its administration directly. The British General Staff considered the tribes of Waziristan "the best umpires in the world as they seldom allow a tactical error to go unpunished."[18] In 1937 the Mahsud caught an entire British brigade in a classic guerrilla ambush in the Shahur Tangi, killing nine British officers and forty-five soldiers and wounding a further forty-seven. In the 1930s the British had more troops in Waziristan alone than in the rest of their Indian Empire. Even to the very end, Waziristan remained an unpredictable area for the British.

Curzon constantly wrestled with finding a solution for Waziristan: "No patchwork scheme—and all our present recent schemes, blockade, allowances etc., are mere patchwork—will settle the Waziristan problem. Not until the military steam-roller has passed over the country from end to end, will there be peace. But I do not want to be the person to start that machine."[19]

The Political Agent: The Key to Tribal Administration

In 1901, not satisfied with the Punjab government's method of dealing with these border tribes, Lord Curzon created a new province out of the old Punjab:

the North-West Frontier Province (now called Khyber Pakhtunkhwa). Under the Frontier Crimes Regulation passed the same year, Britain gave the province's administrators almost unlimited powers (this, too, has been amended recently in Pakistan). Curzon thus concentrated on the caliber of the officers administering the new agencies along the border that were under central government authority and contiguous to the new province.

Curzon had come to the conclusion that his first line of defense on the sensitive northwest frontier would not be British regiments but British political officers. A great deal rested on their shoulders, and Curzon was clear as to the type of person he had in mind: "A good Political is a type of officer difficult to train. Indeed, training by itself will never produce him, for there are required in addition qualities of tact and flexibility, of moral fibre and gentlemanly bearing, which are instinct rather than acquisition. . . . It is upon such men that our security rests, not on the number of battalions we put there."[20]

Curzon's quest for a certain kind of officer sprang from his personal interest in, and knowledge of, tribal societies in the region. Curzon himself had written studies of tribal societies. The second volume of his book *Persia and the Persian Question* (1892) contains ethnography on the Bakhtiari and other tribes of the Zagros Mountains in southern Iran. Not unlike Ibn Khaldun, Curzon was impressed with the nomads he encountered, finding their "virtues of character" in stark contrast to the "foul debaucheries" of the Persians living in the cities. Curzon balanced the virtues of the nomads with their "frank and unrepented vices" and described them as "rough, ignorant, and sometimes fierce."[21]

As the head of the newly created agency, Curzon's political officer represented the governor general himself, the highest official in British India, and was thus designated political agent, or agent to the governor general. Given the nature of his duties, he was best described as "half-ambassador and half-governor," who reported directly to the central government.[22] Under the law, the PA had complete administrative authority and up to my time was called the *Badshah* (king) of Waziristan. The British invariably selected the PA from either the prestigious Indian Civil Service (ICS) or the military. Many of the agents came from an elite cadre within the ICS, the Indian Political Service. A majority of them were educated at Oxford and Cambridge Universities and were versed in the humanities, including the Greek and Latin classics. If India was the jewel in the crown, this elite cadre was the sparkle in the jewel.

As the key representative of the Raj, the PA was always exposed to danger. In the half-century that the British administered the Tribal Areas, five PAs in South Waziristan Agency lost their lives in the line of duty. One was shot by a Mahsud in May 1948 in the PA's winter residence in Tank, just when he was preparing to leave for home after the creation of Pakistan. The young assassin had been told that if he wished to take revenge for the death of his father, who lost his life in a skirmish with the British, he had better get on with it because before long there would be none in the area as they were leaving it forever. In keeping with their charge, the PA's bodyguard, comprised of Wazir and Mahsud tribesmen, instantly shot the assassin.

British political officers had served their country well. They were aware of the enormous responsibilities resting on their shoulders. At their best, they represented a civilization that to them was sophisticated, advanced, progressive, and above all, inclusive. They were the tip of the spear, the first point of contact for the tribal elders and jirgas. Their knowledge of local tribes, customs, and the language would stand them in good stead. Indeed, when I first met Sir Evelyn Howell, who had once been in charge of Waziristan, in the mid-1960s at Cambridge shortly before his death, he was working with Caroe on a translation of the poems of Khushal Khan Khattak. An effective political agent, it was said, knew not only when the cat was about to jump, but precisely where it would land. Considering the volatile nature of the tribes and the incessant interference of outside forces, this was an unpredictable game at best.

These officers believed they embodied the honor of the Raj, as demonstrated by the fate of Major J. O. S. Donald, the political agent in South Waziristan. In 1946 Donald was kidnapped by the Shabi Khel, in the manner of a tribal petition. Having come to know the Shabi Khel so intimately, Donald perhaps developed what is now called the Stockholm syndrome, that is, sympathy for his captors. He promised that their grievances would be met and there would be no retribution for his capture. Once released, however, he saw to his dismay no change in the attitude of the central government. When he learned that the British had actually persecuted and bombed the clan, he believed his honor was compromised. He shot himself in the study of the PA's bungalow at Tank. When Lord Wavell, the viceroy of India, inquired about the incident, Caroe, then governor of the province and classmate of Major Donald from Winchester College, one of Britain's elite schools, replied, "Sir, I am pretty sure you as a Wykehamist [from Winchester College] like me, in that position, would have done the same."[23]

The lot of the political officer was not an easy one. Howell, who admired and was even fond of the Mahsud and wrote a small but excellent monograph on them, nevertheless found his job trying: "A trans-border agency is a charge which imposes upon the holder a heavy strain, physical, mental, and, we may perhaps add, moral. It is not every officer, even amongst members of a picked corps, who is fit or by temperament apt to carry the burden, and even amongst the few who are there are fewer still who can stand the strain for long at a time."[24]

Beneath their high learning and important colonial posts, these officers often displayed a humanity that embraced the people once under their charge, irrespective of differences in race and religion. Sir George Cunningham, for example, was so attached to the region that he gave up his post as rector of the

University of Saint Andrews and returned with alacrity to take up his old position as governor of the North-West Frontier Province in the newly independent Pakistan when invited back by its founding father, Muhammad Ali Jinnah. In my own case, I am sure partly because I was a member of the Civil Service of Pakistan (CSP) that succeeded the renowned Indian Civil Service to which he belonged, Caroe called me a "friend" in the epilogue to his celebrated book *The Pathans* (2000), provided the excellent foreword to *Mataloona,* my little book of Pukhtu proverbs, and in a handwritten letter, sent not long before his death, wrote: "I would like to tell you of my appreciation of what you have done, and are doing. Sincerely, Olaf Caroe."[25]

Notwithstanding the positive aspects of the British in the Tribal Areas, European colonization took varied and changing forms. Other European colonial powers—the French and Italians in North Africa, the Germans in southwest Africa, and the Russians in the Caucasus—dealt with the peoples they encountered in quite a different manner from that of the better British political officers (see chapter 4).

After the great uprisings of the late 1850s that shook the Raj to its foundations, Britain's changed attitude and administrative reforms ensured that the revolt of the Indian masses was effectively over. Until the emergence of Mahatma Gandhi, Jawaharlal Nehru, and the mass mobilization of the Indian National Congress in the 1920s, there was little serious cause for concern on the part of the British. The new class of Indian lawyers and entrepreneurs in the cities, the small farmers in the provinces, and the aspiring civil servants and soldiers wanted to be part of the British system. By then, Indian demand was not to reject Western modernity, but to benefit from it. In contrast, the Tribal Areas, to the last days of the Raj, were determined to keep modernity at bay. Colonial intervention in the Tribal Areas was perhaps best summed up by a senior British officer upon reading Howell's *Mizh:* "What a record of futility it all is!"[26]

Waziristan in Pakistan

In 1947 Muhammad Ali Jinnah, known as Quaid-e-Azam, or the "great leader," faced overwhelming challenges as Pakistan's first head of state. Tension with India on the eastern borders over Kashmir threatened to plunge the new nation into war, millions of destitute refugees arriving from India needed to be settled, and new administrative structures had to be created. By this time, Jinnah was old, exhausted, and terminally ill; he would die the next year.

Nonetheless, he acted swiftly in the Tribal Areas, taking the extraordinary step of deciding "in consultation with my Commander-in-Chief and the Governor of the North-West Frontier Province, to withdraw all regular troops of the Pakistan army from Waziristan at an early date."[27] As a further show of confidence in the periphery, he promised that the government would honor agreements with the tribes, respect their customs and traditions, and not bring change without consulting them. The following year, speaking in Peshawar to a grand jirga from the Tribal Areas, Jinnah declared:

> Keeping in view your loyalty, help, assurances and declarations we ordered, as you know, the withdrawal of troops from Waziristan as a concrete and definite gesture on our part—that we treat you with absolute confidence and trust you as our Muslim brethren. . . . Pakistan has no desire to unduly interfere with your internal freedom. . . . We want to put you on your legs as self-respecting citizens who have the opportunities of fully developing and producing what is best in you and your land. . . . I agree with you that education is absolutely essential, and I am glad that you appreciate the value of it. It will certainly be my constant solicitude and indeed that of my Government to try to help you to educate your children and with your co-operation and help we may very soon succeed in making a great progress in this direction.[28]

Alam Jan Mahsud recounted the meeting between a Waziristan jirga, which included his father, and Pakistan's first prime minister shortly after the creation of the country:

> Soon after Partition, Mir Badshah, my father, led a jirga from Waziristan to meet the Prime Minister, Mr. Liaqat Ali Khan. The main issue was the army garrisons, at Ramzak, Wana, etc. The PM told them that Mr. Jinnah, the Quaid-e-Azam, had ordered that all these troops were to be withdrawn, as also from other parts of the Tribal Areas. He felt that with independence of the country and the departure of foreign power, there was no longer any need of stationing army in those areas. . . . The tribesmen took it on themselves and faced cross-border challenges but never posed any problem for Pakistan.[29]

Jinnah, born in Karachi, educated in London, and practicing law in Bombay, had instinctively understood the best strategy to deal with the Tribal Areas. The tribesmen believed that Jinnah was acting honorably; they would respond accordingly.

Tensions with India had already flared over the fate of Kashmir, which the tribes of Waziristan, now seeing themselves as part of Pakistan, felt the need to defend. Besides, Kashmir had been part of Abdali's Afghan kingdom, and Pukhtuns felt a special affinity with it. When they heard of the atrocities being committed against the majority Muslim population by the Hindu ruler's troops, emotions ran high. Groups from Waziristan traveled hundreds of miles with their own weapons to prevent the massacre. Even up to my time, many a jirga called to account for some transgression would start with a ritual recitation: "Sahib, we have sacrificed much for the cause of freedom. We lost lives in our struggle to free our brethren in Kashmir. How can we be blamed for breaking the law?"

The tribesmen paid no taxes or rents and decided their conflicts on the basis of their own tribal customs, and peace was generally maintained in the Tribal Areas. But in many respects it was also an enforced stagnation. In 1947, when Waziristan became part of the new nation of Pakistan, it had virtually no schools, hospitals, or development schemes. Poverty there was perhaps the highest and literacy the lowest in the country. Because political parties were prohibited in the Tribal Areas and outsiders were forbidden to enter, the entire region was kept outside mainstream political and cultural developments.

Independence came to mean different things to the center and the periphery. The center's main priority was to consolidate and establish its authority in all its parts. The periphery assumed that its state of semi-independence would be preserved, and that its own unique identity would be left untouched. From the birth of the nation, the divergence in the two points of view began to show, and before long the relationship between the center and periphery fluctuated between a working, if not entirely amicable, partnership and a rupture with attendant conflict.

In the first few decades after independence, the central government left the Tribal Areas more or less in the hands of its political agents, many of them hand-picked officers from the CSP cadre. Omar Khan Afridi, one of my predecessors in South Waziristan Agency, who won the Sword of Honor at the Pakistan Military Academy as the top cadet and was subsequently inducted into the CSP, is a good example of one of these outstanding political officers. He was remembered with affection by the tribes even during my time. The first generation of Pakistani military leaders had been trained by the British, and they looked at the Tribal Areas through the affectionate prism of the "noble tribesman." Some of them, like Ayub Khan, who had also been to Sandhurst, affected English airs in dress, speech, and mannerisms. They derided religious clerics as "bloody mullahs," drank whiskey at the club in the evening, played golf, and went shooting on the weekend. Many had fond memories of the time they served with the British regiments and remembered their fellow officers now serving in the Indian army with some nostalgia. Temperamentally, they were more in sympathy with the West than with the emerging Soviet Union opposed to it.

The election of the popular Z. A. Bhutto as prime minister in the early 1970s heralded the first significant signs of change in the Tribal Areas.[30] Bhutto assiduously cultivated the Tribal Areas as part of a flanking political maneuver to check rivals who dominated the North-West Frontier Province—the Jamiat-e-Ulema-Islam (JUI), the religious party, and the National Awami Party (NAP), the Pukhtun nationalist party. With this in mind, Bhutto attacked the privileges of the tribal chiefs and elders, initiated a series of development projects in the Tribal

Areas, promised adult franchise, and became the first prime minister to visit all the agencies in one prolonged tour.

Before I went to Waziristan, I was in charge of Orakzai Agency to the north and in that capacity welcomed the prime minister to the agency on this, the first visit of its kind. The agency was in the process of transformation and experiencing some unrest. I had just moved its headquarters from the settled areas deep into Tirah, almost as legendary as Waziristan in its inaccessibility and reputation for hostility to change. The process had not been smooth, particularly as many elders resented the idea of schools and offices in their midst that would inevitably alter their status. Not surprisingly, my camp in the new makeshift headquarters was fired upon several times. I was fortunate to be alive.

I took what the elders told me about the thistle-like prickliness of Tirah seriously. In an annual event only a generation ago, tribesmen would bring a radio from a city in the settled areas, place it ritually at the end of a valley, and then invite young and old to shoot at it. The symbolism was explicit: they were rejecting modernity and driving home the point that they could survive without the modern age. They were shrewd enough to recognize that change does not occur in a vacuum, that one thing leads to another. Radios convey new ideas, and suddenly people have new demands. The old order is then threatened. The idea of a new full-fledged government presence in the midst of this tribal society was revolutionary.

With the headquarters barely established, my challenge was to organize a peaceful grand jirga representing all of the agency's tribes to receive the prime minister. I used my skills and knowledge of tribal society to the fullest to craft a temporary one-day, one-off truce between the clans. Some had been at war with one another for decades, and my task was to get them all to sit in peace together to listen to the visitor. Having learned of the tribal custom of *teega,* or formal truce, which literally means a stone placed between feuding parties as a symbol of agreement, I called in the various tribal leaders so that everyone was represented and after long negotiations had them agree to a *teega* for the day. Bhutto, who was aware of the momentous nature of the visit, flew in with three helicopters. Following his speech, we presented him with a tribal dagger and turban as a traditional gift on behalf of the tribes, which pleased them no end (a photograph of the event appeared in the Pakistan press and international media, including *Time* magazine in its December 27, 1976, issue). Their guest had been suitably honored. I then escorted Bhutto to the rest house for lunch. There, I noted with consternation that the large gathering of tribesmen had not dispersed. Although they were passively seated, we had announced that the program was over and they were free to leave. Apprehensive in case someone planned mischief, I sent an assistant to check. "Sahib," they told him, "we enjoyed watching these helicopters land, and we want to see them take off. We have seen nothing like this in our agency." When Bhutto's helicopters left for Wana, in South Waziristan Agency, I was not surprised to learn that his entourage had been fired on at night. I thought the use of the Waziristan equivalent of the *teega* would have helped.

Before Bhutto's changes could take effect in the Tribal Areas, he was toppled in a military coup organized by General Mohammed Zia-ul-Haq in 1977, just before the Soviet invasion of Afghanistan. A consciously religious man, Zia-ul-Haq responded to the invasion with a call to jihad against a "godless" enemy. In this, he found natural allies in the United States and Saudi Arabia, both eager to foster an Afghan resistance for their own purposes. Pakistan's Inter-Services Intelligence (ISI), backed by the U.S. Central Intelligence Agency (CIA) and Saudi intelligence, threw its weight behind the Afghan mujahideen in the 1980s. The Afghans received military aid and were hailed as "freedom fighters" by President Ronald Reagan and the world's press.

Pakistan's rhetoric, that Islam was under threat in Afghanistan, and its mobilization of the religious networks with the mullahs and their madrassahs invariably involved Waziristan. The mullahs, the second pillar of authority in the Tribal Areas, now had weapons and money, and thus the means of mobilizing fighting men. The government would often bypass the other two pillars of authority—the nikkat-based elders and the PA—and go directly to the religious leaders. Almost overnight, the mullahs had been elevated to a primary leadership role in Waziristan in the most significant war in the region in living memory.

What Pakistani and their allied foreign intelligence agencies quickly discovered was that the networks of madrassahs run by the mullahs were a ready-made pool of zealous soldiers straining to fight for Islam. The Islam of the madrassahs was of a rough and ready kind. It was shorn of the mystic verses of a Rumi or the academic rigor of an Ibn Khaldun. This Islam demanded obedience and a willingness to sacrifice life and property in the cause of Allah without a moment's hesitation; in short, it was informal or tribal Islam.

For the young students in the madrassahs of Waziristan, the 1980s and 1990s were an exhilarating time. Many of the *taliban*, literally students (*talib* is the singular), were from junior lineages, impoverished families, and even orphans. They now found themselves not only at the forefront of a great war for Islam, but also blessed and supported by the highest religious authority in the Muslim world—the clerics of Mecca and Medina. Their tribal instinct for revenge combined with their zeal for Islam as they threw themselves into the jihad in Afghanistan. In the process, many of them came to see the traditional tribal customs practiced by their elders as un-Islamic and frowned on them, even suggesting they be set aside. The mullahs, who once looked to the elders for support were now seen as the guardians of Islam and dominated the political agenda of the agency. This new society began to upset the delicate balance between the three pillars of the Waziristan model—the elder, the mullah, and the political agent.

As the first Soviet troops moved into Afghanistan in late 1979, the disruption among Pukhtun tribes, especially just across the border, quickly became visible in my area. In 1980 thousands of refugees crossed into my agency, escaping Soviet tanks and helicopters and worrying about the honor of their women. In jirga after jirga, when I asked the refugees what they wanted most, assuming they would say medicine, food, and provisions for their families, they would demand guns. "Give us guns," they would reiterate. "The Soviets have dishonored our families, and we will never let them stay in our country."

The tribes of Waziristan threw their emotional and political support behind the Afghan mujahideen. Because the Wazir tribe lives in both Afghanistan and Waziristan, its members on the Pakistan side felt a special relationship with their kin fighting the foreign invaders. The Mahsud, on the other hand, had no border with Afghanistan and few Mahsud lived in that country. Therefore their incentive to join battle was largely in the spirit of fighting against injustice and to express solidarity.

As varieties of mujahideen from different ethnic backgrounds began to appear in Waziristan, new ideas of religious war, indeed religion itself, emerged in Waziristan. Arab fighters, in particular, defined Islam in a more orthodox manner than the tribes of Waziristan and found much to criticize in local customs. Joined by men from faraway places—Uzbeks from Central Asia and Uyghurs from Xinjiang—they framed the struggle in Afghanistan as an Islamic war against a ruthless and godless invader. Many local Pukhtuns welcomed them according to their traditions of hospitality. Some of these foreigners even struck roots by marrying Pukhtun women.

Once the Soviet forces were driven out in the late 1980s, largely through the support of American arms, the United States appeared to lose interest in Afghanistan. At a time when Afghanistan desperately needed to rebuild its schools and institutions, its great benefactor in war, the United States, by seeming to abandon them, disappointed the Afghan population. In the political vacuum that followed, groups of taliban with little traditional backing banded together to maintain law and order, initially in their local community in Kandahar. They soon earned themselves a name that would become internationally known—Taliban. Given the widespread chaos evolving in the early 1990s, neighboring communities invited them in, and soon they headed for Kabul to capture the country itself. Once in power, the limitations of the Taliban were painfully apparent in the administration of the state, especially their tribal prejudices against women and those not belonging to their ethnic group. The civil war that spread across Afghanistan in the 1990s reflected a clear-cut ethnic division between the Pukhtun-dominated Taliban and the non-Pukhtun Northern Alliance.

The inevitable chaos in Afghanistan was matched by political and social turmoil in Pakistan in the 1980s and 1990s. In these decades, some 5 million Afghan refugees sought shelter across the Durand Line in Pakistan. They brought with them two things that would change the nature of Pakistani society: Kalashnikovs and drugs. Once hailed as heroic fighters for Islam by Pakistan, the United States, and the Saudis, in the eyes of many Pakistanis they were now a danger to society. As a result, these desperate refugees faced increasing discrimination at the hands of Pakistani officialdom.

Meanwhile regimes in Islamabad had their own problems, rising and falling with dismaying regularity on charges of corruption and incompetence. Both Nawaz Sharif and Benazir Bhutto served as prime minister twice, and their governments were dismissed each time. The general decline infected the caliber and texture of the civil service, including the political officers serving in the Tribal Areas. That is why people expected that the inexorable descent into chaos would be arrested when the army's commander-in-chief General Pervez Musharraf declared martial law and promised a clean administration based in integrity and justice.

Musharraf's generation of military officers was unlike the officer corps trained by the British. They were young boys when Pakistan was formed in 1947. Their first defining memory would have been the dismemberment of Pakistan in 1971, which they would blame on India and its determination to "finish the job" of breaking up Pakistan. They would always retain a suspicion of India's intentions, as reflected in the drive to acquire nuclear weapons as a deterrent against India's nuclear program and to create "strategic depth" in Afghanistan to prevent India from flanking Pakistan's army on both the eastern and western fronts. That is why in the past few decades the Pakistan military has supported any group, including the Taliban, that it feels will represent its interests in Kabul.

With their focus on the eastern borders facing India, Musharraf and his officers showed little interest in the history and society of the Tribal Areas in the west. When they had to be dealt with, the tribes were treated like pawns by the Pakistani leadership to be moved about in the interest of the center with little appreciation of their local needs and regional standing. Besides, the urban-based leadership, keen to develop the bigger cities of Pakistan, viewed the tribal societies of Baluchistan and the Tribal Areas as backward, primitive, and even opposed to the national interest. The leadership did not understand the vital importance of being able to influence the tribes in their favor in order to promote stability and maintain the center's integrity. These tribes have consistently shown their capacity to impact political events outside their tribal boundaries—from playing kingmakers in the late 1920s when they successfully installed Nadir Khan on the throne in Kabul, to their incursions into Kashmir, which complicated relations between India and Pakistan, to their support of the Haqqani group, at first against the Soviet forces in Afghanistan and later against the Americans. After 9/11, the importance of the tribes of Waziristan to the Afghanistan and Pakistan region was once again evident.

WAZIRISTAN IN FLAMES

Just like the Soviet invasion, the U.S. arrival in Afghanistan had an immediate, widespread, and negative impact on Pakistan. Thousands of people streamed across the border into Waziristan fleeing U.S. bombings, including some individuals being sought in connection with the 9/11 attacks on American soil. Like Safar Khan, they disappeared into tribal networks. Given that so many Pukhtun tribes were related and lived on both sides of an international border that only existed on a map, it was inevitable that they would, as in the past, use it to their strategic advantage.

When President Musharraf launched a clumsy full-scale invasion of Waziristan, and the Americans began their equally maladroit drone strikes, Waziristan, always a hornet's nest, was unnecessarily stirred. Once again, arrogance combined with ignorance proved the undoing of a military adventure in the region, revealing the truth of the British General Staff's warning: any mistake in Waziristan would be punished.

In apparently ignoring the cultural and historical context of the region, those assaulting Waziristan failed to appreciate the principles of cause and effect. The already uncertain fate of the war on terror in Afghanistan was sealed once the fighting spilled into Waziristan. This was the inescapable lesson of history.

The Rise of the Taliban in the Tribal Areas

Musharraf's invasion was preceded by several events. With Afghanistan in turmoil, Pakistan was urged by the United States to capture Taliban and al Qaeda members crossing its borders. This it could not do unless the tribes of Waziristan cooperated. In June 2002 Pakistani army officers met with a Wazir tribal jirga, traditionally the role of the PA, and pledged that the military would allow the tribesmen the opportunity to handle the situation themselves before taking any action against the wanted men. In reply, the Wazir elders warned that any military operation in the Tribal Areas would be tantamount to a declaration of war on the Pukhtun tribes.[31]

Under intense American pressure for military action in the Tribal Areas, Pakistan broke the agreement with the tribes and launched a succession of large-scale military operations in Waziristan for the first time in Pakistan's history. This tactic was in direct opposition to that of Jinnah, the father of the nation, who had withdrawn the military garrisons from Waziristan and given its people respect and dignity. In October 2003, 2,500 commandos were airlifted into the village of Baghar, near Angoor Adda in South Waziristan, along with twelve helicopter gunships.[32] Within a few months, Musharraf was the target of two assassination attempts. He identified his potential assassins as Taliban supporters from Waziristan. In March 2004 the Pakistan army launched a military invasion of South Waziristan after

Musharraf mentioned a "high-value target" on television, alluding to al Qaeda's top leader after Osama bin Laden, Ayman al-Zawahiri. Employing gunships and 6,000 Pakistani troops, the Kalusha Operation targeted camps of Wazir and Uzbek fighters from Afghanistan in a fifty-square-kilometer area near Wana. The contingent hoped for a short, surgical strike, but quickly found itself ensnared in Waziristan. The army then changed its strategy, signing a series of hastily constructed peace agreements, now with the Mahsud, now with the Wazir. Following one of these agreements in South Waziristan with Baitullah Mahsud, who would emerge shortly afterward to lead one of the most deadly groups in the region, Pakistani general Safdar Hussain, in an exhibition of excessive unctuousness, called Baitullah a "soldier of peace."[33] In September 2006 the Waziristan Accord—a peace agreement between the Pakistani government, Wazir elders, and members of the Taliban—was signed in Miranshah, North Waziristan.

During this period, military operations expanded into the rest of the Tribal Areas, continuing to destroy the balance of the Waziristan model as a new generation of young leaders claiming to speak on behalf of Islam emerged in every tribe, calling themselves Taliban after their kin in Afghanistan. Members of the Mahsud tribe, described not entirely without an element of admiration by Caroe as "wolves" and the most "dangerous" of the Pukhtun tribes, assumed a leadership role in the periphery's resistance against a predatory and relentless center. Headed by Baitullah, a former low-level Taliban commander in Afghanistan and a bodybuilder, the Tehrik-e-Taliban Pakistan, or Movement of the Taliban in Pakistan, would strike terror in the hearts of Pakistanis at the very mention of its name.

The Tehrik-e-Taliban Pakistan: The "Wolves" of Waziristan

The TTP arose from the most thistle-like clan of the most thistle-like tribe— the Shabi Khel branch of the Mahsud tribe. The history of modern Waziristan virtually began in 1905 when a Shabi Khel Mahsud killed Lieutenant Colonel Richard Harman, British commandant of the South Waziristan Scouts. The British also had to contend with insurgencies fomented by another prickly Shabi Khel Mahsud, Mullah Powindah, dubbed a "first-class scoundrel" by Lord Curzon and "pestilential priest" by Lord Kitchener, then commander-in-chief of the Indian army and later secretary of state for war. The clan proved a thorn even in the last years of British rule. In 1946 the Shabi Khel kidnapped PA Major Donald and in 1948 killed Britain's last political agent, P. T. Duncan, as he prepared to leave after the creation of Pakistan. Mullah Powindah's grandson, Shahzada, was a source of anxiety during my tenure as PA until I was able to extract a promise of "good behavior" from him.[34] It is hardly surprising, then, that the TTP leadership, including Baitullah Mahsud and his successor Hakimullah Mahsud, is from the Shabi Khel.

Hakimullah Mahsud, leader of Tehrik-e-Taliban Pakistan after Bait-ullah's death in a U.S. drone strike in 2009 (fbi.gov).

It was President Musharraf's decision to launch a military strike on Islamabad's Lal Masjid, or Red Mosque, in July 2007 that more than anything else was responsible for the creation of the TTP in December of that year. Although the Red Mosque was not in the Tribal Areas, 70 percent of its madrassah students were from the Tribal Areas and the North-West Frontier Province.[35] These students had been detaining individuals, including policemen they thought to be "un-Islamic," and setting up sharia courts in Pakistan's capital. At one point, following a gun battle with Pakistan security forces, many of the students and teachers barricaded themselves inside the mosque complex. Abdur Rashid Ghazi, the head cleric at the Red Mosque, warned that he had the support of the Waziristan Taliban and any attack on the madrassah would result in an "appropriate response."[36] Government authority was now in shambles.

The antics emanating from the Red Mosque, a stone's throw from the Presidential Palace, had provoked Musharraf beyond endurance. He had to maintain the writ of the state. The question was how he would set about it. "We have been patient," he intoned. "I want to say to the ones who have been left inside: they should come out and surrender, and if they don't, I am saying this here and now: they will be killed."[37] In the end, elite Pakistani commandos stormed the complex, leaving an unknown number dead, thought to be anywhere between 100 and 1,000.

The assault on the mosque created an outcry in Pakistan. Attacking and killing people, especially young female students, in a mosque has an emotional resonance far beyond matters of law and order and politics as it involves deep sociological as well as theological issues. Within a matter of days, the peace agreements in the Tribal Areas were annulled in the wake of a string of revenge attacks and suicide bombings throughout Pakistan. Within the same month, a group of about seventy men stormed a mosque and shrine in Mohmand Agency and renamed it Lal Masjid—the Red Mosque. Their leader, Omar Khalid, distanced himself from the Taliban and al Qaeda, declaring, "We are locals. There is no single non-local in our ranks. Our struggle is to carry on the Ghazi Abdur Rashid mission," and he vowed to open a girls' seminary for those displaced by the army's Lal Masjid operation.[38] Khalid would become the top Taliban leader in the region associated with the TTP. Several months after the siege, the eighteen-year-old brother of a female student killed in the operation blew himself up in the army's Tarbela Ghazi mess south of Islamabad, taking with him twenty-two commandos of the Special Services Group that had participated in the Red Mosque raid.[39] In Orakzai Agency, former Lal Masjid madrassah students formed the Ghazi Force, named after the mosque's imam, in order to "avenge" his death. Like the tribesmen in Mohmand, the Ghazi Force would become associated with the TTP and be blamed by Pakistani authorities for numerous deadly attacks across the country.[40]

In the year following the siege, more than eighty-eight bombings across Pakistan killed 1,188 people and wounded a further 3,209.[41] In one notable incident in Waziristan, Baitullah Mahsud and a few dozen men ambushed a seventeen-vehicle army convoy and captured 260 soldiers, including a colonel and nine other officers, without a shot being fired. In response, the Pakistan army moved large concentrations of troops into Waziristan supported by helicopter gunships, fighter jets, and ground artillery.

When the TTP was established in December 2007, it was to be a union of Taliban from various tribes that temporarily transcended traditional tribal agnatic rivalries. Baitullah was dubbed "emir" of a forty-member central council with representatives from all seven agencies in the Tribal Areas. However, the Mahsud were clearly driving the organization. Even traditional cousin rivals, the Wazir and Mahsud, put aside their enmity in the wake of the Red Mosque tragedy and presented a common front. The brief unity soon fell apart, however, ostensibly because the members were fighting for different objectives. The Wazir's number one goal was to target NATO forces in Afghanistan. Thus they threw their support behind their Wazir kin across the border and related tribes like the Zadran, in which the Haqqani group was based. The Mahsud, on the other hand, were determined to focus on activities in Pakistan. They differed, it seemed, not only on the question of military strategy but also on how to reinterpret agnatic rivalry in this new context.

The Wazir came under the influence of Mullah Omar, head of the Afghan Taliban, who had opposed the formation of the TTP and asked Pakistan's Taliban to remain focused on the war in Afghanistan. Mullah Omar also asked the Wazir to expel foreign Uzbek fighters because they were launching fierce attacks against Pakistani security forces and local tribal leaders, turning the population against the Taliban and thus having an impact on the Afghan Taliban crossing into Waziristan for the winter. When Baitullah defied Mullah Omar by supporting the Uzbeks, he aroused not only the mullah's ire but also that of the Wazir. The Utmanzai Wazir of North Waziristan (under Hafiz Gul Bahadur, a direct descendant of the anti-British insurgent leader Mirza Ali Khan) and the Ahmadzai Wazir of South Waziristan (led by Maulvi Nazir) formed the Muqami Tehrik-e-Taliban, the Local Movement of Taliban, also referred to as the Waziri Alliance. Its aim was to oppose the TTP and support the Pakistan government. The Wazir soon became known in Pakistan as the "good" Taliban.

Despite the agreements between Pakistan and the "good" Taliban, violence between the two remained constant. In May 2012 the body of Maulana Naseeb Khan Wazir, a leading cleric from North Waziristan, was found in Peshawar after he was kidnapped in the Nowshera district a few days earlier by unknown persons. A spokesman for Hafiz Gul Bahadar declared, "We will revenge the killing of Maulana Naseeb."[42] Three days later, the Wazir Taliban attacked a Pakistani security post in Miranshah, killing and beheading nine Pakistani soldiers. The army responded the same day with artillery fire, destroying three houses and a mosque and killing three civilians and wounding twenty more. The military also raided a suspected militant hideout, during which the local Taliban kidnapped five of the soldiers and escaped into the night. The next day, the severed heads of two of the soldiers appeared on poles in the center of Miranshah, and the beheaded bodies were dumped in the town's bazaar. The same day, the army responded with helicopter gunships, attacking a weapons bazaar and a mosque, injuring a dozen people and killing thirty "militants."[43]

The TTP Timeline of Terror

After the Red Mosque incident, the TTP, what Pakistanis identified as the "bad" Taliban, entered a period of terror unrelieved by any peace agreements with Pakistan. A pattern of retaliation and revenge ensued involving the tribes of Waziristan, especially the Mahsud and the Shabi Khel clan, and the central government. Wave after wave of suicide bombers struck any target that the TTP perceived as representing central government authority or a threat to the group. It is no coincidence that an estimated 80 percent of all suicide bombers in Pakistan came from South Waziristan.[44]

TTP revenge strikes included a March 2009 attack on the Sri Lankan cricket team and, a day later, the police academy in Lahore. "We did it as a retaliation for U.S. missile strikes off drones inside the Pakistan territory," Baitullah Mahsud announced.[45] After a May 2011 attack on a paramilitary post in Charsadda that killed ninety newly trained cadets, a TTP spokesman declared, "This was the first revenge for Osama's martyrdom."[46] In June 2012 the TTP released a gruesome video showing the severed heads of seventeen Pakistani soldiers, and in late August 2012 they overran a military post north of Wana, claiming to have killed twelve soldiers, beheading some. In the same month, following a Pakistan military operation in the Bajaur Agency, the TTP released a grisly video showing the severed heads of a dozen Pakistani soldiers displayed in a field while men in tribal dress and with a rusty ax and assault weapons stood over them. The TTP said the soldiers had been killed in "revenge" for the actions of the Pakistan army.

Pakistan, blood-soaked and battered by violence, was still shocked by the audacity of the TTP's actions and capacity to strike at will across the land. In 2008 they kidnapped Pakistan's ambassador to Afghanistan, Tariq Azizuddin, in the Khyber Agency on his way from Peshawar to Kabul. He was held for ninety-seven days in Waziristan before being released. The same year, the TTP killed Lieutenant General Mushtaq Ahmad Baig, the surgeon general of Pakistan and most senior official to be killed by a terrorist strike. The general was a *hafiz-e-Quran,* a title of respect given to those who memorize the entire Quran by heart. In October 2009 the TTP stormed Army General Headquarters in Rawalpindi and came within 100 meters of the army chief, who was sitting in his office. They killed, among others, the brigadier general in charge of security for military intelligence. The TTP topped this with a daring assault on Mehran Naval Station in Karachi in May 2011, in which it used rocket-propelled grenades to destroy two of Pakistan's four P-3C Orion antisubmarine and maritime surveillance aircraft. The TTP onslaught outside the Tribal Areas continued with a view to hurting Pakistan as much as possible. The group claimed, for example, to be behind an attack on a prison in Lahore in July 2012 in which nine police officers died and three were wounded, claimed as a revenge attack for torture experienced by TTP members while in custody. Three days earlier, it ambushed an army unit in Gujarat, killing seven soldiers and one police officer. In the next month, it attacked one of Pakistan's largest military air bases at Kamra, not far from Islamabad, killing ten people, including two soldiers, and seriously wounding the base commander. The TTP rampage continued into late 2012, when in December the Pakistan air force base inside the international airport in Peshawar, where helicopter gunships used in the Tribal Areas are based, was attacked by ten sui-cide bombers with rockets and grenades. International commentators expressed concern that Pakistan's nuclear assets might fall into the "wrong hands."

Pakistani soldiers, no less than the tribesmen, have been known to seek revenge for raids on their units, for their fallen brethren in arms, and for the deadly bombings in which wives, mothers, daughters, and sons are lost. In per-sonal interviews for this study in 2012, Brigadier Abdullah Dogar, who com-manded a brigade along the international border in North Waziristan Agency, remarked that "revenge is in the DNA of all Pakistanis." Indeed, the soldiers of the Frontier Corps serving in the Tribal Areas are almost exclusively Pukhtun, while a significant percentage of the Pakistan army is also Pukhtun. So when these soldiers are deployed in the Tribal Areas, they are fighting their ethnic brethren. This has caused intense psychological problems as both sides are moti-vated by similar codes of revenge. The TTP has also intimidated local clerics and prohibited them from performing Islamic rituals over the dead bodies of Paki-stani soldiers they consider to be *kafir,* or nonbelievers.

Due to agnatic rivalry, the Wazir gave the TTP more limited support than groups in Bajaur, Orakzai, and Swat, which remained loyal followers. The Tal-iban movement under the TTP umbrella in Swat was headed by Mullah Fazlullah, known as Radio Mullah because he had a radio station that attracted a wide circle of listeners. In 2008 Swat became the only district of Pakistan in which the Taliban had complete administrative control, handed over to them by the government. While the Taliban in Swat had a reputation for piety, austerity, and honesty—qualities much appreciated by the general public—they also terror-ized men and women. The men were checked for attendance at prayers, growing beards, and general comportment and the women to see if they were properly covered and accompanied by their men. Girls' schools were closed either by the Taliban or because parents were too frightened to send their children to them considering Taliban attitudes toward women. Stories circulated of cruel punish-ments for minor transgressions and summary execution for major ones. A fearful population was not sure of what the morning would bring and was unwilling to speak out.

The TTP, like its affiliate, the Afghan Taliban, was harsh and unbending with anything considered morally corrosive—such as the use of drugs, lack of beards on men, and improper clothing for women. The TTP members vented their fury on video shops, blaming them for promoting pornography. Even some of the price-less Buddhist statues of Swat were not spared, just like those in Bamiyan, Afghani-stan. The statues were destroyed for two reasons: to strike a blow against idolatry and to cause the authorities intense discomfort by inviting bad international pub-licity. Once the Taliban were removed by the army in Swat in 2009, the sense of fear and uncertainty surprisingly remained, despite the continuing presence of some 30,000 to 40,000 Pakistani soldiers. Civilian populations simply do not trust large numbers of men in authority who carry guns—in or out of uniform.

Despite losing control of Swat, remnants of the Taliban continued to terrorize the local population for what they saw as transgressions against Islam, particularly women. In October 2012 members of the Taliban shot fourteen-year-old Malala Yusufzai in the head for speaking out about life under the Taliban and for demanding education and women's rights, as chronicled in her diary published by BBC Urdu. She survived the ordeal and was flown to Britain for treatment. The TTP, which claimed responsibility for the attack, threatened that if she survived, it would continue to target her.[47] The incident sparked outrage in Pakistan and around the world.

Whether in attacking defenseless school girls or military and political officials, the nang Pukhtun targets individuals as symbols of something bigger that the victim represents, such as the state itself. That is why the Pukhtun shows little deference to or little fear of attacking senior officials. The TTP's attacks in this regard were in line with traditional tribal strategy. In 1872 an Afridi, seeking revenge for what he perceived as an attack on his honor by the British, killed the viceroy of India, Lord Mayo, one of several in high office who lost their lives in such attacks over the years. Primary targets after the creation of the Tribal Areas included the PA, who was the head of the civil administration and the commandant of the paramilitary forces. In 1937 the Mahsud killed nine British military officers in an ambush in the Shahur Tangi pass, and in 1946 the elderly Mehr Dil of the Manzai clan, cousins of the Shabi Khel, lunged at Nehru to strike him in Razmak, thereby rallying other tribesmen for the creation of Pakistan. Nehru, who would become prime minister of India the next year, had come to the Tribal Areas to canvas support for his party but went back a disappointed man. The span and intensity of the TTP's attacks were unprecedented, however, and did much to bring down the shaky pillars of the Waziristan model.

Destruction of the Waziristan Model

The TTP sought to demolish the entire structure of traditional society pillar by pillar—the genealogical charter, elders, nikkat, mashar, jirgas, Pukhtunwali, *ulema* (respected traditional religious scholars and figures), and the political administration—and aimed to replace it with the organization's own amorphous idea of an Islamic state. Declaring himself the emir or caliph (king) of this new state, Baitullah Mahsud exposed how out of touch he was with his own nang society, with its base of fiercely independent-minded individuals. But he was intoxicated with power, making grandiose pronouncements such as suicide bombers "are my atom bombs. If the infidels have atom bombs, I have them too."[48] Baitullah was known to send his intended victim 1,000 rupees, a spool of thread, a needle, and then a note instructing him to make a *kafan* (burial shroud) within twenty-four hours, and, invariably, the person was found murdered. This was more Hollywood mafioso than Islamic emir.

Relying on hyperbole normally associated with revolutionary groups and the bravado of the nang Pukhtun tribes, the TTP talked of destroying Pakistan and defeating the United States. It declared its leaders the rulers of Islam, and appropriated the functions of an Islamic court by pronouncing which Muslims had become *kafir*, or heretics, and which ones were *wajib-ul-qatal*, that is, legitimately deserving of death. Brigadier Dogar summed it up when he described the TTP as suffering from "delusions of grandeur."

The lineage-based authority of tribal elders became the TTP's primary target. The elders represented the clearest threat to TTP dominance, despite having lost a great deal of their authority after the Pakistan military invasions. The TTP's anger and frustration against the elders, or mashar, reflected an already existing antipathy toward them in the kashar. According to some estimates, close to 400 elders have been assassinated in Waziristan, some with their entire families, making a total of about 800 elders killed in the Tribal Areas overall.[49] One was Malik Faridullah Khan Wazir, a former senator and federal minister and an acknowledged Wazir leader, who was killed in 2005 while on an officially supported peace-making initiative to the Mahsud area. Considering the small population of these tribes and the limited number of elders in each, the cumulative effect of these assassinations was like a virtual decapitation of the tribe itself.

The bloodiness of these attacks on elders is in wide evidence. In October 2008 the TTP beheaded four tribal elders in Bajaur Agency after they attended a jirga that had decided to take action against the Taliban. The next day in Orakzai Agency, a suicide bomber drove his bomb-laden car into an anti-Taliban gathering of elders just as they agreed to form a *lashkar*, or tribal war party, killing more than 100 people. On another occasion, the TTP kidnapped the majority of a twenty-eight-member jirga of the Bhittani tribe in South Waziristan Agency, convened to negotiate peace, and executed twenty-two of its members.[50] The elders representing tribal authority were given the choice of submitting to the TTP, thereby relinquishing their authority, or being killed as collaborators of the government and enemies of the TTP. Some chose to leave their areas altogether and find shelter in one of Pakistan's bigger cities.

Even the idea and practice of nikkat, the very basis of tribal identity, were not immune to the changes taking place amidst the chaos. "Share," or nikkat, "is not determined by tribal divide anymore," noted Ghulam Qadir Khan, a prominent Wazir civil servant writing about Waziristan. "It is determined by affiliation to militant groups." Qadir Khan berates the resulting loss of traditional balance in society: "At the end of day, those who had no worth have become worthy and those who were noble are disrespected and disregarded."[51]

Religious clerics, the second source of authority, also found their status as the sole legitimate representative of Islam being challenged by the TTP. Clerics seen to be close to tribal elders or government authority became sure targets. In August 2010 a suicide bomber killed Mullah Noor Muhammad, a former Wazir member of the National Assembly and prominent in my time, along with twenty-five others in a Wana mosque. Attacks on mosques became part of the TTP's method of deliberately challenging the authority of religious leaders, and one such assault by a suicide bomber in 2011 killed and wounded about 200 worshippers in a Khyber Agency mosque. Because most clerics relied for their livelihood on the meager income from the mosque or handouts from tribal elders, the prospects of escaping to the bigger cities of Pakistan were poor. Their only option in effect was either to challenge the TTP and most likely be killed or to acknowledge the group's authority.

The third pillar, that of the political agent and his administration, had been drastically weakened by the so-called civil service reforms of President Musharraf, which dismantled the district structures that had served Pakistan well. The offices of commissioner and deputy commissioner were abolished. Ambiguity remained about the political agent's role, with his title changed and rechanged, powers reduced, and future thrown into uncertainty. In 2004, with the office almost reduced to impotence, Musharraf ordered his army into Waziristan.

Once the army arrived, the PA was made irrelevant. The commanding general not only had the men, weapons, and resources to impose his decisions but now became the man dealing directly with the tribes—the tip of the spear in the Tribal Areas, the point of contact for the tribesmen, as the PA had once been. Not trained for political administration in these areas, however, the commanding general invariably proved erratic in his policymaking, oscillating between bombing Waziristan one day and drawing hastily written agreements of short duration the next.

Always quick to seize an opportunity in a fluid environment, tribesmen ignored the PA and went to the military officers instead. Ironically, although emasculated, the PA remained a symbol of authority from the past and therefore a constant target of the TTP. Many PAs had a narrow escape and several junior political officers lost their lives. Given the breakdown of authority and the security concerns, the PA could not work or live in the agency any longer. He could only visit it under military protection. The PA had been reduced to an appendix of the commanding officer, and like that organ, he was quite useless.

While the TTP targeted primarily the three pillars of authority, some attacks were directed at other religious sects represented by different tribal groups. The Shia living as a minority in Kurram and Orakzai Agencies were among the victims of such assaults, which effectively isolated them from the rest of the country for long periods of time. The Sufis were not spared either. In March 2009 a bomb was detonated near the grave of Rahman Baba, perhaps the most famous Sufi poet of the Pukhtun, who may be considered their Rumi. He lies buried on the outskirts of Peshawar, and his shrine attracts fellow poets and Sufi mystics who gather to recite their poetry. Although the TTP denied that it was responsible, its members had threatened to destroy the shrine, because like other Sufi centers, it attracted women. No one was killed in the blast, but his grave and mausoleum were severely damaged. In July 2010 suicide bombers at the Lahore shrine of Data Ganj Baksh, the most famous Sufi saint of Pakistan, killed 44 people and injured 175. In April 2011 two suicide bombers targeted the Sakhi Sarwar Sufi shrine in Dera Ghazi Khan, where thousands of devotees had gathered for the annual Urs celebration. Fifty people were killed.

The destruction of the Waziristan model depicted here is not merely a metaphor or a literary device: it is a sociological reality of Waziristan today, marked by the actual physical termination of the men who formed its three pillars of authority. "The old system of Pushtunwali is [being] destroyed systematically," Qadir Khan lamented. "It was weakened long before 9/11 by being pitched against religion but after that it has altogether been scrapped. Our sleeping government doesn't have a new system to replace the old one. There is no tribal way of life, the ways of the fathers, and there is no new system of government to replace it."[52] At the end of the decade that began on 9/11, the Waziristan model lies broken and, like Humpty Dumpty, will be difficult, if not impossible, to put together again.

Mutation of Pukhtunwali in Waziristan

Driving the TTP was a hodgepodge of culture and faith—a mutation of elements from Pukhtunwali and from Islam. The TTP took what it needed from Pukhtunwali—the compulsion to take revenge and to embrace agnatic rivalry—and ignored its respect for elders, their role in the jirga, the chivalric attitude toward women and children, among other details. From Islam, the TTP selected verses of the Quran demanding that believers stand up and fight in the way of God and ignored those that underlined God's preference for peace over war in every situation (see the discussion in chapter 3 in relation to bin Laden).

This mutation of the code resulted from the breakdown of the Waziristan model. The elders had been killed, so jirgas were incapable of settling conflicts. There was no effective political administration, and the presence of the army only made matters worse. Military operations had displaced some 1 million people from the Tribal Areas and about 200,000 Mahsud, close to half the Mahsud population. Nearly the entire population of Swat, some 2 million people, was dislocated. Tribal women were subject to molestation, with some reportedly engaging in prostitution to survive in Pakistan's main cities. In the face of social destruction, the tribesmen responded with anger and fury. If the military killed their children, they would kill the children of the enemy too. The tribesmen sought to inflict pain and seek revenge, and there were no limits to their actions.

Responding to the onslaught by the modern state, the TTP increasingly moved to the soft spots of its enemy—the city mosques, bazaars, schools, and offices—and targeted innocent Pakistanis. The TTP perceived these populations as having some connection with the government or tribes that opposed the group. A survivor of a TTP attack on the Parade Lane mosque in Rawalpindi in December 2009, which left thirty-six people dead, including seventeen children, recalled with distress: "They took the people, got hold of their hair, and shot them." They targeted children, yelling, "Now know how it feels when other people are killed in the bombings!"[53] Revenge is the clear motive behind such actions, yet the murder of innocent children is far from honorable behavior for a Pukhtun according to Pukhtunwali and is categorically forbidden in Islam.

The suicide bomber, as an instrument of terror often used by the TTP, is rooted in the war on terror and is specific to the age of globalization. Until the mid-twentieth century, the military tactic of capturing the hilltop to snipe at invading British troops had served the Pukhtun well. The Soviet Union's extensive use of helicopter gunships put an end to this strategy, making the man on the hilltop a vulnerable target himself. Pukhtun tribal tactics had reached an impasse. At this point, the Americans came to the rescue. The Stinger missile gave the tribesmen a fighting chance to even the military balance against the Soviets. With the advent of 9/11, drones appeared on the scene. The tribesmen had no strategy, weapons, means, or method to counter this new weapon. Perched precariously with their Kalashnikovs in their speeding Suzuki jeeps, they looked like dated remnants of the war against the Soviet invaders. Spurred by the need to fight back, resist the new technology, and vent their utter frustration at the unprecedented attacks on their homeland, the tribesmen turned to a new type of weapon: the inhuman, un-Islamic, and deadly suicide bomber. This was the first time the tribesmen of Waziristan had used suicide as an extension of war. Even during the bleakest days of fighting Soviet troops, this tactic was unknown. The body now became a weapon of mass destruction.

The emergence of the female suicide bomber is an example of another level of the mutation occurring in tribal societies. While suicide bombing is alien to both tribalism's emphasis on honor and Islam's respect for life, and in particular motherhood as its source, the idea for such bombings seeped into the fabric of the TTP's tactics. Its leadership preferred at first to use males in suicide bombings, in the guise of macho warriors wreaking revenge on the enemy. Female suicide bombers linked to the TTP, however, began appearing in Peshawar and the northern agencies such as Kurram and Bajaur, although not in great numbers. The first female TTP suicide bomber struck in December 2007, blowing herself up near a Christian missionary school and military checkpoint in Peshawar when she could not get through security. A December 2010 attack by a female suicide bomber took place in a World Food Program center at Khar in the Bajaur Agency distributing food to as many as 41,000 Pakistani families; the explosion killed forty-five people queuing up for food and injured eighty. The TTP claimed responsibility, saying the attack was in response to a move by the local Salarzai tribe, to which most of the victims belonged, to raise a pro-government tribal militia. In June 2011 a husband and wife suicide team, identified as Uzbek, killed ten people at a police station in Dera Ismail Khan. In August 2011 a seventeen-year-old female suicide bomber killed herself and another person and injured three policemen in Peshawar. The TTP again claimed responsibility, saying the attack was conducted to avenge Pakistani military actions in the Tribal Areas.

Drones over Waziristan

American drone strikes caused further devastation in a landscape already in turmoil. Strikes began under President George W. Bush targeting specific figures and multiplied under President Barack Obama, hitting Waziristan at an average of once every four days. In North Waziristan they centered primarily on Mir Ali, Miranshah, and Datta Khel, and in South Waziristan on an area around Wana in Wazir territory and in Makin, the heart of the Shabi Khel Mahsud. Initially the drones focused on South Waziristan and targets like Baitullah Mahsud, who was killed in a drone strike in 2009, and his successor Hakimullah Mahsud. After the Pakistan invasion of South Waziristan in 2009, the Mahsud were dispersed and the drone strikes soon shifted to North Waziristan. Of 118 strikes in 2010, the highest number of attacks up to that date, 104, hit North Waziristan. Between the first drone strikes in Pakistan in 2004 and the time of writing in 2012, only 18 in the Tribal Areas have been outside Waziristan.

The use of drones has thwarted any prospects of peace between Pakistan and the tribes of Waziristan. In June 2004 Nek Muhammad Wazir, the leader of the Wazir Taliban who had signed a cease-fire agreement with Pakistan two months before, was killed in the first CIA drone attack in Pakistan, which Musharraf claimed the Pakistan military had carried out. The agreement with Pakistan soon fell apart, and militant forces regrouped under the leadership of Baitullah Mahsud.

Whenever the Pakistan government took responsibility for drone strikes or remained silent in the face of their deadly attacks, the tribesmen took revenge on anything they thought represented the government. In November 2006 a suicide bomber struck a military camp in Dargai, northwest of Islamabad, killing forty-two Pakistani soldiers and wounding twenty, in response to a drone strike on a madrassah in Bajaur the previous week that killed eighty-five people. The Pakistani government claimed the madrassah bombing to be an air strike launched by the Pakistani military.

The drone campaign has also been a source of public friction between the United States and Pakistan, and the core of the problem lies in North Waziristan's Wazir Taliban, headed by Hafiz Gul Bahadur. Pakistan considered Bahadur's group the "good" Taliban as they maintained a lasting peace treaty with the government in contrast to other tribes. Drone strikes jeopardized agreements between Pakistan and the tribes, so much so that in March 2011 Bahadur threatened to pull out of the peace deal altogether after one of his top commanders, Sherabat Khan Wazir, a key pro-Pakistan leader of the Wazir Taliban, was killed in a drone strike in Datta Khel, North Waziristan, along with forty-three other people. America, on the other hand, viewed the Wazir Taliban as one of its primary enemies because of their involvement in the war in Afghanistan alongside their tribal cousins against NATO forces. The year 2013 began with a series of drone strikes that killed, among others, Maulvi Nazir. There was no "good" Taliban where America was concerned.

From a tactical standpoint, Brigadier Dogar believed that the drone was counterproductive to the elimination of terrorism in the region. "The drone undermined us," he said, noting that the tribes thought the Pakistan military was complicit in the drone strikes. "Each drone strike puts my men in jeopardy," he complained, and pointed out that there was no coordination between Pakistan and the United States in the use of drones. On the ground, he never knew in advance that an American strike was imminent. He would hear an explosion and send his staff to check whether or not it was a drone. Before they could return, he would hear about the strike on television.

Some members of the American military were also aware of the negative impact of the use of drones on any tactical success in the region. In March 2010 Admiral Michael Mullen, the chairman of the Joint Chiefs of Staff, stated, "Each time an errant bomb or a bomb accurately aimed but against the wrong target kills or hurts civilians, we risk setting our strategy back months, if not years. Despite the fact that the Taliban kill and maim far more than we do, civilian casualty incidents such as those we've recently seen in Afghanistan will hurt us more in the long run than any tactical success we may achieve against the enemy."[54]

Beyond targeting the Wazir Taliban who were allied with the central government and opposed to the Mahsud-dominated TTP, as well as individuals they had given shelter to, the long lists of drone casualties stoked further resentment in the larger Pakistani population, which demanded an end to the strikes. Pakistanis believed the victims were innocent people and blamed Islamabad for allowing its allies, the Americans, to launch them. Their anger only mounted in the face of uncertainty as to who was killed, why they were deemed appropriate targets for assassination, and when the strikes would end.

Amid the confusion about the legitimacy of the targets, tribesmen with agnatic rivalry on their minds seemed to be playing their own devious games with the drones. Their duplicity was observed by *Arab News,* which in May 2011 reported that the Mahsud and Wazir were manipulating drone strikes to settle scores.[55] It alleged that tribesmen serving as paid CIA informants were directing American drones against their rivals, falsely claiming that these individuals were terror targets.

Stories of innocent people being killed by drones flooded the media. One account that caught the attention of the international media involved Tariq Aziz, a sixteen-year-old boy from Waziristan. In April 2010 Tariq's cousin was killed by a drone. Believing him an innocent victim, Tariq accompanied a group of elders to Islamabad to tell his story to Reprieve, a human rights group. Neil Williams, a Reprieve volunteer, spent an hour with Tariq. "We started talking about soccer. . . . He told me he played for New Zealand. The teams they played with from the village had all taken names from football clubs, like Brazil or Manchester United," Williams recalled. As recounted in the *Rolling Stone* article,

> Tariq and other teenagers at the meeting told Williams how they lived in fear of drones. They could hear them at night over their homes in Waziristan, buzzing for hours like aerial lawn mowers. An explosion could strike at any moment, anywhere, without warning. "Tariq really didn't want to be going back home," Williams [said]. "He'd hear the drones three or four times a day." Three days after the conference, Williams received an e-mail. Tariq had been killed in a drone strike while he was on his way to pick up his aunt. It appears that he wasn't the intended target of the strike: Those who met Tariq suspect he was simply in the wrong place at the wrong time, especially since his 12-year-old cousin was also killed in the blast.[56]

A recent study of the drone attacks in Waziristan conducted by Usama Khilji of the Foundation for Fundamental Rights in Pakistan confirmed their "psychological, social and economic impact" on the people of the region:

> Drones are said to circle the skies in NWA [North Waziristan Agency] all day and all night, except for cloudy days, with the sound being a lot louder during nighttime, according to locals from the Mir Ali and Miranshah areas. Drones produce a monotonous buzz, almost like the sound of a generator, which together with the uncertainty that comes with the perpetual fear of missile strikes have had an immense psychological impact on the population. Particularly affected are young children who are said to be unable to sleep at night and cry due to the noise. Some children have lost their lives with the impact of the drone missile strikes in their neighbourhoods. Local doctors have declared many adults mentally unfit due to the effect drones have had on them, with the details of the disorders unknown due to lack of, firstly, awareness of mental health and, secondly, expert psychiatrists and psychologists in the area.[57]

These findings were echoed in the September 2012 study conducted by Stanford University's and New York University's schools of law titled *Living Under Drones: Death, Injury, and Trauma to Civilians From US Drone Practices in Pakistan*.[58] Jennifer Gibson, an American researcher for the Stanford and NYU study and a staff attorney for Reprieve, representing drone victims in Pakistan, has visited areas adjacent to Waziristan and talked to dozens of people from the area. She told me that she was appalled by what she heard and learned:

> Drones terrorize the civilian population. They subject whole communities to the constant threat of random annihilation. People imagine that drones fly to a target, strike with surgical precision, and return to a U.S. base hundreds or thousands of miles away. The truth is nothing of the sort. For the communities in Waziristan, drones are nearly as common as the clouds in the skies. As many as six of them hover over villages at any one time. People hear them day and night. They are an inescapable presence, one that fires unpredictably on those living below. The United States refuses to tell these communities who it is targeting. As a result, everyone might possibly be next. This constant fear and the inability to make oneself safe is destroying the very fabric of communities in Waziristan. Parents are afraid to send their children to school. Women are afraid to meet in markets. Families are afraid to gather at funerals for people wrongly killed in earlier strikes. The fabric of daily life is ripped to shreds.[59]

In an interview for the Stanford and NYU study, Noor Khan, whose father was killed in the controversial March 2011 drone strike in Datta Khel, commented on the impact of the drone attacks on his community:

> The community is now plagued with fear. . . . The Tribal elders are now afraid to gather together in jirgas as has been the custom for more than one century. We are scared that if we get together we might be targeted again. The mothers and wives plead with the men to not congregate together for fear that they will be targeted. They do not want to lose any more of their husbands, sons, brothers, and nephews. We come from large families, some joined families, and people in the same family now sleep apart because they do not want their togetherness to be viewed suspiciously through the eye of the drone. They do not want to become the next target. . . . The people of NWA are against these strikes. I am against these drone strikes![60]

Not all Pakistanis disapprove of drones, however. Farhat Taj Andersen, who is based in Norway, has been a vigorous supporter of their use. In her book *Taliban and Anti-Taliban* (2011) and in columns for the *Daily Times* of Pakistan, she argues that the drones are popular in the Tribal Areas and urges the Americans to continue using them.[61] Andersen blames the Pakistan army entirely, in particular its powerful intelligence services, for the chaos in the Tribal Areas and the creation of the TTP. The Pukhtun, she believes, would never permit groups like the TTP to form and are the victim of Pakistan's conspiracies. Andersen's uninhibited enthusiasm for drone strikes has generated multiple conspiracy theories in Pakistan purporting to explain her position.

For Americans, the drones are a crucial part of their war on terror. It is said that they keep American "boots off the ground" while killing the "bad guys." The technological "precision" of the drones is widely celebrated in the media, by think tanks, among politicians, and even by the president's advisers and the president himself. John O. Brennan, President Obama's counterterrorism adviser, stated unequivocally in June 2011 that over the previous year "there hasn't been a single collateral death because of the exceptional proficiency, precision of the capabilities we've been able to develop."[62] In January 2012 Obama explained, "I want to make sure that people understand actually drones have not caused a huge number of civilian casualties. For the most part, they have been very precise, precision strikes against al-Qaeda and their affiliates. And we are very careful in terms of how it's been applied."[63] In November 2012 the secretary of defense, Leon Panetta, described America's war on terror as "the most precise campaign in the history of warfare."[64] Even prominent American commentators tamely reflect the White House position. Journalist Peter Bergen calculated that only a negligible number of civilians have been killed by drones, and none in 2012.[65] Until updated in the fall of 2012, the online database posted by Bergen's New America Foundation did not even include a civilian category of those killed by drones, listing only "militants" and "others."

This assessment has been consistently challenged by influential sources in Pakistan. Two of Pakistan's newspapers, *The News* and *Dawn*, calculated that the vast majority of deaths in the drone strikes were civilians. According to *The News*, between January 14, 2006, and April 8, 2009, sixty drone attacks killed 701 people, 14 of whom were "militants"; and *Dawn* reported in 2009 that only 5 of 708 people killed in forty-four drone attacks were known "militants."[66]

In addition, those associated with the U.S. military like Colonel David Kilcullen, the acknowledged expert on counterterrorism for the United States Army and former adviser to General David Petraeus in Iraq and Afghanistan, and Andrew Exum, a former soldier in Iraq and Afghanistan and fellow with the Center for New American Security, echoed these findings. They pointed out: "Press reports suggest that over the last three years drone strikes have killed about 14 terrorist leaders. But, according to Pakistani sources, they have also killed some 700 civilians. This is 50 civilians for every militant killed, a hit rate of 2 percent—hardly 'precision.'"[67]

When interviewed by my team, Brigadier Dogar also maintained the drone strikes are a "very serious problem" with "significant collateral damage." They

kill people indiscriminately, including women and children, he protested, referring to this as "extrajudicial murder." "Drones resonate beyond the Tribal
Areas," he warned. Because they kill from above, people in Waziristan consider
them a dishonorable weapon: "Even if you have to kill your enemy, you do it in
an honorable way."

Brigadier Dogar contradicted Brennan's claim that collateral damage from
drone attacks has been negligible. In March 2011 he was in his headquarters a
mere ten kilometers away from the drone strike on the tribal jirga in Datta Khel.
The jirga was convened for the purpose of resolving a business dispute involving
payments, Brigadier Dogar told us, and he was aware of the meeting ten days
in advance. Forty-four people were killed in the strike, he said, and then added
with emotion in his voice, "They were totally innocent. I could name each one."

Fog of War

The contradictory statements of John Brennan and Brigadier Dogar make
clear that Waziristan is mired in a state of confusion and disinformation. One of
them has to be right and one wrong. This condition is apparent everywhere. Ask
Pakistani officials how the TTP started and who supports it, they will say: Americans. Ask Americans, and they will say: Pakistanis. High-profile assassinations of
people like Benazir Bhutto are similarly difficult to fathom. Musharraf blamed
Baitullah Mahsud for her death, while Baitullah accused Musharraf.

In Brigadier Dogar's view, the chaos in Waziristan was deliberately created
by "foreign forces"; by this he implied the Americans and Indians. TTP fighters are paid around 30,000 rupees, twice as much as the ordinary Pakistani
soldier's monthly pay, he claimed. Where, he asked pointedly, was the money
coming from? And why does India have seven consulates just across the border
in Afghanistan for a mere 5,000 Indians, when it has only two consulates in the
United Kingdom for a population of several hundred thousand Indians? The
aim of these consulates, he hinted, was to create mischief across the border in
the Tribal Areas of Pakistan.

America's aim, according to many senior Pakistani civil and military officials, is
to "de-nuclearize," "de-radicalize," and "de-Islamize" Pakistan. To this end, they
argue, it has joined India in posing a threat to their nation. The difference between
the two, Pakistanis say, is that America acts out of "stupidity," as its actions have
been counterproductive to its interests. Indians, on the other hand, have promoted their interests with "cunning," knowing exactly what they are doing.

Frustrated Pakistani officials claim that the $750 million President Bush
promised the Tribal Areas never materialized. In any case, most of the money
for aid has been recycled into the wages of Western "advisers" and "experts"
who are in Pakistan to oversee the expenditure of these funds. They also feel
America is ungrateful for Pakistani sacrifices since 9/11, pointing to the 45,000

Pakistanis who have lost their lives and the billions of dollars in destroyed property. America is a "fair-weather friend," Pakistanis complain, pointing out that Americans sidled up to Pakistan when it was needed in the 1980s and then pulled away once Soviet troops left Afghanistan and thus U.S. interests had been served. By contrast, Pakistanis are quick to add that China is an "all-weather friend" and laud its virtues.

For their part, Americans have lost patience with their Pakistani allies. They see the ISI along with the senior civil and military officials, indeed the entire nation, as "pathological liars," to use Richard Clarke's description on Bill Maher's television show in 2011. Americans, said a bitter U.S. official I spoke with who deals with Pakistanis and did not wish to be named, are fully aware of the Pakistani "lies," "bogus receipts," and attempts to "cheat" them. They know that as a result of the American aid being poured into Pakistan and the rampant corruption, property prices in Islamabad are much higher than in Washington; that Pakistan, like other countries involved in the war on terror, has made "terrorism" into a "Ponzi scheme"; and that America is in a predicament, for in order to ensure the success of its mission, it needs to turn a blind eye to Pakistani perfidy. Of the promised $750 million, the American added, Pakistanis could use only about $80 million given Pakistan's limited administrative capacity. In fact, 80 percent of the used funds would not have benefited the tribes in any case because they went to nondevelopmental "administrative" costs such as "buying Brazilian teak wood for offices and expensive land cruisers for government officers." Every bullet "fired by the Pakistan army in the Tribal Areas," the official complained, "costs the American taxpayer 50 cents. . . . With this money, the United States could buy the Tribal Areas."

Furthermore, Americans could not understand why Pakistan was unable to control its own territory in the Tribal Areas. They saw Pakistan's explanations as little more than lame excuses and flimsy lies. The final straw was the discovery that bin Laden was hiding in a huge house just a stone's throw from Pakistan's premier military academy in the cantonment town of Abbottabad. Americans were quick to accuse Pakistan of duplicity and incompetence.

While Americans dismissed Pakistanis' explanations as to why they could not control the Tribal Areas and the international border there, a military expert with a British background who writes for *IHS Jane's Sentinel Country Risk Assessments* countered:

It is absurd to loudly condemn Pakistan for "failing to seal the border," when there are tens of thousands of U.S. troops along Afghanistan's border with Pakistan. If they can't seal it from their side, with all their hi-tech gadgets, how can anyone expect the Pakistan army to seal the Pakistan side? The other thing that U.S. experts might consider is keeping quiet. For the

White House National Security Adviser to pronounce that Pakistan must now conduct military operations in North Waziristan is not simply bizarre, it is insolent. The Pakistanis have had enough of people telling them what to do. Their military operations are being conducted with professionalism. It would be a good thing if a bit of professionalism and discretion were to be exercised by all the clever Washingtonians who drop into Islamabad to lecture those who are trying to cope with an emergency for which the U.S. is largely to blame.[68]

In this atmosphere of distrust and suspicion, even the major blacktop road in South Waziristan from Wana to Makin, constructed with assistance from the U.S. Agency for International Development (USAID), has become a source of controversy. Although it is one of the largest development schemes in the history of Waziristan, tribesmen see the road not as bringing commerce, trade, and visitors to their land but as a means to deploy large numbers of troops across the agencies. To them, it is more than an intrusion—it is a deliberate provocation. Meanwhile the Pakistan army has to constantly patrol the road to keep it open but has little authority beyond it.[69]

Each position vying for dominance in the Tribal Areas has suffered from schizophrenia: the Pakistanis fought the TTP yet flirted with the Wazir Taliban; the Americans continued to use drones with increasing frequency in defiance of Pakistan's requests yet proclaimed Pakistan was a "major non-NATO ally"; the TTP claimed to be the champions of Islam yet attacked and killed worshippers in mosques; and the ordinary tribal people, who no longer had the comfort of a traditional framework and its supporting structures to rely on, felt completely vulnerable for they could trust no one.

Perhaps the most confusion for the United States in its dealings with the Tribal Areas lies in the explanations of al Qaeda's role, which it conflates with the Taliban. Commentators could not even agree on where al Qaeda ended and the TTP began. On 9/11 al Qaeda claimed to be promoting resistance to tyranny and a jihad in the name of Islam. While the tribesmen in Waziristan would not have approved or even appreciated the thought of thousands of innocent people being killed in the United States on 9/11, the idea of resisting tyranny for the sake of Islam would have appealed to them. The invasion of Afghanistan by the American-led coalition forced a few elements of al Qaeda to trickle into Waziristan. Although al Qaeda brought ideas of a global jihad against the United States and perhaps techniques in explosives, it had little or nothing to offer the TTP in terms of leadership, strategy, and policy. Small groups like the Sipah-e-Sahaba and Lashkar-e-Taiba from the Punjab, which at one stage had the tacit blessing of the government but were now escaping the authorities, were similarly incapable of providing leadership to the Mahsud. To anyone who has some knowledge of Waziristan, it is highly unlikely, as some commentators have assumed, that a small number of al Qaeda outsiders who did not know the local language, customs, history, and terrain would be providing leadership to the prickly Shabi Khel Mahsud.

Even more far-fetched is the notion that the TTP is part of a global jihad linking it to the Kanuri in Nigeria and the Tausug in the Philippines. That is sheer fantasy. The universe of the Waziristan tribes is Waziristan. Excursions out of it to assert their role in history have been brief: Kabul and Kashmir are the outward limits of their adventures. Unlike other nang tribes, they have not attempted to establish dynasties in Delhi. It is the attacks of the Pakistan military and the American drones that have turned the cities of Pakistan into targets for the TTP.

Yet commentator after commentator in the West has been influenced by the American metanarrative of the clash between the West and the world of Islam and its associated war on terror that fuses al Qaeda with other resistance movements wherever they happen to be situated on the periphery. Some of the most influential Pakistani journalists and writers have also adopted this narrative. For them the suicide bombers are fundamentalist Muslims seeking martyrdom and the reward of large numbers of virgins in paradise. Since these commentators are affiliated with or are based in what I am calling the center with its national newspapers and think tanks, they invariably reflect its worldview, and therefore their notions are not entirely surprising.

According to Zahid Hussain, a widely respected award-winning journalist and author of *The Scorpion's Tail: The Relentless Rise of Islamic Militants in Pakistan—And How It Threatens America* (2010), the violence and disorder in Waziristan are rooted in the presence and ideological message of al Qaeda.[70] He argues that by 2008 "al Qaeda had come to exert more influence, and the TTP had begun to embrace al Qaeda's message of expanded, global jihad."[71] Imtiaz Gul, director of the Islamabad-based think tank Centre for Research and Security Studies and author of *The Most Dangerous Place: Pakistan's Lawless Frontier* (2009), goes even further, suggesting that "millions" of people look to the men of violence in the Tribal Areas for inspiration in their global war. "It is not the few thousand armed militants and criminals who make FATA the most dangerous place, but those silent millions who look up to these militants as daring followers of God and Islam, out to challenge the wayward and corrupt Western world," concludes Gul. "Unless adequately addressed, this trend over the long run will spell ever greater dangers not only for the country but also for the entire region and the world."[72]

Syed Saleem Shahzad, the Pakistan bureau chief of the *Asia Times Online* who lost his life in 2011 under mysterious circumstances (Pakistanis pointing to the involvement of their own intelligence services), goes even further in his book *Inside Al-Qaeda and the Taliban: Beyond Bin Laden and 9/11* (2011). Shahzad's imagination is vivid, his prose purple of the brightest hue, and his vision apocalyptic. He conjures a global war to end all wars, the arrival of messianic prophetic figures leading armies across continents; and at the heart of it all, directing and moving events at their will, is al Qaeda. Here is a sample paragraph:

> Al Qaeda leaders in Pakistan's tribal areas believe there will be rapid development in this direction by 2012. They are convinced the theater of war will be ready in the Middle East for orchestrating the "End of Time" battles by then. In the meantime, under the traditional black flag with the inscription of the *Kalma* (the first word of faith) the downtrodden Afghans, the Arab-Afghans, and Central Asian Muslim tribes would emerge through the mountain passes to announce a most unexpected victory. Then they would start the new journey of their struggle to the Balad Al-Sham (Syria, Iraq, Lebanon, and Palestine) under the command of the promised messiah, Al-Mahdi, for a final showdown against the Western forces, for the defeat of the anti-Christ and for the revival of a global Muslim Caliphate.[73]

For Shahzad, al Qaeda is responsible for every leaf that stirs and every major event that takes place in the Muslim world: al Qaeda was behind 1993's "Black Hawk Down" in Somalia, killed Benazir Bhutto in Pakistan, organized the rise of the TTP, and brought to prominence its leaders Baitullah and Hakimullah. The problem with this kind of thinking, however, is that it remains devoid of cultural and historical context and is therefore not supported by facts on the ground.

Documents from bin Laden's compound released by U.S. authorities in 2012 on the first anniversary of his death cast doubts on the narrative claiming al Qaeda had influence on the TTP in Waziristan. They reveal that bin Laden and other al Qaeda leaders were unhappy with the tactics and behavior of the TTP. The al Qaeda leadership was appalled at the attacks on fellow Muslims and mosques and dismayed at the clumsy planning and execution of the TTP assaults. Because of these actions, it warned, TTP members would be denied paradise. In effect, the TTP's actions were blatantly un-Islamic.[74] Indeed, TTP attacks were motivated not by thoughts of Islamic virgins but the idea of tribal revenge.

The View from the Periphery

Amid the debates and controversies about what is happening in Waziristan and who is to blame, the lives of ordinary tribesmen there have been thrown into convulsion, and they are telling anyone who will listen. "Mahsud as a tribe are on the run and today living like refugees or fugitives scattered all over Pakistan," says Muhammad Jan Mahsud, from South Waziristan Agency and a senior civil servant in Peshawar.[75] Noor Khan of North Waziristan Agency raises a question about the plight of his people that is difficult to answer: "Most of the people in NWA live in poverty. They have no option but to stay in this area, though many want to leave because of the drones. Plus, we are connected to this land. This is ancestral living place. Why should we have to leave when we have done nothing wrong?"[76]

Wazir writer and civil servant Qadir Khan describes a heart-rending and all too familiar everyday occurrence in his native Waziristan that shattered another family:

> Yaqub Shah, an elderly man, was going to Miranshah bazaar with his two children. On the outskirts of town, an Improvised Explosive Device (IED) exploded when the army convoy was passing and the army started indiscriminate firing. Yaqub Shah took shelter by hiding in a nearby street along with his two children. After a while, when the firing stopped and the area was secured, Yaqub Shah peeped from the street to see if all was over and whether he could come out and proceed towards Miranshah. The army people had seen someone taking shelter in the street and were ready to shoot. As Yaqub Shah brought his head out to see, bang, one clean shot, right between the eyes and Yaqub Shah was collateral damage, still holding the hands of his children. His children were in a shock, they couldn't comprehend what happened. Sitting by their motionless father, motionless children holding each other tight, afraid the same might happen to them, hoping their father will live, knowing he is dead, wishing their mom was there. Like foreign occupational force, the security forces shoot anything that is moving, so no one could come to help the innocent children, to wipe their noses and hold them against their chest. They couldn't clean themselves, couldn't speak to each other just held each other tight. Innocent angels were made to undergo the trauma of their life. They were used to moving only when the father moved and the father wasn't moving any more. It was ages before people were able to reach the children and relieve them from their agony. They were able to cry, only when they reached the lap of their wailing mother.[77]

The irony is that the people of the Tribal Areas desperately want to live normal, stable, peaceful, and prosperous lives, and the majority of them do not approve of the TTP, al Qaeda, or the Americans. In a 2012 survey, about half the population of the Tribal Areas gave priority to education, employment, health, and electricity. Though 79 percent opposed U.S. activities in the Tribal Areas, their negative views of al Qaeda and the TTP were not far behind—at 68 percent and 63 percent, respectively.[78] A survey by the New America Foundation in 2010 recorded similar opinions.[79]

To the people of Waziristan, members of the TTP are as much the perpetrators of violence as the Pakistanis and Americans. If there are any doubts, listen to their civil servant Qadir Khan: "The tribesmen are fighting for their survival against the militants also. The terrorists see them as sympathizers of the government and the

American-led coalition forces. Haven't the tribesmen suffered most at the hands of militancy, haven't we lost all our possessions to terrorism?"[80]

According to Muhammad Jan Mahsud, "America, the West, and even many Muslim states are fighting this war against a nonexistent enemy. . . . Against all these odds and hostile environment, the Mahsud tribe," he continues with a flash of pride, "owns almost eighty percent of the heavy construction machinery currently operating in Pakistan and Afghanistan. These simple-looking people, despite their illiteracy . . . can do such wonders despite the completely negative environment. . . . They would certainly surprise the [world] if provided with the right opportunities."[81] But reactions to his attempts to write about the plight of his people have been so critically negative, he told me, that he decided to withdraw into silence.

General Alam Jan Mahsud, a notable figure in Waziristan in my time, is a good example of what a Mahsud can do when interacting positively with the center. Educated outside the agency, he found employment with the military and acquired property in Pakistan. Members of his family, too, joined the services and now hold high positions. With all traditional leaders currently marked for assassination in Waziristan, Alam Jan is a primary target and therefore lives in Islamabad. In my conversations and communications with him in 2011 and 2012, he emphasized that Pukhtunwali, the mashar, the jirga, and the PA must return in order for the situation to normalize. Yet he also recognized that these institutions are "finished."

Despite his loyalty to Pakistan, a "wonderful country," the general could not contain his anguish and anger at the destruction of the Waziristan model. Some 400 mashar have been killed by "beasts," he lamented, some with their entire families, under "mysterious circumstances," while the PA is powerless—his role "you can multiply by zero." As a result of these developments, the Tribal Areas are "traumatized." He accused the Pakistan army of being "leaderless" and "rudderless," and its tactics "wrong and stupid." The entire "show," he said, has been "handed over to lunatics."

The same tribes that had been so assiduously courted by Jinnah were now being freely assaulted by the central government. Alam Jan lays the blame for the chaos in Waziristan squarely on Musharraf, who "turned tribal society upside down." He described Musharraf as "a person with dubious background, no idea of real soldiering and chivalry, except for flexing his muscles, had not fired a shot in anger, unfortunately became army chief and finally president."[82] When asked to elaborate what he meant by a "dubious background," Alam Jan cited an Urdu phrase implying that Musharraf was born in a "filthy gutter in Delhi"—*Deli ki gandi nali.* Although the phrase loses something of its pungent literary quality in translation and cannot be taken literally, it graphically conveys the idea of low birth. Overcome with emotion at the fate of his beloved homeland, a distraught Alam Jan berated Musharraf as "extremely shallow," full of "complexes," and, when he could contain himself no longer, a *kanjar* (a common colloquial term of abuse meaning pimp). Like all tribesmen, Alam Jan was judging Musharraf in terms of his lineage and the high standard of behavior tribesmen expect of their leaders.

What a nang Pukhtun can achieve through education and perseverance is also exemplified by Mahmood Ayub, a Turi Shia tribesman from Kurram Agency. Ayub obtained a Ph.D. from Yale University and made a career as a senior officer at the World Bank. An accomplished and modest man, he lives in Washington, D.C., but his thoughts are never far from his people across the world. In an interview in 2011, Ayub described the collapse of law and order in and around his agency, which has the largest Shia population in the Tribal Areas. The Shia are besieged by the TTP members, who see them as heretics. He is gloomy about the future, especially in view of the region's basic statistics: the literacy rate in the Tribal Areas is 5 percent for men and 0 percent for women. Only 2 to 3 percent of American aid goes to education in Pakistan, he said, and "very little" of that goes to the Tribal Areas. Khalid Aziz, a former PA in North Waziristan and chief secretary of the North-West Frontier Province, was also pessimistic when asked for his assessment in personal communications in 2012: "Can you imagine what will the future be like for Pakistan? Very bad."

"The beautiful village in which I grew up is dead," pointed out Qadir Khan in sorrow tinged with bitterness:

> We have been declared terrorists on our own land as if we have gone around the world to terrorize people. Everyone knows the reality; no one from tribal areas was involved in 9/11 or 7/7 or any other conspiracy against anyone. Those involved are having a swell time and no action is initiated against them. For a couple of Arabs our whole nation is being destroyed. . . . It doesn't end here; all of those killed are declared terrorists. Life of a tribesman is so valueless that anyone who wants to bleed a human can come and fire at a tribesman and no question will be asked.[83]

Qadir Khan concluded:

> Innocent people are being killed day in and day out. Some are killed by militants to terrorize people, branding them as American spies and friends of Pakistan army; others are killed by Pak army for violating so-called lawful orders or branding them as conspirators and friends of the militants and yet others are killed by drone attacks of the Americans. They are all killing innocent civilians without a fair trial, without a chance to prove their innocence. They are all together in the kill for different reasons.[84]

Putting out the Waziristan Forest Fire

The Waziristan I knew lies in ashes. Gone are the men who walked straight, looked you in the eye when they talked, and traded remarks with wit and subtlety; gone the women who showed their infinite hospitality and patience and the children who were full of energy and laughter. They are all dispersed in a pall of uncertainty. I wondered how many had become "bug splats" in a drone strike or were victims of military action and tribal rivals, intelligence operatives and foreign agents, or of the deluded young men with violence on their minds and revenge in their hearts. Gone forever is the Waziristan I served—gone the people who taught me so much about wisdom, dignity, courage, and honor, and gone their way of life.

With drone and missile strikes and satellite tracking systems bringing death, global media depicting this land as the nursery of terrorists while denying it a voice, national political leaders never visiting or seeming to care for the population's plight, suicide bombers from the community relentlessly tearing it apart, and a world showing little knowledge of or even interest in their suffering—the age of globalization has arrived in Waziristan like a precursor to the apocalypse.

Musharraf set the Tribal Areas ablaze with forest fires, while the drones poured gasoline on them. Agreements, tribal jirgas, and peace initiatives were frantically organized as the forest fires burned—now in Waziristan, now in Khyber, now in Bajaur, and now in Orakzai. Tribal elders formed tribal *lashkars,* backed by the United States and Pakistan to attack groups like the TTP. But they struck back with equal force wherever and whenever they could. The collapse of law and order on the periphery and across the country shows the scale of the problem Pakistan faces, one that bodes ill for its very survival.

While the metanarrative of the clash of civilizations and the war on terror demand the use of force to prevent attacks, there are alternative methods of dealing successfully with terrorists and outlaws within their own societies. As this chapter shows, every act of violence in these tribal societies provokes a counterattack: the harder the attacks on the tribesmen, the more vicious and bloody the counterattacks. That is why contemporary Pakistani and non-Pakistani military officials, administrators, and scholars who know Waziristan have advocated working within the traditional frame of tribal authority. Prominent Pakistanis of this opinion include General Alam Jan Mahsud, Khan Idris, Qadir Khan Wazir, and Khalid Aziz.[85] Among the non-Pakistanis, Colonel David Kilcullen, who is an anthropologist with considerable field experience, has concluded that peace and stability are not possible unless the three pillars of authority in tribal societies are restored.[86] In a recent book called *Waging War in Waziristan* (2010), Lieutenant Colonel Andrew Roe, a British military officer who had to deal with tribal society while commanding troops in Afghanistan, argues that the only way these tribal societies can be won over is through political and cultural initiatives, and that force should only be used as a last resort.[87] Any other method, he believes, is detrimental to stability. British anthropologist Hugh Beattie, in a study of the British in Waziristan, emphasizes their largely successful use of culture and custom to establish relations with the tribes.[88] These authoritative commentaries all stress the role of the traditional sources of authority in maintaining peace and stability in tribal society.

As this chapter makes clear, tribal society, as in Waziristan, which is organized along the principles of the segmentary lineage system, is shaped by the lineage charter, the code of honor, and the three sources of authority—what I have called the Waziristan model. That model, however, has fallen prey to Musharraf's invasions of Waziristan, his destruction of the civil administration, and, as a consequence, the near-collapse of governance in Pakistan. All this was abetted by relentless American drone strikes and pressure to "do more," which forced the Pakistan army to launch repeated assaults on the Tribal Areas and thus pushed the Waziristan model toward ruin. The TTP moved in for the kill. Its primary target was the model itself, and it systematically attacked each and every one of the pillars. Had the pillars remained in place, the TTP would have been effectively contained. The conclusion is clear: in order to check and eliminate the TTP and prevent similar future eruptions, the model has to be painfully, slowly, but surely, recreated, with suitable adjustments for proper democratic enfranchisement.

The Waziristan model provides an idea of the bits and pieces that need to be restored and those that need to be confined to the past. Some things need to change. Rights for women and for those not on the tribal charter need to be introduced and vigorously protected. The Frontier Crimes Regulation that governs the Tribal Areas, the excessive and unchecked powers of political officers, the role of traditional elders who so easily compromised with the administration, the population's limited participation in elections, and, above all, the sense of isolation must go. In any case, little of these past traditions and structures will survive considering the scale of the changes taking place in the region. However, wise and authentic tribal leadership, genuinely educated and scholarly religious leaders, and efficient and honest political officers are crucial to the reconstruction of Waziristan society.

The people of Waziristan are painfully aware that their torment can be traced to the actions of one man, Osama bin Laden. In the next chapter, I focus on bin Laden and the journey that drove him to attack America, which, in turn, brought Americans with their drones to Waziristan and other tribal societies.

3

BIN LADEN'S DILEMMA:

Balancing Tribal and Islamic Identity

In his only television interview after 9/11, Osama bin Laden looked decidedly uneasy. The interviewer was persistent, bin Laden rambling, evasive, and increasingly incoherent. The topic causing agitation to both men was the use of violence against innocent civilians. For bin Laden, the challenge was how to maintain a balance between the compulsions of his Yemeni tribal background and his Islamic faith—which was not unlike the dilemma facing the Tehrik-e-Taliban Pakistan (TTP) among the Pukhtun, Al Shabab of the Somali, and even Boko Haram with its base in the Kanuri tribal people in Nigeria. Tribal codes called for revenge, Islam for balance and compassion.

The setting for bin Laden's October 2001 interview with Tayseer Allouni, Al Jazeera's correspondent in Kabul, was a tent in Afghanistan. Allouni was interviewing the man who had dominated the world's attention for the past month. Yet, for some reason, Al Jazeera decided not to broadcast the tape, and it was not released until CNN quoted excerpts and published the transcript on February 5, 2002.[1]

Dressed in a turban and a military fatigue jacket, bin Laden expounded on the necessity of violence in measured tones, raising his hand slowly to emphasize a point from time to time. Al Qaeda, he explained, was acting as the "conscience" of the ummah (Muslim world), and the nineteen hijackers had set out to take "revenge" on its behalf: "These young men that have sacrificed their selves—may Allah accept them—in New York and Washington, those are the ones that speak the truth about the conscience of this Ummah, and they are its vibrant conscience that sees [it] as imperative to take revenge from the evildoers and transgressors and criminals and terrorists that terrorize the true believers." Bin Laden added, "If killing those who kill our sons is terrorism, let history witness that we are terrorists."[2]

Allouni then raised the question of the killing of innocent civilians. In a discursive response, bin Laden put forth the following argument: innocent Muslim civilians are being killed by the enemies of Islam; therefore the killing of their innocent civilians is justified. An unconvinced Allouni returned to his question: "So you say that this is treatment with the same action? They kill our innocent, so we kill theirs?" "Yes," replied bin Laden, "so we kill their innocents, and that is valid both religiously and logically."

Although bin Laden referred to a religious justification, from a theological point of view, he admitted that such killing was not sanctioned by the ultimate sources in Islam, the Prophet and the Quran: "They say that this is wrong and invalid, and for proof, they say that the Prophet (*sallallahu 'alayhi wasallam*) forbade the killing of children and women, and that is true. It is valid and has been said by the Prophet (*sallallahu 'alayhi wasallam*)."

Sensing he had gotten bin Laden to admit, even if implicitly, that the violence of 9/11 was not justified on the basis of Islam, an excited Allouni interrupted bin Laden: "This is what we are asking about exactly! This is what we are exactly questioning ourselves about!"

Bin Laden would not give in so easily:

> But this forbidding of killing children and innocents is not general and there are other writings that uphold it. Allah's—Glorious and Exalted is He—saying "And if you punish (your enemy), then punish them with the like of that with which you were afflicted [16:126]." The scholars and people of the knowledge said—amongst them "Sahib al-Ikhtiyarat," and Ibn al-Qayyim, and Shawkaani, and a lot of others, and Qurtubi in his tafseer—(they all say) that if the disbelievers were to kill our women and children, then we should not feel ashamed to do the same to them, mainly to deter them from trying to kill our children and women again.

Bin Laden's quandary was painfully apparent: he must either abjure his tribal identity, with its emphasis on honor and revenge, or his Islamic one, with its categorical prohibition of suicide and the killing of innocents. Surprisingly, for a self-proclaimed champion of Islam, he tilted to his tribal identity with the use of the word "but." Faith, with its certainties, as anyone wrestling with these spiritual issues knows, by definition abhors "buts" as they smack of nuance and polemics, and even raise the specter of doubt. As an example of a legitimate target, bin Laden cited the Pentagon.

Once again, Allouni was unconvinced and interrupted bin Laden's flow by asking him about the civilians killed in New York: "What about the World Trade Center?"

Bin Laden used the same argument he had just given:

> As for the World Trade Center, the ones who were attacked and who died in it were a financial power. It wasn't a children's school! And it wasn't a residence. And the general consensus is that most of the people who

were in there were men that backed the biggest financial force in the world that spreads worldwide mischief. And those individuals should stand for Allah—Glorious and Exalted is He, and to re-think and re-do their calculations. We treat others like they treat us. Those who kill our women and our innocent, we kill their women and innocent, until they stop from doing so.

Every Muslim with a tribal background is familiar with bin Laden's dilemma. The context may change, but, in varying degrees, the dilemma remains: how to balance tribal and Islamic identity. The refusal to abjure tribal practice is evident in the actions of men who perpetrate honor killings and female circumcision, and of those who, in relatively less fraught examples, deny female inheritance and support money lending and usury—all against Islamic injunctions.

BIN LADEN—RELIGIOUS REFORMER OR TRIBAL REBEL?

By offering an amendment to the core teaching of Islam itself, bin Laden revealed the order of his priorities: he unequivocally supported the tribal notion of revenge over the unambiguous commands of the Prophet and his companions, including the first caliph Abu Bakr who codified them, against killing innocent civilians even during wartime.

The implications of bin Laden's statements are of immense significance, as he appears to supersede the Prophet, something no Muslim would do unless consciously wishing to operate outside Islam. For Muslims, the Prophet is the embodiment of the Quran, as the Quran itself emphasizes. To reject him is to reject the foundations of faith. By doing so, and by implication rejecting the Quran, bin Laden is indicating that his actions emanate from outside Islam.

Bin Laden scatters clues to this thinking with abandon, beginning with his frequent use of the word "revenge" followed by references to the related notion of honor. Both are key concepts in the tribal code, yet revenge is diametrically opposed to the teachings of the Prophet. Born in a tribal society, the Prophet of Islam fully appreciated the dangers of tribal custom undermining the more universal principles of Islam. He consciously and publicly set aside thoughts of avenging himself for past injuries to set an example. When he returned to Mecca from exile at the head of a triumphant army, he declared a general amnesty. He forgave the old woman who threw garbage on him daily, forgave those who plotted to kill him while he slept, and even forgave Hind, who, before her conversion, cut open and ate the liver of Hamza, a favorite uncle of the Prophet, in a particularly gruesome expression of tribal insult against him. Asking his followers to set aside ideas of revenge, the Prophet said: "Bear wrong patiently, verily, best it will be for the patiently enduring."[3]

While the Quran encourages Muslims to struggle against injustice and to enhance spirituality, a struggle that it calls jihad, it consistently advocates both patience and compassion in the form of forgiving, especially in the face of hatred and aggression:

> But indeed if any
> Show patience and forgive,
> That would truly be
> An exercise of courageous will
> And resolution in the conduct
> Of affairs.
>   Quran 42:43

Commentators rarely associate patience or forgiveness with Islam and often quote the following verses to suggest Islam's violent nature, missing the irony that they echo the Bible faithfully:

> We ordained therein for them
> Life for life, eye for eye,
> Nose for nose, ear for ear,
> Tooth for tooth, and wounds
> Equal for equal.
>   Quran 5:45

However, the following lines of the same verse carry the message to its intended point, namely, that forgiveness as an act of atonement supersedes revenge:

> But if anyone
> Remits the retaliation
> By way of charity, it is
> An act of atonement for himself.

When an act such as murder does occur, Islamic justice, as mandated by the Quran, requires a formal trial employing witnesses and evidence in order to establish a person's guilt or innocence. Responsibility for all actions rests with the individual, which means Islam does not advocate the concept of killing a member of a murderer's family, clan, or those associated with the accused for an act they had no role in. Given the evidence of the sayings of the Prophet and the teachings of the Quran, there should be little doubt about where Islam stands on the taking of revenge.

In his call to hate and fight Christians and Jews, bin Laden also appears to be refuting the Prophet. Bin Laden's views on the matter have been frequently and strongly expressed: "Every Muslim from the moment they realize the distinction in their hearts, hates Americans, hates Jews, and hates Christians. This is a part of our belief and our religion."[4] Yet the Prophet, in a letter to the monks of St. Catherine's monastery in Mount Sinai written in AD 628, declared that every

Muslim was ordered to defend Christian churches, monks, women, property, and freedom of worship, as well as to fight on behalf of Christians themselves. Similarly, the Treaty of Medina in AD 622 guaranteed rights for the Jewish community of the town. The Quran sets forth numerous verses underlying the affiliated nature of Christians and Jews as "people of the Book" and "believers." Therefore, by definition, Muslims cannot hate Christianity or Judaism even when fighting against tyranny and injustice they may believe emanates from people who practice those religions.

Muslims with some understanding of Islam such as bin Laden are aware of the Islamic arguments for compassion. In bin Laden's case, however, the compulsions of tribal identity defined his actions and worldview, however much he tried to bolster his arguments with Islamic references. That identity becomes clear when one examines his lineage.

The Arabian Peninsula is home to two dominant tribal lineages named after two ancestors, Adnan and Qahtan, who lived in ancient times, long before the coming of Islam. Although controversy surrounds their relationship to one another, there is little doubt that they were the eponymous ancestors of the peninsula's two major tribes: the Adnan and the Qahtanis. Tribes descended from Adnan live in the northern, central, and western regions of the peninsula, and the Qahtanis, who are also known as Yemenis, live in the southern region. Every tribesman on the peninsula is aware of his position on this tribal map. The Qahtanis view themselves as the peninsula's original tribe, from which all derive including the Adnan, and support this claim by citing the great Muslim historians Tabari in *Tarikh-e Tabari* and Masudi in *Tarikh-e Masudi*.[5]

Bin Laden was a Yemeni and therefore a descendant of Qahtan. He had heard of the culture, courage, and poetry of the people of Yemen through his Yemeni father, whom he idolized. And he would rely heavily for support on the Qahtani tribes and their code of honor. Bin Laden's awareness of the prickliness and honor of the tribe came from his fascination with his tribal background. He recited poetry in honor of the Yemeni tribes. He would consciously sport a Yemeni tribal dagger at his waist as a traditional symbol of masculine honor. Significantly, he would wear it vertically, which traditionally indicated a warrior lineage, rather than tilted, which would suggest a religious one. He would also display a Kalashnikov placed discreetly somewhere in the frame of his videos, further emphasizing that he saw himself as a modern tribal warrior.

Although his followers took full advantage of modern technology, including aircraft and the Internet, bin Laden favored the language and imagery of epic Arab poetry dating to the pre-Islamic period, which abounded with horses, swords, lances, and heroic deeds. Bin Laden described the 9/11 attacks as "*yaum* New York," or "the day of New York," a phrase that Arabs traditionally used in the context of tribal raids.[6] Bin Laden even spoke about al Qaeda as a kind of

Here you see The Muslim Ummah
aflame seeking avenge.

Still of a video showing Osama bin Laden with the traditional dagger of a Yemeni tribesman (used with permission from intelwire.com).

tribe that engaged in "raids"—a word common in the lexicon of tribal nang societies. In this case, however, the goal would not be to attack caravans and towns but to strike at American targets on the other side of the world. The hijackers are described as "going out" (*kharaju*) from their home base, a term traditionally applied to a tribal group taking up arms. A bin Laden video soundtrack proclaims: "Come towards victory, let us tighten our saddle straps."[7] Other al Qaeda videos show groups of ferocious-looking men waving their weapons high while they charge about on horseback.

Poetry, a highly valued cultural trait of nang societies, was employed extensively by bin Laden, often with tribal rhetoric and themes. In a poem honoring the 9/11 hijackers broadcast on Al Jazeera in December 2001, he framed the attacks in the context of a tribe protecting itself from a threatening oppressor. The hijackers were described as "heroes" living in "meadows" and forced to launch "raids" to defend their lands and independence from a "covetous attacker" who lived in "palaces" that the "heroes" would target in retaliation. Bin Laden identified these "heroes" not by name but by tribe, all of whom descended from Qahtan, as he points out in this introduction to a poem that he would recite: "I'll finish with some lines of poetry in memory of those heroes from the land of Hijaz, the land of faith, from Ghamid and Zahran, from Bani Shahr, from Harb, from Najd."[8] Bin Laden goes on to quote the poem that refers to the hijackers as tribal warriors:

I bear witness that they are sharper than any sword:
how long they faced up to hardship,
how long they attacked and held firm!
They are a breed apart who sell their souls to God
who smile at death, while the frowning sword stares at them,
who bare their chests without asking for shields.
When the dark night was everywhere
and ravenous fangs bit out at us;
when our camp flowed with blood
while the covetous attacker strode through it;
when the flash of lances and horses
was gone from the open plains,
and the wailing was drowned out
by merry songs and drums,
their storms blew and destroyed
his palaces, saying to him:
"We will not stop [our] raids until
you leave our lush meadows."[9]

For bin Laden, the tribes of the Muslim world, too long dormant in the face of oppression, were again rising up as their glorious ancestors did to challenge injustice and tyranny as commanded by God. This was clear from bin Laden's praise of the two main Qahtani tribes that made up the *ansar,* or those that helped the Prophet in Medina in the seventh century: "History saw the actions of Aws and al-Khazraj. Well, Aws and al-Khazraj are back."[10] When bin Laden addressed the Muslim world in his tapes, he typically called on them by their tribes as well as the ancient names of their regions, such as al-Sham for the Levant and al-Kinanah for Egypt. [11]

Bin Laden compared American actions in the Muslim world to the violation of women, always a matter of high sensitivity in tribal society, and applied the tribal idiom of honor as a rationale for the Muslim "raids" as acts of revenge. "The enemy," he said, "invaded the land of our *umma,* violated her honor, shed her blood, and occupied her sanctuaries."[12] To atone for the shame incurred by this "rape" of the Muslim world and to preserve independence, one of the most cherished values in tribal society, its members must seek violent vengeance. This is a common theme in the context of honor as interpreted in so many tribal societies.

The 9/11 hijackers would echo the themes of honor and revenge in the videos they filmed before carrying out their mission. As one of them, Ahmad al-Haznawi, said: "I have sworn that either I live with my honor, with my dignity or else that my bones be crushed . . . we proclaim . . . the breaking of dawn is coming and the rising of the sun of honor is near. . . . We shall bring back the life of honor once more."

To avenge the honor of the ummah, bin Laden argued, men must perform their duties as warriors for they live in "a world of crimes in which children are slaughtered like cows. For how long will real men be in short supply?"[13] "The banner of *jihad*," he announced, "is raised up high to restore to our *umma* its pride and honor."[14] He declared, "Do not expect anything from us but *jihad*, resistance, and revenge."[15] Falling back again on poetic verse, bin Laden warned,

The walls of oppression and humiliation cannot be demolished
except in a rain of bullets.
The free man does not surrender leadership to infidels and sinners.
Without shedding blood, no degradation and branding can be
removed from the forehead.[16]

For bin Laden, the Quranic verses advocating battle held special meaning in the tribal context as they intimated that the world was divided between Muslims and "pagans" and did not contradict his tribal impulse for revenge and violence. Speaking from Tora Bora as American troops closed in on his position, bin Laden exclaimed: "Allah bears witness that the love of jihad and death in the cause of Allah has dominated my life and the verses of the sword permeated every cell in my heart, 'and fight the pagans all together as they fight you all together.' How many times did I wake up to find myself reciting this holy verse!"[17] In the citation of this Quranic verse, bin Laden creates theological problems for himself: the vast majority of Christian and Jewish troops are not "pagan" but in fact believers in God. Besides, once again bin Laden is using the Quran selectively and citing one part of the verse to justify his jihad and ignoring the next part, which advocates peace over conflict: "Hence, fight against them until there is no more oppression and all worship is devoted to God alone; but if they desist, then all hostility shall cease save against those who [willfully] do wrong." (Quran 2:193).

Further evidence of bin Laden's nang tribal ethos lies in his emphasis on egalitarianism, as reflected in his conception of al Qaeda as a group that anyone can join and in which all are equal. He saw himself as a Yemeni tribal *sheikh*, a respected and honored leader chosen by the tribe for his abilities and charisma, who is *primus inter pares*.[18] Bin Laden promoted this philosophy in al Qaeda from its early days in Peshawar at the time Soviet troops were withdrawing from Afghanistan. In so doing, he broke with his teacher and mentor in Afghanistan, the Palestinian Abdullah Azzam, a member of the Muslim Brotherhood who was killed in a car bombing in 1989. Azzam wanted to recruit elite and talented followers and train them in the methods of the Brotherhood, but bin Laden insisted on a vision that was more egalitarian and informal.[19] The two also backed opposite sides in the emerging Afghan civil war: bin Laden supported the Pukhtun

Gulbuddin Hekmatyar and his Pukhtun warriors, with their strong nang tribal identity, while Azzam threw his weight behind the Tajik Ahmed Shah Massoud, who would go on to lead the Northern Alliance representing the non-Pukhtun and non-nang tribes of Afghanistan.

Another clue to bin Laden's esteem for the tribes is provided by the names of the dwellings associated with him. The "Ghamdi House" near Kandahar where the 9/11 attacks were planned in the 1990s was named after a prominent Yemeni tribe from the Asir region of the Arabian Peninsula. The house where bin Laden was eventually killed in Abbottabad, Pakistan, was popularly called "Waziristan House." Had they been named after Mecca and Medina instead, bin Laden would have signaled that his Islamic identity had higher priority than his tribal one. These are, after all, the two holiest cities in Islam and recognized as such by Muslims everywhere. By honoring the names of tribes and tribal areas, he was implicitly acknowledging his regard for the tribes and the sources of his inspiration. Inadvertently, he was also revealing clues to what lay behind 9/11.

Bin Laden's Dilemma and the Sayings of the Prophet

In order to understand why bin Laden and his Yemeni supporters traveled down the terror road, it is essential to look at the position of the Yemeni tribes in early Islamic history. As the Prophet of Islam, himself a descendant of Adnan, is reputed to have said in a widely quoted hadith (a saying of the Prophet), the Yemenis are "the best people on the face of the earth." He is also reported to have said they "are tender-hearted and more delicate of soul. *Iman* [belief] and wisdom are of the Yemenis." Legend has it that the Prophet visited the Yemenis before receiving his revelations. Once he declared his mission, he was visited by Yemenis curious to learn of it. So impressed were they by what they heard that it was said the tribes converted to Islam within the course of a day. When the Prophet needed shelter in Medina, the Yemenis were on hand to receive him. They thus earned the title of *ansar,* or "helper." The Prophet never forgot the Yemenis, and in due course sent his son-in-law, Ali, one of the stars of early Islam, as his special envoy to Yemen.

Little wonder that scholars of Islam constantly refer to Yemenis in glowing terms. Ibn Taymiyyah is quoted as saying: "From [Yemen] came those whom Allah loves and they love Him." Yemeni scholars, of course, glorified in the links to the Prophet and the high expectations of their community: the well-known nineteenth-century Yemeni scholar Muhammad ash-Shawkaani, cited in bin Laden's Al Jazeera interview, wrote that the Prophet's sayings indicate "the exclusivity of Yemen's people to this great quality that Allah, the Almighty, will bring them forth at the time when others apostate from among the Arab tribes that live in the Peninsula and this is to show their high status as they are the party of Allah at a time when others leave this religion."[20] Another saying many Yemenis know by heart predicts that the final triumph of Islam will be brought about by the people of Southern Arabia, that is, the Yemenis. "An army of twelve-thousand," said the Prophet, "will come out of Aden-Abyan. They will give victory to Allah and His messenger. They are the best between myself and them."

Like so many Muslims throughout the world, bin Laden was also familiar with one of the Prophet's more common sayings to the effect that the body of the Muslim community is an integrated whole, and if one part of it is in agony, the entire body will feel that pain. In view of the Yemenis' special place in Islamic history, bin Laden and others of Yemeni background would have thus felt compelled to defend the ummah, wherever Muslims were being persecuted.

But a less well-known hadith of the Prophet states that "the ink of the scholar is more sacred than the blood of the martyr," which clearly emphasizes knowledge, rationality, and understanding over destructive thoughts of anger, revenge, and violence. This directive features prominently in the Quran, which makes some three hundred references to the importance of using the mind and studying the universe in which humans live. "Knowledge" is the second most used word in the Quran after the name for God. That is why the Prophet emphasized scholarship as the highest form of human activity and knowledge over martyrdom.

By focusing on the saying about the pain of the ummah, bin Laden was able to tap into a universal Muslim sentiment. But he explicitly rejected the Prophet's exhortations on knowledge and compassion over martyrdom and conflict, as is evident in his statements mentioned earlier about the Prophet's injunctions against killing innocent people. If it was the West and its supporters among Muslims who were slaughtering innocent Muslim women and children, then bin Laden concluded that their women and children should also be slaughtered. Strictly speaking, such dangerous theological arguments had opened bin Laden to the charge of blasphemy. For a man claiming to fight on behalf of Islam to explicitly reject a basic principle of the faith and yet not be fully taken to task for it by religious clerics is a mystery. It can only be explained by the strength of emotions released by the Prophet's reference to the palpable suffering of Muslims throughout the world in his sayings. Bin Laden's own arguments about the plight of the Muslims found a certain resonance in the Muslim community, which would have blunted criticism against him even from those who otherwise condemned him for his actions associated with 9/11.

Had bin Laden clung closer to the Prophet's vision embodied in his sayings about knowledge, he could have moved history in a positive direction instead of leading a global jihad and, as a consequence, plunging Muslim societies across the world into chaos. After his Afghan adventure in the 1980s, had he invested his considerable energy and resources in constructing schools and colleges, he would have created a vast pool of educated Muslims. He could have helped the Muslim world meet its desperate need for doctors, engineers, teachers, lawyers, administrators, and other professionals. That would have been in keeping with the Islamic ideal, especially in the weight it places on knowledge. By setting aside this crucial precept of Muslim behavior—indeed, by standing it on its head—bin Laden and his cohorts were rejecting the very basis of the Islamic cosmological and sociological order. The tension and opposition between the tribal codes and Islamic principles had not been resolved even in the Prophet's lifetime. This tension continues to fester in Muslim society today and underlies the crisis between center and periphery.

The Breakdown and Mutation of Tribal and Islamic Systems

The mutation—reflected in the actions of Muslims like the Taliban, bin Laden, and other al Qaeda leaders from the 1990s onward—emanated from the breakdown of both the tribal and Islamic systems, triggered by what they saw as overwhelming attacks on Muslim lands and peoples. Taking bits from each system, they devised a philosophic basis to justify their acts, combining the notion of revenge from their tribal background with Islamic concepts applied carelessly and with abandon. In their free interpretation of jihad, for example, they included attacks on congregations in mosques and schoolchildren in classrooms.

As for revenge in the tribal context, tradition does not call for violence for the sake of violence or bloodshed. However, if someone's brother is killed, he may, failing attempts at resolution through the council of elders, try to take revenge and kill the murderer's brother, but that does not authorize him to launch a murderous rampage against innocent people. If anything, such a response indicates excess and therefore a breakdown of the code. The council of elders will do everything in its power to prevent an escalating cycle of violence. It will suggest blood money as compensation or may even arrange a marriage between the aggrieved party and a close relative of the assailant. In this way, enemies may be converted to allies. The ultimate aim is to uphold the code, not to disrupt it.

Bin Laden's actions clearly fall into the category of excess and are alien to the categorical imperative laid down by the Prophet, by Abu Bakr, and others about killing innocent people. Unprecedented in their scope and scale, the killings of diplomats and visitors at American embassies or innocent passersby in East Africa or thousands of ordinary men, women, and children in New York, Washington, and Pennsylvania reflect a breakdown and mutation of both the tribal code and Islam. To reiterate, such actions have no basis in the sense of honor and balance at the heart of the tribal code or the compassion and restraint central to Islam.

9/11 AND THE TRIBES OF ASIR

Bin Laden was joined in his movement primarily by his fellow Yemeni tribesmen. According to his former bodyguard Nasir al-Bahri, a Yemeni born in Saudi

Arabia, "95 percent of the al Qaeda activists were Yemenis," meaning they were either from Yemen, were ethnic Yemenis whose families had moved to Saudi Arabia, or were from ethnic Yemeni areas in Saudi Arabia, most prominently from the Asir region, or indeed elsewhere.[21]

Although Mohammad Atta of Egypt has become the best known of the 9/11 hijackers, and investigators were quick to pick up his Muslim Brotherhood antecedents and therefore look in that direction for possible motivations, in reality he was not the driving force behind the plot, and his participation was almost accidental. An idealist and an architect, Atta was frustrated about the condition of ordinary people in his native Cairo and blamed the corrupt national leadership with its western support for their miserable situation. When he arrived in Karachi, still searching for a cause, he met members of bin Laden's group and was brought to Afghanistan. It did not take much to persuade him to join bin Laden.

While Atta became the poster child for the nineteen hijackers, the group was essentially Yemeni. Ten were from the tribes of Asir, whose role in the 9/11 operation was acknowledged by bin Laden himself: "Asir's tribes formed the lion's share [of the 9/11 perpetrators], [including] those from Ghamed, Zahran and Bani Shahr [all Asir tribes]."[22] The largest single tribe represented in the group was the Ghamdi tribe of Asir, with four members: Ahmed and Hamza al-Ghamdi who were brothers, Saeed al-Ghamdi, and Ahmad al-Haznawi. Others from Asir were Abdul Aziz al-Omari al-Zahrani of the Zahran tribe, the brothers Wail and Waleed al-Shehri, and Mohand al-Shehri of the Shahran tribe, and Hani Hanjur, who can be identified with the village of Hanjur in the area of the Abidah tribe in Asir, which is a subclan of Asir's Qahtan tribe, named after the Yemenis' common ancestor.[23] Ahmed al-Nami was described by the 9/11 Commission Report as being "from Asir" and by bin Laden as "from Abha," the capital of Asir; the al-Nami tribe is a subclan of the Qahtani Harb tribe.[24] In addition, Fayez Banihammad, who was born in the United Arab Emirates (UAE), may have had family ties to Asir as he attended university there and was also commonly identified as Fayez Ahmed al-Shehri, which would indicate an affiliation with the Shahran tribe of Asir.[25] By providing their full names, they were giving a clue to their tribal identity and lineage.

The other ethnic Yemenis included Khalid Muhammad Abdallah al-Mihdhar, whose family was from Yemen, although he grew up in Mecca. Marwan al-Shehhi of the United Arab Emirates was from the mountainous Shihuh tribe of the UAE territories and Oman, which, although the population is mixed and local culture and language contain Persian and Baluch influences, claimed descent from Qahtani tribes. Ziad Jarrah of Lebanon may be connected to the Jarrah tribe, part of the larger Qahtani Shammar tribe.[26] Majid Muqid Mushan bin Ghanim can be identified with the traditionally nomadic Ghanim tribe of the Taif area, which is a branch of the Qahtani Thaqif tribe.[27] The three remaining hijackers, Satam al-Suqami and the brothers Nawaf and Salem al-Hazmi, are probably Yemeni as their family names are place names in Yemen, although they were born in Saudi Arabia. In all probability, keeping in mind Mohammed Atta's Egyptian nontribal background, eighteen of the nineteen hijackers on 9/11 were Yemeni tribesmen, or descendants of Qahtan.

The additional relevance of the sons of Qahtan, and specifically those from Asir, to the war on terror can be seen in the prisoner list at Guantánamo Bay, where, at the time of writing, about half of the remaining detainees were from the modern state of Yemen and many others were ethnically Yemeni. Yemenis incarcerated included Jaber Hasan al-Qahtani, Jabran Said bin al-Qahtani, Khalid Mallah Shayi al-Qahtani, Abdul Rahman Uthman al-Ghamdi, Saeed al-Farha al-Ghamdi, and Rashid Khalaf Awad al-Ghamdi.

In its report, the 9/11 Commission identified other men selected by bin Laden, including a number of Yemenis from Asir, "who, for various reasons, did not end up taking part in the operation."[28] These included Muhammad Mani Ahmad al-Qahtani (the so-called twentieth hijacker who was intended for the plane that crashed in Pennsylvania and is now in Guantánamo Bay), Saeed Abdullah Saeed al-Ghamdi, Ali Abd al-Rahman al-Faqasi al-Ghamdi, and Khalid Saeed Ahmad al-Zahrani.

The lineage details of the nineteen hijackers and their immediate operational cadre serve an important purpose in the context of this study. They inform its main argument that tribal groups adhering to a segmentary lineage system constitute themselves as a raiding party, based on the genealogical charter and motivated by notions of revenge and honor, and set out to avenge the dishonor of the tribe singing war songs and waving weapons. The Islamic element is conspicuous by its absence; the source for killing innocent civilians resides in bin Laden's convoluted reasons for rejecting Islam described earlier in the chapter, as well as the hijackers' Yemeni tribal background, their emphasis on honor and revenge, and the centrality of Asir's tribes.

But like a brash tribal raiding party led by a delusional tribal leader, the group had not considered the possible consequences of its actions—the principles of cause and effect. The horrific killings of innocent Americans on 9/11, some of them Muslims, plunged an entire nation into trauma and grief. The terrorists' actions also showed their ignorance of the wider consequences in the context of world affairs. What they did that day has increased the scale and intensity of Muslim suffering a thousandfold.

In order to better explain why and how bin Laden and his Yemeni supporters did what they did, a closer look at their homeland in the Asir region is required. In the same way, as seen in chapter 2, that the TTP cannot be understood without examining Waziristan and its relationship with the central government of

Mountains of Asir (photo by Alex Sykes).

Pakistan, al Qaeda cannot be understood without examining Asir and its relationship with the Saudi government.

The Land of Asir

There are notable similarities between Asir and Waziristan. Like Waziristan, which is known as *ghair ilaqa* or land beyond the pale, the very name Asir translates as "inaccessible" or "difficult to reach." Asir, too, is an isolated land of contrasts, with high mountain peaks, beautiful meadows, desolate deserts, and vast wastelands, which one author has described as "barren and featureless, like a moonscape."[29] Asiri poems reflect the same gritty realism as Pukhtu literature, some about the transience of life: "The world is a few days of nothingness. Its beginning is nothing and its end is nothing."[30] According to a British government study commissioned during World War I, "In no part of Arabia are the tribal elements more sharply defined or their boundaries more immutably fixed than in Asir."[31] A senior American diplomat who served in Saudi Arabia from 1999 to 2002 and spent time in Asir observed that its tribes approach life with a "manic gusto" and are "fiercely independent."[32] Furthermore, they have "for millennia resisted advances by outsiders while quarreling incessantly with one another." Asir tribes have a reputation for fighting, and in the early twentieth century it was the custom of some to "cut a notch on the stock for each man killed."[33]

Like the Pukhtun of Waziristan, the Yemeni tribes in Asir are organized around a segmentary lineage system, with elders and councils, a spirit of egalitarianism, and a code of honor guiding society that emphasizes courage, loyalty, hospitality, and revenge. Here, too, isolation has helped to preserve the independence of the region's thistle-like tribes, most of which dwell in small settlements or in the several urban hubs. In addition, some tribal groups still maintain a nomadic style of life.

The tribes of Asir are all linked through subclans and clans to the larger Yemeni tribe tracing their descent to Qahtan. Tribes with a common ancestry in Asir also live beyond its borders. The most populous Somali clan, the Darod, claims it has a direct ancestral link with the tribes of Asir, believing its eponymous ancestor, Darod Ismail, to be the brother of the ancestor of the Asir tribes.[34]

As it did between the Wazir and Mahsud in Waziristan, tribal cousin rivalry defines Asir politics, for example, between the Ghamdi and the Zahran tribes. As in Waziristan, the central government has attempted to keep the balance and the peace between these tribes in order to prevent conflict. And, as in Waziristan, the major tribes in Asir—the Ghamdi, the Zahran, the Shahran, and the Qahtan (named after the larger Qahtani tribe of Yemen)—have shown a propensity to live more by the tribal code than by Islamic theology.

Asir in Modern Times

For more than a thousand years after Islam arrived in the seventh century, history had stood still for Asir. Its glory days were long over. The empires, kings, and captains of Islam with a connection to the Arabian Peninsula no longer played their part on the world stage. Pomp and power had shifted and for centuries lay in distant Muslim capitals: Istanbul, Isfahan, and Delhi. The land of the Prophet had become a backwater, and Asir was a backwater in that region. Distinctly pre-Islamic practices, characteristic of tribal Islam, survived up to modern times, many of which have been recorded.

British travel writer Rosita Forbes, for example, once described witnessing a trial by ordeal that involved both fire and water (for more details of trial by ordeal, see chapter 1).[35] More recently, Ahmed Abodehman, a native of Asir and a member of the Qahtan tribe, presented an account of tribal life in the 1960s in his autobiographical novel, *The Belt* (2002), which was banned in Saudi Arabia for its frank description of tribal customs. At one point he recounts his mother's encounter with a bat, a common animal in his house, found under stairs and other dark places:

> Mother picked up the creature and stroked it as tenderly and respectfully as she would her own child. She fetched butter and rubbed it all over her hands and lost herself in a strange ceremony. She seemed to be counting every hair on that bat's body. Her gestures were accompanied by prayers and strange words I had never heard before. . . . Without taking her eyes

off the bat, she asked me to light the fire and open every window in the house. . . . At dawn, the bat opened its eyes and began to stir. And Mother was her old self again.

"We saved it!" she cried. "Now, it can go to Heaven."

"Heaven? Isn't Heaven for human beings?"

"This bat is the tormented soul of one of your ancestors. And God granted it one last chance to come among the living to cleanse itself of sin. I made a vow and took all the sins upon myself, even those I didn't entirely understand. . . . God picked me to save this soul, and saving one soul, in God's eyes, is tantamount to saving all humanity. I have been blessed with splendid luck, a chance to save my soul from Hell. It was sublime, like witnessing the Night of Destiny. Your mother, my son, is Heaven-bound."[36]

Events early in the twentieth century entangled the men of Asir in world affairs and changed the area forever. Muhammad al-Idrisi, the great-grandson of the widely known and respected Sufi Islamic scholar Ibn Idris, known for winning public debates against the orthodox Wahhabis, formed a state in Asir in 1906 after being invited to settle a dispute between warring tribes. His state, linked to the Sanusi Sufi Order in North Africa, grew quickly as local tribes wished to associate themselves with a descendant of the Prophet, a sayyed who had a reputation for just and honorable behavior.

Rosita Forbes, who claimed to be the first European to whom Idrisi had granted an audience and was permitted to travel in the region in the early 1920s, observed the traits that made him so popular with the tribes. She noted that in Asir "luxury is forbidden" and gold considered so sinful that "Idrisi will not even have it in his house."[37] Idrisi, Forbes writes, was known as the "Hermit of Arabia," and was reputed to be the "most learned man in Arabia," having acquired degrees at Islam's oldest university, the Al Azhar, in Cairo. She described King Idrisi as "disinterested, just, sincere, and fabulously generous, he had a great reputation amongst the Bedouin." He also had a "critical appreciation of British administration" and told Forbes at one point that "at heart the English are sound."

In 1912 Idrisi published in Cairo a manifesto, *Bayan,* that outlined his philosophy of the world. In emphasizing justice and compassion for the poor, he contrasted his vision with the behavior of the Ottoman Turks, who attempted to conquer Asir with cruel force in the late nineteenth century. Idrisi, who led the tribes in resisting the invaders, refers to the Ottomans as "evildoers" burning homes and subjecting people to "mutilation, torture, and caning." "Do you think," an exasperated Idrisi asked in *Bayan,* "that it is still possible for the Bedouin to believe that his rulers are Muslims?"[38]

Following the collapse of the Ottoman Empire, Idrisi cast his lot with the British to preserve Asir's independence, which was short-lived. Following the

"Flower men" of Asir with their tribal daggers (photo by Charles Roffey).

death of King Idrisi in 1922, Asir grew isolated and vulnerable. Expansionist Arab neighbors had designs on it, and lacking a common enemy, the tribes of Asir began to fight one another. In addition, Britain was shifting its geopolitical interests away from Asir, instead courting the Saudis for their oil. Asir was soon ripe for the plucking. Yet like a true thistle, it would not be easy for the plucker.

In the late 1920s, Abdulaziz bin Saud, a bold and energetic tribal leader with a shrewd eye for the main chance, emerged virtually unknown from the deserts of the Arabian Peninsula to piece together a new kingdom under his rule. Formally consolidated in 1932, the new country was named Saudi Arabia, after bin Saud's tribe, the Saud, who, unlike the Asiris, were descended from Adnan. Continuing his aggressive drive to capture as much territory as he could, bin Saud annexed Asir in 1934 after bitter fighting, taking most of the region but leaving some of it with Yemen. The costs of consolidating the Asiris and other tribes of the peninsula into the new kingdom were enormous. Historians claim that some 400,000 people were killed in this period alone.[39]

The worst possible fate for a tribesman is to see his territory forcibly annexed by neighboring tribes. The annexation of Asir was followed by an invasion of religious clerics imposing their own interpretation of religion onto local people. Seeking to suppress and crush the old tribal customs, the Saudi clerics were bent on teaching the tribes of Asir what is known as Salafi or Wahhabi Islam—a literal interpretation of the Quranic text; its implementation, by force if necessary, was the duty of these clerics.

A great deal in Asir culture was permitted and protected by the tolerant King Idrisi, but would have sent the Wahhabi clerics arriving with their Quran and prayer beads into paroxysms of rage. The Asir men wore skirt-like apparel revealing much of their legs, and they went without socks. Famously known as "flower men," they kept their hair long and adorned it with flowers. Even their turbans were decorated with flowers, grass, and stones. Women were clothed in spectacular explosions of color, and their headdress glittered with coins and jewelry. They used henna to paint intricate patterns on their hands and feet. Indeed, their manner of dress showed few hints of Islamic design. Even their houses were painted with flamboyant stripes of color not normally associated with Islam, such as bright blue, yellow, and red.

As a first task, the Wahhabi clerics set out to destroy the traditional shrines of the Asiri holy men, which were a focal point and symbol of Asir religious identity. Young Asiri males were forced to cut their "un-Islamic" long locks and remove their traditional dagger, a long-recognized symbol of masculinity and manhood. Women were forced to adopt the veil in place of the traditional headscarf. As if this were not bad enough, it was rumored that the Saudi elite was arranging for the abduction of Asiri women, known for their beauty, to be kept as concubines.

Within a few decades, the people of Asir found themselves transformed from masters of their home to despised and degraded strangers in it. Yet it took the Saudis many years to fully incorporate the region, and even then much of the population was still restless and dissatisfied. Always conscious of their links to the Prophet, Yemeni tribesmen of Asir often quoted the sayings of the Prophet that cast themselves in a positive light and their new Saudi rulers representing the central government in a negative one. Because the Saud tribe came from the Najd region of the Arabian Peninsula, the Yemenis are fond of quoting Imam al-Bukhari, who cited a saying of the Prophet about the people of that region:

> "O Allah! Give us Baraka in our Sham, O Allah! Give us Baraka in our Yemen." They said: "And in our Najd?" and he said: "O Allah! Give us Baraka in our Sham, O Allah! Give us Baraka in our Yemen." They said: "And in our Najd?" and I believe that he said on the third occasion: "In that place (Najd) are earthquakes and seditions, and in that place shall rise the devil's horn."

Whatever opinion the Asiris had of their new Saudi rulers, or complaints about the human rights violations they suffered, few in the outside world were listening. Instead, Western nations were tripping over themselves to tap the newly discovered oil in the kingdom, and they were prepared to humor the Saudi rulers at all costs. To make matters worse for the Asiris, the region was soon caught up in the political enmity between the king of Saudi Arabia and the charismatic leader of Egypt, Gamal Abdel Nasser. These two leaders represented an even larger global conflict between the United States, allied with Saudi Arabia, and the Soviet Union, which backed Nasser's Egypt. This confrontation drew in tribes across the state of Yemen and plunged the nation into a bloody civil war. At one stage, Nasser, as part of his intervention in Yemen to check those elements supported by the Saudis, bombed Asir. Even so, the Saudis suspected the Asiris were fifth columnists and arrested large numbers, especially among the Ghamdi.

Alarmed at Nasser's aggression, dissatisfied with the situation in Asir, and backed by his American advisers, the Saudi king ordered the building of a major highway—"Highway 15"—through the heart of Asir and up to the Yemeni border. The project would also include air bases, garrisons, and missile facilities and would help integrate the Asir periphery into the Saudi state. To implement these projects, the king turned to one of the most prominent construction tycoons in Saudi Arabia, Muhammad bin Laden, the father of Osama bin Laden.

Highway 15

The rise of bin Laden's family from poverty to vast riches is a story worthy of the Arabian Nights. The ancestral home of the bin Ladens is in the Hadhramaut region of eastern Yemen, a vast land of sand and rocks that translates as "death has come." They belonged to the Yemeni Kenda tribe, a powerful ancient tribe with roots stretching back to the pre-Islamic era, but by the early twentieth century it had declined significantly in strength and prominence. The bin Ladens' path out of Hadhramaut began when Muhammad's father, Awadh, borrowed an ox from a member of another tribe. When it died, Awadh fled from his village: he was too poor to pay compensation for the animal. Thus began a journey that would bring his son Muhammad to Saudi Arabia and grandson Osama onto the world stage.

In Saudi Arabia, Muhammad found a job with the Arabian American Oil Company, or Aramco, but soon established his own construction company with the help of American patrons. Before long, his company, fueled by the oil and development boom, was the richest in Saudi Arabia. Muhammad was responsible for renovating the major holy sites in Mecca and Medina, including the Prophet's mosque, as well as expanding the Grand Mosque in Mecca to accommodate tens of thousands of additional pilgrims. Muhammad also renovated the Dome of the Rock in Jerusalem, labor that he performed gratis for the sake of God. These actions would earn him the respect and love of many, including his son Osama.

Highway 15 was Muhammad's most lucrative project and also the most dangerous owing to the harsh terrain. It claimed hundreds of lives every year and became known as the Road of Death. In the end, Muhammad himself would die in Asir in a plane crash in 1967. Osama was then a young boy and never quite got over the trauma of losing his father.

Muhammad had come to feel at home in Asir. He loved its tribes, its ways, its history, and its cultural ambiance. One of his favorite wives was from Asir. In turn, the tribes of Asir accepted Muhammad as one of their own. Not only was he a fellow Yemeni, but they were won over by his easy charm as he held court sitting in a large white canvas tent with brightly colored cushions and carpets covering the floor. Muhammad received tribesmen who would petition him to settle disputes or for other assistance. He had become more than a mere construction worker. He had become their sheikh. The tribes would respond with loyalty when Muhammad's son Osama would come to them for support. Twelve of the 9/11 hijackers were from towns along Highway 15.

While the oil boom made the Saudi royal family and its supporters very rich, little was done for the people of Asir. The large, extravagantly built holiday villas owned by the Saudi elite in Asir seemed to add nothing but salt to their wounds. In 1980 the poverty-stricken province had only 535 hospital beds for a population of about 700,000.[40] Besides, given their religious background and its emphasis on austerity, the Yemenis disapproved of the Saudis' arrogance and vulgar displays of wealth. Poor Yemeni tribesmen desperate for work looked for jobs in the Saudi cities. Typically, they could only find employment in the military or as cooks, gardeners, or drivers. After the kingdom began to invite immigrant workers from the Philippines and India, the Yemenis could not even obtain those menial positions. Their resentment against the Saudi centers of power remained a constant undercurrent of Asir society.

Indeed, men from Asir were prominent in one of the most serious challenges to Saudi central authority when in 1979 Juhayman al-Otaibi led a bloody takeover of the Grand Mosque in Mecca. Al-Otaibi had become convinced that one of his students, Mohammed Abdullah al-Qahtani from Asir, was the Mahdi sent to release Muslims from the hold of the Sauds. So impressed was al-Otaibi by al-Qahtani that he divorced his own wife and married al-Qahtani's sister so he could be the Mahdi's brother-in-law. Al-Qahtani had been working at a Riyadh hospital when the Saudi police arrested him on a false charge of stealing money and subjected him to torture, pulling his fingernails out in order to extract a confession. Later he was exonerated and freed from jail when the actual culprit was accidentally apprehended with the stolen money.[41]

It was this simmering resentment of the periphery against what it saw as the corrupt and indifferent center failing to live up to Islamic ideals that provided the background to the siege of the Grand Mosque. During the siege, al-Qahtani fought hand-to-hand combat against the Saudi security forces but was killed by a grenade. Those who died in the attack included 127 Saudi security forces and 117 members of al-Otaibi's group. A further 63 were beheaded after being captured, including al-Otaibi. The incident sent shock waves throughout the Muslim world as many were forced to ask what was going wrong at the very heart of Islam. The answers pointed to the royal family and their system of governance. By drawing negative attention to the Saudis, al-Otaibi had achieved what he had set out to do.

The Asiris Find a Leader and a Cause

Several factors explain why the Ghamdi and Zahran along with other Asir tribes were in the forefront of the movement that culminated in 9/11 and in time had consequences for the Muslim world as well as the entire globe. First, like the Pukhtun of Waziristan, the tribes of Asir are part of a segmentary lineage system and, in addition, have an unparalleled Islamic pedigree going back to the Prophet that gives them a strong sense of tribal and religious identity. Second, relations between Asir and the central government of Saudi Arabia had become increasingly tense owing to Asiri complaints about the lack of opportunities, miscarriage of justice, and ignored pleas. For their part, the Saudis felt Asiris were not much better than heretics and needed to be forcibly converted to their version of Islam. Saudi rulers trampled on the honor of the Asiris and deprived them of justice, one of the highest precepts of the tribal code, the Quran, and the Prophet. Third, dramatic changes under way in the region were having a profound effect on people in Asir, starting with the first Gulf War and the stationing of American troops on the Arabian Peninsula. Anger and discontent were mounting throughout Asir, but its tribes were leaderless and without a rallying cause. With the appearance of Osama bin Laden, they found both.

The men of Asir now found international outlets for their political passions, first in Afghanistan and then in places like Chechnya. In the 1980s Asir was one of the central recruiting areas in Saudi Arabia for the war against the Soviet invaders of Afghanistan. Many Asiris would also join the organization that bin Laden formed in Peshawar in 1988—which he named al Qaeda (meaning "the base"). In the following decade, Asiris became active in operations against Saudi Arabia's central government and its American backer. The Gulf War was a turning point in the region. Religious figures, or *ulema*, led a fierce opposition against the practices of the Saudi royal family and the involvement of the United States in Saudi affairs. This movement was dubbed the "Islamic awakening" (*Sahwa*), and it was soon joined by younger men who were not schooled exclusively in the Wahhabi doctrine and who had also been influenced by ideas from other sources such as the Muslim Brotherhood.

Of all the religious leaders supporting the movement against the Saudi establishment, none was more respectable than Safar al-Hawali of the Ghamdi tribe, who had been dean of the Islamic Studies Faculty at Umm al-Qura University in Mecca and had his Ph.D. research supervised by Muhammad Qutb, brother of Sayyid Qutb, the founder of the Muslim Brotherhood. As U.S. troops began arriving in 1990, al-Hawali proclaimed that the United States was the foremost threat to Saudi Arabia, with plans to take over the kingdom. Al-Hawali argued that the West's strategy was to help modernize and thus undermine Islamic society from within, and he issued blistering attacks on the Saud and Wahhabi establishment for its complicity. The Saudis arrested al-Hawali after he addressed the tribes in Asir.

Bin Laden, who by the mid-1990s had been stripped of his Saudi citizenship for his outspoken opposition to the royal family, was outraged by the arrests of al-Hawali and other religious scholars. In 1996 he issued a declaration of war on the United States in which he "bemoaned" these arrests. In an interview with CNN the following year, he said: "When the Saudi government transgressed in oppressing all voices of the scholars and the voices of those who call for Islam, I found myself forced, especially after the government prevented Sheikh Salman Al-Awda and Sheikh Safar Al-Hawali and some other scholars, to carry out a small part of my duty of enjoining what is right and forbidding what is wrong."[42]

Bin Laden was not the only admirer of these religious leaders. They fired the imagination of those Muslims seeking an Islamic cause. Their speeches proved a recruiting boon for al Qaeda. The 9/11 hijacker Saeed al-Ghamdi praised al-Hawali in his videotaped will, and it was revealed that Mounir el-Mottasedeq, a Moroccan accomplice of Mohammad Atta in Germany, made repeated calls to al-Hawali's office in Riyadh in the months before 9/11.

By the middle of the 1990s, the actions of al Qaeda and its supporters, particularly from Asir, were undergoing a distinct mutation in behavior, by engaging in the killing of civilians, diplomats, and military personnel during peacetime. The Asiri, Muslih al-Shamrani, for example, had returned from fighting Soviet forces in Afghanistan to learn that he was refused his old post in the Saudi army and had to sell produce from a street cart to make ends meet. In 1995 he was involved in the bombing of a U.S. military contractor training Saudi security forces; seven people including five U.S. officers were killed, and al-Shamrani was executed for his action the following year. According to U.S. authorities, the Saudi-Yemeni border area was most likely the location of the planning for the 1998 bombings of the U.S. embassies in Kenya and Tanzania; it is also the area through which those linked to the plot are thought to have escaped. U.S. officials also confirmed that the rubber boat carrying the bomb that rammed the USS *Cole* was purchased in the port of Jizan in the Asir region and then smuggled into Yemen.[43]

Over the 1990s bin Laden himself was transformed in the public imagination from a warrior heroically fighting against a brutal occupying force in Afghanistan to a plotter designing the murder of civilians. In spite of the compulsions of Pukhtunwali, the Afghans had already begun to see him as a guest who had overextended his welcome. Bin Laden gave the impression that somehow he personally engineered the defeat of the Soviet empire, thus belittling Afghan sacrifices and thousands of years of history resisting invading forces. Despite the changing circumstances, bin Laden began to believe that the title of sheikh, an honorific given to established religious scholars and bestowed on him by his followers, entitled him to issue religious decrees. Suffering from what Brigadier Dogar of Pakistan called "delusions of grandeur," bin Laden now wished to turn his attention to vanquishing the other remaining empire—that of the United States. The attacks on 9/11 and resulting deaths of close to 3,500 innocent people would represent the culmination of bin Laden's transformation.

The elder bin Laden pushed the people of Asir into modernity, the son into globalization; neither action was sanctioned by the Asiris or implemented on their terms. Father and son proved to be catalysts of change that would ultimately prove disastrous for the Asiris, however well intentioned their aim. If modernity meant being forced into a subordinate position in your own land, having ancestral homes bulldozed to make way for highways, losing tribal lands to missile bases, and seeing the arrival of a police force ready to pull out your nails to force a confession, then globalization was a greater disaster. People simply vanished into a dark world of rendition, secret prisons, and obliterated identities, where no one seemed to know who you were or if you even existed. The people of Asir were transformed from proud carriers of tradition who were secure in their identity to a despised, dazed, and angry underclass. Their various sources of identity—tribal, religious, and national—were thrown out of joint. Now clinging to one, now another, they were no longer sure of who they were. If modernity posed challenges for identity, globalization threatened to exterminate it altogether. Maintaining a balance was proving difficult. Even those with millions of dollars at their disposal and familiar with the ways of the world faltered; Osama bin Laden was a prime example.

Asiris Abroad after 9/11

After 9/11, Asiris, particularly tribes like the Ghamdi, engaged in a wide variety of terror attacks around the world. A Ghamdi was among the Saudi citizens jailed in Morocco in 2003 for plotting attacks on Western warships. Also arrested were two other Saudi nationals (one of whom was Hilal al-Asiri) and their Moroccan wives.[44] The most prominent Arab fighter in Chechnya was Abu al-Walid al-Ghamdi, known as the emir of the Arab Mujahideen and killed in 2004. He was the scourge of the Russian troops, who accused him of orchestrating the deadly 1999 Moscow apartment bombings and announced his death at least seven times.

The Ghamdi tribesmen also traveled to Iraq to fight the United States following its 2003 invasion. After native Iraqis, the greatest number of the Iraqi insurgency consisted of Saudi "foreign fighters," which included those of Yemeni descent like the Ghamdi.[45] In 2004 a twenty-year-old Ghamdi tribesman blew himself up in a U.S. mess hall in Mosul, Iraq, killing fourteen U.S. troops, four Halliburton employees, and four Iraqi soldiers while injuring seventy-two, including fifty-one U.S. soldiers.

British writer John R. Bradley recently found strong tribal allegiances among Ghamdis living abroad, even those who had never been to Asir. The son of a senior Saudi Ghamdi diplomat in London, having spent little of his life in Saudi Arabia and speaking poor Arabic, told Bradley he was nonetheless "proud of his Al-Ghamdi tribal characteristics: generosity, loyalty, a refusal to judge anyone on any basis other than their merits, even if he comes from the same tribe." Another Ghamdi tribesman who had never been to Asir said that on the anniversary of September 11 he had "heard about his 'cousins' holding celebratory dinner parties" across the tribe's home region and was "acutely aware of the role the Al-Ghamdi tribe had played in various conflicts and attacks the world over, and he beamed with pride as he listed them, one by one. 'Look what we managed to do with just a few of our members on September 11,' he declared on one occasion. 'Imagine what we could do if a million of us rose up together!'"[46]

Inside Asir after 9/11

In the years after 9/11, Saudi Arabia became a war zone and Asir a hotbed of resistance against the central government and its security services, which by then were obtaining a massive influx of funds and weaponry from the United States. The government completely shut the province to journalists and visitors. Gunfights and bombings wracked every major city across Saudi Arabia as "militants" under ethnic Yemeni leaders took on the security forces. The Yemenis included strategist Yusuf al-Ayiri, Khaled Ali al-Hajj, and Salih al-Awfi of Asir. The security services, run by the Interior Ministry, were widely blamed for the torture and execution of citizens.

In late 2003, in the midst of a widespread U.S.-backed crackdown by the Saudi security services, Riyadh-based lawyer Abdul Aziz al-Tayyar spoke by phone to Al Jazeera about the social and economic conditions inside Saudi Arabia: "All tribesmen are now willing to fight this government—we will protect the rights of our people. This is not the kingdom of Saudi Arabia any more. It is a jungle full of monsters. The Saudi people are suppressed. They suffer poverty and unemployment."[47] Just minutes later, Saudi security forces that had been monitoring the interview burst into his home and arrested him on live television.

Once again in 2003 the Ghamdi were implicated in attacks against the central government and Westerners who supported it. Two, and possibly three, of the "al Qaeda" members who conducted the Riyadh bombings of Western compounds that year, killing thirty-five people, were Ghamdi, including the accused mastermind of the operation. When his capture was announced on Saudi television and in newspapers, no mention was made of his Ghamdi tribal affiliation. Instead, over the next month news outlets issued daily reports and official photographs of tribal leaders from Asir and Hejaz meeting with Crown Prince Abdullah and Interior Minister Prince Naif.

In 2004 the Saud governor of Asir, Prince Khaled al-Faisal, appeared mystified by the revolt on his hands, with its vehement uprising against the central government. Writing in an Asir newspaper, he described the province's people as usually full of fun and optimism: "What happened to them? Who scared the children away from laughter, play and joy? Who scared the adults from life? . . . Who convinced our sons and daughters to call their fathers and mothers infidel? Who teaches children in orphanages that Saudi Arabia is not their home, that their only home is Islam? That their future vocation is jihad? . . . Who did this to us?"[48]

The answer to the Saudi prince's anguished questions came from a Zahrani tribesman from Asir, described as "the leading Saudi theorist of al-Qaeda" and whom the Saudi government called "the most wanted terrorist" in the kingdom at the time of his arrest in Asir's capital in 2009.[49] In a widely circulated letter entitled "Saudi Nationality under my Foot," he introduces himself as Faris ibn Ahmad ibn Juman ibn al-Shuwayl al-Hasani al-Zahrani al-Azadi. In stating his name in this fashion, he underscored his identity as a member of the Zahran tribe, whose members, like the Ghamdi, are descended from Azd, one of two branches of the Qahtan. In the letter, he asserts that he does not recognize Saudi nationality:

> I am a Muslim among Muslims. I read history and did not find something called nationality (*jinsiyya*). Each Muslim must operate in the realm of Islam (*dar al-Islam*) wherever he wants and without borders restraining him or passports confining him and without a despotic nation (*taghut watan*) to worship. My fathers are known, my family is known, my tribe Zahran belong to the Azd. Therefore I do not belong to Al Saud, who have no right to make people belong to them.[50]

With the rebellious Yemenis under relentless attack in Saudi Arabia, it was decided in 2009 to merge the Saudi Arabian al Qaeda organization with that of their ethnic cousins in Yemen. The leadership for both was now to be located in Yemen under the protection of local tribes. Presiding over the merger between the two groups was the Yemeni Nasir al-Wuhayshi, who had been Osama bin Laden's secretary in Afghanistan. After 9/11, he fled from Afghanistan to Iran, thence to Yemen. Jailed in Yemen without charges, he escaped from a maximum security prison in 2006. As head of Al Qaeda in the Arabian Peninsula (AQAP), he ordered the 2009 Christmas Day "underwear bomb" attack over Detroit, attempted by Umar Farouk Abdulmutallab, a Nigerian with a Yemeni mother. Speaking in a 2009 video, alongside al-Wuhayshi, AQAP's deputy commander, Said al-Shiri of the Shahran tribe of Asir, who had spent nearly six years in Guantánamo Bay, affirmed: "I say: By Allah, the tribes of Qahtan, Utaibah, Harb, Ghamid, Zahran, Banu Shihr, Dawasir, Juhainah, and other tribes of the land of Haramain [Mecca and Medina] have not deserted you. Here are their children setting off for Jihad in the Cause of Allah to aid you and your sisters all over the world."[51] It was reported that al-Shiri was killed by a U.S. drone in September 2012.

The maker of the underwear bomb, Ibrahim Hassan Tali al-Asiri, had an Asiri tribal background. Four months before that attack, the bomb maker's brother, Abdullah Hassan al-Asiri, had gained an audience with the Saudi head of counterterrorism, Prince Mohammad bin Naif bin Abdul Aziz al-Saud, during Ramadan under the ploy of having been "rehabilitated" from terrorism. Al-Asiri exploded a suicide bomb concealed inside his body and believed to have been triggered by a cell phone; the bomb killed him but left the prince with light injuries because al-Asiri's body absorbed the brunt of the blast.

The continuing turmoil in the region and lack of any sign of resolution explained the continued approval the hijackers still have at home among some Asiris. When contacted on the tenth anniversary of the 9/11 attacks, the father of one of the Ghamdi hijackers expressed support for his son and "fury" at the United States, berating it for the wars in Iraq and Afghanistan and for taking many more civilian lives than were taken on 9/11: "America is the first enemy of all Muslims. . . . I am proud of my son as is all his family."[52]

The history of Asir may be best summed up in the contrasting messages of the two men who had the most profound impact on its people in the past century: King Idrisi and Osama bin Laden. They could not be more different. Idrisi promoted the idea of a compassionate and scholarly Islam allied with friends from the West, particularly the British, and opposed the colonial rule of fellow Muslims, the Ottoman Turks. He was a man with an eye to the future. To bin Laden, on the other hand, the most relevant interpretation of Islam required violence aimed at civilians, and his enemies were very much the dominant Western powers. The two men disagreed most on how to interpret the core of Islam. King Idrisi was inspired by the example of the Prophet and his emphasis on knowledge, whereas bin Laden challenged that interpretation, emphasizing the honor and revenge of the tribal code, where it so easily mutated into acts of wanton violence involving innocent civilians, both Muslim and non-Muslim. While King Idrisi was successful in balancing tribal and Islamic identity and maintained his integrity as a Muslim, bin Laden and his followers were unable to do so, with the result that both sources of their identity underwent a mutation. It is an irony of history that few have heard of Idrisi, while bin Laden has become a household name.

The sequence of events that unfolded with increasing rapidity in Asir propelled its tribes into modernity and then, before they had recovered their balance, beyond that into the age of globalization. From locating links to ancestors in the form of bats to flying planes into the World Trade Center and the Pentagon in one generation is as great a leap in mastering technological skills as it is in imagination.

REVENGE, MUTATION, AND FEMALE SUICIDE BOMBERS

The mutations of the traditional tribal codes of Waziristan and Asir from which emerge excessive and wanton acts of violence extend far beyond these regions—as traditional structures of similar Muslim tribal societies elsewhere are now breaking down. Each person in these societies faces the same dilemma as bin Laden did, expressed within their particular political and social contexts. No one is immune, not even women. If anything, women have become the primary targets of the turmoil and thus for the first time in history have adopted suicide bombing to avenge the wrongs they believe have been inflicted on them, as illustrated by examples among the Pukhtun in the Tribal Areas of Pakistan cited in chapter 2. In September 2012 a female suicide bomber blew herself up with at least thirteen people at Kabul airport as "revenge" for the offensive American film attacking the Prophet of Islam. In Iraq between 2007 and 2008, twenty-seven suicide bombers in Diyala Province were women.[53] Similar incidents in other segmentary lineage societies illustrate the far-reaching impact of the mutation of tribal honor and revenge. Chechnya offers a prime example.

In June 2000 two teenage girls, seventeen-year-old Khava Barayeva, the niece of a prominent Chechen rebel leader killed the previous year, and her best friend Luiza Magomadova, age sixteen, became the first known Chechen suicide bombers when they drove a truck full of explosives into a Russian army base in their home village of Alkhan-Yurt. Khava's *cri de coeur* expressed her anger and frustration in a prerecorded video with Luiza and could be that of any of the other female suicide bombers:

> Sisters, the time has come. When the enemy has killed almost all our men, our brothers and husbands, we are the only ones left to take revenge for them. The time has come for us to take up arms and defend our home, our land from those who bring death to our home. And if we have to become *shakhids* for Allah we will not stop. *Allah Akbar!* . . . Our forefather[s] would have killed anyone who tried to [touch] their women but today Muslim women are getting attacked and raped in front of those who claim to be men—they have no sense of jealousy for their Muslim sisters honour to the extent that they sit and drink tea while listening to this appalling news!! Do you consider yourselves men? . . . This life is not worth anything—every person will die and leave this life behind. . . . So why do we not choose the best way to die, martyrdom, the highest most eminent way? We have chosen this way for ourselves and hope you will choose this way too inshallah.[54]

President Vladimir Putin, the macho man, about to bag a tiger in Siberia (photo by premier.gov.ru).

The Caucasian Case

Khava and Luiza's words demonstrate the place of women in *Nokhchalla,* the Chechen code of honor, and illustrate how the code has mutated with the destruction of traditional society. Under *Nokhchalla,* if a man takes the life of a woman or rapes her, male members of her family have the right to kill two members of the offender's family. Khava and Luiza's anger is directed as much against the Russians, whom they accuse of rape, as against their own men, whom they blame for failing to defend their honor. The duty of men to protect the honor of women is illustrated in a Chechen story about a man who accidentally brushed his little finger against the hand of the woman in whose home he was staying as a guest. To protect her honor, the man cut off his finger.

The bloodshed that followed Russia's all-out attempts to crush Chechnya's bid to secede after the collapse of the Soviet Union threw Chechen society into ferment. In 1996 Chechens succeeded in expelling the Russians, but in 1999 the Russians returned with more than 90,000 troops and killed between 30,000 and 40,000 Chechen civilians. Entire families were decimated. Eleven close relatives of the Chechen leader Shamil Basayev, including his wife, daughters, and brother, were killed in May 1995.[55] In 2000 Basayev stepped on a landmine and needed to have his foot amputated. The operation, conducted under local anesthetic, was taped and televised with Basayev watching dispassionately. Undaunted, later that year Basayev challenged Vladimir Putin to a duel. "The choice of weapon we leave to you," he taunted. In spite of promoting himself as a macho man of action—with internationally circulated photographs of him shirtless, with rippling muscles and holding a rifle, or taking aim to shoot a tiger—Putin believed discretion was the better part of valor and did not take up the offer.

In all, Russian operations in Chechnya after 1994 killed about 100,000 Chechens out of a population of only 1 million. With the complete devastation wrought by the two Chechen wars, increasingly desperate Chechens like Khava and Luiza sacrificed themselves to take revenge and terrorize the Russians, hoping to make them experience the pain the Chechens had felt. In September 2004 thirty men and two women wearing suicide bomb vests took more than 1,100 people hostage in a school in Beslan, North Ossetia, an operation that led to the deaths of 334 people, including 186 children. Basayev claimed responsibility. One member of the group was reported by a hostage to have said that a Russian plane from Beslan's airfield had killed his entire family, and now his sole purpose in life was to seek revenge, even if it involved murdering women and children.[56]

A number of suicide bombers followed Khava and Luiza, many of them women. In November 2001 Elza Gazuyeva, a twenty-three-year-old woman who had lost sixteen of her relatives to the Russians, including her husband, two brothers, and a cousin, walked up to General Gaidar Gadzhiyev and asked, "Do you still remember me?" She then blew herself up, killing the general and his bodyguards. Before this incident, Gadzhiyev had personally summoned Elza to witness her husband's torture and execution, during which the general had slashed open her husband's stomach and forced Elza's face into the gaping, gory wound gushing blood. In October 2002 nineteen Chechen women wearing explosive vests along with twenty-two men took 800 people in a Moscow theater hostage, with 170 people losing their lives. In August 2004 two Chechen women whose brothers had been killed blew themselves up on two separate airliners nearly simultaneously, killing ninety people, while the sister of one of them blew herself up at a Moscow metro station the following week, taking the lives of ten people. Out of a total of 110 Chechen suicide bombers between 2000 and 2005, 47 were women.[57] Studies have shown that nearly all of these women had lost at least one relative in the war with Russia, some had been raped, and others had been kidnapped and tortured. While some were linked to groups and leaders like Basayev and Umarov, a great number had no organizational link at all.

When Rizvan and Muslimat Aliyev, a brother and sister aged twenty-three and nineteen, respectively, blew themselves up in the capital of the Republic of Dagestan, Makhachkala, in May 2012, killing 13 and injuring 101, they were signaling a similar breakdown to the one across the border in Chechnya. The instability and resulting violence in Dagestan began after Putin asserted direct control of the region in 2004, ending local autonomy. Dagestan, meaning the

Land of the Mountains, is home to a number of segmentary lineage societies, including the majority Avars, Lezgins, and Dargin peoples. The region has a long history of violent resistance against Russian rule, particularly by the Avars under the famous Imam Shamil in the nineteenth century. Since 2004 suicide bombings have been a constant threat. They have targeted the police and other representatives of Russian authority in the region in acts of revenge for torture, humiliation, and the killing of family members. Many in the police force are now too frightened to even wear their uniforms as so many are being killed by unknown assassins who follow them for days before striking. Every traffic officer in the Dagestani capital is accompanied by a riot policeman in camouflage with a Kalashnikov. A thirty-year-old police officer told the *New York Times* that even when he and his colleagues stopped to help an ordinary woman who had fallen on the ground, she told them that she hoped all of them would be murdered.[58]

Following in the fashion of the nang Pukhtun, the Caucasian tribes have brazenly targeted top government officials. In 2004, after a number of failed attempts, the Chechens killed the Moscow-backed Chechen president, along with a number of other senior government officials, when they bombed a stadium ceremony commemorating Russia's victory in World War II. A Russian general was killed in Dagestan in 2008, while in 2009 the Avar minister of internal affairs for Dagestan, known for combating the rebellious groups and often employing the slogan "Take no prisoners," was killed by a sniper in broad daylight while attending a wedding party at a restaurant. In September 2011 the deputy director of the federal prison system in Dagestan was shot dead.

The Russian government subjected the other Caucasian republics to the same ruthlessness and was met by similar revenge attacks, not only on Russian security forces but also on anyone associated with the government, even imams and other religious figures. In June 2009 in the Republic of Ingushetia, a female suicide bomber critically injured the president of the republic and his brother, the region's head of security, while killing his driver and bodyguard. In 2010 the top cleric in the majority Circassian republic of Kabardino-Balkaria was murdered, and there were 108 attacks on law enforcement personnel that year, during which forty-two were killed.[59] In a February 2011 trial of fifty-eight terror suspects in Kabardino-Balkaria, a lawyer who worked with their families contended: "What these lads did came after months and years of provocations by the security services on the basis of their religion. They were beaten, they were sodomized with bottles. Some had crosses shaved into their heads. Some were forced to drink vodka."[60] An Ingush suicide bomber in January 2011 blew himself up in Moscow's international airport, killing thirty-seven people. In October 2012 a suicide bomber detonated a bomb at a police checkpoint on the border between Ingushetia and North Ossetia Province, killing a policeman and wounding three others.

The Kurdish Case

On June 30, 1996, Zeynep Kinaci, a twenty-four-year-old Kurdish woman, walked into a group of Turkish soldiers singing the Turkish national anthem in a military parade in Tunceli Province of eastern Turkey. Masquerading as a pregnant woman, she blew herself up along with ten soldiers, thus becoming the first suicide bomber among the Kurds. Kinaci was married, had a college degree, and worked in a state hospital as an X-ray technician.

According to the Kurdistan Workers' Party (PKK), which she had joined the year before, Kinaci had conducted the suicide mission to "avenge" an attempt by Turkish intelligence to kill the head of the PKK, Abdullah Ocalan. Just before she took action, Kinaci had written a public message outlining the reasons for her action. She began by stating her name, village, and tribe, the Mamureki, and revealed that her husband had been captured by the Turks. She continued: "I believe that my support for the PKK and the liberation movement had its roots in the fact that my family was concerned to preserve their Kurdish identity."[61] Addressing the head of the PKK, she declared: "Your life gives us honour, love, courage, confidence, trust and belief. . . . I shout to the whole world: 'Hear me, open your eyes!' We are the children of a people that has had their country taken away and has been scattered to the four corners of the world."[62]

Not long before her suicide, Kinaci's region of Tunceli, known as one of the least accessible areas of Kurdistan with its snow-capped mountains and deep ravines, and whose tribes had remained effectively independent from central government control for centuries, had been characterized as "Turkey's largest prison."[63] It had been the target of a Turkish military campaign in the late 1930s that left as many as 70,000 people dead in the face of burgeoning Turkish nationalism under Mustafa Kemal Ataturk, and tension continued to boil under the surface for decades after. In 1994 and 1995 the army carried out extensive operations in Tunceli Province to counter the PKK, which had emerged during the 1970s in opposition to ongoing "Turkification" of the Kurds. These operations resulted in the partial or complete destruction and forced evacuation of around one-third of the villages in the mountainous province. The pattern was repeated throughout Turkish Kurdistan, where some 200,000 troops were stationed. By 1999 Turkish policies and the resulting war with insurgents had left 35,000 dead and roughly 2.5 million to 3 million Kurds displaced.

In response to these operations, Kurds launched a wave of suicide bombings. Between 1996 and 1999, the PKK, which described itself as a "revolutionary revenge organization," carried out fifteen suicide bombings, with a further six bombers intercepted before they could detonate their bombs.[64] It is notable that 66 percent of the bombers were women.[65] In 1996 Ocalan, whose name in Turkish means "he who takes revenge," declared that "each and every Kurd can become a suicide bomber."[66] Although the PKK stopped its attacks in 1999, suicide bombings continued. In an interview after a suicide bombing at an Istanbul police station in January 2001, the Istanbul police chief stated: "[This is] revenge. What else can a suicide bombing be?"[67] Believing that Turkey was uninterested in peace, the PKK revived its campaign against the government in 2004. A series of suicide bombings followed throughout Turkey, including a suicide bombing in Ankara in May 2007 that killed nine people and an October 2010 suicide bombing in Taksim Square in central Istanbul that injured thirty-two. In October 2011 a female suicide bomber blew herself up near an office of the ruling AK Party in Bingol in eastern Turkey on the anniversary of the founding of the nation, killing two people.

The Somali Case

Late on a Friday night in June 2011, Haboon Abdulkadir Hersi Qaaf, a veiled Somali teenage woman, entered the Mogadishu home of her uncle, Abdi Shakur Sheikh Hassan Farah, Somalia's minister for the interior and national security. Nothing seemed out of the ordinary about the visit. Farah had been paying Haboon's tuition at the local medical school, and she was a frequent guest at his home. The guards knew her well, and this night, as on so many other visits, they let her pass by without so much as a second glance. But this visit was different. Strapped to Haboon's body was a vest of explosives that she detonated after getting close to her uncle, blowing her to pieces and killing him. The Somali group Al Shabab claimed responsibility for the attack, calling Farah an "apostate official" and vowing to continue to target those who associated themselves with the U.S.-backed central government in Mogadishu.

The Somali traditional code of honor and practice of Islam had begun to mutate by the time the country collapsed into civil war after the fall of General Siad Barre in 1991. The ensuing and unprecedented clan-on-clan bloodshed killed 25,000 people in Mogadishu in a mere four months. Somali tribal society mutated further with suicide bombings. Three months before an American-backed Ethiopian invasion in December 2006, the first Somali suicide bomber targeted the Somali president, missing him but killing five people, including the president's brother. Suicide bombings accelerated following the Ethiopian occupation and intervention of several other African countries. In March 2007 a suicide bomber named Adam Salad Adam drove his Toyota past a checkpoint at an Ethiopian military base in Somalia and detonated the explosives in his vehicle, killing sixty-three Ethiopian soldiers and wounding a further fifty. A Somali group called the Young Mujahideen Movement claimed responsibility for the bombing, saying it was in revenge for the rape and torture of a Somali woman named Suuban Maalin Ali Hassan at the hands of Ethiopian troops.

By the time Haboon decided to blow herself up, Al Shabab was regularly launching suicide attacks, often against innocent civilians. The twenty-five victims of a suicide bombing at a Benadir University graduation ceremony in December 2009 included three government ministers, while most of the others were graduating students. In July 2010 Somali suicide bombers killed seventy-four people watching the World Cup in Uganda, the week after Al Shabab had vowed to take "revenge" against Uganda for its military support of the Somali government and for committing the "massacres" of Somalis. An October 2011 suicide strike on a government building killed more than 100 people, most of them students who had come to check examination results for scholarships to Turkey.

This suicide attack, declared the bomber in a video, "will be a big blow to the heart of the enemy."[68] Those who go abroad to college, he said, "never think about the harassed Muslims. He wakes up in the morning, goes to college and studies and accepts what the infidels tell him, while infidels are massacring Muslims."[69] Al Shabab was ruthless with those it felt were collaborating with the government or spying. Ordinary people were petrified with fear. "We wake up with beheaded bodies on the streets every day," a Mogadishu resident told the Associated Press in August 2011. "They call themselves Muslims while doing what Allah banned! Everyone is trying to leave here because people are being killed like goats."[70]

As in the cases discussed earlier, Somalis often targeted the highest possible officials, as seen by Haboon's murder of her uncle. In June 2007 a suicide bomber attacked the home of Somalia's prime minister, missing him but killing seven others. In June 2009 a suicide bomber killed thirty-five people at a hotel in central Somalia, including the Somali minister for national security and several Somali diplomats, one being the former ambassador to Ethiopia. In September 2009 two suicide bombers attacked the African Union military headquarters in Mogadishu, which also housed the offices of DynCorp International, a U.S. military contractor supporting the Somali government, killing twenty-one people. Among those who died was a Burundian major general, the second-highest-ranking African Union commander. In April 2012, just as the prime minister of Somalia was beginning to address an elite Mogadishu gathering in the newly opened Somali National Theater, a female suicide bomber detonated her explosives, narrowly missing him but killing the head of Somalia's Olympic committee and the head of the nation's football federation.

The Nigerian Case

In January 2012 a female suicide bomber from Bauchi State in northeastern Nigeria attempted to gain entrance to the headquarters of the Federal Capital Territory Administration (FCTA) in Abuja, the capital of Nigeria. The FCTA runs Abuja, and its offices house the senior government ministers and thousands of government workers. Although she was stopped before she could detonate the bombs strapped to her body, the emergence of this female suicide bomber in Nigeria, Africa's most populous nation, again points to a breakdown in traditional society and the resulting mutation. Although suicide bombings have been frequent in the region, this was the first known example of a female suicide bomber. It may well be a harbinger of things to come.

Over the previous three years, the group popularly known as Boko Haram had struck fear into Nigerians with its ferocious attacks on both government and civilian targets. Many commentators translate Boko Haram in its literal sense as "book forbidden," implying a rejection of "book" or Western education. The group identifies itself as People Committed to the Propagation of the Prophet's Teachings and Jihad. It was founded by a Kanuri, Ustaz Mohammed Yusuf— "Ustaz" meaning teacher—in 2002 in Maiduguri, the capital of the northeastern Borno State, as a nonviolent microfinance Islamic organization opposed to what it saw as a corrupt government. Its members were drawn from the lower economic classes and students of Quranic schools. The group was dominated by the historically segmentary lineage Kanuri people, who previously had their own independent kingdom until British colonialism.

In July 2009 violence erupted when Boko Haram's meeting place in Bauchi State was raided by Nigerian national police and nine of its members were arrested. Within a couple of hours, reprisal attacks occurred against the police. Riots then erupted, eventually spreading to three other states in the northeast. The fighting lasted for five days. During this time, the military was filmed executing suspected members of the group in public. According to the Red Cross, 780 bodies were found in the streets of Maiduguri alone, with hundreds more killed throughout the northeast.[71] The government targeted the group's affiliated mosques for destruction. After the riots, Mohammed Yusuf, the founder of the group, was captured and shot, and his body was later found dumped in Maiduguri in full view of its residents, his wrists still in handcuffs. The government claimed he died while attempting to escape custody, an incident later cited by Boko Haram as provocation for revenge attacks against the security services.

After Yusuf's death, Abubakar Shekau, also a Kanuri, became leader of the group. To show solidarity with Yusuf, he married one of Yusuf's four wives and adopted their children. The group began to recruit other ethnic groups, such as the Fulani, another segmentary lineage people in northern Nigeria. The first suicide bomber in Nigerian history, who Boko Haram announced was Fulani, blew himself up in the national police headquarters in Abuja in June 2011. His target was the inspector general of the Nigerian national police, who the day before had declared in Maiduguri that "the days of Boko Haram are numbered."[72] Another suicide attack followed a few months later, this time on the United Nations headquarters in Abuja, killing twenty-one people and injuring seventy-three.

Boko Haram also began to target fellow Muslims, particularly those associated with the central government. In September 2011 Babakura Fugu, Mohammed Yusuf's brother-in-law, was shot outside his house in Maiduguri two days after attending a peace meeting with the former president, Olusegun Obasanjo. In July 2012 a teenage suicide bomber blew himself up in the central mosque of Maiduguri, killing five and injuring a further six. His main targets, who escaped from the blast uninjured, were the deputy governor of Bornu State and the shehu of Bornu, Abubakar Umar Garbai el-Kanemi, both Muslims.[73] The previous year, the shehu's younger brother was killed by gunmen. The shehu is one of the main religious leaders of the Kanuri, and the position of shehu was also the former ruler of the Kanuri Kanem-Bornu Empire, which was absorbed into the British colonial government. The current shehu is directly descended from the shehus of the Kanuri Empire. One month later, a suicide bomber targeted the emir of Fika, another religious figure who had spoken against violence and in support of the security forces; this attack occurred during Friday prayers at the central mosque in Potiskum in Yobe State, missing the emir but injuring dozens of people.

In adopting an Islamic identity, the group was also concerned about matters outside the tribe such as the status of Muslims in Nigeria, a country largely divided between a Muslim north and Christian south. In January 2012, in the wake of the 2011 Christmas-day bombings in which several churches were attacked in Abuja, Jos, and in the northeastern Yobe State, Shekau, the leader of Boko Haram, announced, "We are also at war with Christians because the whole world knows what they did to us. They killed our fellows and even ate their flesh in Jos."[74]

Shekau was referring to several incidents in 2011 in which Christian Berom tribesmen ate the charred flesh of Muslims they had killed and roasted in the Plateau State of the Middle Belt region in Nigeria. In a widely circulated online video, voices can be heard telling a young man who is hacking apart a charred and headless body with a machete, "I want the heart" and "Did you put some salt?" as youths proudly hold up severed heads blackened by fire for the camera. Several policemen can be seen standing back and watching the cannibalistic feast. There is an air of festivity about the gathering, as if the revelers were enjoying a special celebration.

The volatile Middle Belt region, which serves as the border between Muslim north and Christian south and where different religious and ethnic groups live side by side, has for the past decade been caught in a vicious cycle of attack and counterattack between the tribal communities. Revenge attacks between Christian and Muslim tribal groups remain a constant threat in the region, such as in Kaduna State, bordering Plateau State, where a number of assaults killed dozens of Christians in the fall of 2012, including a November suicide bombing of a military base church killing eleven.

Large-scale violence erupted in Plateau State on September 7, 2001, when the palpable tension between the communities led to the Jos riots in which more than 1,000 people were killed over a six-day period. By 2004 nearly 54,000 people had been killed in Plateau State, according to a Nigerian investigative commit-tee.[75] At the heart of the conflicts are the nomadic Muslim Fulani herdsmen who moved south in increasing numbers and in the process clashed with other tribal groups in the area. Once again, the actions of the Fulani reflect the mutation of both Islam and *Pulaaku,* the Fulani tribal code.

Fulani migrations south accelerated as the grazing routes for their herds dis-appeared in the north, mainly because of the Sahel drought of the late 1960s and 1970s. The move was also encouraged by the development of new farming prac-tices in the Middle Belt region from the 1970s onward that decimated the tsetse fly population harmful to their cattle.[76] With the removal of the barrier that the tsetse fly formed, more and more Fulani began to move their grazing routes and their camps farther south, coming into conflict with the region's resident farm-ers over land use. The largely Christian farmers, especially the Berom who are the dominant ethnic group in the Plateau State, complained of the destructive presence of Fulani cattle herds on their land and would often kill or steal them.

For the Fulani herdsmen whose very existence depends on cattle, these attacks were devastating, threatening not only their livelihood but also their identity in *Pulaaku.* A nang Fulani can be nothing but a cattle herder. The Fulani organiza-tion Miyetti Allah stated in February 2011 that herdsmen had lost about 8 mil-lion heads of cattle in the preceding decade.[77] The young Fulani boys who often tend the herds, an important way to demonstrate manhood in traditional society, frequently became the victims of ethnic hatred. Inasmuch as the Muslim herders and Christian farmers are both motivated by codes of revenge and honor, any violent act is certain to trigger a series of bloody counterattacks.

Just before dawn on Sunday, March 7, 2010, for example, a group of machete-wielding Fulani herdsmen descended upon the Christian Berom villages of Zot, Ratsat, and Dogo-Nahawa in Plateau State. The Fulani began to fire into the air in order to draw the Berom farmers out of their homes. As the Berom emerged into the streets, the Fulani hacked them to pieces. Most of the victims were those least able to run away: women, small children as young as three months old, and the elderly. The Berom villages were then set on fire with people still inside their homes. After a few hours of bloodshed, some 500 victims lay dead. These acts of savagery were perpetrated in revenge for attacks on the Fulani by Berom youth from the same villages earlier that year, when over 350 Muslims, mostly Fulani, were killed in riots that arose out of objections to the construction of a mosque in a Christian-majority neighborhood in Jos.

The Fulani are also subject to discrimination by the central government and risk being arrested, tortured, killed, and deported on the slightest pretext. The government of Plateau State, headed by a Berom governor, has denied the Fulani any recognition as citizens and has attempted to expel them from the region. In May 2009 it was announced that 20,000 Fulani had been expelled from Plateau

State into other northern states.[78] The state government often justified these actions on security grounds, referring to the Fulani herdsmen as "terrorists." Ahmed Idris, a representative from Plateau State in the Nigerian House of Representatives, referred to these deportations as "ethnic cleansing."[79] According to the Fulani leader of Miyetti Allah, "The race was facing extinction."[80]

In July 2012 another case of ethnic violence in Plateau State hit international headlines, this one directly involving central government security forces. A Fulani herdsman had been accused of killing a member of the Nigerian security forces, the Special Task Force (STF), in Plateau State, and the STF responded by burning fifty Fulani homes to the ground. Three days later, Fulani herdsmen launched revenge attacks on nine Berom villages in Plateau State that they associated with the STF, killing at least 63 people, many in the home of a Christian pastor. During their funeral the following day, the Fulani again attacked, killing about 20 of the mourners, among them two senior Berom politicians, a Nigerian federal senator, and the majority leader of the Plateau State Assembly. The next day, Berom tribesmen retaliated by killing anyone they identified as a Fulani in the area, bringing the weekend's death toll to more than 200.[81] After these incidents, the Berom community called for the expulsion of all Fulani from Plateau State.

Farther east in Nigeria, the Fulani herdsmen have come into similar conflict over land with the Tiv farmers who are Christian and organized along the segmentary lineage system. The nomadic Fulani have also run into problems with farmers across West Africa as the Fulani ethnic group extends over half a dozen countries, where they are variously known as Fulani, Fulbe, Fula, or Peul. In Ghana as the Fulani shifted their herds south owing to changing environmental conditions, bloody battles erupted pitting the Fulani herdsmen against local farmers and the security forces, as in Nigeria. One Ghanaian member of parliament reflected the mood against the Fulani when he publicly announced in December 2011, "If in the course of defending ourselves they have to die then it is justified. So killing them I personally support it."[82] In May 2012 deadly violence erupted along the Burkina Faso and Mali border, pitting Fulani herdsmen against Dogon farmers, a primarily animist ethnic group living in Mali.

Extent of the Breakdown

The frequency of the suicide attacks and their geographical span, especially the advent of female suicide bombers, should have alerted the world that something has gone horribly wrong in peripheral societies and that governments far from resolving the problems have exacerbated them. In response to these tribal actions, the central government, the third pillar of the Waziristan model outlined in chapter 2, has responded with unthinking force that routinely includes rape and in some instances even abets cannibalism. Despite their fearsome reputation

throughout history, the tribes have traditionally associated revenge with satis-
fying honor and not with committing murder for its own sake. Revenge is a
measured response meant to address an injustice—and not meant to lapse into
excessive violence, which is considered dishonorable. Tribal elders seeking to
maintain the code and the religious leaders appealing to Islam both work toward
balance and stability. The actions of the suicide bombers in their indiscriminate
killing are thus devoid of both tribal honor and religious compassion. The fact
that many of the suicide bombings are conducted by women, whose protection
is considered a matter of honor for the tribesmen, is further evidence of the devastation being wrought on the community, with too many of the women being
raped and their husbands arrested, tortured, or killed.

The depth of the dilemma faced by individuals under such circumstances
cannot be fully appreciated without measuring the suicides against Islam's ideals.
Islam not only categorically prohibits suicide—only God gives and takes life—
but it considers the idea of female suicide especially reprehensible. Women in the
ideal have the highest possible status in Islam, both theologically and sociologi-
cally. The sayings of the Prophet and his behavior toward women confirm this
position. When asked the best way to reach paradise, the Prophet thrice replied,
"Under the feet of the mother," pointing to the importance of the elevated position of the mother as a child-bearer and role model. The Prophet's household
provided some of the leading role models for Muslim women, which would have
been known to each of the female suicide bombers mentioned in this chapter.
Khadijah, Aisha, and Fatima—successful businesswomen, scholars, military
commanders, and carriers of the sacred lineage—each of these extraordinary
women embodies compassion, courage, and balance in her life and serves as a
guide to Muslim women. By abandoning their example and taking her own life,
the female suicide bomber is saying she is prepared to negate her Islamic heritage
and duty. Yes, something has gone terribly wrong.

As the cases just described demonstrate, every member of a tribe faces bin
Laden's dilemma within a particular cultural, social, and historical context: each
must weigh the Prophet's words against the unchecked desire for revenge. This
dilemma is a product of the disruption of the relationship between state and
tribe, center and periphery. In the ensuing mayhem, a new, cruel, and revengeful
leadership has emerged bent on destroying whatever remains of the traditional
model. It promotes bloodshed, ironically in the name of Islam. For the women
who face this dilemma, the burden is even heavier, knowing that they need to
preserve and perpetuate life. With the traditional models broken and without
efforts to reconstruct them, these societies will find it difficult to emerge from
the current state of pain, cruelty, and violence. Chapter 4 examines the history
of these societies and their interactions with the center to show how they have
come to this sorry state.

4

MUSHARRAF'S DILEMMA:

Balancing Center and Periphery

A century after perhaps the most erudite viceroy of the British Raj, Lord Curzon, had expressed reservations about sending the "steamroller" across Waziristan to crush and pacify its fierce tribes, Pervez Musharraf ordered the Pakistan army into Waziristan. He then launched military operations in the rest of the Tribal Areas as well as in Baluchistan. These were the actions not of a foreign imperialist but the president of Pakistan. Musharraf, in a dramatic display of hubris, was reversing the policy toward the Tribal Areas and Baluchistan established by Muhammad Ali Jinnah, the founder of the state of Pakistan, who had reached out specially to the tribes in these areas. Musharraf was faced with the dilemma of balancing the writ of the state with the demands of the periphery, a dilemma familiar to the modern state.

Musharraf was in fact battling the two most formidable Pukhtun tribes, the Wazir and the Mahsud, as well as the toughest Baluch tribes, the Marri and the Bugti. Musharraf had already dismantled the administrative structure of the districts in Pakistan and disrupted the civil service that Jinnah had called the "steel frame" holding the country together. The collapse of law and order inevitably followed. When Musharraf attacked the people of the Tribal Areas and Baluchistan, they reacted by striking civilian targets throughout the country, turning all of Pakistan into a battle zone. The resulting instability directly challenged U.S. policy both in Pakistan and in Afghanistan. Musharraf had not learned from the mistakes of his role model Napoleon Bonaparte: the folly of fighting on multiple fronts simultaneously.[1]

Born in Delhi, raised in Karachi, and educated in Lahore—all big cities—Musharraf had little instinctive sympathy for tribesmen, viewing them as primitive and backward folk. The image he cultivated for himself was that of a tough-talking, muscular, aggressive, and even reckless soldier, in keeping with the dominant Punjabi culture of bravado and machismo that permeated the Pakistan army. He joined the commando units to emphasize this image. He projected a vigorous and confident Pakistani nationalism. When Musharraf took over, I,

President George W. Bush, who described his relationship with President Musharraf as "tight," receiving him at the White House in September 2006 (photo by Eric Draper, courtesy of the George W. Bush Presidential Library and Museum).

like many Pakistanis, hoped that he would improve the condition of Pakistan and provide it good governance. The previous governments had brought the country to the brink of disaster with their incompetence and corruption. Alas, it was not to be. Musharraf's government proved equally inept, and as he was head of a powerful army, it was not easy to challenge or dislodge him.

Very early after 9/11, Musharraf saw an opportunity to strengthen his domestic position and gain international legitimacy by establishing ties with the United States and joined its war on terror as a full-fledged ally. He had cleverly convinced Washington that if he were removed, the dreaded Muslim fanatics with long beards, wearing *shalwar-kameez* and brandishing Kalashnikovs, would take over Pakistan's nuclear assets; in effect, al Qaeda would have access to nuclear bombs. In the United States, the ideal "good guy" among Muslims was like Musharraf—beardless, wearing expensive suits and ties, and speaking English. The "bad guy" had a beard, wore a turban and traditional ethnic clothes, and was proud to speak his tribal language. As a consequence, large sums of money, the latest weapons, and advanced training for his officers were lavished on Musharraf and his government. Americans set aside their reservations about military dictators and embraced him. He was invited by Jon Stewart on *The Daily Show* and handled himself adroitly. The love affair with America reached a peak when President George W. Bush, the most powerful man in the world, described their relationship as "tight." The two appeared at Camp David—Bush's way of showing special honor to his guest. Musharraf now felt himself unassailable.

With his newfound confidence, Musharraf set his sights on the Bugti tribe and Nawab Akbar Bugti, its chief. The center had always been at odds with the Bugti over the government's exploitation of the Sui gas fields located in the Bugti Agency, whose inhabitants felt they were not getting their fair share of the natural resources found in their lands. Moreover, they were treated with indifference and even contempt in their own agency by the central government.

What actually sparked the confrontation between Musharraf and Akbar Bugti was an incident involving a woman and her honor. A female doctor living in the Bugti Agency (now a district) was raped by an officer of the Pakistan army, and the *nawab* demanded justice, claiming that Baluch honor had been violated. Although the woman was not a Baluch herself, she was a "guest" and therefore protected under the Baluch code of honor. Musharraf dug his heels in and backed his fellow officer, who was tried by a military court and found innocent. Adding insult to injury, Musharraf made public statements that Pakistani women were deliberately inviting rape in order to get visas to Western countries so that they could migrate and that the doctor was among them. The doctor's life fell apart as she attempted to escape from the humiliating national spotlight. Akbar Bugti, too, stuck to his guns and demanded justice for the doctor. The matter quickly spiraled out of control, and the nawab took to the hills, with the Pakistan army in close pursuit.

In a television interview on January 4, 2005, Musharraf issued a stern warning to the Baluch: "Don't push us. It is not the 70s, when you can hit and run, and hide in the mountains," he threatened, referring to a military campaign to suppress a Baluchistan insurgency in the 1970s. "This time, you won't even know what hit you."[2] Akbar Bugti was killed in 2006 in a military operation that, according to the Baluch, employed U.S. weapons meant for fighting "terrorists." Akbar Bugti's death confirmed the cowardice and perfidy of the general and immortalized the courage and honor of the Baluch. Akbar Bugti was now depicted as a lion in folk culture. The Baluch had their nationalist martyr.

In the wake of Akbar Bugti's death, an already simmering Baluch movement for autonomy blossomed into a drive for independence from Pakistan. To counter it, the authorities adopted a torture, kill, and dump policy that saw far too many Baluch bodies appearing mysteriously in their home villages. Unspeakable things had been done to them. Engraved on their bloodied chests with sharp knives, for example, were messages such as "Pakistan Zindabad," or "Long Live Pakistan." Baluch scholars, journalists, and leaders were being deliberately targeted. This was akin to the decapitation of an entire society. In retaliation, individuals who had settled in Baluchistan, especially from the Punjab, were being harassed, kidnapped, and killed. Trains and buses were being attacked. The safety of the passengers depended on their ethnicity. For Baluchistan, these attacks marred celebrations during Pakistan's Independence Day on August 14, 2012, which Baluch nationalists declared "Black Day." The irony of Akbar Bugti's killing, noted the Baluch journalist Malik Siraj Akbar, was that "Akbar Bugti was the only link with Pakistan, and by killing him Pakistan has effectively cut off links to the Baluch people."[3] "Let it be reflected," Sir Evelyn Howell had mused when contemplating Waziristan, "how great a diversion of the ship follows from a slight deflection of the rudder."[4]

The Bugti tribe has put a price on Musharraf's head of 1 billion rupees and a 1,000-acre plot of land. Musharraf, in self-imposed exile in London, condemned the Baluch in 2012 as "terrorists" and "militants." Akbar Bugti was never far from Musharraf's mind, meriting five full paragraphs in a brief article that called the nawab—and other Baluch chiefs—"very vicious, unforgiving and decadent." Musharraf accused them of "killing people of other ethnicities (especially Punjabis), blowing up and damaging national infrastructure . . . and challenging the writ of the government." He singled out the Marri and Bugti as the main sources of "agitation," dismissing them as insignificant for their combined population amounted to a mere 400,000 or .25 percent of the population of Pakistan. Musharraf is on record giving several different explanations as to how Bugti died, including suicide. In the article just mentioned, Musharraf claimed that an explosion in the cave inadvertently killed him. "This," he argued, hoping that it would close the discussion of Akbar Bugti's death and thereby exonerate him, "is a clear case of a self-inflicted casualty."[5]

Trumpeting his successes in Baluchistan, Musharraf went on to list development projects there, yet five of these, as the Baluch would immediately point out, were highways intended to move Pakistani military personnel in the province. Musharraf believed his greatest contribution to Baluchistan was the "new deep-sea port at Gwadar." The port project, however, has become a sore point with the Baluch, who complain that most of the jobs and plots of land are being given to outsiders. Musharraf gave a list of several important education projects that he had initiated and he now claimed had stalled under the new government. He roundly condemned those commenting on Baluchistan, particularly the media "with their half-baked knowledge," "groups like Human Rights Watch" for "meddling," and "foreign agencies" and "anti-Pakistan elements" with "their nefarious designs." Once again, Musharraf reiterated Baluchistan "needs to be dealt with an iron hand."

While Musharraf denounced the Bugti tribe and publicly threatened the nawab, Jinnah had a different approach, apparent in his address to the Sibi

Nawab Akbar Bugti, in western suit, receiving Muhammad Ali Jinnah, governor general of Pakistan in Baluchistan in 1948 (wikipedia.org).

Durbar on February 14, 1948. Dating back to British times, the Sibi Durbar was a grand ceremonial gathering of the most influential leaders of Baluchistan in which they expressed their loyalty to the central government, and the government, in turn, recognized them with honors. Now called Mela, or festival, a word that is more demotic and less stately than Durbar, the annual event is the most colorful, biggest, and noisiest of its kind in Baluchistan.

Jinnah was by then terminally ill and had just half a year more to live. But he had to make the trip to Sibi to express his appreciation of the Baluch. Jinnah opened his address by acknowledging that his "personal connection with Baluchistan extends over a long period. I can now look back with satisfaction to the days when the people of this Province fought shoulder to shoulder with me in our struggle for freedom."[6] He then apologized for not coming earlier as he was preoccupied with the problems of the new nation, including the arrival of millions of refugees and the undeclared state of war with India over Kashmir: "You will, therefore, forgive me if I was not able to attend to the affairs of Baluchistan as speedily as I would have wished. Let me assure you, however, that I have not for one moment allowed the affairs of Baluchistan to slip out of my mind."

Jinnah's aim, he said, was to listen to the people of Baluchistan and then discover "the ways and means of improving the lot of our people in this Province." He acknowledged the decision of the tribes to join Pakistan through a referendum and promised to honor all agreements that would safeguard their integrity. To underline his regard for the people of Baluchistan, Jinnah made the unprecedented announcement that henceforth the governor general, Jinnah's own office as head of state, would directly oversee the rights and privileges of the Baluch and ensure their autonomy. Jinnah concluded with a rare exhibition of emotion: "I wish you my brethren of Baluchistan, God speed and all success in the opening of this new era. May your future be as bright as I have always prayed for and wished it to be. May you all prosper."

If Musharraf's words reeked of derision for and hostility to the Baluch, Jinnah's reflected respect and affection for them. Here, in the two leaders of Pakistan, one sees Musharraf dishonoring the Baluch and Jinnah honoring them. It is well to keep in mind that the same Akbar Bugti who Musharraf treated with contempt and hounded to his death, was in the audience at Sibi cheering Jinnah. There is a historical photograph of a young Bugti in a smart Western suit and tie receiving Jinnah along with other Baluch leaders. Today, the Baluch feel there is little "connection," personal or otherwise, with Pakistan.

Like Musharraf, I faced a dilemma in connection with Nawab Akbar Bugti. As commissioner of Sibi Division, I was aware of the importance the people of Baluchistan attached to the chief of a tribe, nawab or *sardar:* he was the very symbol of the tribe's identity and honor. There is a Baluch saying, "The Baluch will swear on the Holy Quran but never on the head of the sardar."[7] I had heard of Akbar Bugti's difficult reputation and recognized that he had to be kept in line with the administration as much as possible if I was to succeed in my assignment. Yet I needed to balance my authority as the most senior field officer representing the state with the demands of the periphery.

My charge included the two Baluch tribal agencies, named after the dominant tribes, Marri and Bugti, and I was aware of the strained relations between them and the center. While the Marri and Bugti had opted to join Pakistan at the outset, the Khanate of Kalat in south Baluchistan, which incorporated many Baluch tribes but not the Marri and Bugti, declared itself an independent state. In late March 1948, Pakistani troops crossed into Baluchistan, and the khan (leader) agreed to join Pakistan, but his brother Prince Abdul Karim Khan vowed to fight for independence: "From whatever angle we look at the present Government of Pakistan, we will see nothing but Punjabi Fascism. The people have no say in it. It is the army and arms that rule. . . . There is no place for any other community in this government, be it the Baloch, the Sindhis, the Afghans or the Bengalis, unless they make themselves equally powerful."[8]

When the One Unit Policy in 1955 put all of West Pakistan under central rule to offset East Pakistan, anger spread throughout the periphery. Faced with growing unrest, Pakistan declared martial law across the nation in 1958 and sent troops into Baluchistan to arrest the khan of Kalat. This sparked an insurgency led by the ninety-year-old leader of the Zehri tribe, Nawab Nauroz Khan, who was arrested and died in prison. His son and five others were executed. Incensed by the government's removal of local autonomy and oil and gas explorations in the tribe's territory intended for exploitation by the center, the Marri tribe continued its rebellion through the 1960s. The nawab of the Marri tribe declared: "I can coexist with a pig but not with a Punjabi."[9] In 1973 a new rebellion broke out against Prime Minister Z. A. Bhutto's government. In response, the center targeted villages for destruction in which it was aided by Iran, whose own restive Baluch population similarly feeling marginalized and oppressed by the center was in revolt. By the time the war ended in 1977, nearly 10,000 Baluch had been killed in Pakistan.[10] Anger among the Baluch tribes in both Pakistan and Iran remained high as they continued to feel neglected and humiliated by the center.

By the mid-1980s the world's attention was fixed on Afghanistan, but Baluchistan was a powder keg ready to explode, as I discovered on my arrival. Decades of economic and political neglect combined with the posting of arrogant Pakistani officials ignorant of local culture to key positions had alienated the population. Outside events were also causing a stir. Ideas of separatism were being fomented by the Soviet Union, which was retaliating for Pakistan's role in Afghanistan, and by India, equally angered by Pakistan's support of the uprisings in Kashmir. Following the bloody Islamic revolution in Iran, which shared a long border with Baluchistan, Iranian agents were busy promoting the message of the Shia clerics among the Shia population, especially the Hazaras in Quetta. At the same time, General Mohammed Zia-ul-Haq's so-called Islamization of Pakistan was alienating Baluch tribal society, as was the growing presence of army officers in government positions traditionally reserved for the civil service. Zia would not be the first or last dictator to undermine the civil service in order to establish his authority. I understood even then that the days of the neutral administrator ensuring peace between tribes and clans while maintaining law and order were numbered; officials were ever more frequently selected on the basis of their ideological or political support of the regime.

Some Baluch tribal chiefs had had enough. They flirted with outside forces and even talked of separating from an unjust Pakistan. Fortunately for Pakistan, the charismatic and volatile Akbar Bugti was one of the few who were not advocating separation, in spite of what he perceived as a long list of provocations by the center, including imprisonment.

Soon after taking charge, I reached out to the nawab, and he responded with courtesy. He had not only heard of me but had read my books on tribal societies. In a rare gesture to an official—remember this was the man who refused to shake the hand of a powerful governor of the province who was also martial law administrator—he invited me for dinner in his traditional home in the Bugti Agency. I turned up with my full complement of bodyguards and was ushered into his presence. There was only one other guest, his brother and at that time a

Author when commissioner of Sibi Division in Baluchistan with his son, Umar, at the commissioner's house (author's collection).

cabinet minister of Pakistan, who barely spoke in deference to the nawab. I was seated on the nawab's right as a mark of honor. The man serving food was none other than his elder son, a member of the provincial assembly who would go on to become the education minister of Baluchistan.

We talked late into the night about Baluch tribes and their history, and I listened with great interest to the nawab's animated description of his ancestors and the importance of honor and lineage to the Baluch. The nawab admired Ibn Khaldun and read him when he was locked in the Sahiwal jail by the Pakistan government. The nawab, who had studied at Oxford University, was clearly not a stereotypical tribal chief. The grandson of Sir Shahbaz Khan Bugti, he held some of the most important posts in the country, including that of governor, chief minister, and federal minister. Tall, erect, and slim—he told me he controlled his diet strictly and exercised regularly—he cultivated a mystique about himself. A smitten American female anthropologist wrote that the nawab told her he had killed his first man at the age of twelve.[11] I had described the nawab as looking like Sean Connery playing a Berber tribal chief in *The Wind and the Lion*.[12]

After dinner, as a mark of respect for his guest, the nawab walked me to the door of my car. The dozens of men in the compound, all bristling with their

Nawab Akbar Bugti, known as the "Lion of Baluchistan" (used with permission of Malik Siraj Akbar).

weapons, who had either accompanied me or who were part of the nawab's entourage, observed the symbolism. Here was traditional Baluch hospitality and humility. I knew the word would spread like wildfire that the nawab had honored the commissioner. But soon after our dinner, a crisis in the Bugti Agency threatened to disrupt the newfound and delicate relationship. It involved the nawab's son; and no subject is more sensitive to a tribal chief than how his son is treated.

The political agent in charge of the Bugti Agency had rung me, as his immediate superior, to complain that Akbar Bugti's son had set up roadblocks at the main entrance of the agency and was stopping traffic to relieve passengers of their valuables. I was told he had done something like this before my time and should not be allowed to get away with it. My official was at his wits' end as he was aware that if he used force to discourage the activities of Bugti's son, it could lead to an immediate confrontation with the tribe and the nawab that could generate attacks on the Sibi headquarters and attempts to blow up the gas pipelines. Matters would then spread beyond the agency and become further complicated drawing in other tribes allied to the Bugti. If the official did nothing, however, the administration would lose credibility and become ineffective.

I rang Akbar Bugti in Quetta. In one of the more difficult telephone conversations of my tenure in Baluchistan, I laid out the alternatives before him. If I arrested the nawab's son for highway robbery and extortion, it would bring dishonor to his name. If I did nothing, it would dishonor mine. I therefore appealed to the nawab's sense of honor by suggesting that I would take an appropriate course of action that would maintain his own honor and at the same time resolve the problem. I asked that the nawab have confidence in my judgment and support it.

The nawab heard me out without saying much. He did not agree or disagree. I took it as a tacit approval of my intended action and immediately rang my official in the Bugti Agency and told him to go ahead with his plan to have the nawab's son picked up and deported out of the province for a specific period of time. The expulsion orders meant that the young man could no longer terrorize the local population and that the authority of the administration had been reestablished. Word spread among tribesmen that if the nawab's son could be dealt with so severely, swiftly, and fairly, no one was above the law. Still, we held our breath to see how the nawab would respond. Given the volatility within the province, if I lost the nawab, my administration would have started unraveling. Nothing was heard from him, and I had no problem with the Bugti or their area after that. In this course of action, I maintained the balance between the writ of the state and the integrity of the periphery.

After 9/11, I often wondered how the nawab would fare in a world so indifferent to notions of tribal identity and honor codes. I was particularly concerned as I knew his temperament would clash with that of the man Washington was fully backing in Pakistan—President Musharraf. Besides, Americans had little idea or interest in Baluchistan, as summed up by Henry Kissinger when sent to Pakistan by President John F. Kennedy in 1962 on a fact-finding mission: "I wouldn't recognize the Baluchistan problem if it hit me in the face."[13]

The story of Musharraf and Bugti is an apt allegory of the deadly encounters between the center and the periphery evident throughout the world today, with the strong men at the center focused on the security and integrity of the state and those in the periphery on honor. One thing is clear: with some honorable exceptions, leaders at the center are devoid of wisdom and compassion and too ready to use the "steamroller" that Curzon rejected as an all too enticing alternative—with disastrous results.

The war on terror cannot be understood without some knowledge of the historical background of the Muslim peoples involved. To accomplish this, one must examine the roots of Muslim tribal societies as they have encountered or coexisted with assorted authorities, from Islamic emirates to colonial powers. Such societies now face further challenges presented by the turbulent modern state. The following pages will help to trace this arc of history.

ISLAMIC EMIRATES AND TRIBAL SOCIETIES

In many minds, the spiritual and temporal center of Islam over the last thousand years—whether in Damascus, Baghdad, Cairo, or Istanbul—was the caliph's palace, marked by opulence and abundance. Harems and concubines were at hand to cater to the caliph's every whim. Great scholars and calligraphers gathered in his capital, and wondrous buildings and parks were built there. Vast armies and bureaucracies supported the caliph and his empire. Powerful courtiers and aristocrats swaggered about in fine robes. The nobility owned vast tracts of irrigated lands, and the bazaars sold goods from all over the world. For the peasants toiling in the fields, it was difficult to distinguish between the caliph and the Roman or Byzantine emperors who had gone before.

In reality, the first caliphs (caliph originally meant the successor to the Prophet) were unlike those who later ruled from the great cities of the Middle East. They were called the Righteous Ones, and their mosques and dwellings were made of mud and clay. Easily approachable, they lived and dressed like ordinary folk, and their women worked like other women. Their livelihood depended on camels, goats, and horses. These caliphs preached and practiced austerity, in keeping with the example of the Prophet of Islam. Thus the original model of Islamic rule was the small tribal emirate. The ruler was the emir, a title that derives from "chieftain" or "commander." If the caliph came to represent the ultimate power, wealth, and authority of Islam, the emir represents tribal, folk, or informal Islam. For many of the tribes examined in this study, the emirate was the only form of central rule they would know until the modern era and the arrival of the European colonialists.

The Islamic emirates existed for the better part of a thousand years across vast expanses of Africa, the Middle East, Central Asia, and in the Far East in Malaysia, Indonesia, and the Philippines. Hundreds of such emirates of varying size and power operated throughout early Islamic history. Each emirate was formed by a loose federation of alliances between tribal societies who otherwise may have been in conflict with one another. The rulers' titles reflected their cultural region: the Africans called them sultans and emirs in response to Arab influence, the Central Asians called their rulers khans after the famous Genghis Khan, and in the Far East they were rajas, owing to a strong Hindu influence.

Some emirates dissolved into independent tribal enclaves under strong assertive clans; others expanded into sizable kingdoms under charismatic rulers, many with ill-defined borders. At their peak, they gave rise to vast trading networks, most notably through Sufi brotherhoods that integrated different tribes and cultures. The Tijaniyyah Sufi network across North and West Africa was astonishing in its embrace of different peoples, bringing them commerce and peace. The Sanusi of Cyrenaica in North Africa established an extensive network that combined Sufi teachings, administration, trade, and learning. The Sufi scholars and traders who brought Islam to the Far East added to the richness of a culture already permeated with ancient Hindu and Buddhist wisdom and ways. In these societies, religious and temporal authority rested in the same person. The rhythm of life was colored by the traditions of sharia and tribal customs that fused and overlapped. Most important, the emirate gave these rural and tribal societies a sense of continuity, stability, and certainty.

These early kingdoms—using kingdom for lack of a better word—identified themselves as "Islamic" societies. They fostered Islamic schools, scholars, and sharia courts that dispensed impartial, immediate, and visible justice. The rulers included some who were religious figures from outside the tribe and others who were tribal leaders. Both attempted to balance tribal traditions with Islamic learning. The sayings of the Prophet, phrases from the Quran, and Islamic law informed their administration. The better of them attempted to live in the Prophet's image as accessible and compassionate rulers, patrons of Islamic scholarship, and champions of swift and open justice. Some, like Usman dan Fodio of the Sokoto Caliphate, even opposed tribal customs such as female circumcision and honor killings and brought the weight of Islamic arguments against them, though not always successfully.

A thousand years ago, names like Timbuktu in West Africa and Fez in North Africa, and a mere half millennium ago, Bukhara in Central Asia, became widely known as centers of learning with their libraries and hospitality that attracted scholars from far and wide. Africa produced towering names like Ibn Battuta, Ibn Khaldun, and, of course, dan Fodio and his daughter, Nana Asmau, who played the role described today as a "public intellectual." It is ironic that Europeans arriving in the nineteenth century, in their ignorance of history, called Africa "the dark continent."

As Islam spread across the Middle East, parts of Africa, the subcontinent, and Central Asia, great Muslim empires sprang up—the Ottomans, Safavids, and Mughals—with the tribal emirates persisting on their margins or being fully absorbed by them. Because many such emirates inhabited remote and impoverished areas, imperial rulers tended to leave them alone. Far from the overbearing presence of central governments, the segmentary lineage system flourished. Its egalitarian nature and tribal politics found full play on the periphery, while maintaining some loose and generally unspecified relationship to the empire.

The Zaydi Imams of Yemen

The best Muslim ruler, the Prophet is supposed to have said, would be from his kin community, the Quraysh. Indeed, his direct descendants, widely known as sayyeds, provide the first example of the Islamic emirate that is discussed in this study. In the ninth century, a sayyed named Yahya ar-Rasi living in the Hejaz was invited to mediate between feuding tribes in the northern highlands of Yemen, just as the Prophet himself had been invited to do in Medina, and, as seen in chapter 3, King Idrisi was invited to Asir. Yahya was a well-known and respected Islamic scholar and a proponent of a Shia sect known as Zaydi Islam, named after Zeid, the grandson of Hussein who himself was the grandson of the Prophet. Yahya was particularly respected among the Yemeni tribes as a direct descendant of the Prophet (see chapter 1) and was so successful in settling their feuds that with the assistance of the major tribes of the region, he was able to establish the Zaydi Imamate of Yemen with its seat at Sadah. He was intent on bringing new laws to the tribes based in Islam, yet he faced a dilemma as the tribesmen were loath to abandon their tribal code and customs. Yahya, representing a weak center, was thus forced to work within the tribal structure, serving in the vital role of mediator between clans. This imamate would last until the 111th imam fell to a military coup in September 1962.

With his success at mediation, Yahya began appointing officials to interact with the tribes' leaders. These were either fellow sayyeds or *qadis* (Islamic judges or legal scholars). They were nonetheless knowledgeable and respectful of tribal codes and traditions. They slaughtered animals in the manner of the tribes, for example, as a gesture of moral and honorable reconciliation to end conflict. Eventually the tribes entered into alliance with the imam and provided him with fighting forces. When the officials were successful in their dealings with the tribes, the center and periphery maintained a working balance; when they failed, violence and rebellion followed.

The tension between *urf,* tribal law, and sharia persisted throughout the past thousand years of Yemeni history. Like Yahya at the beginning, the imams who followed him were aware of the tribes' many un-Islamic practices and beliefs. The Zaydis often described urf as "rule of the *taghut*," meaning idol or devil.[14] Some referred to tribesmen as "dogs" or "depraved," "corrupt," and "wicked" men with "no religion."[15] When Yahya was told that a particular Yemeni tribe offered visitors a type of sexual hospitality, he declared such people more deserving of jihad than the Christian Byzantines.[16]

To become the Zaydi imam, it was necessary to hold sayyed status and be elected by the religious establishment. Imams extended their authority through pledges of allegiance by tribal leaders. The imam's "conquest" of a given area amounted to an agreement with its tribes. Imams gained this allegiance by offering money or land, by playing on tribal fears, or by joining with allied tribes against nonallied tribes. Intrigues were common as imams struggled to keep "their" tribes as allies; hence tribal allegiances shifted constantly. Despite such agreements, the authority of the imam invariably ran into problems with the tribes, which might decide to block a vital road or vent their anger in some other way. Successful imams were those who could induce the tribes to keep the roads open.

In this atmosphere of delicate relations, tribes had to be handled with great tact even when they failed to meet the informal terms of participation in the imamate, such as paying their taxes and contributing soldiers to the imam's army. Instead of paying their taxes, the most recalcitrant tribes often ended up receiving subsidies from the imam in order to prevent them from breaking away or causing trouble. Any that felt he was violating their ideals of good governance would switch allegiance to a rival power or rebel against the weak center. Zaydi historians frequently blamed the tribes for the fall of various imams. It was difficult for the Zaydi imamate to act against the tribes, militarily or otherwise, because its armies were constituted of the tribes themselves. The steamroller was, thus, not an option.

Throughout history, the imams' strength waxed and waned in accordance with their ability to effectively maneuver within the tribal system so as to gain and hold allies. At their peak, they controlled all of Yemen, including the Sunni southern regions, which, when not subject to Zaydi rule from the north, established their own sultanates. That was the case in 1728 when Fadl Ibn Ali, the chief of the powerful Abdali tribe, threw off the Zaydi yoke and declared himself sultan of Lahej, a large oasis some twenty miles north of Aden. Other southern tribal sheikhs followed suit, confining the imam's rule to the north. In 1735 the sultan of Lahej gained control over Aden and annexed it to his sultanate, ruling the territory until the British established control in 1838.

Establishing Tribal Emirates

Unlike the Zaydi imam, who established his rule from outside the tribe by virtue of his sayyed status, many emirs originated within a particular clan or tribe, as did the sultan of Lahej. Over time, these tribally based emirates adopted the structure and identity of an Islamic state. For a thousand years, Somalia's coastline was dotted with tribal sultanates of this nature. Though primarily engaged in international sea trade, they turned their attention on rare occasions to the nomadic territory in the interior to extend their administration to some degree. In the late thirteenth century, for example, the Warsangali clan of the Darod, one of the four major Somali tribal groups, established the Warsangali Sultanate on Somalia's northern coast. Another notable emirate in the region was the Adal Sultanate, which flourished in the fifteenth century with historic cities like Zeila, Berbera, and its capital from 1520, Harar, in present-day Ethiopia. The late sixteenth century was the golden age of Harar and became the center of traditional Islamic scholarship in the region—and remained so for hundreds of years. Dating perhaps to the seventh century, Harar was considered Islam's fourth holiest city after Mecca, Medina, and Jerusalem and possessed nearly 100 mosques.

When the renowned traveler-scholar Ibn Battuta visited the coastal sultanate of Mogadishu in the fourteenth century, he was impressed with the "exceedingly large city" there, presided over by a sultan with his *wazirs,* qadis and legal experts, commanders, and royal eunuchs.[17] Battuta wrote of the high value placed on knowledge and scholarship in Mogadishu and the surrounding coastal sultanates. These communities offered students and scholars from afar, such as Battuta himself, both food and lodging, often without payment, just as student hostels did in Damascus, Baghdad, Medina, and Mecca.

Battuta noted that Mogadishu was ruled by sharia, and that its judiciary council—which included the qadi, the wazir, the sultan's private secretary, and four chief emirs assembled every week to listen to the public's complaints: "Questions of religious law are decided by the *Qadi;* others are judged by the council. If a case required the views of the Sultan, it was put in writing for him. He sends back an immediate reply, written on the back of the paper, as his discretion may decide. This has always been the custom among these people."[18]

Perhaps the largest and most sophisticated rule in Somali history was that of the Ajuuraan Sultanate under the Ajuuraan, a subclan of the Hawiye. From the fourteenth to seventeenth century, this sultanate extended its authority from the coast into the interior and took control of the southern agricultural region, constructing large stone wells that attracted nomads and their livestock. Government officials occupied these sites and represented the central authority in dealing with the nomads, allowing the officials to exact tribute. Even so, the Ajuuraan risked opposition from agnatic rivals, notably the Darandoolle subclan of the Hawiye.

Similar emirates under the leadership of local tribes emerged in the Caucasus, there called khanates. The Avar Khanate, for example, was established in the thirteenth century by a group of Avars who claimed descent from earlier Arab governors of the area. The Avar leader, whose title was *nutsal,* was a member of the noble clan and elected by an assembly of elders. Despite having an acknowledged leader in the khan, mountain clans preserved their independence. As one chronicler observed, "The Avars . . . have a Khan whom nobody obeys."[19] The Avars produced sophisticated scholarship in Arabic, Islamic law, and Islamic sciences, and their scholars were renowned throughout the Caucasus and beyond in the greater Middle East. Local Arab scholars in Mecca and Medina were sometimes astonished by the quality of the works coming out of Dagestan and the command of literary Arabic by the authors.

Sufism and the Emirates

While emirates differed in their origins—some were sayyeds from outside the region, some came from dominant tribal clans—the presence of Sufi orders cut across all the variations of the emirate networks. Sufis even provided a ruling family to the Pukhtun, through the descendants of the Akhund of Swat in the nineteenth century, proving the exception to the general Pukhtun principle that only warriors can rule them. While the Akhund himself refused the crown, the Akhund's grandson became the first Wali of Swat and was recognized as such by the British, as discussed in chapter 2.

Another Sufi ruler emerged in the Fulani kingdom known as the Sokoto Caliphate in present-day northern Nigeria. Its founder, Usman dan Fodio, claimed descent from the Prophet and was a noted religious cleric of the Qadiri-yya Sufi order. Besides his religious pedigree, he was also a member of the Toronkawa clan of the Fulani. Prior to establishing his rule, dan Fodio embarked on preaching tours throughout the region to bring religious reform and sharia to a center dominated by the Hausa people, a settled Muslim ethnic group that dan Fodio accused of being Muslim only in name.

Dan Fodio eventually rose up against the Hausa states when they resorted to violence in an effort to stem the tide of his growing influence. Upon being elected Amir-al-Muminin, commander of the faithful, by his followers dan Fodio rallied those sections of society that had been suppressed by the Hausa center and launched an attack against it that came to be known as dan Fodio's jihad. Unlike dan Fodio, many of his supporters sought to overthrow the government not for the ideals contained in an Islamic vision but for more mundane economic, political, and cultural reasons. Yet in making Islam the basis of the "jihad," he acquired an air of spiritual authority that spanned the various groups, clans, and classes behind the movement.[20]

Acting on that authority, dan Fodio established standards for the conduct of the war against the Hausa states, denouncing indiscriminate killings and plundering as being antithetical to Islamic law. However, many of dan Fodio's fighters were nomadic Fulani whose traditional practices and code proved resilient despite his orders. Witnesses to their raids during the jihad noted that they "spared neither Muslim nor pagan and that any town or village in their way was looted quite impartially."[21]

After establishing the Sokoto Caliphate in 1809, dan Fodio named his Toronkawa clan the royal clan and moved to consolidate his power even further by establishing positions of authority from within his own clan.[22] Drawing on his clan, he formed a council of electors to recruit candidates for administrative positions. At the same time, he left the Hausa ruling structure by and large in place, even retaining the Hausa language as the lingua franca and the state's cattle tax on the nomadic Fulani herdsmen, which they continually tried to avoid.[23] The nineteenth-century German scholar Heinrich Barth described the Fulani rulers of the Sokoto Caliphate as the "most ingenious, intelligent, cultured and politically sophisticated."[24]

The Sokoto Caliphate was notable for the educational and leadership opportunities afforded to women. Dan Fodio argued that it was a lesser evil to mix the sexes than to leave Muslim women ignorant of Islam. Nana Asmau, one of Usman dan Fodio's daughters born before the jihad, is revered for her efforts to educate the caliphate's women as well as for the poetry and theological tracts she wrote in Arabic, Fulfulde (the Fulani language), and Hausa. In one poem she wrote, "Women, a warning. Leave not your homes without a good reason/You may go out to get food or to seek education./In Islam, it is a religious duty to seek knowledge/Women may leave their homes freely for this."[25] Many Fulani women today consider her a role model who inspired them to seek knowledge as a necessary pursuit in their lives. Under her educational system, *jajis,* or female scholars, would travel the country and teach women at home. This allowed women in villages or remote areas to gain an education while fulfilling their familial obligations, a practice that continues into the twenty-first century.[26]

Just as dan Fodio's Sufi vision influenced large areas of West Africa, that of the sayyed Ibn Idris, the Moroccan scholar who taught his brand of Sufism in Mecca, gained prominence in large parts of North and East Africa. King Idrisi of Asir, who was discussed in chapter 3, came from a line of Sufi leaders descended from Ibn Idris. Among the several students selected by Ibn Idris to spread his teachings, one, the scholar Mohammed Uthman al-Mirghani al-Khatim, went on to found the Khatmiyya order, which became influential among tribes in Sudan, Egypt, Eritrea, and Ethiopia. Al-Khatim also established the first school for women in the region in the nineteenth century near the port city of Suakin in present-day Sudan.

Besides al-Khatim, Idris's other favored student was Muhammad Ali al-Sanusi, a scholar trained at Al Azhar in Cairo who in the 1840s founded the Sanusi order in the Cyrenaica region of eastern Libya. The Sanusi united all Cyrenaica tribes under a common religious and political banner—a difficult achievement in a segmentary lineage society that until then was virtually untouched by central authority. Al-Sanusi, known as the Grand Sanusi, established the seat of the order in the desert oasis of Jaghbub in eastern Cyrenaica.

Like King Idrisi of Asir, the Grand Sanusi had a keen understanding of how tribal society functioned and was able to spread his authority among tribes deep in the south and the west through a system of Sanusi lodges. Each Sanusi lodge had a mosque, schoolrooms, guest quarters, apartments for the religious scholars, and small gardens. The lodges served as law courts, forts, social and commercial centers, banks, storehouses, houses for the poor, and burial grounds. In Jaghbub, the Grand Sanusi built a university that became the most prestigious and important educational institution in Africa after Al Azhar.

Each tribe came to have a lodge, which linked it to other tribes, thereby creating a kind of informal nation with the Grand Sanusi as its head. By the 1940s, there were forty-five Sanusi lodges in Cyrenaica, twenty-one of them established before 1860.[27] Strong cohesive tribes had only one lodge, while more fractured and feuding tribes had many to act as seats of mediation. The tribes themselves sought lodges after seeing one established by their rival tribes and petitioned the Sanusi leadership to send a sheikh to teach their children, cater to their religious needs, and settle tribal disputes. Eventually the Sanusi order in Cyrenaica "embraced in its network of lodges the entire tribal system of the country."[28]

The major center of Sufism in Central Asia, and home to a number of prominent Sufi orders, was Bukhara, which meant "full of knowledge." Owing to its location on the Silk Road to China and its trading networks, it became the hub of Islamic culture and political power amid the nomadic tribes of the region. It drew Muslims from distant lands, many of whom came to study with its Sufi sheikhs. In turn, Bukhara's Sufi orders spread Islam throughout Central Asia and the wider Muslim world. In particular, the Naqshbandi order, whose founder was born in Bukhara in the fourteenth century, took root everywhere from Kurdistan to Kyrgyzstan, from the Caucasus to Xinjiang. Sufi religious leaders educated in Bukhara established emirates by marrying into the families of prominent tribal leaders.

One of the largest tribal ethnic groups in the world, the Kurds, developed a variety of emirates, some ruled by a dominant clan, others by sayyeds, and yet others by outsiders descended from prestigious and legendary figures of empires. The rulers of the Hasankeyf Emirate in present-day Turkey were descended from the Ayyubid Empire founded by Saladin, while the Bitlis Emirate, renowned for its patronage of the arts, was ruled by the Ruzagi tribal confederation. Botan, among the most famous Kurdish emirates, was governed for many centuries by a family that claimed descent from Khalid ibn Walid, one of the Prophet's most illustrious commanders. Most of these emirates came under Ottoman rule in the sixteenth century and were allowed a degree of autonomy. However all emirates were required to provide soldiers for military campaigns when demanded by the Ottoman center. The Kurdish tribes gained immense power under the emirates and, when dissatisfied with a particular ruler, could depose him.

The Sultanates of Southeast Asia

In contrast to the emirate system, which emerged as a new political and administrative structure among the tribal societies of the Muslim world, the sultanates of Southeast Asia—including the Sulu Sultanate in present-day Philippines, the Patani Sultanate in South Thailand, and the Aceh Sultanate in Indonesia—arose from a different social and historical context. Many of them began as trading kingdoms under the influence of Hinduism, Buddhism, and other local religions that converted to Islam after interactions with Arab traders and Sufi missionaries.

The Tausug of the Sulu Sultanate trace their roots to Muslim traders and scholars who were believed to have arrived as early as the tenth century. In the mid-fifteenth century, a Hadhramaut Yemeni named Sayyed Abu Bakr married the daughter of the local ruler and subsequently founded the Sulu Sultanate. Abu Bakr shaped institutions along Islamic lines and introduced Quranic study, slowly converting the broader Tausug population through peaceful means.

The Sulu Sultanate soon became the largest and most powerful political entity in the Philippines with highly developed trade links across the region. Islam then spread to the island of Mindanao and took root among the dominant Maguindanao people, who then formed the Maguindanao Sultanate. Some Tausug became literate in Arabic and adapted the Tausug language to the Arabic script, along with their indigenous oral traditions, histories, and epic literature. The Tausug became literate in Islamic tradition having obtained copies of the Quran, some hadiths, books on *fiqh*, mysticism, and other Islamic writings. Prominent Tausug kept *tarsilas* (from the Arabic *silsilah*, for chain or link) describing their descent from sultans or *datus*—nobles in the sultan's government—going back to the Prophet. Not unlike the Zaydi imams, no man could become a sultan or a royal *datu* without proof of his holy lineage. Some *tarsilas* traced descent to Muslim dynasties from elsewhere in the Muslim world, including Sumatra and North Africa.

As in the Zaydi imamate of Yemen, the Sulu sultan was elected by the *datus* or nobles who made up his council of advisers. A wazir and other ministers presided over various offices that oversaw naval expeditions and customs. The Tausug sultan relied on one of the wisest qadis in the sultanate for advice and also consulted the *ulema* in making decisions. A body of sharia courts administered Islamic law.

The Malay sultanate of Patani lying to the south of Siam (present-day Thailand) began as a prominent trading kingdom with Malay Hindu-Buddhist roots, then converted to Islam in the fifteenth century through contacts with Muslim traders from outside, as did the Tausug of Sulu. The sultanate reached its golden age at the end of the sixteenth and beginning of the seventeenth century under four successive queens. It became a center of Islamic learning and culture with a network of Patani scholars. Snouck Hurgronje, a Dutch scholar of Oriental cultures and languages who had converted to Islam, remarked on the extensive network of Patani scholars in Mecca on a visit to that city in the 1880s. The writings of these scholars, noted Hurgronje, were significant, judging by the regularity with which various Meccan presses printed them.[29]

On the coast of western Sumatra in present-day Indonesia, a series of trading kingdoms began converting to Islam from the eighth century onward as a result of contacts with Arab traders and scholars. By the early sixteenth century these kingdoms, in the face of the growing threat of a Portuguese invasion, were united to form the Aceh Sultanate. Aceh reached the height of its power in the early seventeenth century with the ascension of Sultan Iskandar Muda and remained an important trading power, which by the 1820s was providing half of the world's pepper supply, with strong commercial links to the Ottoman Empire, India, England, the United States, and France.[30]

Under Muda, the interior tribes became part of a feudal system governed by the *uleebalang,* a new "nobility" in control of various sultanate regions and directly loyal to the sultan, helping Muda to strengthen his power. He himself concentrated his rule in the ports and along the coast, where the wealth, strength, and prestige of the sultanate resided, and had minimum control, if any, over the indigenous government and the administration of justice in the interior. Even the most powerful of sultans did little more than claim a certain and limited right of interference in the governance of the divergent villages and Acehnese chiefs, serving largely as a supreme court of arbitration between feuding tribes.[31] The divide between the sultan, surrounded by the ruling elite and influential families of the coast, and the interior Acehnese people was made all the deeper by the fact that the ruling elite were primarily of foreign origin, a number being sayyeds.

Although the various kingdoms just discussed are not widely known and have garnered little interest from the wider world, they have long carried the torch of Muslim civilization with dignity and honor. Despite their flowering, vast swaths of tribal societies ensconced in difficult terrains and strongly adhering to the segmentary lineage system remained outside the purview of a central author-ity—these included Somalis, the Sahrawi of Western Sahara, the Tuareg of West Africa, the Rifian Berbers of northern Morocco, the Kurds of Turkey, isolated tribes of the Caucasus, and the Pukhtun of the Tribal Areas of Pakistan. Interac-tion with an emirate, khanate, or sultanate compromised the ideal of the segmen-tary lineage system. For most, their first interaction with central authority came in the form of a European military officer brandishing a gun and asserting ideas of European civilization and the nation-state. Although the tribes would resist in spite of facing superior economic and military power, their rulers, schools, elders, courts, and councils would all be affected. In the next phase of history, their identity as an Islamic and tribal people would be challenged. It would be a slow and painful destruction of an entire way of life wrought by the collapse of the immediate clan, the kingdom it was associated with, and the larger Islamic community to which both belonged.

Colonization

In the distant past, great empires and dynasties learned to live with the peoples of the periphery. Central authority usually acknowledged the periphery's autonomy, if not independence, often offering bribes to secure passage through a tribal ter-rain. Local tribesmen believed a small payment was more in the nature of a legiti-mate toll that would help them survive in an environment of meager resources. Even the greatest generals of history, like Alexander the Great and Babar, the founder of the Mughal Empire, paid Afridi tribesmen guarding the Khyber Pass a toll to allow them passage into India. When they attempted to force their way through, imperial armies often discovered, as did the Mughal emperor Aurang-zeb, the descendant of Babar, that it would have been more expedient to pay the Afridi and thus have saved thousands of lives, great expense, and shame.

The woes of the thistle-like tribes began in earnest with European colonialism in the nineteenth century. From then on, they followed a trajectory of disruption, displacement, assaults, fragmentation of tribal life, and loss of territory. During this period, central authorities applied two broad approaches to governing the periphery and its tribes: indirect rule through tribal chiefs and elders, which allowed maximum autonomy and left the genealogical charter and codes of behavior more or less in place, as demonstrated by British rule; and straightforward conquest through massive force and all-out warfare aimed at demolishing the traditional structures, in some cases bringing entire communities to the point of extermination. As an example of the latter, Imperial Russia's armies wiped out half the Circassian population and drove the other half into the Ottoman Empire, while French rule in Algeria over four decades of the nineteenth century brought death to 2 million, or two-thirds of the population, and Italian rule in eastern Libya reduced the Cyrenaican population by two-thirds through death and displacement. Other European empires were not far behind in their acts of brutality. In the early twentieth century Germany sought to exterminate the animist, segmentary lineage, nomadic Herero people of Namibia, killing up to 100,000, or 75–85 percent of the population, in addition to wiping out thousands of people from other tribes.[32] The Belgians, mirroring German tactics, killed about 10 million people in the Congo between 1885 and 1908 by means of murder, famine, disease, or forced labor.[33] Even Muslim empires joined in the destruction of the periphery: the Ottomans in the nineteenth century abandoned their more laissez-faire attitude toward the periphery for ruthless cruelty similar to the European colonialists. As many as 300,000 Armenians were killed in the mid-1890s during the Hamidian massacres, while an estimated 1.5 million Armenians were killed between 1915 and 1922.[34]

European powers—most notoriously and brutally the French and Italians—occupied large parts of Africa and created the myth that these areas were really an extension of the motherland, treating Algeria as just another province of France, or Libya and Somalia as part of Italy. European settlers in the thousands were encouraged to farm in these African lands, and their protection became a matter of vital interest for colonial troops. Invariably, local people reacted angrily and even violently, emotions on both sides running the gamut from aggravation and dismay to fury.

While the French and Italians relied heavily on military conquest, at times they employed British-like indirect rule in their tribal policies if expedient and also contributed to the study of the tribes. Some influential ethnographic contributions came from scholar-administrators like Italy's Enrico Cerulli, who studied Ethiopian and Somali society, or France's Robert Montagne, author of *The Berbers: Their Social and Political Organization*.[35] The French actually accepted a system of Grand Qaids, or grand leaders, in Morocco, allowing Berber chiefs to deal with their own tribes with minimal interference. Tribal law remained in effect under the supervision of a military officer who spoke the local languages. One of these colonial officers was Robert Montagne, whose work on the Berbers has received high praise from no less an authority than the anthropologist Ernest Gellner who had also worked in Morocco:

> The brilliance of his ideas, the thoroughness and perceptiveness of his documentation, the range of his historical and comparative vision, and (a trait not always found in scholarly writing on North Africa) the simplicity and vigour of his style, all help to make plain that we have here a social thinker and observer of the very first rank, and one who deserves to be far better known outside the French-speaking world than he is at present.[36]

But there were far too few Montagnes. General Hubert Lyautey, France's first resident-general of Morocco, admitted ruefully when taking a comparative look at the British administrative system: "Before us rises the admirable English organisation: large, supple, commanding, directed from top to bottom by gentlemen or men who live and act like gentlemen, whatever their origins, who practise a humane code. They have the personnel, we do not."[37] The British, however, had learned the hard way; and their tutors were the nang Pukhtun tribes.

What the British Learned about Tribal Societies from the Fate of William Brydon

On a freezing January day in 1842, British sentries on duty at Jalalabad Fort in Afghanistan looked with disbelief at the sight of a lone bedraggled British soldier on an emaciated horse. Covered in blood, part of his skull slashed open, and bleeding from several wounds, William Brydon was the sole surviving member of the Grand Army of the Indus that had marched several years before to occupy Kabul. Forced to abandon Kabul, the army was slowly destroyed on the return journey by deadly Afghan fighters occupying the heights of the passes. It was estimated that as many as 16,000 British troops and civilians, including women and children, had been killed by the tribesmen. It was one of the worst massacres in the history of the British Empire and is captured in a painting by Lady Butler that today hangs in London's Tate Gallery. The tribesmen had let the Scottish doctor live so that he could relate the terrible tale to his fellow countrymen. Barely conscious when asked where the rest of the army was, the good doctor replied, "I am the army."

As the dominant central authority based in Delhi, the British faced a dilemma in deciding how to deal with the Pukhtun tribes on the northern marches of their Indian Empire. Much was happening in the region to concern the British. Not only were the tribes along the frontier proving troublesome, but the Russians were pushing to extend their influence into Persia and Afghanistan. As every

Remnants of an Army by Lady Butler, portraying Dr. William Brydon outside Jalalabad, the sole survivor of the British army after its defeat by the Afghan tribes in 1842 (Tate Gallery, London, wikimedia.org).

British political officer knew, Russia was aiming to reach the warm waters of the Persian Gulf and thereby threaten India, the jewel in Britain's crown. This was the era of the "Great Game," the struggle for primacy in Central Asia between imperial Britain, Russia, and China, and, as always in the region, the prickly Pukhtun tribes were caught in the middle.

After decades of military failures and countless deaths at the hands of the tribes, including those that befell Brydon's army, the British eventually adopted a policy of annual subsidies in Afghanistan and treaties with the Afghan king. On the frontier of British India, they established a system of indirect rule over the most independent-minded of tribes like the Wazir and Mahsud (see chapter 2).

The British realized perhaps more than any other European power that an efficient and minimal administration providing a semblance of justice in maintaining law and order would be far more effective than the gun and the whip. While constantly on the verge of giving in to what Lord Curzon had called the steamroller, they rarely ever used it. By the time the British moved toward the frontiers of northern India and up to the borders of Afghanistan in the late nineteenth century, their attitude was even more pragmatic. Faced with some of the most turbulent tribes in Asia living in the most difficult of terrains, the British devised a system of administration that was far ahead of what any other imperial power was able to design. Its neatness and economy were conceptually breathtaking. They would select the finest of their officers and invest in them complete authority, both political and military, and allow them to administer, with a mixture of diplomacy and force, a specially designated frontier area. Notions of dignity, honor, and service to the people in their charge mattered to this elite corps, as pointed out in chapter 2. One of the more successful political officers, Robert Sandeman in India, enunciated what became the British philosophy of tribal administration: "To be successful on the frontier a man has to deal with the hearts and minds of the people, and not only with their fears."[38]

This system provided almost a century of relative—and everything to do with tribal societies on the frontier is relative—stability. Throughout Britain's Indian empire, and wherever possible outside it, Muslim tribes were administered through the political agent—in the Tribal Areas of the North-West Frontier Province and in Baluchistan, in the Gulf emirates, among the tribes of southern Persia, in Yemen, and in Somalia. There was even a political agent in Kashgar in Xinjiang.

Beginning in 1838, the Indian Civil Service also supplied officers to British colonies in Yemen and across the empire to administer tribal societies. The British established their Yemeni capital in the port of Aden, an ancient city and the seat of the Rasulid dynasty, the Yemeni successor to Saladin's Ayyubid Empire. Stafford B. Haines, the first political agent, tried hard to win the respect of the surrounding tribes, as he knew they could interfere with trade and supplies on which Aden depended. He was so successful that as late as the 1920s, more than eighty years after he took over, interior tribesmen still affectionately referred to the people of Aden and the surrounding area as "the children of Haines."[39]

British administrators attempted to use and reinforce existing tribal structures and traditions to ensure stability. The political agent in Yemen dealt with the tribes through the "treaty chief," either a tribal or religious leader already endowed with authority in the tribe who entered into a treaty of protection with the British.[40] The British soon found, however, that providing stipends to sheikhs and sultans was not enough to prevent attacks. The Abdali tribe, ignoring their own sultan of Lahej who had allied with the British, entered into alliances with other tribes, attacking the British and those working for them.

The most successful political agents were those who recognized the egalitarian nature of the tribes and approached them through their customs and traditions. Harold Ingrams, who left a mark as a political agent in Yemen, succeeded, for example, in one of his major missions by working within traditional culture. His task was to bring a tribal area in the Hadhramaut region under British control, which he set about by meeting with the tribal elders while his wife met with tribal women. He quickly discovered that the treaty chiefs of two rival tribes were "anxious that I should help to bring to an end a state of tribal warfare which had lasted, with brief intervals of strong chiefs, for over a thousand years and which was in the 1930's particularly acute. I was persuaded by them and other leaders that this could only be done by direct approach to the tribes."[41] So Ingrams toured the area holding meetings and thereby obtained a three-year truce agreed to by between 1,300 to 1,400 tribal leaders. As Ingrams observed, "Sultans were generally disregarded not only by the tribes but even by other local rulers and peace could not have been secured in any other way than personal intervention and the help of men of influence. There were in fact not two governments to deal with but nearly 2,000."[42] The British, Ingrams thought, needed to understand that the Arabs and Europeans had a very different mentality and approach to administration: "It is curious that after more than 2,000 years of experience of the futility of trying to endow Arabs with the European character, Westerners should still think Arabs can make a Western-pattern state work."[43]

Across the Gulf of Aden in Somalia, the British system of indirect rule began in 1884 and was administered by officers from the Indian Civil Service coming from Aden. They were able to extend some degree of authority from their base at Berbera on the northern coast over the interior Somali clans using a "light footprint," recognizing clan leaders on the lineage charter and giving them small stipends as a sign of respect. However, periodic attempts to strengthen British influence by expanding education and introducing a script to enable Somali to become a written language, for example, were strenuously and even violently opposed by the clans.

As in Waziristan, the role of British administrators was made complicated by agnatic rivalry. The Somali clans constantly sought to play different sections of the administration and personnel against each other in order to gain advantage against their agnatic rivals, always complaining of unjust representation. The senior British commissioner in the Somali port city of Kismayo cautioned the chief native commissioner of British East Africa that, with the Somalis, "you are dealing with the most advanced brain on the East Coast."[44]

The first British administrator in British Somaliland was the political agent Major Frederick Mercer Hunter, author of *A Grammar of the Somali Language* (1880).[45] Alluding to Hunter's philosophy on the extent of force to be used by a political agent, one of his junior officials, Langton Prendergast Walsh, the vice-consul of Berbera in Somaliland, noted:

> Apart from my local knowledge, one of his reasons for selecting me to deal and negotiate with the Somali akils [chiefs] and tribes was that he had heard me assert that a good Political Agent always deprecated the use of force, aiming at conducting operations by skill rather than by fighting. With this view Hunter entirely agreed; and he knew that if he entrusted to me any dealings with the Somalis, I would avoid to the best of my ability all warlike acts.[46]

When Walsh was searching for a qadi for Berbera, he stipulated what kind of man he wanted, stating that he "should prefer that he knows no English, and has had no Western education. He should be well versed in the Koran. . . . He must also be tolerant . . . good-natured."[47] Under this system, the British found that they could control the coastal area with just 100 regular police armed with rifles, as well as an irregular armed force to protect caravans traveling in the interior.

The interior tribes still proved dangerous to such caravans and a headache for the British. In one instance, a tribal leader stole 1,500 camels from Berbera. Consul Walsh knew that military force would be futile and only make matters worse, yet as the representative of British authority, he had to respond. Walsh vowed to use other forms of "pressure." Relying on traditional tribal tactics, he detained a number of the chief's clansmen and seized his child and wife, but treated them with respect and honor while in custody. Making contact through a cousin of the chief's wife, Walsh successfully established a peace agreement with the chief involving both the return of the camels and the release of his wife, child, and clansmen. At the ceremony marking the exchange, the chief's wife publicly exclaimed to her husband: "We owe a debt of gratitude to this Christian officer. I felt much safer while in his charge than I would have done if I had been in the custody of a Moslem official." Berbera, Walsh reported, was afterward "peaceful and prosperous" and "none of the tribes of the interior directly interfered with, or levied tolls on, caravans."[48]

This system promoted stability only insofar as the British administrator maintained his neutrality toward the feuding clans. In many instances, however, the British failed to maintain neutrality. One political officer among the Kurds in Iraq, C. J. Edmonds, arrived in the wake of a controversy involving his predecessor, who, according to Edmonds, on the surface appeared to have done everything right. He wore Kurdish clothes and developed close personal relations with *aghas* (tribal leaders) and ordinary people alike. His post, Darband, had no town or village, so visitors would stay in the official guesthouse, where they would get to know the political officer. "But," said Edmonds, "in a factious country like Kurdistan such familiarity, useful as it may be in many ways, is full of pitfalls for the young and inexperienced political officer: before he knows what is happening he will find himself identified with one of the factions . . . the result is that the adherents of the other faction will become aggrieved and show what seems to them their righteous indignation in ways that will blacken their record with the administration still further, until they become 'hope-less' and come out openly against the Government."[49] The political officer in this case was attacked with a dagger after running afoul of a rival faction. A loyal pro-British agha stepped in to save him and was injured when the dagger missed its mark and plunged into his shoulder. The officer drew his revolver and shot the attacker dead, sparking a blood feud, and was promptly evacuated.

The British system of indirect rule was far from formulaic. Despite the best efforts of its administrators, unforeseen incidents could quickly spin out of control, threatening to upset the balance of what has been called the Waziristan model, with its three pillars of authority. The British invariably faced problems when charismatic religious leaders were able to convince the tribes that they faced a common enemy and a threat to Islam in the form of Christian colonialists. Mullah Powindah, for example, led an all-out rebellion of the Pukhtun tribes against the British as did Mahmud Barzanji leading the Kurdish tribes. Mohammed Abdullah Hassan of Somalia, dubbed the "Mad Mullah" by the British, led a two-decade struggle against the British, Italians, and Ethiopians.

For all their civility and flexibility toward tribal society and their talk of civilization, the British could react with violent fury when the interests of the empire seemed to be threatened. In their response to the early nineteenth-century Uva-Wellassa Rebellion in southeastern Sri Lanka, the uprisings throughout north India in the late 1850s, and the Mau Mau insurgency in Kenya in the middle of the twentieth century, the British reached the levels of savagery attained by other European colonial powers. Even a peaceful gathering, as in Jallianwala Bagh in 1919 in India, resulted in the massacre of more than 1,000 innocent Indians.

The Steamroller

Apart from the use of military force for specific objectives and against tribal uprisings, British colonial rule rested in the hands of the civil service, which by and large viewed military options as an administrative and political failure. By contrast, all other European colonizers—the Russians, French, Italians, Spanish, and Dutch—relied almost exclusively on the steamroller approach in dealing with tribal societies.

RUSSIA. When Tolstoy's narrator in *Hadji Murad* encountered the thistle that would not submit, he was reflecting the tribal reactions to Imperial Russia's efforts to expand into the Caucasus during the eighteenth and nineteenth centuries. Russia's invasion of the Caucasus was the second prong of its imperial ambitions which covetously eyed the independent Muslim nations on its periphery, the first being the expeditions into the ancient khanates and kingdoms of Central Asia, such as Bukhara and Khiva. Because of the difficult mountainous nature of the terrain in the Caucasus and the developed segmentary lineage system of its tribes, this region proved far more difficult to conquer for the Russians.

While the region's tribes, such as the Chechens and Avars, pushed back vigorously, the Circassians proved to be the prickliest. Living in remote and difficult mountain terrain, they were the most isolated and therefore the most independent. The harder the Russians attacked them, the fiercer their resistance. A song composed following an eighteenth-century massacre at the hands of the Russian army revealed the extent to which they were prepared to fight to uphold their code of honor, *adyghe xabze*. The Circassians sang: "Our time-honoured customs and revered way of life, we have been deprived of/ . . . Our sheep herds used to graze in the vast Qwrey Steppe/ . . . Our herds of horses had their pasturelands in the Setey Steppe/ . . . Our past glorious life in this world has been wilting and drooping,/That it is verily more fitting for us to die with our honour intact, than to endure such a miserable life!"[50]

When General Alexei Yermolov, the lauded military commander of the southern tsarist forces, arrived in the region in 1816, he explicitly stated Russia's military strategy: "I desire that the terror of my name should guard our frontiers more potently than chains or fortresses, that my word should be for the natives a law more inevitable than death. Moderation in the eyes of the Asiatics is a sign of weakness, and out of pure humanity I am inexorably severe."[51] True to his word, he and his troops killed civilians mercilessly, annihilated villages, and destroyed the crops of the tribesmen. In response, the Circassians resolved to unify and established a Circassian federation of all tribes in the region, all the while desperate for British assistance that would never arrive.

At the time of the Circassian campaign, the Russians were also fighting the Chechens and the tribes of Dagestan, led within an Islamic frame by Imam Shamil, an Avar from the ruling lineage of the Avar Khanate and an esteemed Naqshbandi sheikh. The Russians hoped to force Shamil to surrender, believing that once the leadership fell, tribal resistance would crumble. When Shamil was finally captured in 1859 and declared an end to the war, the Russians treated him as a valiant foe deserving great honor.

To the isolated Circassians who had little interaction with any emirate or Sufi order and were not organized under religious leadership, Shamil's defeat meant little. Their fight was based in their code, and the only way to crush that thistle, the Russians decided, was to adopt a policy of extermination. Prince Kochubei, a leading Russian statesman and diplomat, had told one of the first Americans to visit the area: "These Circassians are just like your American Indians—as untamable and uncivilized . . . and, owing to their natural energy of character, extermination only would keep them quiet."[52] According to the Russian general Rostislav A. Fadeyev, the Circassians were incapable of becoming Russian: "The re-education of a people is a centuries-long process, but in the pacification of the Caucasus the time had come for us, perhaps for the last time, perhaps only for a brief time, to complete one of the most vital tasks in Russian history."[53] The Russians, he explained in the clinical manner of a medical doctor prescribing relief for the common cold, intended "to exterminate half the Circassian people in order to compel the other half to lay down their arms."[54]

One by one, the Circassian tribes, which to a man refused to surrender, were annihilated by the full onslaught of the Russian military. Thousands were massacred and entire villages burned to the ground. The population of the Shapsugh tribe was reduced from 300,000 to 3,000 tribesmen, who managed to escape into the plains and forests. The 140 Shapsugh who remained were sent to Siberia.[55]

Russian troops destroying a village of the Shapsugh, a Circassian tribe, in the Caucasus in 1853 (personal files of Zakaria Barsaqua).

In 1864 the Ubykh tribe fought the Circassian "last stand" at Sochi on the Black Sea. Knowing they were doomed, the tribe members withdrew to Khodz, a "rough mountainous area."[56] The women threw their jewelry into the river, took up arms, and joined the men in a fight to the death. The objective was to die honorably. The Russians approached with heavy artillery and, under the relentless blanket of modern military gunfire, slaughtered every man, woman, and child. "The bodies of the dead," wrote a Circassian chronicler, "swam in a sea of blood."

Those who survived the larger Russian campaign were herded by soldiers onto boats, ill designed to take so many passengers, that were then cast into the frigid waters of the Black Sea. Russian historian Adolph Petrovich Berzhe witnessed the misery of the Circassians as they awaited their fate:

I shall never forget the overwhelming impression made on me by the mountaineers in Novorossiisk Bay, where about seventeen thousand of them were gathered on the shore. The late, inclement and cold time of year, the almost complete absence of means of subsistence and the epidemic of typhus and smallpox raging among them made their situation desperate. And indeed, whose heart would not be touched on seeing, for example, the already stiff corpse of a young Circassian woman lying in rags on the damp ground under the open sky with two infants, one struggling in his death-throes while the other sought to assuage his hunger at his dead mother's breast? And I saw not a few such scenes.[57]

Many boats sank and their passengers drowned. For those who survived, conditions in Turkey were no less miserable. The Russian consul in the Turkish coastal city of Trapezund reported that 240,000 Circassians had arrived, but that 19,000 of them died shortly afterward. An average of 200 people were dying every day.[58] In all, the Russians had killed about 1.5 million Circassians and expelled a similar number, mostly to the Ottoman Empire.[59]

The only Circassians remaining in the Caucasus in any substantial numbers were the Kabardians, who corresponded to the tribes I have described as qalang. They escaped the worst of the Russian military campaigns, reserved for the nang mountain tribes. The Circassian communities, now shattered and suffering humiliation, lived in pockets separated from one another by a sea of Cossacks, Slavs, and other settlers, with not a single town having a Circassian majority.[60] The Shapsugh tribe saw its capital city renamed after the Russian general who committed atrocities in the area, and a massive victory statue erected to him. By 1897 only 217,000 Circassians remained in the Caucasus.

In James Fenimore Cooper's novel *The Last of the Mohicans,* the warrior Chingachgook is the last remaining member of his tribe on the American frontier. My team and I interviewed someone who also represented the last of his people—Zakaria Barsaqua, president of the Circassian Cultural Institute and member of the International Circassian Council. Zakaria came to see us in Washington, D.C., with Iyad Youghar, chairman of the council. Both organizations are based in New Jersey, where most of America's 5,000 Circassians reside. Although both were European in appearance and dressed in western clothes, they spoke animatedly and with pride of their tribes and the honor of their people.

Zakaria is among the last of the Ubykh, the Circassian tribe that inhabited the Black Sea coast and once numbered a quarter of a million people. Today the Ubykh no longer exist in the Caucasus, but about 40,000 live in Turkey with a handful of families in other countries. Their language is extinct—the last remaining Ubykh speaker died in 1992—and Zakaria and Iyad both fear the Circassian culture and identity may soon be "exterminated."

The Circassians have been particularly outraged by the selection of Sochi, now a Russian resort city, to host the 2014 Winter Olympic Games. Sochi was the site of the Circassian capital and the Ubykh tribe's last stand in 1864. The Olympics will be held on the 150th anniversary of the mass killings there. Iyad told us that hundreds of thousands of corpses lay just beneath the ground, and those digging in the area are already finding human remains.

The Russian government, said Iyad, does not recognize the "genocide" of the Circassians. Nor does it appear to recognize that Circassians even lived in Sochi.

Leaders of the Circassian community being interviewed at American University (from left to right): Iyad Youghar, the author, Frankie Martin, and Zakaria Barsaqua (author's collection).

When President Vladimir Putin spoke to the International Olympic Committee in 2007 to secure Russia's bid, he described Sochi as a place inhabited by ancient Greeks with no mention of the Circassians. The Winter Olympics, noted Iyad with pain and sorrow in his voice, would symbolically close the chapter on his people once and for all. The world would gather at the Circassian capital of Sochi and celebrate the games and their Russian hosts, all the while unaware of the horrors that lay beneath the ground. The Olympic Games thus represented the "final nail in the coffin" of the history of the Circassians.

FRANCE. The Russians were not the only European colonial power using the steamroller in dealing with Muslim tribal societies in the nineteenth century. France, for example, moved aggressively into Africa, beginning with Algeria in 1830, where it placed colonial administration in the hands of the military under a governor general.[61] With one-third of the entire French army posted there, the colonial government became known as *régime du sabre* or "government of the sword."[62] As French settlers took over the farm lands of Algeria, its traditional small-scale agrarian economy was overrun by large-scale, settler-owned enterprises. In addition to land distribution, the famous French love of wine transformed large expanses of cereal-producing land into vineyards for wine production and export, creating widespread famine among Algerians. When the Algerians rose in protest, the French adopted a "scorched earth" policy, systematically destroying villages, livestock, crops, and forests and frequently burning tribesmen alive.[63] Torture and massacres were commonplace.

The stiffest resistance came from segmentary lineage tribes such as those in the Berber mountainous region called Kabylie, from the Arabic word meaning "tribe." In June 1845, 800 Kabyle Berbers of the Ouled-Riah tribe who had refused to acknowledge French authority sought refuge in a cave in the Dahra Mountains and were killed by asphyxiation when French troops blocked the entrance with raging fires. Two months later, French troops killed another 500 tribesmen in the same fashion. Reports of the incidents speak of dead infants found clinging to their mothers' breasts, mothers trying to protect their small children from the smoke in the folds of their clothes, and a man's corpse rigid from the moment of death trying to shield his wife and child from a smoke-maddened ox.[64]

These massacres were not moments of excess but official government policy relating to the tribal periphery. Thomas Bugeaud, the governor general of Algeria, deemed the actions "necessary to strike terror among these turbulent and fanatical montagnards [mountain people]" and to show them that there was no escape from state power, even in caverns. Members of parliament in France openly advocated a "war of extermination."[65] In the first forty years of French rule, 2 million of Algeria's 3 million people were killed as a result of the colonial policy of violence, which also resulted in mass starvation and disease.[66] A member of a French government investigation committee for French policy in Algeria remarked, "We have surpassed in barbarism the barbarians we came to civilize."[67]

In 1871 French attempts to assert greater central authority were met with a major Kabyle rebellion involving 250 tribes, almost a third of the Algerian population.[68] In response, the French seized 500,000 hectares of Kabyle land and exiled the tribes' leaders to the South Pacific island of New Caledonia.[69] Kabyle rebellions erupted again in 1876 and 1882. Eventually Algerians were allowed to become citizens of France, but to do so they had to renounce *au fond* their tribal, ethnic, and Islamic identities, with the result that only 2,500 Algerians had acquired French nationality by 1936. In 1945, on the very day France celebrated the surrender of Germany, Berber tribesmen demonstrated for independence in the Kabyle town of Setif and were met with a vicious crackdown in which as many as 45,000 people were killed. During the Algerian war of independence against France, in which Berber tribes played a key role, between 1 million and 1.5 million people were killed, including one-tenth of the entire Kabyle population.[70] Two million Algerians were imprisoned in French concentration camps.[71]

France's policy of conquest and of striking terror in unyielding peoples extended south to the sparsely populated Tuareg tribes of West Africa. After an early French incursion into Tuareg territory from 1880 to 1881—the disastrous Flatters expedition in which almost ninety men were killed—the French vowed after a twenty-year wait to return in full force and conquer the Tuareg tribes. The Tuareg, who preferred to fight with swords, were no match for modern

French weaponry, which included early machine guns. In one noteworthy but not untypical episode, in 1917 at the time of a major Tuareg revolt, the French invited a Tuareg tribe to cast votes of support for their chief in order to honor him. On that glorious day, the Tuareg tribesmen, dressed in their finest attire, were called out of their camp to cast a secret ballot for the chief. As each man prepared to leave, he was pushed to the ground and his turban ripped off. If he had long and braided hair signifying noble status, the French would slash his throat and the body, stripped of weapons and jewelry, would be thrown onto a growing pile of the dead. Only the religious figures, identifiable by their shaved heads, were not killed. The chief, Ikhesi, the man whom the French promised to honor, was shot and decapitated, and his head stuck on a pole. About 200 Tuareg were killed in one day.[72]

Unlike the British, with their indirect rule, the French chose to dismantle and restructure traditional society. The French forced the tribes to shift local loyalties from fellow tribesmen to their colonial power, which projected itself as the natural "father" of the tribes. Their policy ultimately centered on resettling the Tuareg on the plains, driving them from their mountains and deserts with a view to "civilizing" them and other natives along the model and culture of their "fathers," the French. Even after independence up to the 1970s, many history books in Niger, a former French colony with large numbers of Tuareg, spoke of "our ancestors the Gauls."[73] French rule favored the settled southern farming regions, which in Mali and Niger had been the centers of civilizations to peoples such as the Hausa, Songhai, and Mande. The Tuareg, who saw themselves as lighter-skinned and their way of life as superior to that of the settled people, were now being asked to abandon their lifestyle and conform to that of people they had traditionally looked down upon.

In another contrast to the British who installed the "cream of the crop" as political agents, the accepted French practice was to have the country's less than admirable characters serve in its colonial backwaters like the Sahara as administrators. A 1911 pamphlet declared that "a barber, a peanut vendor, a navvy with the right connections, can be named an Administrator of Native Affairs without the slightest concern for his abilities, his intelligence, his attitudes or his aptitudes."[74] Before 1914 not even half the recruits for the French colonial administration held a secondary education, and 22 percent were deemed incompetent by their supervisors.[75]

SPAIN. In 1912 the Treaty of Fez gave the French control over Morocco, adding an important region to their colonial expansion in West Africa. Later that year, however, they ceded the northern coast to Spain, including the Rif region and its Berber tribes. Spain had already made incursions into the Rif region in the late nineteenth century and clashed with the Rifian Berbers, with one notable casualty in General Juan Garcia y Margallo, the military governor of the nearby

Spanish troops with the heads of Rifian Berbers in the 1920s (wikipedia.org).

Spanish possession of Melilla, who was shot in the head by a Rifian sniper in 1893. After the Spanish Protectorate of Morocco was established in 1912, the Spanish military columns began to move into the interior of the Rif Mountains. An adjutant to the commanding Spanish general, Manuel Fernandez Silvestre, publicly stated, "The only way to succeed in Morocco is to cut off the heads of all the Moors."[76]

After encountering Rifian Berbers in 1921 under Abd-el-Krim, an Ait Wary-aghar tribal leader, General Silvestre ordered his army of 20,000 Spanish troops to retreat to the coast. En route, 3,000 to 4,000 Rifians decimated the panic-stricken Spanish, killing as many as 15,000 of them in a period of two weeks, including General Silvestre himself.[77] All territorial gains of the past decade were lost.

The Spanish responded with bombing raids and gas attacks from airplanes, often indiscriminately striking villages. The high commissioner of Spanish Morocco, the senior-most colonial administrative officer, had written to the Spanish minister of war in August 1921, "I have been obstinately resistant to the use of suffocating gases against these indigenous peoples but after what they have done, and of their treasonous and deceptive conduct, I have to use them with true joy."[78] King Alfonso XIII of Spain stated that the purpose of the aerial gas campaign was "the extermination, like that of malicious beasts, of the Beni Urriaguels [Abd-el-Krim's tribe] and the tribes who are closest to Abdel Karim."[79] In 1924 at Dar Aquba, the Spanish military was again attacked by the Rifian Berbers, who killed a further 10,000 troops of the already shaken Spanish ranks. Over the next five months Spanish planes retaliated by dropping 24,104 bombs in the Rif.[80]

In April 1925 Abd-el-Krim, whose men were facing supply shortages and starvation, invaded the French-controlled part of the Rif, killing 1,000 French soldiers.[81] The French then united with the Spanish and applied the steamroller to the Rif: approximately 325,000 French troops with 400,000 reinforcements invaded from the south, aided by air and artillery support, and almost 140,000 Spanish troops approached from the north.[82] The Rif war ended with the surrender of Abd-el-Krim in May 1926, with approximately 30,000 Rifians killed and wounded.[83]

Spanish operations in the Rif were part of a long tradition of colonial rule through military conquest, beginning with the Tausug, Maguindanao, and other Muslim tribal groups in the southern Philippines in the sixteenth century. The Spanish had arrived in the Philippines fired with imperial zeal following the expulsion of Muslims from Spain in 1492. They considered the Muslims they encountered there part of a larger war Christians had been fighting against Muslims since the Crusades. Recalling their struggle against the Moors in Spain, they called these Muslims Moros, perceived to be a pejorative term. In 1578 the Spanish waged their first military expedition against the Tausug and the Maguindanao. Calling Islam an "evil and false" religion, the Spanish governor instructed his captain to "begin the Hispanization and Christianization of the Moros" with the arrest of all preachers and destruction of all mosques.[84]

Stiff resistance from the Muslim groups, particularly the Tausug, prevented the Spanish from carrying out their objectives, but plunged the area into three centuries of continuous warfare. In expeditions manned by Christian Filipinos, the Spaniards attempted to wipe out the Muslims by burning their settlements and lands and enslaving them for service on Spanish galleys. The Spanish spread terror, decapitating Muslims and putting their heads on pikes. The capital of the Maguindanao Sultanate fell to the Spanish in 1637 and the Sulu Sultanate's capital in 1638, both of which were on the coast. Undeterred, the Tausug and the other groups fought on from the interior of the country. Constant battles and raids on Spanish territories continued into the 1700s, though on a smaller scale as the Muslims sensed a decline in Spanish power, most starkly witnessed in the British occupation of Manila in 1762. A Spanish army officer writing to the Philippine governor general in 1893 still felt that the Muslims "will ever be our eternal enemy," and that force "is the only argument they can understand." He advocated they be "promptly and severely punished" if they "antagonize" the Spanish.[85]

ITALY. Italy was a latecomer to the European scramble for colonial territory in Africa but wasted little time in establishing itself on the continent after becoming a unified country in 1861. Italy encountered the segmentary lineage system in both Somalia and Libya, where it too embarked on a bloody campaign of military conquest. Italian ventures in Africa began in the 1880s in Somalia where

Italy came to focus on establishing an agricultural settler colony. In 1920 Italy launched a plan to develop the massive Societa Agricola Italo-Somala (SAIS) plantation, with the hope of turning Somalia into a plentiful El Dorado. Its grand dreams failed, partly as a result of the Somali tribesmen's refusal to toil as slave labor in the fields. As a consequence, Somalia fell into economic stagnation and was plagued by constant tribal rebellions.

With the rise of Mussolini, Somalia entered a new era. In 1923 Somalia's first Fascist governor, Cesare Maria De Vecchi, arrived in Mogadishu. De Vecchi was one of Mussolini's close confidants and had been commander general of the Blackshirts, the Italian equivalent of the Nazi SS. He and the Fascists thought it intolerable that so little of Somalia was under central control with fewer than 1,000 Italians living in the colony. Plans were made to expand this number substantially, and as with the French in Algeria, the population would be separated into European "citizens" and native "subjects."

The Fascists used military officers to rule the Somali clans with terror, frequently resorting to arbitrary arrests and summary killings or assorted penalties such as tying suspects to moving trucks. An internal Italian government report evaluating the colonial effort found that the military governor of the city of Merka, who was especially notorious in his methods and actions—at times killing religious leaders—was harming Italian objectives: "This system of arresting people and leaving them to die, or having them killed in prison . . . has put in the hearts of the population a dumb terror, mingled with a desire for revenge, which results in an overwhelming hatred of our domination."[86]

The British entering the Italian areas of Somalia during World War II were greeted as liberators, as described by a British officer who was present at the southern port of Kismayo: "All the populace were out in the streets to welcome us, clapping their hands."[87] British officers were shocked to learn of Italy's treatment of the Somalis and the condition of the prisons.

In Libya, then part of the Ottoman Empire, Italian incursions consisted of two major waves, the first beginning in 1911. The war against the Libyans and Ottomans stretched out through the years of World War I, during which time Italy continued to control strongholds on the Libyan coast but failed to penetrate into the interior. The second wave began in 1922 with the ascension of the Fascist government of Mussolini, who vowed to intensify the occupation and gain direct control of the Libyan interior, including the Cyrenaica tribes. This military conquest was to be the first step of Mussolini's plan to settle between 10 million and 15 million Italians in North and East Africa.[88]

The Italians aimed to eradicate the very structure of tribal society, as Cyrenaica's Italian governor, General Rodolfo Graziani, made clear: "Direct rule will not be an empty phrase, because chiefs and sub-chiefs are going to be abolished; I have withdrawn them from circulation."[89] His successor as governor reiterated the message: "Chiefs do not exist any more—there are only citizens with equality of duties and rights." The Italian goal was to turn the tribesmen into "peasant-tenants of the State and wage-labourers."[90]

The tribes were to bear the brunt of the Italian military campaign as the people in the settled areas of Libya put up little resistance. The same was true of some qalang tribes near the settled areas, which had learned to deal with the foreign administration of the Turks. But the more rural nang tribes, motivated by honor, refused to submit. What the Italians called the "rebellion" in both wars was waged exclusively by these tribesmen.

The tribesmen struck incessantly at the Italians for nine years, with a battle taking place every few days.[91] Attilio Teruzzi, an exasperated Italian governor of Cyrenaica, complained:

> Against 200, 500, 1,000, 2,000 rebels, dressed in picturesque rags and badly armed, often 5,000 or 10,000 of our soldiers are not sufficient, because the rebels are not tied down to anything, are not bound to any impediment, have nothing to defend or to protect, and can show themselves to-day in one place, tomorrow 50 km. away, and the following day 100 km. away, to reappear a week later, to vanish for a month, to disperse to fire from afar on an unarmed shepherd, on a patrol of inspection, or on a column which files along the edge of a wood, or at the foot of a hill.[92]

"In this semi-darkness of suspicion and uncertainty," observed E. E. Evans-Pritchard, the British anthropologist who studied the Cyrenaica tribes, "this twilight of confidence, when every human being was a foe, the friend behind no less than the enemy in front, every thicket an ambush, and every crag and boss a sniper's nest, the campaign became distorted to unreality. It was a fantastic shadow-show in which dozens of unrelated episodes were thrown at the same time on to a gigantic screen."[93]

In spite of Italy's harsh policy—with its summary executions, wells sealed, tribesmen dropped from airplanes, and other reprisals—the insurgency did not cease. In response, the Italians regularly bombarded the oases of the resisting tribes with phosgene and mustard gas. In 1930 the Italians made a desperate attempt to break the will of the population by herding entire communities into concentration camps. That summer, 85,000 men, women, and children were interned. Suffering from hunger and disease, some 50,000 of them died within three years.[94] By 1932, with the population of Cyrenaica reduced by as much as two-thirds owing to death and displacement as a direct result of the colonial policy, the insurgency was finally defeated.[95] Not long afterward, World War II would see the victorious British entering the Italian colonies, eventually preparing them for and granting independence.

THE NETHERLANDS. On the other side of the Indian Ocean, the Dutch were contemplating the military conquest of the Aceh region in Indonesia. For centuries, the Dutch had been watching the trading power of the Aceh Sultanate from their Dutch East Indies colony. They were not the only European power to do so. The first British governor of the Straits Settlements in southeast Asia, Robert Fullerton, anticipating Lord Curzon's unwillingness to deploy the steamroller in Waziristan, wrote in 1825, "With respect to the future establishment of European influence over Acheen, it may be observed that such an arrangement on our part was long considered a desirable object, but it has been found *utterly impracticable without employing a large military force to overawe the inhabitants*."[96] The British opted to sign a trade treaty with the Acehnese sultan. The Dutch, however, set out to conquer Aceh and its interior tribes.

In April 1873 Dutch forces landed on the shores of Aceh with 3,000 men but were quickly driven back to their boats. The following December another 13,000 troops arrived and captured the coast but made little headway in the interior. By the end of 1878, 7,000 Dutch troops lay dead, with large numbers being felled by cholera and other diseases. During the 1880s, Dutch positions were constantly under attack.[97] By the 1890s, the Dutch began to employ scorched-earth tactics, which included massacring entire villages, to crush the Acehnese resistance. The war lasted until 1903, when the Aceh sultan and military leadership surrendered to the Dutch, although a guerrilla resistance continued in the interior for another ten years. The war resulted in the deaths of approximately 100,000 Acehnese, with 16,000 on the Dutch side killed.[98] General J. B. van Heutsz, the Dutch military commander during the Aceh-Dutch War and later governor general of the Dutch East Indies, reflected, "Atjehnese will never be defeated except by force, and then only someone who shows himself to possess power to make his will respected shall be the master whose orders they will obey."[99] Even after the resistance was finally defeated, the Dutch were often the target of dagger attacks, known as *Aceh moord*.

Under Dutch rule Aceh was divided into districts, each administered by the uleebalang, the hereditary leader in a hierarchy established under Sultan Iskandar Muda in the seventeenth century, under constant supervision by Dutch civil servants. The 102 officially recognized uleebalang received large allowances from the Dutch, at times equal to half the income of their entire district.[100] With their Dutch backing, which included a strong military force to keep locals at bay, the uleebalang alienated the wider Acehnese population. After World War II, the exhausted Dutch took Indonesia back from the Japanese but did not even attempt to reenter Aceh, with memories of decades of warfare fresh in their minds and facing a growing independence movement elsewhere in the country. Once the Dutch were gone from Aceh, many rose up against the uleebalang, with dozens being killed. By 1946 the uleebalang establishment had been completely decimated.[101]

THE OTTOMANS. The Christian European powers were not alone in the colonization of tribal societies in the Muslim world, as the example of the Muslim Ottoman Empire in the nineteenth century illustrates. In decline and under pressure from Europe to reform, the Ottomans moved to centralize their administrative structure and reverse the policies of autonomy for its peripheries. Among the Kurds, they radically overhauled the autonomous emirate system, replacing tribal leaders, emirs, and aghas with central government officials. Unfamiliar with local traditions and viewed as illegitimate rulers, the new governors were unable to keep tribal conflicts and feuds in check. In the ensuing social chaos, the emirates broke apart into quarreling tribes led by chieftains eager to grab as much power as the new situation allowed. Bedir Khan, the ruler of Botan, who represented the only remaining autonomous Kurdish emirate, fiercely battled the Ottoman state for independence and even some of the tribes formerly a part of his emirate. Bedir Khan and other former emirate ruling families also played a prominent role in the Kurdish nationalist movement that developed during the First World War.

It was in Yemen in the mid-nineteenth century, however, where the Ottoman Empire sought to duplicate the European steamroller in its battles with the Yemeni tribes who had successfully resisted an Ottoman invasion in the sixteenth century. Much like the Europeans, the Ottomans now attempted direct rule over the tribes, which included infrastructure projects and bringing modern "civilization" to the periphery, but were met with a ferocious insurgency. For four decades, the tribes would bleed the Ottoman invaders. Yemen became known as the "Cemetery of the Turks." For Turkish troops, serving in the Yemeni tribal areas, which included Asir, was a death sentence—some recruits had to be chained and forcibly transported on board troop ships, so great was their terror of their fellow Muslims in Yemen. An old Ottoman folk song captures the sentiment of a parent who mourns the loss of a son in Yemen:

> Yemen, your desert is made of sand
> What did you want from my son?
> I don't know your way or your sign
> I am just missing my son
> O Yemen, damned Yemen.[102]

In 1892, 70,000 tribesmen laid siege to Sanaa, under Ottoman tutelage and their administrative capital, and in 1905 another tribal assault on the city caused widespread famine, forcing its residents to eat dog, cat, rat, and human flesh to survive. Fifty percent of the population perished.[103] Sanaa, which in 1900 was described by a foreign visitor as "the most impressive city [in the Ottoman

Empire] after Baghdad," was destroyed in the fighting.[104] Turkish battalions were annihilated in the mountains, with as many as 1,000 Turkish troops killed in a single ambush.[105] In 1905 alone, 30,000 of 55,000 Turkish reinforcements sent to aid the war effort died.[106]

In the wake of the Ottoman defeat in World War I and continued tribal resistance, the Turks pulled out of Yemen. The last Ottoman pasha in charge of Yemen administration in Sanaa mused frankly, "In my opinion, this is what happened, from the day we conquered it to the time we left it we neither knew Yemen nor did we understand it nor learn [anything] about it, nor were we, for that matter, able to administer it."[107]

THE MODERN STATE AND ITS STRUGGLES WITH THE PERIPHERY

Seeing the backs of the departing European colonialists and the rise of new independent states, tribesmen on the periphery joined in the general euphoria, only to discover that the Europeans had left behind a poisoned chalice. Colonial officers with maps, charts, rulers, and red pens had drawn straight lines through ravines and mountains to create the boundaries of the new states in Africa and Asia. These boundaries, now international borders, sliced through tribal communities that had lived as integrated ethnic communities for centuries. I am not referring to the odd anomaly like the railway station that in 1947 found itself physically situated on the international boundary between India and Pakistan, the platform in one country, the ticket office in another. Rather, entire tribal nations—the Somali in the Horn of Africa, the Pukhtun in the northwest of the Indian subcontinent, the Kurds in the Middle East, the Bedouin in North Africa, and the Albanians in the Balkans—woke one morning to find their kin separated from them by an international border. Some, like the Kurds and Somalis, were cruelly divided into four or even more modern states. Visiting each other now involved cumbersome visa regulations and passports. Besides, relations quickly soured between the neighboring nations, making it more difficult for relatives to maintain contact.

This poignant sense of the individual being cut off from the family is captured by the Somali who yearns in verse for his brother across the border in Ethiopia:

My brother is there
I can hear the bells of his camels
When they graze down in the valley,
And the leaves of the bushes they browse at
Have the same sweetness as the bushes near my place
Because the rain which

Makes them grow comes from the same sky.
When I pray, he prays,
And my Allah is his Allah.
My brother is there
And he cannot come to me.[108]

International border posts and guards now blocked the annual migration of nomadic tribes who had roamed freely across different cultures and empires—in effect pronouncing a death sentence on their way of life from North Africa to Central Asia. Up to my time in Waziristan, the nomadic Sulaiman Khel, a Ghilzai Pukhtun tribe, would cross the international border from Afghanistan into Waziristan and onto the Punjab to escape the harsh winters of Afghanistan in search of pasture for their flocks and then return once the heat became unbearable in the plains.[109] This cycle has now been stopped with helicopters, drones, and national and international armies battling for the very passes and routes that the Sulaiman Khel once frequented.

A startlingly large percentage of the Muslim world's population—perhaps as high as one-third—found itself in non-Muslim nations. Here, too, by accident of geography and the sheer power of the new political dispensation, tribal communities confronted an unsettling reality. Whether they liked it or not, some had become part of the highly centralized communist states of the Soviet Union and China, which aimed to obliterate religion altogether, while at the other end of the political spectrum, some found themselves in noisy and sometimes politically chaotic democracies like India, Kenya, the Philippines, and Israel, where they were relegated to the position of unimportant and even despised minorities.

The modern nation-state, at least in its Western variety, assumes a healthy working democracy, efficient and honest bureaucracy, an incorruptible justice system, and rights for all citizens, so that they can participate in the nation to improve their lives through education, employment, and the pursuit of prosperity. Muslim populations on the periphery became attached to or annexed by one or another modern state that gave them few, if any, of these rights. The promises of human rights, democracy, women's rights, stability, or economic progress proved hollow, as much in the Muslim states as in the non-Muslim ones.

Besides, modern Muslim nations in which Muslim tribes now lived were vastly dissimilar. The rulers of some called themselves emperors and cast themselves in the role of historical figures: the shah of Iran, for example, saw himself as a modern-day Cyrus or Darius, the ancient Persian emperors. Others patterned themselves on communist leaders like Joseph Stalin of the Soviet Union, complete with a personality cult and sadistic all-intrusive secret service, as in the case of Hafez al-Assad of Syria. There were also straightforward military dictators ruling the state as a personal fiefdom in the most eccentric and bizarre manner, a prime example being Muammar Gaddafi of Libya. Still others claimed kingship because of their descent from the Prophet, as in Morocco and Jordan, or through tribal conquest, as in Saudi Arabia. In each and every case, the ruler assigned key posts in the state to members of his own group or clan.

Nation building is never a smooth or easy task. It amounts to a tectonic shift for the communities involved. Indeed, millions of people lost their lives in these upheavals: almost 2 million died in the 1947 partition of India and creation of Pakistan; some 2 million were killed in Nigeria's civil war of 1967–70; half a million died in the Indonesian bloodbath of 1965–66 involving the communists and Chinese; and according to Bangladeshi government sources, about 3 million were slaughtered in East Pakistan in 1971 at the hands of the Pakistan army before it broke away to become Bangladesh. Though the scale of such killing was biblical, the sheer momentum of the national movements carried the day, and in most cases the state survived (Nigeria); in other cases it did not (Pakistan).

The Founding Fathers and the Dawn of a New Era

The founding fathers of the newly formed modern states embodied hope and promised a new order. They loomed like titans on the horizon—extraordinary men of charisma who were literally changing history and, in some cases, the world map. Jinnah of Pakistan, for example, created a country where one did not exist. In the jubilation of achieving nationhood and closing the colonial chapter, something that looked impossible to their fathers, the founding generations glossed over the deep ethnic and religious divisions in their societies. Their success depended on their appearing to be all things to all men and women.

National unity was more assumed than real. The warm and evocative phrases of the independence movement were broad and ambiguous—"common struggle," "nationhood," and "a new dawn." In the exhilaration of gaining freedom from the colonial masters, everyone—regardless of race or religion—could identify with a future that promised a fresh beginning. Communities with different ethnic, sectarian, and even religious backgrounds saw what they wanted to see in this vision of the coming time.

Many of these founding fathers came out of a European educational system with its ideas of the Enlightenment, democracy, equality, and nation building. Take some examples of the most prominent names of the independence era: Gandhi and Jinnah were educated in the law courts of London; Nehru of India, Tunku Abdul Rahman of Malaysia, Liaquat Ali Khan and Khawaja Nazimuddin of Pakistan attended Oxford or Cambridge Universities; Jomo Kenyatta of Kenya, Kwame Nkrumah of Ghana, and Krishna Menon of India went to the London School of Economics; and Leopold Sedar Senghor, the first president of Senegal, studied at the Sorbonne.

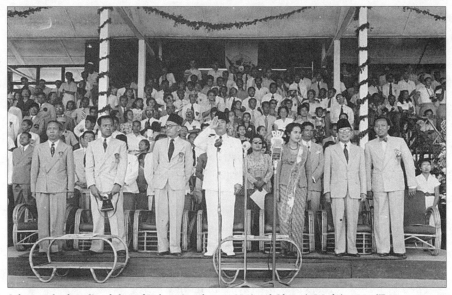

Sukarno, the founding father of Indonesia, salutes at National Olympic Week in 1951 (Tropenmuseum of the Royal Tropical Institute, Amsterdam).

Perhaps no one better in the illustrious list of founding fathers captured the exuberant sense of inclusivity than Sukarno of Indonesia. "I am a follower of Karl Marx," Sukarno had announced and then without pause, in his characteristic manner, offered a contradictory idea, "I am also a religious man." Later he pronounced: "I have made myself the meeting place of all trends and ideologies. I have blended, blended, and blended them until finally they became the present Sukarno."[110]

The rhetoric of the founding fathers consciously included the peoples of the periphery. Sukarno visited Aceh in 1948, seeking to simultaneously acknowledge its distinct history and culture while trying to incorporate it into the larger Indonesian nation, particularly given its prominent role in the independence movement against the Dutch. In a gathering of hundreds of thousands of people in Koetaradja, Sukarno was effusive in his praise of Aceh:

> I know that the people of Atjeh are heroes. Atjeh has always been an example of the independence war, an example of the struggle for independence of all the people of Indonesia. Brothers and sisters, I know this, in fact, all of the people of Indonesia look to Atjeh, they seek to strengthen their inner spirits from Atjeh, and Atjeh continues to be the flame that guides the struggle of the people of Indonesia, in the same manner, I also hope that the people of the entire Republic will become examples, will become the vanguard of the struggle of the people of Indonesia.[111]

Jomo Kenyatta, the first president of Kenya, was determined to see the Somali areas remain part of the new nation, and, in a meeting with Somali elders, he welcomed them and their tribal followers into the fold: "It is a great joy to hear that Somalis are now prepared to join other black Africans in order to form a new Union with them, and to become one people."[112] He also told the elders that he believed his ruling party, Kenyan African Union (KAU), should be reorganized so that Somalis would be able to join it. In reply, a Somali elder appreciated Kenyatta's words and recognized that Kenyatta was working not just for black people but for "all mankind." He hoped Kenyatta would tell other blacks in Kenya to respect Somalis and accept their inclusion in society.[113]

In Burma, General Aung San led the movement for independence from the British, who helped him appoint an executive council as the interim government consisting not only of ethnic Burmese but also a leader of the Karen ethnic group, a Shan chief, and Adul Razak, a Muslim leader from Mandalay.[114] Unfortunately, this was a short-lived period of participation for the ethnic minorities. Aung San and six of his council members were assassinated on July 19, 1947, by a group working under U Saw, a former Burmese prime minister under the British and a political rival of Aung San. As a result of his murder, Aung San is seen as a martyr and has become a *nat,* "the spirit of a powerful person who died a violent and untimely death."[115] The room where he was killed has become a shrine. His daughter, Aung San Suu Kyi, now embodies the hope for a democratic Burma, now known as Myanmar.

The euphoric masses looked on these founding fathers with high expectations, anticipating miracles, along with a sense of familiarity within a family: Gandhi was called Mahatma, the Great Soul, or Bapu, father; Nehru was Panditji, or learned sage; Jinnah was the Quaid-e-Azam, the Great Leader, or Baba-e-Qaum, meaning father of the nation; Sukarno was Bung Karno, or brother Karno; Tunku was Bapa Malaysia, or father of Malaysia; Nkrumah of Ghana was Osagyefo, or redeemer; Jomo Kenyatta among his people was known as Mzee, or respected paternal elder; and Mustafa Kemal was known as Ataturk, the father of the Turks.

But the honeymoon did not last long. The high expectations could not be met, and the consequent disappointments soon turned into anger and frustration. To many in the independent nations, the arrogant, aloof, and culturally alienated white sahib of the colonial administration was replaced by an equally arrogant, aloof, and culturally alienated black sahib of the new administration. Many in the rural and tribal areas were discovering that little had changed in spite of the promises of the founding fathers, who themselves were now the object of people's wrath. Gandhi in India was shot by a Hindu, Liaquat Ali Khan by a Muslim, Aung San was killed by fellow Burmese, Bandaranaike of Sri Lanka was assassinated by a Sinhalese Buddhist monk, and Sheikh Mujib-ur-Rahman of

Bangladesh by Bengalis. Jinnah survived a knife attack by a Muslim. King Abdullah I of Jordan, King Faisal II of Iraq, and King Faisal of Saudi Arabia were all assassinated by fellow Arabs.

People in the millions had followed these individuals as if they were the Pied Piper. These very founding fathers now turned on their own communities. Any signs of unrest or insistent demands were met with fierce force: Kenyatta in Kenya, Sukarno in Indonesia, King Mohammad V in Morocco, and Ataturk in Turkey—all used the same brutal strategy and terror tactics as their colonial predecessors. The next generation of leaders was even more ruthless, with many emerging from military coups and too inclined to use military force to solve civil and political problems. Hafez al-Assad, for instance, in February 1982 slaughtered up to 40,000 people in just over a fortnight in Hama, Syria.

In February 1971, when confronted by Bengalis with legitimate demands, the president of Pakistan, General Yahya Khan, not quite a founding father but part of the founding generation, responded with these chilling words: "Kill three million of them and the rest will eat out of our hands."[116] The army launched a military operation at the end of March 1971, killing 30,000 people in a week. Over the course of the nine-month conflict, Bangladesh's official estimate is that as many as 3 million people were killed, with millions displaced and 200,000 women raped.[117]

However, it is unfair to assume that all army officers are in the mold of military dictators like Yayha Khan. I have known younger Pakistani officers like Major Shabbir Sharif and Major Sabir Kamal who lived simple and honest lives, cared deeply for the problems of the ordinary people, and readily sacrificed their lives for their nation in acts of extraordinary valor in war in spite of being aware of the caliber and failings of the senior leadership. Their motivation, courage, and idealism are second to none compared with that of any officer cadre of any army in the world. In war, Pakistani officers are known to lead their men by example. Since 9/11, a disproportionate number of these younger officers have been killed in action in the Tribal Areas. It is largely because of officers of this kind that the public continues to harbor affection for the army as an institution in Muslim countries.

When the army has appropriated political power, in Pakistan as well as in other states, it has invariably been an unmitigated disaster for the countries involved. Seniority allows officers to cast covetous eyes on accumulating property.[118] With every promotion, they acquire more plots of land and businesses and, in inverse proportion, lose their edge as soldiers and the respect of the people. They thus compromise their moral standing and become vulnerable to attacks by critics like Asma Jahangir, one of the leading human rights lawyers of Pakistan who called them "duffers," used colloquially to mean dunces.

A ruling military can wreak national catastrophe: Colonel Nasser and Hafez al-Assad, an air force officer, lost large swaths of their countries to Israel; General

Yahya Khan lost half his country in 1971; and Colonel Gaddafi, General Omar al-Bashir, and Saddam Hussein emerged from the military or security forces to lead their potentially rich countries to economic and political ruin. The generals strut about, their chests festooned with so many colorful medals from imagined victories that they resemble peacocks in a tropical jungle. They have given themselves the highest military title—field marshal—on par with Second World War British and German generals like Bernard Montgomery and Erwin Rommel who actually commanded divisions on the battlefield. They may not have won wars against a foreign enemy but have been outstandingly successful in launching military assaults to butcher their own people, and some of them could be readily admitted to the twentieth-century pantheon of psychopathic mass murderers like Adolph Hitler, Joseph Stalin, Mao Zedong, and Pol Pot.

The Modern Muslim State and Its Different Models

The modern Muslim state emerged in a complex range of forms, but each one struggled to strike a balance with the tribes on its periphery. These forms can be divided into five distinct categories or models to depict the relationship between the center and the periphery. The center's policies toward the periphery ranged from attempts at forced assimilation or annihilation to calculated neglect, as the cases below will illustrate. The breakdown became apparent early on after independence. For the most part, little but cruelty and contempt passed between the center and the periphery.

Although each case is different, and this is by no means a comprehensive exercise, they all have one thing in common. The dominant group at the center, having taken the reins of power and possessing the arsenal of a modern nation, is then legitimized in the eyes of the West and the international community, as well as in its own eyes as it becomes the "government." In Western political theory, legitimate violence resides in the hands of the state, with the result that the ruling group of the modern Muslim state has been free to use excessive force or otherwise marginalize traditional rivals with impunity, often with the blessing of Western powers.

In the first model, the state has a strong Muslim center formed by one dominant ethnic group confronting a Muslim segmentary lineage society on the periphery. This model is typified by Turkey. Emerging from the shattered Ottoman Empire, it was the first of the modern Muslim states and has always evoked a special pride among Muslims. Turkey is home to the majority of the world's Kurds, and its dealings with them reflect the problems associated with this model. Others that fit this model are the Kurds in Iran, Iraq, and Syria; the Kabyle Berbers of Algeria; the Nuba of Sudan; the Tuareg of Mali and Niger; the Lezgins and Avars of Azerbaijan; the Jola of Senegal; the Acehnese of Indonesia; the Karakalpaks of Uzbekistan; and the Sinai Bedouin of Egypt. Pakistan, as discussed earlier, is another Muslim nation in which one ethnic group, the Punjabis, dominates the all-important civil, military, and economic structures at the center while the tribes on the periphery of its western borders remain neglected.

The second model consists of tribal monarchies with members of a clan or religious lineage forming the center. Examples here are the tribal kingdoms of Afghanistan, Albania, Saudi Arabia, and the Gulf Emirates. Kingdoms with dynasties that have a sacred lineage traced directly to the Prophet include Jordan and Morocco. While each kingdom is different, its organizing principle is to promote loyalty to the royal dynasty irrespective of the tribe or even religion.

The third model is that of a state in which several ethnic groups, including segmentary lineage systems, jostle to control the center. Libya and the unstable centers of the West African nations, best exemplified by Nigeria, are good examples of this category.

Modern Muslim states of the fourth model are dominated by one segmentary lineage system, and include Somalia, Yemen, and Turkmenistan. In this category, clans within a dominant tribal group compete for political power in the tradition of agnatic rivalry.

The fifth model consists of states with non-Muslim centers and Muslim segmentary lineage peripheries, such as the Uyghurs in China, the Oromo of Ethiopia, the Somali of Kenya, the Caucasus tribes in Russia, the Bedouin of the Negev Desert and Palestinian territories, the various Palestinian clans, and Albanians in Kosovo and Macedonia. Additional material is presented on non-Muslim centers dealing with segmented Muslim tribal peripheries (the Tausug and "Moro" groups of the Philippines and the Malay Muslims of Thailand) and settled Muslim peripheries (the Cham in Cambodia and the Rohingya of Myanmar), which also demonstrates the breakdown between center and periphery.

Model One: Strong Center Confronting a Segmentary Lineage Society on the Periphery

In this first category of cases, a center dominated by one ethnic group used the European concept of nationalism to extend its authority over tribal peripheries with differing ethnicities, cultures, and histories. In contrast to the tribes on the periphery, the nationalist centers consisted of settled hierarchical societies, with a population willing to pay taxes, a strong agricultural base, an army ready to defend the nation, and, through their drive to modernize, a nation prepared for the age of globalization. Coming out of the colonial era, there was no doubt which group would be the center and which the periphery. For the new centers, the all-important goals were economic development and trade links with other nations, establishment of international telecommunications networks, technological innovation, and cooperation with multinational corporations. The dominant population supported educational programs in order to be able to successfully interact with and live in the modern world, thus separating the center even further from segmentary lineage peripheries; to the periphery, education meant the imposition of the dominant ethnic identity, language, and culture. For the centers, it seemed natural to want to "civilize" their tribal peripheries, which they saw as a hurdle to their modernizing ambitions.

The first modern Muslim state was Turkey. Its founder, Kemal Ataturk, was once seen as the role model by nationalist leaders who emulated him in the Muslim and non-Muslim world. Turkey also provides the first case in this model of the study.

TURKEY AND ITS KURDISH PERIPHERY. On coming to power in 1923, Turkey's founding father, Ataturk, set out to mold his new state in the image of a modern European nation, emphatically rejecting anything that smacked of tradition and the past. The caliphate, women in hijab, men with beards, and traditional Ottoman dress were all swept aside. In this effort, the Kurdish tribes living in remote mountains and valleys were seen as nothing more than a relic of the past.

Ataturk's plans for the Kurds soon became clear, and he expressed his opinion of the Kurds in unambiguous terms. "Within the political and social unity of today's Turkish nation, there are citizens and co-nationals who have been incited to think of themselves as Kurds, Circassians, Laz or Bosnians. But these erroneous appellations—the product of past periods of tyranny—have brought nothing but sorrow to individual members of the nation, with the exception of a few brainless reactionaries, who became the enemy's instruments."[119] In short, Ataturk pronounced there was no such thing as Kurdish identity. In Turkey Ataturk's word was law.

Although many Kurdish leaders hoped for an independent Kurdistan and European leaders made promises to this end, no such state came into existence after World War I. By the time the Ottoman Caliphate was abolished, the final link between Kurds and Turks was broken. Kurdish nationalist organizations, schools, and presses had already been shut down by the Young Turks, the nationalist reform party. Religious schools were closed, the only source of education for most Kurds. Steps were taken to detribalize the Kurds, banning their language along with the word "Kurd" itself, which was replaced with "mountain Turk." The Kurds, who it was said were actually Turks, would be taught to "relearn" this fact that they had forgotten. Turkish scholars supplied "proof" that the "tribes of the East" were purely Turkish, as was their language, which had been corrupted owing to the proximity to Iran.[120]

The Turkish government appropriated massive tracts of land in the Kurdish areas to be given to Turkish settlers and those who had a Turkish background, such as the Muslims from the Balkans who had migrated to Turkey after 1923. In articulating the Kurdish policy, Ataturk's prime minister, Ismet Inonu, himself half Kurdish, declared: "We are openly nationalist. Nationalism is the only cause that keeps us together. Besides the Turkish majority, none of the other [ethnic] elements shall have any impact. We shall, at any price, turkicize those who live in our country, and destroy those who rise up against the Turks and Turkdom."[121] In May 1925 a Turkish journal remarked, "There is no Kurdish problem where a Turkish bayonet appears."[122]

The Kurdish response was not long in coming. In 1925 a large number of Kurdish tribes rose in revolt under the Naqshbandi Sheikh Said. The Turks met the rebels with devastating force. Between 1925 and 1928, 206 Kurdish villages were destroyed with 8,758 houses burned and 15,206 people killed.[123] Thousands of Kurds were slaughtered without a trial, and the populations of entire districts were deported to western Turkey. The British ambassador in Istanbul reported in June 1927 that the same tactics were being used against the Kurds as against the Armenians in 1915.[124] In 1934 the Turks formally abolished the very idea of the tribe with their Settlement Law. Kurdistan was divided into three zones: one reserved for habitation of those possessing Turkish culture, one in which people with non-Turkish culture were to be moved for assimilation, and finally, areas to be evacuated. All villages where Turkish was not the native language were to be dissolved and their residents forcibly moved to Turkish areas.

The Turkish army moved the steamroller relentlessly through the Kurdish areas until the late 1930s, when it was forced to halt in the Dersim region, one of the most inaccessible and least explored parts of Kurdistan with high, snowcapped mountains, narrow valleys, and deep ravines. The fact that the same ruling family had been able to remain in position over a thousand years through the eras of Genghis Khan, Tamerlane, and others attested to Dersim's isolation and resilience. The region had never been subdued by any previous government in history.

The Turkish army, widely recognized as one of the most professional armies in the world with a reputation for fearlessness, now set out to conquer its own civilian population. What happened to the Dersim Kurds in 1937 and 1938 was nothing short of a massacre. While tribesmen were fighting, the women and children hid within deep caves. The army bricked up the entrances, permanently trapping them, while setting fire to the entrances of other caves and bayoneting anyone who attempted to flee the suffocating smoke. Forests were surrounded and burned to exterminate those who had taken refuge there. Thousands of Kurdish women and children were killed, many of them thrown into rivers to drown. Many women and girls threw themselves from high cliffs into ravines to avoid falling into Turkish hands. Others were rounded up, doused with kerosene, and set alight. The inhabitants of some villages were killed by machine gun and artillery fire. Even pro-Turkish Kurdish tribes were not spared, as their chieftains were rounded up, tortured, and shot dead while their women and children were locked in barns that were set on fire.[125]

At least 10 percent of the population was massacred during the operation, with estimates placing the number killed in Dersim in the span of a year as high as 80,000. The population scattered following the massacres, and there are now far more Dersim Kurds elsewhere in Turkey and Europe than in Dersim itself. By a special law, the name Dersim was changed to the Turkish name Tunceli, meaning "bronze hand." The Dersim massacre by and large halted Kurdish resistance for several decades, although there continued to be sporadic rebellions. In 1960 the president of Turkey, Cemal Gursel, who took power after a military coup, declared while standing on a tank in one of the main Kurdish cities, Diyarbakir: "There are no Kurds in this country. Whoever says he is a Kurd, I will spit in his face."[126]

In the comparatively "quiet" decades that followed the Dersim massacres, a new generation of Kurds grew up speaking Turkish in Turkish schools. Over time, these young Kurds began to raise the question of their Kurdish identity. It was in school that they realized they were different from the Turks, as Mahmut Altunakar, a well-known Kurdish intellectual, recalled while attending secondary school: "Until I arrived in Kutahya I did not know I was Kurdish. We used to throw stones at those calling us Kurds in Diyarbakir. We came to Kutahya and they called us Kurds. They baited us with 'Where is your tail?' Going to school was an ordeal. Then we understood our villagers were right, we were Kurds."[127]

Kurdish anger and a renewed sense of identity and purpose gave rise to leftist student movements among the Kurds in the 1960s that were met with a security crackdown, resulting in mass unrest. Turkish operations and tactics against the Kurds were similar to those of four decades earlier. A Turkish commando report of 1970 described a land war that was under way in Kurdish regions "under the guise of hunting bandits":

> Every village is surrounded at a certain hour, its inhabitants rounded up. Troops assemble men and women separately, and demand the men to surrender their weapons. They beat those who deny possessing any or make other villagers jump on them. They strip men and women naked and violate the latter. Many have died in these operations, some have committed suicide. Naked men and women have cold water thrown over them, and they are whipped. Sometimes women are forced to tie a rope around the penis of their husband and then to lead him around the village. Women are likewise made to parade naked around the village. Troops demand villagers to provide women for their pleasure and the entire village is beaten if the request is met with refusal.[128]

In the 1960s and 1970s, Kurdish student movements in Turkey, coming at a time of broader social unrest in the country, developed into the Kurdistan Workers' Party (PKK) under Abdullah Ocalan, which waged a brutal guerrilla war against the state. The PKK was based in the eastern mountains, particularly the Cudi Mountains, the area of the Botan Emirate, now known as Cizre. By the mid-1990s Turkish Kurdistan had become the most militarized part of Turkey, with close to 200,000 troops stationed there. Around one-fourth of NATO's second largest army was deployed fighting the PKK.[129] A village would often be raided by government security forces one night and then the PKK the next night.[130] As the campaign escalated, 3,500 Kurdish villages were evacuated and many destroyed. By the mid-1990s, 35,000 people had been killed and 3 million Kurds displaced, many of them moving to overcrowded Kurdish cities like Diyarbakir with high unemployment rates and abominable living conditions. As a result, the population of Diyarbakir alone grew from 380,000 in 1991 to 1.3 million in 1996.[131]

Recep Tayyip Erdogan's landslide victory in 2002 in Turkey and his appointment as prime minister the next year not only opened a new chapter in relations between the civilian administration and the military, particularly after the unprecedented trial and sentencing of over 300 military officers for political interference, but also between the center and the Kurds on the periphery. Erdogan's Justice and Development (AK) Party granted Kurds greater cultural rights than ever before under what came to be known as the "Kurdish opening." These measures included broader access to Kurdish language television, the right to give political speeches in the Kurdish language, and bringing an end to the torture of Kurds in Turkish prisons. Erdogan took the bold step, considering how sensitive the Turks are to issues of national pride, of apologizing for the actions of the central government in the massacre of the Kurds at Dersim in the late 1930s.

Even these actions, important in themselves in a country where the very mention of the word "Kurd" was enough to land a person in jail, are far from resolving the decades-old mistrust, grievances, and prejudice that have poisoned relations between the center and the periphery. In April 2012 it was announced that 50,000 students had scored a zero on Turkey's university entrance exam, answering all questions incorrectly. Cities like Ankara reported the highest scores and the Kurdish cities of Van, Hakkari, and Sirnak reported the lowest, showing the stark differences between opportunities for the center and those for the periphery.[132] Scores also indicated that Kurdish students were implicitly rejecting the use of the Turkish language, as well as expressing their opinion of the educational system. With opportunities such as education remaining closed for the Kurds, the unrest and violence continued. The same year, the war between the security forces and the PKK escalated and was complicated by the instability in Syria. From March to September 2012, the Turkish military conducted about 1,000 operations against Kurdish targets. In September Prime Minister Erdogan announced that in the preceding month security forces had killed "500 terrorists" among the Kurds.[133] Violence has remained frequent in spite of the recent efforts to settle the Kurdish issue peacefully and withdrawal of the PKK's demand for an independent country. In Turkey, where military service is compulsory for all males from the age of twenty, 2.5 million Turkish soldiers who have served in the Kurdish areas are reported to have "Southeastern Anatolia Syndrome," a local term for post-traumatic stress disorder. One Turkish soldier remarked, "I served 19 months in the army. I came back alive. But I don't have a soul. My soul is broken."[134]

Turkey's new identity as a confident, democratic, modern Muslim nation acting as a leader in the Muslim world and as a champion of human rights abroad—for example, in its initiatives in Somalia, Gaza, and Syria and its general support of the Arab Spring—is tarnished and incomplete as long as its own Kurdish problem remains unresolved.

THE KURDS IN IRAN, IRAQ, AND SYRIA. The Kurds in Iran faced pressures similar to those in Turkey. When the modernizing Persian military leader Reza Shah overthrew the Qajar monarchy in 1925, he, too, was bent on reducing the power of the influential Kurdish tribal chiefs, killing some and detaining many permanently in Tehran. Inspired by Ataturk, he imposed a single language, Persian, on the country, and changed its name from Persia to Iran to reflect its ethnic base in the Aryan people. The Kurds now became known as "Mountain Iranians."[135]

Reza Shah also launched military campaigns to bring not only the Kurds but also other diverse and largely independent tribes under central rule, including the Qashqai, the Bakhtiari, the Ahwazi Arabs, the Shahsavans, the Baluch, and Turkmen. The campaigns were brutal and humiliating for the tribes—one official ordered "Qashqai women to feed his puppies with their breast milk."[136]

In another tactic, entire tribes were relocated and settled far away from their homes where they were forcibly sedentarized by the army. Deportation to central Iran in 1941 decimated the Kurdish Jalali tribe, for example, driving its numbers down from 10,000 to only a few hundred.[137] On top of this, new dress requirements were instituted, in particular the obligatory Pahlavi hat, which enraged the tribes, some of which retaliated by forcing government garrisons out of their territories.[138]

In the instability following World War II, the Kurds were able to set up an independent state in Mahabad in northwestern Iran, but this republic did not last a full year after the Persian army moved against it. The Kurdish press was banned in Mahabad, as was the teaching of Kurdish. All education in Kurdistan had to be in Persian, and all senior figures appointed from Tehran.[139]

The 1979 Islamic Revolution did not bring respite for the Kurds, with around 10,000 dying in battle against the Revolutionary Guard in the first two years of Ayatollah Khomeini's rule. Many were executed upon the orders of the central government's administrator in Kurdistan, an ayatollah.[140] Although Khomeini declared that Islam had no minorities for there were no differences between

Muslims, the main Kurdish party, the Kurdistan Democratic Party of Iran (KDPI), was outlawed as the "party of Satan" and called "corrupt and [the] agent of foreigners."[141] In another example, a prominent Kurd who had been elected to the Council of Experts was barred from taking office and was described as "seditious." By 1993, 200,000 Iranian troops were deployed in the Kurdish areas.

While the Kurds in Turkey faced an aggressive campaign of "Turkification" and in Iran one of "Persianization," Kurds in Iraq and Syria were forced to undergo "Arabization." Following a series of coups that disrupted British plans for the former Ottoman province of Iraq and saw the Hashemite king overthrown, Saddam Hussein of the Arab Bani al-Nasiri tribe took power in 1979. Under Saddam's "Arabization" policy, the Kurds were marked for either assimilation or elimination. The Kurds had already been a target of Saddam's Arab predecessors in the 1970s, with at least 600,000 and probably many more Kurds sent to Iraqi concentration camps throughout the decade.[142] The government evacuated all Kurdish villagers along the Iranian and Turkish border and resettled them in camps or towns surrounded by guard posts. Anyone caught attempting to return home was shot, regardless of age or sex. Within months, a new guerrilla war had begun.

Saddam resolved to bring the full weight of the modern state against the Kurdish resistance. He targeted the Barzanis who provided the dominant Naqshbandi sheikhly family and led the resistance under their famous leader Mustafa Barzani. Saddam seized 8,000 Barzani males, many of them boys, and paraded them through the streets of Baghdad before executing them, afterward declaring, "They went to hell."[143] One million Kurds were relocated and their lands settled by Arabs.[144] Arabs were paid to take Kurdish wives to dilute the ethnic group. Saddam destroyed nearly 4,000 Kurdish villages, and 45,000 of the 75,000 square kilometers of Iraqi Kurdistan were cleared of all Kurds. In 1988 alone between 150,000 and 200,000 Iraqi Kurds were killed, thousands of them by chemical weapons.[145] However, Saddam's campaign came to a halt with U.S. involvement in the first Gulf War, when a Kurdish autonomous region was established in the north under the protection of a U.S. no-fly zone.

The situation was not much better for the Kurds in Syria. Of the roughly 1 million Kurds in Syria, most were of nomadic stock, which meant their forebears would have moved with the seasons and happened to be on the Syrian side of the border when the modern states in the Middle East were being formed. Others were refugees fleeing from Ataturk's repression who settled among Arabs in Syria's Jazira region.

On a wave of anti-Kurdish Arab nationalism in the 1950s, Syria purged the government of mid- to high-ranking Kurdish officials. Then in 1960 the authorities went on to arrest Kurdish leaders and outlaw the Kurdish language. Celebrations like the main Kurdish festival of Nowruz were prohibited and the names of places altered from Kurdish to Arabic. In 1962, 120,000 Kurds were stripped of their citizenship. A 1963 report produced by the head of Syrian internal security ominously read:

> The bells of Jazira sound the alarm and call on the Arab conscience to save this region, to purify it of all this scum, the dregs of history until, as befits its geographical situation, it can offer up its revenues and riches, along with those of the other provinces of this Arab territory. . . . The Kurdish question, now that the Kurds are organizing themselves, is simply a malignant tumour which has developed and been developed in a part of the body of the Arab nation. The only remedy which we can properly apply thereto is excision.[146]

In 1973 Syria created an "Arab belt" in the north, confiscating Kurdish lands running along a 180-mile strip and settling Arabs on them. Bedouin of Arab stock were brought from the northern Syrian town of Raqqa and settled in Kurdish territory, the official explanation being that the Bedouin land had been flooded under the Tabqa Dam. Tensions between the Arab and Kurdish populations remained high for decades, with periodic eruptions of violence, as in 2004 when Syrian security forces opened fire on a crowd of Kurds in the northern Syrian town of Qamishli, killing 30 and wounding a further 160. When a local Baath Party headquarters was burned to the ground and a statue of former president Hafez al-Assad toppled, the government bore down swiftly on the Kurdish population, arresting hundreds.[147] With the 2011 uprisings against the Syrian central government, Bashar al-Assad, like his father, Hafez, willingly slaughtered his civilian population: by the start of 2013, over 60,000 Syrians had been massacred by the Syrian army and air force. Amid the turmoil caused by this uprising, the Kurds declared autonomy. Their first step was to reinstate the banned Kurdish language.

The Kabyle Berbers of Algeria. In North Africa, the Berbers of Algeria were also subject to harsh policies of assimilation at the hands of an Arab-dominated government. Its Kabyle Berbers had led the fight for independence from France and were outraged when the country's first president, Ahmed Ben Bella, declared upon returning from exile, "We are Arabs, we are Arabs, we are Arabs!" The regime, ruled by the military elite, forbade the use of the Berber language in schools, government offices, or the press and banned Berber names for Berber children. Berber leaders were systematically arrested and killed, including the revolutionary hero Krim Belkacem, who had advocated a federal model for Algeria.

Kabyle rebellions against the central government broke out only a year after the celebration of independence in 1962, and it took two years for the military to quell the revolt. Suppression continued into the next decade with arrests for crimes such as possessing Berber language books. In March 1980 the government banned a

Kabyle Berber academic's lecture on ancient Kabyle poetry. When hundreds of Berber activists, including students and doctors, protested the lecture's ban, the government ordered a clamp down, killing thirty-six people and arresting many others.[148]

The trajectory of the Kabyle region, indeed Algeria itself, in the era of the modern state can be seen in the life of Mustafa Bouyali, a Kabyle Berber. Born in 1940, Bouyali fought the French in the war for independence as a captain in the resistance army. Like so many Berbers of the revolutionary era, he resented the emerging Arab military dictatorship and in 1963 returned to the mountains to fight the Arab-dominated central government. When the insurgency was defeated, the government promised that it would incorporate the Berbers into Algeria and persuaded Bouyali to take a government post in Algiers. With the imposition of overt military rule in 1965, however, he began to publicly oppose the regime in favor of an Islamic state. Security forces then shot and killed one of his brothers in front of his brother's children and attempted to seize him. Bouyali escaped to the Kabyle mountains, where he reconnected with fighters from the past under the banner of the Armed Islamic Movement (MIA) and waged a five-year insurgency until he was killed by security forces in 1987, becoming a folk hero for tribesmen opposed to the government.

In October of the following year, students rioted across Algeria, demanding reform. In what became known as Black October, security forces fired on the protesters, killing 500 people and arresting 3,500.[149] Outraged, two of Bouyali's associates, Abassi Madani and Ali Belhadj, formed the Islamic Salvation Front (FIS), whose goal was to compete in elections that the West was pressuring the Algerian military to permit.

When it appeared the FIS would win the second round of national elections in 1992, the military canceled the vote and declared martial law. Several groups led by men who had been affiliated with Bouyali then launched an insurgency out of which emerged the Armed Islamic Group (GIA), known for its deadly strikes. These garnered world headlines but alienated fellow insurgents when they involved the wanton killing of opponents, noncombatants, and civilians in particular. In response, Hassan Hattab, a Kablye Berber, broke away to form a new group, the Salafist Group for Preaching and Combat (GSPC).

Algeria descended into a particularly destructive civil war in which as many as 250,000 people lost their lives. Security forces began arresting anyone with a beard, while soldiers subjected captured "terrorists" to assorted cruelties and humiliation—water torture and sexual abuse, gang raping women, ripping out prisoners' nails, drilling open their legs and stomachs, and carrying out secret executions. Government forces exterminated the entire populations of many villages by slashing people with blades, all the while pinning the blame on the rebel "Islamists" who were, in the mean time, targeting anyone associated with the government. It was not long before the imprint of Algerian security forces in such operations became clear as information trickled into the international press. A woman working in the Algerian security forces told journalist Robert Fisk that over a period of months she had witnessed the torture of at least 1,000 men, as many as twelve a day, with some shouting, "We're all the same, we're Muslims like you." Anyone could be arrested and jailed for "terrorism." In 1998 a former Algerian minister was asked if such tactics compared with those used by the terrorists. "To compare a rape in a police station to a rape by a GIA terrorist," he replied, "is indecent."[150]

These counterterrorism measures were supplemented with renewed "Arabization" rules and regulations making Arabic the only official language and banning both Berber and French. Several weeks before such a law was to take effect in July 1998, the famous Kabyle singer Lounes Matoub, a prominent activist who had staunchly opposed it, was killed in mysterious circumstances, and in response 100,000 Kabyles took to the streets in violent riots. On the first anniversary of Matoub's death, protesters broke into the courtroom in the Kabyle capital of Tizi Ouzou, tearing down its scales of justice.

In April 2001 Massinissa Guermah, a nineteen-year-old Kabyle student, was arrested by Algerian security forces in the town of Beni Douala and shot dead in police custody. Riots erupted across a vast area lasting months that killed as many as 200 people and injured 5,000, as security forces beat, tortured, and opened fire on Kabyle protesters. Mobs attacked symbols of state authority such as town halls, tax offices, and offices of political parties, and taunted police by praising Hassan Hattab.[151] The uprising became known as the Black Spring. In June 2001 a new Kabyle organization, Mouvement Citoyen des Aarchs (Citizens Movement of the Tribes), which was based on a revival of traditional councils of elders, staged a rally in Algiers against repression and injustice with half a million people participating. It was Algeria's largest protest since independence. In 2005 the Kabyle and the central government signed a deal promising economic aid to the Kabyle region and greater recognition for the Kabyle language. The Kabyle believed these measures did not go far enough, and tension remained between center and periphery.

THE NUBA OF SUDAN. When Sudan emerged from British colonialism in 1956, "Arabization" policies were part of the Arab center's attempt to impose its authority over the nation's different ethnic and religious groups. Located in between Sudan's Muslim north and Christian, non-Arab, south were the majority Muslim, non-Arab, Nuba tribes—described by Winston Churchill as a "mountain people who cared for nothing but their independence."[152] Under the British, the tribes of the Nuba Mountains in the South Kordofan region had been administered through "indirect rule" and given autonomy. They therefore remained isolated from the Arabs, but the new central government, dominated by the northern Arabs, reversed British policy and began evicting the Nuba from their lands, distributing the lands to Arab settlers and loyal officials. The Nuba rebel leader and politician Yousif Kuwa captured the alienation and pain of his people when he wrote that he believed he was an Arab until secondary school: "That is what we were taught. As I understood what was happening and became politically conscious, I recognised that I was Nuba, not Arab."[153]

By the mid-1980s, the Nuba had been drawn into Sudan's civil war between the central government and the mainly Christian and animist south, which killed 2 million people. After attacks against the government in South Kordofan by the southern Sudanese People's Liberation Army (SPLA), the government armed local Arab tribes against the Nuba, pushing the Nuba into an alliance with the SPLA.

In 1989 Omar al-Bashir of the Bideriyya Dahmashiyya clan of the Arab Jaalin tribe seized power in a military coup, and with his fellow clansmen now in key posts, he stepped up the campaign to quell the Nuban rebels and impose an Arab identity on the population. The policy was promoted as a jihad against nonbelievers, despite the fact that the majority of Nuba were Muslim. Pro-government Islamic leaders declared that any "insurgent who was previously a Muslim is now an apostate," that "Islam has granted the freedom of killing."[154]

The commander of a powerful government-backed militia announced his intention to "cleanse every stretch of territory sullied by the outlaws."[155] The government blocked access to the mountains and began a campaign to starve the Nuba population. In addition, hundreds of thousands of men, women, and children were held in so-called peace camps in which men were conscripted to fight against fellow Nuba, women were raped in order to dilute the ethnic group, and children were forcibly taught both Arabic and the center's official interpretation of Islam. Villages were systematically bombed and Nuba intellectuals and community leaders arrested and killed. By the time international mediation put a halt to the war, half of the Nuba population, some half million, lay dead. Similar assimilation policies against other non-Arab Sudanese peripheries were also implemented, including in the Muslim Darfur region, where some 400,000 people were killed and 2.5 million displaced.

When Sudan was partitioned in 2011, the oil-rich South Kordofan region was not included in the new nation of South Sudan and remained as part of the north. This left the possibility that the region could emerge as a battleground between the north and south that could become an African version of Kashmir in South Asia. The government of Sudan declared that the final status of the region was to be decided by "popular consultations," but no such consultations were held. A gubernatorial election was held in which a Nuban rebel leader was defeated by Ahmed Haroun, a prominent government bureaucrat wanted by the International Criminal Court for war crimes in Darfur. President al-Bashir declared that if the Nuba did not accept the results of the election, "we will force them back into the mountains and prevent them from having food just as we did before."[156]

A campaign was launched to extend central authority to the Nuba mountains in order to defeat the "terrorists." As a result, half a million Nuba were displaced, with hundreds of thousands seeking safety from government bombardment in mountain caves. The Nuba did not have access to food and water and were forced to eat bark and leaves, while the government blocked aid from reaching them. Diplomats and analysts warned of a full-scale famine. From June 2011 to June 2012 the central government launched over 1,000 aerial bombings in the Nuba region.[157] In a video aired by Al Jazeera in October 2011, Haroun instructed his troops preparing to enter Nuba territory to battle rebels: "You must hand over the place clean. Swept, rubbed, crushed. Don't bring them back alive. We have no space for them." The governor also vowed in other comments, "We will kill in order to purify this state . . . eat them raw."[158]

THE TUAREG OF WEST AFRICA'S SAHEL. In the Tuareg areas of Mali and Niger at independence, the tribes were likewise subjected to aggressive assimilationist policies from faraway centers dominated by different ethnic groups. These measures included a ban on the Tuareg language and administration by the heavy hand of the military. Just three years after the independence of Mali, the response to the center's policies came in the form of a rebellion led by Elledi ag Alla, who was from one of the most powerful clans of the Kel Adrar tribal confederation. His father had been a thorn in the side of the French, who condemned him for his "banditry" and refusal to submit to their authority. When Elledi was seven years old, his father was decapitated by the French and his head displayed to the Kel Adrar. "I became a rebel," Elledi explained, "to avenge my father, killed by the French administration, and to personally avenge myself for what the security agents of the Malian security post at Bouressa kept repeating at me—that if I did not stay quiet I would be slain like my father had been."[159]

In checking the rebellion, northern Mali was shut off from the outside world and put under military rule, led by Mali's commanding officer in the region, Diby Sillas Diarra. Captured Tuareg, including respected religious leaders and tribal elders, were shot and dumped in desert pits filled with blazing embers, known as "Diby's ovens," and then covered with sand. Mali security forces systemically targeted herdsmen and their herds and poisoned wells, the only source of water in the desolate desert. Tuareg women and children were imprisoned and subjected to forced labor, with Tuareg women ordered to marry Mali soldiers. The following year the rebellion was crushed, and the Mali government proudly announced victory over the "feudal" Tuareg people, "an anarchist society without attachments and without sedentary spirit."[160]

The Mali government's tactics were aimed at the livelihood of the nomadic herdsmen—which included poisoning wells, killing herds, and destroying trees—and contributed to a devastating drought in 1973 that led to the deaths of 200,000 people across the Sahel. Around 500,000 Tuareg fled to Niger, while

Veiled Tuareg tribesman (photo by Florence Devouard).

some 500,000 people from Niger, including Tuareg, sought refuge in Nigeria.[161] To outside observers, the Mali government's actions regarding the Tuareg constituted a deliberate policy of starvation as reported in a 1973 cable from the U.S. embassy in Mali: "There is evidence piling up that GOM [Government of Mali] is hoarding grain in government warehouses at distribution points . . . think GOM is doing only small amounts of food and hoarding rest to keep fiercely independent and sometimes hostile desert nomads, i.e. Tuaregs, under government control in towns."[162] Tuareg in exile composed poetry about the anguish of their people and their desire for revenge, addressing the Mali government in one: "Beware! You will soon burn!/ [The Tuareg] have spent years sleeping with this anger/ Because of those elders you killed/ Those animals you burnt."[163]

The situation for the Tuareg in Niger was not much better: with increasing marginalization in the 1970s and 1980s, hundreds of thousands of people had become entirely dependent on food aid. In 1990, after a clash with police in the town of Tchin Tabaradene, the Tuareg launched an open rebellion against the government. Police retaliated by destroying Tuareg camps and hanging nomads, hacking them to pieces, and burning and burying them alive. As many as 1,700 people were killed in the rampage.[164]

Tuareg anger arose in large measure from the government's exploitation of the natural resources on their lands, specifically on the environmentally damaging uranium mines in the hands of the French government–owned nuclear company AREVA. The Tuareg demanded a greater share of uranium wealth, which came to account for 72 percent of Niger's exports.[165] AREVA had built two cities around its uranium mines, Arlit and Akokan, to house the 80,000 workers required to run the mines and AREVA operations, in the process appropriating Tuareg land and thus reducing available pastures for their herds. Tuareg activists complained that increasing numbers of people were becoming mysteriously ill, particularly individuals who worked for AREVA and were subsequently taken to AREVA-owned hospitals that denied any link between the illnesses and radiation exposure during uranium mining. A Tuareg woman whose husband worked in the uranium mine and died in 1999 of a strange illness felt "it was because of the dust. There was something evil in the dust." The general Tuareg population in the region and their meager crops are exposed to dust blown from a massive hill consisting of 35 million tons of waste material that retains 85 percent of its radiation.[166]

In 2007 another Tuareg rebellion erupted in both Niger and Mali. Insurgents in Niger attacked one of AREVA's mines, shutting down production for a month, and the government imposed a state of emergency. Tuareg rebels explained that they had to organize the Niger Movement for Justice (MNJ) "because nothing has been done by the government. There is no work, no schools, not even drinking water in all Niger. It's terrible, it's a genocide, and the government is corrupt, taking money from people and leaving them to live in poverty."[167]

AZERBAIJAN AND ITS TRIBAL PERIPHERY. The northern mountainous periphery of Azerbaijan is home to Lezgin and Avar tribes organized along the principles of the segmentary lineage system. When the state gained independence from the Soviet Union in 1991, the tribes became subjected to Ataturk-style ethnic nationalism by the Azeri-dominated center. As if to drive home the point, the first elected president frequently wore a button on his lapel bearing Ataturk's image. The Azeris, a Turkic Shia people, consolidated their nationalism in early violent conflicts with Christian Armenians over territory in the new post-Soviet states. The Lezgin and Avar tribes, already having had their clans split and herds decimated by the imposition of a new international border between Azerbaijan and Russia, were frequently accused of collaboration with Armenia. Both peoples, with a population of about 1.2 million Lezgins and 200,000 Avars, were forced to register as "ethnic Azerbaijanis" and faced severe restrictions on their native culture and languages, policies also imposed on other minorities like the Muslim Persian-speaking Talysh people. Assimilation began at the time of the Soviet Union when ethnic Azeris actively settled the northern periphery. This process continued into the 1990s, with the government, led first by a former Soviet Politburo member and then by his son, opening Lezgin lands to more than 100,000 Azeri refugees from the conflict with Armenia over the Nagorno-Karabakh region, in which a large number of Lezgins were forcibly conscripted to fight. This helped fuel a Lezgin nationalist movement led by the Sadval (meaning "Unity") nationalist group. Sadval was blamed for a series of terrorist attacks in the 1990s, including a 1994 bombing of the Baku metro that killed fourteen people. In 1996 Ali Antsukhskiy, an Avar MP and one of the most prominent Avar leaders, was assassinated in Baku, and in 2002 security forces killed the Avar guerrilla leader Haji Magomedov.

In 2008 an advocacy group of Avars sent an open letter to the president of Dagestan, an Avar, urging him to put pressure on the Azerbaijani leadership to end the "physical and moral genocide" against the Avars of Azerbaijan. Most local officials in Azerbaijan's Avar areas are ethnic Azeris, they said, who "organize the destruction of the entire non-Azerbaijani material heritage and raze to the ground anything that may be reminiscent of the presence of other ethnic groups."[168]

THE JOLA OF SENEGAL. In Senegal, the majority Muslim segmentary lineage Jola tribesmen of the heavily forested Casamance region in the south, numbering roughly 500,000, have long complained of oppression by the settled Muslim Wolof population in the north. The Wolof were favored by the French during Senegal's years of colonization, and after independence their language was adopted in administrative affairs and commerce. Other ethnic groups endeavored to assimilate into Wolof culture in order to participate in the central government and economy. The Jola of Casamance, known for their resistance to the French, received little economic and political attention, in large part because the hierarchical Wolof did not know how to deal with the distinctly egalitarian Jola in matters of governance and were unable to locate effective leaders for the region, thereby appointing non-Jolas. To many Wolof, the Jola were Niak, meaning "forest people" or "savage." During the 1970s, the Jola complained of "Wolofization" as a growing number of northern Wolof, especially merchants and settlers, in addition to northern administrators, moved to the region. With the passage of the National Domain Law in 1964 under which the government assumed rights over all land that did not have a legal deed, these new settlers were able to procure land at the expense of the local population.[169]

Unrest began in 1980 when a northern police officer killed a Jola student in a protest against both nationwide cuts by the government in education spending and an unpopular high school administration with a non-Jola principal from the north. In December 1983 military forces fired into a crowd of demonstrators in Ziguinchor, the main town of the Casamance region, killing as many as 200, mainly Jola, and arresting hundreds. This action was followed by armed resistance and calls for independence, under the Movement of Democratic Forces of Casamance (MFDC) led by Augustin Diamacoune Senghor, a Catholic priest who questioned France's right to attach Casamance to Senegal at independence: "Casamance has no link with Senegal, neither a historical link, nor an economic link nor an ethnic link. It was simply for bureaucratic convenience [for the French] that it was administered together with Senegal."[170] Given wide powers to crush the rebellion, the military retaliated with arbitrary arrests, summary executions, and torture and went on to destroy crops and clear entire villages. The government was determined to hold onto the region because of its natural resources and the fear that Casamance's Jola population could unite with The Gambia, led by a Jola president, and Guinea-Bissau to the south, allowing that country to rival Senegal's regional dominance. By 2007 roughly 5,000 people had died in the conflict.

THE ACEH REGION OF INDONESIA. The Acehnese, one of some 300 ethnic groups in Indonesia, faced brutality and marginalization from the Javanese center, as did other minority peoples. The central government on the island of Java relied on military force to suppress any dissent, some of which had roots in the colonial era under the Dutch. Acehnese complained that even after the Dutch recognized Indonesian independence in December 1949 a form of colonization remained, as attested by Jakarta's move to absorb the province of Aceh into the government of its southern neighbor, the province of North Sumatra, in spite of strong local resistance.

With the loss of self-governance, the Acehnese found voice for their discontent in 1953 in the national Darul Islam movement, formed in the 1940s, which sought the establishment of an Islamic State of Indonesia. Like the Berbers of Algeria, the Acehnese had played a prominent role in the independence movement but soon found themselves fighting the center they had helped to make possible. When the Indonesian government responded with a large military force, it met stiff resistance from the Acehnese.[171] Fighting largely ceased in Aceh in 1957 when the government reestablished the province of Aceh and two years later granted it autonomy in religion, culture, and education.

In 1974 military leader General Suharto, who replaced Sukarno in 1967, began appointing regional leaders who were accountable to Jakarta, thus putting an end to Aceh's autonomy. The following year he implemented a new settlement policy in Aceh for Javanese settlers so as to "absorb as many transmigrants as possible" and allow Aceh, considered backward, to "catch up" with the rest of the nation. Over the next twenty-four years, 160,000 such "transmigrants" were settled in 126 all-Javanese settlements.[172] This policy was instituted in a boom economy resulting from the exploitation of Aceh's rich oil, natural gas, timber, and mineral reserves. By the mid-1980s the province's per capita GDP had risen to 282 percent of the national average, the third highest in Indonesia.[173] Most of the profits, however, landed in the coffers of Jakarta and the state-owned oil company, Pertamina, while 70 percent of the population of Aceh continued to live off the land, largely through subsistence farming, and fewer than 10 percent of the Acehnese villages had a steady supply of power.[174]

These factors prompted Tengku Hasan di Tiro, the grandson of a hero of the Aceh-Dutch War, to found the Free Aceh Movement (GAM) in 1976 to fight for independence, arguing that Aceh "had always been a free and independent sovereign State since the world begun. . . . The Javanese are alien and foreign people to us Achehnese Sumatrans. We have no historic, political, cultural, economic, or geographic relationship with them. . . . 'Indonesia' was a fraud: a cloak to cover up Javanese colonialism."[175] The conflict between the GAM and the Javanese center continued for many years, accelerating in the early 1990s after the government declared Aceh a military operations area (DOM).

Military tactics included nighttime raids, house-to-house searches, arbitrary arrest, routine torture, the rape of women suspected of being associated in any way with GAM, and extrajudicial executions. Between 1989 and 1993 approximately 2,000 civilians, including children and the elderly, were killed by the military, some in public and others in secret, their mutilated bodies dumped in mass graves or left to decompose in public as a warning to other "suspected rebels."[176]

Major General R. Pramono, the Indonesian military commander in Aceh from 1990 to 1993, urged the community, "If you find a terrorist, kill him. There's no need to investigate him. Don't let people be the victims. If they don't do as you order them, shoot them on the spot, or butcher them. I tell members of the community to carry sharp weapons, a machete or whatever. If you meet a terrorist, kill him."[177]

In September 1999, as an act of goodwill, the central government implemented sharia law in Aceh, but this did not stem the tide of the violence.[178] In 2002 the government had 40,000 security personnel stationed in Aceh, nervously awaiting the imminent independence of East Timor and concerned about losing another part of the country. In the wake of the deadly 2004 tsunami, the GAM and the central government declared a cease-fire and the following year the center granted Aceh autonomy, abruptly bringing the conflict to an end.

THE KARAKALPAKS OF WESTERN UZBEKISTAN. The Karakalpaks, the traditionally nomadic tribes of Karakalpakstan, a region of western Uzbekistan, provide another example of a people neglected and marginalized by the center, in this case, the settled Uzbeks who inherited power from the Soviet Union. As a result of government policies, the Karakalpaks have lost their traditional tribal structure, and their lands are facing catastrophic environmental damage. The Karakalpaks, closely related to the Kazakhs, settled south of the Aral Sea in the seventeenth and eighteenth centuries. They came to rely on the sea for their livelihood, which included fishing and agriculture. Under the Soviet Union, they were absorbed into the Uzbek Soviet Socialist Republic. After Uzbekistan gained independence following the collapse of the Soviet Union, Karakalpakstan, an "autonomous" region, was placed under the tight control of the authoritarian Uzbek president Islam Karimov. The region was cut off from outside influence with no foreign reporters able to enter the region. The capital city of Karakalpakstan, Nukus, was surrounded by security checkpoints. The migration of Uzbek and Kazakh settlers since the fall of the Soviet Union has steadily diluted the Karakalpak culture and language, with the outsiders now forming the majority of the region's population.

Karakalpakstan is also a poverty-ridden area, greatly affected by the shrinking of the Aral Sea, which was down to 10 percent of its original size as of 2010. This has been called "one of the planet's worst environmental disasters."[179] Nearly 2 million hectares of farmable land have been lost due to decades of failed irrigation projects under both the Soviet Union and Uzbekistan, as well as from mass contamination by pollutants, forcing the Karakalpaks to rely entirely on the central government. This environmental crisis has created disastrous rates of unemployment, serious public health concerns, and mass emigration from the region, yet the Uzbek government has done little to address these issues.

An English journalist, Jack Shenker, interviewed for this study in 2011, who visited Karakalpakstan undercover, described the condition of the region and its people with horror and sorrow. He drew a picture of total oppression, fear, and complete economic stagnation. He was shocked to discover that even those who were passionate about preserving their Karakalpak language and identity were barely able to remember their native language after decades of official neglect and assimilation.

THE SINAI BEDOUIN. The Bedouin in Egypt's Sinai Peninsula provide another example of the center's brutality against the periphery and its successful policy of depriving the local community of the benefits accruing from the economic boom in that region. Between 1949 and 1967 Sinai was administered by the Egyptian military until it was lost to Israel in the Six-Day War of 1967. After Sinai was returned to Egypt in 1982, the Bedouin saw their lands settled by outsiders from the Nile Valley and Delta coming to Sinai to work in the growing tourist industry, particularly in southern Sinai. The number of tourist establishments jumped from 17 in 1994 to 274 in 2003, and they were primarily concentrated around Sharm el Sheikh.[180] The Tourism Development Authority of the Egyptian government opened the land for sale to private investors, and barred the Bedouin from being able to purchase land. This policy thus shrank the geographic sphere in which the Bedouin could practice their traditional economy as in any case rights to their own lands were not recognized. The Bedouin unemployment rate reportedly reached a high of 90 percent as they were shut out from hotel jobs, except as security guards.[181] The growth of tourist resorts also reallocated the scant resources of the desert, primarily water. In this harsh environment many Bedouin turned to traditional smuggling practices to survive.

Many in Egypt view the Bedouin with mistrust, suspecting them of being Israeli sympathizers given that the border between Israel and Egypt split their tribes between the two countries. A small portion got "lost" between the two nations, such as members of the al-Azazma tribe, one of the largest groups in the Israeli Negev Desert. A number of them were expelled into Sinai upon the creation of Israel in 1948. Egypt denied the 12,000 al-Azazma tribesmen in Sinai citizenship, arguing that because part of the tribe held Israeli citizenship they were ineligible. They are among the nearly 75,000 Bedouin with no citizenship rights in Egypt.[182] The Bedouin of Sinai, even those who held Egyptian citizenship, were denied the right to own land for fear that they would sell it to Israelis. The Bedouin increasingly resorted to kidnapping foreign tourists for short periods of time to raise awareness of their plight or to appeal to the government to free their clansmen in Egyptian jails. In their frustration, some attacked symbols of Egyptian economic development, such as the gas pipeline in North Sinai. Only as late as October 2012 were Sinai Bedouin granted permission to purchase the land they lived on, and that after rigid procedures demanding proof of their Egyptian citizenship and that of their parents.

In Sinai, the Bedouin were largely seen by government officials through the prism of security and as a threat to the state. This was made evident by the center's response to the bombing in 2004 of a Hilton hotel and other tourist sites in Taba in southern Sinai in which 34 people were killed and 171 injured. Having already named nine suspects, Egyptian security services began mass arrests of Bedouin throughout North Sinai. Egyptian human rights organizations reported nearly 3,000 people arrested and held without charge, with many subjected to torture. Women and children were arrested "as pawns to force men to turn themselves in." The security forces targeted any individuals with beards as "presumed adherents of Islamist congregations."[183]

The fall of President Hosni Mubarak in February 2011 during the Arab Spring did not alter the prism through which Sinai was viewed. In August 2011, six months after Mubarak resigned, the Egyptian military, in cooperation with Israel, deployed two Special Forces brigades to the Sinai Peninsula to combat "militancy" and maintain law and order. In December 2011 a further 2,000 troops were sent to bolster these forces.

One year after Cairo sent the military into Sinai, the tension erupted into violence when sixteen Egyptian border guards were killed by what the Egyptians were calling "Islamist militants." In retaliation, the Egyptian army launched a massive strike using helicopters to fire missiles that killed twenty "terrorists." This was the biggest military action of its kind in the region since the war with Israel in 1973. The fact that it was ordered against so-called Islamists by President Mohammed Morsi, a member of the Muslim Brotherhood, confirms that this had less to do with religion and more with the structural breakdown between center and periphery.

Model Two: Tribal Monarchies

Unlike states defined by ethnic nationalism and assimilation, a number of modern states emerged with a monarch at the center symbolizing the state and its unity. Some of these had ancient lineages that had ruled for centuries. The monarchies were based either in a dominant tribe that had established itself at the center, as in Afghanistan and more recently Saudi Arabia (see chapter 3), or claimed legitimacy and authority through a religious lineage traced to the Prophet, as in Jordan and Morocco.

These nations, many of them home to a wide array of peoples, were held together by the legitimacy vested in the king and his family, with loyalty to the state judged by loyalty to the monarch. The peripheries of these countries did not face the same pressures of assimilation as those in the preceding model. Monarchs operating within a tribal context were sensitive to the honor and dignity of tribes and their elders. Even so, their governments still faced the dilemma of keeping the needs of the center and periphery in balance within their own historical and social contexts.

Kings based in a single clan faced problems on three levels: agnatic rivalry, as cousins vied for power; the collision between the egalitarian ethos of the nation's tribes and the center's hierarchy and principle of dynastic succession; and the need for political skill, diplomacy, and appropriate strength in dealing with communities on the periphery. Their affairs were also complicated by the interests of international powers looking for economic opportunities or furthering their geopolitical influence.

THE KINGDOM OF AFGHANISTAN. The kingdom of Afghanistan was founded by Ahmad Shah Abdali in the eighteenth century. A successful young military commander, generous and compassionate leader, and poet of the Pukhtu language, Abdali won support across clan and religious boundaries. While still under Persian rule, he advanced to a position of leadership over his agnatic rivals with the granting of landholdings. He was named head of the Abdali tribe at a jirga in the Kandahar area after the Shah of Persia's death in 1747 and, now independent from Persia, established his own kingdom. The Abdalis assumed the title of Durrani, which corresponds to the "pearl of the age" or "pearl of pearls," titles given to Ahmad Shah. He adopted the major outlines of the Persian system of administration and effectively incorporated the other Durrani tribal leaders into the new state by entrusting all major positions of power to them.[184] The Durrani kings would incorporate Uzbek areas to the north, as well as Punjab and Kashmir in the Indian subcontinent to the southeast. Ahmad Shah's kingdom became known as Afghanistan, or the land of the Afghan.

The Uzbek Khanates, which came under Durrani rule in 1751 and submitted a nominal tribute to Kabul, remained more or less independent and maintained their cultural ties to Bukhara and Samarkand. Although dominated by the Pukhtun, there were many Persian-speaking settled communities in Afghanistan of artisans, tradesmen, merchants, bureaucrats, and farmers, identified by their locality. They held important positions in the Durrani administration because the language of the court and governance was Persian. These settled people were known as Tajiks and formed the majority of Kabul's population.

The Afghan king ruled through a combination of Islamic and tribal practice. A nineteenth-century American visitor observed royal custom at the general court convened before the king on a Friday, Islam's holy day: "The gateway . . . was thrown wide open and the doorkeeper withdrawn. Every one who had a cause to urge or curiosity to gratify might come into the presence without impediment. The Ameer heard all complaints in person, attended by the Cauzee."[185] Moreover, another observer wrote, "any man seeking for justice may stop him on the road by holding his hand and garment, once his beard, may abuse him for not relieving his grievances, and the Amir will continue to listen to him without disturbance or anger."[186] Despite the appointment of qadis to implement laws based on sharia, Pukhtunwali always remained strong among Pukhtuns, even in the urban areas. In Kandahar, for example, the family of a murder victim was permitted to take revenge against the family of the murderer to settle the matter.[187]

The Afghan king had a particularly difficult position to maintain because he had to balance the international machinations of the Great Game with internal tribal politics. Afghanistan was always an important piece on the Central Asian chess board with the great imperial powers—Britain, Russia, and China—competing to extend their influence in that country at the cost of the other players. It took all the skill of the king to keep Afghanistan independent while having its indispensability acknowledged by each player of the Great Game in order to extract benefits.

The Afghan kings administered the kingdom as a tribal confederation, granting the tribes their freedom except to require them to submit to different forms of taxation and supply tribal fighters for military campaigns. The king asked the same of the chiefdoms on their periphery, such as those of the Uzbek khans in the north. As a tribal kingdom, the Durrani kings were constantly faced with challenges from their agnatic rivals, particularly the more thistle-like Ghilzai and Karlanri tribes found on the eastern borders. The Ghilzai believed their conquests of Persia and India just before the ascent of the Durranis made them the kingdom's rightful rulers, and they posed a constant threat, especially when the Durrani attempted to curtail the power and influence of their leaders. In 1801 a Ghilzai leader of the Hotak clan, the same clan that had conquered Persia in the previous century and established the short-lived Hotaki dynasty, declared himself king in a rebellion that was crushed the following year. The Durrani king ordered the leader and two of his sons blown out of a cannon and had a minaret constructed out of Ghilzai skulls.[188]

Unlike the Ghilzai, the border Karlanri tribes never had pretensions to the throne of Kabul, wishing to remain independent in their mountains. These tribes, chief among them the Wazir, were the most difficult for the Afghan kings to deal with despite receiving handsome sums and only being expected to furnish soldiers for the king's army, an obligation that was not always forthcoming.

The border tribes launched many rebellions in the nineteenth century, often hinging on revenue collection as well as matters of honor. When the Afghan governor abducted three local women in the border region of Khost, for example, the tribes of Khost, along with the Wazir, besieged the king's fort from 1856 to 1857. The tribes expelled the central government's revenue officials "naked and disarmed."[189] The exasperation of Yaqub Khan, who reigned for less than a year in 1879 before abdicating and seeking refuge with the British, would have found a resonance in most of the rulers of Kabul: "I would rather be a grasscutter in the English camp than ruler of Afghanistan."[190]

Afghanistan entered the modern era in 1919 with the kingship of Amanullah Khan, who succeeded in casting off British influence after the Third Anglo-Afghan War. Another ruler inspired by Ataturk, Amanullah embarked on a series of reforms mandating Western dress, bringing traditional religious courts under government control, increasing taxation, introducing compulsory secular education for girls and boys, establishing national registration and identity cards, and abolishing subsidies for tribal chiefs. He also established conscription, which challenged the authority of tribal leaders, who had previously controlled military recruitment.

The results were constant uprisings, beginning with the Mangal Karlanri insurrection in Khost Province in 1924. In November 1928 the Shinwari, who along with the Durranis descend from Qais Abdur Rashid's son Saraban, revolted in Jalalabad and then, uniting with various Karlanri clans, marched on Kabul. They deposed the king in January 1929, although the Durranis regained the throne shortly thereafter. In 1945 the Safi tribe of Kunar Province launched a rebellion after capturing a detachment of Afghan troops that had been sent to collect conscripts. Angered by government attempts to build roads in its region, the Mangal tribe rebelled once again in 1959.[191] In 1973 tarboorwali finally ousted the Durrani king when his cousin, Daoud Khan, staged a coup and established a secular republican government, declaring himself the first president of Afghanistan. Five years later, he was overthrown in a military coup led by Ghilzai communist leaders and was killed, along with his family, and dumped in a mass grave.

In the following months, the majority Ghilzai government under Nur Muhammad Taraki set about targeting its rivals and executed some 500 of an opposed communist faction dominated by Durranis and Tajiks. The government then instituted a brutal Marxist campaign of land reform that caused yields to plummet, abolished Islamic laws, and launched female education programs. Between April 1978 and December 1979 it also executed some 27,000 people, targeting mullahs and elders who opposed both secularization and modernization

202 *Musharraf's Dilemma*

efforts.[192] An insurgency began brewing across the country as Taraki appealed to the Soviet Union for assistance.

Taraki was killed by a rival Ghilzai in the communist government, and in December 1979 the Soviet Union installed Babrak Karmal, who had a Tajik background, and invaded Afghanistan with thousands of soldiers to back his government. They met their stiffest resistance from the nang Ghilzai and Karlanri tribes. The war left roughly 2 million Afghans dead and 7 million displaced. Following the Soviet withdrawal from Afghanistan in 1989 and the collapse of the communist government shortly afterward, a civil war erupted pitting the Ghilzai Gulbuddin Hekmatyar, along with other Pukhtun mujahideen, against the predominately Tajik and Uzbek Northern Alliance. In the ensuing chaos, the Taliban took Kabul in 1996, establishing their rule over much of the country. The Taliban were firmly based in the Ghilzai tribe, with their head, Mullah Omar, and much of the Taliban leadership belonging to the Hotak clan of the Ghilzai.

ZOG, KING OF THE ALBANIANS. The second example of Muslim tribal kingship comes, unexpectedly, from Europe. After majority Muslim Albania gained independence from the Ottoman Empire in 1912, the influential powers of Europe—the United Kingdom, Austria-Hungary, France, Germany, Russia, and Italy—selected a young German prince, William of Wied, to head the country as its monarch, establishing it as a principality. William immediately faced a rebellion, forcing him to leave the country after only six months. He did not, however, relinquish the crown, and a state of civil war persisted over the next decade. Coups, countercoups, and general upheaval followed. Between 1920 and 1922, for example, Albania had seven heads of government.[193]

Central authority was not established until Ahmed Zog, the leader of the Mati tribe in central Albania and whose grandfather had led an uprising against the Ottomans at the end of the nineteenth century, took the reins of power, eventually being proclaimed king of the Albanians. Zog first emerged as the powerful minister of the interior and then as the prime minister in 1922. In order to keep the tribes from attacking the government, he relied upon "peace money" and appointed tribal chieftains as colonels in the Albanian army. These chiefs emphasized *besa,* the traditional Albanian code of honor, in setting aside blood feuds in the interests of unity and the state. They swore loyalty to Zog personally, however, and not the government as such, viewing him as a kind of super-chieftain who would then be called upon to arbitrate between tribes.[194] When he moved to consolidate his power, Zog found it necessary to rotate the position of the minister of interior between members of the cabinet every seven days, so as not to appear to be favoring one clan over another.[195] In 1928 Zog was declared king. In a reflection of his ecumenical spirit, Zog used both the Bible and the Quran in the ritual swearing-in ceremony and broke off an engagement with a Muslim girl to marry a Christian woman who was half Hungarian and half American. After becoming king, Zog forbade civilians outside his own Mati tribe and its allied tribes to carry arms. He placated many of the tribal chiefs by appointing them to prominent military posts, a move that also served to strengthen the army and the authority of the central government.[196]

In spite of these efforts, Zog's rule was marked by constant tribal intrigue and violence—he survived fifty-five assassination attempts.[197] In constant fear of his life, he would only leave his residence accompanied by his mother, since the murder of women in Albanian blood feuds was prohibited, and by a personal guard of cavalry consisting of members of his Mati tribe. He treated rebellious Gheg tribes from the north that revolted following attempts to disarm them harshly, burning their villages and conducting large-scale hangings and imprisonment.[198]

After one assassination attempt in February 1924 when he was shot several times as he entered the parliament building, Zog calmly walked to his seat, pistol in hand and covered in blood, and told the members of parliament—who were all armed and heard the exchange of gunfire in the foyer—"Gentlemen, this is not the first time this sort of thing has happened. I ask my friends to leave it alone and deal with it afterwards."[199] His response was to kill Avni Rustemi, a political rival, whom he blamed for orchestrating the attack. Rustemi's party withdrew from parliament and along with a number of northern chieftains declared open revolt against the government. Zog was forced to flee, and Fan Noli, the founder of the Albanian Orthodox Church and ally of Rustemi, organized a new government. Two years later, Zog retook Tirana with a fighting force of loyal tribes. He killed those who opposed him and used "peace money" to win over those who had remained neutral.[200]

Zog ruled until the Italian invasion of 1939, when he escaped the Fascists and went into exile, formally abdicating his throne in 1946. He eventually settled in France. A brutal communist government had emerged under Enver Hoxha in Albania in 1944, which targeted the traditional tribal structure and its leaders. Under Hoxha, a dark cloud descended over Albania, and it was effectively cut off from the rest of the world until the 1990s. In November 2012 Zog's remains, after his death in France in 1961, were finally repatriated back to Albania with full military honors and placed in a newly constructed mausoleum for the royal family.

THE KINGDOMS OF THE ARABIAN PENINSULA. Saudi Arabia, founded by the Saud tribe of the Najd region, typifies the tribal monarchies in the Arabian Peninsula. The alliance between the tribal chief Muhammad Ibn Saud and the cleric Muhammad Wahhab in the eighteenth century resulted in the eventual adoption of what came to be called Wahhabism as the Saudi national ideology when the kingdom was unified in 1932 under Abdulaziz bin Saud. In time all others were forced to assume this identity. The Saud tribe reinforced its tribal dominance through legal means such as prohibiting the marriage of any woman from Najd to men from peripheral regions such as Asir, Hejaz, or al-Hasa. The key government positions, including governorships of provinces with a non-Saud majority population, were reserved for the Saud.

After consolidating the Najd tribes into feared fighting units known as the Ikhwan (or "Brotherhood"), King bin Saud persuaded them that the security of the state depended on their participation in his campaigns across the peninsula. The Ikhwan were, however, determined to thwart Saud's centralization policies, including settlement of the tribes, as they threatened the tribes' autonomy and ability to raid as they wished. The Ikhwan also objected to taxation of the tribes and the introduction of technology such as automobiles, telephones, and telegraph systems, sabotaging telephone lines that Ibn Saud used in Mecca. In the late 1920s the Ikhwan mounted a rebellion in an attempt to preserve their tribal structure and customs. King bin Saud, who had by now achieved sufficient strength and was allied with Western powers looking for oil concessions, crushed the insurgents. Their final showdown with King Saud came in the Battle of Sabilla in 1929, when his forces turned their automobile-mounted machine guns on Ikhwan astride camels, slaughtering more than 1,000 of them. A member of one such tribe, Juhayman al-Otaibi, would go on to lead the 1979 siege of the Grand Mosque in Mecca, as discussed in chapter 3.

As for the Shia of Saudi Arabia, who make up 15 percent of the country's population, they faced many challenges. The Shia were not part of the Saud segmentary lineage charter, and religious figures influenced by Wahhabi thinking considered them heretics. When, for example, the Shia of al-Qatif in the Eastern Province, inspired by Ayatollah Khomeini in Iran, decided in November 1979 to openly mark Ashura, the traditional Shia ritual commemorating the death of Imam Hussein, even though Saudi authorities had banned the practice, security forces fired on and killed several in the procession. Rioting spread to other Shia cities in the region in which thousands were arrested and twenty-four killed.

A sign of the neglect of the Shia in the Eastern Province is the fact that the first modern hospital in al-Qatif, one of its main Shia cities, opened as recently as 1987. The Shia commonly work as manual laborers, often for oil companies, and have virtually no political or economic influence in their own region. They have neither a strong tribal base to give them a sense of identity nor a place in the dominant Sunni sect of the country.

In contrast, the large numbers of Shia of the Ismaili sect living in Najran Province, which borders Asir and is populated mainly by the Yemeni Yam tribe, have a developed tribal identity. During bin Saud's efforts to incorporate the region between 1916 and 1928, approximately twenty-six rebellions rose against his authority, in which some 7,000 people were killed.[201] After Najran was officially annexed to the kingdom in 1934, opposition to the government continued to simmer for years. In April 2000, following the tribes' decision to celebrate Ashura openly for the first time, Saudi religious police stormed an Ismaili mosque, seized many of its religious texts, and arrested its Yemeni imam for "sorcery." Within an hour, 30,000 tribesmen carrying Kalashnikovs had sealed off the area, opened fire on security forces in a battle that killed several people, and laid siege to a Holiday Inn where the Saudi governor was living. Hundreds of tribesmen were arrested and tortured.[202]

Elsewhere on the eastern board of the Arabian Peninsula, other tribes came to dominate the Gulf monarchies that had either a long nomadic history on the peninsula or moved about in response to pressures from other tribes. In the eighteenth century some clans established a presence on the coast, attracted by the pearl and oasis date palm trade. Over time, the leading clans adopted a sedentary lifestyle and formed states, and tribal sheikhs were transformed into hereditary monarchs. The British were instrumental in this process in that they bestowed status and privileges on tribal leaders, calling them Trucial sheikhs.

When these sheikdoms were granted independence from Britain in the 1960s and 1970s and the discovery of oil ensured that vast funds would flow into the treasuries of the ruling clans, they were able to demonstrate their power and authority as they built modern states with skyscrapers, luxury hotels, and even new islands, seemingly overnight. The royal clans ran the emirates and inevitably monopolized the top government and business positions. This can be seen in Bahrain ruled by the al-Khalifa clan, Qatar run by the al-Thani clan, Kuwait dominated by the al-Sabah clan, Oman ruled by the al-Said clan, and the seven clans that united to form the United Arab Emirates. Many of the ruling clans of the United Arab Emirates share segmentary affiliations: for example, Dubai's royal Maktoum clan and Abu Dhabi's ruling Nahyan are part of the larger Bani Yas tribe. Even if those not belonging to the ruling families form the majority in the country—the Shia in Bahrain, for example, constitute about 60 percent of the population—they have virtually no economic or political power and complain of oppression.

With the discovery of oil, immigrant labor from around the world, including Bedouin from different tribes in the region, swelled the populations of these Gulf States. In Dubai, the population jumped from around 58,000 in 1968 to 2 million in 2010. Foreign laborers soon found that since they were not on the lineage charter of the ruling clans, they were vulnerable to a host of human and civil rights abuses. Many are so desperately poor that they have resorted to selling human organs.

Kuwait has 120,000 such people called Bidoon, literally meaning "without" or someone devoid of identity or citizenship, effectively signifying that they do not officially exist. They appear to have no semblance of rights. The problem is that Kuwait melded the principle of patrilineal segmentary descent with the Western notion of citizenship, requiring citizens to prove their family was in the country before 1920 and mandating that citizenship be passed exclusively through the male line. Thus in 2005 Kuwait had only 139,000 eligible voters out of a population of almost 2.5 million.[203]

THE HASHEMITE MONARCHIES. Other monarchies in modern Muslim states claimed legitimacy through their descent from the Prophet of Islam, as in the case of the Hashemite monarchies of Iraq and Jordan established in the first half of the twentieth century. When the British carved up the former Ottoman Empire, they selected two sons of Hussein bin Ali, who was the sharif of Mecca and king of the Hejaz until he was driven out in 1925 by King Saud, to reign over these kingdoms under a British mandate: King Faisal over Iraq and King Abdullah over Jordan, then known as Transjordan. King Faisal had briefly been king of Syria before he was deposed by the French and then installed by the British as the king of Iraq. While Iraq had existed under the Ottoman Empire, Transjordan was a new political entity carved out of greater Syria, a creation of European colonial officers.

These monarchies would be challenged by the forces of socialism and Arab nationalism, which found expression in military leaders such as Gamal Abdel Nasser and their international backers, in his case the Soviet Union. None of these systems suited the Hashemite kings as their rule was legitimized by descent from the Prophet. It was a shaky base of authority, made shakier by the predilection of the tribes to resist the center. The kings themselves understood their predicament well, as attested by the title of the autobiography of King Hussein of Jordan, *Uneasy Lies the Head* (1962).[204] While the Iraqi monarchy fell to a military coup in 1958, the Jordanian monarchy survived, and the country gained international recognition largely because of the leadership of King Hussein, who ruled from 1952 to 1999. It was only through his charisma and personal qualities that the monarchy and indeed the state itself were able to survive in the face of a restless tribal periphery and the turmoil of the region. The king had the support of the East Bank Bedouin tribes, who were given important positions in the military and government. The strength of the Bedouin's loyalty to King Hussein was such that the country was often referred to as the Bedouin Kingdom.

THE MOROCCAN KINGS AND THEIR TRIBAL PERIPHERIES. Like the Hashemite monarch of Jordan, the Moroccan Alaouite dynasty, the current ruling family, maintains its legitimacy through its descent from the Prophet, but unlike the Jordanian monarchy, it is rooted in Moroccan history going back centuries. The Alaouite dynasty, which consolidated its rule over the country in the seventeenth century, was the second Arab-dominated kingdom of what is today Morocco. It followed a series of Berber dynasties beginning with the Almoravids in the eleventh century. In the manner of the Islamic emirates discussed earlier in this chapter, the Alaouite sultans dealt with the Berber tribes through their chiefs, known as qaids, who were rewarded handsomely for their loyalty. As long as the tribes paid taxes and provided troops for the sultan's campaigns, they were left alone. Whenever overbearing central rulers encroached on tribal sovereignty, as the second Alaouite sultan Moulay Ismail did in his numerous campaigns, bloody battles ensued. The tribesmen, however, differentiated between the state and the person of the sultan. While they were prepared to resist the former and fight to the death if their freedom or honor was threatened, they still revered the sultan as a descendant of the Prophet. During lulls in battles between the sultan's forces and tribes in the late nineteenth century, for example, Berber women would kiss the sultan's cannons and ask them for benediction in order to defeat the sultan's forces, as the cannon had the *baraka,* or blessing, of the sultan and thus the Prophet.[205]

Following more than four decades of French colonial rule, Morocco gained independence in 1956 with the Alaouite sultan Mohammed V as head of state. The entire country rallied behind him, including the nationalists, represented by the Istiqlal Party and dominated by urban Arabs as well as Berber tribes. Mohammed V's policy was one of inclusion, which ranged from appointing Jews to key government positions to magnanimously pardoning powerful Berber chiefs who had worked with the French to expel him from the country shortly before independence. The Berbers of the Middle and High Atlas mountains would become the king's staunchest supporters at a time when nationalists were overthrowing monarchs across North Africa and the Middle East.

The king adroitly handled his Berber population by incorporating the tribes into the modern state. A political party closely connected with the monarchy, Mouvement Populaire (MP), was created for them, and Berbers associated with it were given senior posts in the sultan's cabinet. Although officially the old system of having tribal leaders deal directly with the sultan was abolished in favor of state administration, a system of "communes" was adopted in which small regional bodies with access to state funds could decide policy. Tribal bonds remained strong, however, and communes inevitably came to be dominated by certain clans. Tribal law proved resilient and councils of elders often continued to decide matters of land, water, and pasture in the areas the government had preserved for the tribes' flocks. At the same time, Mohammed V reinforced state authority by utilizing the age-old method of marriage alliances, arranging, for example, a union between his son, Crown Prince Hassan, and the daughter of a major Berber leader of the Middle Atlas Zayyan tribe. In this case, the king also appointed the chief to the Upper House of the Moroccan parliament.[206]

The importance of the king for the Berbers was reflected in a 2011 interview with Mohamed El Manouar for this study. El Manouar, a Berber from Kelaat Mgouna in the High Atlas Mountains, is the director of the language department at the Institut Royal de la Culture Amazighe (IRCAM) in Rabat, which was opened by King Mohammed VI, the grandson of Mohammed V, in 2001. El Manouar emphasized that the Berbers have not contested the religious authority of the king, but the relationship with temporal state authority has often been tense and limited. When asked to define Amazigh, which is how Berbers describe themselves, El Manouar said that the word has many meanings, including "fiérté, fidélité, révolté, and libérté"—"pride, loyalty, revolt, and liberty." The most common definition of Amazigh, he said, is the "proud man." El Manouar explained that in spite of setbacks with the government, the Berbers in Morocco had achieved several victories in recent years, beginning with King Hassan's 1994 proclamation introducing Tamazight, the Middle Atlas Berber language, in primary schools. El Manouar said that Mohammed VI has been more sympathetic to the Berbers than his father, King Hassan. In addition to creating IRCAM and promoting the teaching of Tamazight in primary schools, the king introduced constitutional changes in July 2011 naming Tamazight an official Moroccan language.

What has been more problematic for the dynasty is its relationship with the Berber tribes of the Rif in the north and the Sahrawi tribes of Western Sahara in the south. These tribes have faced severe marginalization and been subjected to major military operations. For different historical and cultural reasons, both have become isolated and distinct from the rest of Morocco.

What sets the Rif apart is its mountain tribes, which are among the most thistle-like in the region, and its status as a former Spanish colony that had been joined to independent French Morocco. While the Rifians were active in the anticolonial uprising that led to independence, they soon felt sidelined and disillusioned, especially after the government began filling the Rifian administration with Arabic- and French-speaking bureaucrats when the locals spoke only their native Berber language, Tarifit, which is distinct from the language spoken by the Berbers of the Atlas, in addition to passable Spanish.

Violence erupted in October 1958 when members of the Ait Waryaghar tribe, which had resisted the colonial Spanish under the leadership of Abd-el-Krim, began to attack markets and Istiqlal party offices. The tribesmen then escaped into the mountains, killing envoys sent to meet them. Although they were fighting the state, as Berbers had in the previous century, they were quick to profess their loyalty to Mohammed V because of his holy lineage.

In January 1959 King Mohammed V sent 20,000 troops of the newly formed Forces Armeés Royales (FAR), over two-thirds of the entire army, led by Crown Prince Hassan, to carry out what the king called a "cruel punishment." The Moroccan troops, with full air and artillery support, faced 5,000 Rifian tribesmen, primarily of the Ait Waryaghar tribe. When the crown prince's personal plane was landing in the Rif Mountains, he was greeted by fire from Rifian sharpshooters hidden at the edge of the airfield.[207] The FAR reacted in fury and indiscriminately bombed entire villages and raped Rifian women.[208] The tribesmen were slaughtered with casualties exceeding 10,000.[209] The uprising came to an end in February 1959 with the region being placed under military administration for the next three and a half years.

After ascending to the throne in 1961, the newly crowned King Hassan avoided visiting the Rifians, whom he later described as "savages and thieves."[210] The Rif would remain largely neglected by the central government and as a result suffered from high levels of poverty, its people forced to survive on hash cultivation and smuggling. In the 1960s the region's infant mortality rate exceeded 50 percent within a week of birth.[211] Many Rifian Berbers emigrated to the slums surrounding Casablanca and other large Moroccan cities or to Europe as migrant laborers. The majority of Moroccan immigrants in Europe are from the Rif. The 1971 failed coup against King Hassan was led primarily by Berber officers from the Rif and Middle Atlas Mountains, and as a result large numbers of Berbers were removed from the security services and other sensitive positions within the government.[212]

Western Sahara, the other troubled region of Morocco, was also a former Spanish colony. The Sahrawi tribes of the area had been under colonial rule from the 1880s until 1975, when Spain transferred sovereignty to Morocco without consulting the tribes. Morocco had claimed Western Sahara as part of what it called Greater Morocco, which was based on the Almoravid borders extending south to the Senegal River. On November 6, 1975, Morocco, to establish ownership of the region, sent 350,000 Moroccan citizens accompanied by 20,000 soldiers on what it called the Green March into Western Sahara—the color green being the primary color associated with Islam. The Moroccans subsequently met with Sahrawi resistance led by the Polisario Front, dominated by the Reguibat tribe, which had been in the midst of fighting for Sahrawi independence from Spain. Moroccan troops brutalized the local population, raping women, poisoning wells, destroying food supplies, burying land mines on desert nomadic paths, and burning homes and grazing lands upon entering Sahrawi settlements and villages. Moroccan planes strafed and bombed refugee camps, at times with napalm. According to an eyewitness account of the siege of Amgala in the eastern part of Western Sahara in January 1976, Moroccan soldiers killed the camp's women and children with machine gun fire as they fled helter-skelter from their tents.[213] By 1978 Moroccan armed forces in Western Sahara included 80,000 men with sixty-one combat planes, armored cars, tanks, transport planes, and helicopters. The fighting, which lasted until 1991, resulted in the deaths of as many as 24,000 people.

As a result of these ruthless measures, more than 65,000 Sahrawis fled to refugee camps in the Tindouf region of western Algeria barely a year after the conflict began. Thousands, especially children, never reached the camps, dying in the desert from thirst, fatigue, hunger, exposure, or illness.[214] In the squalid Algerian camps, the Sahrawi refugees formed a state in exile, the Sahrawi Arab Democratic

Refugee camp in Tindouf, Algeria, in 2012, in which Sahrawi refugees from Western Sahara have languished for over thirty years (wikimedia.org).

Republic (SADR), under the leadership of the Reguibat. At the time of writing, the sovereignty of the Sahrawi nation has been recognized by fifty-two countries and it has been welcomed as a full member of the African Union (AU). Morocco refuses to recognize the SADR and as a result is the only African nation excluded from the AU. Although the United Nations called for a plebiscite for the Sahrawi nation as part of the 1991 cease-fire, decades later, the people of Western Sahara still await news of their homeland.

In the 1980s Morocco built a 2,500-kilometer "defensive" wall running along the eastern border of Western Sahara surrounded by one of the longest continuous minefields in the world. These structures separated the Sahrawi population of Western Sahara from its kin living as refugees in Algeria. Those remaining in Western Sahara were subjected to "Moroccanization" policies making Moroccan Arabic the official language and prohibiting the use of Hassaniya Arabic (the Sahrawi dialect) in public. Sahrawi children were made to wear Moroccan-style clothing in school, and young Sahrawi males were encouraged to marry Moroccan women in order to bring them into Moroccan culture.[215] Moroccans were given incentives to settle in Western Sahara, such as double wages, tax exemptions, and subsidized housing and soon made up the majority of the population. By 1997 the population of Western Sahara consisted of 200,000 soldiers of the Forces Armeés Royales, approximately 200,000 Moroccan settlers, and roughly 65,000 Sahrawi.[216]

Model Three: Multiple Tribal Societies in One State

The third model reflects new nations that emerged from the colonial period with various ethnic groups, segmentary lineage and otherwise, some with their own centers of power, thrust together but with no certainty as to which would constitute the national center. Most of the African nations fall in this category. As a result of this ethnic complexity, founding fathers found it particularly difficult to maintain the unity of the nation. To complicate matters further, some of the ethnic groups that formed the new state belonged to different religions. As many leaders found to their cost, the nation's center could shift overnight, transferring power to a different center and a different ethnic group. Those that were successful in taking over the center could be merciless with other groups that resisted them. The outlines of this model, with all its inherent internal tensions, can be clearly seen in Libya, the first example presented below.

Libya and the Cyrenaican Tribes. Before independence, Libya consisted of three distinct and ancient regions that represented historical centers in their own right: Cyrenaica in the east, Tripolitania in the northwest, and Fezzan in the southwest. The British, who took over the administration of the country after the defeat of the Italians in World War II, incorporated the regions into the modern state of Libya, which became independent in 1951 under King Idris, the reigning head of the Cyrenaica Sanusi Order. It was not a natural union. An authoritative commentator of the region described the boundary between eastern and western Libya as being "without dispute one of the most decided frontiers, natural and human, to be found anywhere in the world."[217] Exactly the same division in the region was observed as far back as over two millennia ago by the Greek historian Herodotus.[218]

King Idris, identified with the east, was toppled by Colonel Muammar Gaddafi in a military coup in 1969. Gaddafi, ignoring the tribal and ethnic divisions of the region, immediately began a transformation of Libyan society, marginalizing the old center of the Cyrenaica tribes in favor of his own tribe, the Gaddafa from central Libya, and the major tribes in Tripolitania and Fezzan. Thus Gaddafi's inner core at the new center came from the Gaddafa, who were given monopoly of the Libyan air force. Under the influence of Nasser's Arab nationalism and Soviet communism, Gaddafi created his own ideology, called Jamahiriya or "state of the masses," and made his "Green Book," which contained his philosophy of the state and meaning of citizenship, compulsory reading for every Libyan. He even went so far as to rename the months of the calendar, replacing August named after Augustus Caesar with Hannibal, and July named for Julius Caesar with Nasser.

Gaddafi reserved special vitriol for the Sanusi. He hunted down Sanusi figures, smashed Sanusi graves—scattering their bones in the desert—and disinterred the body of the Grand Sanusi himself, removing it to an unknown location to prevent Sanusi followers from finding and preserving it.[219] In 1988 Gaddafi razed the celebrated Sanusi University in Jaghbub to the ground. Ahmed Zubair Ahmed al-Sanusi, the nephew of King Idris, was arrested and condemned to death, and spent nine years in solitary confinement as part of a sentence that stretched over

King Idris of Libya, who had close relations
with Britain, meets Sir Winston Churchill in El
Adem, Libya, in 1962 (Danny McL/flickr.com).

three decades. He was frequently tortured by Gaddafi's men: at times he was
strung up by his hands and legs and had his feet broken, battling cockroaches
for sleep and rats for food. He became the world's longest-serving political prisoner, incarcerated for thirty-one years, four years longer than Nelson Mandela.
"I envy Mandela," al-Sanusi would say in 2011, because at least Mandela could
read and be visited by his family, while al-Sanusi had no visitors and only one
book to read.[220] This was compounded by the psychological torture of expecting
execution at any waking moment.[221]

In 1980 open hostilities began developing against Gaddafi with the mutiny
of troops in the eastern port city of Tobruk. In the 1990s many of the former
Sanusi tribes of Cyrenaica formed anti-Gaddafi resistance groups, including the
Libyan Islamic Fighting Group associated with veterans of the war against the
Soviet troops in Afghanistan. From its base in the eastern mountains near the
Egyptian border, the Libyan Islamic Fighting Group attacked government positions. Gaddafi responded brutally by launching bombing raids, closing mosques,
and arresting clerics. Keeping a long beard or going to the mosque regularly
could arouse the suspicion of the security services.[222] From 1995 to 1998 Gaddafi
locked down the Jebel al-Akhdar mountain region, the heart of tribal resistance
during the Italian era, with security forces manning checkpoints and roadblocks

every ten kilometers.[223] In 1996 Gaddafi's regime killed more than 1,200 prisoners, primarily Cyrenaica tribesmen, in Tripoli's Abu Salim jail, the government's main detention center for suspected "Islamist" militants.

While attacking the Cyrenaica tribesmen, Gaddafi targeted the Berber tribes in the western Nafusa Mountains along the Tunisian border for assimilation. In promoting Arab nationalism, Gaddafi argued, as recounted by a Berber writer, that the Berbers were "ancient Arabs who migrated from Yemen and Palestine in the pre-Islamic era, and that the Amazigh language [the Berber language] is an ancient Arabic dialect unsuitable for modern times and an obstacle to progress."[224] The Berber language was outlawed, the names of Berber towns changed, and Berbers forced to register under Arab names. Under Gaddafi's rule, even the Nafusa Mountains, a Berber name, were known only as the Western Mountains. Shortly after assuming power, Gaddafi stated that for Berbers to study the Amazigh language was like drinking "poisoned milk from their mother's breast."[225] Gaddafi told Berber leaders, "You can call yourselves whatever you want inside your homes—Berbers, children of Satan, whatever—but you are only Libyans when you leave your homes."[226]

On February 17, 2011, a "Day of Rage" was organized in Benghazi, the capital of Cyrenaica, and other places in the region. The date commemorated events in the past, particularly one in 1987 in which Gaddafi had publicly executed people from Cyrenaica in Benghazi's sports arena and shown the spectacle repeatedly on television. The Day of Rage began a movement that would lead to the toppling and death of Gaddafi. The Cyrenaica rebels were joined by other tribes including the Berbers in the west who demanded autonomy. Cyrenaica too now reasserted its distinct ethnic identity, and there was even talk of total independence. Harking back to the time of King Idris, the people of eastern Libya resurrected symbols of the Sanusi leader. Ahmed Zubair Ahmed al-Sanusi emerged from the dark and long night of prison to provide leadership to his region.

Ethnic Conflict in Nigeria. In West Africa, many nations emerging from the colonial era faced the same centrifugal forces as Libya. Additional pressures were felt by those straddling the border between Muslim and Christian Africa and reflected the increasing tensions between these two global religions. The ethnic group favored by the colonial authorities would inevitably hold the initial reins of power in the newly established state, and there would be a predictable backlash by rival ethnic groups, often possessing their own historical centers. Inherently politically unstable due to religious and ethnic tensions and lacking a single dominant group with an overriding ethnic majority, different ethnic groups representing different religions and regions assumed power and enacted policies in their own self-interest, before being overthrown themselves.

A good example of such instability in Africa is provided by Nigeria, the most populous nation on that continent. Nigeria was cobbled together by British colonialists from different kingdoms in the early twentieth century and emerged as an independent state with three different centers: the first in the north comprised of the Hausa and Fulani (the former largely and the latter overwhelmingly Muslim and often viewed as a single ethnic group with a shared history of once belonging to the Sokoto Caliphate); the Christian Igbo in the southeast; and the Christian Yoruba in the southwest. Each of these has had its own historical kingdoms, complete with its own tribal peripheries. With the creation of Nigeria, these peripheries found themselves caught between the three centers, particularly in the vast Middle Belt region that serves as the border between the largely Muslim north and Christian south. The peripheral groups of this region include the nomadic Muslim Fulani herdsmen and the Christian Tiv, Angas, and Berom tribes, but almost a hundred more groups live here.

Nigeria's history as an independent state has been one of constant conflict as the different centers of power struggle for political control and fighting rages both between tribes on their peripheries and between tribes and the center, based in Abuja since 1991. In the late 1960s the Igbo region of Biafra attempted to break away from the country, resulting in a bloody civil war and famine that killed about 2 million people. Nigeria has since experienced a series of military coups and countercoups as the different ethnic groups and centers have jockeyed for dominance. In the Middle Belt region, the conflict between Muslim and Christian segmentary lineage tribes is largely a result of land conflicts and tribal codes of revenge, as discussed in chapter 3.

Since 1999 Nigeria has seen a gradual and general power shift away from the Muslim areas in the north to the Christian areas of the south, represented notably by the Yoruba president, Olusegun Obasanjo, and the current president, Goodluck Jonathan, a Christian Ijaw from the far south. Tensions between the different centers and peripheries in Nigeria continue to simmer, constantly erupting into bloodshed. The central government, regardless of which group holds power, has failed to stem the tide of violence and, indeed, often contributes to it with short-sighted and brutal policies toward the opposition.

CAMEROON. Similar tensions are evident in neighboring Cameroon. Here, power is contested between the Christian tribes of the south, the largely animist Bamileke people of the west, and the Muslim Fulani in the north. The first Cameroonian president in 1960, Ahmadou Ahidjo, was a northern Fulani who favored the northern groups in the government. He immediately faced a Bamileke-dominated insurgency, which was finally suppressed in 1971 with the help of France and resulted in some 400,000 Bamileke deaths.[227] Ahidjo ruled until 1982 before handing over power to a southern Christian, Paul Biya, an ethnic Bulu, who withstood an uprising following a 1984 coup attempt by northern Muslims (reportedly instigated by an order from Biya to remove all guards at the palace who came from the north). Over 1,000 people were killed in the fight-ing.[228] Biya remains Cameroon's president.

IVORY COAST. Tensions between the Christian south and the Muslim north can also be seen in Ivory Coast. From 1993 to 1999 its president was Henri Konan Bedie, a member of the Baoule subgroup of the dominant and settled Christian Akan people of the south, who was overthrown in a military coup. He had implemented a policy of "Ivoirite," defining the Christian southerners as the only true Ivorians. The northern Muslims, according to Bedie's government, were foreigners from Burkina Faso. And the northern Muslim population, including communities like the Jula, descendants of the Kong empire, was excluded from government and civil society. (The Kong empire had been established when its rulers, the Ouattara, came to power in the early eighteenth century.) The policy of exclusion extended to the country's former prime minister, Alassane Ouattara, a Muslim Jula, preventing him from run-ning for president in 2000. The banning of Ouattara and the further denial of rights to the northern population sparked a civil war beginning in 2002 that killed 3,000 people and displaced 700,000.[229] A United Nations–backed international interven-tion led to a peace agreement in 2007, and Ouattara took power in 2010.

GUINEA. Since Guinea's independence from France in 1958, the nation had been ruled by dictators, including Ahmed Sekou Toure, a Mandinka Muslim of the Mande people, who killed an estimated 50,000, thousands of them in concen-tration camps.[230] In Guinea the tension between its majority Muslim population and the Christian minority, which constitutes some 10 percent of the popula-tion, became more pronounced in 2008. For the first time, a Christian from a minority tribe, Moussa Dadis Camara, became head of state in a military coup. To protest Camara's junta, a largely Fulani crowd of 50,000 opposition support-ers held a political rally in a stadium in Conakry, the capital, on September 28, 2009. The Fulani now hoped to move away from military rule, which excluded and terrorized them, toward an open democracy. Just as party leaders were about to address the crowd, however, security forces entered the stadium and sealed off most exits. They opened fire into the crowds while men in civilian dress attacked with knives, machetes, and sharpened sticks, bludgeoning and executing even elderly political leaders. The security forces began gang-raping Fulani women, declaring, "We are going to exterminate you Fulani."[231]

One young woman, Fatoumata Barry, a graduate student in economics, spoke of her terrifying ordeal at the hands of the Guinea security forces:

> In front of us, another group of girls were being raped on the lawn of the stadium, a place usually used for prayer . . . they pulled my legs and dipped their hands in my pants. They tore off my pants and my underwear throw-ing them on the ground under my feet. . . . A police officer, after raping

me, decided to urinate in my mouth, as if it was part of their program. I received streams of urine all over my face. After, they used sticks to rape me again with these objects. Then, finally, one tried to stab me in front, on the private parts. . . . The blood began to flow and I was so exhausted that I could not scream or cry. Then they lifted me wet with blood to put me into a truck filled with bodies."[232]

While Fatoumata survived, although left infected with HIV, other women were killed when security forces fired weapons inside their vaginas.[233] A soldier was heard saying that there were "clear orders to rape and kill today. We must obey orders."[234] In all between 150 and 200 people were killed, although a UN panel investigating the massacre found that the death toll was likely far higher and that security forces had disposed of many bodies in mass graves. At least 1,500 people were wounded.

Camara's rule did not survive long after this incident, and he was removed from power in December 2009, after barely surviving an assassination attempt. Since then Guinea has seen two presidents in office, both Muslim Mandinka, illustrating the fragile and shifting nature of politics at the center.

THE GAMBIA. In The Gambia, which has a similar religious division of population to that of Guinea, the conflict over the center is between Muslim groups—the settled Muslim Mandinka (the largest ethnic group in The Gambia, making up 42 percent of the population) and the Muslim segmentary lineage Jola (who constitute 10 percent of the population). Mandinka rule ended in 1994 when Yahya Jammeh, a Jola tribesman, came to power in a military coup. Jammeh then took control of the media, the judiciary, and legislature and filled the senior ranks of the government with Jola tribesmen and members of his Jammeh clan. Jammeh targeted the Mandinka, claiming that they were not Gambians as they had come from elsewhere in West Africa.[235]

Jammeh developed a personality cult incorporating aspects of Islam to solidify his rule and implementing his philosophy of "Jammehism," which was opposed to "laziness" and "Baboon work."[236] In 2012 he vowed to "wipe out almost 82 percent of those in the workforce in the next five years starting this Friday unless they change their attitudes."[237] Jammeh, who constructed a giant arch in the capital that only he was allowed to drive through, announced he had pioneered a cure for AIDS administered personally by him live on television, which according to his official biography was "based on traditional medicines, powered by the Glorious Holy Quran."[238] "Jammeh's treatment is free of charge," the book reveals, but "his healing powers for HIV/AIDS are only available to him on Thursdays" while "he can also cure asthma on Saturdays."[239]

In February 2009, believing his aunt had died from a spell cast by a witch, Jammeh ordered his paramilitary police to arrest 1,000 people, who were then stripped naked and transported in military trucks and buses to the Jammeh clan's village of Kanilai, while hundreds fled into Senegal. In Kanilai, the villagers were forced to take hallucinogenic potions, after which they began defecating, urinating, and vomiting on themselves while crying out for help amid beatings. They were later paraded in the village courtyard and forced to make confessions of cannibalism, revealing how many people they had eaten using supernatural powers and asking Jammeh to forgive them.[240]

Jammeh's opponents have accused him of relying on the support of Jola tribesmen across the border in the Casamance region of Senegal to illegally swing elections in his favor. One Casamance Jola described the process: "There are supporting committees that work in many villages in Casamance for the re-election of Jammeh. The members of the committee come to the village on the eve of the elections by bus. Then after they have voted, they are taken back to their villages."[241] Immediately after the 2001 elections, opposition supporters, human rights activists, and journalists were arrested, and draconian media laws were passed in 2004—a leading journalist who opposed the restrictions was shot to death days after their passage. Jammeh was dismissive of the high-profile killing: "Listen to me: Is he the only Gambian who died? Is he better than Gambians who die in accidents, Gambians who die at sea, Gambians who die on their way to Europe?"

Jammeh declared in 2011 he was ready to rule The Gambia for "one billion years." He struck a defiant note aimed at his national and international critics: "I will not bow down before anybody, except the almighty Allah and if [human rights groups] don't like that they can go to hell."[242]

Model Four: Modern States Dominated by One Segmentary Lineage System

In this category, the modern state is superimposed on a population dominated by one segmentary lineage system and sharing a common ancestor and heritage. Inevitably, the center comes to consist of one dominant clan and its allied clans confronting agnatic rivals in the pattern of the segmentary lineage system. Because this rivalry, pitting cousin against cousin, permeates the entire society, this center is the most unstable of all. The epitome of this model is Somalia and its different tribes all descended from a common eponymous ancestor, Samale.

THE CLANS OF SOMALIA. Despite Somalia's foundation of European-style democracy and nationalism when British and Italian Somalia were joined into an independent state in 1960, Somalia soon began to unravel along lines that explicitly suggested agnatic rivalry, with 150 political parties emerging after independence. Even amidst the rejoicing on Independence Day, clan riots led to the deaths of two people and made for a bloody celebration.[243] The state was found to be an empty concept as politicians were more motivated by the interests of their clans rather than that of the state. The politics of the new nation came to be dominated by the nationalist Somali Youth League (SYL), based in the Darod clan. The year following independence, the Isaaq clan in the north launched a coup by Sandhurst-trained officers, which ultimately failed.

Despite its shaky foundations, Somalia's democratic system endured, and in its 1967 presidential election the president peacefully handed over power to a democratically elected successor, Abdirashid Ali Shermarke of the Darod Majeer-teen subclan, the first leader in postcolonial Africa to do so. In 1969, however, President Shermarke was assassinated by one of his own bodyguards, and the military under Siad Barre, a member of the rival Darod Marehan subclan, swiftly seized control. Most of the power under Barre was reserved for three Darod subclans: Barre's Marehan, his mother's Ogaden, and his son-in-law's Dulbahante (collectively known as the MOD). Barre's armed forces were usually commanded by his closest kin such as his son and son-in-law. Barre ensured loyalty among rival clans by striking alliances with their small, politically powerless lineages through rewards of contracts and jobs.

Barre arrested members of the former government, banned political parties, dissolved the parliament and the Supreme Court, and suspended the constitution. One year after taking power, he announced that henceforth Somalia would be governed by an ideology of "scientific socialism." This ideology was a confused mixture of Islam, tribalism, nationalism, and Marxism. In an attempt to overcome clan divisions, the regime called everyone comrade or *jaalle* (a friend or playmate) and promoted a socialist identity that superseded kinship and aimed to put an end to the clan. In the name of Marxist progress, Barre forcibly relocated whole populations of herders into collective settlements and communal farms. As part of his urbanization and modernization efforts, he concentrated virtually all government development and investment in the center at Mogadishu, which had the country's only universities and hospitals.

By the late 1970s and 1980s, virtually every major Somali clan, in addition to rival subclans within Barre's Darod such as the Majeerteen, were in revolt against his government. In 1978 Barre troops smashed reservoirs to deny water to the Umar Mahamuud lineage of the Majeerteen subclan and their herds, resulting in the deaths of 2,000 tribesmen and the loss of 50,000 camels, 10,000 cattle, and 100,000 sheep and goats. Large numbers of women were raped.[244] In 1987 Barre's son-in-law, the Darod general Mohamed Said Hersi Morgan, targeted the Isaaq clan, declaring he wished to "liquidate the Isaaq problem."[245] In 1988 Isaaq clans launched a military campaign against the government, capturing the northern city of Hargeisa. Government forces bombarded the Isaaq, forcing the rebels to withdraw and causing around 300,000 Isaaq to flee to Ethiopia. As many as 60,000 Isaaq died in the fighting, including women and children. A thousand were allegedly bayoneted to death by Barre's forces.[246] At the same time, Barre massacred Hawiye clans on the coast.

With Somalia now in the grip of all-out internecine tribal warfare, movements representing the various clans were brought together in Ethiopia in 1990 to present a united front against Barre. In December 1990 General Mohamed Farah Aideed of the Hawiye fought his way into Mogadishu, causing Barre to flee to Kenya. According to an agreement among the clans, a post-Barre Somalia would come under their joint rule. But Aideed's faction, the United Somali Congress (USC), was ripped apart in violence between two of its Hawiye subclans. In May 1991 the Isaaq in the north seized the opportunity to declare an independent Somaliland, which corresponded to the old British colony, and withdrew from the emerging chaos in the south. The Darod clans to the east of Somaliland would also declare autonomy later, calling their region Puntland.

In Mogadishu's battlefield hell, ordinary people paid the highest price. Warfare between the clans killed 25,000 civilians in the first four months of fighting.[247] Tribal affiliation became the paramount identifying factor during the war. Reuters correspondent Aidan Hartley described the significance of tribal identity during the war's worst days:

> A queue of civilians was huddled at a roadblock before a gang of rebels. As each person was waved through, another came forward and began uttering a litany of names. My guide with the flaming red hair said the people were reciting their clan family trees. The genealogies tumbled back generation after generation to a founding ancestor. It was like a DNA helix, or a fingerprint, or an encyclopedia of peace treaties and blood debts left to fester down the torrid centuries. I was thinking how poetic this idea was, when *bang;* a gunman shot one of the civilians, who fell with blood gushing from his head and was pushed aside onto a heap of corpses. "Wrong clan," said my flaming-haired friend. "He should have borrowed the ancestors of a friend."[248]

This devastation came with a heavy price: famine. 300,000 Somalis died of starvation in 1992 and about 1 million fled to refugee camps in neighboring countries like Kenya and Ethiopia. With the influx of aid, the various clans sought to obtain and maintain control over the ports and distribution routes through which supplies passed. Control over aid was very profitable for a clan and its leading "warlord."

The UN mission, led by the United States, intervened to organize food distribution. The U.S. strategy was to intimidate the clans into allowing in food aid by sending a large force as a "warning." General Colin Powell, chairman of the Joint Chiefs of Staff, made it clear that American troops would not only defend themselves but launch preemptive attacks if necessary: "We are just not going to ride shotgun, waiting for people to shoot at us and then shoot back." With characteristic gusto, Powell announced that the United States was sending enough soldiers to "dominate the entire country."[249]

The United States soon found itself swimming in choppy waters. After the United Nations charged General Aideed with crimes against humanity for interfering with its mission, the United States attempted to target him with conventional military strikes, but these antagonized his clan and others. A fragile unity seemed to emerge along segmentary principles against the foreign invader. The 1993 disaster of "Black Hawk Down," in which eighteen U.S. soldiers were killed, needs to be understood in the context of the chaos of the time. The deaths of the American soldiers effectively marked the end of international intervention.

Left to its own devices, Somalia, bereft of central authority, was divided into clan-dominated regions. Some areas returned to tribal law and rule by elders, while many nomadic clans simply resumed their traditional way of life, seeking pasture and water for their flocks and clashing with other clans over sparse resources. Other areas succumbed to anarchy as rival "warlords," many of them former officials in Barre's government, battled over resources and territory.

YEMEN AND ITS TRIBES. Modern Yemen society similarly consists of one segmentary lineage system, with common descent from Qahtan. After more than a thousand years of rule, the Yemeni Zaydi Imamate was finally toppled in a 1962 coup launched by military officers loyal to Nasser and his vision of a modern socialist Arab state. The deposed imam fled to the northern mountains and organized a tribal resistance to the new state, beginning a civil war in Yemen. The two most powerful tribes, the Hashid and Bakil, known as the twin wings of the imamate, were drawn into the conflict on opposing sides, with the Hashid at the core of the socialist republican forces and the Bakil backing the imam. The war was a brutal affair that killed 200,000 people, mainly Yemeni tribesmen.[250]

The socialist military rulers were backed by 70,000 Egyptian troops. The Yemeni civil war, which has been described as "Egypt's Vietnam," cost Egypt 20,000 casualties.[251] Nasser's Field Marshal Abdel Hakim Amer, in an echo of the Ottoman pasha's lugubrious assessment of Yemen in the early twentieth century, summed up Egypt's mistakes in Yemen: "We did not bother to study the local, Arab and international implications or the political or military questions involved. After years of experience we realized that it was a war between the tribes and that we entered it without knowing the nature of their land, their traditions and their ideas."[252]

In 1969 the military defeated the deposed imam and the tribes loyal to him. They formally submitted to the new government's authority in 1971, pledging allegiance on the condition that tribal law and tradition would be respected and modern development projects initiated such as roads, schools, and a telegraph system "so people with grievances can notify the authorities."[253]

The transition from imamate to modern state without an intervening colonial era left Yemen largely devoid of a Western-educated middle class familiar with parliamentary democracy. Its first president, Colonel Abdullah al-Sallal, had never slept in a bed and was so confused when confronted by a pair of trousers that he wore them as a shirt.[254] The government ultimately found it needed to govern through traditional tribal structures knowing that if it pushed too hard there would be a violent backlash among the tribes. When in 1981 the government more than doubled customs fees on oil that tribesmen were bringing from Saudi Arabia, for example, the tribesmen refused to pay and clashed with soldiers the government had stationed on the border to enforce payment. The tribal truckers assaulted several officers guarding the border, including the nephew of the local governor, and took their weapons, putting the honor of the government and the tribes at stake. After a series of tense negotiations and accompanying threats, the governor agreed to a traditional settlement. He received the weapons taken from the border officers along with additional weapons and bulls and sheep slaughtered to restore the honor of the government. In return, the government lowered the customs on oil to a level even lower than before.[255]

In 1978 a consultative body that included tribesmen elected Ali Abdullah Saleh, a Hashid tribesman, as president. To extend his power base, Saleh incorporated the tribal sheikhs into the government, building a relationship with Yemen's tribes that in many ways resembled the tribal policies of the Zaydi imams. Saleh was adept at navigating the tribal landscape and often remarked to visiting journalists that his position as president was like "dancing on the heads of snakes."

After securing his power base in the north, Saleh wished to extend his authority into the independent nation of South Yemen, a Soviet client state. When the British pulled out suddenly from South Yemen in 1967, both the pro- and anti-British tribes were abruptly left at the mercy of the new communist government. South Yemen, with its large population of settled peasants, was committed to replacing the tribal system with communist ideology and subjected the tribes to a ruthless security regime. The traditional tribal leaders saw their large landholdings appropriated by the government. Many of the tribesmen fled to Saudi Arabia, with some later continuing to Afghanistan to fight the Soviets, seeing the Afghan jihad as revenge against communism. After the Soviet withdrawal from Afghanistan, many of these Yemenis sought to return to South Yemen to continue their fight against the communists in their homeland.

In May 1990, with the impending collapse of the Soviet Union, Saleh was able to merge North Yemen with South Yemen, creating the Yemen of today. Of the two, the north was more powerful and wealthy, the south beset by shortages of daily items such as food and cigarettes, as well as cars and spare auto parts. The perception in the south was that the union was a northern success and rule by the

Yemeni central government amounted to an occupation waged by the northern tribes of the old imamate.

Under a strong Saleh and his subtribe, the other tribes complained of increasing marginalization and neglect. Steven Caton, an anthropologist who conducted fieldwork in Yemen in 2000, noted, "The government had not been forthcoming in channeling such resources to Khawlan [the large northern tribe Caton studied] because of its uneasy political relationship with the region. . . . [T]he cynical adage of twenty years ago still applied: 'Yemen is the Republic of the Sinhan (Saleh's Hashid subtribe).'"[256]

TURKMENISTAN AND THE TEKE TRIBE. The Turkmen of Turkmenistan, who, like the Somali and Yemeni in the previous examples, are descended from a common ancestor, in their case Oghuz, achieved independence following the collapse of the Soviet Union. The first president of Turkmenistan was Saparmurat Atayevich Niyazov, known as Turkmenbashi, or Father of Turkmens. Turkmenbashi was a member of the Teke, the largest and most powerful Turkmen tribe, which had led the resistance against the Russian invasion in the nineteenth century. The Teke of Akhal Province saw themselves as "the first among Turkmen."

After taking power, the Akhal Teke tribe dominated the government and laid claim to its largesse. Turkmenbashi focused his economic and development programs primarily in the capital city Ashgabat and Akhal Province, which included the capital city, neglecting all other provinces. With absolute power vested in him, he developed a personality cult with its accompanying eccentricities. Turkmenbashi changed the names of the months after his family; banned ballet, opera, and music on car radios and at weddings and other public events; forbade men from having long hair and growing beards; dismissed 15,000 medical personnel in hospitals across the country and replaced them with soldiers; built a golden statue of himself in the capital, which turned to always face the sun; and in response to a 2004 outbreak of bubonic plague in eastern Turkmenistan, declared the word "plague" illegal. The Akhal Teke continued to dominate after Turkmenbashi's death in 2006. Under his successor, Gurbanguly Berdymukhammedov, also an Akhal Teke, eighteen of twenty-two ministers, four of seven deputy chairmen, and the parliamentary speaker were Akhal Teke, with the tribe completely monopolizing law enforcement agencies.[257]

Model Five: Non-Muslim Centers with Muslim Segmentary Lineage Peripheries

In the first model, a dominant Muslim center responded to its Muslim tribal periphery with policies of forced assimilation, settlements designed to shrink or dilute the local population, and outright massacre. In states where a dominant non-Muslim center faces a Muslim tribal periphery, the same tension is evident between the two but is exacerbated by the religious factor.

CHINA AND THE UYGHURS. Over half a century ago, the Turkic Uyghurs of Xinjiang Province in northwest China, like so many others of China's peripheral communities, fell under the steamroller of the communist central government in Beijing, represented overwhelmingly by the Han Chinese. In contrast to the foregoing cases, the Uyghurs have a history of interaction with the Chinese center dating back more than 2,000 years, although central rule over the Uyghur tribes and kingdoms was often weak, and for about 1,000 years entirely absent. In addition, the historically segmentary lineage Uyghurs have been settled for centuries and once constituted a center of their own, with the result that their clan allegiances gradually diminished in favor of identity based on the oases of Xinjiang in which they lived.

The relationship between the Uyghurs and the Chinese center is embodied in the legend of the Fragrant Concubine. An eighteenth-century campaign in Xinjiang by the forces of Emperor Qianlong of the Qing Dynasty resulted in the capture of a Uyghur girl called Iparhan. She was the grandniece of Apakh Khoja, the *khoja* or emir of the Sufi Kashgar Emirate, one of the most revered figures in the history of Xinjiang and a descendant of the Prophet of Islam. Iparhan was exquisitely beautiful, and her body was said to give off a mysterious and intoxicating scent.

When the emperor heard about her irresistible beauty, he commanded his general to kidnap Iparhan for his royal harem in the Forbidden City in Beijing. She was taken from her husband, a prominent Kashgar leader who had resisted the Chinese. Every day on the journey to Beijing, her body was washed in camel's milk and lathered with butter. When the emperor laid eyes on Iparhan, he was enraptured and renamed her Xiang Fei, or the Fragrant Concubine. The story of the Fragrant Concubine is famous in China, and she features in films, television series, paintings, operas, books, and even on cigarette packs and perfumes.

For the Chinese, the Fragrant Concubine is a symbol of the conquest of the exotic western lands and of their barbaric people finally being civilized under Han rule. The Chinese believe that although she was homesick, she eventually came to love the emperor when he sent for her favorite things from Xinjiang, such as a jujube tree with golden fruit and silver leaves, and built her a mosque and a magnificent garden. By the tomb of Apakh Khoja, among the holiest pilgrimage sites in Xinjiang and also said to be Iparhan's final resting place, the Chinese government placed a sign proclaiming that Iparhan is an example of "the good wish for unity and mutual love between different nationalities since ancient times. . . . Love between this Uyghur maid and the emperor is evidence for great unity among different ethnic groups in China."[258]

Uyghur accounts of Iparhan, however, vary substantially from the Chinese, painting her as a forlorn prisoner, anxiously pacing her apartment in the Forbidden City and pining for home. Iparhan planned to kill the emperor as revenge for his conquest of her homeland and concealed daggers in her sleeves for this purpose. At the winter solstice when the emperor was away at the Temple of Heaven, the emperor's mother warned Iparhan that if she did not submit to him, she would be put to death. In the end, Iparhan chose to die, thus preserving her own honor and that of her beloved people, the Uyghurs. While this story has become a blend of mythology and history, it captures both the Chinese concept of a harmonious society stretching beyond its civilizing Han center to include its western periphery, just as the emperor did with his Fragrant Concubine, and Uyghurs' resistance against an imperial power that challenged their honor.

In the late nineteenth century Xinjiang officially became a full province of China under the authority of emerging Han military leaders. General Zuo Zong-tang, a Han of the declining Qing Dynasty, initiated a policy of forced assimilation to Han culture and language, reversing a previous policy of cultural autonomy. In the anarchy that followed the fall of the Qing Dynasty in the early twenti-eth century, the Uyghurs found themselves enjoying de facto independence as the center in Beijing crumbled, which resulted in the establishment of the East Turkestan Republic in 1944. In 1949, however, the republic was absorbed into China when People's Liberation Army troops marched into Xinjiang after the victory of Mao Zedong's communist forces in China's civil war.

The structure of Uyghur society was completely overturned under the communists. Massive tracts of land were redistributed, and the Communist Party attempted to destroy the power of the traditional village headmen. Members of the Uyghur establishment were divided into the categories of "goats" and "sheep." The leading "goats"—politically powerful Uyghurs with land, such as the Muslim nobles with hereditary status—were summarily shot. Smaller land-lords and middle-class "enemies" were given a chance for reformation. The "sheep" were either middle-class "friends" or proletarians who were tasked with creating a new communist China. The Communist Party assumed control of Islam, seizing mosque lands and training and appointing imams. Portraits of Chairman Mao were hung in mosques, and imams were instructed to give sermons about "the international solidarity of the working class."[259]

During Mao's Great Leap Forward from 1958 to 1961, Xinjiang's population was corralled into 450 communes of approximately 20,000 people each, under a nationwide central government policy of agricultural collectivization.[260] The resulting famine devastated Xinjiang; up to 42 million people died across China. It was the deadliest famine in the history of the world. In 1964 the Chinese began testing nuclear weapons at the Lop Nor test site in Xinjiang, where reportedly 210,000 Uyghurs have been killed by nuclear radiation, although Uyghur sources put the number at half a million. There have also been untold numbers of Uyghurs born with birth defects and increased rates of cancers.[261]

The Cultural Revolution carried the Great Leap Forward even further, with its official attack on the "four olds" (old ideas, customs, culture, and habits). There was a wholesale closure of mosques and madrassahs, many of which were turned into stables, barracks, or slaughterhouses. Clerics "were arrested, tortured and given menial jobs, such as cleaning sewers."[262] Uyghurs had their names "twisted in Mandarin."[263] Xinjiang remained bubbling with discontent through the 1980s, with a Uyghur student, Urkesh Doulat (whose Chinese name was Wuerkaixi), leading the Tiananmen Square protests in 1989.

In the 1990s the central government accelerated its policy of settling Han in Xinjiang to fully develop its infrastructure and extract its natural resources of oil, coal, and gas reserves, arguing that this was an effort to modernize the region. Han numbers jumped from 300,000 in 1949, at which point the Uyghur constituted 90 percent of the population, to 7.5 million in 2000, a figure that did not even include the 1 million soldiers and police, the 2.5 million working for the Xinjiang Production and Construction Corporation, or the "professional advisers," who brought the number of Han closer to 12 million.[264] By 2012 the Uyghur population had dropped to 45 percent, with the Han rising to 40 percent in the entire province and 70 percent in Xinjiang's capital, Urumqi.[265] While marriages between Han and Uyghurs were banned until 1979 and are today extremely rare, they eventually gained official state sanction, with the government providing money to mixed couples.[266]

Severe restrictions were imposed on the Uyghur language and culture. No Uyghur under the age of eighteen was permitted any religious education.[267] In any case, those working for the Communist Party, which employs 80 million people, were not permitted any religious expression at all. Uyghur children were required to attend state-controlled schools teaching in Mandarin, and no Uyghurs could send their children out of the country to study.[268] Proud of their literature going back to eleventh-century scholar and poet Mahmud Kashgari, Uyghurs faced difficulties in publishing in their own language. Turgun Almas, the author of one of the books banned, *The History of the Uighurs,* was put under house arrest in 1991.[269] In February 1996 Chinese authorities raided an evening *mashrap,* a Sufi gathering in which poetry, prayer, dancing, and singing occur, and arrested the participants. Ensuing protests led to the deaths of 120 Uyghurs and the arrest of over 2,500.[270] According to human rights groups, in 1997 government forces killed hundreds and possibly thousands of Uyghurs marching in the city of Gulja against the banning of the *mashrap* and the arrest of religious leaders.[271]

The 1990s were filled with high tension and violence as a bus bombing campaign hit both Xinjiang and Beijing. There were periods of riots followed by further crackdowns in which thousands were arrested at a time. Amnesty International reported 190 executions in Xinjiang from 1997 to 1999, primarily of

Kekenus Sidik, a Uyghur, interviewed by the author (center), and Dean Emeritus Louis Goodman at American University (American University/Annie Lyon).

Uyghurs found guilty of political and religious "crimes."[272] Imprisoned Uyghurs commonly faced the Chinese labor camp system. The communists had developed two types of labor camp: "reform through labor" camps in which inmates often worked until they died, and "re-education through labor" camps, which instead of punishing "crimes" were structured to correct "mistakes."[273] In the 1990s and early 2000s, many mullahs were sent to "re-education" camps, where "an endless process of verbal abuse, written and verbal self-denunciation, and brainwashing" eventually led prisoners "to believe that their thoughts are crimes."[274] Uyghur exiles in the early 2000s claimed that 250,000 people were in Xinjiang labor camps and prisons, three-fifths of them Uyghur.[275]

The life, fears, and aspirations of Kekenus Sidik, a young Uyghur woman, could reflect those of any young woman from the other case studies in this volume. I was introduced in 2012 to Kekenus through my daughter, Nafees, when both were students at Georgetown University, and my team and I were impressed by her confidence and composure, particularly after hearing her profoundly moving story.

Kekenus is the daughter of Rebiya Kadeer, a witness of what became known as the Gulja massacre and a well-known human rights activist who is currently president of the World Uyghur Congress. Kekenus was born in Urumqi. In our discussion, she said her mother, father, and two brothers were arrested for "political activity" and disappeared into the jail system for many years where they were subjected to torture. Her mother was locked in solitary confinement for two years. Though ten years have passed since her father was released from prison, he is still terrified whenever he sees a dog because it reminds him of his ordeal in prison.

Kekenus spoke with pride of the customs of the Uyghurs, especially their hospitality, sense of community, and identity as a Muslim Turkic people. But she is a realist. She described the steady changes in society from the time she was a child, lamenting the plight of the young who will "within a generation" have forgotten to speak Uyghur under current educational, cultural, and employment pressures. Since worthwhile employment is impossible without fluent Chinese, large numbers of Uyghurs are without work. The only jobs Uyghur girls are offered, she told us, are in faraway Chinese cities where they are hired as prostitutes. The Chinese policy, she added, is "to assimilate and exterminate" the Uyghur, whom they see as "inferior," "second-class," "thieves," and "dirty." She described the situation as "very, very bad." Everyone secretly wants independence but is "too scared" to say it—"scared to go out, scared to be picked up, and being killed." Tragically, Kekenus lamented, the Uyghur have no great leader like the Dalai Lama to speak for them on the world stage. To make matters worse, she said, the world is so anxious to please China that it avoids discussing the issue of human rights. Unlike President George W. Bush, neither President Barack Obama nor Secretary of State Hillary Clinton had met her mother to talk about the human rights of the Uyghurs.

Emma, another Muslim woman from China who was interviewed for this study in 2012, had nothing in common with Kekunus; the former is the classic insider, and the latter, in the opposite direction, the ultimate outsider as far as China is concerned. Emma was a deputy director in the Center for Religious Research of the Ministry of Religious Affairs of the Chinese government in Beijing, a proud representative of a world power. Unlike Kekunus, Emma had several names reflecting her different identities. She called herself Emma— a nice English name that could have come out of Jane Austen and was quite appropriate in the English setting in Cambridge where she was conducting official research. I met her when she came to attend my public lecture delivered for the Woolf Institute, one of the premier organizations promoting interfaith dialogue. Apparently she had come with the intention of offering to have my book *Journey into Islam* translated into Chinese. She said she had been reading my works and "loved" them. It soon transpired that Emma was in fact a Hui Muslim—an ethnic group that lives largely in northwest China and has an autonomous region named after it. Her Muslim name was Hajilai, and she had recently performed the Hajj in Saudi Arabia. She also had a Chinese name, Jianping Jia. Emma was joining three great civilizations—Western, Islamic, and Chinese—in her identity. This could be a tricky business or it could be a rewarding and exhilarating one. Emma seemed to see no conflict between them; her Chinese identity took primacy over her Muslim one, her loyalty to the center

Emma (Jianping Jia), the author, and Harrison Akins in idyllic Cambridge by the River Cam (author's collection).

over her identification with the periphery. Unlike Kekunus, she appeared at peace with herself.

Apart from the majority Han, there were fifty-five minorities in China, Emma told us, ten of which were Muslim. Centrifugal tendencies were severely discouraged, and there was no negotiation on the question of the integrity of China. Emma referred to the majority Han with an awe that derived from the knowledge that it was the supreme, not-to-be challenged ethnicity of China. Once that fact was accepted, the minority groups were able to coexist in ease and even harmony.

The Hui Muslims live primarily in the Ningxia Hui Autonomous Region in northwestern China but are also found spread throughout the nation. The Hui ethnic group, which numbers over 9 million of the 23 million Muslims in China, is the largest Muslim group according to official figures. They speak Mandarin Chinese and have fully assimilated into the majority Han culture after centuries of intermarriage and interaction with the Han. Hui Muslims are today free to practice Islam and have been granted a degree of political freedom. The Ningxia region has over 400 mosques, religious schools that have trained nearly 7,000 imams, and a thriving *halal* food industry that exports goods to Central Asia and other Muslim regions. Beijing clearly does not see the assimilated Hui Muslims as any kind of threat to the authority of the state.

This was confirmed by Emma, who claimed, "The Chinese government holds firmly the policy of ethnic equality and religious freedom." She described the varying and distinctive architecture of mosques throughout China with some pride; there were seventy mosques in Beijing alone. She continued on the theme of privileges given to the minorities:

> The minorities of China are equal in various aspects with the majority. Besides that, the Chinese government provides some special priority to the minorities. For example, in some areas, minority couples can have two or even more children while the others only one. And the minority students can enjoy extra scores for the College Entrance Examination, which is a big issue in China, and extremely important to young people and their families. Furthermore, the Chinese government had and has been doing a great deal for the minorities' economic development.

Emma believed that,

> Chinese Muslim minorities have the same rights and obligations as the other Chinese, they enjoy the same priority as the other minorities, and they have religious freedom. They can be Chinese and be Muslims as well. The Chinese Muslims have a good tradition; that is, they love both their country and their faith. In November 2010 and in May 2012, my colleagues and I did fieldwork in northwest of China. We visited about 50 mosques, Sufi shrines altogether, and we talked with local Imams, committee members of mosques and Muslims there. They all spoke highly of the Chinese policy towards them and they all believed that, since China's reforms and opening-up, they have been in a golden age.

She felt the Uyghur were different from the Hui. They were more beautiful and had lighter skin, she said with a shy smile. They were Turkic, or "foreigners." They had their own ancient culture with their own script and language, of which they were very proud. Today, unfortunately, too many of them are seen as urchins and "thieves" in the cities. She believed the Uyghur were "relatively backward in economic and educational condition, which will be a problem in the long run." However, "the Chinese government has been aware of this and is taking efforts to make it up." A more serious problem, as Emma saw it, was that the Uyghur—only some of them, she quickly added—talked of independence. That, she said, shaking her head, was "not good."

Emma was aware that "Chinese Muslim minorities are of great help to China's foreign policy with Muslim nations." She had examples of Muslim scholars being part of Chinese delegations visiting the Muslim world and making a big impression. She was particularly proud of Imam Da Pusheng who accompanied "our beloved" ex-premier Zhou En-Lai when he attended the Asian-African

Conference in 1955. She told us of "Imam Da's fluent Arabic, beautiful Quran reciting and respectable manner that won the hearts of many Muslim leaders for China."

When I told Emma about my meeting with Lebin Zhang, the vice minister in Emma's ministry, she could barely contain her joy. Zhang had led a high-powered delegation to the United States in July 2011 consisting of twenty-three senior government officials dealing with religious affairs. The trip was organized by the Berkley Center at Georgetown University, and I had been invited to give a lecture to them on Islam in America. The deputy director of Xinjiang Province Ethnic and Religious Affairs Committee was a member of the delegation and asked in the question-and-answer session what should government policy be in cases where local custom clashes with central state law, a matter that clearly weighed heavily on his mind. I responded that a good administrator needs to act as a just and compassionate mediator between the two positions and accommodate local custom, thus underlining the importance of officials on the periphery in the mold of the political agent with which I was familiar and a subject that has formed part of the discussion in this study. I also referred to the tradition of Confucius and his ideas of administration including that of the scholar-administrator whose success in the field ensured that there was prosperity and peace in the district, and therefore calm and stability at the center.

Once the Chinese discovered my Pakistani background, they were extremely friendly and gave me presents, expressing how much they enjoyed my lecture. We continued talking over lunch, and Vice Minister Zhang invited me and my team to visit China, and the official from Xinjiang specifically invited us to his province, promising to receive us at the border between Pakistan and China. Spending part of a full day with the Chinese, my impression was that this was not some third-world delegation, wide-eyed and grateful to be allowed a brief glimpse of the American paradise and easily seduced by a mere trip to the United States. They were the representatives of a world power with their own specific ideas of how to do things. Hierarchy, control, authority, and critical awareness of their surroundings were apparent in the Chinese delegation.

As we had two different Muslim perspectives from the periphery, it was appropriate that we place them in the context of a scholar's analysis from the point of view of the Chinese center. I therefore interviewed the eminent professor, my friend and colleague, Quansheng Zhao, a Han Chinese and a noted authority on China currently teaching at American University in Washington, D.C. In underlining the vital importance of the center to Chinese politics and culture, Zhao reflected the views of the Han population, today constituting more than 90 percent of China's 1.3 billion people. By contrast, the Uyghur are a tiny minority—official figures put their number at about 8 million, although Uyghur estimates are much higher. For two thousand years, the Han have held power

Lebin Zhang, the vice minister of religious affairs of the People's Republic of China, presents the author with a gift after the author's lecture to a Chinese delegation at Georgetown University (author's collection).

in this land. There was, according to Zhao, "no chance of the Uyghur getting independence." The matter is under "firm central control."

Zhao explained the philosophy underlying Chinese history and civilization: the closer to the center, the more civilized the people; the further from the center, the less civilized. Because the Uyghur are at the outer rim of China, they are thought to be barely civilized. They look "Western," have colored hair and "big noses," and have their own language. Of course, Zhao explained, people living beyond the boundaries of China, like the British or the Americans, are normatively considered irredeemably uncivilized. Zhao admitted the destruction of mosques and temples during the Cultural Revolution of the 1960s, when "everyone suffered." These days things are much better, more relaxed. The Uyghur are now considered useful because through them relations with neighboring countries like Afghanistan and Pakistan and those in Central Asia are improved. Zhao also pointed to the "benefits" the Uyghur are now enjoying in the wake of China's economic success. As long as there was no demand for independence, the Uyghur would be part of the "Chinese family."

To Beijing, its relationship with the Uyghurs, the Tibetans, or Mongolians is not about the moral, religious, or human rights of communities on the periphery;

it is about the compulsions of the center. Any compromise on the territorial authority of China is seen as a direct threat to the integrity of the nation. The definition of Chinese nationalism, however, has an ethnic underpinning: to be Chinese means to be Han. The state and Han identity intertwined and overlapped to a point where they appeared to be one and the same thing.

ETHIOPIA AND THE OROMO PEOPLE. Like the Han Chinese, the Amhara of Ethiopia inherited an ancient civilization, the Christian Aksum Empire, with roots going back 2,000 years. The Ethiopian state was personified in the figure of the emperor, who carried the legacy of Aksum and Ethiopian Christianity. The former emperor Haile Selassie, meaning Power of the Trinity, would personify this ideal while leading Ethiopia into modernity.

To better understand the Ethiopian center and its relationship with the Muslim periphery, which accounts for about 40 percent of the population, I spoke with His Imperial Highness Ermias Sahle Selassie, the grandson of Haile Selassie. In an interview in Washington, D.C., in February 2012, he said that the Ethiopian government has officially sanctioned his royal title and that he is free to return when he wants to. A sophisticated man, dapper in his dress with the influences of his British education evident in the intonations of his speech, Ermias displayed a humanist approach to the problems of his country. He explained that the once "harmonious relations" between Christian Ethiopians and the Muslim tribes are now "breaking down," noting that his grandfather had relied on "building affinity and using minimum force" in dealing with the troubled eastern Ogaden Province and its majority Somali population. He reminisced about the time when Ethiopia's Somali territory displayed its own flag and the local population spoke its own language and enjoyed its own culture. Referring to Ethiopia's earliest encounters with Islam in the seventh century, he said, "Ethiopians revered Islam. Muslims were people who believed in one deity. Islam and Muslims were always protected and treated as honored guests." Even subsequent raids by Muslim tribes into Ethiopia did not spoil this relationship, although it created fear in the hearts of the Ethiopians.

In certain cases, he explained, the existing Muslim sultanates "had to be destroyed," as in the example of the Harar Sultanate, where Ermias's father was governor. Other sultanates, such as the one under the Afars and the Jimma of the Oromo, were allowed to continue and their sultans given court titles and brought into a larger Ethiopian aristocracy. There was give and take, push and pull between the center and the periphery. Contemplating the chaos of ethnic and religious conflict in his homeland, he believed the solution was to view each side through its own culture and with respect, and to involve tribal elders to make peace. Today the appearance of "Wahhabi elements" has made Ethiopians "defensive." Nonetheless, he believed that Ethiopia must "start the healing process."

Of course, the modern Ethiopian state did not exist before the nineteenth century, which is when the Amhara, with access to large quantities of modern weapons and European advisers, began to conquer other ethnic groups and consolidate them under one center. Many of these groups were segmentary lineage tribes, including the Somalis of the Ogaden region and the Afars in the Awash Valley in the northeast. The largest and most important of these groups, however, was the Oromo. A majority Muslim people concentrated in the south with a current population of 30 million, the Oromo are among the largest ethnic groups in Africa. Their name derives from Orma, their eponymous ancestor. The Amhara claimed that in conquering the Oromo, they were restoring a mythological "greater Ethiopia" that had existed before the invasion of the Oromo's Islamic armies.[276]

The Oromo, fighting with spears and arrows, were no match for the Amhara and emperors like Menelik II, who finally conquered them through a policy of total devastation. Between 1868 and 1900, around 5 million Oromo were killed, half of the total population.[277] The Arsi Oromo, who claim descent from a common ancestor called Arse, live in the mountainous Bale region and offered Menelik the fiercest resistance. Their Bale region contains the site of the shrine of the thirteenth-century Sufi sheikh Hussein, considered one of the most important in the Horn of Africa. Following the defeat of the Arsi in 1886, Menelik's general ordered the right hands of all strong men severed and tied to their necks, and the breasts of the women sliced and borne in a similar fashion.[278] Other tribes, including the Somalis of the Ogaden, were subjected to the same brutal policies. One battle alone, south of Jijiga in 1899, claimed the lives of some 9,000 Somalis.[279]

The Amhara government sent hundreds of thousands of settlers, known as *naftanya* (a gun carrier), into fortified towns in Oromo areas. Amhara landlords appropriated vast tracts of land and were assigned Oromo for use as forced labor. At times, a single Ethiopian Orthodox church was given as much as 5,000 hectares of the community's best land.[280] Oromo place names were changed to Amharic, the Oromo language was banned, and all expressions of Oromo tradition and identity were prohibited. The Oromo were called the derogatory name *Galla,* or lowly "outsiders." Their status in Amhara culture as savages or worse is reflected in Amhara phrases such as *Gallana sagara eyadar yegamal* (Galla and human feces stink more every passing day) and *Saw naw Galla?* (Is it human or Galla?)[281]

The ascendancy in 1930 of Emperor Haile Selassie, who was himself part Oromo, marked a new phase of centralization, modernization, and "Amharization," though it was interrupted by an Italian invasion that killed 760,000 people in the region and the Second World War. Multinational corporations were given large Oromo landholdings, which forced out local tribes and further decimated their populations. With the appropriation of Oromo grazing land by the Dutch sugar company HVA, for example, the Oromo Karrayyu clan numbers dropped from more than 200,000 to less than 10,000.[282] Such policies led to constant rebellions against the central government: five alone occurred in the Oromo Hararghe Province between 1900 and 1908, and among the Raya Oromo in 1928, 1935–36, 1943, and 1948.[283]

The largest antigovernment rebellion took place in the 1960s, launched by tribes of the Bale region. One of its leaders explained that the Oromo were fighting because their history "has been of deprivation and misery, a story of endless tragedy. In our own country we have lived as aliens and slaves, deprived of our lands and discriminated against on the grounds of our tribal and religious identities."[284] As the Bale threat increased—the insurgents drove out large numbers of Amhara settlers and assassinated two district governors—the area was put under martial law. By the time the rebellion was suppressed in the early 1970s, close to half a million Oromo had been killed, 200,000 had been wounded or mutilated, and about 5 million animals eliminated.[285] Bale rebels, however, would play a key role in forming the Oromo Liberation Front (OLF) in 1973, which remains among the most prominent Oromo nationalist movements.

The overthrow of Haile Selassie and ascension of the military Marxists under Mengistu Haile Mariam, known as the Derg, in 1974 only heightened the tension between the central government and the Oromo. In 1978 about 80,000 Oromo were reported killed in Hararghe Province, and the government began to implement a plan that had originated with Haile Selassie's government to resettle mass numbers of northerners in the Oromo areas.[286] By the mid-1980s the program was in full swing, resulting in a devastating famine that killed more than a million people and shocked a world largely unaware of its root causes. From 1984 to 1985 about half a million people were forcibly moved into settlements in Oromo areas, most of them located along Oromo rebel access routes, with as many as 100,000 settlers killed in the process.[287] The Oromo were forced to assist the new arrivals with labor, food, tools, and furniture.[288] Under a "villagization" effort during the same period, about 8 million Oromo were relocated to what were effectively military-run concentration camps.[289] An Oromo female refugee told the journalist Robert Kaplan how the program worked:

> When the Amhara soldiers first came to our village . . . they ordered every wife in the village to sleep with another husband, not her own . . . the soldiers made intercourse compulsory. Then [they] went into every *gambisa* [mud hut] to watch. They said, "Do it, do it." Those who did not were beaten with fists. The prettiest girls were taken by the soldiers. . . . The soldiers said no one could read the Koran, because it is Arab politics. The mosque was turned into an office for the soldiers. Seventeen sheikhs in the area were shot. . . . Then our maize was collected by the soldiers and taken for storage. We never saw it again. . . . We were marched three hours by

foot eastward where we were made to build new *gambisata* in a straight line. The new town was called Gamaju [Oromo for gladness]. . . . The men were taken every day to work in a place called Unity farm. We were hungry and complained to the soldiers. They said, "Eat your flesh."[290]

After the fall of Mengistu's government in 1991, following the demise of the Soviet Union and relentless assaults by the OLF and other ethnic rebel groups, the Oromo were once again able to practice their culture, with more material published in the Oromo language in 1993 and 1994 than from 1880 to 1992.[291] There was hope the nation was entering a new era of inclusion and democracy.

However, the new rulers of Ethiopia, Christian Tigrays who were also ethnic successors to Aksum and spoke a related language, continued the Amhara policy of marginalizing and persecuting the Oromo. From 1992 to 1994 as many as 50,000 Oromo suspected of association with the OLF were imprisoned in four concentration camps, and 3,000 died.[292] Between 1992 and 2001 an estimated 50,000 Oromo were killed and 16,000 "disappeared," a euphemism for secret killing.[293] The Oromo were conscripted to fight in the 1998–2000 war with Eritrea, which killed more than 100,000 Ethiopian soldiers, the majority of them Oromo.[294]

THE SOMALI OF KENYA. The Somali peoples were forcibly divided into four independent modern states, one being Kenya, where they were subjected to the brutal policies of a Christian center. In 1963 an insurgency erupted in Kenya's Somali-majority Northern Frontier District (NFD), now known as the North Eastern Province, when its Somali tribes were stopped from joining the newly independent Somalia. Tribesmen launched raids on government posts and assassinated officials, including one of the first Kenyans to achieve the post of district commissioner.

By 1967, large numbers of the Somali population in Kenya were forcibly moved into fourteen "protected villages" guarded by Kenyan troops, where they were required to give up their nomadic lifestyle and witnessed the destruction of their herds. The same policy was implemented for the nomadic Borana Oromo of Kenya, who were also forced into large camps.[295] The long-term goal of these "villages" was to "rehabilitate" the Somali nomads and transform them into settled citizens of the state. Instead they served to populate Kenyan towns and cities with a destitute Somali underclass. The Kenyan government replaced traditional tribal chiefs with those whom it nominated. Somali leaders were put in prison and remained incarcerated over the next decade. Somalis were commonly called *shifta,* or bandits, a highly derogatory term, and the 1960s conflict, which claimed the lives of 10,000 Somalis, came to be known as the Shifta War. Even after the war, Kenya's security forces could be brutal in dealing with Somalis, as attested by a series of massacres in the early 1980s. In November 1980 in the

Garissa district, Kenyan government forces, in pursuit of a Somali who had killed four Kenyan civil servants while seeking revenge for his torture and castration by security forces, set fire to homes, executed residents, raped women, and moved the entire local population to a primary school playground for three days with no food and water, an operation in which 3,000 Somalis died.[296]

In a February 1984 attempt to stop "banditry" among the Degodia subclan of the Hawiye clan, as well as warfare between clans, the Kenyan army surrounded nomad settlements and ordered the residents to leave their homes, seizing Degodia Hawiye whom they blamed for the unrest. Thousands of tribesmen were transported to a military airfield, told to strip naked, and then forced to lie on the tarmac in the heat of the blazing sun. Clan elders were separated, their clothes piled on top of them and set alight, burning to death as their clansmen watched. While this was happening, Kenyan soldiers descended upon their homes, gang-raping women and looting and burning their property.

For five days, the security forces kept the men lying on the airstrip, sometimes lighting them on fire with petrol. Those who refused to follow orders, including imams, were shot. Denied water, the men drank urine, with many dying in the merciless temperatures soaring above 100 degrees Fahrenheit. Soldiers went through the lines of men, killing them with "bayonets, knives, sticks, and their boots."[297] The bodies were dumped in the bush to be eaten by hyenas. In the end, an estimated 5,000 Somalis lay dead.

One woman who as a primary school student witnessed this "security operation" described the sight: "First, I see images of grown men in Tarbaj in broad daylight, stripped of all dignity, of all their clothing, in front of women and children, being whipped and herded like animals to the centre of the town. The naked men beg for mercy as the *nyahunyos* [whips] cut into their flesh in the blistering sun."[298] The episode, which came to be known as the Wagalla massacre, was described as "the worst episode of human rights violations in Kenyan history" by the United Nations.[299] Such repeated incidents have kept the Somali population on edge, and there is constant tension between the center and the periphery.

THE CAUCASUS REGION OF RUSSIA. A similar collapse between center and periphery marked by violence is reflected in the Caucasus, which, like Xinjiang in China, fell under the juggernaut of the modern communist state with the establishment of the Soviet Union. Thousands of Muslim scholars were detained, sent to gulags, exiled, or simply shot. In an effort to "Sovietize" the region's tribes, the government closed or destroyed most Islamic institutions—mosques, schools, libraries, and Islamic foundations—and banned the local languages. Sufi locations of worship and pilgrimage were destroyed and the tombs of holy sheikhs ploughed over. Worshipping at such holy places was declared illegal. As a consequence of Stalin's agricultural collectivization program in the late 1920s and early 1930s, a famine killed 1 million people in the North Caucasus from

1932 to 1933. These policies, which resulted in violence and disease along with the famine, also felled more than 1.5 million Kazakhs in Kazakhstan, one-third of the region's entire population, along with 80 percent of their herds, effectively destroying what was left of their tribal structure.[300]

The Chechens, in particular, faced wholesale deportation in the 1940s. Stalin's chief of Soviet Secret Police, Lavrenty Beria reported clinically: "The eviction of the Chechens and the Ingush is proceeding normally: 342,647 people were loaded onto special trains on February 25, and by [February 29] the number had risen to 478,479, of whom 91,250 were Ingush and 387,229 Chechens."[301] The Chechens were packed in cattle cars with no food or water and deposited in the frozen steppes of Kazakhstan and other Central Asian republics in the middle of winter. Up to half of the population deported died either in the process or within a few months after deportations began in 1944.[302]

The collapse of the Soviet Union in 1991 brought much celebration among the tribes of the Caucasus. Boris Yeltsin told the periphery "to take as much sovereignty as they could swallow."[303] Almost all of the Caucasus republics opted for autonomy. In Dagestan, the tribes developed an innovative power-sharing agreement, balancing the different ethnic groups to ensure that none gained dominance. For Chechnya, however, autonomy was not sufficient. When it declared independence in November 1991, Russia responded with a military invasion that culminated in the First Chechen War in December 1994. At the height of the violence, the Russian army shelled Grozny at a rate of 4,000 detonations an hour.[304] The war resulted in the deaths of 46,500 people, 35,000 of whom were civilians.[305]

A Russian soldier who served in the war described the actions of a Russian military unit upon entering a Chechen village:

> Around the main square were large crosses upon which Russian soldiers had been crucified. They'd been nailed up by their hands and each had a few bullet holes in his chest. They had all been castrated. The commander ordered them to do a sweep through the village. All the men who could be found were herded into the square. They were thrown down in piles and then our soldiers started to hack them up. One guy pinned a Chechen to the ground with his foot while another pulled off his pants and with two or three hefty slashes severed his scrotum. The serrated blade of the knife snagged the skin and pulled the blood vessels from his body. In half a day the whole village was castrated, then the battalion moved out.[306]

A peace treaty was eventually signed in August of 1996, officially ending the war. The Russians, experiencing heavy losses, withdrew, granting de facto independence to Chechnya while it remained de jure within the Russian Federation. The Second Chechen War began in 1999 with another Russian invasion that was similarly devastating for the civilian population: the two Chechen wars resulted in

Mass grave in Chechnya in 2000 (photo by Natalia Medvedeva).

the deaths of 10 percent of the entire Chechen population of 1 million people. As of April 2008, there were fifty-seven known mass graves in Chechnya.[307]

Unlike Yeltsin, who spoke of crushing an independence movement, the new Russian leader, Vladimir Putin, justified war with Chechnya through the 1998 Struggle against Terrorism Law, which permitted the use of the army for counterterrorist operations. In September 1999 during a televised interview, Putin stated his intent to destroy Chechnya as a "terrorist state" and "an outpost of international terrorism." As for the Chechens, his policy was "to waste them in the shithouse."[308] In 2000 the Russians instituted direct rule in Chechnya and in 2004 in the rest of the North Caucasus republics, removing entirely the autonomy that Yeltsin had allowed. Putin's move triggered widespread unrest and violence in the region as discussed in chapter 3.

THE NEGEV BEDOUIN OF ISRAEL AND THE PALESTINIANS. In the foregoing cases, the central governments enacted mass settlement or collectivization policies, including the use of internment camps, to "civilize" the tribes in accordance with the center's conception of a modern state. Turkey adopted a similar practice under its Settlement Law, which abolished the concept of the tribe and relocated mass numbers of Kurds into Turkish "villages." Upon becoming a state in 1948, Israel as well enacted a settlement policy that focused on its nomadic Bedouin in the southern Negev Desert. David Ben-Gurion, Israel's first prime minister, wrote of the government's objective: "Negev land is reserved for Jewish citizens whenever and wherever they want. We must expel the Arabs and take their place."[309] Accordingly, 85 percent of the Bedouin population was expelled from the Negev, with only nineteen of the original ninety-five tribes remaining. Many were pushed into Gaza, the West Bank, or across the international borders into Sinai or Jordan.[310]

The entire Southern District incorporating the Negev was placed under military administration, which claimed ownership of all Negev land for the Israeli state. The remaining Bedouin tribes were relocated to settlements within the Siyag (meaning "fence"), a reservation-like area in the northern Negev of 1,000 square kilometers, about one-tenth of the region.[311] They were relocated for the ultimate purpose of settling and establishing them as an urban population. Moshe Dayan, the southern military commander during this period, stated:

> We should transform the Bedouins into an urban proletariat. . . . This will be a radical move which means that the Bedouin would not live on his land with his herds, but would become an urban person who comes home in the afternoon and puts his slippers on. His children would be accustomed to a father who wears trousers, does not carry a Shabaria [traditional Bedouin knife] and does not search for vermin in public. This would be a revolution, but it may be fixed within two generations. Without coercion but with government direction, this phenomenon of the Bedouins will disappear.[312]

While they were eventually granted Israeli citizenship and even served in the Israeli military, the Bedouin, residing in impoverished villages, continued to complain of marginalization and the lack of government services. Many chose to remain on their traditional lands in illegal settlements that were constantly destroyed by the Israeli government. One such village, al-Araqib, in the Negev Desert was demolished in 2012 for the thirty-ninth time, the Bedouin living there rebuilding it each time.[313] As in so many of the other cases discussed in this volume, "settlement" has meant poverty, neglect, and the loss of identity.

The Bedouin in Gaza and the West Bank faced similar problems as their cousins in the Negev, including marginalization, the loss of herds and livelihood, lack of economic opportunities amid a life of squalor, forced population relocation and destruction of "illegal" villages, and sharp restrictions of movement. In late 2011, for example, controversy erupted over the Israeli government's planned expansion of a Jewish settlement that involved relocating about 2,300 members of the Bedouin Jahalin tribe, children making up two-thirds of the total, in the West Bank to a site adjacent to a landfill on the edge of Jerusalem.[314]

The Jahalin had been expelled from their ancestral lands in the Negev in 1948 and forced to relocate in the West Bank. Now, they faced further displacement. Eid Khamis, the head of a Jahalin community in the West Bank, complained that "every time we go near [the settlements], our sheep are stolen or killed, and our children are beaten by settlers." He was fatalistic about the future after being informed that their homes would be destroyed as a result of this expansion, "I cannot even count how many times the Israeli authorities have demolished our homes and structures." He expressed his fears for his community's survival, "We are refugees and my fear is that [the Israeli authorities] will make us refugees once again. We already know what's coming, but we don't know when. It's like a man on death row. He knows he will die but he doesn't know when his execution will happen."[315]

Gaza and the West Bank, parts of which passed to Palestinian administration following the 1993 Oslo Peace Accords, have, in addition to the Bedouin, a plethora of tribal and clan groups of various sizes and in varying states of sedentarization and urbanization. All governments that have ruled the area, including the Ottomans, British, Jordanians, Egyptians, and the Israelis after 1967, administered it through their contacts with clans and their leaders, known as *mukhtars*, who lived according to urf or tribal law.

The 1987 Palestinian Intifada against Israeli rule set younger clan members, many of whom had migrated out of their areas in search of work and became associated with Palestinian nationalist movements, against the *mukhtars*. Numerous clan leaders were marked for assassination as Israeli collaborators and were among the more than 1,000 Palestinians killed by other Palestinians during the uprising, which was about the same number of Palestinians killed in clashes with Israeli soldiers. With the coming of Palestinian rule and its efforts to deal with violence and clan rivalries, instability resurfaced in Gaza and more tribal parts of the West Bank like Hebron. Problems were exacerbated by the proclivity of officials to recruit members of their own clan to the government office or department they led; consequently, different agencies soon became associated with different clans.[316]

When Palestinian police killed a teenage member of the Jaabari clan in Hebron in 2006, the clan openly challenged the Palestinian government, storming police headquarters, kidnapping thirty-four officers, and torching fourteen jeeps after the police refused to turn over the offending officer to the tribe.[317] Farid Khader el-Jaabari, the clan's powerful head sheikh and the nephew of the former mayor of Hebron who took office in 1948, was a vocal advocate of coexistence with Jews on the grounds that Jews had lived with the tribes in the area from time immemorial and belonged to a kin religion. He emerged as one of the most vocal Palestinian opponents of the Palestinian Authority. "The governments of Israel," he argued, "made a mistake in that instead of talking with the sheikhs, they talked with the leaders from Tunis. . . . Israel did not contact the real leadership, which knows the street and the Palestinian population. All the political organizations—Hamas, Fatah and the Popular Front—are no more than 5 percent of the Palestinian people."[318]

In Gaza, which has less arable land, the clans were generally stronger and more prominent than in the West Bank. Following the election of Hamas in the vacuum created when Israel withdrew from the territory in 2005, battles broke out between the clans and the government as Hamas moved to disarm the clans and institute sharia over urf. Prominent Hamas religious leaders like Marwan Abu Ras attacked the tribal code, declaring, "Revenge is *haram* [sinful]. No one has the right to take the law into his own hands."[319] Araf Shaher, a clan leader in the south and known for settling disputes between smugglers on the border between Sinai and Gaza, echoed the feelings of many elders: "I have nothing to do with the Hamas police and their version of the law. My rulings are based more on my own traditions, and Gaza's traditions, than they are on Islam. There are many times when they clash directly with Islamic principles, especially when I am ruling on a murder. But I won't change."[320]

The difficulties Hamas encountered in centralizing its authority can be seen in its bitter conflict with clans such as the Dughmush. In December 2006 two members of the Dughmush clan were shot dead at a checkpoint by the Dira, a Hamas-affiliated clan, triggering a blood feud involving numerous tit-for-tat killings. The Dughmush opened fire on the house of Mahmoud Zahhar, the cofounder of Hamas, killing three of his Dira bodyguards, which provoked the Dira further. Both clans refused to erect mourning tents, indicating the necessity for revenge as Dughmush elders demanded that Hamas turn over its members to be tried according to urf. "We don't care if it brings down the government," declared a Dughmush fighter. "We just want honour for our boys."[321] A prominent Dughmush group even dubbed itself the Army of Islam, challenging Hamas's Islamic credentials. In March 2007 the blood feud came to a head when the Army of Islam kidnapped BBC journalist Alan Johnston, after which Hamas attacked the Dughmush quarter in Gaza City. The clan finally agreed to release Johnston after 114 days in captivity. Around the same time, the Army of Islam announced it had transferred into Hamas custody another high-profile prisoner it had captured the year before, Israeli soldier Gilad Shalit.

THE ALBANIANS OF KOSOVO AND MACEDONIA. Although situated in Europe, the final case of this model reflects the same tensions between non-Muslim center and Muslim tribal periphery as in Asia and Africa. Though similar, the relationship between the Balkan states and their Albanian populations can only be understood in the context of their own history and culture.

The Albanian segmentary lineage communities of this region under the Ottoman Empire were united until the modern age, at which point the newly devised borders of four nations cut through them. Over the past century, the Albanian tribes that found themselves on the periphery of a non-Muslim state dominated by Serbs were the targets of sustained campaigns of violence and assimilation. Their conflict has centered on Kosovo, the heartland of the medieval Serbian kingdom that was also inhabited by Albanian tribes, known as Kosovar Albanians. In events that have become shrouded in myth, the Serbs lost the region to invading Ottoman Turks in the late fourteenth century, after which most of the Albanians converted to Islam while the Serbs, granted religious autonomy by the Ottomans, preserved their Orthodox church.

In 1912 the Serbs, along with neighboring ethnic groups, succeeded in driving the Ottomans out of Kosovo and following World War I annexed it to a new nation uniting southern Slavs, or Yugoslavs, under a Serbian king. In the process, large-scale massacres were committed against Albanians who refused to submit to a Serbian king, and some 25,000 of them were killed between 1912 and 1913.[322] The central government denied the ethnicity of the Albanians, often calling them "lost Serbs" while simultaneously classifying them as subhuman creatures. In 1913, for example, former Serbian prime minister Vladan Djordjevic asserted that Albanians had monkey-like tails as recently as the previous century.[323] The Albanian language was banned in schools and in publications and Albanian names were "Serbicized." The government expelled half of the Albanian population of Kosovo and settled around 70,000 Serbs in the area.[324] The tribes rose in rebellion but were crushed by the government's modern weaponry. More than 6,000 Albanians were killed in January and February 1919 alone.[325]

During the Axis occupation during World War II, Albanian tribes became famous for saving Jews, to whom they pledged their *besa*, or word of honor according to their code, to protect all those in need. Yet even Albanians who resisted the Nazis along with the Serbs found themselves targets of Serbian forces. In Bar, Montenegro, in 1945, for example, as many as 4,300 Kosovar Albanians, who had been conscripted to fight the retreating Germans, were reportedly executed by Serbs. Yugoslav communists, coming to power shortly after the end of the Second World War, launched a large-scale military campaign to consolidate their rule in Kosovo. The center of the tribal resistance was the inaccessible Drenica Mountain region—an area that saw many rebellions in the Ottoman period—where around 2,000 tribesmen resisted a Yugoslav army of 30,000. In six months of fighting, an estimated 48,000 Albanians were killed in total.[326]

The new communist government of Yugoslavia run by Josip Broz Tito, who was not a Serb, gave some autonomy to the provinces, although Kosovar Albanians still complained of a Serb-run security apparatus. In 1974 Tito introduced majority rule in Yugoslavia's six republics and two provinces, which left Kosovo largely in control of its own affairs and included a local assembly, police force, and Albanian-language schools, among them a prominent university.

In March 1981, however, the year following Tito's death, student protests in Kosovo, which had the highest unemployment rate of any area of Yugoslavia, were met by a security crackdown resulting in the deaths of 1,000 people.[327] Over the next eight years, 584,373 Albanians, around half of the adult population, were "arrested, interrogated, interned, or reprimanded."[328]

As Yugoslavia collapsed in the late 1980s, the communist leader Slobodan Milosevic emerged to lead the Republic of Serbia. His vision was to unite the Serb regions into a new Yugoslavia under strong central authority. In 1989 Kosovo's autonomy was removed, and 130,000 Albanian employees, including teachers, police, and doctors, were fired and replaced with Serbs appointed by Belgrade. The use of the Albanian language in education was banned, Albanian place names were changed to Serbian, and tens of thousands of Serb settlers were brought to settle in the region. In response, the Albanians, under Ibrahim Rugova, who advocated nonviolent and peaceful resistance, boycotted Serb-run institutions, led labor strikes, and formed an unofficial parallel shadow government. Tribesmen gave their homes freely to be used as underground schools, pledging their *besa* that instruction would continue until Kosovo was free. Every member of the local community contributed to the schools.[329]

The conflict erupted into widespread violence in February 1998 when Serb antiterrorist units attacked the Jashari clan in the volatile Drenica region. Their target was Adem Jashari, a leader in the Kosovo Liberation Army (KLA), a murky insurgent group that had been attacking Serb targets for a number of years. Security forces shelled a clan village, killing more than eighty people. All males detained by the security forces were executed, many in view of their spouses and children. The attack electrified the tribes as elders mobilized clan fighting units across Kosovo, which often went by the name KLA whether or not they were associated with the organization.

The central government cast such actions as "counterinsurgency" operations, and the Albanians were almost exclusively referred to as "terrorists" by Serb media.[330] In its public statements, the government warned the West that Muslims in both Albania and Bosnia were attempting to set up an Islamic state in the heart of Europe. When U.S. deputy secretary of state Lawrence Eagleburger, for example, challenged Milosevic on Kosovo, Milosevic insisted the Serbs must protect themselves against "Islamic fundamentalism."[331] For the central government, the solution was clear. "We know how to deal with the problem of these Albanians," Milosevic told the American General Wesley Clark, "we've done this before. . . . In the Drenica region in central Kosovo in 1946. . . . We killed them. We killed them all. It took several years, but eventually we killed them all. And we had no problem."[332]

Milosevic was true to his word. In the midst of its war against the "KLA" insurgents, the central government implemented a plan to "cleanse" Kosovo of all Albanians. The Albanians were stripped of any proof of their identities, with the government seizing ID cards, birth certificates, passports, and license plates.

Nearly a million Albanians were loaded on trains or cast out of the country on forced marches. Simultaneously the government launched a campaign of terror in which entire villages were massacred, women raped, children set on fire, and men hacked to pieces with their body parts left in the streets, while others were conscripted to dig mass graves.[333] In all, 10,000 to 15,000 Albanians were killed, and 80 percent of the population was displaced.[334]

International outrage over Serb actions brought tens of thousands of people out in protests across the United States and Europe in March 1998. The United States under President Bill Clinton led NATO in a military intervention. The 1999 NATO air war destroyed the Serbian government's capabilities to attack Albanians, halting Milosevic in his tracks. A NATO force of 50,000 entered Kosovo to keep the peace, and the United Nations took over its administration. Milosevic was turned over to the United Nations to be tried for war crimes. In 2008 Kosovo declared independence from Serbia. The following year, Bill Clinton attended the unveiling of a statue of himself in Pristina, Kosovo's capital.

At the same time that NATO was intervening in Serbia, a crisis was raging across the border in Macedonia, another former Yugoslav republic with a large number of Albanians and, like Serbia, dominated by a Christian Orthodox Slavic people, the Macedonians. Nearly a quarter of the population of Macedonia is Albanian (Albanians claim it could be as high as 40 percent) and have clan connections with fellow Albanians in Kosovo. The Slav-dominated government had, from 1980 onward, moved to assimilate the Albanians into Macedonian culture and limit any signs of Albanian identity and nationalism. The curriculum of Albanian schools was revised in 1981 to require the teachers to use the Macedonian language only; those who refused to comply lost their jobs. In 1988 policies were put into place to curtail the Albanian birth rate.[335] In an attempt to eradicate religious identity, the Macedonian government destroyed Islamic libraries, took over Islamic buildings for use by the government, and built roads through Muslim cemeteries in Gostivar and Tetovo, the two main Albanian cities.

The situation was not much different following Macedonia's independence from Yugoslavia in 1991, with Albanians holding only 4 percent of state jobs and their mother tongue taught in university only as a foreign language. In 1997 the Macedonian government ordered an end to the flying of the Albanian flag over the municipal offices in Gostivar and Tetovo. When the local government refused, the Macedonians sent in the police, and three people died and seventy were wounded in the resulting clash.

In 1999 the National Liberation Army (NLA) emerged under the leadership of Ali Ahmeti, one of the founders of the KLA and a member of the Zajas clan in Macedonia, which had close relations with Kosovo's Jashari clan. By January 2001 the NLA was openly fighting the Macedonian government. In March 2001 the NLA issued a statement explaining that it was fighting in response to

"Macedonia's ignorant view and hypocritical disrespect of the demands and the patience of the Albanians has surpassed all limits. Our people have for decades been insulted, discriminated against and banned from all civilisation traditions in Macedonia. These are the main reasons that forced the Albanians to take up weapons and fight for their rights . . . we decided not to allow further humiliation and trampling on our dignity."[336] In a series of clashes between Albanian fighters and Macedonian security forces, nearly 250 people were killed over a period of six months along with a further 650 wounded and 140,000 people displaced.[337] Albanian shops and homes were burned, often with police actively participating, and mosques were vandalized with swastikas painted on their walls and the phrase "death to the *shiptars*" (as already mentioned, a derogatory term for Albanians).[338] The fighting ended with the signing of the Ohrid Agreement in August 2001, which gave Albanians broader language rights and guarantees for greater participation in the government. As part of the agreement, the NLA would be disbanded and disarmed by NATO forces. However, Albanians still complain of marginalization as tensions between the non-Muslim center and Muslim tribal periphery continue to fester and cause sporadic violence.

Non-Muslim Centers with Muslim Non-Segmentary Lineage Peripheries

While the focus of the five models discussed above is on Muslim segmentary lineage groups, other countries have strong non-Muslim centers that have not been able to deal justly and amicably with Muslim groups on the periphery that are, however, not organized along the principles of the segmentary lineage system. These examples are important as they serve the purpose of pointing out the principle that, whether segmentary lineage or non-segmentary lineage, the relationship between the center and the periphery is as equally troubled as in the five models, reflecting the failure of the modern state to provide its citizens security and justice.

Several cases of Muslim peripheral groups are presented below to illustrate two different types of non-segmentary lineage groups—the first of which could be described as tribal with a developed code of honor and the second with characteristics of agricultural peasantry. The Maguindanao of the southern Philippines and the Malay Muslims of South Thailand fall in the same category as the Tausug, identified as segmented early in this study. All these peoples are organized on the basis of clans and practice a code of honor and revenge. However, in the case of these segmented societies, the genealogical charter with its eponymous ancestor, descent from whom defines social and political status, does not have the same mythical relevance and therefore importance to the community as in the segmentary lineage system. These societies have seen continuous violence in offering resistance against the aggressive policies of the central government, which has too often resorted to the steamroller. The second category discussed below is that of peasant communities, which lack a defined code of honor and revenge, like the Cham of Cambodia and the Rohingya of Burma/Myanmar. In their cases, resistance to the onslaught of and systemic oppression by the central government has been conspicuous by its absence.

THE MUSLIMS OF THE SOUTHERN PHILIPPINES. For the Tausug and other Muslim tribal groups in the southern Philippines like the Maguindanao, resistance against the central government began with Spanish colonization and continued through four decades of American colonial rule, which ended with the independence of the Philippines in 1946. The Muslims considered their inclusion in a central state dominated by Christian Filipinos merely a new era of colonization. A Muslim sultan of the Maranao people in the south stated plaintively, "The Moro people want to set their house in order but how can they when the very key to their own house is not in their possession."[339] With little economic development and high unemployment on the Tausug island of Jolo, the Tausug took to piracy and looting, traditional occupations demonstrating their bravery and honor. In response, the central government based its largest command of security forces, both police and army, among the Tausug.

The spark that ignited open war with the center was the Jabidah massacre in 1968 by the Philippine army. The massacre occurred when Tausug military recruits training for a secret mission refused to follow orders upon discovering that their objective was to invade the Malaysian island of Sabah, which included a Tausug population. Between 60 and 100 Tausug were driven to a remote airstrip where they were executed by machine-gun fire. The following year, an independence movement calling itself the Moro National Liberation Front (MNLF) took shape and engaged central government forces, claiming a "genocide" was being carried out. In one operation in February 1974, the government completely flattened the main city on Jolo Island by gunfire from its warships; in one night alone, the bombardment left 2,000 dead and 60,000 displaced.[340] In 1976 the MNLF and the government reached an agreement to grant the Muslim areas autonomy, but subsequently this was not fully implemented.

The Moro Islamic Liberation Front (MILF), a splinter organization dominated by the ethnic Maguindanao on Mindanao Island, refused to accept autonomy and continued to fight for independence. For them, autonomy was unsatisfactory because Christian settlers were taking more and more of their land and might continue to do so unless Mindanao gained independence. As it was, the total population had changed dramatically, from 76 percent Muslim in 1903 to 72.5 percent Christian by 2000.[341] During the war, the government armed militias of Christian settlers. In June 1971 the most notorious Christian militia, the Ilaga, killed seventy Muslims in a mosque while at prayer. The conflict between these groups and the central government cost about 120,000 lives over four decades. In October 2012 the government and the MILF signed an agreement that provides a roadmap to create a new autonomous region in the south in order to end the conflict, though tensions still remain.

THE MALAY OF SOUTH THAILAND. When the Malay Muslims of the Patani Sultanate were annexed by Siam (later Thailand) in 1902, the Malays found themselves on the southern periphery of a Buddhist nation. After ascending to power in 1938, Prime Minister Phibun Songkhram, the third prime minister since the 1932 coup against absolute monarchical rule, began to implement the first aggressive policies toward modernization, which focused in part on integrating and assimilating minority groups into the modern Thai state. Known for admiring Ataturk who created Turkey for the Turks, his regime bore the slogan "Thailand for the Thai." He renamed the country "Thailand" and redefined the Malays as "Thai Muslims." Like Ataturk, he rejected traditional culture, from which emerged the "cultural rules" of 1940. All Thai citizens, regardless of ethnicity, were required to wear Western clothes, which included brimmed hats, and traditional dress was banned. The use of the Malay language, Islamic courts, and Malayo-Arabic names was banned as well. Individuals were required to eat with fork and spoon while sitting in a chair at a table. Fines were imposed for any violations of these rules. When the clothing rules were disobeyed, the enforcing Thai officials were also known to rip the clothing off the backs of individuals in broad daylight.[342] In January 1944 a Malay religious leader complained that the Buddhist governor of the Patani Province, one of the three Thai provinces of the Muslim majority "Patani" region, "compelled all Malay leaders and ulema to pay homage to the image of Buddha."[343] Malay children were forced to bow to a statue of Buddha in school.

During a visit to South Thailand in September 1947, Barbara Whittingham-Jones, an English newspaper correspondent in Malaya, observed that the Patani region "is nailed down by a skeleton network of Siamese commissioners, police and other officials. Everywhere I went it was the same tale of systematic oppression and of a deliberate campaign to de-nationalise the population. Deepest resentment is aroused by the ban on Malay education."[344] She went on to expose the Thai officials' treatment of the Malay: "For alleged harbouring of gang robbers, though without preffering a charge in court, the Siamese people burn *kampongs* [villages] to the ground, blackmail the wealthier class of shopkeepers into paying thousands of ticals in 'protection money,' force their way into Malay homes, beat up their women and carry off such of the smaller and moveable goods as they fancy. Individuals are constantly shot out of hand or simply disappear and are never heard of again."

On April 28, 1948, a large crowd of Malays armed with knives, spears, and whatever makeshift weapons were available attacked a police station in the village of Dusun Nyor in the southern Muslim majority Narathiwat Province, killing 30 policemen but losing 400 of their own members.[345] This event sparked a resistance movement in the 1950s and 1960s led by the religious and scholarly elite, which called for separation from Thailand and Patani independence. Violence subsided under Prime Minister Prem Tinsulanonda's efforts in the 1980s to abandon assimilationist policies and establish an administrative structure that allowed for Malay participation and respect for their language, culture, and religion.

The resurgence of violence in 2004 had its roots in Prime Minister Thaksin Shinawatra's reversal of the administrative arrangements in the south. Under Thaksin's highly centralized government, the extremely unpopular police and military were granted greater powers in conducting operations, which included immunity for their actions. On April 28, 2004, groups of Malays attacked a number of military and police posts in which 111 people were killed. Afterward, some of them sought refuge in the Kru-Ze mosque, a 425-year-old landmark in the Patani Province considered to be the holiest mosque in the south. The military surrounded and stormed the mosque with machine gun fire, while the Malays were armed only with knives and a single gun.[346] In all, thirty-two Malays were killed in the incident. A Thai colonel later commented, "If I agreed not to storm Kru-Ze, I'd be agreeing to give up our Thai land."[347] The violence of 2004 culminated in an October incident at Tak Bai, Narathiwat, where seventy-eight unarmed protestors died of suffocation while in military custody after being piled into the back of army trucks.

The Malays lashed out in revenge attacks against anyone working in or associated with the central government, effectively shutting down all state services in a number of areas. According to a 2011 report of the Southern Border Police Operation Centre in Thailand, 5,243 people had been killed in the southern border region since 2004. The deaths were largely a result of small-scale attacks conducted by decentralized groups, with no organization taking credit. A Malay postal worker recounted, "We don't wear postal uniforms any more when we deliver the mail—it's too dangerous. Sometimes we wear sarong and cap as though going to the mosque to pray, carry letters on our motorbikes where they are not conspicuous. Most of the post office men killed were wearing uniform."[348] During an interview conducted deep in the jungle and wearing a garbage bag over his face to conceal his identity, a Malay fighting against the government told Al Jazeera, "What we do is a reaction to what government troops do to us. They always blame the violence on us, but that is not true. We only kill civilians who work together with the troops."[349] In December 2012 classes were suspended at 1,200 schools due to attacks on children and teachers. Thailand's National Security Council announced it will send a further 4,000 policemen to the Patani region by April 2013, reinforcing the 60,000 members of the security forces already present in the south.

The Thai national mood concerning the Malay periphery was captured by the revered Queen Sirikit in a 2004 nationally broadcast speech at Chitralada Palace in

Bangkok: "Even at the age of seventy-two, I will learn how to shoot guns without using my glasses." She called for the Thai Buddhists in the three Muslim majority provinces of the south to remain in the area and to begin taking shooting lessons.[350]

THE CHAM OF CAMBODIA. For the settled Cham of east Cambodia, incorporation into the modern state nearly led to their extermination. The Cham, the historical inhabitants of the Champa Kingdom in present-day southern Vietnam, were conquered by the Vietnamese in the fifteenth century with many of their numbers driven into present-day eastern Cambodia. Split between Cambodia and Vietnam, they were the target of assimilationist policies by both in the era of the modern state in the twentieth century. In South Vietnam, President Ngo Dinh Diem, its first president from 1955 to 1963 after French colonization, relocated large numbers of Vietnamese settlers into the Cham regions and imposed Vietnamese institutions, language, and culture. Materials in the Cham language were banned and, at times, burned if found by Vietnamese officials.[351]

In Cambodia, the situation was far more desperate. The Khmer Rouge, a communist regime led by Pol Pot that lasted from 1975 to 1979, targeted the Cham because of their religious beliefs and ethnicity. Thus while the entire country of Cambodia and all its various ethnic groups suffered under Pol Pot's Khmer Rouge, the Chams were singled out in an attempt to eradicate both Islam and the Cham themselves.

Under Pol Pot, the Cham, located primarily in the Eastern Zone, were collectively labeled "Khmer bodies with Vietnamese minds," due to their origin in Vietnam, and were classified as "new people," despite the fact that a Cham population had existed in the country for nearly five centuries. The regime began a program of persecution: it executed religious leaders and teachers, destroyed mosques, and banned any religious literature. In addition, it imposed bans on the Cham language, even in the privacy of their homes. Militia reportedly sneaked about the villages at night, eavesdropping on people's conversations. If they heard individuals speaking Cham, they would shoot them.[352] In one village, Koh Phol, after Khmer authorities collected all copies of the Quran, the Cham armed themselves with knives and swords, killing six Khmer troops. In retaliation, the entire village was destroyed with artillery fire and over 1,100 Cham were killed.[353] When the Cham attempted to rebel against these policies, the government targeted them for extermination.

Every individual in the Eastern Zone, including women and children, was forced to wear a blue and white checked scarf, identifying them as marked for death in the killing fields.[354] One Cham village, Po Tonle, was turned into an execution center where 35,000 people, including 20,000 Cham, were reportedly killed.[355] Among the Cham religious leadership, Grand Mufti Res Lah and the two deputy muftis were executed, and only 21 of 113 imams, 20 of 113 *hakims*, and 25 of 226 deputy *hakims* were left alive, and only 20 of the 113 mosques in

Cambodia survived.[356] All the Cham *hajjis* were killed in 1977.[357] By the end of the Khmer Rouge rampage, out of a population of 250,000, approximately 100,000 Cham, or 40 percent of the total population, were killed.[358]

The Cham, like the rest of the country, struggled to put their lives together after the fall of Pol Pot's regime. Many Muslim countries and aid organizations were hesitant to support the Cham community in Cambodia because of the lack of support for the Vietnamese-backed communist government that replaced the Khmer Rouge. After the UN-brokered democratic elections in 1993, the international Islamic community began to play an active role among the Cham population in Cambodia, helping to finance the construction of mosques. In the 1990s many Islamic nongovernmental organizations (NGOs) also became increasingly involved in providing humanitarian aid to the Cham and helping them rebuild their religious institutions.

THE ROHINGYA OF BURMA/MYANMAR. Like the Cham, the Rohingya of western Burma/Myanmar, a population of about 1 million with a further 1 million refugees scattered across South Asia, faced an unsympathetic and violent central government that denied them their existence as part of the modern state. The government, dominated by Buddhist Burmese, deliberately and incorrectly labeled them illegal Bengali immigrants and took steps to drive them and their culture out of the nation. When that failed, it moved to eradicate them entirely.

The Rohingya, originally part of the independent kingdom of Arakan, were conquered by the Burmese Kingdom in 1785, with thousands of captives sent to the Burmese capital as slaves to labor on infrastructure projects. As a result of the First Anglo-Burmese War, ending in 1826, the Rohingya were split from what remained of Burma for nearly sixty years until the Burmese center was fully conquered and colonized by the British in 1885. This led the Burmese to side with the Japanese during World War II while the Rohingya remained loyal to the British. There was Rohingya interest in joining East Pakistan after the war, and leaders of the community even discussed this with Jinnah, who was supportive of the Rohingya. However, Aung San, the founding father of Burma, assured Jinnah that the Rohingya would be an integral part of the independent Burmese state established in January 1948.

After a coup in 1962 under General Ne Win, military rule was declared over the entire country. Ne Win sought to define the nation as one for the Buddhist Burmese and enacted "Burmanization" policies. The Rohingya were declared to be ethnically related to South Asians and no longer considered part of the nation. The 1974 constitution did not recognize the Rohingya as one of the nation's 135 indigenous ethnic groups, with a law issued in 1982 officially denying them citizenship.

In 1978 the military attempted to expel the Rohingya population into Bangladesh through mass arrests, destruction of mosques and villages, and confiscation of lands. These measures ultimately pushed a quarter of a million Rohingya into Bangladesh in only six months.[359] In July 1978 Bangladesh and Burma agreed to the repatriation of the refugees over the objections of the Rohingya back to Arakan, which by this time had been renamed Rakhine after the majority Buddhist population.

After student uprisings broke out in 1988, the military renamed the country Myanmar and refused to relinquish its rule after being voted out of power in the 1990 civilian elections. It again began operations to displace the Rohingya population, settling Buddhists in their place and relocating the Rohingya into "strategic villages" near military bases. As part of these operations, the Burmese government implemented the "Four Cuts" strategy, which denied the population "land, food, shelter, and security."[360] Roughly 250,000 Rohingya again fled across the Naaf River into Bangladesh.

A new border security force, known as the Nay-Sat Kut-kwey Ye (NaSaKa), was formed in 1992. Under the NaSaKa, the Rohingya were subjected to slave labor for the purpose of building villages for Buddhist settlers on Rohingya land. They were also forced to work on infrastructure and agriculture projects as well as maintain government and military buildings. Rape and forced prostitution of Rohingya women were widespread.

The government, still unsuccessful at casting out the entire Rohingya population, enacted policies intended to halt the Rohingya's ability to practice and transmit their culture, which included measures to stop procreation. The Rohingya were unable to participate in the army, civil service, or media, prevented from owning businesses or getting loans, and barred from building new mosques and madrassahs, or even repairing existing ones. The government also implemented severe travel restrictions that required the Rohingya to obtain a rarely granted government permit even when visiting a neighboring village. The travel restrictions severely limited their ability to obtain medicine or adequate medical treatment as travel to the health facilities of Sittwe, the state's capital, was denied. As the Rohingya were not permitted to work for the government because they were considered noncitizens and the staff of local clinics could not speak the Rohingya language, this further hampered their ability to receive medical treatment. In 1994 the Burmese government stopped giving Rohingya children birth certificates and in the late 1990s began requiring government permission for Rohingya to marry, which was rarely granted without a substantial bribe that few could afford. Cohabitation, sexual contact, and pregnancy outside of wedlock became arrestable offenses. Couples who married without government permission were sent to separate prisons where the woman was subjected to gang rape and the man to torture. Many women who became illegally pregnant fled the country or died after complications from abortions conducted under the most unsanitary conditions and unsafe procedures, including the "stick method." Many of the deaths were a result of the inability to receive medical attention owing to the severe travel restrictions or fear of having an illegal pregnancy discovered by the government. Furthermore, if Rohingya children were born, they were considered noncitizens and thus not permitted to attend state-run secondary schools or obtain any state services.

The ethnic basis and strength of this prejudice against the Rohingya is clearly seen in remarks made to reporters by the Burmese consul general to Hong Kong, Ye Myint Aung. In December 2009, responding to media attention on the Rohingya "boat people" attempting to flee the country by sea, the consul general sent an official letter to media and foreign officials denying that the Rohingya were Burmese. He pointed out that the "dark brown" Rohingya complexion contrasted with the "fair and soft" skin of the Burmese people, who he added were "good looking as well." He went on to explain: "(My complexion is a typical genuine one of a Myanmar gentleman and you will accept that how handsome your colleague Mr Ye is.) It is quite different from what you have seen and read in the papers. (They are as ugly as ogres.)"[361]

Of the hundreds of thousands of Rohingya who fled to Bangladesh, only 28,000 were recognized as refugees and placed in two camps in the Cox's Bazar District, where meager government and NGO food rations and aid were provided, their only form of subsistence. Facing corruption or cruelty at the hands of local officials, the refugees could not count on these rations as they could be taken away at will. Some 200,000 unrecognized refugees were dispersed throughout Cox's Bazar and the surrounding hills in makeshift camps where they struggled to survive on their own, constantly in danger of arrest, exploitation, violence, starvation, and disease.[362] Bangladesh even rejected international aid for the Rohingya refugees to prevent more of them from crossing the border. In 2011, for example, the Bangladesh government blocked $33 million in UN humanitarian aid for the Rohingya refugees.[363]

As part of this study, my team and I met with Wakar Uddin, one of the prominent leaders of the Rohingya community, chairman of the Burmese Rohingya Association of North America, and the director general of the Arakan Rohingya Union. He was born in 1954 in the Arakan state of Burma. I was surprised when he spoke to me in fluent Urdu, and I discovered the many links between the Rohingya and Pakistan. His views on Jinnah, whom he clearly admired, impressed me. He said his father accompanied a Rohingya delegation to meet Jinnah twice in Dacca. His father described Jinnah as being "very handsome, a man of integrity and one who cared for Muslims." The possibility of joining Pakistan in 1947 was discussed. It looked hopeful. One year later, when Wakar Uddin's father heard that Jinnah had died, he said it was over; the Rohingya cause was lost.

Wakar Uddin is passionate about the plight of his people, existing as they do in a penumbral state, neither quite fully dead nor quite fully alive. On both sides of the international border, they live in extreme squalor, under oppression, and in constant fear of the future. The Burmese government, he avers, has launched a "policy of extermination." Without a developed sense of tribal identity or unity or code of honor, without support, without leaders to inspire them, the Rohingya have lost the will to fight. They fear their own families and friends might report on "troublemakers." They also live in terror of the ubiquitous and sadistic army and police, awaiting their fate with resignation.

There was widely reported violence against the Rohingya by the Buddhist Rakhine people in June 2012 in which over 1,000 Rohingya were reportedly killed, although official numbers were much lower as is often the case, with entire Rohingya villages burned to the ground. This incident is further evidence of the ongoing oppression of the Rohingya, as well as the attitudes of those associated with the center against the periphery. The violent actions of the Rakhine were committed with the complicity and, at times, direct participation of the security forces in the region.[364]

The new democratic reforms that gained Myanmar international praise have not altered this perception of the Rohingya, as reflected in President Thein Sein's announcement in July 2012 that he would not recognize the Rohingya or their rights and wished to turn over the entire ethnic group to the United Nations High Commissioner for Refugees.[365] Buddhist monks staged a number of anti-Rohingya marches in September of the same year to declare their support for this proposal. The following month, the government blocked the Organization of Islamic Cooperation (OIC) from opening an aid office in Burma/Myanmar to assist displaced Rohingya. In 2013 an investigative report by the BBC revealed that Thai officials were selling to human traffickers Rohingya refugees fleeing the recent violence by sea.[366]

Like so many of the communities on the periphery, the Rohingya are under assault from all elements of society. The armed services, the social and religious leaders, the media, the main opposition leaders, and even the president have united in declaring that the Rohingya are not Burmese and therefore should not be in the country in the first place. Condemned in the court of public opinion, the Rohingya are held wholly responsible for the atrocities that happen to them.

Even their last hope, Daw Aung San Suu Kyi, has remained strangely silent on their suffering and predicament, preferring to court the majority view rather than fight openly for justice. In a BBC interview in which she discussed the Rohingya and the current violence, she stated that it was not her place to champion one side over the other and that "I am urging tolerance but I do not think one should use one's moral leadership, if you want to call it that, to promote a particular cause without really looking at the sources of the problems."[367] She added that she had not seen any "statistics" to show that the Rohingya were being denied citizenship.

In contrast and to his credit, President Obama on his historic visit to Burma/Myanmar in November 2012 spoke out unambiguously and boldly about the "dignity" and the suffering of the "innocent" Rohingya people. By merely mentioning the Rohingya in his speech at Yangon University, Obama had almost single-handedly given them legitimacy and, equally important, provided them a ray of hope.

As this chapter has made clear, an overwhelming dilemma for the modern states discussed in this study lies in how to successfully balance the writ of the center with the needs of its periphery. Experience far and wide demonstrates that these states have consistently tilted against the latter and denied it the basic prerequisites of citizenship—and humanity. Indeed, the center has all too frequently resorted to brutal and unnecessary military action. With the advent of 9/11, the center found a natural ally in the United States. Together, they worked to track down al Qaeda and affiliated terrorists in the periphery and in the process compromised fundamental human rights and civil liberties. This created a dilemma for the United States itself, which is the subject of chapter 5.

5

OBAMA'S DILEMMA:

Balancing Security and Human Rights

From the time of George Washington to that of George W. Bush and Barack Obama, the American president has faced a dilemma not very different from the kind that confronted President Musharraf in Pakistan or the leaders of other countries. At its heart, the problem has been how to maintain the writ of the center while ensuring that marginal and peripheral groups are fully included as citizens of the state and their rights and privileges firmly safeguarded. But the United States has tackled it quite differently from the rest of the world. America's approach has been anchored in the clarity and unequivocal resolution that its Founding Fathers arrived at after grappling with the same issue. Their vision gave form and content to the world's first democratic state. It also created high standards that succeeding American leaders could aspire to but not always attain.

As the Founding Fathers of the United States were acutely aware, a government's security interests must be kept in balance with those of human rights, civil liberties, and democracy. That is why they underwrote the supremacy of the latter in their founding documents—the Declaration of Independence and the Constitution. However, the exigencies of the state—dealing with civil wars, world wars, and terrorist attacks on the homeland—have consistently challenged that balance, tilting it toward security, which is precisely what happened in the United States after 9/11. American presidents and administrators increasingly favored security over human rights. Not to do so was considered not only weak but also anti-American. As security gained precedence, the use of the drone was almost a logical next step for nations equipped with the tools of globalization. This and other aspects of the imbalance between security and human rights are having enormous consequences for the tribal societies that are the subject of this book.

The use of the drone overturned notions of justice and the rule of law laid out in America's founding documents, which themselves were based on centuries of precedents in Western legal practice and thought. The right to a trial by jury is at the core of the U.S. judicial system and enshrined in the Sixth Amendment of the Bill of Rights. The power of the president to extrajudicially execute anyone, even U.S. citizens, with a drone strike from his "kill list," the details of which are unknown, is a clear violation of the right to trial under both U.S. and international law. The actions become even murkier when there is no international agreement on what constitutes a crime. Yet the drone strikes and their violation of the law seem justified to Americans because the deadly weapon is thought to keep America safe.

This is contrary to the ideals on which the United States was founded. Paramount among these ideals were the concepts of justice, equality, and rule of law—the formula for liberty. In his first Inaugural Address as president, Thomas Jefferson stated that the "essential principles of our Government, and consequently those which ought to shape its Administration" must begin with "equal and exact justice to all men, of whatever state or persuasion, religious or political."[1] The antithesis of this conception of law and civilization was torture. Jefferson believed government "shall not have power . . . to prescribe torture in any case whatever."[2]

These ideals were absolute and could not be compromised, even for the sake of security. Benjamin Franklin, the sage of Philadelphia, warned his countrymen, "Those who would give up essential liberty to purchase a little temporary safety deserve neither liberty nor safety."[3]

George Washington, in outlining what he saw as America's mission at home and abroad, declared, "The bosom of America [was to be] open to receive . . . the oppressed and persecuted of all nations and religions."[4] Indeed, Washington's words would be echoed in the message displayed on one of the main symbols of America, the Statue of Liberty, which has inspired millions of people all over the world.

Until recently this vision of Washington and the other Founding Fathers had wide appeal among the tribesmen of the Muslim world, who viewed the United States as a nation that would challenge the tyranny of their central governments and as a sanctuary within which they could find peace and dignity. In 1946, for example, the renowned Kurdish leader Mustafa Barzani confided to the U.S. ambassador in Tehran that the Kurds wished to leave Iran. The ambassador later recounted: "When I asked where he thought of going, he said, 'We'd like to go to the United States.' I asked, 'Do you mean all the Kurds? That means many hundred thousand.' He nodded affirmatively."[5] Barzani, who said he "trusted no other major power," frequently told the U.S. government that if his cause was successful, his people were "ready to become the 51st state."[6] Following the U.S. intervention in the first Gulf War, Barzani's son, Massoud Barzani, became head of the autonomous Kurdish region of northern Iraq.

Before 9/11 the United States had intervened frequently to save thousands of Muslim tribesmen on the basis of its concern for human rights. It was this temperament and momentum to do something good and positive on the world

Somalis, including women and children, seek shelter under the tree of life representing America in a painting by a Somali in a refugee camp before 9/11 (photo by Frankie Martin).

stage that led Americans to help those being persecuted or in need. The Pukhtun of Afghanistan fighting the Soviet forces in the 1980s, along with their clansmen across the border in Pakistan, were grateful for American support in their war of liberation. President Ronald Reagan, who helped arm and train them, welcomed Pukhtun tribesmen to the White House and declared them the "moral equivalents of America's Founding Fathers."[7] In the 1990s the Kurds being brutalized by Saddam Hussein in northern Iraq saw the Americans as their main benefactors once the no-fly zone was created for them. The Somali confronted with starvation and looking for outside aid saw Americans arriving with assistance; the Black Hawk misadventure came from the noble idea of helping starving people in the midst of a civil war. In Kosovo, American intervention halted the massacres in which Muslims tribesmen were the main victims.

Even Hollywood depicted the Muslim tribesmen as heroes and freedom fighters, as seen in the films *Rambo III* and *The Living Daylights* when both John Rambo and James Bond join the mujahideen fighters of Afghanistan against the Soviet Union. Earlier, in the 1950 film version of Kipling's *Kim*, Mehboob Ali, the Pukhtun horse trader, was played by none other than Errol Flynn, the very embodiment of the swashbuckling hero. One could imagine the periphery of countries where the center was particularly brutal repeating such doggerel as "Muslim tribesmen have no fear/ Uncle Sam is here."

AMERICA TURNS AGAINST THE TRIBES

After 9/11, the doggerel changed: "Muslim tribesmen you need to fear/Uncle Sam is here." Americans had now become suspicious and fearful of these same tribal societies, viewing them as a threat. Central authorities had whispered in American ears, "Lurking among these tribes are the ubiquitous Islamic terrorists." In response, the United States threw itself without reservation into the pursuit of al Qaeda and its affiliates wherever it believed they were to be found.

U.S. attitudes after 9/11 cannot be understood without examining the context of American culture and history, as I discovered after a year's fieldwork in the United States.[8] From earliest times, starting in the early seventeenth century with the foundation of Plymouth and its vulnerable settlers who shaped America's primordial identity, American society has exhibited a strong and clear impulse to retaliate with full force at any perception of threat. This tendency can be summed up in the phrase "zero tolerance," which exposed a predatory strain in American society. It was precisely to check this impulse that the perceptive Founding Fathers outlined a vision of society based in knowledge, justice, civility, and respect for all religions that formed its pluralist identity. The tension between American predatory and pluralist identity provides the dynamic propelling history after 9/11.

When George W. Bush declared on September 20, 2001, to a cheering joint session of Congress, "Our grief has turned to anger and anger to resolution," he committed America to a policy informed by emotion and colored by the spirit of revenge. He had triggered underlying notions of "zero tolerance" that would become the motto for American policy in its war on terror. What was needed was "infinite tolerance." Without this change, it would be impossible to win hearts and minds in different cultures with their different customs and problems. In that sense, the American enterprise in Iraq and Afghanistan—and in several other Muslim lands—after 9/11 was doomed to failure from the start.

The attitude of America, which the periphery looked to for justice and mediation against the excesses of the center, reminded me of a story I was told in the Tribal Areas of Pakistan. The tribesmen said nothing is worse than when the person who is the final arbiter of justice himself commits an injustice against the person who has appealed to him. The belief is embodied in this popular story about a daughter-in-law of an important tribal chief who was raped regularly and beaten mercilessly by her husband, the son of the chief. She complained to her father-in-law, who, instead of stopping the injustice, raped her himself. That left her with no more doors to knock on in order to seek redress and justice. It was the ultimate betrayal. After 9/11, when communities on the peripheries desperately sought American intervention, they were horrified to learn that their potential benefactor had not only turned away from them, but was directly or indirectly a major source of their misery. They had nowhere else to turn.

The kind of America they were looking for had changed—the America so well represented by characters played by film actor Gary Cooper such as Longfellow Deeds, Sergeant Alvin York, Robert Jordan, and Sheriff Will Kane, who were decent, strong, down-to-earth, kindly, champions of the poor and the "little man," and who stood up to bullies. Cooper had come to symbolize these quintessential American characters he played so well. In contrast, the popular post-9/11 characters in the media reflected a different kind of American. Take two in the popular TV series *24* and *Two and a Half Men.* Jack Bauer in *24,* played with gusto by Kiefer Sutherland, is the manic counterterrorist agent who suffocates terror suspects with plastic bags, slices open stomachs, and applies electric shocks to them in order to thwart terror attacks against the United States. Charlie Harper in *Two and a Half Men,* played as self-parody by Charlie Sheen, lives for the excesses of the consumerist society in a drug-ridden, alcohol-soaked, and prostitute-dependent haze. Jack and Charlie did not appear from nowhere: they are a product of the social environment formed by the sadism of Dick Cheney and the corrupt executives of Wall Street. Both are a far cry from Gary Cooper.

Cooper and the people of the periphery would have seen much to respect and admire in each other. He would have instinctively wished to champion their cause against the tyranny of central predatory armies; the people of the periphery would have respected his chivalry, courage, and compassion. The new post-9/11 heroes, on the other hand, represent mainstream American culture: Jack on seeing a tribesman would impulsively reach for his pliers and electric prod, while Charlie, who devoted his life to the pursuit of prurient pleasure, would say he could not care less about the state of the world, let alone that of hairy, smelly men speaking a strange language from across the world. Few of the young American generation in the age of globalization have even heard of Cooper and the values he so successfully represented on the screen and are therefore unaware of the scale of the loss.

For Muslim societies on the periphery, the present phase of history, this age of globalization, begins with 9/11 and the intrusion, directly or indirectly, of the United States into their lands. The United States has thus slipped into the role of a global center in confrontation with the Muslim periphery throughout the world. It is difficult to predict how this phase will end, but easy to see its widespread turmoil and chaos. No longer isolated as they once were, Muslims on the periphery moved to the eye of a global storm as the United States, allying with the central government, hunted for al Qaeda and its associates in the periphery's communities. The United States scoured the world for "terrorists" as if they were a malignant tumor that needed to be removed surgically, not quite realizing the trauma the operation was creating for the body.

The U.S. solution to terrorism was twofold: first, to capture or kill the "terrorists" through military operations as part of its war on terror; and second, to extend central government authority to the "ungoverned spaces" of the tribal periphery. To do so, it needed to link up with the central governments and adopt their policies toward the periphery, which included the use of torture. With the United States openly promoting torture "to keep America safe," other central governments were encouraged to do the same without compunction as the erst-while champion of human rights, the United States, had changed its position on the matter. In the newly minted war on terror, all Muslim tribal societies were now viewed as either infested with terrorists or offering a potential safe haven for them. Once America saw the specter of al Qaeda in any of these places, its com-mitment to the center knew no bounds. The same tribesmen it would have once supported in their genuine demands for democracy, human and civil rights, and dignity, were now targeted. Under the all-encompassing American metanarra-tive, no Muslim tribe, or even any Muslim community, was immune, as central governments were quick to use it to their benefit in the ongoing confrontation with their peripheries. Central governments cynically manipulated the United States in their suppression of the Muslim periphery.

The entanglements with Muslim tribal communities on the periphery of many nations, both Muslim and non-Muslim, began soon after 9/11, and one by one they grew: the invasion of Afghanistan followed by Iraq, a military training mission in West Africa, a missile strike in the Kurdish region of Turkey, a unit of Special Forces in the Far East, and drones buzzing over the theaters of conflict where Muslim tribesmen lived. But America was not fighting an established army equipped with heavy artillery and tanks, an air force, or a navy. It was striking at individuals or small groups, attacking now a police station, now a bus stop, without pause. Bushfires had burst out around the world, and the harder the Americans hit the tribes, the harder the tribes hit back. Frustrated, angry, and exhausted after a decade of war, America continued to lash out as it was wont to do under threat. But it was not just taking a hammer to squash a mosquito; it was using bunker-busters.

The lack of military and political objectives, the poorly thought out and exe-cuted tactics on the ground, and the shifting alliances of the U.S.-led campaign soon threw the periphery into anarchy. Few seemed to have any real idea of why the war they were involved in was really being fought, how long it would last, and who was allied to whom. America's chosen weapon in the war was the drone, its targets the tribes of Yemen, Somalia, and Turkey, and the Tausug tribes of the Philippines, not to mention those in Waziristan (as discussed in chapter 2) and Afghanistan. What was clear was that, imperceptibly and inexorably, America's war on terror had become a global war against tribal Islam.

Targeting the Tribes of Yemen

On May 12, 2012, the Yemeni air force dropped leaflets into Abyan Province in South Yemen encouraging people to evacuate and stay clear of areas where "al

Qaeda" fighters were gathered. All roads leading into the province were blocked by the government. Close to 150,000 people had already been displaced, escaping the daily violence between tribes and Yemeni troops. Three days later, in the town of Jaar in Abyan, a missile fired from a U.S. drone struck an alleged meeting of insurgents. A second missile quickly followed, hitting the people who had gathered to pull the bodies from the rubble of the house. Twelve civilians were killed and a further twenty-one injured. In the previous month, President Obama had approved the use of these "signature" drone strikes, as used extensively in Waziristan, which allowed for attacks to occur on unidentified groups at alleged "militant" locations without clear evidence of their activities. Anyone thus killed was in retrospect categorized as a "militant" and therefore a legitimate target. Abyan Province had become Yemen's Waziristan.

Under President Obama, the drone strikes focused largely on the two southern provinces to the east of Aden: Abyan Province and Shabwa Province. Of the nineteen drone strikes in 2011, ten took place in Abyan and a further six in Shabwa. By the following year, their use had dramatically increased. Over a two-day period in June 2012, for example, these provinces were the site of at least fourteen strikes.

Before these "signature" strikes, drones in Yemen had been primarily a tool of assassination, as demonstrated in the 2011 high-profile killing of Anwar al-Awlaki, an American citizen from the Yemeni Awalik tribe of the Shabwa Province. In a separate drone strike two weeks later, the United States killed al-Awlaki's sixteen-year-old son, also a U.S. citizen, along with a teenage friend and several others. The Obama administration stated that al-Awlaki's son was a "military-aged male traveling with a high-value target."[9]

Despite the media's blanket statements that the drones, concentrated in the south, were targeting al Qaeda, the reality is that such assessments overlook the local context of the history of South Yemen over the past five decades and its impact on today's tribesmen. A good example of the trajectory followed by many Yemeni tribesmen in the south is Tariq al-Fadhli, the son of the head of the Fadhli tribe, one of the tribes under British colonial rule. His father was the last British-backed sultan of the Fadhli Sultanate. When the subsequent Marxist government appropriated the land of the old feudal families, al-Fadhli and his clan escaped to Lebanon and then to the Asir region in Saudi Arabia, where he grew up. At the age of nineteen, he traveled to Afghanistan, where he became close to bin Laden and was wounded in Jalalabad.

After the war in Afghanistan, al-Fadhli returned to South Yemen for the first time since he was a child to be elected chief of his tribe in a traditional ceremony. He soon gathered a large force of Afghan war veterans that he called the Islamic Jihad. The Islamic Jihad fighters trained in camps in tribal areas in the south, with backing from bin Laden and the support of President Ali Abdullah Saleh, who wanted to use the tribesmen to purge the remnants of the old Marxist state

Tariq al-Fadhli, front and center, and fellow Yemeni tribesmen stand at attention before the American flag in 2010 (youtube.com).

from within his own government. In 1994 al-Fadhli and allied tribes supported Saleh in the civil war that broke out after former communist rulers had second thoughts about the south's 1990 union with the north and tried to secede. In July that year, al-Fadhli's forces took Aden, sending southern leaders fleeing the country. Al-Fadhli was rewarded with a prominent government position on Saleh's advisory council. By 2004, however, he had grown disillusioned with the Yemen union. He even told the British journalist Victoria Clark he would welcome the colonial British back in Aden. As his father had pointed out, "In British times there was the rule of law; no one could be imprisoned for more than forty-eight hours without charge."[10] In 2009 al-Fadhli broke with Saleh and vowed to fight the central government to create an independent South Yemen, which he called South Arabia, stating that the Yemeni state "was born deformed, grew up disabled and now is thankfully buried."[11] He soon became the Yemeni Ministry of Interior's most wanted man.

An important source of friction for this southern independence movement was the seizure of vast tracts of land by northerners at the expense of southerners following unification. The managing editor of the most widely read newspaper in South Yemen, the Aden-based *Al-Ayyam,* informed Clark that the government military commander in charge of the south, a northerner, "had helped himself" to land "nearly the size of Bahrain" over the previous four years.[12] In 2009 the central government closed down the paper for promoting "separatism."

Saleh then claimed that al-Fadhli was an al Qaeda operative. To show that this was not true, al-Fadhli shot an Internet video from his home in Zinjibar, the capital of Abyan Province and the center of the Fadhli tribal area, that showed him raising the American flag to the tune of "The Star-Spangled Banner" as he and a group of tribesmen stood to attention. In a 2010 interview with the *New York Times,* he said that his connections made him a potential asset to America: "I can be a mediator between America and Al Qaeda. We can be allied with the United States against terrorism, and we will achieve the interests of the United States, not those of the regime."[13]

By January 2011, however, he had turned firmly against the United States, presiding over a burning of the same American flag he had previously saluted. Al-Fadhli now blamed America for killing women and children in the south, referring specifically to the December 2009 U.S. cluster bombing of the mountain village of al-Majalah in Abyan, which killed forty-one people, including twenty-one children and fourteen women, and he decried U.S. support for Saleh.[14] In April 2010 the Yemeni government attacked his compound, and in 2011 six drone strikes hit Zinjibar. Driven like Baluchistan's Nawab Akbar Bugti by actions against the periphery, al-Fadhli went in a few short years from being pro-government and actually part of the administration to the foremost advocate of splitting the nation apart. Following the trajectories of so many who began as loyal citizens and were converted to rebel leaders, al-Fadhli now finds himself under arrest in Aden as of November 2012 with his future uncertain.

Before his arrest, al-Fadhli had announced his support for the organization Ansar al-Sharia, an additional name for Al Qaeda in the Arabian Peninsula (AQAP) adopted in 2011 in order to associate AQAP with sharia, which its members believed was the solution for Yemen. AQAP had been originally formed in 2009 when tribesmen from Asir, fleeing the Saudi steamroller, moved into southern Yemen and took refuge among increasingly antigovernment tribes. Mentioning the Yemeni government assault on his house in Abyan, al-Fadhli, whose sons were with him during the attack, said, "When my sons saw what happened to me and their country and the creation of Ansar Al-Sharia, they joined Ansar Al-Sharia and fought with them, and I'm proud of that . . . if I had one thousand sons I wouldn't chose [sic] for them any other way but this path."[15]

Ansar al-Sharia was making international headlines with its daring operations, which included the takeover of entire cities and vast swaths of territory, and soon became a target of U.S. drones. In one such operation in March 2012, Ansar al-Sharia attacked a military base just south of Zinjibar. Two suicide bombers blew up the gate of the base; then Ansar al-Sharia fighters unleashed mortar and rocket attacks and stormed inside. They seized armored vehicles, artillery, assault rifles, and rockets, which they used against the Yemeni army inside the base, killing 185 soldiers, wounding 150, and capturing 73. In May 2012 Ansar al-Sharia again attacked a military base, killing 32 soldiers, capturing 28, and stealing a tank following a U.S. drone strike that had occurred only hours earlier. Two weeks later, an Ansar al-Sharia suicide bomber blew himself up in a military parade rehearsal in Sanaa that marked Yemen's national day celebrating the 1990 union between the north and south and was attended by Yemen's defense minister. Some 100 soldiers were killed and 300 injured. Ansar al-Sharia announced that the attack was "revenge" for the central government's war in Abyan Province. In June 2012 a suicide bomber killed the Yemeni general in charge of operations in southern Yemen in the city of Aden, blowing himself up next to the general's car. In August 2012 groups of armed men with rocket-propelled grenades and automatic weapons stormed the government intelligence headquarters in Aden, killing twenty intelligence officers and security forces while injuring thirteen. In November 2012 a suicide bomber blew himself up inside a government building in Zinjibar, killing three local militiamen allied to the central government.

The following month, the Yemeni army, in response to tribesmen blowing up the nation's principal oil pipeline and sabotaging power lines, launched a major assault with thirty tanks in Maarib Province in central Yemen. Days later, the Yemeni general who commanded forces in central Yemen was killed in an ambush in Maarib along with seventeen Yemeni officers and soldiers, with the assailants making off with weapons and six army vehicles.[16] The Yemeni government announced that the general had been killed by "al Qaeda" and stepped up its campaign to attack the tribes.

The turmoil in Yemen can be traced directly to 9/11 and events following it. In November 2001 Saleh had visited Washington and vowed to support President Bush in the war on terror. The United States pledged Saleh millions of dollars in aid, helicopters, weapons, and a hundred Special Forces trainers. It also supported the National Security Bureau (NSB) in Yemen, an intelligence and internal security force that became notorious for torturing prisoners. Saleh, in return, gave the United States secret authority to conduct "targeted killings" in the country. In 2002 the United States launched its first drone strike in Yemen, killing the accused mastermind of the 2000 USS *Cole* attack, who had been under the protection of local tribes, in addition to a U.S. citizen of Yemeni descent with him.

In this post-9/11 environment and with the backing of the United States, Saleh changed tactics in favor of more direct and brutal methods against the two main insurgencies, the southern independence movement and a new Shia Zaydi imam and his allied tribes in the north, known as the Houthis, who declared independence in 2004. Like Pervez Musharraf, Saleh found himself fighting on two tribal fronts with the full support of the United States. And like Musharraf, he was destined to fail and fall.

The northern Houthi rebels represented the revival of the millennium-old Zaydi Imamate and its ideals for the first time since it was overthrown in the 1960s. In 2004 violence broke out when the central government attempted to arrest Hussein al-Houthi, a former Yemeni member of parliament and a Zaydi sayyed. Since his father provided the impetus behind the movement, he was considered a supporter of Zaydi revivalism. The government, placing a bounty on his head, accused him of attempting to reestablish the Zaydi Imamate, opening unlicensed religious centers, and staging violent anti-American protests. Ten weeks into the fighting, al-Houthi was killed by the Yemeni military, after which his octogenarian father and then his brother stepped into his shoes to lead the Zaydi resistance.

Bolstered by American military aid, Saleh invaded the northern tribal areas in an aggressive military campaign that violated local practices such as the traditional role of mediation in solving disputes and upset the historical balance with the tribal periphery.[17] Although U.S. Special Forces had been dispatched to train Yemeni security forces, government troops were immediately bogged down against the warlike tribes in the difficult terrain that the tribes knew so well.

Despite the deployment of 20,000 Yemeni troops and additional tribal forces against the ragtag rebels, about 6,000 Houthi tribesmen fought the government to a standstill, with an estimated 1,000 Yemeni troops killed and 3,000 wounded in May 2008 alone.[18] Fighting soon spread to areas just twenty miles from Sanaa. In August 2009 Saleh, not unlike Musharraf opting for the steamroller in Waziristan, launched Operation Scorched Earth to crush the mountain tribal rebels. In December of that year, the Houthis claimed the United States bombed Zaydi tribes, killing 120 people and wounding 44 in areas that included markets and refugee camps.

Although the central government banned all reporting from the mountainous tribal region, it soon became clear that a massive humanitarian crisis was occurring. Over 340,000 people were internally displaced in the sparsely populated area, and an estimated 25,000 people had been killed in six years of warfare.[19] In March 2011 the Houthis successfully cast off government authority from Sanaa in three northern provinces and achieved de facto independence. Saleh, facing millions of protesters, was forced to step down as president the following year.

Under the new president, Abd Rabbuh Mansur Hadi, the war on terror continued to rage unchecked. A Houthi spokesman said that drones hovered overhead "always, day and night."[20] In October 2012 three people were killed in a U.S. drone strike in the Houthi-controlled mountainous region of Sadah. Shortly thereafter, thousands of people took to the streets to protest U.S. drones, with the Houthi leader condemning the "U.S. crime."[21]

The United States and Somali Tribes

In 2011, as drone strikes in Waziristan and Yemen increased, drones were used for the first time in Somalia, with deadly effect. In June of that year a drone targeted Al Shabab leaders in Kismayo, a port city in the south, where, it is worth pointing out, local tribesmen had welcomed British troops after they expelled the Italians. A series of drone strikes followed around Mogadishu and across Somalia's south, targeting areas controlled by Al Shabab, which the United States accused of being linked to al Qaeda.

The roots of Al Shabab lie in the chaos of Siad Barre's collapse. In the late 1980s religious leaders from various clans formed an organization known as Al-Itihaad Al-Islamiya (AIAI) with the idea of creating order on the basis of Islamic law. AIAI's ranks were initially filled with mujahideen returning from Afghanistan, where more than 1,000 Somalis had taken part in the war effort. They slowly began running ports and making business connections and launched small-scale attacks on Ethiopia in support of Somalis in Ethiopia's Ogaden region, who had long complained of marginalization and persecution. These resulted in Ethiopian incursions into Somalia, such as one operation in March 1999 in pursuit of AIAI members who had staged a kidnapping and stolen medical supplies.

In the 1990s religious leaders of Hawiye subclans in the south started a separate movement overlapping with the AIAI to set up Islamic courts with the aim of bringing order to the chaos of warlord rule. Sheikh Hassan Dahir Aweys, a Hawiye and part of AIAI's leadership, established one such court in Mogadishu and another in Merka. The Islamic courts, based in separate subclans and reflecting religious and tribal support, maintained militias and received the backing of businessmen. As the number of Islamic courts increased, a sixty-three-member Sharia Implementation Council, which became known as the Union of Islamic Courts, was formed, with Sheikh Ali Dheere, a Hawiye who set up the first Islamic court, as chairman and Sheikh Aweys as secretary-general.

After 9/11 the United States began to view AIAI and the country's informal and traditional financial networks—known as *hawala* and used throughout the Muslim world, particularly in the Middle East—as an increasing threat. President Bush placed AIAI on America's terrorist list and imposed financial sanctions on the organization and its leaders, accusing it of links to al Qaeda. U.S. law enforcement agencies believed AIAI was receiving funds from a Somali remittance company known as Al-Barakaat, literally meaning "blessings," and distributing them to bin Laden.[22]

The United States accused the *hawala* organizations of financing terrorism, most prominently Al-Barakaat. Al-Barakaat was a collection of loosely connected

firms that formed a significant part of Somalia's economy as it was the conduit
for funds streaming from the global Somalia diaspora back to the impoverished
homeland. It became the largest business group and employer in Somalia, with
subsidiaries engaged in construction, banking, and telecommunications and
Internet services. It ran the only water-purification plant in Somalia and had 60
offices in the country and 127 offices in forty nations around the world.[23] The
United Nations used Al-Barakaat to fund Somali relief operations.

In November 2001 President Bush, standing alongside Secretary of State Colin
Powell, Attorney General John Ashcroft, and Treasury Secretary Paul O'Neill,
declared that Al-Barakaat would be shut down as "another step in our fight
against evil."[24] Bush said the United States had "solid and credible" evidence that
Al-Barakaat raised "funds for Al Qaida; they manage, invest, and distribute those
funds. They provide terrorist supporters with Internet service, secure telephone
communications, and other ways of sending messages and sharing information.
They even arrange for the shipment of weapons." Al-Barakaat, Bush argued,
operated "at the service of mass murderers." These allegations were proved false
by the 9/11 Commission, which found "no direct evidence at all of any real link
between al-Barakaat and terrorism of any type."[25] By then, however, the damage
had been done, and the allegations had adversely impacted the lives of countless
Somalis around the world.

Along with the American assault on Somalia's economy, the Central Intelligence Agency worked to curtail and defeat the Islamic courts, whose influence
was spreading, by supporting "warlords" against them. The United States accused
the Islamic courts of harboring several suspects implicated in the 1998 embassy
bombings in Kenya and Tanzania. The warlords organized themselves into a
group known as Alliance for the Restoration of Peace and Counter-Terrorism
and gained American backing. Nonetheless, the Islamic courts defeated them in
2006, gaining control of most of the south.

The United States, however, kept up its campaign to target the Islamic courts.
In December 2006 Ethiopia, working closely with the United States, invaded
Somalia with tanks and ground troops. The United States deployed Special
Forces in the region and began airstrikes. In a matter of months, the invading
forces had killed more than 8,000 members of the Islamic courts.[26] The presence
of thousands of Ethiopian occupying troops and the return of the "warlords"
from the Barre era, now organized by the United Nations and Western powers into the Somali central government based in Mogadishu, caused a furor in
Somalia. Many fighters for the Islamic courts, with their base in the Hawiye clan,
blended into the population and launched an insurgency against the weak central government, which controlled only a few city blocks in Mogadishu. Battles
between insurgents and Ethiopian troops, their ranks expanded by Ugandan and
Burundian forces, had killed thousands of Mogadishu residents. In the chaos,

Somali children suffering from malnutrition due to famine wait for food assistance (wikimedia.org).

Somali pirates resumed operations that had been curtailed by the Islamic courts, staging dramatic raids on ships in international waters.

By now, the youth wing of the Islamic courts movement, Al Shabab (meaning "the Youth"), had emerged as the most tenacious fighters in the insurgency. They began operating their own courts, formed an administrative structure, and took over more territory in the south and central region than the Islamic courts had controlled before the invasion. Hoping to check the violence, the United Nations and Western powers formed a new government headed by a former member of the courts, but this had little impact on the ground.

As a result of the collapse of law and order, clan warfare, foreign interventions, and famine, the Somali population was devastated. In the first two years following the American-backed Ethiopian invasion, approximately 80,000 Somalis died and nearly 1 million were displaced.[27] By the time of the escalating drone strikes in 2011, the instability had led to another famine, with 29,000 Somali children under the age of five dying in just ninety days and a further 640,000 children acutely malnourished.[28]

U.S. operations in the region, under Operation Enduring Freedom—Horn of Africa, relied heavily on the regional governments, especially the security services, and in turn they were the beneficiaries of American assistance. The Puntland Intelligence Service, for example, of the declared Somali autonomous region, was established with help from the United States in 2001. It is funded by

U.S. and Western intelligence agencies and reportedly receives 50 percent of the budget of the entire state of Puntland.[29]

The United States increasingly relied on the central governments of Somalia's neighboring countries—Djibouti, Ethiopia, and Kenya—that had their own Somali populations. Djibouti became the site of the only U.S. military base in Africa, while Ethiopia and Kenya took the lead in providing the Americans intelligence and logistical support. In late 2011 Kenya, the strongest economic power in East Africa, invaded southern Somalia, claiming that Al Shabab was launching cross-border attacks on Kenyan security forces and kidnapping tourists. The Kenyan military "live-tweeted" its invasion on Twitter so as to warn Somalis of imminent attacks.

The United States had poured millions of dollars into training and funding Kenyan security forces, which since 9/11 had been launching wide dragnet operations against their own Somali periphery. The Kenyan troops were accused of indiscriminately shelling Somali border towns and raping Somali female refugees fleeing the ongoing famine.[30] The number of Somalis arrested by security forces was 1,000 in 2002 (these included hundreds designated as refugees by the United Nations), while 300 were arrested in a single operation in 2010 (including twelve Somali members of Kenya's parliament).[31] Bombings, shootings, grenade attacks, and riots involving Somalis, often leading to mass arrests, became increasingly common in Kenya following its invasion of Somalia.

The Kenyan ethnic Somali town of Garissa, where security forces killed 3,000 people in one incident in 1980 (see chapter 4), became a flashpoint in confrontations between Somalis and the Kenyan central government. In July 2012 masked gunmen attacked two churches in Garissa simultaneously, killing seventeen people, including two policemen, and injuring fifty. In November 2012 three Kenyan soldiers were shot dead in Garissa, and immediately after the killings, the army surrounded the town, beat, detained, and opened fire on civilians, and raped local women.[32] The army set Somali businesses on fire, causing widespread devastation. Shortly thereafter, security forces opened fire on residents protesting the army's behavior, killing a chief who had been working for the government administration and leaving high school students and women with gunshot wounds.[33]

The main Somali neighborhood of Eastleigh in Nairobi also became increasingly volatile, with an IED targeting a civilian bus in November 2012, killing ten people, after which riots broke out. In December 2012 an ethnic Somali member of parliament (MP) in Kenya narrowly escaped with his life when a grenade exploded as he was leaving a mosque in his constituency after evening prayers. The attack killed five people, including a ten-year-old child and a teenager, with thirty-seven people injured, along with the MP, whose legs were fractured. In the days after the attack, Kenyan security forces arrested more than 600 Somalis.

Later that month, the Kenyan government declared that due to an "unbearable and uncontrollable threat to national security," all Somali refugees and those seeking asylum must report to Dadaab refugee camp in the northeast of the country, which already held 400,000 people. An ethnic Somali MP from Garissa and former major general criticized the measure: "This means that the government is saying refugees should be put in to concentration camps. That can't work and is against international law."[34] Relations seem to have completely broken down between the Kenyan center and the Somali periphery.

The United States similarly funded and equipped the security forces in Ethiopia, as well as operated a drone base at Arba Minch in the country's south. Ethiopia received in excess of $2 billion in U.S. funds in the two years following the 2010 national elections, in which the ruling party won 99.6 percent of the parliamentary seats.[35] In 2009 the Ethiopian government passed the Anti-Terrorism Proclamation, which was soon invoked in the arrests of numerous journalists and opposition politicians, including prominent Oromo leaders. A blogger was arrested in September 2011 after criticizing the antiterror laws and calling on the government to respect freedom of expression and end torture in prisons; he was sentenced to eighteen years for "disseminating terrorist ideas." In April 2012 Ethiopia's president told the parliament that al Qaeda was operating in the country's Oromo Arsi and Bale provinces. Ten days later, four people were killed in Arsi when security forces arrested an imam who, the government claimed, was attempting to "instigate *jihad*."[36] In September 2012 Muslims throughout Ethiopia protested against their treatment by the government and called for the release of seventeen Muslim leaders arrested in July 2012 in a security crackdown.

Ethiopia also claimed that its Somali population in the vast region of Ogaden in the east, which had only thirty kilometers of paved roads in 2007, was collaborating with Al Shabab. In particular, it singled out the Somali Ogaden National Liberation Front (ONLF), which had been fighting for Ogaden independence since the 1980s. After 9/11, when Ethiopia invaded Somalia, the ONLF increasingly staged daring strikes, including attacks on government targets and foreign oil workers. The Ethiopian government embarked on a policy of population relocation in the region, giving Somalis two to seven days to move. To ensure compliance, public executions were staged and livestock killed. Civilians who remained in evacuated villages or settlements were in danger of being tortured, raped, or killed if seen by security forces. Between June 2006 and August 2007, at least eighty-seven villages and nomadic settlements were partly or completely burned or forcibly evacuated. The central government planned to forcibly resettle 1.5 million people in four Ethiopian regions by 2013, including those populated by Somalis and Afars.[37]

While the U.S. State Department in 2008 implicated the ONLF in "widespread human rights abuses," it glossed over the crimes of Ethiopian soldiers as occurring when "forces acted independently of government control."[38] In August 2011 the BBC reported that billions of dollars in development aid the West was giving to Ethiopia was being used, in a time of famine, to systematically starve Somalis who opposed the government. An Ogadeni woman told the BBC that Ethiopian security forces had seized her along with 100 people from her village and placed them inside a shipping container, then took them out nightly to be tortured or raped: "They raped me in a room, one of them was standing on my mouth, and one tied my hand, they were taking turns, I fainted during this. . . . I can't say how many, but they were many in the army."[39]

The Kurds, Drones, and the War on Terror

In 2011, the year the drone came into its own as an advanced weapon of war, it found yet another target in the thistle-like Kurds. In December, along the Iraqi border, Turkish media reported the use of U.S. Predator drones in a strike that killed thirty-four Kurdish "smugglers," many of them children as young as twelve, who were members of the Goyan tribe, which had been divided between Turkey and Iraq when the modern international border was drawn.[40] As the Kurds were returning from Iraq to Turkey, laden with food and gasoline and attempting to avoid Turkish soldiers who would confiscate their haul, they were spotted from above by a U.S. drone patrolling the border. Missiles were launched at the Kurds, mistaking them for terrorists. This strike was dubbed the Uludere massacre after their home area and location of the strike.

After 9/11, Turkey sought to associate its war against the Kurdistan Workers' Party (PKK) with the U.S.-led war on terror. Just two months before the Uludere massacre, Turkey's minister for European Union affairs had declared, "What al-Qaeda is to the West, the PKK is to Turkey."[41] This comparison had struck a chord with the United States. The State Department had already appointed retired Air Force general Joseph W. Ralston, a former NATO supreme allied commander and vice chairman of the Joint Chiefs of Staff, as special envoy for countering the PKK in 2006. Drones had been based in Turkey since 2007, when the Bush administration set up a Combined Intelligence Fusion Cell in Ankara, a dimly lit complex where U.S. and Turkish officers, sitting side by side, monitored Predator drone video feeds.[42] In January 2008 President Bush, alongside the Turkish president at the White House, declared the PKK "a common enemy."

In the years following 9/11, Kurds escalated their attacks against the central government. In 2003 suicide bombers struck in Istanbul, targeting synagogues and foreign installations, including banks and the British consulate. Many of the "al Qaeda" operatives that Turkey implicated in the attacks were Kurdish.[43] In 2004 the PKK, which renounced violence in 1999 and hoped to work within the Turkish system for Kurdish rights, renewed its armed campaign after stating that the government was not committed to seriously addressing the concerns of the Kurds. A series of ensuing strikes, including suicide bombings against symbols of the state, were variously blamed on the PKK, al Qaeda, or other groups. In December 2007 Turkey, working with U.S. intelligence, had sent in fifty aircraft to strike at PKK camps in northern Iraq. By 2011 the Turkish army was once again in full counterinsurgency mode. In September of that year, for example, the army announced it had launched an operation against the PKK involving 2,000 troops in the snow-covered mountains of Tunceli.

In addition to its military operations, Turkey enacted draconian antiterrorism laws that accounted for roughly one-third of all global terrorism convictions after 9/11.[44] In 2010 a Turkish court sentenced Mayor Aydin Budak of Cizre, formally the center of the Botan Emirate, to seven and a half years in prison for "committing a crime on behalf of a terrorist organization."[45] The mayor's crime was joining a rally protesting the conditions of PKK head Abdullah Ocalan's incarceration. He could clearly be seen on video stopping youths from throwing stones, but this was not sufficient to lessen his stiff sentence. In March 2012 half of the Cizre city council's twenty-five members were either in prison or fleeing from arrest warrants. In the preceding several years, 630 officials of the locally popular Peace and Democracy Party, including at least 24 mayors and dozens of city council members, were jailed on charges of terrorism and separatism.[46]

Many of the "terrorists" arrested by Turkey were children. Between 2006 and 2007, 1,572 minors were detained and tried under the Anti-Terror Law, with 174 of them convicted.[47] "I never thought I could go to prison for throwing a stone," said a Kurdish teenager who faced twenty-eight years in prison for participating in a protest against Ocalan's prison conditions.[48] These Kurdish children come from a population of between 1 million and 4 million internally displaced Kurds, most living as an urban underclass in cities like Diyarbakir with thousands of abandoned children roaming the streets. Despite government programs designed to facilitate the return of Kurds to their villages, many barriers remained, including the presence of some 1 million land mines in Turkey's southeastern border area.

The United States and the Tausug of the Southern Philippines

Five weeks after the strike on the Kurdish smugglers, U.S. drones were reportedly used in a strike that killed fifteen people on the Tausug island of Jolo in the southern Philippines, the target being accused leaders in the Abu Sayyaf and Jemaah Islamiyah, formed by Indonesians of Yemeni descent in the 1990s. It was not the first reported drone strike in the area's jungles; a Predator drone had launched "a barrage of Hellfire missiles" at an accused "militant camp" in 2006.[49]

Following the 9/11 attacks, the United States sent over 1,000 troops to the Tausug areas to battle Abu Sayyaf, which America linked to al Qaeda. In 2003 the

Bush administration designated the Philippines a major non-NATO ally, equipping and training its security forces as part of Operation Enduring Freedom—Philippines. U.S. troops served in a support capacity, staying out of combat. Still, two U.S. troops were killed in a roadside bombing on Jolo Island in 2009. The United States accused Abu Sayyaf of not only having al Qaeda links, but also of providing a "safe haven" to foreign terrorists.

Abu Sayyaf was established in the early 1990s by a charismatic Tausug preacher, Abdurajak Abubakar Janjalani, whose speeches attracted angry young men in a community rife with orphans owing to the previous decades of war. Abu Sayyaf was subsequently blamed for kidnappings, bombings, and beheadings, gripping the nation with sensational headlines. Despite constant coverage in the Philippine and Western press, there are serious questions as to whether Abu Sayyaf exists. The Philippine military, writes scholar Eduardo F. Ugarte who conducted a study of Abu Sayyaf, "is often quick to ascribe many crimes and virtually all acts of terrorism in the region to the 'Abu Sayyaf' without evidence."[50]

In an interview, Ghalib Andang, described as a senior member of Abu Sayyaf and known as Commander Robot, stated that "Abu Sayyaf is just a name." Humanitarian workers kidnapped in 2009 reported that their "Abu Sayyaf" captor told them "I can be ASG [Abu Sayyaf], I can be MILF, I can be Lost Command [MILF or MNLF breakaway group]."[51] Another question surrounds the number of fighters cited by government and media sources. Abu Sayyaf has been described as consisting of variously anywhere between 11 fighters and 300, 500, 1,000, 3,000, 5,000, and so on.[52]

In Ugarte's assessment, Abu Sayyaf is nothing more than what anthropologists refer to as a "minimal alliance group," or a clan, of Tausug kinsmen. In this case, Abu Sayyaf represented the clan of the group's founder. The most obvious example in support of this position is the founder's brothers, who were all associated with the group. Uncles and nephews were involved in one high-profile kidnapping in 1993, and in her memoir of her captivity with Abu Sayyaf from 2001 to 2002, Gracia Burnham observed that two brothers and their nephew were among her captors.[53] Ugarte wrote that these groups have been "a staple of the unsettled conditions in the Philippine South for over a century."[54]

The Philippine security forces have been noted for brutality in their operations against Abu Sayyaf suspects, justification for their actions falling within the frame of the war on terror. In March 2005 Philippine Special Forces were called after a group of alleged Abu Sayyaf detainees barricaded themselves inside the Camp Bagong Diwa prison near Manila following the killing of three guards in an alleged escape attempt. Special Forces stormed the prison and killed twenty-two prisoners. In spite of this blatant misuse of authority, President Gloria Macapagal-Arroyo praised the security forces for showing that "terrorism will never win in the Philippines." Her press secretary, Ignacio Bunye, added, "The terrorists got what was coming to them."[55] However, an investigation by the Philippine Commission on Human Rights condemned the security forces for summarily executing prisoners and found the entire operation unnecessary because no life was in danger at the time of the assault.[56]

Drone strikes have shattered entire Muslim tribal communities, and there is no sign of the campaign abating. On the contrary, every indication is that the frequency and span of drone strikes are increasing. For these communities, their overriding idea and impression of the United States comes through the deadly contact made when a drone blows them apart.

THE U.S. TERROR NETWORK

Drones were, however, only one part of the American strategy in the war on terror. Another was to operate through national governments across the world and their all-too-pliable leaders. Together, the United States and these governments formed a global terror network involving drones, rendition, and comprehensive initiatives to shore up the central governments, especially their security and military capacities.

What came to be known as rendition became one of the most widely discussed, sinister, and controversial aspects of the war on terror. National governments found the vulnerability of their own peripheral communities an easy way to collect reward money from Americans who had placed bounties on the heads of any suspected terrorist while also gaining U.S. favor. American gullibility and the venality of national leaders combined to destroy the lives of millions of ordinary people on the periphery.

If there was any doubt in my mind about the role of Muslim leaders in this regard, former president Musharraf removed it in his interview with Stephen Sackur on the BBC's *HARDtalk* in November 2011. Sackur accused Musharraf of "playing both sides." Cut to the quick, an angry Musharraf retorted that he had successfully killed the entire range of the "terrorist" leadership from number three downward and captured and handed over large numbers destined for Guantánamo Bay. In this emotional exchange, Musharraf exposed himself perhaps more than he wished. He admitted on record that he was responsible for the deaths of many without trial and the capture of even more to be sent for torture in the dark maze that is the U.S. terror prison network. Musharraf did not have to tell the audience about the reward money he collected in handing over the so-called terrorists. He had done that in his autobiography.[57] Musharraf had confirmed what I had heard about Pakistan having one of the worst human rights records, especially in dealing with unsuspecting Muslim visitors to the country. Whether they were genuine Somali students, Yemeni visitors, or Chinese waiters at a restaurant, they were peremptorily picked up, hooded, and chained as Muslim terrorists and handed over to Americans to be flown to unknown destinations. In its inefficiency and transparent unfairness, this was an operation worthy of the Keystone Cops, except that it was no laughing matter. The violation of justice never is.

Musharraf's position on drone strikes in Pakistan was equally ambiguous. Publicly he denied giving permission to the Americans for their use but privately handed over the Shamsi Airfield in western Baluchistan to the United States as a base for drones. The policy of Pakistani duplicity was continued by Musharraf's successors. "I don't care if they do it as long as they get the right people," former prime minister Syed Yusuf Raza Gilani reportedly said in August 2008, according to documents released by WikiLeaks. "We'll protest in the national assembly and then ignore it."[58] Gilani was reflecting the position of President Asif Ali Zardari, who was described as a "numbskull" by the British air chief marshal Sir Jock Stirrup in the same documents.

Pakistanis who still cared for their national honor were appalled by what they saw as the perfidy of their leaders. "The Musharraf years were so shameful," Imran Khan, the Pakistani cricket star and politician, told the *New York Times*. "The Westoxified Pakistanis have been selling their souls and killing their own people for a few million dollars. And then the Americans come in with shady deals to bring Benazir Bhutto back and let crooked people like Zardari go scot-free. I was so disgusted, and if I hadn't been in politics I would have left Pakistan."[59]

The actions of the Pakistani leaders were impacting Pakistanis everywhere, including someone like me in Washington. An amiable Uyghur driver and his companion, driving me home in a taxi late at night, suddenly transformed when they heard I was from Pakistan. They said Pakistan, of all the Muslim countries, was the worst as it captured anyone from their community who escaped persecution in China and returned them to certain torture and death. What sort of Muslims are you Pakistanis, they said bitterly, leaving me speechless and uncomfortable. No doubt had I been driven by an Afghan, a Chechen, Somali, or Yemeni driver, they would have expressed similar sentiments about Pakistan. It was clear to me that Pakistan's zealous rounding up of virtually all "foreigners" after 9/11, declaring them to be "terrorists" and handing them over to Americans for payment, did not go unnoticed and earned it loathing and anger in the Muslim world.

Torture and the Black Hole of Rendition

Shortly before 9/11, Uyghurs fleeing from Chinese persecution had established a community in the Tora Bora region of southern Afghanistan. According to reports and testimony from the Uyghurs, it was an expatriate village populated by people with a wide variety of backgrounds, including educators and businessmen. There was limited weapons training in the event that some of the Uyghurs would return in the future to Xinjiang to fight the Chinese. Some later reported that they had either never fired a gun or had only one or two lessons. One Uyghur, Abdul Nasser, claimed the entire camp had only one gun: "I don't know if it was an AK-47. It was an old rifle, and I trained for a couple of days."[60]

When the United States invaded Afghanistan after 9/11, it identified the Uyghur village as an al Qaeda training camp. U.S. planes bombed the camp and sent the unarmed Uyghurs fleeing toward Pakistan. While hiding across the border, the Uyghurs were first welcomed and then betrayed to Pakistani authorities by Shia villagers who had heard of American bounties for al Qaeda suspects. The United States paid the villagers $5,000 for each Uyghur, who was then flown to Guantánamo Bay as an "enemy combatant." Twenty-two Uyghurs were soon imprisoned there.

While the United States accused the Uyghurs of being al Qaeda operatives, the detainees claimed they had never heard of al Qaeda until they arrived in Guantánamo.[61] The Uyghurs were confused as to why they were there as they admired the United States. As one detainee explained, "From the time of our great-grandparents centuries ago, we have never been against the United States and we do not want to be against the United States. I can represent for 25 million Uighur people by saying that we will not do anything against the United States. We are willing to be united with the United States."[62] Another Uyghur said he entered Afghanistan "to escape from the torturing, darkness and suffering of the Chinese government," and "wanted to go to some other country to live in peace." He further stated, "The [Chinese] government, if they suspect us for anything, would torture and beat us, and fine us money. Lately, the young Uighurs would get caught just doing exercising. They would stop us and say it was not our culture, and put us in jail for it. For the females, if they have [more than] one child, they open them up and throw the baby in the trash."[63]

The Chinese government and the United States worked together to interrogate the Uyghurs in Guantánamo. Before the arrival of the Chinese, U.S. interrogators kept the Uyghurs from sleeping for long periods, deprived them of food, and exposed them to freezing temperatures for hours on end.[64] After U.S. troops had "prepared" the Uyghurs for interrogation, the Chinese arrived to threaten them with torture. Chinese authorities informed one detainee that he would be "beaten, and eventually killed" when they were allowed to take him back to China. After years of interrogating the Uyghurs and subjecting them to conditions their lawyer described as "nightmarish," the United States admitted it had no case against them.[65] Yet many countries would not take in the high-profile detainees, fearing retaliation from China if they did. China was not a possibility as U.S. law, ironically, considering what was happening in Guantánamo, forbids sending anyone to a country where they could be tortured or killed. Six were resettled in Palau in the Pacific, four in Bermuda, five in Albania, two in Switzerland, and two in El Salvador. Three Uyghurs were still in Guantánamo at the time of writing.

When the Obama administration announced it was considering resettling Uyghur detainees in the United States, there was a public backlash. Prominent U.S. politicians like Newt Gingrich, the former Speaker of the U.S. House of Representatives, called the Uyghurs "trained mass killers," contending that they were "instructed by the same terrorists responsible for killing 3,000 Americans on September 11, 2001" and possessed the "ideology of mass killing."[66] When Senator Lindsey Graham was asked if there were lawmakers advocating for the release of the Uyghurs in the United States, he replied bluntly: "The Uyghur caucus is pretty small."[67]

Apart from the Uyghurs, other tribal peoples caught in Pakistan's bounty dragnets included the Kabyle Berbers of Algeria. Djamel Ameziane was one such Kabyle Berber. He had fled Algerian oppression against his people first to Austria, where he was a chef at an Italian restaurant, and then, when his visa was not renewed, to Canada, where he sought asylum but was rejected. In 2000 he went to Afghanistan because he believed that as a Muslim he would not face discrimination. When the U.S. bombing began, he fled to Pakistan, where he was subsequently captured by Pakistani police and sold to the United States for a bounty. Ameziane was then sent to Guantánamo Bay, where his lawyers reported he was tortured by U.S. troops. In one instance, "guards entered his cell and forced him to the floor, kneeing him in the back and ribs and slamming his head against the floor, turning it left and right. The bashing dislocated Mr. Ameziane's jaw, an injury he still suffers. In the same episode, guards sprayed cayenne pepper all over his body and then hosed him down with water to accentuate the effect of the pepper spray and make his skin burn. They then held his head back and placed a water hose between his nose and mouth, running it for several minutes over his face and suffocating him, an operation they repeated several times. Mr. Ameziane writes, 'I had the impression that my head was sinking in water. I still have psychological injuries, up to this day. Simply thinking of it gives me the chills.'"[68] He was never charged with any crime and was still imprisoned at the time of writing.

The extent of linkages between the U.S. terror network and central governments around the world and the depth of U.S. misunderstanding of its enemy can be best demonstrated by the case of Cyrenaica tribesman Ibn al-Sheikh al-Libi (born Ali Mohamed al-Fakheri) of Ajdabiya, Libya, formerly a major Sanusi center on the Mediterranean coast. Al-Libi had gone to Afghanistan to fight the Soviet forces in the 1980s.[69] After the war, he joined the Libyan Islamic Fighting Group, which waged an insurgency against Gaddafi from the mountains of Cyrenaica. In the 1990s he became the head of a training camp in Afghanistan called Khaldun, where he trained mujahideen from around the world.

Following the U.S. invasion of Afghanistan, al-Libi crossed into Pakistan, where he was captured in November 2001 by Pakistani forces. Musharraf turned him over to the Americans, who imprisoned him in Bagram Air Base in Afghanistan. During FBI interrogations, it was revealed that al-Libi disagreed with bin Laden over the targets, believing that only nations that had invaded Muslim countries should be included. Yet just as al-Libi was warming to a devout Christian FBI agent, a CIA official ran into the cell, screaming, "You're going to Egypt! And while you're there, I'm going to find your mother, and fuck her!"[70] Shortly thereafter, CIA and U.S. military personnel tied him down on a stretcher and duct-taped his mouth. He was put in the back of a pickup truck, transferred to a plane, and flown to the USS *Bataan* in the Arabian Sea. From there, al-Libi was renditioned to Egypt.

In Cairo, al-Libi and two Egyptian nationals whom the CIA had picked up from an airport in Sweden were sent to the Scorpion maximum-security prison. The two Egyptians have since said through lawyers and family members that "almost immediately upon disembarking from the U.S. jet, they were tortured with excruciatingly painful jolts of electrical charges to their genitals, under the watchful supervision of a medical doctor."[71] One of them stated that "he was forced to lie on an electrified bed frame." Other prisoners renditioned by the CIA to Egypt were hung from metal hooks, had their fingers broken, and were submerged in water up to their nostrils.[72]

CIA director George Tenant wrote that al-Libi was renditioned to Egypt to receive such treatment because "we believed al-Libi was withholding critical threat information," and thus a "further debriefing" was necessary.[73] It emerged that the United States, then putting together a case to invade Iraq, wanted al-Libi to provide a connection between al Qaeda and Saddam Hussein, despite the fact that he had never been to Iraq. Under torture at the Scorpion prison, he was pressured by the Egyptians to provide information on such a relationship. When al-Libi insisted he knew of no connection, they locked him in a tiny cage in what has been described as a "mock burial" for more than eighty hours. Although he still said he knew of no connection, they "knocked him over and punched him for fifteen minutes." When they again asked him about connections between Saddam Hussein and al Qaeda, he made up a story, as he later admitted, to stop the torture. He told the interrogators that three al Qaeda figures, whose names he knew, had traveled to Iraq "to learn about nuclear weapons."[74]

The Egyptians were not satisfied and "pressed him about Saddam Hussein supplying al Qaeda with anthrax and other biological weapons." Al-Libi "knew nothing about the subject and didn't understand the term 'biological'" so was unable to make up a further story. He was beaten once again. He then made up further details, which were sent to the office of Vice President Dick Cheney and used in the crucial months leading up to the U.S. invasion of Iraq. In October

2002 President Bush cited al-Libi's fabrications to an audience in Cincinnati: "We've learned that Iraq has trained Al Qaeda members in bomb making and poisons and deadly gases."[75]

In February 2003 Secretary of State Colin Powell used this same citation in a globally televised speech to the United Nations Security Council, making the argument that America must wage a preemptive war against Iraq. Powell stated that "a senior terrorist operative" who "was responsible for one of Al Qaeda's training camps in Afghanistan" had confessed that Saddam Hussein offered to train two al Qaeda members in the use of "chemical or biological weapons." Powell asserted confidently that "every statement" of his was "based on solid intelligence . . . from human sources."[76]

After "confessing," al-Libi was sent back to Afghanistan. Almost a full year after Powell's speech, the CIA confronted al-Libi with information from other detainees that contradicted his claims, and he admitted that he had made the whole thing up. Al-Libi then disappeared. In April 2009 a team from Human Rights Watch was stunned to discover al-Libi in Tripoli's Abu Salim prison during a fact-finding mission to Libya. Two weeks later, he was dead. The Gaddafi government announced that al-Libi had hung himself. It soon emerged that the United States had flown him to Libya in 2006. Before this, al-Libi had reportedly also been transported by the CIA to Morocco, Jordan, and Mauritania before reaching his final destination of Tripoli.[77] Al-Libi was buried in May 2009 in his Cyrenaica home of Ajdabiya. His funeral was attended by thousands.

Cooperation between Gaddafi and the United States began shortly after the 9/11 attacks. Just weeks afterward, Musa Kusa, the Libyan intelligence chief who was accused of coordinating the 1988 Lockerbie bombing, met with CIA agents in London and provided intelligence on the Libyan Islamic Fighting Group and its connections to Afghanistan. The Bush administration put the Libyan Islamic Fighting Group on its list of terrorist organizations. Libya's new relationship with the United States meant that any Libyans who were captured in countries like Egypt or Pakistan could be renditioned back to Libya.[78] Libyan agents were also granted access to captured Libyan suspects in Guantánamo Bay.

With the alliance of Gaddafi and President Bush, tribal fighters from Cyrenaica branched out around the world to fight American interests in places like Iraq. Libyans formed the third-largest group of "jihadists" there, behind Iraqis and Saudis, a startling statistic given Cyrenaica's small population.[79] Of these, more than half came from one eastern Cyrenaica city, Derna, which is surrounded by mountains with deep caves, and it is from where the Libyan Islamic Fighting Group drew heavily for its membership.[80] Of the roughly 1,200 people killed by Gaddafi at Tripoli's Abu Salim jail in 1996, 100 were from Derna.[81]

Other figures from Cyrenaica prominently involved in the war on terror include the Islamic scholar Mohamed Hassan Qaid, also known as Abu Yahya al-Libi, who was associated with the Libyan Islamic Fighting Group and went to Afghanistan in the 1990s. After 9/11 he was captured by the Pakistanis and handed over to the United States and imprisoned in Bagram Air Base. In 2005 he escaped and is believed to have crossed into the Tribal Areas, where he issued videos on behalf of al Qaeda, frequently commenting on what he described as injustices facing Muslims across the Islamic world from Libya and Somalia to Xinjiang. Yahya al-Libi's view of America, which he called on Muslims to fight, was shaped by his experience in prison. Abu Ghraib, he said in one video, is "insignificant" compared with what happens to "the Mujahid brothers in the American prisons." Yahya al-Libi explains the ordeal prisoners face: "First of all, methods of torture are unlimited. That is, the primary goal of the interrogators is extracting information, and their hands are free when it comes to the way they extract this information—i.e., they stop at nothing. And everything you could possibly imagine has been suffered by the Mujahideen. The worst thing we could possibly mention in this regard is violation of honor."[82] In June 2012 he was killed in a U.S. drone strike in Waziristan. At the time of his death, he was described as "Al Qaeda's No. 2."

Central Asian governments as well became important allies in the war on terror, particularly given their proximity to Afghanistan. Islam Karimov, the president of Uzbekistan, firmly allied himself with President Bush, who saw Uzbekistan as a strategic partner directly bordering Afghanistan to the north. In 2001 the United States established an air base in Uzbekistan to support its operations in Afghanistan. The two presidents signed an agreement in Washington in March 2002 giving Uzbekistan security guarantees in strengthening "the material and technical base of [their] law enforcement agencies." That year, Uzbekistan received $500 million in U.S. aid. Of this amount, $79 million went to the Uzbek police and intelligence services known to use "torture as a routine investigation technique," and at a time when it was estimated that 6,500 political prisoners were in custody, with numbers of them dying, including two who were boiled to death in August 2002.[83] The country was long known for its medieval interrogation methods, which included, in addition to boiling people, raping prisoners with broken bottles and ripping off fingernails and toenails with pliers.

Tashkent, the Uzbek capital, became a major thoroughfare and site of CIA rendition, which turned over terror suspects to Uzbek government officials for interrogation. Craig Murray, the former British ambassador to Uzbekistan, stated that during 2003 and early 2004 "C.I.A. flights flew to Tashkent often, usually twice a week."[84] The U.S. air base at Manas International Airport near Bishkek, Kyrgyzstan, established in December 2001 to support operations in Afghanistan, had also been reported as a transit site for flights carrying terror suspects to rendition facilities.[85]

In 2004, however, the United States placed restrictions on military aid to Uzbekistan as a result of the country's consistently poor human rights record.

The following year an estimated 1,500 civilians were killed by Uzbek security forces firing directly into a peaceful protest, an incident that came to be known as the Andijan massacre. U.S. bases in Uzbekistan were closed the same year. There the matter stood, until in December 2011 the U.S. Congress removed restrictions on military aid to Uzbekistan. In October that year a State Department official accompanying Secretary of State Hillary Clinton to the country told reporters that "President Karimov commented that he wants to make progress on liberalization and democratization, and he said that he wants to leave a legacy of that for his — both his kids and his grandchildren." When a reporter questioned the sincerity of this statement, the official replied, "Yeah. I do believe him."[86]

This glowing endorsement of Karimov came just months after the State Department released a report on the deplorable human rights situation in the country. It stated, "Sources reported that torture and abuse were common in prisons, pretrial facilities, and local police and security service precincts. Reported methods of torture included severe beatings, denial of food, sexual abuse, tying and hanging by the hands, and electric shock." The report also cited a letter from 121 prisoners in Uzbekistan to a human rights group that claimed, "Guards routinely raped the prisoners with a club, subjected prisoners to enemas with red pepper solutions, and beat their heels until they bled."[87]

The war on terror and acts of rendition saw the United States working with governments it was not normally associated with. The Gambia, led by President Yahya Jammeh, established itself as a loyal ally of President Bush after 9/11 and became a site of rendition. Just as Jammeh was committing a series of outrages against Gambians that would include torture and dragnets to capture "witches" (see chapter 4), Bush would, unaware of the irony, offer him high praise:

> Let me also take this opportunity to express my appreciation for The Gambia's steadfast support for the ongoing war against terrorism. President Jammeh has sent a powerful message that the fight against terrorism is a cause embraced by all freedom-loving people around the world. . . . We note The Gambia's improved human rights record, and hope that your country continues on the path of protecting the rights of all your citizens. The Gambia has also [focused] during the past year on fighting corruption and improving governance.[88]

In November 2002 Gambian authorities, as part of their involvement in the U.S. war on terror, arrested three U.K. residents, Bisher al-Rawi, Wahab al-Rawi, and Jamil al-Banna, on terrorist charges at the airport in the Gambian capital, Banjul. Bisher and Jamil had been previously detained at London's Gatwick Airport after being discovered with what was thought to be a component of an explosive device, an incident the U.S. intelligence was informed of. This device was later determined to be a battery charger, and the men were released to continue their journey to The Gambia. The United Kingdom sent a second message to U.S. intelligence, giving the men's flight details and associating them with the Muslim cleric Abu Qatada, whom the British accused of terrorism links. In the message, however, the United Kingdom stated, "This information is being communicated in confidence . . . should not be released without the agreement of the British government. It is for research and analysis purposes only and should not be used as the basis for overt or covert action."[89] After the men were arrested in Banjul, the Gambian National Intelligence Agency and U.S. officials questioned them for the next month in several undisclosed locations in the city. The United States accused the men of coming to The Gambia to establish terrorist training camps, while they claimed to be legitimate businessmen seeking to invest in a peanut oil factory. Wahab, a U.K. citizen, was released, but Bisher and Jamil had their clothes ripped off, had diapers put on, were blindfolded and gagged and taken to a plane in chains, then flown to the CIA's "Dark Prison" in Kabul. They were imprisoned in isolation and darkness, held in leg shackles for twenty-four hours a day, starved, and beaten.[90] While interrogating Jamil about possible links between Abu Qatada and al Qaeda, an American official screamed, "I am going to London. You know why? I am going to FUCK your wife! Your wife is going to be my BITCH! Maybe you'll never see your children again."[91] Bisher and Jamil were then flown to Guantánamo Bay in early 2003.[92] In 2007 they were released to the United Kingdom without any charges having been brought against them.

The United States found itself in dalliance with other strange bedfellows, including Malawi, Zimbabwe, and Sudan, which became willing partners in the U.S. terror network. In June 2003 Khalifa Abdi Hassan, a Kenyan scholar of Somali background working as a teacher in the small southeastern African nation of Malawi, was arrested at his home. In the middle of the night, dozens of security agents seized him, and he disappeared along with two Turks, one Saudi, and one Sudanese. The wife of Arif Ulusam, one of the Turks arrested, was distraught when her husband disappeared and said their daughter, not yet three, "misses her father so much, she puts on his shoes, kisses his shirts. . . .They said Arif would be released the next day, but when we went to the police station he wasn't there and nobody could tell us anything."[93] The Malawian lawyer hired by the families declared, "I've never been as depressed on a case as this one. No evidence was ever produced."[94] A Malawi high court judge barred the deportation of the men, ordering the government to charge them or release them on bail, yet by this time, they had already disappeared into the U.S. terror network. Malawi's director of public prosecutions, exasperated, asked the court, "Who can I produce in court now? Their ghosts? These people are out of reach for us. It's the Americans who know where they are." The abductions caused violent unrest among Malawi's Muslim community, which necessitated the deployment of the army to quell the rioting.

It soon emerged that the CIA had renditioned the men to Zimbabwe, where they were held for one month. They were subsequently flown to Khartoum, Sudan. They were questioned about connections to al Qaeda and bin Laden before being released after U.S. officials concluded they had no association with terrorists.

Macedonia, which was quick to label any unrest in its own tribal Muslim Albanian periphery as the work of "terrorists" or "Wahhabis," also became linked with the U.S. rendition network. In 2002 the Macedonian government submitted a seventy-nine-page report to the U.S. National Security Council on al Qaeda activity among the Albanians in the northwest of the country, which included the presence of "foreign fighters" from Turkey, Saudi Arabia, and other places who, the government said, had trained in Afghanistan.[95] In December 2003 Macedonian officials arrested Khaled el-Masri, a German citizen of Lebanese descent who was in Macedonia on vacation. He was questioned for twenty-three days in Skopje, where he was accused of attending a terrorist training camp, holding a fake passport, and being Egyptian.[96] He ended up in the custody of the CIA, eventually being sent to a secret prison in Kabul. After being tortured for four months, during which time he claimed to have been sodomized, el-Masri was flown to Albania and released on a desolate road in the middle of the night without money, resources, or even proper clothes. Khaled el-Masri's only crime, it appears, was that his name sounded similar to that of someone on some terrorist list.

For those caught within the U.S. terror network's dragnets, age and citizenship did not matter. Omar Khadr, a Canadian citizen, was captured in Afghanistan in 2002 at the age of fifteen and transferred to Guantánamo Bay. Khadr was born in Toronto and divided his childhood between Peshawar and Canada. His father, an Egyptian Canadian, had brought his family to Afghanistan in 1996. The United Nations' special representative for children and armed conflict referred to Khadr as the "classic child soldier narrative: recruited by unscrupulous groups to undertake actions at the bidding of adults to fight battles they barely understand" and stated that he should be returned to Canada.[97]

A surveillance video declassified by a Canadian court shows his interrogation by Canadian intelligence officials while in Guantánamo. In the interrogation video, Khadr refers to his treatment in captivity. When one of the interrogator asks him, "So everything you told the Americans was because they tortured you?" his response was, "Yes . . . everything is not true." He then lifted his shirt to show bruising from his treatment at the hands of the Americans. He cried out, "I can't move my arms and all of these. . . . Is this healthy? I requested medical over a long time. They don't do anything about it."[98] When left alone in his cell after a particularly aggressive interrogation session, Khadr broke down in tears, covering his face with his hands, and whimpered repeatedly like a child, "*amee, amee,*" a widely used term for mother. In September 2012 Khadr was repatriated to Canada to serve out the remainder of his sentence after 3,619 days in captivity at Guantánamo Bay.

These are but a few examples of how the United States abandoned its foundational principles dedicated to upholding human rights, civil liberties, and the rule of law in pursuit of "terrorists" and in that regard implemented misguided security measures.

The Ever-Expanding Universe of the Terror Network

The U.S. terror network is not confined to drones and rendition. It includes a range of direct U.S. involvement with central governments, including providing military aid, deploying U.S. Special Forces, forming regional security alliances, training local security forces, providing military technology, sharing intelligence, and otherwise aiding and bolstering central governments in assaulting their periphery. In addition, by joining the terror network, governments are given the added benefit of accessing the benefits of globalization. As noted earlier, cooperation between the United States and central governments surrounding Somalia, for example, included drones, the presence of U.S. Special Forces, and an extensive rendition network between the countries, under which terror suspects were held on ships off the coast. West Africa had a similar network among the Sahel countries, formed after 9/11. Algeria is a pivotal nation in this network as it is a central power in the Sahel battling what is known as "Al Qaeda in the Islamic Maghreb," with its base in the mountainous Kabyle Berber region. The tribes of this area have remained a troubled periphery to the Algerian Arab-dominated center ever since independence.

The strongest organization after the violence subsided in the Algerian civil war in the late 1990s was the Salafist Group for Preaching and Combat (GSPC) led by Hassan Hattab, a Kabyle Berber. From their bases in the Kabyle mountains, Hattab's fighters, including many who had battled the Soviet invaders in Afghanistan, continued attacks against Algerian security forces. Algeria declared its support for the U.S. war on terror after 9/11, and several weeks later President Bush included the GSPC on a list of groups that "commit, threaten to commit, or support terrorism."

Algeria's significance also derives from its nomadic Tuareg population in the south, which extends deep into the Sahel widely considered an "ungoverned space" par excellence. In November 2002 the United States announced the Pan-Sahel Initiative (PSI) to assist in improving the border security and counterterrorism capabilities of Mauritania, Mali, Niger, and Chad, equipping their militaries, and enhancing intelligence sharing.

The United States began to focus on Algeria, however, when in 2003 thirty-two European tourists were kidnapped and half of them moved to Mali and then northern Chad by the shadowy Amari Saifi, or El Para, associated with GSPC.

U.S. Special Forces took swift action, flying U.S. aircraft over the Sahel and forming an unprecedented team of security forces from several regional countries that scoured the desert in search of El Para.

Following the incident, the United States relaxed its arms embargo on Algeria, which was still under martial law, and announced the sale of counterterrorism equipment to the country. William Burns, assistant secretary of state for Near Eastern Affairs, had stated in Algiers in 2002, "Washington has much to learn from Algeria on ways to fight terrorism."[99] By 2004 U.S. Special Forces were stationed on Algerian soil to train, equip, and assist local forces in the pursuit of the GSPC.

In 2005 the United States expanded its regional engagement further with the creation of the Trans-Sahara Counterterrorism Initiative (TSCTI), enlarging the PSI with funding of $500 million to cover five additional countries—Algeria, Morocco, Nigeria, Senegal, and Tunisia—and with the support of 1,000 U.S. Special Forces soldiers. In 2007 the United States created an African command at the Pentagon, called AFRICOM, tasked with containing threats like the GSPC, and launched Operation Enduring Freedom—Trans Sahara. The FBI opened an office in Algiers with the bureau's director of international relations describing the relationship between the United States and Algeria, as well as France, as "an extended family."[100] By this time, though, media outlets were casting doubt on the very basis of the relationship between the United States and Algeria by questioning the identity of El Para. An investigation by the French newspaper *Le Monde diplomatique* concluded that El Para was an agent of the Algerian government.[101]

GSPC, which took the name Al Qaeda in the Islamic Maghreb (AQIM) in early 2007, had already established roots in the Tuareg region, where its members had ingratiated themselves with local tribes. GSPC leader Mokhtar Belmokhtar, for example, had married the daughter of a Tuareg chief in the 1990s after returning from Afghanistan and was reported to have taken additional wives from other tribes, whose allegiance helped secure smuggling operations. Despite the presence of certain people associated with GSPC, such as Belmokhtar in the Sahel, most of the attacks blamed on the group were located in and around its original base in the Kabyle mountains. These included the December 2007 bombing of UN headquarters in Algiers that killed thirty-seven people and an August 2008 suicide bombing of a police academy in Issers that killed forty-three people, most of them civilian recruits, with an attack the following day on the regional military command center and a hotel in the Kabylie Bouira region that killed eleven people. Following a July 2010 suicide bombing that killed thirty-six Algerian soldiers in Tizi Ouzou, the center of Kabyle culture and society, the group announced it had targeted the soldiers "in revenge for the deaths of our Kabylie brothers and children" in the town of Beni Douala, where a 2001 killing of a teenager by security forces had led to massive riots (see chapter 4).[102] Even as this instability in

A U.S. soldier trains Malian troops to use an automatic grenade launcher in 2006 (Department of Defense).

the Kabyle region continued, most international attention focused on the small number of operatives who had been kidnapping Western tourists in the deserts of the Sahel.

Across the border in Mali, a country that is part of the United States' TSCTI, the Tuareg launched yet another rebellion in 2006, led by Iyad Ag Ghali of the Kel Adrar tribal confederation of Kidal. The area is one of the most inhospitable of the Sahel and was the launching pad for the rebellions in 1963 and 1990. The 2006 rebellion began following the violation of Tuareg women by government security forces.[103] The role of the United States in backing the central governments of the region was demonstrated when, during a Tuareg siege of a remote Mali army outpost on the Algerian border in 2007, Mali troops called for American support. A U.S. Air Force C-130 aircraft arrived to drop some 14,000 pounds of food to the beleaguered Mali garrison. The Tuareg opened fire on the plane, inflicting minor damage.

In early 2012 the Tuareg again rebelled and began to take control of the vast area of north Mali, roughly the size of France. Battles with security forces displaced 200,000 people. The United States attempted to aid Mali troops with C-130s, but this time the security forces could not hold out, and the government fell in a military coup, leaving the Tuareg to declare their own independent state, which they named Azawad, "land of transhumance," after their tribal territory and identity. Two Tuareg groups emerged, the nationalist National Movement for the Liberation of Azawad (MNLA) and the religious group Ansar Dine. The MNLA was led by Mohammed Ag Najm, whose father had been killed by the Malian army in 1963, and Ansar Dine was led by Ag Ghali. On October 12, 2012, the UN Security Council adopted a resolution to begin preparations for an international military intervention in northern Mali in early 2013, with the support of the African Union. France, taking a leading role, announced shortly afterward the deployment of French surveillance drones to the region. In December 2012 the Obama administration announced that the U.S. military was working with surrounding nations to plan an offensive against "al-Qaeda and affiliates."[104] In 2013 France launched airstrikes in Mali.

In Azerbaijan, security forces also began to crack down on "terrorists" and "Wahhabis" in the country for links with al Qaeda, many of them from the northern Lezgin and Avar periphery. A number of those arrested were sent to Russia. In the months after 9/11, Azerbaijan, working with the United States, rendered "dozens of foreign citizens with suspected ties to terrorists."[105] In January 2002 President Bush waived U.S. restrictions for aid to Azerbaijan in the interests of counterterrorism. Azerbaijan allowed the United States to use its air space and airports for military operations in Afghanistan. The U.S. State Department declared that "Azerbaijan is a logical route for extremists with ties to terrorist organizations."[106]

Rovsan Novruzoglu, the director of the Azerbaijani Public Center to Combat International Terrorism, cautioned in April 2005: "The spread of Wahhabism has reached threatening proportions in six Azerbaijani districts—Balakan, Zaqatala, Qax, Qabala, Saki, and Qusar," all areas on the northern periphery with substantial numbers of Lezgins and Avars.[107] In 2007 the Azerbaijan government announced the capture of a terrorist network and named the U.S. embassy in Baku as one of its potential targets, along with "several state structures in Baku, embassies and missions of the countries which are members of the international anti-terror coalition."[108] Many Islamic charities were also shut down in the antiterror operations. The government demolished, closed, or raided mosques, and seized religious literature. There were reports of mass arrests, torture, and the forcible burning or shaving of beards.[109] In Zaqatala, many tribesmen were required to come to police stations daily for "beard check-ups" to ensure they did not have beards.[110]

In June 2011 Azerbaijan sentenced a group of seventeen "militants" to jail terms stretching to life in prison for "links to al Qaeda."[111] In April 2012 security forces conducted operations across the country in which weapons and "literature that promotes terrorism and jihad" were seized, with the majority of those arrested having Lezgin names.[112] The government announced that the Zaqatala-born Vugar Padarov, who the government claimed led a terrorist group trained by al Qaeda, had been killed during the operation, despite reports circulated by the political opposition claiming that Padarov had been dead for five years.[113]

In 2003 America's terror network even implicated the Cham in Cambodia. Many of the Islamic and Arab NGOs that arrived in Cambodia to help rebuild religious institutions lost during the Khmer Rouge period found themselves on the U.S. list of organizations accused of supporting al Qaeda and terrorism. These included the International Islamic Relief Organization and the al-Haramayn Islamic Foundation.[114] A school near Phnom Penh sponsored by one of these NGOs, Umm al-Qura, was shut down after American intelligence reports linked its Egyptian director and two of the school's Thai teachers with Jemaah Islamiyah and al Qaeda, "possibly even Osama bin Laden."[115] The three men were arrested by Cambodian police in May 2003. The remainder of the school's foreign teachers—twenty-eight in all from Egypt, Nigeria, Pakistan, Sudan, Thailand, and Yemen—were deported along with their families. In June 2003 Sman Ismael, a Cham from Kampot, was arrested for connections with this school.[116] A non-American diplomat, quoted anonymously the same month just before a national election, summed it up: "There are only four things the Americans care about in Cambodia: Wahabis, Wahabis, Wahabis, and the elections—in that order."[117] The arrest of Ismael came days before U.S. Secretary of State Colin Powell was scheduled to attend a meeting of the Association of Southeast Asian Nations in Phnom Penh. A Cham leader believed the arrests were a political maneuver to "woo the Americans." The efforts of the central government to close down schools accused of "terrorism" angered the Cham, with Cham MP Ahmad Yahya referring to Cambodian prime minister Hun Sen, a former member of the Khmer Rouge, as a "second Pol Pot," because "he used to close schools as well."[118]

In 2006 the FBI caused controversy in Cambodia when it gave a medal for counterterrorism to General Hok Lundy, Cambodia's chief of police. Lundy was widely despised and feared in Cambodia and referred to by foreign diplomats as a "thug." He was responsible for extrajudicial executions of political rivals and torture, allowed protesters to burn the Thai embassy in 2003, returned refugees to nations where they faced persecution, was connected to drug trafficking, and was denied a visa by the U.S. State Department on the grounds of his suspected involvement in human and drug trafficking. Not only did the FBI bestow the medal on Lundy the month after the State Department denied him a visa, but the U.S. ambassador to Cambodia publicly praised Lundy's cooperation in combating human smuggling.[119]

In 2007 the United States opened an FBI office in Phnom Penh. Earlier, it had assisted in forming a Cambodian government National Counterterrorism Committee, where Prime Minister Hun Sen's son served as head of the anti-terrorism department and commander of the special forces. In 2008 the U.S. ambassador announced that "there are some organizations here that are very radical and that are very intolerant, and they are trying very hard to change the attitude and the atmosphere of the Muslim population here in Cambodia."[120] In 2012 it was reported that U.S. Special Forces were training the Cambodian military in counterterrorism.[121]

THE SPECTER OF AL QAEDA IN THE PERIPHERY

Painting their peripheries as associated with al Qaeda, many countries have sought to join the terror network because of the extensive benefits that it brings. They use the rhetoric of the war on terror to both justify their oppressive policies and ingratiate themselves with the United States and the international system. This is the new global paradigm. Burma/Myanmar is a good example of the absurd lengths countries will go to in order to join this system. In its burgeoning efforts to build a democracy and open up to the West, the government adopted the rhetoric of the terror frame, referring to the still-persecuted and crushed Rohingya as "Taliban." Violence in June 2012 against the Rohingya was quickly blamed on the Rohingya themselves and the presence of "1,000 terrorists."[122]

Spotting al Qaeda has become a favorite sport of security agencies throughout the world. Even countries with no significant Muslim populations such as those in Latin America claim to have located al Qaeda in their midst or warn of potential ties between al Qaeda and drug cartels. It was reported in April 2011 that "security agencies are looking into reports that a frontier triangle linking Argentina, Brazil, and Paraguay has become a nexus for al-Qaida activities with alleged armament of Latin American youths and planning of cross-border attacks."[123] New Zealand, across the world from the theaters of conflict, got in on the act and passed the stringent Terrorist Suppression Act of 2002, arresting a number of individuals from its own segmentary lineage periphery in the mountains, the Maori, and accusing them of running terrorist training camps, with an accompanying outcry from the community.[124] When the U.S. government refuses to link peripheral Muslim groups with al Qaeda, as desired by some central governments, many others, from national and international journalists to academics to security "experts," will not hesitate to do so. Today, even a single line of conjecture by one of these commentators is enough to damn an entire people in the eyes of the international community and set in motion a series of actions calculated to condemn and harm them.

The emerging giants on the global stage after 9/11—China, Russia, and India—were equally swift in adopting this new paradigm. It made excellent strategic sense. It not only served their own interest in establishing the legitimacy of their harsh dealings with their already restive periphery, but it also bolstered their economic, commercial, and political credibility with the United States and its allies. Bush famously reached out to leaders irrespective of their human rights record as long as they backed his war on terror. In this manner, countries gained entrance to and reaped the benefits of globalization, whatever their history in dealing with their peripheries. For the purposes of this discussion of U.S foreign policy and the war on terror, mention must be made of Israel and the effect of the war on its relationship with the Palestinians at its "periphery." Although Israel is not in the same league in terms of population or landmass as China, Russia, or India, its importance in the United States rivals that of any of these countries.

China and the Uyghurs

In the days after 9/11, China officially shifted its rhetoric against the "Uyghur threat." For many years, protests and unrest in Xinjiang had gone unreported in China or were described as "hooliganism," "accidents," or "sabotage" and blamed on separatists. The Communist Party now blamed Islamic fundamentalists and al Qaeda.[125] In November 2001 the Chinese government released a list of terrorist acts it said had been committed in the province during the previous decade, retrospectively labeling incidents of violence as the work of Islamic terrorism. The list included explosions, assassinations, arson, poisonings, and instances of public disorder.[126] The Chinese government also published a long paper outlining a new policy toward Islamic terrorism in the post-9/11 age just before a visit by President Bush to Beijing.[127] Uyghur separatists had been trained and financed by bin Laden, the Chinese claimed, as part of a "holy war" to establish an Islamic state in Xinjiang. China announced it had arrested more than 100 such "terrorists."

In August 2002 the U.S. government declared the Uyghur group East Turkestan Islamic Movement (ETIM)—a mysterious organization that China claims was founded in the 1990s—a terrorist organization, despite the fact that no one seemed to have ever heard of ETIM and no Uyghurs had ever threatened the United States in any way. According to the Chinese government, however, ETIM had sent "scores of terrorists" from Afghanistan into China in the late 1990s and established a dozen training bases in Xinjiang. It was also said that the Xinjiang police had discovered a number of underground ETIM training centers and "confiscated large numbers of antitank grenades, hand-grenades, detonators, guns and ammunition."[128] The FBI soon opened an office at the American embassy in Beijing to support counterterrorism efforts.

The U.S. Jamestown Foundation reported that China was already using ETIM as an "all-purpose descriptor for those responsible for any militant activity."[129] Western news outlets, academics, and politicians recently reached a similar conclusion about ETIM, with the *Christian Science Monitor* pointedly observing that "questions exist as to whether ETIM existed as China described it."[130] In June 2009 Representative Bill Delahunt of Massachusetts called a hearing on ETIM, noting that the United States cited 162 deaths in 200 incidents as justification for placing ETIM on the terror list, the exact figures provided by China, adding, "It appears to me that we took substantial intelligence information from the communist Chinese regime and then used that questionable evidence as our own."[131] The Congressional Research Service reported that the first mention of ETIM anywhere occurred in 2000, despite China retrospectively blaming it for attacks in the 1990s.

ETIM and the "Uyghur threat" also factored heavily in China's increasingly close ties with Pakistan. China has always had a special place in the affections of the Pakistanis, with the slogan "Chini-Pakistani *bhai bhai*" ("Chinese-Pakistanis brother brother") embodying it, and this relationship was strengthened after 9/11 in the context of the war on terror. In December 2001 the Chinese invited President Musharraf to Beijing, and the two nations pledged to jointly fight terrorism. Endorsing China's crackdown in Xinjiang, Musharraf vowed, "Pakistan will wholeheartedly support China's battle to strike against the East Turkestan terrorist forces."[132] China was concerned about the Tribal Areas of Pakistan, where it said that ETIM had its military headquarters. China also asserted that most of the Uyghur terrorists in Xinjiang had "close links" with similar groups in Pakistan.[133] In 2003 the Pakistan army killed the accused head of ETIM, Hasan Mahsum, and seven others in an attack on a suspected "al Qaeda hideout" in South Waziristan. In 2010 a U.S. drone strike in North Waziristan killed Abdul Haq al-Turkistani, Mahsum's alleged successor.[134]

With the new justification provided by America's war on terror, thousands of Uyghurs were detained in China, and a number of them were given long jail sentences or were executed. The Chinese government also launched a crackdown on Uyghur schools because, according to a Communist Party committee, "religion, illegal religious activities and extremist religious thought" had "severely influenced, disturbed and infiltrated society, and villages and in particular education."[135] Many of those arrested in the crackdown were sentenced in public in large, prominent locations in Xinjiang, sometimes forty at a time, with some being sentenced to death and executed just after the public sentencing concluded.

By January 2002 the city of Kashgar had in effect been put under martial law, with large numbers of military and police forces patrolling the city, checking vehicles and people's identity cards. Amnesty International described the Chinese post-9/11 measures as "reminiscent of those held during the Cultural Revolution."[136] In March 2008, 1,000 women in the city of Khotan of western Xinjiang took to the streets to protest a Chinese ban on the headscarf, as well as to demand an end to torture and the release of political prisoners. The Chinese government described the women as adhering to the "three evil forces," a Chinese saying that refers to separatism, religious extremism, and terrorism. Following the deadly Urumqi riots between Uyghurs and Han in 2009, state-run media reported, "Evidence shows Uygur separatists who orchestrated the July 5 riots in Urumqi, capital of the Xinjiang Uygur autonomous region, have close relations with the Afghanistan-based Al-Qaida."[137] A massive crackdown with thousands of security forces was subsequently launched in Urumqi. Many Uyghur men disappeared, with the main Uyghur advocacy group in Washington claiming that 10,000 people disappeared in one night.[138] The *Financial Times* reported that prisons were so full in Urumqi that Uyghurs were being moved to Chinese army warehouses.[139] Several dozen death sentences were announced.[140] The Internet in Xinjiang, which is the size of Western Europe, was shut down for months, and it was not restored until nearly one year later.

As well as cracking down on the Uyghurs in the country, China pursues a vigorous policy beyond the region of exposing any possible link between terrorism and the Uyghurs. In October 2012 a Chinese anti-terrorist official stated, "After receiving orders from al-Qaida, terrorists from China came to Syria to meet with jihadists already on the ground before forming groups on the front lines." A spokesman from China's Foreign Ministry went on to state that groups from Xinjiang "not only damage China's state security, but threaten other countries' peace and stability."[141]

"China is a sleeping giant; when it awakes the world will tremble," Napoleon is reputed to have said. His prediction was right. China is awakening and the world watches transfixed. The sheer scale of China with its ancient history and the world's largest population is staggering and difficult to comprehend. It has emerged from almost nowhere in the modern world to become an economic superpower. China has launched astronauts into space. It provides designer clothes, electronic goods, and luxury items for world markets. China's rapidly growing influence in Africa, Asia, and Latin America will make it a major player in the global arena in the coming decades.

China has much to be proud of. But its triumph will carry a blemish unless it is able to fulfill its own essential philosophy of life—the desire for what it calls a "Harmonious Society." China's test will come in its dealings with its periphery where ancient peoples such as the Uyghurs, Tibetans, and Mongolians, among others, live on vast tracts that are identified with their ethnicity. The neglected people on the periphery must be part of China's success story while being able to preserve their cultures and identities. Similar arguments, in different ways, can be made for other major nations with problems on their peripheries—like Russia and India.

Russia and the Caucasus

When 9/11 occurred, Russia had already adopted the rhetoric of the Islamic terror threat to justify its brutal actions in the Caucasus. President Vladimir Putin projected the concept of a war on terror, arguing that Chechens were part of global Islamic terror networks. Four days after President Bush officially declared the war on terror, Putin called Bush, the first head of state to do so, to express his support for the United States. Putin repeatedly invoked connections between al Qaeda and the Chechens to Americans, who in return softened their rhetoric against Russian actions in the Caucasus. Putin would take every opportunity to impute a global terror network behind the actions of the Russian tribal periphery. Following the Beslan school siege in 2004 perpetrated by tribesmen from the Caucasus, Putin claimed that nine of the hostage-takers were from the "Arab world," a claim that was never corroborated.[142] The often frosty relations between Russia and the United States have not discouraged close cooperation in counterterrorism matters between the two. In May 2012 the two powers conducted joint antiterror military training involving paratroopers and Special Forces in Colorado.

The contrast between the pre- and post-9/11 U.S. government policies toward Russia could not have been starker. In 2000 in Moscow, U.S. secretary of state Madeleine Albright said, "We have made quite clear that we think that there has been an incredible amount of misery injected upon the civilian population of Chechnya. . . . Civilians have been indiscriminately targeted in a way that has broadened and widened the problem."[143] In contrast to this attitude toward Russia, Bush, upon meeting Putin just before 9/11 and foreshadowing the relationship they would have in the war on terror, gushed, "I looked the man in the eye. I found him to be very straightforward and trustworthy and we had a very good dialogue. I was able to get a sense of his soul."[144]

While the Russians and Americans trace the cause of the violence in the Caucasus to radical Islam and Wahhabism, Muslim leaders fighting Russia in the region contradict this claim. The Russian and American governments along with international media sources have portrayed Dokka Umarov, the Chechen leader of the insurgent group Caucasus Emirate, fighting the Russian state, as a "militant Islamist" and "Russia's bin Laden." Though he claimed responsibility for several deadly attacks, many utilizing suicide bombers, including the 2010 and 2011 attacks on the Moscow metro and international airport, Umarov declared himself a "traditionalist." "Before the start of the first war in 1994 when the occupation began and I understood that war was inevitable, I came here as a patriot," Umarov said in a 2005 interview. "I'm not even sure I knew how to pray properly then. I can't remember. It's ridiculous to say I'm a Wahhabist or a radical Muslim."[145] Dismissing claims that the Chechen separatist movement is linked in any way to al Qaeda or the "global jihad," he stressed that his focus is on independence from Russia and peace for the Caucasus. He hoped that "reasonable people will come to power" in Moscow. The United States placed a bounty of $5 million on his head.

With the steamroller crushing Chechnya, other republics in the Caucasus also experienced the heavy hand of Putin's Russia, now fully involved in the fight against "terrorism." The contrast in the 1990s between largely peaceful, stable

Dagestan and its war-torn neighbor Chechnya was striking and confounded analysts. Dagestan's stability was largely due to the fact that Dagestanis never adopted a position of total independence, instead opting to work within the framework of autonomy permitted by Yeltsin and devising a unique power-sharing democratic system among its disparate ethnicities. Though rickety and imperfect, the system worked. Yet the removal of autonomy and implementation of direct rule in 2004 resulted in increased violence throughout Dagestan and other republics, accelerated by the 2004 Beslan school siege. Following Beslan, decisions affecting the Caucasian republics would only be made from Moscow. Local political parties were essentially annulled in favor of federal parties like Putin's United Russia. Expressions of Islam were targeted as "Islamist terrorism," just as what the Russians had called "Wahhabism" had been banned in 1999. Then, the Russian government blamed Avars for involvement in a series of apartment bombings that killed nearly 300 people; security forces arrested and tortured thousands of young men in Dagestan, accusing them of being "Wahhabis." After years of controversy, a credible study concluded in 2012 that it was manifestly clear that Russian intelligence had carried out the apartment bombings, which served to bring Putin to power and provided the impetus for the Second Chechen War.[146]

The policies of the security forces in republics like Dagestan are widely hated by the population. These forces were known to capture Dagestanis and hold them for ransom, charging their families tens of thousands of dollars to set them free. Because authorities have lacked enough evidence to put so-called Wahhabis in jail for long periods, detainees are commonly set free following months of torture in Russian prisons and detention camps. Over the past decade, thousands of Dagestanis have been made "physical and psychological cripples."[147] Russian tactics have also included using tanks to blow up or crush individuals, destroying homes, and firing on and dispersing peaceful rallies. Entire villages have been displaced by the actions of the security forces, with residents spending years away from their homes. Crosses are frequently shaved into the heads of young men in custody. In a 2011 BBC interview, Dagestan's deputy premier and the man in charge of the police and security forces described the enemy as "non-people" who "like animals they just crave blood and want to fight—they will be dealt with briefly by the necessary power agencies."[148] Then, proudly grasping his iPad, he showed the BBC journalist his Facebook page.

Moscow should understand the consequences of treating peoples brutally and denying their identities. The numerous regions that broke away from the Soviet Union, including non-Muslim states like Ukraine, Georgia, and Estonia, attest to this troubled relationship between center and periphery. If Moscow's leaders are to promote the modern, multiethnic, and inclusive "new Russia" they cite as their vision, they must extend to all citizens their full human rights, dignity, democratic representation, respect for identity including language and religion, and economic opportunities. Only this will ensure a progressive and stable Russia. Such a vision would be in the tradition of classic Russian humanist writers like Pushkin, Turgenev, and Tolstoy. Using cruel, brutal methods in the periphery will not serve to stabilize Russia but may well have the opposite effect. The old tactics of Imperial Russia and the Stalinist era will not stand in the twenty-first century.

India and Kashmir

India similarly adopted the frame of the war on terror and the threat of al Qaeda in its ongoing conflict in the Muslim mountainous area of Kashmir, the territory disputed between India and Pakistan since partition in 1947 and the source of their three wars. In spite of UN resolutions passed over half a century ago promising a free and fair plebiscite that would allow Kashmir to choose its future with either India or Pakistan, Kashmir remains divided between the two. By linking Kashmir to the war on terror, India was able to translate this move into several important economic, military, political, and nuclear agreements with the United States. As a consequence, the Kashmir issue was effectively put in the deep freeze, India's traditional foe Pakistan was sidelined, and India was recognized as a major player on the world stage.

In early 2002 Indian intelligence informed the CIA that bin Laden was hiding in Kashmir. American and British Special Forces were deployed to the region in a manhunt. Later that year, U.S. secretary of defense Donald Rumsfeld stated in Delhi, after meeting with Indian leaders, "I have seen indications that there are al-Qaeda operating near the line of control, but I do not have hard evidence of precisely how many or who or where," a position he later softened after meeting with Musharraf as the Pakistani government denounced these claims as Indian propaganda.[149] This speculation was followed by an offer of U.S. military technology to guard the India-Kashmir border and an agreement between the two countries for sharing intelligence and "joint Indo-U.S. military action."

Kashmir's population of less than 5 million in small agricultural communities resides in the most militarized region in the world today, with nearly 700,000 Indian military and paramilitary troops located in the part controlled by India and 300,000 Pakistani troops across the border in the part controlled by Pakistan. The "official" purpose of the massive Indian military presence is to halt Pakistani incursions, yet this force has been occupied fighting the Kashmiri resistance. A vicious insurgency began in 1989 following disputed elections two years before, and India quickly blamed Pakistan and its Inter-Services Intelligence (ISI) for arming, training, and funding the insurgents. Most of the victims are, however, Muslim civilians killed in either insurgent strikes or counterattacks by Indian security forces. According to Kashmiris, the death toll has reached 100,000 since 1989.[150] It is also estimated that 70,000 Kashmiri women have been raped, although the actual figures may be much higher as many women refuse to share their ordeal, believing it will bring shame to their families.[151] One middle-aged Kashmiri mother recounted a February 1991 incident in which as many as 100 women in the village of Kunan Poshpora were gang-raped by Indian troops over a period of almost twelve hours: "There were too many of them. Our lawn was filled with the army. They broke lamps, drank alcohol. . . . We were violated. The army entered our houses at 10 in the evening and left at 9 in the morning. . . . There were screams everywhere—from almost every house in the village."[152]

The cruel irony is that Kashmir, with its snow-covered mountains and placid lakes, was once widely known as "paradise on earth." It was a favorite resort for the Mughal emperors and British officials in India seeking escape from the heat of the plains during the summer. The people there were predominately Muslim, but a culture of tolerance prevailed with ample evidence of Hindu, Buddhist, and Islamic traditions drawing from one another. Kashmir was always a periphery to the dynasties of Delhi, but an important one.

Although the turmoil in Kashmir is widely attributed to a religious clash between India's Hindu majority and Muslim minority, India has also had long-running problems with non-Muslim peripheries like the Nagas, who are mainly Christian, and the Bodo and the Adivasi, who are Hindu and animist. These conflicts, too, have involved wars and human rights abuses that have left thousands of people dead. According to India's prime minister, Manmohan Singh, the country's "biggest internal security threat" resides in the "Maoists" and in the Adivasi and their armed struggle, which has claimed over 10,000 lives in the past three decades. Adivasi men have reportedly disappeared without charge or trial if suspected of insurgency, and the central government is said to be arming vigilante squads, which are widely blamed for rape and extortion.[153]

India's failure to resolve the long-simmering issues on its periphery is surprising considering the moral stature and vision of its founding fathers, particularly Mahatma Gandhi. It was Gandhi who rested his spiritual and political philosophy on the twin pillars of *satyagraha,* meaning insistence on truth and passive resistance, and *ahimsa,* or nonviolence. Gandhi believed that "the most distinctive and the largest contribution of Hinduism to India's culture is the doctrine of *ahimsa.*"[154] He had said that that "India's acceptance of the doctrine of the sword will be the hour of my trial," and "India's mission is different from that of others . . . India is less in need of steel weapons, it has fought with divine weapons, it can still do so. Other nations have been votaries of brute force . . . brute force is as nothing before soul force."[155] In the excitement of observing India emerge as an economic power in the post-9/11 era, people sometimes overlook the fact that India's real strength lies in its rich spiritual legacy. This land has produced some of the world's greatest religions—Hinduism, Jainism, Buddhism, and Sikhism—which have contributed richly to the global discourse in modern political thought. Perhaps by rediscovering its own legacy India will be in a better place to resolve issues with its periphery through the vision of its sages.

Israel and the Palestinians

Along with Kashmir in South Asia, Britain's hasty and chaotic withdrawal from its colonies after the Second World War left another great unresolved problem—that of the Palestinians in the Middle East. The politics of both the Kashmiris and Palestinians have drawn in regional and international powers. Both peoples evoke high emotions among their supporters and detractors. The former see both Kashmiris and Palestinians as symbols of an oppressed people deprived of their lands and their rights, and the latter view both as terrorist infected and backward. The continuing confrontation between the center and the periphery in both cases has threatened the security and stability of the center, preventing its citizens from settling down to the normal rhythm of life while disrupting the lives of the periphery.

Israel has been in the eye of the storm of Middle East politics since its birth six decades ago, as attested by several wars with its Arab neighbors over the fate of the Palestinians. Following 9/11 Palestinian actions were viewed through the prism of the war on terror—with Israel's frequent operations in the West Bank and Gaza described as "antiterrorist" activities. As early as 2002 Palestinian areas were suspected of harboring al Qaeda operatives, while American charity organizations associated with the Palestinians, such as the Holy Land Foundation, and even academics supporting Palestine were targeted and implicated in terrorism. Whatever sympathy the Palestinians had from the United States and hope they had for justice and a fair deal were now set aside as the United States courted Israel in its bid to strengthen allies in the war on terror. It became almost impossible after 9/11 to even sustain the idea of genuine Palestinian demands for their own state in this changed and unsympathetic environment as more Jewish settlers moved into Palestinian lands.

Suicide bombers and rockets fired from the Palestinian side sealed their fate as far as Israel, America, and their allies were concerned. Being painted with the brush of terrorism has done irrevocable damage to the Palestinians, leaving millions still living in appalling conditions and facing an uncertain future. Their lackluster leadership, often marked by corruption and mediocrity, has not helped their cause.

Israel made frequent use of the primary weapon of the war on terror, the drone, mainly in the Gaza strip, the most tribal of the Palestinian regions. Drones—nicknamed *zenana* by the local population, meaning "buzz" but also slang for a nagging wife—are a constant presence in the area. In late 2011 a Gaza mechanic and father of eight told the *Washington Post* that since the summer of

2006, when he watched a drone kill three men in front of him, reducing one to an armless torso, he has seen at least one and sometimes several drones circling above every day: "It's continuous, watching us, especially at night. You can't sleep. You can't watch television. It frightens the kids. When they hear it, they say, 'It is going to hit us.'"[156] Israel, which had pioneered the world's first drones, deploying them in the 1982 war in Lebanon, stepped up their use after the Second Intifada begun in 2000 and after it withdrew from and sealed off Gaza in 2005. Over a three-week period between December 2008 and January 2009, for example, Israel launched forty-two drone strikes in Gaza.[157]

Clan groups were among those targeted by drones. In November 2010 two leaders of the Army of Islam, based in the Dughmush clan (see chapter 4), were reportedly killed in a drone strike. In justifying its strikes, Israel stated that the Dughmush group was "affiliated with the Global Jihad terror movement."[158] In 2011 the United States used similar language when it officially declared the Army of Islam a terrorist organization that "subscribes to a Salafist ideology of global jihad."[159]

In November 2012 Israel, accusing the Palestinians of firing rockets into south Israel, launched a full-scale military attack on Gaza that cost more than 160 lives. The sequence of events began with the assassination of Ahmed Jaabari, Hamas military chief and a member of the Jaabari clan, when a missile fired from a drone killed him. The military operation, which ended with a cease-fire after eight days of fighting, used drones extensively. Journalists present during the conflict commented on the fact that the distinct buzzing sound of the drone was a constant and disturbing presence. Sara Hussein, a journalist who covered the Gaza war for Agence France-Presse, wrote on her Twitter feed, "The sound of what is apparently drones overheard has not stopped in hours. Sound like lawnmowers in the sky." Several days later, she added, "And the drones are still here. The sound of them feels like it is permanently implanted in my head at this point."[160]

Ahmed Abu Hamda, a Palestinian radio producer in Gaza City, described what the Israeli drones meant for the people of Gaza: "Their drones hover like invisible demons above us." Hamda also quoted his Palestinian friend, "They watch us from their drones and they peer right into our homes. They know what we are doing all the time. They like to hunt people. We are like chess pieces and they are just playing with us."[161]

In spite of this bleakest of periods in relations between Israelis and Palestinians, well-wishers of both should promote harmony between the two as a strategic and moral imperative. With the stakes as high as they are in the Middle East, it is to the benefit of Israel and all of its Arab neighbors to work toward a lasting peace. Israel has much to offer the region—a thriving democracy and free press, exciting and substantial progress in technology, industry, and agriculture, and one of the best educational systems in the world. In turn, the Arabs can provide Israelis security and, equally important, express their acceptance and welcome of Israelis as good neighbors, thus moving the region to closer integration, especially in areas such as commerce and trade. Unfortunately, Arab communities cannot benefit from these Israeli developments, nor can Israel expect its neighboring Arabs to allow them to participate effectively or constructively in the region because its troubles with the Palestinians overshadow all other issues.

As the preceding pages make clear, modern societies with tribal peripheries face dilemmas of an exceedingly complex nature occurring at several levels—the tribal, the national, and the international. As long as these dilemmas remain unresolved, antagonisms between the center and the periphery will deepen, with increasingly violent results. U.S. involvement since 9/11 has further devastated peripheral communities. Why the United States did so and where it should be proceeding in the future are discussed next.

6

How to Win the War on Terror:
Stopping a Thousand Genocides Now

Tall, young, blonde white females elegantly dressed received us with a clinical charm. This could have been the hospitality room of Fox News. But it was President George W. Bush's White House. We were briskly ushered into a medium-sized room with no natural light. The high-level officials sat on one side of the table, we, the "experts" on Islam, on the other side. I noted that I was the only Muslim present in a gathering of less than a dozen. There was a structure here, with a senior member of the administration presiding, one who reported directly to the president. He asked questions, and when we answered, the subordinates discreetly but studiously took notes. He went around the table inviting each one of us to speak, allowing us to develop our points.

The frame in which the discussion took place was firmly defined by a set of binaries: "the good guys" versus "the bad guys," "us" versus "them," "Americans" versus "the terrorists." Everyone assumed they knew who the former were and who the latter. There was no doubt about the resolve of the officials pursuing "the bad guys" to the bitter end, no matter what the costs. The atmosphere was somber, the mood earnest. The content of the meeting was infused with Bush's ideology.

Tall, young, African American males elegantly dressed received about forty of us in President Barack Obama's White House. They hugged some guests and exchanged pleasantries and business cards with others. I met Muslim leaders from different parts of the United States. We were asked to move to a large room with large windows letting in the sunlight. The tables were arranged in the form of a square emphasizing the egalitarian nature of the gathering. The atmosphere was informal and relaxed as different senior officials came to address us and left. We had been called to discuss Afghanistan and Pakistan, but the focus on these countries quickly dissolved as participants representing different interest groups brought up their special projects, vying for attention. To make matters worse, we were asked to take turns speaking, for only one to two minutes each. There was a spirited representation of Latinos and then an equally energetic one on behalf of lesbians from the West Coast. The focus and structure of the meeting soon fragmented into several discussions, which, however important in themselves, were not even remotely related to the subject of the meeting, Afghanistan and Pakistan.

The first time around no one seemed to understand me; the second time no one seemed to listen. Bush's administration, I felt, was spectacularly wrong because it was imposing a prefabricated ideological frame on different cultures and societies, an exercise that was predictably bound to run into trouble. Obama's administration was spectacularly unsure, and I looked in vain for a coherent frame. It gave the impression of lurching dangerously from one crisis to another as events on the ground developed and it reacted to them. Neither approach helped the United States and the Muslim world resolve the problems that plagued them after 9/11. Both administrations were driven by issues almost wholly on a political level, neglecting the moral and social dimensions and their implications.

The purpose of these high-level official meetings was to discover solutions to the problems surrounding the vexed relationship between the United States and the Muslim world. The style and content during President Bush's and President Obama's tenures were different. The end results were the same. I was no wiser about the challenges facing the United States in its dealings with Muslims and how to solve them leaving either of these White Houses than when I had entered. And yet, this is the engine room, the cockpit, that drives the war on terror, indeed, the United States and through that the age of globalization.

My impression at these and other government meetings that I attended in Washington was that in spite of the vast data and information available to the participants, they understood little of Muslim tribal societies even though the United States had been intimately involved in the recent past in supporting dozens of them across the globe and championing their cause. The events of 9/11 seemed to have erased that American memory and replaced it with raging emotions. This was a dangerous development. Even more curious was the fact that Americans had their own legacy of dealing with tribal societies in the example of their Founding Fathers. A century before elite British political officers were devising effective ways to deal justly and humanely with tribal societies, the American Founding Fathers were already contemplating the same approach.

AMERICA'S FOUNDING FATHERS AND TRIBES

The Founding Fathers envisaged a largely accommodating, mutually beneficial relationship between the U.S. government and the Native American tribes of the American frontier. President George Washington, in his 1792 State of the Union address, announced his intention to create a cadre of officers much akin to what would become the British political agents. He wished "to enable, by competent rewards, the employment of qualified and trusty persons to reside among [the Indians] as agents," which "would also contribute to the preservation of peace and good neighbourhood. If in addition to these expedients, an eligible plan could be devised for promoting civilization among the friendly tribes, and for carrying on trade with them, upon a scale equal to their wants, and under regulations calculated to protect them from imposition and extortion, its influence in cementing their interests with our's could not but be considerable."[1] But first, Washington argued, "outrages upon the Indians" by the center must stop, "without which all pacific plans" would be useless.

For Thomas Jefferson, too, the military solution was not advisable in dealing with the Native Americans. In his 1804 Annual Message to Congress, the year after the Louisiana Purchase, President Jefferson argued against "an augmentation of military force proportioned to our extension of frontier." Instead, he advocated a "moderate enlargement of the capital employed in that commerce, as a more effectual, economical, and humane instrument for preserving peace and good neighborhood with [the Indians]." If the United States declined to use the military and had this "humane" policy toward the tribes, Jefferson declared, the safety of Americans among the Indians "will become their interest and their voluntary care."[2]

The Founding Fathers also showed an admiration for and understanding of Native American culture and their egalitarian system of government. Benjamin Franklin, who would head the Committee on Indian Affairs under the Continental Congress, noted that America had a model of federalism in the Iroquois Confederacy. A number of related tribes, including the Mohawk and Seneca, were united in the confederacy, which dated back to the fifteenth century. Each tribe controlled its own affairs, but clans selected elders to represent them at a grand council that made decisions on behalf of the entire confederation. Tradition had it that the confederacy was formed when a chief of the Onondaga tribe sought to break the cycle of revenge and unite warring tribes. Studying the example of the Iroquois, Franklin asked in 1751 if they could create "such an Union," why not the colonies?[3] In 1754 Franklin submitted a plan to the colonies to create a "grand council" consisting of representatives from each colony. Two centuries later, in 1987, the U.S. Senate passed a resolution acknowledging "the historical debt" that the United States owed to the Iroquois "for their demonstration of enlightened, democratic principles of government and their example of a free association of independent Indian nations."[4]

Franklin wrote that there was much for Europeans to learn in the tribal system of government, which was based on "the Counsel or Advice of the Sages": "There is no Force, there are no Prisons, no Officers to compel Obedience, or inflict Punishment. Hence they generally study Oratory; the best Speaker having the most Influence."[5] Franklin admired the "Order and Decency" with which the council of elders conducted themselves, noting that when an elder is speaking, "the rest observe a profound Silence. When he has finished and sits down, they leave him five or six Minutes to recollect, that if he has omitted any thing he intended to say, or has any thing to add, he may rise again and deliver it. To interrupt another, even in common Conversation, is reckoned highly indecent."[6] The tribal elders, always practical, refused to "contradict, or deny the Truth of what is asserted in their Presence," instead listening to all opinions before reaching decisions. Franklin continued:

How different this is from the Conduct of a polite British House of Commons, where scarce a Day passes without some Confusion that makes the Speaker hoarse in calling *to order;* and how different from the mode of Conversation in many polite Companies of Europe, where if you do not deliver your Sentence with great Rapidity, you are cut off in the middle of it by the impatient Loquacity of those you converse with, & never suffer'd to finish it.[7]

Franklin summed up the difference between the two systems by quoting a Native American elder who had been offered the opportunity to have members of his tribe educated at a local college by the government of Virginia. After thanking the government "heartily," the elder explained that he must decline:

Our Ideas of this Kind of Education happen not to be the same with yours. . . . Several of our Young People were formerly brought up at the Colleges of the Northern Provinces; they were instructed in all your Sciences; but when they came back to us, they were bad Runners, ignorant of every means of living in the Woods, unable to bear either Cold or Hunger, knew neither how to build a Cabin, take a Deer, or kill an Enemy, spoke our Language imperfectly; were therefore neither fit for Hunters, Warriors, or Counsellors; they were totally good for nothing. We are however not the less obliged by your kind Offer, tho' we decline accepting it; and to show our grateful Sense of it, if the Gentlemen of Virginia will send us a dozen of their Sons, we will take great Care of their Education, instruct them in all we know, and make *Men* of them.[8]

Franklin's respect for tribal traditions and the tribesman's insistence on letting his people be "men" like their forefathers anticipates Sir Evelyn Howell in Waziristan. When Howell speaks of the political agents as "custodians of civilisation dealing with barbarians," he sums up the response of the Mahsud elders:

A civilisation has no other end than to produce a fine type of man. Judged by this standard the social system in which the Mahsud has been evolved must be allowed immeasurably to surpass all others. Therefore let us keep our independence and have none of your "qanun" [law] and your other institutions which have wrought such havoc in British India, but stick to our own "riwaj" [custom] and be men like our fathers before us.

"After prolonged and intimate dealings with the Mahsuds," concludes Howell, "I am not at all sure that, with reservations, I do not subscribe to their plea."[9]

The Founding Fathers believed that relations with tribal societies in America should be based on several principles. Concerned about creating a viable administration for the new nation, they advocated the use of specially trained officers to interact with the tribes and to avoid the use of the military to solve their problems. They emphasized the promotion of a healthy relationship between the center and the tribes that would be mutually beneficial. On a more philosophic level, the Founding Fathers expressed their respect for the culture of Native Americans and the worth of their system of government, especially in the conduct of the council of elders, as would Howell and other British officers in their dealings with the Pukhtun. While subsequent generations often forgot or ignored these ideas, the views of the Founding Fathers have endured both in providing a possible model for tribal engagement and in being evident in the very structure of American democracy. Current ideas about the clash of civilizations and the war on terror have, however, marginalized these seminal approaches of the Founding Fathers.

The Failure of the "Clash of Civilizations" Metanarrative

Considering the extraordinary influence of the historian Bernard Lewis as the father of the concept of the clash of civilizations, I looked forward to discussing and debating Islam with him at the World Affairs Council in Washington, D.C. We met on a cold fall evening in 2010, before a full house. The atmosphere was cordial as Bernard and I had known each other for several decades since I was a visiting professor at Princeton's Institute for Advanced Study.

For me, as a scholar of Islam, a discussion with Lewis, hailed by the *New York Times* as "the doyen of Middle Eastern studies," could not have been more urgent or interesting. I wished to engage with Lewis in order to draw out what I believed to be the neglected part of his work on the Muslim world, that is, the importance of promoting dialogue, understanding, knowledge, and science in interactions with that world. Lewis, both in the dialogue at the World Affairs Council and in his book *What Went Wrong?: The Clash between Islam and Modernity in the Middle East*, recognized that the clash of civilizations is not an inevitable outcome of history, but a sign that communication and exchange between civilizations have broken down.[10] I pointed out that commentators focused on only one aspect of Lewis's ideas, the clash of civilizations, and ignored the rest.

In response, Lewis pointed out that the Muslim world was not a monolith, noting the tensions between tribal customs and the Islamic faith. "Islam should not be held responsible for the tribal customs of tribal societies that accepted

Islam," he emphasized. Lewis argued that the teachings of Islam reject tribal customs, such as female genital mutilation and honor killings. Lewis rejected the association of Islam with terrorism: "Islam expressly condemns terrorism," he explained, and "Islam is governed by a system of laws. There was tolerance even for deviants among Muslims." Lewis cited the Quranic verse in Arabic meaning "there is no compulsion in religion."

A Muslim journalist attending the event captured the content and form of the discussion that evening:

> A clash of civilizations is what some would like you to believe is happening in the world today. But, if you were at the World Affairs Council a day after the elections, you would not have seen any nuclear exchange between the Jews and the Muslims. . . . [The] Special Briefing . . . began with friendly gestures like Professor Akbar Ahmed helping the 95-year-young Professor Bernard Lewis climb the stage. During the pleasant discussion, Professor Ahmed even opened a water bottle when Professor Lewis seemed to choke. And, the warmth continued in the cool November evening.[11]

The Instant Terror "Experts"

It is often the fate of influential writers to see their central ideas distorted by zealous followers in their own lifetime. Thus it was with Lewis. Searching for an explanation for the events of 9/11, the emotional, angry, and frightened commentators reduced Lewis's complex ideas to a caricature, that of the clash of civilizations, or a war between the West and the world of Islam with only one victor. Western and Islamic civilizations, the thinking went, had been battling since the coming of Islam in a zero-sum game, and 9/11 was the latest blow in Islam's war to destroy Western civilization.

A new species of instant "experts" emerged in U.S. think tanks, security centers, government, and the media, influenced by scholars such as Lewis, to define, explain, and give direction to the war on terror. They focused on Islam as the root cause driving the enemy. For proof, they pointed to verses in the Quran and the writing of Islamic scholars like Ibn Taymiyyah and Sayyid Qutb. The experts would have benefited from reading works on tribal Islam by Ibn Khaldun, Ernest Gellner, Clifford Geertz, I. M. Lewis, Lawrence Rosen, or Steven Caton. These scholars have provided invaluable insights into Muslim tribal society, which include the subject of war and conflict. None of these genuine scholars of Muslim society would consider theology alone as a motivating factor in social action, but would instead point to the importance of lineage, custom, tradition, codes of honor, and other social factors. Unfortunately, the experts took little advantage of their analyses as they did not fit into the metanarrative of the clash. Thus they focused entirely on groups that they identified as "Islamic terrorists" or "support-ers of Islamic terrorism," cold designations devoid of a tribal or cultural context.

These experts were overwhelmingly white males and came from eclectic back-grounds. Some were from business or financial circles, while others were simply party loyalists who worked on political campaigns and were rewarded for their service. Whatever their background, they defined and set the agenda on how America, and its allies, viewed and dealt with the war on terror and terrorists. What these experts quickly and impressively put together was a vast array of statistics—data and images gathered largely through new technology—and a global network of like-minded colleagues. But all this information existed in the here and now. From the experts' viewpoint, the societies that were supposedly producing terrorists were devoid of history and possessed one-dimensional iden-tities. The experts could not hope to understand these societies without some knowledge, however cursory, of their history, culture, customs, and traditions.

Armed with little knowledge and much power, the instant experts too often assumed to speak on behalf of the "American people." They were frequently called on to explain Islam and the actions of Muslims in the media and to assist the administration and Congress in formulating policies toward Muslims, includ-ing recommendations for the military and intelligence services. They determined who was a "good" Muslim and who a "bad" one, who was to be "taken out" and who merely "rendered," perhaps to be released at some later date. Immediately following 9/11, even the normally assertive American media, with some honor-able exceptions, meekly took their cue from the experts, keeping their doubts to themselves and thereby compromising their integrity.

The insatiable interest in Islam after 9/11 provided a platform for the "pseudo-experts on Islam," as they were called in a report published by the Muslim Pub-lic Affairs Council (MPAC), such as Frank Gaffney and Robert Spencer. The media gave them a megaphone beyond their wildest expectations. The details and impact of their activity were documented in *Fear, Inc.: The Roots of the Islamophobia Network in America*.[12] Keep in mind that before 9/11 few of them were considered experts on Islam or even had any degree, let alone in Islamic studies.[13] With their predictions of doom unless the towering menace of Islam was crushed, they gained a Cassandra-like fame in some sections of society. They churned out ill-researched and mean-spirited material with sensationalist and apocalyptic titles.

With their capacity to influence policymakers and public opinion, some com-mentators assumed the sinister role of a self-appointed inquisitor in the Spanish Inquisition. Those who disagreed with their interpretation of events were cast as "anti-American," a "secret Muslim," or a "stealth jihadist." A campaign in the summer of 2012, promoted by U.S. Representative Michele Bachmann, sought to expose the "deep penetrations" by the Muslim Brotherhood into Congress, the

Pentagon, the Department of Homeland Security, and the State Department; the extent to which they had "infiltrated and influenced" the government was based on the "research" of Frank Gaffney.

Huma Abedin, senior aide to Secretary of State Hillary Clinton, was accused of assisting the Muslim Brotherhood in infiltrating the U.S. administration in order to "destroy Western civilization from within." Even the president of the United States was not above suspicion. In a particularly vitriolic attack on Obama on the eve of his reelection as president for a second term, Gaffney wrote, "President Obama, from his first months in office, has been enabling in this country an insidious effort by Islamic supremacists to keep us from engaging in speech, videos, training or other forms of expression that offend Muslims, their god, prophet and faith." He also accused Obama of appointing "persons with extensive ties to the Muslim Brotherhood" in places of power.[14] The president was thus labeled a "stealth jihadist." These terms were devoid of meaning or context and only served to further keep a fearful and befuddled America in a high state of fearfulness and befuddlement.

The insidious work of the Islamophobes had, not surprisingly, penetrated pop culture. Muslims provided a rich harvest of villainy in adventure stories on television and in films. The hit television drama series *Homeland,* produced by Fox and aired on Showtime, and reportedly President Obama's favorite TV show, focused on the suspicions of a CIA agent that a returning Marine prisoner of war from Iraq, who had converted to Islam during his captivity, had been "turned" by al Qaeda and was plotting an attack on U.S. soil. One of the villains in the show attempting to harm the United States was named after the Yemeni Ghamdi tribe. The show underlined the idea that Islam is linked to terrorism, and that even conversion to Islam, in effect, equates to becoming an al Qaeda terrorist. Tony Stark, in the 2008 movie *Iron Man,* is abducted by an Afghan terrorist group with international links so that he can construct a deadly missile for them. In Marvel Comics' 2011 movie *Thor,* an unknown stranger appears out of nowhere in the American West and is able to effortlessly defeat a group of highly trained U.S. troops in hand-to-hand combat. He turns out to be the Norse god of thunder banished to Earth from Asgard in a distant universe. The incredulous government agent who finally secures Thor's capture asks him, in spite of his blue eyes and flowing blond locks, "Why don't you tell me where you received your training? Pakistan? Chechnya? Afghanistan?" The 2012 film *Act of Valor,* starring active duty U.S. Navy SEALs, pits a SEAL team against a group of international "jihadis" composed of Chechens, Muslims of the Philippines, and Somalis, whom they also call "skinnies," teaming up with Mexican drug cartels to smuggle suicide bombers into the United States. Note that each of these groups cast as villains represents the main tribal societies of this study: Yemenis, Pukhtun, Chechens, Muslims of the Philippines, and Somalis.

Such portrayals of Muslims feed into a larger Islamophobia and is seen in the doubts younger Americans have about Islam. A survey conducted ten years after 9/11 found that about 50 percent of young American adults between the ages of eighteen and twenty-four believed that Islamic and American values were incompatible.[15] Abdullah Antepli, the Muslim chaplain at Duke University, compares the social climate in the United States to McCarthyism. If left unchecked, he fears, the Islamophobia "has the potential to evolve into something dangerous."[16] The Islamophobic terror experts were proving effective in putting pressure on the Muslim community in the United States. "These attacks are real and hurt people's lives," complained Haris Tarin, director of the MPAC's Washington, D.C., office: "Public servants have been forced out of jobs, with suspicion shadowing them. Very few public officials have had the courage to publicly condemn the escalating witch hunt." Referring to the attacks on Huma Abedin and others, he goes on to say, "Will this latest absurdity finally force our politicians and policy-makers to not only defend someone like Huma Abedin, whose public service needs no defense, but also all American Muslims who serve this country every day?"[17]

Anti-Islamic laws influenced by the experts have been passed in Arizona, Louisiana, Oklahoma, South Dakota, Tennessee, and Kansas. Of the seventy-eight bills or amendments designed to thwart Islamic religious practices and considered in thirty-one states and the U.S. Congress in 2011 and 2012, sixty-two of them had lifted language from David Yerushalmi's American Laws for American Courts model legislation. Yerushalmi's Society of Americans for National Existence (SANE) called for the prompt deportation of all Muslims who did not hold citizenship. He advocated that Congress declare war against the "Muslim nation," identified by SANE as "all Muslims," and pushed to make "adherence to Islam" a criminal offense subject to twenty years in prison. The Southern Poverty Law Center (SPLC) called Yerushalmi a member of the "anti-Muslim inner circle." He has served as legal counsel to Frank Gaffney and others in the Islamophobia network. Although Yerushalmi's Islamophobic comments have been singled out for quotation, his equally malicious remarks on women's rights, minorities, and his own Jewish community have not made similar headlines. Yerushalmi has said, "There is a reason the founding fathers did not give women or black slaves the right to vote."[18] He has also claimed that members of the Jewish faith destroyed "their host nations like a fatal parasite."[19]

The Islamophobic environment has repeatedly provoked attacks on Muslims, their mosques and schools, and their supporters. Anders Breivik, the Norwegian who murdered seventy-seven men, women, and children in cold blood in July 2011, cited Robert Spencer 54 times and Spencer's website 112 times in his manifesto.[20] Breivik's aim was to kill those Norwegians who were tolerant of foreign immigrants, especially Muslims.

In August 2012 the American-Arab Anti-Discrimination Committee issued an "urgent release" titled "Attacks on Places of Worship Increase: Alarming Rate of Attack Is Reason for Concern" pointing to cause and effect in the statements of a member of Congress, Joe Walsh, and an attack on an Illinois Muslim school:

> It is not a coincidence that after the remarks by Rep. Walsh were made that there was a homemade bomb directed at an Islamic school in his district. The facts are clear—By proclaiming to the public that 'Muslims are trying to kill Americans every week,' Walsh raised suspicion of the American Muslim community and incited fear. Rep. Walsh is responsible for the assailants actions, and would have been responsible for any injuries from the attack.[21]

Perhaps these Muslim voices were right to be concerned, considering the widespread Islamophobia. The analysis of the experts who were influencing public figures like Representatives Walsh and Bachmann was colored by a hyperpatriotism tinged with prejudice against, or dislike of, Muslims. When they scrutinized the Quran, it was not to generate interfaith understanding; when they probed into the Muslim community, it was not to add to their knowledge of human society; and when they made inquiries about the persecution of Muslims, it was not to expiate or atone: they believed this information would be useful in their assault on Islam. Yet their ideas influenced policy, and, in that sense, they are partly responsible for the predicament the United States finds itself in and the cataclysm in tribal societies abroad.

America's Islamic Frame

What had become widely influential in America was the idea that Islam, or an interpretation of it, was the root cause of terrorism, and the war on terror, therefore, could not be successfully concluded without dealing with the religion itself. Americans seemed to be falling mainly into two camps—in one, the aim was to "eradicate" Islam, in the other, to promote "moderates" and through them to defeat the "radical" Muslims. Both camps reflect the metanarrative of the clash of civilizations in different ways.

The proponents of the first approach were prominent in American public life and frequently seen and heard in the media. In 2007 former U.S. senator and future presidential candidate Rick Santorum defined Islam as the enemy in the war on terror and offered this tactical approach: "We must educate, engage, evangelize, and eradicate. . . . We are in a war, and theology is its basis."[22] Former Speaker of the House Newt Gingrich, another presidential candidate, compared Muslims to Nazis when discussing the proposed controversial Islamic center near Ground Zero. Instructors at the Pentagon were teaching that the only solution for Islam was the "final" one—nuclear obliteration of Mecca and Medina.[23]

Many Americans, however, wished to distinguish the "bad" Muslims from the "good" ones and used terms like "radical" Muslims versus "moderate" ones. The tone was set by President Bush in his first major address to the joint session of Congress just days after 9/11, in which Bush appears wise and tolerant in comparison to his fellow Americans cited above:

> I also want to speak tonight directly to Muslims throughout the world. We respect your faith. It's practiced freely by many millions of Americans and by millions more in countries that America counts as friends. Its teachings are good and peaceful, and those who commit evil in the name of Allah blaspheme the name of Allah. . . . The enemy of America is not our many Muslim friends. It is not our many Arab friends. Our enemy is a radical network of terrorists and every government that supports them.[24]

If the enemy was associated with a certain interpretation of Islam, which was of the "extremist" or literalist kind, then the more religious a Muslim, the voices in the second camp argued, the more likely that he or she could fall under the influence of terrorism and al Qaeda. From this perspective, any Muslim was still a possible terrorist, a "potential walking bomb," as Thomas Friedman observed, speaking of Muslims in the West.[25] Friedman's writing provides a good example of this common conception of the enemy in the war on terror. To him America's war was against "radical Islamists" and "a jihadist death cult."[26] Thus it was important to identify and support "moderate" Muslims in order to defeat the extremists. Every effort should be made to promote "secularism" in Muslim society and check the growth of religious political parties advocating sharia.

Just as mainstream American figures like Friedman were failing to comprehend the root cause of the conflict, so were prominent American Muslims like Fareed Zakaria, editor of *Time* magazine and a CNN television host. Instead of looking at the shortcomings of the center in its dealings with the tribal periphery and the nature of tribal society, they borrowed from the experts and blamed extremists within the religion. "Victory in the war on terror will be won," Zakaria argued, "when a moderate, mainstream version of Islam—one that is compatible with modernity—fully triumphs over the world view of Osama bin Laden."[27] Muslim think tanks whose charter was to study the subject were also using the simplistic binary formulation. The British-based Muslim Quilliam Foundation described itself on its website as "the world's first counter-extremism think tank" seeking "to counter the ideological underpinnings of terrorism."

Both camps, however, agreed that the threat of terrorism coming from Islam would be diminished if attempts were made to promote an Islam compatible with Western culture and wean Muslims away from their orthodox religious sensibilities. I observed this approach in its most bizarre form when one of the experts in my White House meeting during the Bush presidency suggested dropping hundreds of thousands of copies of *Baywatch* into Taliban territory to destroy their commitment to Islam, and no one challenged it. The argument of the expert was based on America's experience confronting the Soviet Union during the cold war when it was believed the attractions of American culture undermined Soviet society. Granted the allure of Miss Pamela Anderson's jiggly bits in slow motion, this was exactly the kind of thing that would infuriate local tribesmen, whether they supported the Taliban or not. It was another scheme destined to waste large sums of money and have the opposite effect of what was intended. Of course, as clearly established in the preceding chapters, none of these approaches will resolve the problems at the heart of which lies the troubled relationship between the center and the tribal periphery.

Given the fact that experts in both camps were predisposed to view Islam in terms of a global clash between the West and Islam, a flood of books were written claiming to link "jihadi" terrorism with an apocalyptic vision of religion. These books were produced by major publishing houses, many of them academic presses associated with prestigious universities. Titles of such books published after 9/11 have included *Apocalyptic Realm: Jihadists in South Asia*, *The Globalization of Martyrdom: Al Qaeda, Salafi Jihad, and the Diffusion of Suicide Attacks*, *The De-Radicalization of Jihadists: Transforming Armed Islamist Movements*, and *God's Terrorists: The Wahhabi Cult and the Hidden Roots of Modern Jihad*.[28]

In *Apocalypse in Islam*, Jean-Pierre Filiu argues that the "Great Battle" between Western and Islamic civilizations will take place—or is taking place—in the Tribal Areas of Pakistan and Afghanistan. If that is the case, then the world needs to know something of their tribes and peoples. Since the experts were neglecting tribes and customs in their analysis, as I have pointed out, it is not surprising that Filiu makes no mention of Waziristan or its major tribes, the Mahsud and the Wazir, or indeed any other major Pukhtun tribe. The index is largely devoted to such topics as the anti-Christ, the Hidden Imam, the Mahdi, Sayyid Qutb, and Wahhabism—standard references that one has come to expect of such works.[29] The explanation of terrorism as the result of an apocalyptic struggle between civilizations has even taken root in the Muslim world, as in the example of Pakistani writers Syed Saleem Shahzad, Imtiaz Gul, and Zahid Hussain noted in chapter 2.

Some American scholars attempted bravely, if unsuccessfully, to move the discussion of Muslim violence away from theology to other sociological and political factors. American political scientist Robert Pape, in *Dying to Win: The Strategic Logic of Suicide Terrorism*, examined every known case of suicide terrorism, 315 in all, between 1980 and 2003 and concluded that the driving force of the terrorist was "an extreme strategy for national liberation."[30]

But the clash of civilizations metanarrative was too powerful and would not go away. It dominated even the most authoritative studies of the 9/11 attacks. Because attention has focused on Wahhabi-like literalist theological interpretations of Islam and their apocalyptic vision, the roots of 9/11 in bin Laden's tribal identity and the relationship between the Yemeni tribes and the Saudi central government have been missed. The cause for the attacks is thus rendered incomprehensible. The fact that ten hijackers came from the Yemeni tribes of Asir and that all but one had a Yemeni tribal background, as discussed in chapter 3, has not been raised by commentators of the war on terror, which left them looking for clues in the wrong places. Sayyid Qutb and the Muslim Brotherhood are examined in exhaustive detail in Lawrence Wright's Pulitzer Prize–winning study *The Looming Tower: Al-Qaeda and the Road to 9/11*, but the word "Asir" does not appear once.[31] Similarly, in Steve Coll's *Ghost Wars: The Secret History of the CIA, Afghanistan, and Bin Laden from the Soviet Invasion to September 10, 2001*, also winner of the Pulitzer Prize, the name Asir is never mentioned.[32] It is only in *The Bin Ladens: An Arabian Family in the American Century* that Coll mentions Asir. Yet Coll identifies only five hijackers as being from Asir (half of my count) and relegates the point to a trivial footnote noting the fact that the plane that killed Osama bin Laden's father crashed in Asir and was piloted by an American, while the 9/11 planes crashed in America and were flown by Asiris. He observes a "striking symmetry in these air crashes involving Americans and Asiris, which took place during two Septembers thirty-four years apart."[33]

Even the few analysts who recognize that the majority of the hijackers were from Asir reach the wrong conclusions, attributing this prevalence to Asir's reputation as a bastion of Wahhabist ideology. The journalist Stephen Schwartz, for example, sees the high number of Asiri hijackers as a manifestation of the "cruel and fanatical" character of Wahhabism in Asir. The boasts of local tribesmen that the "sons of Asir" committed 9/11 were, Schwartz thought, "pure expressions of the Wahhabi traditions from which they sprang, geographically as well as religiously."[34]

Yet this was the exact opposite of the reality of the Asiris. The Asiri hijackers did not conform to the Wahhabi caricature. A brother of two of the Ghamdi hijackers said, "You have to understand my brothers were not Islamic purists. They were young, they were bored, and we have no idea what happened to them. To be very honest, neither one of them was very smart, nor very motivated to do anything."[35] Another Ghamdi hijacker was a singer and played the *oud,* a traditional Arabic lute, and smoked tobacco from a waterpipe.

As writers and commentators have failed to satisfactorily explain the nature of Islam's relation to terrorism and the reason for 9/11, Americans continue to see Islam as a threatening presence in their lives, and they view al Qaeda as the main agent of Islam itself. Every Muslim is therefore a potential terrorist and, by the same logic, a potential supporter of al Qaeda. He or she could be "turned" just as the nineteen hijackers were. While no one can doubt the deadliness of al

Qaeda's method and capacity to deliver it, or that of its allies, no one should also doubt that its influence has been overblown beyond any semblance of reality.

Americans tend to inflate their heroes and villains in popular culture. Al Qaeda is depicted as an almost supernatural evil, a comic book villain like Lex Luthor or Magneto, with instant global reach and the ability to change shape—now an American Muslim promoting sharia and bent on overturning the U.S. Constitution, now a Uyghur set on dismantling China, now a Somali disrupting shipping on the East African coast, or a Mexican smuggling terrorists into the United States in order to destroy it. Al Qaeda seemed everywhere and could assume any form.

The American perception of al Qaeda and Islam was not lost overseas. The president of Nigeria, Goodluck Jonathan, with an eye on American aid, explained the activity of Boko Haram after the violence had claimed another 250 lives in January 2012 in one phrase, as did Libya's president, Mohamed al-Magariaf, later that year regarding the violence in Benghazi that killed several American diplomats, including Ambassador Christopher Stevens—"al Qaeda." Exactly the same explanation has been repeatedly given for similar violence around the world. It echoed precisely what other heads of government had been repeating to Americans for a decade: Musharraf in Pakistan, Putin in Russia, Mubarak in Egypt, Gaddafi in Libya, Saleh in Yemen—the list could go on. Al Qaeda had become an instant explanation for every kind of eruption everywhere in the world. The perception of al Qaeda as a super villain is now an established cultural fact, and Americans are conditioned to overreact to any hint of its activities, or even mention.

How to Damn a Community without Even Trying

In this heated environment, any expert or commentator can level the vaguest and the most baseless accusations against a Muslim or the Muslim community and trigger a sequence of tragic events, ultimately borne by Muslim families. The language of these accusations throughout the press and in political speeches, scholarly literature, and government and think tank reports employs words such as "alleged," "accused," "linked," "said to be associated with," "probably," and even "inspired by" to connect some Muslim or Muslim group with the amorphous and ever-present al Qaeda or its affiliates. These articles and accusations are picked up, circulated, and legitimized within the network of experts, as the following case illustrates.

The dispirited Rohingya of Burma/Myanmar, who are not fighting their oppressive central government, were implicated in the war on terror and accused of having al Qaeda "links" by the Thailand-based Swedish journalist Bertil Lintner. Beginning in 2002 Lintner published a series of articles asserting that some Rohingya had teamed up with al Qaeda, as well as the Taliban, as part of the global jihad, and traveled to Afghanistan. His claims were picked up by a number of other sources as evidence of Rohingya involvement in terrorism and were heavily cited, as in the Library of Congress's Congressional Research Service reports, or included in think tanks reports, as in one by the Center for Strategic and International Studies (CSIS) in Washington, D.C., in which Lintner repeats verbatim his same arguments from previous articles associating the Rohingya with terrorism.[36] Such reports were being widely circulated when, in 2012, the Burmese government, pushing to open up to the West, increased its efforts to label the Rohingya "terrorists" and "Taliban." According to documents released by WikiLeaks, the Burmese government had already approached the U.S. government with claims that Osama bin Laden had personally met with Rohingya "Muslim Terrorist-Insurrection groups."[37]

In his articles, Lintner made little more than vague assertions about bin Laden and others. In one of the articles used for the CSIS report, Lintner wrote, "In an interview with the Karachi-based newspaper, *Ummat,* on September 28, 2001, bin Laden said: 'There are areas in all parts of the world where strong jihadi forces are present, from Bosnia to Sudan, and from Burma to Kashmir.' He was most probably referring to a small group of Rohingyas on the Bangladesh-Burma border." Lintner did not provide a source for this claim, a glaring omission given that Burma/Myanmar is home to a number of other Muslim groups besides the Rohingya. He compounded this claim with another, also without citation: "There is little doubt that extremist groups have taken advantage of the disenfranchised Rohingyas, including recruiting them as cannon fodder for Al Qaeda in Afghanistan and elsewhere."[38]

In another article, he quotes a CNN interview with the American "Taliban" fighter John Walker Lindh in which Lindh says the Taliban forces are divided along linguistic lines between "Bengali, Pakistani (Urdu) and Arabic." Even though the Rohingya do not speak Bengali, Lintner states that Lindh's quote "suggests that the Bengali-speaking component—Bangladeshi and Rohingya—must have been significant." He follows this assertion by citing the words of the Afghan foreign minister: "We have captured one Malaysian and one or two supporters from Burma."[39] In a 2002 article in *Far Eastern Economic Review,* Lintner mentions this same quotation by the Afghan foreign minister, following it up with, "It seems clear that these were Rohingyas from Bangladesh."[40]

Distorting History

It is enough of a stretch to apply the metanarrative of the clash of civilizations to current events around the world, but many scholars have even attempted to apply it retrospectively to Islamic history, blaming various actions by Muslims in the past on "jihadi Islam." Consider the example of Sher Ali Khan, an Afridi tribesman from Tirah in the Tribal Areas and a prisoner in the penal colony on the Andaman Islands in the Bay of Bengal, who in 1872 assassinated Lord Mayo, the viceroy of India, on an official visit. It created a sensation throughout the British Empire. Nothing like this had happened before.

Sher Ali had no personal animosity against Lord Mayo. In his dying confession, he explained that he wished to kill a "European of high rank" because he had been wrongly punished for a murder back in the North-West Frontier Province. Sher Ali had been a member of the Punjab Mounted Police working for the commissioner at Peshawar and, as such, was a man of some standing in his community. He had been convicted of murder as he had killed someone in a blood feud that he believed was justified by the tribal code. The victim was his tarboor, or cousin, and had he acted in his own area in Tirah, along the Durand Line, he would have got away with it. But this murder was committed in the cantonment area of Peshawar, and he was immediately arrested, tried, and sent to the penal colony.

Clearly Sher Ali's actions were in keeping with the code of revenge of nang tribesmen, yet the experts after 9/11 cast him as a forerunner of contemporary Islamic "jihadis." Scholar Charles Allen describes Sher Ali as a terrorist motivated by his understanding of Wahhabi Islam.[41] Helen James interprets Sher Ali's act of tribal revenge as a blow for Islamic supremacy, summing up her thesis in the title of her article: "The Assassination of Lord Mayo: The 'First' Jihad?"[42]

The retrospective application of the frame of "jihadi Islam" has even reached as far back as the Muslim Almoravid Kingdom that ruled in northwest Africa and southern Spain a thousand years ago. In a report issued by the Combating Terrorism Center at West Point, "AQIM's Objectives in North Africa," Geoff D. Porter, who holds a Ph.D. in Middle Eastern and Islamic Studies, believes the Almoravids hold the key to Al Qaeda in the Islamic Maghreb (AQIM). Porter argues that AQIM is fighting the same jihad of conquest as the Almoravids did, noting that "references to the Almoravids abound in AQIM messaging, mostly through noms de guerre and the names of AQIM's Saharan battalions." The Almoravids, Porter explains, came from two Berber tribes, the Sanhaja and Lamtuna, whose men veiled themselves, and "the practice is now the name of AQIM leader Mokhtar Belmokhtar's unit, Katiba al-Mulathimin, or 'The Battalion of Veiled Men.'" Porter seems unaware that the present-day Tuareg men of the region veil themselves in the same fashion as the Almoravids—and indeed as do other peoples living in the Saharan region in order to provide protection from the harsh winds, intense heat, and fierce sand storms. Porter then links the Almoravids from a millennium ago to the current threat: "The Almoravids stressed personal moral comportment and the responsibility of the individual for the Islamicness of the whole community—a notion echoed eight centuries later by Sayyid Qutb. . . . These strong Almoravid overtones . . . are in line with Salafi-jihadi narratives of restoring a caliphate and returning Islamic authority to lands that it once ruled."[43]

Given this kind and quality of expertise where anything Islamic sounding becomes a matter of suspicion, it is not difficult to speculate on conversations at high-level secret U.S. intelligence headquarters: In a dimly lit office deep in the bowels of a counterterrorist center, the commanding officer, in the hunt for Islamic jihadists, looks to the officer on his right, a muscular, rosy-cheeked young man with closely cropped hair:

"Anything for me, Joey?" he asks.

"I think I may have sir. I may have identified two al Qaeda affiliates. It's come up in terrorist chatter and the monitoring of jihadist websites. But I need to look closer."

"What are they?" the officer asks.

"Al-Gebra and al-Chemy."

"These sons of bitches sound dangerous. I know I've heard of them somewhere. It's all part of the Global Jihad. Good work, boy!"

"Rozi Laggi Hai"

The government, private companies, universities, and think tanks set up special units and centers to allow the newly minted and well-funded experts to develop their ideas and spread their influence. Because they tapped into deep American fears, their funding and their jobs were secure at a time of high unemployment and economic uncertainty. The scale of the network was staggering. According to an extensive 2010 *Washington Post* report titled "A Hidden World, Growing beyond Control,"

> Some 1,271 government organizations and 1,931 private companies work on programs related to counterterrorism, homeland security and intelligence in about 10,000 locations across the United States. An estimated 854,000 people, nearly 1.5 times as many people as live in Washington, D.C., hold top-secret security clearances. In Washington and the surrounding area, 33 building complexes for top-secret intelligence work are under construction or have been built since September 2001. Together they occupy the equivalent of almost three Pentagons or 22 U.S. Capitol buildings—about 17 million square feet of space. . . . Analysts who make sense of documents and conversations obtained by foreign and domestic spying share their judgment by publishing 50,000 intelligence reports each year—a volume so large that many are routinely ignored.[44]

By exaggerating the nature and ubiquity of the danger every American faces, the experts and the participants and beneficiaries of this vast network succeeded in ensuring that no member of Congress could suggest in public that funds be withheld from the efforts at protecting America. In the process the experts succeeded in protecting their jobs. Yet in private, even the experts have reservations about the al Qaeda threat. In a high-level conference on security in Washington late in 2011, at which I presented a paper, Peter Bergen, one of the smartest and best-informed commentators on the war on terror, exploded the myth of al Qaeda as a global force. Al Qaeda, Bergen said, is "not ten feet tall" and "their bench has been obliterated." He pointed out that since 9/11 there have been 180 cases of what he calls "jihadi" terrorism resulting in seventeen American deaths, most of those at Fort Hood. Bergen emphasized that the "transnational" al Qaeda of the past no longer exists and what people are identifying as al Qaeda at present is nothing more than a number of local groups, even ones that call themselves al Qaeda, fighting for their own reasons.

The influential participants, reacting to Bergen's presentation, generally agreed that the American public was not quite ready to be told that the threat from al Qaeda does not exist anymore, and it may have been overblown all along. They wondered how to get the message through to the public and especially politicians who have political reasons to continue talking about the war on terror and al Qaeda. Despite the private misgivings of some experts, such frank assessments rarely see the light of day, and therefore the American public continues to remain in a state of fear and confusion.

The American lack of understanding of the forces at play in Muslim tribal societies was puzzling considering the resources diverted to the armies of experts and the countless think tanks to study the terrorist problem set as it was in tribal societies. Ambassador Touqir Hussain, former Pakistani ambassador to Japan and at present adjunct professor at Georgetown University in Washington, D.C., believed he had the answer. In an August 2011 interview, Hussain said he had worked with ten American ambassadors over his career, attended meetings at the highest levels, including those with Prime Minister Z. A. Bhutto of Pakistan and U.S. secretary of state Henry Kissinger, and was now self-consciously part of the think tank circuit. It gave him an extraordinary position to observe American policymakers closely. His assessment of the current situation was irrevocably pessimistic. American foreign policy, he said, was driven by a mixture of ignorance, arrogance, and prejudice. In describing the security experts, he believed "a new nexus has emerged consisting of academia, journalists, the media and think tank community, advocacy groups, lobbyists and consultants that has become a powerful adjunct to the policymaking."

Hussain blamed the crass materialism driving the security industry: "That is where the money is. Almost 80 percent of academics have sold their soul to this new cult as this is leading them to write 'best sellers' and make fabulous money as consultants. That is why Afghanistan and Pakistan have been messed up and the government does not even realize it."[45] Hussain described the work of the experts as *rozi laggi hai*—an Urdu expression using the word *rozi* (daily earnings), which implies that as long as the problem persists, their jobs are secure and so is their "bread and butter"; therefore they have no real interest in or commitment to solving it. American journalist Nathan Lean, coming from a different perspective, seems to echo the same concept of *rozi* in his use of the word "industry" to describe the professional output of the experts on Islam in the title of his book, *The Islamophobia Industry: How the Right Manufactures Fear of Muslims.*[46]

When Secretary of Defense Leon Panetta publicly admitted in 2011 that no more than ten to twenty al Qaeda leaders were left in the entire world and that "we're within reach of strategically defeating al Qaeda," it appeared that the large numbers of experts were no longer needed.[47] Their jobs would soon be redundant as the war on terror was winding down. But Panetta's assessment of an almost exterminated al Qaeda was perhaps a brief moment of candor that quickly passed. Ignoring his previous statements and whatever misgivings even some experts had begun to develop about al Qaeda, Panetta outlined an ambitious and rejuvenated security campaign after Obama's re-election as president in 2012. In doing so, Panetta gave a new lease on life to those who depended on the war on terror for their *rozi*.

In a November 2012 speech at the Center for a New American Security in Washington, D.C., Panetta outlined American strategy for the new term. He now argued that "the threat from al-Qaeda has not been eliminated." Despite the U.S. conduct of what he called "the most precise campaign in the history of warfare," especially in Afghanistan and Pakistan, Americans could not rest. "We have slowed a primary cancer," Panetta warned, "but we know that the cancer has also metastasized to other parts of the global body." The cancer had spread first to Yemen and Somalia, he said, and was now spreading even further across the Middle East and North Africa. Panetta singled out Nigeria, Mali, and Libya as being infected by al Qaeda, thereby adding the Kanuri and Fulani, the Tuareg (and by mentioning Al Qaeda in the Islamic Maghreb, the Kabyle Berbers), as well as the Cyrenaica tribes, to the list of societies in which the United States was planning to engage more directly. To meet these threats, Panetta announced an increase in the number of special operations troops and drones in the U.S. arsenal, in addition to a continuing close engagement with central governments in providing "security assistance, economic development, strengthening democratic institutions, [and] advancing political reforms."[48]

Panetta had rightly identified the tribal societies in turmoil—the very same peoples that formed the focus of this study—but he had offered little that was new in the way to resolve the conflicts that were consuming them. More than a decade after 9/11, the experts had failed to understand Muslim tribal societies, and therefore the problems persisted. The consequences for Americans were trillions of dollars sunk in a bottomless pit, hundreds of thousands of American and non-American lives lost, fundamental values and human rights compromised at home and abroad, the global image battered, and entire nations thrown into upheaval. The experts had led them into a blind alley.

Return to Anthropology

With 9/11 it seemed anthropology's time had arrived. People began to ask questions that were the staple, the very core, of the subject—why men and women from small communities did what they did, who led them, and how they dealt with issues of war and peace. Anthropology was the only discipline that offered a comprehensive picture of the entire "universe" the anthropologist was studying, often no more than a village or a tribe, including its economics, politics, society, religion, kinship patterns, leadership, culture, and customs; it provided cross-cultural comparisons between different communities—the one in this valley compared with those across the mountains—and their relations with the state; and the discipline also offered the kind of fine-grained ethnography characteristic of its research methods, which relied on extended periods of fieldwork. Because anthropologists spend time living with usually remote groups of people—the discipline's famed methodology of participant observation—and recording the voices of ordinary people in the field, they are able to present an authentic picture of social reality.

As it turned out, anthropology's moment came and passed swiftly. Anthropologists were unsuccessful in fielding an authoritative name on par with public intellectuals who constantly appeared on television and in the media such as journalist Thomas Friedman, historian Niall Ferguson, or economist Jeffrey Sachs. They were not called on to help explain to the public how tribal societies functioned within the framework of the war on terror.

To compound matters, the new breed of instant terror experts monopolized the commentary on Muslim societies and was unwilling to accommodate anthropologists. The experts conflated and confused religious and tribal customs, doctrine and practice, theology and anthropology. Their ill-defined and shoddy concepts of "security" and "terrorism" became substitutes for legitimate scholarship. Looking through the post-9/11 prism, they had little patience, empathy, or desire to learn about the tribal communities that they were forced to deal with. Besides, men with beards who wore turbans and traditional dress were too reminiscent of al Qaeda to evoke interest or sympathy.

When the experts invited anthropologists to share their expertise, it was to act as guides whose task was to present their knowledge of Muslim societies so that their "vulnerable" points could be exploited. As Muslims were averse to pig meat because it is ritually forbidden, the prison guards would place slices of bacon on the food and faces of the prisoners; as Muslims consider the Quran the word of God and revere it, their captors made sure its pages were torn and flushed down the toilet in front of them. Reports emerging from American prisons overseas describe "beatings and various forms of sexual humiliation. In some cases, an interrogator would place his penis along the face of the detainee while he was being questioned. Other inmates were raped with sticks or threatened with anal sex."[49] This, the advisers guiding the interrogations calculated, would break the spirit of the prisoners. In short, anthropological knowledge could have helped the world better understand events engulfing entire nations but was either misused or in the main remained largely ignored.

At the time when it was needed most, anthropology could not contribute with confidence to the larger world because those involved in the discipline were unsure about the nature and direction of their scholarship. I got a glimpse of this debate at a lecture by Claude Imbert from Paris given at Cambridge University's Department of Social Anthropology on November 1, 2012, and at the dinner that followed. The conversation and debate that evening would continue at Trinity College over a formal, candle-lit dinner, both hosted by the distinguished anthropologist Henrietta Moore, the current head of the department at Cambridge. The dinner was the kind that only a Cambridge or Oxford college can boast because of academic pedigree: Sir Isaac Newton, Sir Francis Bacon, Lord Byron, Lord Tennyson, at least three signatories to the American Declaration of Independence, Allama Iqbal, and Jawaharlal Nehru—these are just some of the names produced by Trinity College over its history stretching half a millennium.

In her lecture, "From Philosophy to Anthropology and Back: A Puzzling Trade That Never Finished," Imbert argued for studying visual arts, philosophy, and anthropology in one conceptual frame. Names like Ludwig Wittgenstein, Jacques Derrida, and Michel Foucault flew about, along with those of Claude Levi-Strauss, Bronislaw Malinowski, E. E. Evans-Pritchard, and Meyer Fortes. It was difficult to discern where anthropology ended and other disciplines began. A French professor explained his work on robotics and its relationship to anthropology, and a British art historian did the same for his subject. Ideas were merging and clashing, shifting and changing in a veritable display of fireworks, but failed to illuminate the nature of the discipline.

An audience member voiced concern that in anthropology departments, people ask each other "What theory are you applying?" and noted that a "centrifugal proliferation of theories" existed in the discipline. Anthropology, she said, had gotten away from its strength in comparing cultures across different societies, and anthropologists should return to this approach. Later, Frankie Martin, my research assistant who had joined the department in Cambridge, spoke with me about the lecture. "Several of my fellow masters students were there and the consensus was that we were lost," he told me. "We had no idea what the lecture was about."

The further it moves from its own traditional discipline, the less anthropology resembles itself. It risks losing its form as a distinct discipline and ending up as something tacked onto other areas of study that overlap with it. While the debate within anthropology shows vitality, it also reveals that some of the issues I came across when I first began my studies four decades ago have remained unresolved.[50] The debate gives the subject a sense of internal unease about itself, raising doubts about its place among the various disciplines, even whether it is a science and to be taken seriously.

It was Caroline Humphrey, another leading light in the discipline and recently honored by the Queen of England with an award, who, at the lecture, provided a ray of clarity with a call to return to basics, to reclaim and reinforce boundaries within anthropology. Humphrey felt that the pendulum had swung too far the other way, and it was time to recognize the work of the founding fathers—and mothers—of anthropology such as Evans-Pritchard and Fortes. She argued that it was precisely the foundational concepts of anthropology such as structure and function that gave it its distinction. She pointed out that the use of Foucault, Eduardo Castro, and Derrida was "half-understood." There was a "headlong rush to philosophy as it is broadly understood," and as a result anthropology was compromising its distinct character.

Humphrey was right. Anthropology was assuming different, exciting, but amorphous forms—philosophical, poststructuralist, postreflexive, postmodernist, ontological, phenomenological—and was also influenced by gender and minority studies and the fine arts. An example of the trends within the discipline is provided by the brilliant but controversial study *The Headless State*, recently published by David Sneath and based on his work in Mongolia.[51] Sneath, who teaches in the department at Cambridge, rejects the traditional ideas of anthropology about tribes and segmentary lineage systems altogether. Instead, he has been promoting what he calls "technologies of the imagination" as an alternative way to study society.

This new approach contrasts with the workmanlike and explicit nature of the titles of the studies of the older generation of anthropologists—*The Nuer, The Sanusi of Cyrenaica,* or *The Kingdom of the Zulu of South Africa*—and their contents. The titles conveyed exactly the subject matter and each study contained standard information that allowed the reader to draw his or her own conclusions: the introduction to the group, its history, the terrain in which it lived, social organization, kinship groups, leadership, rites of passage, and its relations with its neighbors, including the state. The base of anthropology was solid ethnography, relying on fieldwork. It offered concrete material about real societies, not reified ideas formed by currently fashionable theories.

Anthropologists today not only appeared to be constantly on the defensive about their subject but also treated what in fact was the pride of the discipline— the study of tribes and their varieties such as the segmentary lineage system— as if it were radioactive. They had rejected their founding fathers and mothers because of their colonial association and wished to prevent the shadow of that era falling on the subject. Even the word "tribe" had been tacitly dropped from the lexicon (the concept was said to be a colonial invention) and replaced by various substitutes, such as "ethnic community" or "ethnic group." As my South Asian background makes me acutely aware of colonialism, I can fully understand and sympathize with the sentiment that expresses its aversion to it. But by rejecting the work of the early anthropologists in this wholesale and unthinking manner, I am afraid they may be guilty of having thrown the baby out with the bath water. While anthropology, in their case, has left the safe shores of its traditional base, its destination or direction is far from clear.

For purposes of this study, then, by applying anthropology to current affairs, I not only stand on the shoulders of the giants of anthropology but also hope to draw attention to the merits of the discipline and point to its relevance in today's world. Far from being an outdated and obscure handmaiden of colonialism, as many in and outside the discipline believe, anthropology has the capacity to be at the cutting edge of contemporary commentary on society, politics, religion, and international affairs. It can only do so if it overcomes its internal confusion and uncertainty.

This study represents an attempt to contribute to the epistemology of the discipline. Its method has been to examine the events that led to 9/11 and developments afterward through the prism of anthropology by employing the traditional tools of the subject now gathering dust in the basements of its departments. It has shown the importance and relevance of this traditional approach to the discipline. This study offers not only the construction of a new paradigm to understand the war on terror but is in fact a step toward reconstructing a new paradigm for anthropology by giving it greater integrity and bringing it closer to its own identity. Anthropology is thus able to fulfill its purpose of explaining the reality of societies that are different from Western ones and yet profoundly similar in that they are fully formed and complex human societies with which Washington, London, and Paris are inextricably linked and involved.

SOCOM and the Segmentary Lineage System

If civilians appeared muddled and unsure of the direction of the war on terror, the American armed services were spending time and energy in thinking pragmatically about the subject. They were after all on the ground and on the frontline facing the enemy. They were the ones losing lives in the line of duty and aware that it was a result of how little they knew of people abroad whose land was the theater of war. Speaking with a candor and intelligence that should have been heeded by U.S. policymakers, General Stanley McChrystal, the former commander of the coalition forces in Afghanistan, admitted: "Most of us—me included—had a very superficial understanding of the situation and history, and we had a frighteningly simplistic view of recent history, the last 50 years."[52]

To give the U.S. Army credit, however, as the Afghan operation dragged on, becoming the longest war in American history, the army gained a greater understanding of the importance of tribal culture and encouraged commanders to interact with tribal elders, a policy influenced by the U.S. experience in Iraq. In that conflict, U.S. military leaders had come full circle, at first seeing tribes as an impediment to efforts to establish democratic institutions, and then working with them as partner, especially in efforts to restore a modicum of stability in the midst of sectarian bloodshed and a breakdown of law and order.[53] But the strategy came too late and ultimately remained ineffective because of the very nature of the war itself. The United States did not have the time, the resources, or the temperament to create an effective and neutral tribal administration—the Waziristan model—at the district or local level that was crucial to peace and stability. The strategy was therefore haphazard, short term, and shifting. It relied too heavily on bribing elders who were often more interested in extracting as much as they could from the Americans while using them to their advantage against tribal rivals.

In my dealings with the American armed services, I found great interest in discussing various aspects of tribal administration. The audiences were educated, courteous, inquiring, and eager to understand, as was the case during my lectures delivered over two days in 2010 at U.S. Special Operations Command (SOCOM) in Tampa, Florida, at the invitation of its commander, Admiral Eric Olson. He was in charge of the SEALs, the elite striking force of the American military, which gained instant celebrity in America after the force's strike against bin Laden in Abbottabad in 2011.

Admiral Olson, a scholarly and thoughtful commander, commenting on future relations between the United States and tribal societies early in 2011, presented an image of the earth taken from space at night.[54] Olson explained the correlation that was clear at a glance: the dark spots—having no or very few lights—were the potential trouble spots. The light areas in the image gave the fewest problems. The dark areas, Olson explained, were ungoverned areas with porous borders: "Our strategic focus has shifted largely to the south . . . certainly within the special operations community, as we deal with the emerging threats from the places where the lights aren't." He identified fifty-one dark countries, which generally overlap with the dark regions, to be of "high-priority interest in the global campaign against the extremist threat." And it is precisely those dark areas that pinpoint the tribal communities I have discussed in this volume.

"We don't know them, and they don't know us," Olson admitted frankly, talking about the challenges that accompany close partnerships with central governments with which the United States has historically had no military relationship. "We generally don't speak their languages, we don't understand their histories, we don't know their families, we don't know how work is done, we don't know how money is made, we don't know all the nuances, we don't know the effects,

T. E. Lawrence, famous as Lawrence of Arabia, in Bedouin dress with Bedouin dagger (wikimedia.org).

truly, of climate, of terrain, of religion, of culture, in these regions. And it takes time to get there from here."

As if this admission was not interesting in itself (many Americans do not take much interest in cultures outside their own), the admiral displayed a capacity to think outside the box and went on to propose a solution. What the military needed, Olson suggested, were figures like T. E. Lawrence, or Lawrence of Arabia, the legendary British officer who had served in World War I and had successfully rallied the Arab tribes of the Arabian Peninsula against Ottoman rule. Lawrence lived among Arabs, spoke their language, wore Arab dress, understood their tribal codes and customs, and was accepted by them. What SOCOM needs, Olson concluded, were "Lawrences" of Afghanistan, Pakistan, and other places. These Lawrences would not be restricted to Americans and could include local people. Officers who could bridge the cultural gap that exists between American soldiers and local people were desperately needed and would ease the problems for both. Olson was therefore promoting "Project Lawrence."

Olson's remarks made an interesting contrast with those of Panetta. Although the areas identified by Olson on his map were precisely the same as named by Panetta, Olson's approach could not have been more different. For Panetta, the civilian, the war on terror is about exterminating the enemy; for Olson, the admiral, it is about understanding the society in which the enemy resides and building bridges and alliances in order to reduce the threat to America and promote its interests.

But Olson's ideas contain a contradiction if they are to be carried to their logical conclusion. His strategy rests on two prongs: the usual direct activity of the SEAL in the field, what Olson calls "man-hunting," and the offer to help central governments build their security and military capabilities. Both approaches involve working closely with central governments. Lawrence, on the other hand, took the opposite approach. In terms of my study, Lawrence saw himself as a champion of the tribes that formed the periphery against the central authority of the Ottoman Empire; he would lead the tribes to their independence so they could live according to their customs and traditions. Lawrence admired the tribesmen of the periphery as much as he despised the officials who represented the center as corrupt and brutal. While he tended to turn a blind eye to the exasperating internal squabbles of his Arab tribesmen, he could be cruel and vindictive with the Turks. For Lawrence, the Arab Bedouin was an approximation of the "noble savage"; for the SEAL, he was a "militant" or "terrorist," or potentially one. For Lawrence, the center was the problem; for Olson, it was the solution.

Olson and those who succeeded him at SOCOM, therefore, need not only to produce many Lawrences, but also to provide them with a map of the local tribal cultures and their historical relations with the central government. Local culture is more than just learning the language. It is also learning about the centrality of the tribal charter, the code emerging from it, and the way in which members of the tribe weigh the different features of that code. Not coincidentally, a map that Lawrence designed and is on display at the Imperial War Museum in London has an alternative vision of Middle Eastern nations based on tribal identity, and not on the arbitrary lines drawn by the European bureaucrats who were so supremely indifferent to tribal boundaries.

But even the most ardent of Lawrences would have a problem with the Muslim tribesmen today. Take the Pukhtun. Few of the Afghans' adversaries in history knew as much about them as the Americans: spy satellites picked up the details of every courtyard in every village in the country, soldiers mapped every dirt tract, and intelligence agencies collected files on every Afghan of "possible interest." Yet the Americans had failed to comprehend the central significance of the genealogical charter and the code of honor in tribal society. Had they known of the normative importance of honor and dignity to the Afghan, they would have taken greater care to educate their soldiers about them. It is difficult to escape the conclusion that as far as tribal society was concerned, Americans had information about everything, yet they understood nothing.

As a result, the way the war on terror has been conducted has left the Muslim tribesmen with little respect for Americans and their culture. Inasmuch as Muslim tribesmen see everyone and everything through their particular cultural prism with its emphasis on honor, they find Americans not up to the mark. Too many stories circulating in Afghanistan and Pakistan—for example, of torture, the killing of innocent civilians including children in their homes, of urinating on bodies, desecrating the Quran, and fighting a war with weapons such as the drone, which is not even visible—have created the impression of Americans as a people without honor. Olson's Lawrence would find the task of convincing Muslim tribesmen of the worth of Americans a challenging one.

Yet for anyone who doubts the tenacity, ferocity, courage, and moral purpose of Americans at war, they need to look at them in action in the last century, at Iwo Jima, for example, and in landing on the beachhead at Normandy—where ground was won through hand-to-hand, inch-by-inch fighting, with enormous casualties. During the Second World War the Americans led the allies in a global conflict against the Germans and the Japanese, two of the strongest and most disciplined armies wreaking havoc across continents. While the United States represented democracy, human rights, and civil liberties, the Germans and Japanese were bent on domination based on their notions of racial superiority and the use of concentration and labor camps. To lead the allies to victory, the Americans had to show resolve and honor. In contrast, after 9/11 the United States was fighting in Afghanistan and Iraq, two Asian nations already shattered by starvation, corruption, and civil strife, and steadily expanding the theater of conflict to other similar nations. Even the reasons for the wars in Afghanistan and Iraq appeared weak. America had no clear moral purpose for these wars and was therefore divided and unsure about them.

Without ever officially acknowledging the fact, in its war on terror the United States had crippled its mightiest instrument: the magnificent United States Army. Perhaps the most powerful army in history, like the mighty Soviet army a short while before, was done in by a ragtag group of tribesmen living at a subsistence level in distant valleys and high mountains. The asymmetry in economic and military power between the combatants and the way the war proceeded leaves the mind grappling for answers and explanations. Most Western, especially American, commentators simply refused to face the reality of what was happening in Afghanistan and Iraq. The United States had reached a point where General Colin Powell declared in public in 2006 that its army was "almost broken."[55]

American soldiers were committing suicide at an unprecedented rate, nearly one a day by 2012. Ironically, in 2012 more American soldiers killed themselves in despair than had been killed in combat in Afghanistan. The army so freely used for more than a century to implement U.S. foreign policy had been blunted at a time when the nation needed it more than ever to confront the challenges posed by emerging global powers like China and Russia.

The cyclical processes of empires with their rise and fall are accelerating. While it took the Roman and Ottoman empires centuries to arrive at the period of decline, the collapse of the British Empire, a truly global enterprise on which the sun never set, was quicker, only a few short years after the Second World War, when it seemed to just evaporate. The cycle of the Soviet rise and collapse was even more dramatic and its very existence confined to the twentieth century. While nations with the size and influence of the United States do not collapse overnight, the precipitous rise of the United States as the single hegemon in the late 1990s and its equally precipitous decline into a nation plagued by massive debt, unemployment, uncertainty, and unending overseas wars point to the accelerated pace of the cycle.

In President John F. Kennedy's Inaugural Address in 1961, he identified the "common enemies of man—tyranny, poverty, disease, and war itself." Kennedy's vision of America was inspired directly by the Founding Fathers. It is difficult to imagine that there was an American president only half a century ago who imagined an America in this manner. Recent presidents have compromised the vision of the Founding Fathers, echoed by Kennedy, for the sake of "security." Tyranny, poverty, disease, and war are everywhere since 9/11, and America has directly or indirectly, wittingly or unwittingly, emboldened these "enemies." That is why, when navigating the complicated map of the Muslim world, America needs to treat the different Muslim tribal societies on their own terms with honor and dignity in order to most effectively promote its own objectives.

It is difficult to escape the conclusion that the United States has been fighting the wrong war, with the wrong tactics, against the wrong enemy, and therefore the results can be nothing but wrong. Those who struck U.S. soil on 9/11 could have been brought to justice far more expeditiously, as this book illustrates. Instead, the United States has been sinking deeper and deeper into a quagmire under the weight of vague and changing objectives, all the while compromising its most cherished values. The post-9/11 leadership in America may be characterized as the mediocre leading the confused in pursuit of the dubious.

The United States needs to realign its current paradigm so that it is fighting the right war with the right tactics, against the right "common enemies," which in turn will give it the right results. The United States will fight a cleaner, clearer, stronger, and more successful war if it understands the causes and dynamics of the war and remains true to the ideals defined by its Founding Fathers: human rights, civil liberties, knowledge, justice, and democracy for all. If that were to happen, the men of violence would not only be dealt with through the processes of the law, but also effectively contained. That alone would be victory. That is an objective worth fighting for and to be savored.

Realigning the War on Terror

How a powerful imperial center views the world is visually illustrated in the "snails and oysters" bath scene from Stanley Kubrick's *Spartacus* (1960), famously deleted for its explicit lasciviousness and later restored in the 1991 version. The cold-blooded Roman general Crassus, played by Laurence Olivier at the height of his thespian powers, steps out nude from his bath after being scrubbed by Antoninus, a beautiful, young male slave portrayed by Tony Curtis. Moving to the balcony, Crassus reflects on the glory of imperial Rome stretched out before him with its marble buildings and columns, statues, aqueducts, and parks. A Roman legion in full formation marches out against Spartacus's army, as if to remind the viewer of the base of Rome's imperial power.

. "There, boy, is Rome," Crassus muses in awe. "The might, the majesty, the terror of Rome. There is the power that bestrides the known world like a colossus. No man can withstand Rome. No nation can withstand her. How much less . . . a boy! Hmm? There is only one way to deal with Rome, Antoninus. You must serve her. You must abase yourself before her. You must grovel at her feet." Then the coup de grâce, the final thrust: "You must . . . love her." Crassus turns around to find Antoninus has fled. He has gone to join Spartacus, a former gladiator and chief of a nomadic border tribe (from present-day Bulgaria), and his army of slaves demanding freedom or death. The idea of freedom is powerful and contagious; it will not die easily.

In the prurient discussions about the deleted scene and the debate surrounding the merits of eating snails as opposed to oysters—Crassus slyly hints to Antoninus that he enjoys both—the political metaphor it conveys is lost. But it is in fact reflected, in one way or another, in how every central government with imperial ambitions or temperament views the periphery: not only must you abase yourself before the center but "love" it.

For thistle-like tribes, this was difficult to do. However, over the centuries, an equilibrium, a modus vivendi even, had developed between center and periphery. The center saw the periphery as uncivilized and primitive; the periphery viewed the center as corrupt and effete. From time to time, the former attempted to crush the latter, or the latter raided the former, but on the whole the equilibrium between the two was maintained.

For over a thousand years, tribal Islam survived in the deserts and mountains. Sometimes it flourished, sometimes it developed into Islamic sultanates, and sometimes it even replaced the rulers at the center with its own tribal dynasties. Rites of passage were conducted according to tradition, memory of ancestors on the genealogical character was maintained, and religious ritual observed in the community's own fashion. Madrassahs provided education, sharia courts justice, and tribesmen took advantage of them. Conquering armies moved cautiously through their passes and deserts, rival clans attacked them, their elders lived and died, but not before passing on their traditions, and were succeeded by others who maintained the code and memories of the lineage as best they could. There was a stability and continuity in culture. Most tribes paid no taxes and many recognized no central authority; they were free in every sense. They were the lords of the deserts, masters of the mountains.

With European colonization, the equilibrium between center and periphery was drastically altered. Communities on the periphery woke to a nightmare reality. They had become the despised periphery of some distant, alien imperial power, a power that required their submission, abasement, and "love." Blood and thunder had heralded the arrival of European imperialism; its departure was the same. Perhaps its worst legacy was the haste and insensitivity with which departing Europeans had drawn up national boundaries. One of the most poignantly tragic results was that borders divided clans and communities. Brothers who shared a field or pasture until yesterday, whose children were married to each other, could not visit without papers and passports.

At the end of the era of colonization lay the seductive notion of independence, shimmering and sparkling on the horizon. It was a chimera, conjured up by those with little idea of what that meant in practice. To the tribesmen, independence in the form of a new state meant freedom to maintain their traditional lives and to be part of the modern world; to the city-dweller, it meant the rights and privileges enjoyed by the former European colonizers. In either case, it was something more imagined than real. The reality was the slow and steady erosion of the periphery and the equally slow and steady encroachment by the center.

For some tribes, the modern state was like hitting the jackpot. The dominant tribe now became the state, controlling the levers of power and having access to untold wealth and power, as in Saudi Arabia. Others, following a ruthless personal agenda and a mishmash of foreign ideologies, as Gaddafi did in Libya, ran affairs by appointing their family and clan members to all the key jobs. These tribesmen were the beneficiaries of modernity, just as their offspring would be of globalization.

In the next decades, the relationship lost its balance and transformed into an asymmetry as tanks, fighter planes, and modern military technology made the center more than capable of crushing the periphery. Besides, the center discovered that it need not be too concerned about the bad publicity surrounding human rights abuses as few outside were interested in the remote tribesmen. It was easy to cast the attacks on the periphery as a legitimate exercise in maintaining the writ of the state. The tribesmen were called rebels, miscreants, and after 9/11, terrorists. The anticipated benefits of independence had vanished for the tribesmen even before they could savor its joys. The exuberant moment or two that they felt at the birth of the nation had passed. After 9/11 the periphery found itself facing another complex predicament. They were now a periphery of what in effect was another periphery: most of these states were reduced to the status of "allies"—some would say "satellites"—looking to Washington and other Western capitals for aid, direction, and guidance on security issues.

The arrogance of Crassus is not unique to the Roman Empire. But because the Roman Empire was the prototype in history of an imperial enterprise, over time military officers, whatever their nationalities, referred back to the Romans and their legions. The Roman eagle was a standard symbol commonly adopted by militaries, and many an officer swaggered about as if he were a Julius Caesar or Marc Anthony. They would have murmured the words of General Crassus approvingly while applying it to their own empire—"The might, the majesty, the terror of Rome." Many a colonial general, whether in Africa or Asia, would have had similar ideas when contemplating the periphery: how to subjugate it while forcing it to "love" them. With the departure of the European imperialists and the formation of the new states, the uniforms and the color of the skin may have changed, but the same central attitudes to the periphery remained.

Core Findings

The juxtaposition of forty tribal societies, all from the periphery but drawn from vastly different political and cultural contexts, provides insights into contemporary tribal societies and their relations with their central governments. The communities exhibit notable similarities despite the diversity of their backgrounds: the dominant notion of "honor" and the tribal lineage charter that defines and shapes them; the idea that each was once, if not free, a freer society; the agony of discovering themselves within countries often dominated by a traditionally hostile ethnic population now in the majority; the sense that they are "voiceless" and "faceless," worse: that they are represented by hostile propaganda from the center; the frustration that they are suffering outright human rights abuses and no one seems to know or care about it; and the knowledge that the United States is directly, through acts of commission, or indirectly, through acts of omission, involved with each and every one of these abuses. The findings from the cases of this study suggest a time of crisis is at hand for tribal societies on the periphery.

THE SEGMENTARY LINEAGE SYSTEM AND THE WAR ON TERROR. First, there is a correlation between the maximum drone strikes and tribes that have the most developed segmentary lineage systems—Pukhtun, Yemeni, and Somali.

A connection also exists between highly developed clan structures and codes of honor and the determination to defend identity: the stronger the segmentary lineage system, the fiercer the resistance to outside aggression. Consider the dramatic difference in approach between the stuporous Rohingya and the excitable Wazir and Mahsud. This insight should be the basis for meaningful and positive negotiations by central governments in resolving the problems of their tribal communities. As a corollary, the groups that practice suicide bombing are all predominantly based in segmentary lineage systems—like the Tehrik-e-Taliban Pakistan (TTP) in the Pukhtun tribes, Al Shabab in the Somali tribes, the Kurdistan Workers' Party (PKK) among the Kurds, Boko Haram in the Kanuri people, and the various groups in the north Caucasus. Al Qaeda itself, my team and I found, is impossible to understand without insight into the culture, history, and relations between the Saudi center and periphery of the Yemeni segmentary lineage system that, in some profound way, is the place where it all began.

THE ROOTS OF TERRORISM. The next finding relates to Islam and terrorism. Despite the popular perception that Islam is at the root of terrorism, the weight of evidence gathered in this study indicates that the problem stems from the relationship between center and periphery—and that Islam actually has very little to do with terrorism. As Bernard Lewis has said, Islam is opposed to any form of terrorism. While the men of violence in Muslim society are aware of this fact, it appears that the experts on Islam are not.

The violence the tribes are caught up in, therefore, does not come from a religious compulsion, but as a result of the failure of the modern state to deal effectively and peacefully with the periphery. The center is marked by poor governance, corruption, and incompetence. It is applying short-term callous tactics to exterminate "terrorists." But the center has no long-term strategy to maintain its own integrity while including the periphery in the nation with its identity and rights respected. For all its rhetoric about national identity and unity, the center is too quick to dismiss the periphery as excrescence. The modern state has not lived up to its promise of providing prosperity, security, peace, education, and participation to all its citizens. Worst of all, it has repeatedly compromised civil liberties, human rights, and the practice of democracy. Based as they are in the urban and settled areas, the leaders of the center remain disdainful of the tribes, with their elders and codes.

As relations between center and periphery collapsed into violence, tribal society broke down, and everything that held up its structure—elders, families, religious leaders, and representatives of the central government—was destroyed. As a consequence, the foundations of society based in tribal and Islamic traditions began to mutate and assume alien forms. Not only were men blowing themselves up in suicide attacks that targeted representations of the central government and innocent civilians, but women had also begun to do the same. The periphery had descended into a vortex of violence that did not spare school children on a bus, officials in an office, or congregants in a house of worship. The case studies of this volume provide endless examples confirming the mutation and its extent and indicating that the problem is far from over and demands urgent attention.

Although this book is about tribal societies, a comment on what is called homegrown terrorism in the West needs to be made in the context of the war on terror, even if in parenthesis. The causes of terrorism in the West and that of Muslim tribesmen seeking revenge according to their custom or fighting to defend their territory are fundamentally different. The phenomenon of the homegrown terrorist was covered in some detail in my previous study of Muslims in America, *Journey into America* (2010). Terrorism—or plans to commit terrorism—among Muslims in the West is a product of several factors: living as a marginalized and often despised minority, confronting an environment of Islamophobia, concern that the global ummah is under siege with Palestine and Kashmir usually on top of the list, criticism of American foreign policy, the wars in Afghanistan and Iraq and the use of the drones in Pakistan and elsewhere in the Muslim world, and the absence of influential elders in the community and the lack of knowledge on the part of the parents of the cultural context within which their children are growing up. Given this background, many young Muslims find the answers that they are seeking from forceful Islamic voices, either in person or on the Internet, preaching hatred of the West and quoting certain selective verses of the Quran. Muslim organizations in the Middle East or South Asia may influence these young Muslims with ideas of global jihad and violence on behalf of the ummah. Yet, the sources of Muslim action in this case would not be based in the genealogical charter and the code, as it would in the example of the tribal societies that have been examined in this book.

THE UNITED STATES AND ALLIED CENTRAL GOVERNMENTS. Instead of attempting to rectify the failure of the relationship between the center and the periphery in the modern state, U.S. intervention is exacerbating it through the war on terror. As in the past, the tribes will not surrender and will continue to fight in the face of violence perpetrated against them, and the conflict will only escalate unless the paradigm is altered. Because trust for the time being has dissipated, there is little communication between the two.

Each center has used the war on terror to promote its own strategic interests, often at the expense of the periphery. It has done so using the appropriate language and symbols in subtle ways so that the adjustment would not be too obvious. Take the examples of India and Pakistan. After 9/11 both countries found themselves allies of the United States and ostensibly supporting the war on terror. Yet both adjusted American assistance and agreements to their own specific national interests. For India, this meant putting pressure on Pakistan by accusing it of being a source of terrorism and therefore forcing it to back away from supporting the insurgency in Indian-controlled Kashmir; for Pakistan, it meant taking military and economic assistance to battle the Taliban on the western front but diverting it to its eastern front facing India.

More than a decade after 9/11, central governments around the world still cannot provide a satisfactory explanation for the violence or are merely manipulating the United States into supporting their efforts against the periphery. If after all the time, expense, and deaths, governments are unable to see the reason for this consistent violence and dismiss it as al Qaeda, they are, in other words, resigned to the idea that the only solution is continued killing of anyone suspected of being al Qaeda. This study, however, has established that virtually entire tribal communities, wherever they live, could be assigned an al Qaeda link. This is lazy and dangerous thinking. It could lead to the next logical step involving nuclear weapons—the ultimate steamroller. The idea is not far-fetched. It can be seen in the statement of Lord Gilbert, a former defense minister of Britain, given in the House of Lords in November 2012. He suggested the use of the neutron bomb in the Tribal Areas. The action would create an impassable border between Pakistan and Afghanistan due to radiation and thus end terrorism in the region. As if this were not enough, Lord Gilbert went on to suggest that similar action could be taken "along various borders where people are causing trouble."[56]

THE INTOLERANCE OF THE CENTER. Small, isolated, largely illiterate, economically impoverished communities face the overwhelming military, economic, and political force of the center. The voice of the periphery is barely heard over the din and propaganda emanating from the ministry of information at the center. Tribal people have become despised strangers in their own homes, and in the cities vagrants and paupers. When I asked a smart, articulate Turkish student, someone who could pass as a white American, about the Kurds, her face suddenly distorted in anger. "They are so dirty," she said in disgust. "Their children have no clothes. We feed them. And they demand their own language!" Then she said with all the force of youthful vigor: "They should be wiped off the map of the earth."

The irony that she spoke with such contempt of not only fellow nationals but also fellow Muslims escaped her. But because she was a student on the campus of an American university, she spoke with candor. There is little doubt, however, that many of the world's young people living at the center, self-consciously connected to the age of globalization, and talking of human rights and democracy, feel the same about members of the periphery. When a Turk, suspected of having a Kurdish background, won Turkey's first gold medal at the London Olympics in August 2012, the following toxic tweet was trending on Twitter and went viral: "The best Kurd is a dead Kurd."

Let me underscore the point: as anecdotal evidence suggests, societies have a blind spot when contemplating the despised smaller community on their nation's periphery. Talk to the most cordial, enlightened, and intelligent Pakistanis, Indians, Israelis, Russians, Moroccans, Turks, Egyptians, Kenyans, Thai, Burmese, or Chinese from the center, and ask them about their countrymen—respectively, the Baluchis, Kashmiris, Palestinians, Chechens, the Sahrawi, Kurds, Bedouin, Somalis, Malays, Rohingya, or Uyghur—and too many will suddenly be transformed into either fire-breathing nationalists, coldly indifferent citizens, or close-minded bigots. They are not prepared to see any good in these people and will assail them as backward, primitive, thieving, and violent elements of society, or simply terrorists. They are anathema, they will say, holding back or outright harming the development of the nation. These amiable companions become chauvinistic nationalists at the mere mention of a name, reminding one of Samuel Johnson's dictum, "Patriotism is the last refuge of a scoundrel."

If the majority population at the center treats the Muslim periphery cruelly and unfairly, it will do the same to other minorities. If Iran treats the Kurds, Baluch, Ahwazi Arabs, Turkmen, and Azeris harshly, it does the same to the Jews and Bahai. Take Pakistan as another example. Its recent treatment of its periphery in the Tribal Areas and Baluchistan is far from satisfactory and compromises the vision of the founder of the nation, Muhammad Ali Jinnah, but its handling of Hindus and Christians and even sects like the Shia and Ahmadis is not much different. The Ahmadis, for instance, have been officially declared "non-Muslims" and are openly discriminated against. The tombstone of Abdus Salam, the only Nobel Prize winner from Pakistan and an Ahmadi, has been defaced because it described him as a Muslim. In 2010 two of their places of worship were attacked in Lahore, with 94 people killed and over 100 injured. The injured were then attacked in the hospital, whereupon another twelve died. The failure of the modern state extends beyond Muslim centers and Muslim peripheries: the Nagas and Adivasis in India, the Tibetans and Mongolians in China, and the Georgians, Ukrainians, and Estonians in the Russian-dominated former Soviet Union have had much to complain about.

The unrelenting cruelty of the center has driven millions of tribal people from their ancestral homes. Branded "potential terrorists," many of these displaced persons find it next to impossible to settle permanently and with honor. A popular song from my youth in the 1950s—sung by Talat Mahmood in the Indian movie *Taxi Driver*—contained a refrain that captures what communities living at the periphery are feeling around the world: "If I flee where do I go? One small boat and a hundred storms ahead. Who will understand the anguish of the broken heart?" The avenues of escape have closed for the people on the periphery. If the tribesman escapes with his family from Waziristan, or the hinterland in Kurdistan, Somalia, or Yemen to a big city, he is vulnerable to being picked up as a "terrorist" by the local police on the lookout for a promotion or a reward. If he crosses an international border, he is likely to land in some foul prison-like camp and be forgotten. If by some miracle he manages to arrive at a Western airport seeking asylum, the chances of getting through are not good. And if he does make it and is settled in some drab part of a big city, he then faces the backlash of being perpetually under a cloud of suspicion as a potential homegrown terrorist. One by one, with every step of the journey that takes the individual farther from home and family, a layer of dignity is peeled off, until in the end nothing is left but faded memories of the past and a dying hope for the future.

AUTONOMY IN THE PERIPHERY AND PEACE. My case studies show a clear correlation between peace and autonomy in the periphery, especially when autonomy includes cultural and language rights. Conflict invariably follows when autonomy is removed. Central governments need to understand that most of the communities discussed in this volume do not want outright independence as long as they are treated with respect and given the rights due to citizens.

To find peace, the central governments in the cases mentioned in this study face two choices, both requiring major changes. One unrealistic and unlikely option would be to redraw the present national boundaries, so carelessly and arbitrarily established at the creation of the modern state, and grant complete independence to the periphery. The other is to grant autonomy to the periphery with full participation in the political process and respect for the local culture and rights protected by the state. This second more viable alternative would require not only a change of heart of the leaders at the center but also a change of direction. If they cannot see the writing on the wall in the bloodshed that their soldiers are committing, then they need to look at examples such as liberated Libya. In spite of being part of a modern nation for half a century, one of the first demands of the people of Cyrenaica was the restoration of their identity based in the Sanusi order, which had been systematically crushed by Gaddafi. The flag of post-independent Libya under its Sanusi king was revived in 2011 as the flag of Libya. In 2012 a conference of 3,000 tribal leaders in Cyrenaica, led by the nephew of the former Sanusi king, Ahmed Zubair al-Sanusi, demanded autonomy under a federal system.

At the time of writing, only four of our case studies had found peace with their central governments as a direct result of being granted independence or autonomy: Kosovo and Iraqi Kurdistan, owing to international intervention, and Aceh in Indonesia and the Maguindanao of the southern Philippines because of internal reconciliation. Even when limited autonomy is given to the periphery, as in the case of the Albanians in Macedonia, relations with the center begin to improve.

The impetus for the agreement with Aceh was the catastrophic December 2004 tsunami that struck the Acehnese shores. Of the 230,000 people believed

Libyan protesters in Cyrenaica in 2011 wave the flag of Libya under King Idris and carry his portrait (wikimedia.org).

to have been killed, 170,000 were in Aceh alone, with a further half a million displaced. Out of this tragedy, Aceh and Jakarta found their common humanity. Interviews with then newly elected Indonesian president Susilo Bambang Yudhoyono showed that the only occasion when he "revealed deep personal anguish and emotion was in his descriptions of what he witnessed on his first trip to Aceh after the tsunami."[57] His vice president, Jusuf Kalla, was similarly moved by what he saw firsthand in Aceh. An agreement for Acehnese autonomy was signed in August 2005, allowing for the local recruitment of police, the right to retain 70 percent of revenues from local natural resources, the power to levy local taxes, and the formation of local political parties, which was formerly prohibited. Amnesty was granted to all former Free Aceh Movement (GAM) fighters, many of whom now serve in the Aceh administration and police. The December 2006 elections in Aceh saw a number of former GAM members winning political office, including independent candidate Irwandi Yusuf as provincial governor. In the Philippines, the Moro Islamic Liberation Front (MILF) of the Maguindanao people on Mindanao Island and the central government in Manila signed an agreement in October 2012 that sets the framework for granting autonomy to the Muslim southern region by 2016. The autonomous region will be called Bangsamoro, or Muslim nation.

In Macedonia, President Boris Trajkovski advocated a political rather than a military solution to the demands of the Albanian population and offered to more fully integrate them into the nation while respecting their culture and language in order to end the 2001 conflict. Nationalists opposed to this move besieged his palace, demanded his resignation, and fired shots in the air, as they believed the government needed to destroy the Albanians by force. He narrowly averted a coup, but Trajkovski stood his ground: "There are extremists in every country. My job is to lead the nation on the correct path, not follow the mob. The President has to do the right thing, and that is build peace and prosperity." He reminded the Macedonian people in a televised speech that the path to peace "may be the long way, but it is the right way."[58] Under the Ohrid Framework Agreement adopted in 2001, what was called "decentralized government" was mandated and included the right of Albanians to express their culture and identity and establish their own schools using the Albanian language. Tragically, Trajkovski died in a plane crash in 2004 before the reforms could be fully implemented. But while much remained to be done, Macedonia had taken an important step in dealing with the problems facing the center and the periphery.

Preserving Law and Order Effectively in a Tribal Society. Certain fundamental principles of administration can be drawn from the cases that have been examined, without which there can be no peace between the center and periphery. These principles are in consonance with the thought of those great figures of history who represented the center and pondered issues of governance—Confucius, Akbar the Mughal emperor, President George Washington, and Lord Curzon of British India. Their challenge was to create stability and peace in society. In order to do so, they identified a certain kind of representative official at the district or local level of administration.

The principles of tribal administration are reflected in what has been called in this study the Waziristan model. As this model has established, an efficient, impartial, honest, and culturally sensitive administration working with elders will not only be able to successfully maintain law and order but be widely accepted in tribal society. Trust and reputation are vital in order to win the respect of the tribes, while success in the field enhances those attributes. The Waziristan model, however, can be most effective when the administration is conducted by qualified civilians and not the military. Even in incidents that require force, civilian administration is most desirable because the proceedings are conducted within the framework of the law. In the process, ordinary people along with their tribal elders are mobilized to support the administration in marginalizing criminals in order to make them ineffective. By focusing on the actual criminals, the administration conveys to the general public the importance of maintaining the law at all costs, and such actions demonstrate that the center and periphery are working together to keep order in the region. When the model works, no problem in the field is too great to resolve.

To illustrate best the functioning of all of these principles of tribal administration, I present a case that involved the kidnapping of Mir Noor Muhammad Jamali in June 1986 when I was commissioner of Sibi division in Baluchistan. Noor Jamali, a chieftain of the influential Jamali tribe, was kidnapped from Nasirabad, a district headquarters in Sibi division, by dacoits, or an armed criminal gang. The dacoits headed for their base in the Sind province to the east with their prize. This incident came after a series of kidnappings in which dacoits would cross over from the Sind to kidnap people and take them across the provincial border for ransom. The operations were widespread and becoming increasingly bold. For the dacoits, it was a highly successful criminal enterprise.

I had recently taken over the Sibi division, and the incident became a test for my reputation. Immediately mobilizing all my resources, I followed the gang in "hot pursuit." I instructed one group of my officers to form an advance scouts' party, along with members of the Jamali tribe, and to leave without a moment's delay so as not to lose the trail of the gang. As the second prong of my attack, I gathered whatever armed men I had available to me and crossed into the Sind province. I had an excellent team of field officers, including Sikander Muhammadzai, the head of the police, who personally led his force over the next few days.

As commissioner of Sibi division, I was not authorized to act outside my jurisdiction, and crossing into another province with a raiding party was fraught with dangers. I was constantly in touch, however, with the chief minister, the head of Baluchistan province, who had telephoned his counterpart in Sind, informing him of my imminent arrival in his area, and this gave me administrative cover. As the news spread, anger grew among the Baluch tribes. A tribal war erupting across provincial borders was a real danger. In the meantime, on the national level, the opposition was hammering away at the newly formed elected government in Islamabad about losing control of the law and order situation in the country.

I knew if the trail went cold we would not be able to recover Noor Jamali easily, if at all. We were relentless in our chase. Gunfire was exchanged and several people wounded, but we kept after them. The heat was oppressive and the region desolate. We had virtually no food or water for three days. When I could, I snatched sleep at night in the back seat of the commissioner's car, with my Bugti bodyguard throwing a ring of protection around it. Had I not earned the respect of the Bugti through previous initiatives, they could have easily used the opportunity to kill me in my sleep and disappear into the hills in Baluchistan. In this case, however, my protection became a matter of honor for them. With their fierce-looking appearance and reputation for vendettas, their presence added to the pressure on the dacoits.

The chief minister of Baluchistan (left) honors the author with an award at a public ceremony after he successfully secured the release of a Baluch leader from a criminal gang (author's collection).

Deep in the Sind province, we were in the middle of what I described in my official report later as "no man's land."[59] The people in these villages found it hard to believe that an officer of the seniority of the commissioner was among them. The police locked themselves behind closed doors in their dilapidated police stations in fear of the dacoits. "The Sind Government," I wrote in my report, "cannot even collect revenue from here" and "the local police were demoralized and fearful."

After the intensity of our pursuit, the dacoits felt it was no longer worth keeping Noor Jamali. They told him what was happening was unprecedented and would ruin their business. They could not have senior officers exchanging fire with them and tramping around in their areas, thus exposing their hideouts. They released Noor Jamali unconditionally, and he was brought home safely. Given the national prominence the matter had assumed, it was widely reported in the press. The prime minister and chief minister gave statements to show the extent of control they had over law and order in the country.

Expressing his appreciation, the chief minister of Baluchistan wrote to me: "This is to place on record the appreciation of the Provincial Government for good work done and the high sense of duty displayed by you in giving a hot pursuit to the criminals who had abducted a notable of Jamali tribe namely Mir

Noor Muhammad Jamali and taken to Sind area. But for the untiring efforts and constant pressure put on the criminals recovery of the abducted tribal elder would not have been possible. It is only with such dedication and hard work that these undesirable elements can be controlled and discouraged. I am confident that you would keep up and continue with dedication for the eradication of such elements."[60]

A Baluch chief himself and the former ruler of a Baluch state, the chief minister followed up his generous letter with an equally generous gesture. He convened an all-Baluchistan jirga of chiefs and members of Parliament where in glowing terms he publicly honored me and my key officials with special awards. The word had got out to dacoits in the region: any breach of law would be met by swift and resolute action. I was informed by my police that a saying was circulating among the dacoits that it was best to lie low as the new commissioner was quite mad and capable of turning up with a large force at their doorstep if they broke the law. I would not have any law and order problem for the rest of my tenure as commissioner of Sibi Division.

The actions both of the administration and the dacoits have lessons for us in the post-9/11 environment. It is easy to conjecture how the experts and security officials would have viewed and handled the kidnapping of Noor Jamali. As they would apply the framework of the metanarrative and look for apocalyptic themes and "jihadists," a sequence of events would be set in motion that would take them further and further away from solving the problem. It would also make understanding what was actually happening on the ground increasingly more difficult. "Al Qaeda strikes again," "al Qaeda metastasizes in the Sind," and "drone strikes for dacoits" would become the media talking points. Large numbers of heavily armed security personnel in armored vehicles with no understanding of local culture would have been ordered into the region to seal it off. Anyone who appeared slightly suspicious—which could include virtually every citizen—would be picked up and taken for "interrogation." Some would be "rendered," and some may well have landed in Guantánamo Bay. The media and intelligence communities would be abuzz with accusations of links with al Qaeda groups in other parts of the world. Ordinary people would have been outraged by the disproportionate use of force and the encroachment of the center. And the dacoits would have thrived on local sympathy and waited for things to die down before they were back in business.

PARADOXES. This volume has revealed some interesting paradoxes. The first paradox is that a Muslim group could be rejected by fellow Muslims yet accepted by non-Muslim communities. As the Circassians fled the brutal butchery of their people in the Caucasus, for example, they were treated with indifference or outright hostility by fellow Muslims, yet warmly welcomed by Jews and Christians. Arriving on the borders of the Muslim Ottoman Empire in the hope of finding refuge, they assumed that these fellow Muslims, who in the past had been well served by people from the Circassian nation, would return the hospitality. Instead, as elders of the Circassian community said in an interview in Washington, "The men were given guns and told to go and fight against the enemies of the Ottomans on the frontiers, and the women were sent off to different harems and distributed as sex slaves."[61] Such was the terror that many women preferred to commit suicide, helped in this ghastly endeavor by their own men.

The Circassians I spoke to categorically declared that the best nation for them is Israel—and of course, they added, the United States where they live. Israel in particular has gone out of its way to honor them and their culture. Sensitive as they are to matters of honor and culture, they deeply appreciated the museum of Circassian culture and the schools created for them by the Israeli government. The 5,000 Circassians in Israel, they said, could not be happier. In contrast, they pointed out that in the Muslim nations of Turkey and Syria, they remain marginalized and are barely able to preserve traces of their identity and culture in the face of the center's strong, persistent, and crude attempts to erase them. The Circassians also speak with warmth of Christian Orthodox Georgia, which recognizes their suffering and has given them shelter. In fact, the first monument to commemorate the mass slaughter of the Circassian people was built not in a Muslim country, but in Anaklia, Georgia.

This same paradox can also be seen in the area of human rights regarding the case of the persecuted Ahwazi Arabs of Iran. An Ahwazi Arab who fled Iran for Syria when his family was arrested lamented: "Iran occupies more Arab land in terms of square meters than Israel does. Yet we get more attention from the Dutch than from all the Arab states."[62] In contrast to Muslim lands, the Netherlands hosted the Ahwaz Liberation Organization (ALO) and granted its leader, Faleh Abdullah al-Mansuri, refugee status and Dutch citizenship when he fled from an Iranian death sentence in 1988. On a visit to Syria in 2006 to meet other Ahwazi refugees, he was arrested in defiance of international law and sent to Iran where he was accused of "terrorism." He has since disappeared into the prison system.

The second paradox emerging from this study is that the same group has been both persecutor and persecuted. Pukhtuns, for example, who traditionally treated Afghanistan's non-Pukhtun ethnic groups such as the Hazaras and the Tajiks with disdain, found the shoe was on the other foot after 9/11 when they were routinely suspected of being potential terrorists in both Afghanistan and Pakistan and mistreated. Similarly, the Uzbeks have treated minorities like the Karakalpaks poorly but in Kyrgyzstan are subject to persecution. The Jola on the periphery of Senegal are persecuted by the dominant Wolof center, yet across the border in The Gambia, the Jola dominate and oppress the Mandinka people. And the Azeris in northern Iran complain of Persian prejudice, while fellow Azeris in

Azerbaijan, where they form the center, have been harsh in their dealings with minorities such as the Lezgins, Avars, and Talysh.

Another paradox is that the experts, who have monopolized resources, media attention, and the ears of policymakers, are either blatantly incorrect or logically absurd, and yet the general public relies on them for information, analysis, and guidance. According to the experts, for example, the tribes of Asir are the staunchest Wahhabis; Boko Haram is fighting for the imposition of sharia law; the Rohingya are Bengali and speak the Bengali language; and the Taliban are committed to cultivating poppy. In each and every case, as established in the preceding pages, the reality is contrary to what the experts have said. The Asir tribes are at the opposite end of the ideological spectrum to the Wahhabis and have been their victims ever since Asir became part of Wahhabi-dominated Saudi Arabia in the last century; Boko Haram has no cause to fight for sharia law as it already exists in their region; the Rohingya are not Bengali and have their own language; and the Taliban, far from wanting to cultivate poppy fields, actively target anything that they believe is not Islamic, which includes the use of drugs.

The absurdity of what these experts have related in these examples—and many more are at hand—is almost tantamount to suggesting that the main religion of Canada is Wahhabi Islam, Mexico is a country of Swedish immigrants, and the Quakers promote violence. The mistakes of the experts may be faintly amusing, but they are not harmless. Because their assessments and judgments influence policy, they have deadly consequences for the communities involved. They may lead to the interrogation, torture, or killing of innocent people. This is irresponsible and careless scholarship. Given the lack and level of information, the need to tell the stories of the people on the periphery, as has been done in this study, is imperative for any attempt to create a realistic picture of society.

Tribes in the Age of Globalization

If modernity was a disaster for tribal Islam, globalization was a catastrophe. If modernity meant reduction to third-class citizenship, constant humiliation at the hands of the arrogant and corrupt officials appointed by the center, watching helplessly as the language and culture of the forefathers were suppressed and ancestral lands appropriated by outsiders, then globalization after 9/11 was even worse. Given the significance of the seeming incompatibility between globalization and tribal society, this point merits closer attention.

After 9/11 globalization for tribal people meant the possibility of individuals vanishing into a dark world of rendition and secret prisons, where no one seemed to know why they were there or even who they were or if they ever existed. Perhaps you could end up as a "bug splat" to American drone operators on the other side of the world. It is no coincidence that when the voices from the periphery were heard, faint and dim through the attempts to block them out, they spoke of not being given justice and deprived of their rights. It is well at this point to contemplate Martin Luther King Jr.'s insightful comment: "Justice denied anywhere diminishes justice everywhere." Of course, there were immense benefits from globalization, but these were reserved for the elites and their cronies: villas by lakes and rivers, skiing vacations, children studying abroad, and an extravagant consumerist lifestyle of unprecedented wealth behind high-security walls.

Tribal Islam survived a thousand years of autonomy, the onslaught of European colonization, the disruptions of the industrial and communist revolutions, and the vagaries of nationalist eruptions—Arab here, Iranian there—and even the psychotic "strong men" of the modern state, but may not so easily survive globalization. The tempo and velocity of change have increased exponentially with each one of these stages of history. In the frenetic race of societies for economic betterment, tribal Islam appears out of touch, unsure, dazed, and antiquated. It is at loggerheads with some of the fundamental precepts of globalization—individualism, consumerism, materialism, and the rapacious role of multinational corporations.

Globalization is characterized by several developments that are directly detrimental to tribal societies. Even before 9/11, commentators noted that the globalized economic world order reinforced the authority of the central government and multinational corporations that were usually its partners. Officials in the national capitals eyed the economic potential of the resource-rich lands on the periphery, the exploitation of which would link them to world markets. Representatives of multinational corporations flew in to meet the nation's leaders to negotiate deals that would allow them access to these resources; both spoke the same language and worked within the same globalized economy. The aim of these foreign visitors, therefore, was and is to deal as smoothly and as swiftly as possible with officials at the center. They have little concern or care for the peoples of the periphery who have lived on these lands for centuries. Stories have long circulated of untold and untapped resources in the periphery: phosphate in the Sahrawi areas of Morocco; uranium in the Tuareg lands of Niger; oil in the Cyrenaica tribal areas of Libya; oil, gas, copper, gold, diamonds, coal, and the seaport facilities of Gwadar in Baluchistan; oil, gas, coal, and minerals among the Uyghurs in China; and the rich natural resources of the Nuba and Acehnese.

In order to gain access to these resources on the periphery, the center has made a deliberate and sinister attempt to change the ethnic demographic balance of the region by encouraging and organizing settlers of the majority ethnic group to live in, settle, develop, and exploit these lands. In the process, the demographic percentages that once favored the local community against outsiders have been drastically altered. This is true of Xinjiang, Western Sahara, Baluchistan, South Kordofan, and Mindanao. This demographic engineering has been accelerated with globalization.

It is worth drawing attention to the Ahwazi Arabs of Iran as there is a more than usual urgency in their case. A persecuted tribal group on the periphery, they are on the verge of finally losing their identity as a result of globalization and international political developments. With the war drums beating around Iran, the Ahwazi Arabs may soon find themselves in the eye of a global conflagration.

The greater the pressure from the United States to prevent Iran's nuclear program through economic sanctions, the greater the determination of the Iranians to generate funds for survival. Iran therefore exploits its oil resources, which it sells to the emerging giants of globalization, China and India. But the oil is in the region of the Ahwazi. The relentless drive of the Iranian center to the sources of the oil is therefore accelerated, and the Ahwazi in the process are pushed further aside.

This region was once called Arabistan—the land of the Arabs—and oil was discovered here early in the twentieth century when the region was under the British. Not long after, Persia annexed it and changed its name to Khuzestan, from ancient Persian history. The Arabic language was replaced by Persian. When the modern states of the Middle East were being created, the international border went right through the lands of the Ahwazi Arabs dividing them between Iraq and Iran.

On the Iranian side, the Ahwazi region came to account for 90 percent of Iran's oil and 10 percent—maybe as high as 20 percent—of OPEC's global oil production. Eager to lay claim to the oil without obligation to the Ahwazis, the center adopted a policy of sending waves of Persians to settle in the region and alter its ethnic balance, displacing the Ahwazis from their homes into filthy shanty towns. New towns were built for the Persian settlers who, because of government intervention, were able to buy Ahwazi properties at far below market value. Ahwazis claim that 1.5 million people, one-third of their total population of 5 million, have been driven from Khuzestan since 1979, with 250,000 people displaced by the seizure of lands for use in a sugar cane plantation.[63]

Despite the fact that Khuzestan has one of the highest GDPs of Iran's provinces, 80 percent of Ahwazi children are malnourished. Their living conditions are dire. A UN official who visited Khuzestan in 2005 observed, "There are thousands of people living with open sewers, no sanitation, no regular access to water, electricity and no gas connections."[64] The capital of the province, Ahwaz City, is recognized by the World Health Organization as the most polluted city on earth.[65] Disease rates are high as Ahwazis are forced to drink contaminated water, with Khuzestan water diverted by pipeline projects to government-patronized sugar plantations in the region and the center of the country.

The Ahwazis are deprived of their rights as citizens and are banned from speaking their language. Unrest is met with harsh crackdowns and accusations of "terrorism" and "agents of Zionism," with 25,000 Ahwazis arrested between 2005 and 2006 alone.[66] Ahwazi leaders complain of "ethnic cleansing."[67] In the case of the Ahwazis, globalization and world politics combine to crush further the identity and independence of another already persecuted periphery.

The Ahwazis, like other communities on the periphery, are also subject to the worldview that has formed over the last few decades as a result of globalization of how to conduct global affairs within the international political framework. This view is reinforced by organizations like the United Nations, the World Bank, the International Monetary Fund, and the entire international relations system. Ambassadors and embassies representing national governments coordinate with these organizations. These interactions further reinforce the legitimacy of both the global order and the central authority of the national government. By definition, they sideline the voices and demands of people on the periphery, who are seen as hurdles in the path to global progress. There is therefore little sympathy for them.

Consumerism and materialism, which lie at the heart of globalization, teach people to care only about their own communities and their own selves. There is a remarkable absence of compassion for others in the age of globalization. So the latest story of honor killing in the Tribal Areas of Pakistan, famine in Somalia, an assault on Kurds in eastern Turkey, or the massacre of the Rohingya reaches ears but not hearts. That is why the work for the people on the periphery of a Bono, a George Clooney, or an Angelina Jolie makes such an impact, is so admirable, and is so necessary.

While globalization emphasizes the individual, tribal society constantly underlines the importance of the larger kin group. Everyone is related to everyone else in tribal society. Elders are expected to look after the family, the young pay heed to what their parents say. If only "I" or "me" matters in globalization, "us" or "our community" takes precedence over individuals in tribal societies. As tribal communities are shattered, tribal people find it difficult to continue functioning as one group and yet equally difficult to start seeing the world through the prism of "I" or "me." They have lost what they once were and not sure of what they have become.

Finally, globalization works in opposite ways for the state and the periphery as far as warfare and military technology are concerned. While globalization has aided the center in combating the periphery in significant ways—providing high-tech weapons, surveillance, and communications equipment—it has also highlighted the failure of the periphery. As the center constantly acquires ever more deadly weapons, the impoverished periphery, its primary target, remains preoccupied with the past. Throughout history, tribes have been able to adapt to new challenges and threats, as discussed in chapter 2, yet in the age of globalization they have been unable to adapt to the center's new war tactics, technology, and communications.

The West's advancements in military technology over the past two centuries have given it the capability to inflict mass casualties and cause immense psychological and physical damage among tribesmen. These include the Maxim machine gun in the nineteenth century, the helicopter gunship in the twentieth, and the drone in the twenty-first. The Maxim, invented in Britain by Sir Hiram Stevens Maxim, could fire 600 rounds a minute, and when it was first used as a standard issue weapon by the British in 1893 in the First Matabele War in present-day Zimbabwe, it annihilated an army of Ndebele warriors considered among the finest fighters in Africa. At the end of the war, the British had fewer than 100 casualties, the Africans 3,000. European armies would use the machine gun on other tribal societies with similar results. Soviet forces used the helicopter gunship with equally deadly effect against Afghan fighters in the 1980s. The drones introduced after 9/11 were proving lethal to every member of tribal society wherever used.

While each traditional society, especially those rooted in the segmentary lineage system, attempted to resist the new weapons of war with customary notions of honor and courage and decried the cowardice of the attackers safely out of reach, ultimately these traits proved of little value in the face of advanced technology. Hilaire Belloc, the British scholar, poet, and statesman, summed it up in his oft-quoted verse: "Whatever happens we have got/The Maxim gun, and they have not."[68]

In the case of the drones, tribal communities on the periphery were using nineteenth-century tactics with twentieth-century weapons in order to fight a twenty-first-century war. Aware of their impotence in fighting drones effectively, tribal fighters began to rely on another weapon, previously unused—their own bodies in acts of suicide bombing. Their willingness to resort to suicide indicated the fundamental change that had come to their lives, to the ways they were fighting their wars, and to their assessment of their situation. It was an act of sheer desperation, a reflection of the breakdown of the tribal universe and everything for which it stood. Helpless in the face of modern weaponry, they plunged into an orgy of violence that reflected a mutation of the code—schools, offices, mosques, nothing was sacrosanct. They killed their own elders, religious leaders, and government officials. Systematically, they were dismantling the structures of tribal society. Rejecting traditional notions of honor, the individuals who succumbed to suicide in this way, however horrific in its consequences, believed that it was an "honorable" act. The killing not only of the self but often of completely innocent people has opened serious moral questions for Muslim leaders and scholars that are yet to be answered.

Globalization and the current wars have thus created a crisis for the tribal male once at the center of his society. Because tribal societies emphasize notions of honor, courage, revenge, hospitality, and protection of the family, and associate each of these with "manly" behavior, the inability to perform any of these traditional functions creates a sense of emasculation. The male is simply not able to perform. It is a collapse of a central part of his identity.

These observations about globalization lead one to ask whether tribal society is doomed in this age as it is failing to adapt. Such an idea is easily refuted by the Scots—the prototype thistle. The Scots have demonstrated that communities with a tribal background can succeed, even thrive, under globalization. Scotland's latest high-tech industries, glittering literary and film festivals that attract world-class celebrities, art and the architecture, and economic and commercial activity are all evidence of its embrace of globalization. Some of the prominent names of globalization are Scottish: Sean Connery, for one, is a celebrated voice for Scottish nationalism.

Even the clan structure continues to be celebrated in the age of globalization. In July 2009 the Scottish parliament convened a clan convention made up of more than 400 clan chiefs and elders, the first time such a gathering had been held in recorded history, to discuss their role in the twenty-first century. In addition, the Scottish impact on that quintessential engine of globalization, the United States, is hugely significant. The Scots, widely known as Scots-Irish in the United States, brought their characteristic tribal drive, initiative, courage, integrity, and hard-nosed pragmatism—all qualities evident in the tribal societies examined here, such as the Pukhtun—to help form the American character. As for the impact of globalization on the tribes of this study, its signs are evident among the autonomous Kurds in northern Iraq, which set it apart from other Kurdish communities in the Middle East. Erbil, the capital of the autonomous region, boasts glistening shopping malls and even a skating rink. It is already being called Iraq's Dubai.

Thus one may well ask why tribal identity has not prevented the Scots and certain Muslim groups, like the Kurds in northern Iraq, from benefiting from and participating in globalization. As the present study concludes, it is not due to any innate disability in Muslim tribal character, but largely due to the failure of the modern state to accommodate tribal groups as full citizens and provide them the opportunities to utilize their talents. Globalization after 9/11 has thrown tribal societies off balance.

Tribal societies need to rethink their strategy to preserve themselves not only in national but international terms. Just as the center attempts to block the world from knowing what it is doing on the periphery, it is in the interest of the periphery to bring its stories to the attention of international forums like the United Nations and global media such as CNN, BBC, and Al Jazeera. The world would be sympathetic if leaders in the periphery made serious attempts to improve the position of women and education in their communities. The more the periphery is linked to the globalized world, the greater the pressure on the center to behave with fairness and civility in its dealings. In any case, the periphery will evoke little, if any, sympathy on the global stage until it is able to effectively stop suicide bombers emerging from its ranks. Young people blowing themselves up not only take their own lives and the lives of others, but they destroy the image of their communities.

In the end, the problems of globalization, as it stands today, may outweigh its advantages for tribal society. The citizens of globalization are rightly concerned about the poor health of the planet and the status of natural life on earth—whether the primates in Borneo and the Amazon, the polar bears of the Arctic with the loss of their habitat, or the coral reefs off Australia. Surely they should be just as concerned, if not more so, about endangered human societies.

A Path Forward

The discovery of ways and means to resolve the conflict between center and periphery and conclude the war on terror to pave the way to stability and peace assumes paramount importance. In order for things to change, modern society needs to understand the context and history of conflicts and not impose an artificial external frame or ideology onto them. Given the periphery's response to assaults on its traditions and identity, a federal model of governance with autonomous tribal peripheries is a clear solution. The center also needs to create television and radio stations in the ethnic language, promote it in schools and colleges, and encourage members of the periphery to participate in the center's services and politics. Muslim communities on the periphery and the central governments that have problems with them could learn a lesson from America. This is true for non-Muslim and Muslim nations alike. This may appear paradoxical as many Muslims now look on Americans as invading predators. They refer to the genocidal treatment of the Native Americans and the cruel treatment of the African Americans who were brought to the American colonies as slaves. The United States, however, has a great deal to teach the world today about managing relations between the center and the periphery.

Tiny Hawaii in the midst of the Pacific Ocean, for instance, as part of the United States—absorbed thanks to the U.S. Navy in the nineteenth century—has the rights and privileges of every other state. The indigenous population may complain about cultural imperialism from the mainland, but it is not quite ready to break away. A functioning democracy, free media, and vocal legislators within a federal system allow the people of Hawaii to express their sentiments and sublimate their frustrations. Puerto Rico, a predominantly Spanish-speaking U.S. territory in the Caribbean since 1898, provides another example. It voted in a plebiscite in November 2012 to become the fifty-first state of the United States. It recognized that within the U.S. federal system its people would be able to participate fully and benefit as equal citizens while maintaining their own local culture and heritage. President Obama, reflecting the pluralist vision of the United States in respecting the wishes of the periphery, said in March 2011, "I am firmly committed to the principle that the question of political status is a matter of self-determination for the people of Puerto Rico."[69]

Yet another example from the West is the improved relationship between England and Scotland. In 1997 the United Kingdom granted Scotland its own parliament for broader autonomous home rule through a referendum. In October 2012 First Minister Alex Salmond of Scotland and Prime Minister David Cameron of the United Kingdom signed an agreement in Edinburgh to hold a referendum on Scottish independence in 2014. In this manner the periphery is free to choose whether to remain part of the United Kingdom or not. The United Kingdom thus provides a contemporary model of how to deal with a tribal periphery.

Similarly in northeastern Spain, the segmentary lineage Basque people, having been granted an autonomous region in 1978, used the polls to express their support for the possibility of future independence. For fifty years, Spain had experienced a campaign of bombings and shootings by the separatist Basque organization ETA, an acronym for Basque Homeland and Freedom, which was responsible for nearly a thousand deaths. The ETA declared a cease-fire in October 2011 and sought to take the "historical opportunity to reach a just and democratic resolution to an age-old political conflict."[70] The October 2012 elections in the Basque region saw two pro-independence parties winning almost two-thirds of the seats in the regional parliament. The following month ETA announced that it was prepared to disband and enter into talks with the government.

Perhaps few examples can be as illuminating as a Christian Ethiopian supporting cultural and political solutions rather than military ones when commenting on the Muslim communities in the Horn of Africa. Keeping in mind the sweep of history and the variety of religions and cultures in the area, Ermias Sahle Selassie, the grandson of the former emperor, Haile Selassie, believed that no military approach could solve the problems of the nation; they had to be solved through cultural and diplomatic initiatives and, most crucially, solved by the local people themselves, not outside forces. He was of the view that everyone involved needed to be consulted, including the men of violence: "Al Shabab is part and parcel of the land. These people need to be brought in." Ermias was skeptical about big power politics in the region: "Is the whole debate about al Qaeda in our region," he asked trenchantly, "to protect U.S. interests in Somalia or in the interests of the people of that area?"[71]

These examples illustrate that debates and discussions rather than guns and missiles can improve the difficult relationship between a strong center and a periphery with an equally strong tribal identity. It is vital to stress the importance of deploying educated and understanding civil servants rather than the military in the administration of the peripheries. If force is to be used, then it should be in the form of local police in place of external troops. The imposition of military rule should be avoided at all costs: it sends the message that the periphery is not part of the nation but rather a fringe of troublemakers and outsiders that the government needs to "defeat" or "punish."

An examination of the administration of tribal societies over time and across many societies confirms that intelligent and compassionate political officers were able to ensure justice and stability in tribal societies far more effectively than a military officer using force. There is a problem, however, with the full-blown revival of the "political agent," even if suitably adjusted to modern times. Most Muslims see the office as a relic of colonialism; the British, who created the post, view it as an embarrassing reminder of their imperial past to be consigned to the dustbin of history; and Americans, unaware of the musings of their own Founding Fathers, do not know what to make of it. Yet the idea is significant enough on the basis of our findings to persevere with its promotion.

If my thesis is correct that the fierce contemporary violence stems from a mutation of the tribe's structure and code, a solution to the present impasse— that is, the manner in which the war on terror has evolved—surely needs to be sought in the same source. If the tribal code promotes the notion of revenge, then it just as surely advocates the resolution of conflict through a council of elders based on justice and tradition. Traditional tribal structures and the code of honor that emphasize tribal councils and efforts at reconciliation need to be revived and reconstructed. Those parts of tribal society that are currently in play, such as the imperative to take revenge, need to be firmly countered within the tribal frame. In that manner only can those promoting the bloodshed and anarchy be challenged and marginalized by the community. The periphery, too, needs to draw on the vast resources in its legacy. In recent memory, for example, tribal societies have produced leaders like Ghaffar Khan and his message of nonviolence—a message that he emphasized was rooted in his Islamic and tribal identity.[72] It is well to ponder the fact that if the Pukhtun have produced the Tehrik-e-Taliban Pakistan, they have also given the world the Frontier Gandhi.

These case studies have exposed the weakness of the center and the predicament of the periphery. The center has its legitimate needs and demands, and the periphery must express itself through its customs and traditions. Some accommodation and give-and-take between the two is essential in order to avoid a breakdown in their relations. While the state must express its ideas of nationhood by providing education and other benefits to its peoples, the leaders of the periphery need to encourage their followers to participate in the processes of change and take advantage of them. The state must understand that its components have different customs and traditions, and it needs to acknowledge them, granting the communities on the periphery the full rights and privileges enjoyed by its other citizens. It must understand and work with the segmentary lineage system, particularly with the elders forming the first pillar of the Waziristan model. Somalia took a positive step in this direction in August 2012 when, for the first time, its new parliament was selected by tribal elders and evenly represented the four major clans as well as minority groups in the country. This contrasted with the previous attempts at establishing a central government that relied on the authority of warlords. Hassan Sheikh Mohamud, a member of the Hawiye clan, was elected president by the parliament a month after its formation. Shortly thereafter, Fowsiyo Yusuf Haji Adan of the Isaaq clan was appointed as the first female foreign minister of the country.

All administrative reforms and development need to be implemented within the tribal structure and code. Every time people from these tribal societies have been able to express their views, they have yearned for traditional tribal structures to return.[73] Only in this way will people be able to better their lives and give their children opportunities to connect the future with the past. These reforms must not aim to destroy local culture or to turn people into something that they are not. If the world is to move away from violence, wars, and stories of torture and tragedy, this is the alternative paradigm that needs to be explored.

The process of bringing center and periphery closer together can be greatly facilitated by the United States, which is involved with both in different ways. The United States thus has a potentially vital role in helping these societies move toward democracy and promoting human rights, civil liberties, and education. Instead of pumping billions of dollars into missiles, guns, and torture instruments, American aid should emphasize education, teachers' training programs, health facilities, computers, conferences, and opportunities for tribesmen to develop their talents. This calls for a long-term and holistic strategy in order to defeat the forces of violence and anarchy and to convert America's war on terror into a drive toward a more peaceful, equitable, and just world—one envisioned by Americans like Dwight Eisenhower, John Kennedy, and Ronald Reagan.

However good the intentions on both sides, there is still the matter of how each sees the other. Unfortunately, American perceptions of Muslim tribesmen and vice versa reflect little but contempt and disgust, as the American survey cited in chapter 1 illustrates. Although that survey gave insights into how Americans and Afghans saw each other, it is applicable to all situations where Americans interact with Muslim tribesmen in their tribal lands. This study can offer advice to both on how to behave if they want better relations. Americans need to stop endlessly "passing gas" in public, urinating on dead bodies, burning the Quran, and using foul language every time they speak, stop harassing women, and they must desist from killing civilians. Muslim tribesmen need to bathe from time to time, control their urge to only help their immediate clansmen, stop lying and thieving, and, in the case of Afghans, end the murder of those very comrades-in-arms who have provided them jobs, training, guns, and uniforms. In short, each position must appreciate the perception the other side has of it. This would provide insights into each other's societies, allowing both to make adjustments in dealing with each other. Without this adjustment, relations between the two will not improve.

The suggestions on how to move forward come with a note of urgency. On careful analysis of the cases presented, it is not difficult to offer a prognosis of countries where unsympathetic central governments backed by the United States confront tribal communities on the periphery: disaster awaits. But the war on terror, itself triggered by 9/11, is not the only factor driving the world in this direction. There are two others: xenophobic ideas of racial identity that lie embedded in history and the more contemporary processes of globalization that have set out to "flatten" the world.

The combined impact of these several factors on tribal societies is proving calamitous. Unless the nature of the war on terror changes its purpose and direction, the future appears bleak. Perhaps lessons can be learned from one of the most tragic breakdowns between the government and a minority community— the Holocaust that took place in Europe in the last century.

Genocide by Another Name

The Holocaust was the ultimate act of inhumanity, the very definition of genocide: the entire resources of a modern European nation were mobilized to demonize the Jewish community and then plan and implement its annihilation. Every part of the state joined in this campaign—military, academia, media, and even cultural and religious leaders. Germany was a nation of Nobel Prize–winning scientists, world-renowned musicians and composers, and respected theologians and philosophers, and it possessed a highly industrialized economy. Even 25 percent of the leadership of the most notorious of Hitler's killers—the SS—had advanced academic degrees; many of them possessed a Ph.D.[74] None of this prevented the Holocaust or ordinary Germans from becoming genocidaires, resulting in the deaths of over 6 million Jews. Anyone who was Jewish was a potential target for the concentration camps, though Nazi officers determined who was and was not a member of the community—recall Goering's chilling remark, "I decide who is a Jew."

Knowing something of this background, I could not but be overwhelmed when I visited the U.S. Holocaust Memorial Museum in Washington, D.C., on June 22, 2006, to give a public lecture. At the museum, I saw an exhibition of the actual shoes of those who had died in the concentration camps to remind the public of those terrible events. The display, powerful and mundane at the same time, effectively drove home the plight of those who died. What struck me was the utter helplessness of the Jews as they were led to the slaughter: the United States closed its doors to them, and the Pope was indifferent to their suffering so as not to offend the Nazis. I had not seen anything like this before, and I was grateful that the museum had brought me face to face with the extreme limits of evil that human beings are capable of. This, I believed, could never be allowed to happen again. It was therefore legitimate and necessary to say "never again."

Drawing lessons for humanity at large, the museum officials consciously underlined the need for *all* acts of persecution to be challenged and exposed to the 2 million people who visited the museum annually. This, they stressed to me, included the suffering of Muslims. Although several Muslim ambassadors and leading Muslims had come to my talk, taking pride in the fact that this was the first Muslim speaker at the museum, I discovered later that few Muslims had ever visited the museum. They dismissed it as a "Jewish" museum, suggesting that there was an element of propaganda in it. When I pointed out that, on the contrary, this was a regular American museum, like those of the Smithsonian, Muslims were surprised.

Lessons from the Holocaust

What had particularly impressed me was that the museum's officials—Sarah Bloomfield, the executive director, and Arthur Berger, the senior adviser for external affairs—did not project the Holocaust as only a Jewish tragedy. In a discussion with my team and me about the themes of this project in June 2012, Bloomfield and Berger told us that the first lesson from the Holocaust was to understand it in terms of "a common humanity." Bloomfield underlined the importance of treating the other with dignity, stressing that "our dignity is linked to the other." She warned that human nature being what it is, people need to be constantly alert to the fact that "the unthinkable is thinkable." "Apathy and indifference, demonization of the other, fear of the authorities, political and economic instability," Sarah pointed out, are the "signposts" on the path to genocide.

It was critical, Bloomfield said, to educate the young about the dangers of hatred for the other; to convince society that what happens outside our borders affects us in our communities; and it is important to understand that the relationship between victims, perpetrators, and bystanders is a shifting one, that their roles may change with differing circumstances. When people lack knowledge about the suffering of minorities, Bloomfield and Berger pointed out, propaganda against the other in the media can be dangerous. Hitler, Berger told us, was the first to use live television—ten years before the United States. Hitler's men used the media to deadly effect in promoting hatred of the Jews. By tapping the anti-Semitism in European history, the Nazis were able to make it an accepted part of popular culture. That is why telling the story of the persecuted community, the recounting of what is actually happening to those people through personal accounts, becomes an important element in challenging hatred. People must know that while Hitler's men could boast of their efficiency in killing ten thousand Jews a day in the gas chambers of Auschwitz, the technology available today could kill that number in a second.

In spite of so many having said "never again" to the Holocaust, evidence of anti-Semitism still lurks like a poisonous gas that has not quite evaporated—a synagogue or Jewish cemetery desecrated in one place, the swastika daubed on a Jewish building in another. In 2012 television screens showed sights disturbingly reminiscent of Europe more than half a century ago—thousands of white youths in a soccer stadium during a match between Poland and Ukraine vigorously giving the Nazi salute and chanting in passionate unison *Sieg Heil*—the slogan associated with Hitler and shouted at mass rallies. In August 2012 a nineteen-year-old Jewish student at Michigan State University was viciously attacked at a party by two men who stood over him giving the Nazi salute and repeating "Heil Hitler" just before knocking him unconscious, while the rest of the group stood by without interfering.

On my arrival in Britain's Cambridge in the fall of 2012, I read of objectionable anti-Semitic graffiti painted in several spots across the town.[75] England's Tottenham soccer club, which traditionally draws support from the Jewish community of north London, was the target of a number of anti-Semitic attacks in 2012. Fans of West Ham soccer club, in a November match with Tottenham, chanted "Adolf Hitler's coming to get you" at the opposing fans.[76] Only days earlier, after a match in Rome in which anti-Semitic slogans were shouted at Tottenham players, a Tottenham fan was stabbed in an attack by masked men shouting "Jews."[77]

The same poison that persists against the Jewish community infects views about tribal people. It has already led to acts of genocide of every hue—cultural, economic, and physical—as defined by those who have contributed to its understanding. Raphael Lemkin, who coined the term "genocide," intended it to "describe assaults on all aspects of nationhood—physical, biological, political, social, cultural, economic and religious."[78] The 1948 UN Convention on the Prevention and Punishment of the Crime of Genocide unambiguously stated in Article 2:

> Genocide means any of the following acts committed with intent to destroy, in whole or in part, a national, ethnical, racial or religious group, as such: Killing members of the group; Causing serious bodily or mental harm to members of the group; Deliberately inflicting on the group conditions of life calculated to bring about its physical destruction in whole or in part; Imposing measures intended to prevent births within the group; Forcibly transferring children of the group to another group.

In addition to genocide, "Conspiracy to commit genocide; Direct and public incitement to commit genocide; Attempt to commit genocide; and Complicity in genocide" were all taken to be punishable acts (Article 3). Lemkin and Samantha Power, special assistant to President Obama on human rights, who has also contributed to the subject, did not restrict their definition of genocide to the mass killing of a people. Power wrote, "A group did not have to be physically exterminated to suffer genocide. They could be stripped of all cultural traces of their identity."[79]

According to these definitions, all of the tribal societies presented in this volume, at one time or another, are clearly victims of genocide.

The Holocaust stands as the worst form of genocide. It was the *Glaubenskrieg,* a total war to exterminate a race and religion incorporating all aspects of society. The lessons of the Holocaust point out the ominous signposts on the road to genocide in Muslim tribal societies on the periphery: demonization here, forced migration there, the pervasive fear of brutal authority everywhere, and too many examples of the actual elimination of entire communities. If the directions are not quickly changed in these societies, the end results are not difficult to predict.

Anguished Voices from the Periphery

Genocide is on the minds of the people on the periphery. They use the word "genocide" to describe their condition whether it is the Tuareg and Fulani in West Africa, the Avar of the Caucasus, or the Tausug of the Philippines. So do many others, and the word becomes a distant echo of imminent doom. Here is a Wazir tribesman talking of the genocide facing his people:

> The players are powerful; they have trampled our way of life, our hopes and aspirations. They are trampling our culture and the future of our children, rather our destiny. I ask, where are the people who stood up against tyranny and genocide? Where are the proponents of human rights? Did we harm anyone, do we deserve all this? Allah is not answering our prayers, has He forsaken us or is He testing our resilience? Can a test be thirty years long? I ask the world to stand up for the voiceless, get us out of this quagmire, that we had nothing to do with.[80]

These voices from the periphery haunt me. My team and I heard the word genocide too many times in the interviews conducted with the people of the periphery. The Circassian elders who came to see us in Washington, D.C., spoke in similar tones when describing their experience with the Russians. "The worst part of the genocide," said Iyad Youghar, "is the continuity until today," and he pointed to the government's brutal methods in the Caucasus. Russia, he said, wants to "erase us from existence."

"What is going on is genocide," pleaded Kekenus Sidik, the young girl representing the Uyghur of Xinjiang, in my office. "We want the world to listen. We want independence, because Chinese 'Social Harmony' means total assimilation and the death of our culture. The worst thing to do is to stay silent. The world needs to act now before it is too late and we say 'never again' as we said for the Holocaust."

Genocide is also on the mind of Wakar Uddin when he contemplates his people, "The Rohingya face a policy of extermination." He reflects with pain on the plight of his community:

Rohingya ethnic minority in Burma (Myanmar) is one of the most persecuted people in the world, and their very existence is on the verge of
disappearance. If the purposeful policy designed by the Burmese military
with its ethnic Rakhine ally to remove the Rohingya people through means
of violence and terror from their native land is not a genocide, then the
definition of 'genocide' should be questioned.[81]

Hearing the voices of people from the periphery, one gets the impression of
utterly normal and decent human beings bearing witness to the slow but inexorable destruction of their communities. It is like a Greek tragedy being played
out: the audience knows that ruin awaits the protagonists, and it fears for their
fate; but it also knows that nothing can alter the dénouement.

The formula is as sinister as it is familiar. The central government implements
stringent measures that may include sealing off a town or area, blocking access to
communications, and putting out distorted and turbid statements about quelling
"rebellion." The world, overloaded with a twenty-four-hour cycle of "breaking
news," has little interest in yet another story of human tragedy and little incentive to discover the truth. In any case, the center has a trump card up its sleeve:
by applying the label "Islamic terrorism" or "Islamic militancy" that points to
links with al Qaeda, it guarantees the world will cheer it on in its mission without
asking too many questions. With that cynical maneuver, the center becomes the
legitimate interpreter of what is happening on the ground and seals the fate of the
periphery. Now, with the world looking away, the notorious security and Special
Forces can proceed to do their bloody work without interruption or scrutiny
from prying eyes. Another genocide may be taking place, but, it would appear,
no one really cares.

Acts of genocide not only challenge their victims but all those who must contemplate the consequences of these actions. This was evident in the following letter, sent to me from an anonymous author after reading the op-eds in Al Jazeera
written by my team and myself about the suffering of these beleaguered communities with reference to our project: "I felt ashamed to not have known about
their struggle for existence. I wonder how these people cannot become terrorists
or rebels if faced with such inhumane conditions. The question is how would we
react if faced with a situation they are in. I can only pray to Allah to protect all of
us from this test. For sure, most of us would fail in this test."

The anonymous writer had raised a pertinent question. Genocide had been
taking place in history and was again recurring. What is new is the increased frequency and intensity of genocide as far as tribal societies are concerned; and if,
as I maintain in this study, every tribal community is like a bounded world of its
own, then the obliteration of literally hundreds of worlds becomes possible. The
scale of suffering can be illustrated in numerous examples from these studies.

In the 1860s Russia killed 1.5 million Circassians, half of their population, and expelled the other half from their lands. In the 1940s the Soviet government loaded the entire Chechen population of 400,000 on trains to Kazakhstan, killing half in the process, while more than 100,000 were killed in the wars after 1994, or 10 percent of the entire population. In the first four decades of French colonial rule, 2 million Algerians, two-thirds of the population, were killed. The Italians killed 50,000 Cyrenaica tribesmen in Libya from 1930 to 1933, and, in total, reduced the population by two-thirds as a result of death and displacement. Between 1868 and 1900, some 5 million Oromo, or half the population, were killed in Ethiopia, with an additional half a million killed in the Oromo Bale region in the 1960s. In the 1990s the Sudanese government killed as many as 500,000 Nuba, half of the population, and as many as 400,000 Darfuris in the early 2000s. These figures convey a stark reality: if Muslims are an embattled species in the modern world, Muslim tribesmen are an endangered species in it.

Because these staggering statistics involve hundreds of thousands of people, if not millions, they are numbing and difficult to comprehend. Perhaps individual cases will throw the horror of genocide in sharper relief. Consider the two children in Waziristan who saw their father shot in the head during indiscriminate firing by Pakistani security forces when he took them shopping to a bazaar: "The children were covered in blood and brains of Yaqub Shah, they saw their beloved father, head shattered, lying in a pool of blood with no one to help them. For hours, the terrorized children sat by the dead body of their father, eyes wide open, not able to cry not able to speak." Or consider the Fulani Muslims of the Middle Belt region of Nigeria who became victims of cannibalism by Berom tribesmen making matter-of-fact comments on video while police watched passively: "I want the heart" and "Did you put some salt?" Or hear a Russian soldier describing what his fellow soldiers were doing in Chechnya: "One guy pinned a Chechen to the ground with his foot while another pulled off his pants and with two or three hefty slashes severed his scrotum. The serrated blade of the knife snagged the skin and pulled the blood vessels from his body. In half a day the whole village was castrated, then the battalion moved out." Or listen to Fatoumata, the brave young Fulani woman, who relived her ordeal at the hands of security forces chanting "We are going to exterminate you, Fulani" in the notorious episode at the stadium in Conakry, Guinea: "A police officer, after raping me, decided to urinate in my mouth, as if it was part of their program. I received streams of urine all over my face. After, they used sticks to rape me again with these objects. Then, finally, one tried to stab me in front, on the private parts. . . . The blood began to flow and I was so exhausted that I could not scream or cry." Or hear the courageous Kashmiri woman recalling the night the women of her village were gangraped by the Indian Army: "The army entered our houses at 10 in the evening and left at 9 in the morning. . . . There were screams everywhere—from almost every house in the village." Or contemplate the bodies of dead Baluch men with lettering freshly carved into their chests declaring "Long Live Pakistan."

It is difficult to believe that these are not chronicles and legends of ancient peoples visited by demon barbarians but what is happening today. People on the periphery have been traumatized beyond imagination in recent years: they have been cooked and eaten; their women have been gang-raped in front of them; their young men, elders, and religious teachers have been humiliated, tortured, and killed; their houses of worship have been destroyed; they have been relocated away from their homes and their lands stolen from them. They face widespread famine and disease and are voiceless and friendless in a hostile world. They have been called "insects," "snakes," and "reptiles." They have been robbed of their dignity and honor. They have seen their young men and women transformed into suicide bombers killing women and children, passengers in buses, and worshippers in a mosque in a frenzy of anger. Yet the world seems indifferent to their suffering and is barely aware of its scale. This is indeed the dark side of the soul of man.

After the grim and relentless litany of woes I have just related, it is hard not to cry with Joseph Conrad: "The horror! The horror!" It should give everyone pause to reflect on the fate of humans and ask: is this where they were meant to arrive? In the end, will they be defined by little more than their indubitable capacity to breed and kill?

Healing a Fractured World

The metaphor of the drone for the war on terror in the age of globalization and the thistle for the tribal societies caught up in it brings to light the complexities of several important issues emerging from the interaction of two completely different kinds of societies: the nature of tribes, especially those with the segmentary lineage system, and the central role their identity plays in their lives; the breakdown of relations between the center and periphery; the importance of analyzing tribal peoples of the periphery within the frame of their social structure, lineage, and code of honor and within their perception of Islam, not through theology and sacred texts alone; and the challenges tribal societies face as a result of globalization, exacerbated by developments after 9/11 and the war on terror. This study also provides irrefutable evidence of the strength of primeval emotions in societies today and the weakness of modern political thought with its ideas about democracy, civil liberties, and human rights in checking the violence and corruption of the state. The cases have illustrated the complex interplay between cause and effect in human affairs, which is why my team and I have wandered in the dense thickets of several scholarly disciplines in search of answers. On a philosophic and humanitarian level, the study points to the real possibility that one type of human society may be facing extinction—that of tribes.

All is not lost, however. Young Pukhtun boys—defying drones, suicide bombers, and the guns of the security forces—are still playing football and cricket in the Tribal Areas of Pakistan, the Kurds are still singing the songs for harvest, and in the midst of anarchy Somali and Yemeni parents still want the best possible education for their children to secure their future. These communities still celebrate the great festivals, and the children still expect sweets and toys on these occasions. There is still joy at birth and marriage, sorrow and mourning at death.

Glimmers of light, love, and hope can be seen in this study. The action of the commander of the Philippine forces who was formerly in charge of military operations in the Sulu Province, Major General Ruben Rafael, offers an example of how to proceed. In 2007 the general gave a public apology to the Tausug for atrocities committed by the military. Soon, members of the audience started to cry, including the Tausug mayor of the town, who exclaimed that in the history of the province a military officer had never apologized to them in such a way before. Likewise, the devastation wrought by the 2004 tsunami in Aceh resulted in the outpouring of emotion and prayer accompanied by humanitarian aid and autonomy from the central government. After decades of warfare between center and periphery, peace finally came to Aceh.

Bright-colored flowers still bloomed in the midst of the dark and bleak battle-scarred landscape. I received one such flower in the form of a message from Mahdi Murad, a young Kurd in northern Iraq who had just performed in my allegorical play *Noor* at the American University in Sulaimani; it was produced by Peter Friedrich, a dedicated American professor who inspired his students. We had never met, but Mahdi's heart was overflowing with love as he wrote: "We all prayed for you and expressed our gratitude to you for writing such a great play." Then, from a region plagued by war and genocide, this young student made an offer to a professor safe and secure in Washington, D.C.: "Please let me know if I can assist you in any way." Mahdi went on to write not of revenge and honor lost but of tears and redemption, and in this he conveyed a message of compassion and love for all. Saddam's missiles and mustard gas and the anarchy of the American invasion could not extinguish the Rumi in Mahdi's heart:

As I am writing you this e-mail, my eyes are full of tears. . . . If you could have seen the audience, you would have known that almost everyone lost someone very close to them in a war. I say a war because there have been many of them since the day we were born.

However, none of us have had the opportunity to cry for the people we have lost. We, Kurds and Arabs in the 'Noor' cast, are joining hands together to shed the light of the life of every single person of our country. We gather together to shed our last tears to the sad events our people have experienced so far. We, the cast, stood together, as Kurds and Arabs, to cry for the innocent

sons and daughters we lost. But it would be selfish to do just that. We also
cried for the soldiers, on all sides, who gave their lives. We also cried out
against corrupt politicians and greedy businessmen, to cry out a warning to
everyone who thought someone was evil just because they spoke Kurdish
or Arabic or English. We cried for all these things, but most of all, we cried
for every Noor in every home, wherever she was.

In effect, Mahdi was saying—no more; there must be a different way. Mahdi's
tears in search of Noor, or light, are an apt metaphor to conclude this study.
There could be nothing more human than tears of compassion shed in the yearn-
ing for illumination.

The test is to see a common humanity in the suffering of others. If people can
rise above tribe, race, and religion to reach out to others not like them, it will save
humankind in the twenty-first century. It is a daunting task. Perhaps it is necessary to seek guidance from our ancestors and apply their wisdom to the present
time. If the world is to become safer, more harmonious, more compassionate,
then both the non-Abrahamic and the Abrahamic societies have much to offer.
The path to nonviolence and peace shown by the Hindu, Jain, and Buddhist
sages, the lessons of the great Guru Nanak of the Sikhs to embrace all humanity, the knowledge of the Jewish savants, the commandment of Jesus to love one
another, and the exhortations of the Prophet of Islam, known to his followers as
"a mercy unto mankind," to express compassion at all times—all may be combined and reduced to one universal shibboleth: to go out and "heal a fractured
world"—*tikkun olam.*

APPENDIX
Of Tears and Nightmares

Social scientists consciously strive to keep a distance between themselves and their subjects, otherwise objectivity and neutrality will be compromised, they believe. Anthropologists face a peculiar predicament. Observing and participating in the rites of passage, living, eating, sleeping, and laughing with a small community over a length of time, they invariably form emotional links. It assists many of them in understanding the community better. In some cases it also creates a desire to champion the community, especially when they see it as being persecuted and under threat. Thus I. M. Lewis studying the tribal populations of Somalia, Lawrence Rosen those of Morocco, and Steven Caton those of Yemen have written and spoken extensively on these communities in an effort to explain the context of their culture and politics. This is also true of government officials with an anthropological eye. James Spain, the American diplomat, wrote of the Pukhtuns with admiration and affection. Even imperialist administrators of the British Raj such as Sir Evelyn Howell and Sir Olaf Caroe, who wrote about the Pukhtuns, projected them as people of nobility, courage, and honor.

Aware of the pitfall of dissolving the distance between the social scientist and the community under study, my team and I, too, have consciously attempted to maintain objectivity. But it has been difficult. The exercise of collecting statistics and data and examining case studies and historical narratives is easily overwhelmed by the stories of real women and children being raped and killed. It is difficult then to pretend we are not imbued with human emotions, that we do not feel for the suffering of others, especially if we happen to have met them.

WITNESS TO GENOCIDE

Perhaps I am oversensitive to issues of ethnic hatred as I have myself witnessed its results firsthand in East Pakistan in 1971, when I was deputy secretary to the chief secretary of East Pakistan in charge of the civil administration of the province. I was part of a number of civil servants sent to East Pakistan, while our counterparts were sent to West Pakistan, to act as a bridge between the two wings. We had been initially posted in the field as subdivisional magistrates, the equivalent of assistant commissioner. Like millions of other Pakistanis, Bengalis celebrated the creation of Pakistan in 1947 with high expectations and made immense sacrifices for it. Although East Pakistan had a majority population, the arrogant elite of West Pakistan, with its Punjabi-dominated army and bureaucracy, saw it as the periphery. A gifted and artistic people, Bengalis remained patient in spite of the overbearing West Pakistanis, but the military action in 1971 changed everything. With one devastating stroke, Pakistan undermined its own foundational vision of a pluralist, democratic, and modern Muslim state.

Bengali civilians, who were innocent of any wrongdoing, were picked up by security forces and accused of being "miscreants"—a word that today echoes in "terrorists" and "insurgents"—to disappear in military camps. Stories of women being raped were rife as senior West Pakistani military officials were quoted as saying that "the stock needed to be improved." As a young civil servant, I was confronted with the horrifying spectacle of the breakdown between central government and its periphery, the failure of the modern state to accommodate its citizens, and acts of genocide. It was an almost impossible situation for the civil administration attempting to uphold law and order and the principles of justice as the country was under martial law. In East Pakistan, military officials literally had the power of life and death over the population. In the mayhem, several of my West Pakistani civil service colleagues were killed in their posts in the field, along with many other non-Bengalis. Once my wife and I got back to West Pakistan later in the year, we found the atmosphere charged with ethnic chauvinism. West Pakistanis used derogatory terms for Bengalis, contemptuously calling them "Bingos" and other names. For our attempts to explain the Bengali position with understanding, to condemn the killing, we were labeled "Bingo lovers," and I was warned by my senior officials that martial law was in place and such talk could be construed as anti-Pakistani and I could "disappear." I was too angry and disgusted by the leaders of Pakistan and felt too much empathy for their victims to contain my feelings. I expressed them in the following poem as a catharsis when, in faraway Peshawar, I could contemplate the enormity of what had happened:

"they are taking them away"

sullen shine the stars
the moon in agony aloof
so still stand the palm trees
the seasons are bearing
my dreams away
sanity

suspended
while all the black
horrors of the mind
uncoil
slowly
snakely
settle
over this land

they came by night
they came in shame
they came
to take the weapon and the woman

my throat
was dry
and chilled
my groin, for

they are taking them away
to the slaughter houses

when a house is empty
the family missing
and silence a way of life
the nights get chilly
the nights get lonely
and in the night
strong men break down to cry, for

there is no shame like the shame of
taking them away to the slaughter houses[1]

My words depicting the arrogance and cruelty of those at the helm of the central government's affairs could be applied to the leaders of other nations where similar genocide has taken place:

the lords of men
gods of pain
have taken council:
the unholy juggernaut will move

it is decreed
and none to challenge it
what compulsions drive such men

what fear makes them such savages
while reason, so thin on the breast,
deserts so quickly[2]

Too many leaders and officials in central governments from our case studies, I suspected, have supported "the unholy juggernaut," which has created such misery for the periphery. I suspected, too, that many Pukhtuns, Somalis, Yemenis, Kurds, and others on the periphery have also felt this same anguish.

THE SUFFERING OF OTHERS

Once I began to collect information for this study, my fears were confirmed. The stories of persecuted peoples came to me in different forms and from a variety of sources. In the case of the Rohingya, it came through the story of the young Rohingya girl in a camp in Bangladesh. The story, which was told to me by Melody Fox Ahmed, who is married to my son, Umar, and works at Georgetown University in Washington, D.C., represents the suffering of the Rohingya people. Melody met the girl on a visit to the Lada camp in Bangladesh on the border with Burma/Myanmar. She described the filth and squalor of the camp. Without official papers, the people there could neither be educated nor given employment. Every time Melody talked of the plight of the Rohingya girl, she struggled with her tears.

This young orphan lived a life of utmost squalor in Lada. Suspended between two countries that did not want them, the Rohingya became a non-people. Desperate to earn money for food, the young Rohingya girl found a job in a neighboring town. There, the men in the family sexually assaulted her, according to a doctor's report, and to cover their crime threw her into a fire in the hope that the matter would end there. They were aware that she had no official papers and therefore the authorities would not take any action. The girl somehow managed to survive and returned half alive to the refugee camp. As she was in great pain and without money or medicine, the chances of her survival were slim.

For me, the utter helplessness of the Rohingya girl had become a metaphor for those—Muslims and non-Muslims, tribal or city folk—forcibly displaced from their homes and subjected to injustice and inhuman treatment. In the scheme of things, they, like the Rohingya girl, were voiceless and defenseless, an image of utter desolation.

The Rohingya had been violently driven out of their homes by the Burmese who refused to acknowledge their existence. I could not imagine the Burmese behaving in this manner. As a young boy growing up in Bangkok, I came to know many Buddhist families and was enchanted by their welcoming compassion and gentility. I had also got to know the Burmese through my father who worked at the United Nations. My father's boss, U Nyun, was a distinguished civil servant who had studied at Oxford and was once a member of the elite Indian Civil Service. His wife and family were particularly close to us. They radiated an aura of tranquility. After I got married, U Nyun's wife was most affectionate to my wife Zeenat and said she was her daughter in a previous life. She gave Zeenat exquisite Burmese gifts and called her by a Burmese name, Chit Chit, "Beloved."

Just when I thought there could be no more heart-rendering image than that of the Rohingya girl, I saw a young Somali woman on the *BBC World News* late in 2011. The story was about the widespread starvation in Somalia, and this woman provided the evidence. Her body was a skeleton, and she cradled a starving child in her arms. "Where are the Muslim countries?" she asked, faintly looking into the distance. "We are dying." Facing a slow and painful death, what she still had in spite of seeing her world explode around her was dignity. She was too far gone to be angry or sarcastic about her brother Muslims, some of the richest people in the world, living just across the waters on the Arabian Peninsula and the Gulf States.

Story after story that I heard in relation to this study cast a pall of gloom on my naturally optimistic nature. These suffering people had one thing in common—they were all part of communities living on the periphery and margins of the state. Those who represented the center of the state usually called them "primitive" and "savage." Some said their time in history was up. They were even described with words that had a chilling connotation. I soon discovered I was not alone in my emotional reactions. Those working on my project, regardless of race, religion, or age, were being similarly affected as some examples will illustrate. Here is Harrison Akins on the effect the plight of the Rohingya had on him:

> I was sitting in the back of the room at an all-day conference at the British Embassy with my previous job, before coming on full time to this project. I thought this would be a good opportunity to begin looking through some printed-out material for our research on the Rohingya of Burma. I was told that they were a severely oppressed minority. While one can never truly be acclimated to such things, oppressed groups was not an unfamiliar category of research for me. For the Rohingya, I was completely wrong. Reading through a human rights report on the experience of Rohingya refugees in Bangladesh, I couldn't stop myself from crying in a room full of embassy and government officials, as the report recounted the brutal experiences of rape, murder, and starvation in the camps. I felt cold chills as I read accounts of young girls and boys being born into this world, living a short life, and dying without ever officially existing or being acknowledged by anyone. I was forced to excuse myself to the restroom as the other people in the room began to wonder what was wrong with me.

Harrison was aware of the challenge we faced in communicating the suffering of people like the Rohingya to those living in the West. "I carry an almost overwhelming sense of shame and heartache studying these different groups and not being able to understand their suffering, which is seemingly never ending the deeper we dig into our research," he said. "This lack of understanding presents the biggest challenge of this project for me: humanizing the individuals of the different case studies beyond the words on the page. I think this is not just an emotional challenge for me but a challenge for many people in the West as well."

Aja Anderson, who was especially interested in the Kurds, recounted the case of 300 Kurdish children locked in a cinema hall in Syria and burned alive. The story had a profound effect on Aja and caused her nightmares:

> I woke in a cold sweat to my sister shaking me violently. 'Wake up!' she hissed urgently. 'What's going on?' I asked, disoriented. 'You've been screaming about a fire, about needing to save the children.' Examining the populations in each of the modern states that host the Kurds, I kept expecting that their situation would improve, that it could not be possible for them to have been treated so poorly by Europe, the U.S., and their own countries. From Syria to Turkey to Iraq to Iran, the pattern of abuse was consistent. While Saddam Hussein's al-Anfal campaign in the late 1980s was a sickening example of the center's policy towards its Kurdish periphery, the story of this cinema fire in 1960s Syria personalized their suffering and affected me indelibly.

The encounter with a fellow Georgetown student, a Uyghur, also left my daughter Nafees in tears:

> In my public speaking class last week I heard some five informative speeches on topics ranging from fantasy football, to autism, to the socio-economic problems of momma's boys in Italy. Then Kekenus stood up to give her speech.
>
> I sat in the front row listening to her facts. China had "invaded Uyghur territory" in 1949. The atrocities have been "declared genocide by the UN." Uyghurs have been subject to "arbitrary executions, massacres, forced abortions, forced relocation, and nuclear radiation."
>
> Kekenus then started telling the class about her personal story. Her father had organized a peaceful protest for Uyghur rights when he was in university. He was jailed for ten years. In response her mother launched a campaign to release him. She was jailed for eight years. Her two brothers now serve seven- and nine-year terms, respectively.
>
> The conditions they were subjected to were not merely those of political prisoners. Her father had spent weeks at a time in solitary confinement in

a room not high enough for him to stand up in or wide enough to stretch out his arms. The prison guards considered it a form of entertainment to have prisoners chased down by their German shepherds. To this day, she told us "my father is both claustrophobic and afraid of dogs."

She then spoke of the plight of her fellow Uyghurs. She said: "We are luckier than the seventeen-year-old boy who had a broom repeatedly shoved down his throat after he accidentally stepped on a police officer's shoe. We are luckier than the nine-year-old girl who was raped in front of her family because they had refused to move out of their home. We are luckier than that father who begged to be killed as his four-year-old son was being hacked to death because he could not bear to watch."

This is when Kekenus could not handle it any longer. Her voice started to tremble. Tears fell from her face. She took heavy breaths in between each sentence. This is when a lump grew in my throat and I could not hold back the tears I was restraining. I looked over to my friends who had tears in their eyes. Even the professor was wiping her face. I would later repeat the speech to my mother and at this point we both burst into tears.

Frankie Martin, the veteran of my research projects, summed it up for the entire team:

> I realized that had I been born in Somalia, Pakistan, the North Caucasus, or any of the other societies we are studying, I would be liable to be imprisoned, killed, or made to undergo the grossest humiliations and tortures at any moment. My house could be destroyed, my family members and loved ones raped and massacred, or my limbs blown off. My existence would not matter—and would often be denied completely—and my life rendered useless and meaningless. It is extremely depressing to realize that this is not just one people or another but many. The problem is systemic. : . . I hope with all my heart that the frightening trajectory they are battling can be reversed. I want to help make this happen.

As the pace of research quickened and as these terrible stories of gloom and doom came thick and fast, I had a suggestion for Frankie, half in earnest. Next time we should research the rituals of Oktoberfest in Munich where vast quantities of beer and sausage are consumed and the world's woes are forgotten. Our subject matter would then be jolly, middle-aged, overweight, pink-cheeked Germans dressed in shorts and wearing Alpine hats, singing loud songs while slowly becoming inebriated through the day and into the night. That image of other societies carrying on with their lives acted as a corrective and momentarily checked the descent into despondency.

Perhaps for me the metaphor of the Rohingya girl was particularly moving because I was a father and grandfather; perhaps because I was a Muslim and felt a sense of connection; perhaps as a human being I had seen suffering and was concerned with the pain of others. What about my research team of young scholars? Why should they respond as I did? The answer is not hard to locate. It is there in the vision of America's great Founding Fathers as they dreamed of a new world of justice, civility, compassion, and learning. It is there in the sacred literature of the Abrahamic and non-Abrahamic faiths and informs the finest ideals of humanity. It explains why the young are so quick to fight for justice and against tyranny. They still remember the lessons which the old have forgotten.

In asking God "Am I my brother's keeper?" Cain is raising a question that is at the center of this study. Cain has just killed his brother Abel—committing the world's first murder. God's answer is explicit and repeatedly stated throughout the Bible. It is an emphatic "yes." God is unequivocally laying down the need for compassion and kindness toward all human beings as each and every one is related going back to Adam and Eve. Everyone who believes in the Bible will respond to the suffering of others as a moral duty. The Bible underscores the sacred duty to care for each other. There is perhaps no greater example of showing compassion in the face of cruelty than that of Jesus on the cross. Betrayed by his disciples, tortured and taunted by his adversaries, Jesus turned to heaven and said, "Forgive them for they know not what they do." We also note the same divine attitude toward others in the universal saying, "Do unto others what you would have others do unto you." Every faith thus asks us to become our brother's keeper. Hinduism provides the concept of nonviolence, which has been so effectively translated into political action in modern times, as seen in the examples of Mahatma Gandhi in India and Martin Luther King Jr. in the United States.

What was heartbreaking was that few people had even heard of the communities we were studying, let alone knew of their story of suffering. The ongoing brutalization by their own central governments is little known, and therefore there is little public outcry. We feel privileged to recount their story, to be able to say: you are not alone. We are with you. We feel for you. We cry with you. We will tell your story.

That is why in pursuing this study my team had become like the Apostle Jude, the patron saint of lost causes. They were determined to champion the communities on the periphery that we were studying. Frankie Martin was so dedicated to this study that he was ready to postpone the admission for his postgraduate studies at the prestigious University of Cambridge—for this I was firm as it is one my favorite places on earth and I knew how much he would benefit from and enjoy it. In an even more dramatic expression of his commitment, Harrison Akins actually resigned a well-paid job, saying he would work in a coffee shop if necessary so as to spend his time with the project I was conducting.

As we pursued our study, the juxtaposition between the past and the present, the present and the future, became clearer and clearer. Perhaps it was most dramatically illustrated when Frankie, Harrison, and I were deep in discussion in my office at American University about Wazir and Mahsud war tactics in Waziristan on April 17, 2012, and Harrison jumped up excitedly and pointed to the large window behind me. We turned to see the space shuttle *Discovery* sitting atop a larger plane flying low and majestically on its way to its final resting place at the Smithsonian Institution's National Air and Space Museum. *Discovery* was the future: it evoked images of flights to the moon and exploration of space through the most advanced technology. Waziristan was the past: a male-dominated tribal society riven with cousin rivalry and defined by a code of honor, with an economy of small landholdings and camels, goats, and sheep.

Our hope is that this study will provide an insight that will benefit both center and periphery. Considering the global scale and urgency of the problem, I believe that every one needs to contribute to a better understanding between different peoples and social systems. My team and I have chosen to do so through knowledge and research.

NOTES

CHAPTER 1

1. Michael Hastings, "The Rise of the Killer Drones: How America Goes to War in Secret," *Rolling Stone*, April 16, 2012.

2. Jo Becker and Scott Shane, "Secret 'Kill List' Proves a Test of Obama's Principles and Will," *New York Times*, May 29, 2012.

3. David Luban, "What Would Augustine Do?: The President, Drones, and Just War Theory," *Boston Review*, June 6, 2012.

4. "U.S. Airstrikes in Pakistan Called 'Very Effective,'" CNN, May 18, 2009 (http://articles.cnn.com/2009-05-18/politics/cia.pakistan.airstrikes_1_qaeda-pakistani-airstrikes?_s=PM:POLITICS).

5. Rory Carroll, "The Philosopher Making the Moral Case for U.S. Drones," *Guardian* (Manchester), August 2, 2012.

6. Hastings, "The Rise of the Killer Drones."

7. Nicola Abé, "Dreams in Infrared: The Woes of an American Drone Operator," *Der Spiegel*, December 14, 2012.

8. David Ignatius, "Pakistan Blew Its Chance for Security," *Washington Post*, May 16, 2012.

9. Leo Tolstoy, *Hadji Murad* (New York: Random House, 2003), pp. 4–5.

10. Sir Walter Scott, *Manners, Customs, and History of the Highlanders of Scotland* (New York: Barnes & Noble, 1993), p. 22.

11. Sir Olaf Caroe, *The Pathans* (Oxford University Press, 2000), p. 87.

12. Billy Briggs, "Call of the Warrior Women," *Sydney Morning Herald*, April 6, 2012.

13. Yaroslav Trofimov, "Many Afghans Shrug at 'This Event Foreigners Call 9/11,'" *Wall Street Journal*, September 7, 2011.

14. David Axe, "Insider Attacks Now Biggest Killer of NATO Troops," *Wired*, August 30, 2012.

15. Jeffrey Bordin, "A Crisis of Trust and Cultural Incompatibility: A Red Team Study of Mutual Perceptions of Afghan National Security Force Personnel and U.S. Soldiers in Understanding and Mitigating the Phenomena of ANSF-Committed Fratricide-Murders," George Washington University National Security Archives Electronic Briefing Book, May 12, 2011 (www.gwu.edu/~nsarchiv/NSAEBB/NSAEBB370/docs/Document%2011.pdf).

16. Ibid.

17. Thomas L. Friedman, *The World Is Flat: A Brief History of the Twenty-First Century* (New York: Farrar, Straus & Giroux, 2005); Thomas L. Friedman, *The Lexus and the Olive Tree: Understanding Globalization* (New York: Farrar, Straus, & Giroux, 1999).

18. See, for example, Philip S. Khoury and Joseph Kostiner, eds., *Tribes and State Formation in the Middle East* (University of California Press, 1990).

19. See John H. Bodley, *Cultural Anthropology: Tribes, States, and the Global System* (Lanham, Md.: AltaMira Press, 2011); David Maybury-Lewis, *Indigenous Peoples, Ethnic Groups and the State* (Boston: Allyn & Bacon, 2002); and Barry Sautman, ed., *Cultural Genocide and Asian State Peripheries* (New York: Palgrave Macmillan, 2006).

20. For a seminal study of this kind, see Meyer Fortes and E. E. Evans-Pritchard, eds., *African Political Systems* (Oxford University Press, 1940).

21. Karl A. Wittfogel, *Oriental Despotism: A Comparative Study of Total Power* (New York: Vintage Books, 1981).

22. Ibid., pp. 64–65; *Warrior Empire: The Mughals*, the History Channel, 2006.

23. Wittfogel, *Oriental Despotism*, p. 137.

24. Clifford Geertz, *The Interpretation of Cultures* (New York: Basic Books, 1973), p. 297.

25. Carleton S. Coon, *Caravan: The Story of the Middle East* (New York: Holt, 1952), pp. 264–65.

26. Sir Evelyn Howell, *Mizh: A Monograph on Government's Relations with the Mahsud Tribe* (Oxford University Press, 1979), p. 96.

27. Richard F. Burton, *First Footsteps in East Africa; or, An Exploration of Harar* (London: Longman, Brown, Green, and Longmans, 1856), pp. 174–75.

28. Howell, *Mizh*, p. 96.

29. Ibn Khaldun, *The Muqaddimah: An Introduction to History*, translated by Franz Rosenthal (Princeton University Press, 1967).

30. For my critique of Barth's work among the Pukhtun in Swat, see Akbar S. Ahmed, *Millennium and Charisma among Pathans: A Critical Essay in Social Anthropology* (London: Routledge, 1976).

31. Clifford Geertz, *The Interpretation of Cultures* (New York: Basic Books, 1973); Clifford Geertz, *Islam Observed: Religious Development in Morocco and Indonesia* (University of Chicago Press, 1968).

32. Thomas M. Kiefer, *The Tausug: Violence and Law in a Philippine Moslem Society* (New York: Holt, Rinehart and Winston, 1972).

33. Gerard Rixhon, "Tausug and Corsican Clan Feuding: A Comparative Study," in *Rido: Clan Feuding and Conflict Management in Mindanao*, edited by Wilfredo Magno Torres III (Asia Foundation, 2007), p. 310.

34. *Mataloona: Pukhto Proverbs*, translated by Akbar S. Ahmed (Oxford University Press, 1975), p. 35.

35. Lord Rennell of Rodd, *People of the Veil: Being an Account of the Habits, Organisation and History of the Wandering Tuareg Tribes Which Inhabit the Mountains of Air or Asben in the Central Sahara* (Oosterhout N. B., Netherlands: Anthropological Publications, 1966), p. 163.

36. Isabel Hilton, "Letter from Pakistan: Pashtun Code," *The New Yorker*, December 3, 2001.

37. Rosita Forbes, *El Raisuni: The Sultan of the Mountains* (London: T. Butterworth, 1924), p. 73.

38. Rodd, *People of the Veil*, pp. 236–37.

39. Marie Benningsen Broxup, "The Last *Ghazawat*: The 1920–1921 Uprising," in *The North Caucasus Barrier: The Russian Advance towards the Muslim World*, edited by Marie Benningsen Broxup (New York: St. Martin's Press, 1992), p. 130.

40. Yuri Yu. Karpov, "The Dagestani Mountain Village: From the Traditional *Jamaat* to Its Present Social Character," *Anthropology and Archeology of Eurasia* 48 (Spring 2010): 54–55.

41. Ahmed, *Mataloona*, pp. xvi–xvii.

42. Lale Yalcin-Heckmann, *Tribe and Kinship among the Kurds* (Frankfurt am Main: Peter Lang, 1991), p. 235.

43. Amineh Ahmed, *Sorrow and Joy among Muslim Women: The Pukhtuns of Northern Pakistan* (Cambridge University Press, 2006).

44. Ahmed, *Millennium and Charisma among Pathans*; Akbar S. Ahmed, *Pukhtun Economy and Society: Traditional Structure and Economic Development in a Tribal Society* (London: Routledge, 1980); also Akbar Ahmed, "The Code of the Hills," *Foreign Policy,* May 6, 2011.

45. Martin van Bruinessen, *Agha, Shaikh, and State: The Social and Political Structures of Kurdistan* (London: Zed, 1992), p. 112.

46. Ibid., p. 65.

47. Ernest Gellner, "Doctor and Saint," in *Islam in Tribal Societies: From the Atlas to the Indus,* edited by Akbar S. Ahmed and David M. Hart (London: Routledge, 2008), p. 35.

48. Salman Rushdie, *The Satanic Verses* (New York: Viking, 1988).

49. Thomas M. Kiefer, *Tausug of the Philippines* (New Haven, Conn.: Human Relations Area Files Press, 1972), p. 13.

50. Ronald Cohen, *Dominance and Defiance: A Study of Marital Instability in an Islamic African Society* (Washington: American Anthropological Association, 1971), p. 47.

51. John Mercer, *Spanish Sahara* (London: George Allen & Unwin, 1976), p. 101; Rosita Forbes, *Adventure: Being a Gypsy Salad—Some Incidents, Excitements and Impressions of Twelve Highly-Seasoned Years* (London: Cassell and Co., 1923), p. 104; Thomas M. Kiefer, *The Tausug: Violence and Law in a Philippine Moslem Society,* p. 134.

52. Akbar S. Ahmed, "Trial by Ordeal among the Bugtis: Ritual as a Diacritical Factor in Baloch Ethnicity," in *Marginality and Modernity: Ethnicity and Change in Post-Colonial Balochistan,* edited by Paul Titus (Oxford University Press, 1996); the custom was also mentioned by Anatol Lieven in *Pakistan: A Hard Country* (New York: PublicAffairs, 2011), p. 361.

53. See Joseph Ginat, *Bedouin Bisha'h Justice: Ordeal by Fire* (Brighton: Sussex Academic Press, 2009).

54. Nira Sherman-Sides and Elia Sides, producer and director, *Bisha: The Awesome Fire Test* (New York: Filmmakers Library, Inc., 1995).

55. Forbes, *Adventure,* pp. 107–08.

56. Akbar Ahmed, *Journey into Islam: The Crisis of Globalization* (Brookings, 2007).

57. Akbar Ahmed, *Journey into America: The Challenge of Islam* (Brookings, 2010).

58. Ahmed, *Pukhtun Economy and Society*; Ahmed and Hart, *Islam in Tribal Societies.*

59. Akbar S. Ahmed, *Resistance and Control in Pakistan* (London: Routledge, 2004).

60. Ahmed, *Resistance and Control in Pakistan,* p. 175, n. 6.

CHAPTER 2

1. For a detailed account, see Akbar S. Ahmed, *Resistance and Control in Pakistan* (London: Routledge, 2004), pp. 112–14.

2. Ibid., p. 110.

3. Colonel of the Zhob Militia, Demi Official Letter 207-6/100/A, Zhob Militia Headquarters, Zhob Agency, Pakistan, January 10, 1980.

4. Inspector General Alam Jan Mahsud, Secret Letter PF /4933/1, Office of the Inspector General, Frontier Corps, Baluchistan, February 14, 1980.

5. Sir Olaf Caroe, *The Pathans* (Oxford University Press, 2000), p. 398.

6. Ibid., pp. 390–91.

7. Ahmed, *Resistance and Control in Pakistan.*

8. Arthur Bonner, *Among the Afghans* (Duke University Press, 1987), p. 29.

9. *Mataloona: Pukhto Proverbs,* translated by Akbar Ahmed (Oxford University Press, 1975), p. 57.

10. Ibid., p. 1.

11. Ibid., p. 52.

12. Ahmed, *Resistance and Control in Pakistan*, pp. 153–55.

13. Caroe, *The Pathans*, p. 391.

14. Ibid., p. 393.

15. John F. Richards, *The Mughal Empire* (Cambridge University Press, 1995), pp. 50–51.

16. James W. Spain, *The Pathan Borderland* (The Hague: Mouton, 1963), p. 33.

17. Christian Tripodi, *Edge of Empire: The British Political Officer and Tribal Administration on the North-West Frontier 1877–1947* (Surrey: Ashgate, 2011), p. 80, n. 27.

18. General Staff of India, *Military Report on Waziristan 1935* (Calcutta, India: Government of India Press Confidential, 1936), p. 163.

19. Sir Evelyn Howell, *Mizh: A Monograph on Government's Relations with the Mahsud Tribe* (Oxford University Press, 1979), pp. 35–36.

20. Tripodi, *Edge of Empire*, p. 26.

21. George N. Curzon, *Persia and the Persian Question*, vol. 2 (London: Longmans, Green, and Co., 1892), p. 271.

22. James W. Spain, *The Way of the Pathans* (London: R. Hale, 1962), p. 25.

23. Ahmed, *Resistance and Control in Pakistan*, pp. 177–78, n. 26.

24. Howell, *Mizh*, p. 98.

25. Olaf Caroe, personal communication, July 12, 1979.

26. Howell, *Mizh*, p. 95.

27. Z. H. Zaidi, ed., *Quaid-i-Azam Mohammad Ali Jinnah Papers: Pakistan: Pangs of Birth, 15 August–30 September 1947* (Islamabad: National Archives of Pakistan, 2001), p. 309.

28. Syed Farooq Hasnat, *Global Security Watch—Pakistan* (Santa Barbara, Calif.: ABC-CLIO, 2011), p. 148.

29. General Alam Jan Mahsud, personal communication, May 2012.

30. Akbar Ahmed, *Social and Economic Change in the Tribal Areas* (Oxford University Press, 1977).

31. Syed Saleem Shahzad, *Inside Al-Qaeda and the Taliban: Beyond bin Laden and 9/11* (London: Pluto, 2011), p. 5.

32. Ibid.

33. Zahid Hussain, *The Scorpion's Tail: The Relentless Rise of Islamic Militants in Pakistan—And How It Threatens America* (New York: Simon and Schuster, 2010), p. 79.

34. See Ahmed, *Resistance and Control in Pakistan*, pp. 174–75, n. 4.

35. Hussain, *The Scorpion's Tail*, p. 114.

36. Syed Shoaib Hasan, "Profile: Islamabad's Red Mosque," *BBC News,* July 27, 2007 (http://news.bbc.co.uk/1/hi/6503477.stm).

37. "Pakistani Colonel Killed in Clash," *BBC News,* July 8, 2007 (http://news.bbc.co.uk/1/hi/world/south_asia/6281404.stm).

38. Riaz Khan, "Militants Seize Shrine in Pakistan," Associated Press, July 30, 2007; "Jirga to Discuss Taliban Action," *Daily Times* (Pakistan), July 31, 2007.

39. Amir Mir, "Pakistan: The Suicide-Bomb Capital of the World," *Asia Times Online,* September 16, 2011 (www.atimes.com/atimes/South_Asia/MI16Df04.html).

40. "Five Most Wanted Militants," *Dawn* (Pakistan), August 18, 2011.

41. Hussain, *The Scorpion's Tail*, p. 120.

42. "Has Taliban Pulled Out of the Peace Deal in Pakistan?" *Rediff News* (India), May 9, 2012 (www.rediff.com/news/report/).

43. "NWA Operation 'in the Offing' as 13 Troops Beheaded," *The Nation* (Pakistan), May 8, 2012.

44. "Tackling the Other Taliban," *The Economist*, October 15, 2009.

45. Imtiaz Gul, *The Most Dangerous Place: Pakistan's Lawless Frontier* (New York: Viking, 2009), p. xv.

46. "Scores Killed in Pakistan Twin Bomb Attacks," Al Jazeera, May 13, 2011 (www.aljazeera.com/news/asia/2011/05/201151322834765706.html).

47. Essa Khankhel and Javed Aziz Khan, "Nation Prays for Malala," *The News* (Pakistan), October 10, 2012.

48. Gul, *The Most Dangerous Place*, p. 130.

49. General Alam Jan Mahsud, personal communication, 2011, 2012; Khalid Aziz, "Conflict & Fata Institutions," *Dawn* (Pakistan), March 16, 2012.

50. Gul, *The Most Dangerous Place*, p. 108.

51. Ghulam Qadir Khan, "Cheegha" (unpublished manuscript available with author in Peshawar, 2011), p. 258.

52. Ibid., p. 261.

53. Hussain, *The Scorpion's Tail*, p. 179.

54. Admiral Mike Mullen, Chairman of the Joint Chiefs of Staff, Remarks at the Kansas State University Landon Lecture Series, Kansas State University, March 3, 2010 (www.jcs.mil/speech.aspx?id=1336).

55. Azhar Masood, "Pakistani Tribesmen Settle Scores through US Drones," *Arab News*, May 23, 2011 (www.arabnews.com/node/378426).

56. Michael Hastings, "The Rise of the Killer Drone: How America Goes to War in Secret," *Rolling Stone*, April 16, 2012.

57. Usama Khilji, "Living under Drones," *Daily Times* (Pakistan), May 10, 2012.

58. *Living under Drones: Death, Injury, and Trauma to Civilians from US Drone Practices in Pakistan*, International Human Rights and Conflict Resolution Clinic, Stanford Law School and Global Justice Clinic, NYU School of Law, September 2012.

59. Jennifer Gibson, personal communication, December 11, 2012.

60. Reprieve, *Statement of Noor Khan* (Islamabad, Pakistan: February 27, 2012).

61. Farhat Taj, *Taliban and Anti-Taliban* (Newcastle upon Tyne, UK: Cambridge Scholars, 2011).

62. Scott Shane, "C.I.A. Is Disputed on Civilian Toll in Drone Strikes," *New York Times*, August 11, 2011.

63. David Jackson, "Obama Defends Drone Strikes," *USA Today*, January 31, 2012.

64. "The Fight against Al Qaeda: Today and Tomorrow," Speech delivered by Secretary of Defense Leon E. Panetta, Center for a New American Security, Washington, D.C., November 20, 2012 (www.defense.gov/Speeches/Speech.aspx?SpeechID=1737).

65. Peter Bergen, "Drones Decimating Taliban in Pakistan," CNN, July 3, 2012 (www.cnn.com/2012/07/03/opinion/bergen-drones-taliban-pakistan/index.html).

66. Muhammad Idrees Ahmad, "The Magical Realism of Body Counts," Al Jazeera, June 13, 2011 (www.aljazeera.com/indepth/opinion/2011/06/2011613931606455.html).

67. David Kilcullen and Andrew McDonald Exum, "Death from Above, Outrage Down Below," *New York Times*, May 16, 2009.

68. Brian Cloughley, "Defeating the Taliban in Pakistan's Tribal Areas," Reuters, November 22, 2009.

69. Ishtiaq Mahsud, "Journey with Pakistan Taliban Shows Militants' Resilience," Associated Press, December 15, 2011.

70. Zahid Hussain, personal communication, 2012.

71. Hussain, *The Scorpion's Tail*, p. 188.

72. Gul, *The Most Dangerous Place*, p. 222.

73. Shahzad, *Inside Al-Qaeda and the Taliban*, pp. 122–23.

74. "Letters from the Bin Laden Compound," *New York Times*, May 3, 2012 (www.ny times.com/interactive/2012/05/04/world/asia/04binladen-text.html).

75. Muhammad Jan Mahsud, personal communication, 2011, 2012.

76. Reprieve, *Statement of Noor Khan.*

77. Khan, "Cheegha," p. 249.

78. Khalid Aziz, "Insight into the Fata Mind," *Dawn* (Pakistan), March 2, 2012.

79. New America Foundation, *FATA: Inside Pakistan's Tribal Regions* (Washington, 2010) (www.pakistansurvey.org).

80. Khan, "Cheegha," p. 260.

81. Muhammad Jan Mahsud, "The Solution for FATA," *The News* (Pakistan), May 24, 2008.

82. General Alam Jan Mahsud, personal communication, 2011, 2012.

83. Khan, "Cheegha," pp. 248–50.

84. Ibid., p. 249.

85. Khan Idris, *Jirgas: The Pashtun Way of Conflict Resolution* (Richardson, Tex.: Tribal Analysis, 2010); Aziz, "Conflict & Fata Institutions"; Aziz, "Insight into the Fata Mind."

86. David Kilcullen, *The Accidental Guerrilla: Fighting Small Wars in the Midst of a Big One* (Oxford University Press, 2009).

87. Andrew M. Roe, *Waging War in Waziristan: The British Struggle in the Land of bin Laden, 1849–1947* (University of Kansas Press, 2010).

88. Hugh Beattie, *Imperial Frontier: Tribe and State in Waziristan* (Richmond, United Kingdom: Curzon, 2002).

CHAPTER 3

1. "Transcript of Bin Laden's October interview," CNN, February 5, 2002 (http://articles.cnn.com/2002-02-05/world/).

2. Osama bin Laden, interview with Tayseer Allouni, parts 1–6 (English subtitles) (YouTube.com).

3. Syed Ameer Ali, *The Spirit of Islam: A History of the Evolution and Ideals of Islam* (New York: Cosimo, 2010), p. 71.

4. Steve Coll, *The Bin Ladens: An Arabian Family in the American Century* (New York: Penguin, 2008), p. 204.

5. Pirouz Mojtahed-Zadeh, *Security and Territoriality in the Persian Gulf: A Maritime Political Geography* (London: Curzon Press, 1999), p. 66.

6. Denis McAuley, "The Ideology of Osama bin Laden: Nation, Tribe and World Economy," *Journal of Political Ideologies* 10 (October 2005): 277.

7. Ibid., pp. 277–78.

8. Bruce Lawrence, ed., *Messages to the World: The Statements of Osama Bin Laden* (New York: Verso, 2005), p. 156.

9. McAuley, "The Ideology of Osama bin Laden," p. 278.

10. Osama bin Laden, *IntelCenter: Words of Osama bin Laden*, vol. 1 (Alexandria, Va.: Tempest, 2008), p. 98.

11. Brad K. Berner, *Jihad: Bin Laden in His Own Words: Declarations, Interviews and Speeches* (New Delhi: Peacock Books, 2007), p. 250.

12. Lawrence, *Messages to the World*, p. 15.

13. Peter L. Bergen, *The Osama bin Laden I Know: An Oral History of Al Qaeda's Leader* (New York: Simon and Schuster, 2006), p. 371.

14. Lawrence, *Messages to the World*, p. 14.

15. Ibid., p. 164.

16. Coll, *The Bin Ladens*, p. 463.

17. Ibid., p. 565.

18. McAuley, "The Ideology of Osama bin Laden," p. 279.

19. Coll, *The Bin Ladens*, p. 335.

20. "Role of Yemen in Present-day Events in Light of Hadiths of Prophet Muhammad (pbuh)," Kavkaz Center (Chechen), May 31, 2011 (www.kavkazcenter.com).

21. Joseph Kostiner, "The Rise of Jihadi Trends in Saudi Arabia: The Post Iraq-Kuwait War Phase," in Efraim Inbar and Hillel Frisch, eds., *Radical Islam and International Security: Challenges and Responses* (New York: Routledge, 2008), p. 84.

22. Murad Batal al-Shishani, "An Assessment of the Anatomy of al-Qaeda in Yemen: Ideological and Social Factors," *Terrorism Monitor* 8 (March 5, 2010), pp. 7–8.

23. Sheila A. Scoville, ed., *Gazetteer of Arabia: A Geographical and Tribal History of the Arabian Peninsula*, vol. 2 (Graz: Akademische Druck- u. Verlagsanstalt, 1979), p. 199; Fuad Hamzah, "Arab Tribes in the Kingdom of Saudi Arabia," *Near East/South Asia Report* 2798 (Spingfield, Va.: Joint Publishing Research Service, August 11, 1983), pp. 21, 30.

24. National Commission on Terrorist Attacks upon the United States, *The 9/11 Commission Report: Final Report of the National Commission on Terrorist Attacks upon the United States* (New York: W. W. Norton, 2004), p. 232; Hamzah, "Arab Tribes in the Kingdom of Saudi Arabia," pp. 12, 38; Scoville, *Gazetteer of Arabia*, Vol. 2, pp. 205–08; Sheila A. Scoville, ed., *Gazetteer of Arabia: A Geographical and Tribal History of the Arabian Peninsula*, Vol. 1 (Graz: Akademische Druck- u. Verlagsanstalt, 1979), p. 16.

25. Caryle Murphy and David B. Ottaway, "Some Light Shed on Saudi Suspects," *Washington Post*, September 25, 2001.

26. Hamzah, "Arab Tribes in the Kingdom of Saudi Arabia," p. 21.

27. Ibid., pp. 8–9.

28. National Commission on Terrorist Attacks upon the United States, *The 9/11 Commission Report*, p. 235.

29. Coll, *The Bin Ladens*, p. 115.

30. Noura bint Muhammad al-Saud, Al-Jawharah Muhammad al-Anqari, and Madeha Muhammad al-Ajroush, *Abha Bilad Asir: South-western Region of the Kingdom of Saudi Arabia* (Riyadh, Saudi Arabia: N. Saud, 1989), p. 215.

31. Sir Kinahan Cornwallis, *Asir before World War I: A Handbook* (Cambridge: Oleander Press, 1976), p. 11.

32. Mark A. Caudill, *Twilight in the Kingdom: Understanding the Saudis* (Westport, Conn.: Praeger, 2006), p. 121.

33. Cornwallis, *Asir before World War I*, p. 16.

34. Ioan M. Lewis, *Blood and Bone: The Call of Kinship in Somali Society* (Lawrenceville, N.J.: Red Sea Press, 1994), p. 103.

35. Rosita Forbes, *Adventure: Being a Gypsy Salad—Some Incidents, Excitements and Impressions of Twelve Highly-Seasoned Years* (London: Cassell and Co., 1923), pp. 107–08.

36. Ahmed Abodehman, *The Belt*, translated from the French by Nadia Benabid (London: Saqi Books, 2002), pp. 105–06.

37. Forbes, *Adventure*, pp. 102–05.

38. Anne Katrine Bang, "'This Is an Announcement to the People . . .'—The Bayan of 1912 by Muhammad B. 'Ali Al-Idrisi in 'Asir," in *New Arabian Studies, 4,* edited by G. Rex Smith, J. R. Smart, and B. R. Pridham (University of Exeter Press, 1997), pp. 21, 24, 26.

39. John R. Bradley, *Saudi Arabia Exposed: Inside a Kingdom in Crisis* (New York: Palgrave Macmillan, 2006), p. 9.

40. Mordechai Abir, *Saudi Arabia in the Oil Era: Regimes and Elites: Conflict and Collaboration* (Boulder, Colo.: Westview Press, 1988), p. 207.

41. Yaroslav Trofimov, *The Siege of Mecca: The 1979 Uprising at Islam's Holiest Shrine* (New York: Anchor Books, 2008), p. 38.

42. Erick Stakelbeck, "The Saudi Hate Machine," *The National Interest*, December 17, 2003.

43. Charles M. Sennott, "Why bin Laden Plot Relied on Saudi Hijackers," *Boston Globe*, March 3, 2002.

44. "Saudis Jailed for 'al-Qaeda' Plot," *BBC News*, February 21, 2003 (http://news.bbc.co.uk/1/hi/world/africa/2789233.stm).

45. Seth G. Jones, *Hunting in the Shadows: The Pursuit of Al Qa'ida Since 9/11* (New York: W. W. Norton, 2012), p. 154.

46. Bradley, *Saudi Arabia Exposed*, p. 71.

47. Ibid., p. 55.

48. Ibid., p. 59.

49. Ian S. Lustick, *Trapped in the War on Terror* (University of Pennsylvania Press, 2006), p. 134; "Saudis' Most Wanted Is Captured," *CBS News*, February 11, 2009 (www.cbsnews.com/2100-224_162-663581.html).

50. Madawi Al-Rasheed, "The Local and the Global in Saudi Salafi-Jihadi Discourse," in Roel Meijer, ed., *Global Salafism: Islam's New Religious Movement* (Columbia University Press, 2009), p. 311.

51. "The Global Islamic Media Front presents . . . 'From Here We Begin . . . and at Al-Aqsa We Meet' Addresses of the Commanders of Al-Qaeda in the Arabian Peninsula," Youtube.com.

52. Charles M. Sennott, "Highway 15: The Long Road to Rehabilitation," *GlobalPost*, September 6, 2011.

53. Martin Chulov, "Violent Province's 27 Female Suicide Bombers Who Set Out to Destroy Iraqi Hopes of Peace," *The Guardian* (Manchester), November 11, 2008.

54. Paul J. Murphy, *Allah's Angels: Chechen Women in War* (Annapolis: Naval Institute Press, 2010), p. 140; "Conversation between the two sisters who did a martyrdom operation in Chechnya, killing hundreds of Russian soldiers—can be seen in 'NO SURRENDER VIDEO'" (www.terrorisme.net/pdf/chechen.pdf).

55. Steven Lee Myers, "Beslan Organizer Is Killed, Russia Says—*Europe-International Herald Tribune*," *New York Times*, July 10, 2006.

56. Rebecca Leung, "New Video of Beslan School Terror," *CBS News*, February 11, 2009 (www.cbsnews.com/8301-18559_162-668127.html).

57. Anne Speckhand and Khapta Akhmedova, "Black Widows: The Chechen Female Suicide Terrorists," in *Female Suicide Terrorists*, edited by Yoram Schweitzer (Tel Aviv: Jaffe Center for Strategic Studies, 2006), p. 63.

58. Ellen Barry, "With Breakdown of Order in Russia's Dagestan Region, Fear Stalks Police," *New York Times*, March 20, 2010.

59. Mairbek Vatchagaev, "Rebel Attacks in Kabardino-Balkaria Skyrocket," *Eurasian Daily Monitor* 8 (February 4, 2011).

60. Tom Parfitt, "Islamists on Trial," *Foreign Policy*, February 24, 2011.

61. "Zeynep Kinaci (Zilan)," PKK Online (www.pkkonline.com/en/index.php?sys=article&artID=153).

62. Ali Kemal Ozcan, *Turkey's Kurds: A Theoretical Analysis of the PKK and Abdullah Ocalan* (Abingdon, U.K.: Routledge, 2006), p. 176.

63. Martin van Bruinessen, *Kurdish Ethno-Nationalism versus Nation-Building States: Collected Articles* (Istanbul: Isis Press, 2000), p. 246.

64. Ibid., p. 239; Yoram Schweitzer, "Suicide Terrorism: Development and Main Characteristics," in The International Policy Institute for Counter-Terrorism, ed., *Countering*

Suicide Terrorism: An International Conference (Herzlia, Israel: International Policy Institute for Counter-Terrorism, 2001), p. 81.

65. Rosemarie Skaine, *Female Suicide Bombers* (Jefferson, N.C.: McFarland, 2006), p. 81.

66. Michael Biggs, "Dying without Killing: Self-Immolations, 1963–2002," in *Making Sense of Suicide Missions,* edited by Diego Gambetta (Oxford University Press, 2006), p. 184.

67. "Suicide Bomb Blast in Turkey," *BBC News,* January 3, 2001 (http://news.bbc.co.uk/1/hi/world/europe/1099315.stm).

68. "Somali Militants Warn of More Attacks after Bombing," *USA Today,* October 5, 2011.

69. "World Scene—Somalia: Bomber Who Killed 100 Opposed Education," *Washington Times,* October 6, 2011.

70. Abdi Guled, "Somali Islamists Behead 11 Civilians in Capital," Associated Press, August 26, 2011.

71. "Red Cross Finds 780 Corpses in Single Nigeria City," PressTV, August 3, 2009 (http://edition.presstv.ir/detail/102384.html).

72. Ahmad Salkida Maiduguri, "The Story of Nigeria's First Suicide Bomber-Blue Print Magazine," *Sahara Reporters,* June 26, 2011 (http://saharareporters.com/news-page/story-nigerias-first-suicide-bomber-blueprint-magazine).

73. "Suicide Bomber Targets Mosque in Nigeria," Al Jazeera, July 13, 2012 (www.aljazeera.com/news/africa/2012/07/2012713153221739855.html).

74. "Boko Haram: Nigerian Islamist Leader Defends Attacks," *BBC News,* January 11, 2012 (www.bbc.co.uk/news/world-africa-16510929).

75. "World Briefing Africa—Nigeria: 53,000 Killed in 3 Years of Ethnic Conflict," *New York Times,* October 8, 2004.

76. Ann Waters-Bayer and Wolfgang Bayer, "Coming to Terms: Interactions between Immigrant Fulani Cattle-Keepers and Indigenous Farmers in Nigeria's Subhumid Zone," *Cahiers d'Etudes Africaines* 34, Cahier 133/135, L'archipel peul (1994): 214–16.

77. Victor Iluyemi, "Fulanis Lament Loss of 250 People, 8 million Cattle to Jos Crisis, *WorldStage Newsonline,* February 8, 2011 (http://worldstagegroup.com).

78. Jaafar Jaafar, "Nigeria Plateau Deports 20,000 Fulani—Fuldan Chairman," *Daily Trust* (Nigeria), May 9, 2009.

79. U.S. Department of State, Bureau of Democracy, Human Rights, and Labor, *2009 Human Rights Report: Nigeria* (Washington, March 11, 2010).

80. Iluyemi, "Fulanis Lament Loss of 250 People, 8 Million Cattle to Jos Crisis."

81. Ibrahim Garba, "Weekend Clashes Kill 200, as Nigeria Struggles for Control," *Christian Science Monitor,* July 9, 2012.

82. "'I Support Killing of Fulani Nomads'—PC Appiah Ofori," *Citi News* (Ghana), December 16, 2011.

CHAPTER 4

1. Pervez Musharraf, interview with the author in Akbar Ahmed, *Journey into Islam: The Crisis of Globalization* (Brookings, 2007), pp. 171–75.

2. Roedad Khan, "Our Descent into Chaos," *The News* (Pakistan), February 29, 2012.

3. Malik Siraj Akbar, personal communication, 2012.

4. Sir Olaf Caroe, "*Mizh* Book Review," *Asian Affairs* 11, no. 1 (1980): 90.

5. Pervez Musharraf, "Understanding Balochistan Part–I," *The News* (Pakistan), March 14, 2012, and "Understanding Balochistan," *The News* (Pakistan), March 15, 2012.

6. "Quaid-e-Azam Addresses the Sibi Darbar, Balochistan (Pakistan) Part-1" (You Tube.com).

7. Akbar S. Ahmed, *Pakistan Society: Islam, Ethnicity, and Leadership in South Asia* (Oxford University Press, 1997), p. 188.

8. Farhan Hanif Siddiqi, *The Politics of Ethnicity in Pakistan: The Baloch, Sindhi, and Mohajir Ethnic Movements* (Abingdon, U.K.: Routledge, 2012), p. 61.

9. Malik Siraj Akbar, *The Redefined Dimensions of Baloch Nationalist Movement* (Bloomington, Ind.: Xlibris, 2011), p. 313.

10. Rob Johnson, *A Region in Turmoil: South Asian Conflicts since 1947* (London: Reaktion Books, 2005), p. 45.

11. Sylvia A. Matheson, *The Tigers of Baluchistan* (Oxford University Press, 1997), p. 1.

12. Ahmed, *Pakistan Society*, p. 188.

13. Ibid., p. 191.

14. Paul Dresch, *Tribes, Government, and History in Yemen* (Oxford University Press, 1989), p. 184.

15. Ibid., p. 218.

16. Ibid., p. 188.

17. David D. Laitin and Said S. Samatar, *Somalia: Nation in Search of a State* (Boulder, Colo.: Westview Press, 1987), p. 15.

18. Ali Jamale Ahmed, *The Invention of Somalia* (Lawrenceville, N.J.: Red Sea Press, 1995), p. 7.

19. Charles King, *The Ghost of Freedom: A History of the Caucasus* (Oxford University Press, 2008), p. 37.

20. Marilyn Robinson Waldman, "The Fulani Jihad: A Reassessment," *Journal of African History* 6, no. 3 (1965): 347–49.

21. Ibid., p. 351.

22. E. C. Ejiogu, *The Roots of Political Instability in Nigeria: Political Evolution and Development in the Niger Basin* (Surrey: Ashgate, 2011), p. 91.

23. A. G. Adebayo, "Jangali: Fulani Pastoralists and Colonial Taxation in Northern Nigeria," *International Journal of African Historical Studies* 28, no. 1 (1995): 123.

24. Ibrahim Muazzam, *The Citizenship Question in Nigeria* (Kano, Nigeria: Centre for Research and Documentation, 2009), p. 25.

25. Beverly B. Mack and Jean Boyd, *One Woman's Jihad: Nana Asma'u, Scholar and Scribe* (Indiana University Press, 2000), p. 83.

26. Ibid., p. 76.

27. E. E. Evans-Pritchard, *The Sanusi of Cyrenaica* (Oxford University Press, 1949), p. 70.

28. Ibid., p. 73.

29. Peter G. Riddell, *Islam and the Malay-Indonesian World: Transmission and Responses* (University of Hawaii Press, 2001), p. 198.

30. Anthony Reid, *An Indonesian Frontier: Acehnese and Other Histories of Sumatra* (Singapore University Press, 2005), pp. 164, 338.

31. C. Snouck Hurgronje, *The Acehnese,* vol. 1, translated by A. W. S. O'Sullivan (Leiden: Brill, 1906), p. 8.

32. Jeremy Sarkin, *Germany's Genocide of the Herero: Kaiser Wilhelm II, His General, His Settlers, His Soldiers* (Suffolk: Boydell and Brewer, 2011), pp. 1, 137.

33. Philipp Blom, *The Vertigo Years: Europe, 1900–1914* (New York: Basic Books, 2008), p. 119.

34. Michael Bobelian, *Children of Armenia: A Forgotten Genocide and the Century-Long Struggle for Justice* (New York: Simon and Schuster, 2009), p. 3; David P. Forsythe, ed., *Encyclopedia of Human Rights* (Oxford University Press, 2009), p. 98.

35. Robert Montagne, *The Berbers: Their Social and Political Organization*, translated by David Seddon (London: Frank Cass, 1973).

36. Ernest Gellner, preface in ibid., p. vii.

37. Douglas Porch, *The March to the Marne: The French Army 1871–1914* (Cambridge University Press, 1981), p. 144.

38. Christian Tripodi, *Edge of Empire: The British Political Officer and Tribal Administration on the North-West Frontier, 1877–1947* (Surrey: Ashgate, 2011), p. 49.

39. Harold Ingrams, *The Yemen: Imams, Rulers, and Revolutions* (New York: Praeger, 1964), p. 56.

40. Ibid., p. 79.

41. Ibid., p. 80.

42. Ibid.

43. Ibid., p. 105.

44. Catherine Besteman, *Unraveling Somalia: Race, Violence, and the Legacy of Slavery* (University of Pennsylvania Press, 1999), p. 119.

45. Frederick Mercer Hunter, *A Grammar of the Somali Language* (Bombay: Education Society's Press, 1880).

46. Langton Prendergast Walsh, *Under the Flag: And Somali Coast Stories* (London: Andrew Melrose, 1925), p. 201.

47. Ibid., p. 240.

48. Ibid., p. 263.

49. Cecil John Edmonds, *Kurds, Turks, and Arabs: Politics, Travel, and Research in North-Eastern Iraq, 1919–1925* (Oxford University Press, 1957), p. 229.

50. "The Song of the Kabardian Night Assault," sung by Vladimir Bereghwn, translated by Amjad Jaimoukha, and produced by Sanjalay Jaimoukha (YouTube.com).

51. Yo'av Karny, *Highlanders: A Journey to the Caucasus in Quest of Memory* (New York: Farrar, Straus & Giroux, 2000), p. 48.

52. Stephen D. Shenfield, "The Circassians: A Forgotten Genocide?" in *The Massacre in History*, edited by Mark Levene and Penny Roberts (New York: Berghahn, 1999), p. 156.

53. Walter Richmond, *The Northwest Caucasus: Past, Present, Future* (Abingdon, U.K.: Routledge, 2008), p. 78.

54. Shenfield, "The Circassians: A Forgotten Genocide?" p. 157.

55. Amjad Jaimoukha, *The Circassians: A Handbook* (New York: Palgrave Macmillan, 2001), pp. 68–69.

56. Shenfield, "The Circassians: A Forgotten Genocide?" pp. 152–53.

57. Ibid., p. 153.

58. Ibid.

59. Ibid., p. 154; Michael Mann, *The Dark Side of Democracy: Explaining Ethnic Cleansing* (Cambridge University Press, 2005), p. 99.

60. Shenfield, "The Circassians: A Forgotten Genocide?" p. 158.

61. Kwame Anthony Appiah and Henry Louis Gates Jr., eds., *Encyclopedia of Africa* (Oxford University Press, 2010), p. 90.

62. Daniel R. Headrick, *Power over Peoples: Technology, Environment, and Western Imperialism, 1400 to the Present* (Princeton University Press, 2010), p. 166.

63. Appiah and Gates, *Encyclopedia of Africa*, p. 90.

64. Jennifer E. Sessions, "'Unfortunate Necessities': Violence and Civilization in the Conquest of Algeria," in *France and Its Spaces of War: Experience, Memory, Image*, edited by Patricia M. E. Lorcin and Daniel Brewer (New York: Palgrave Macmillan, 2009), pp. 35–36.

65. Benjamin Claude Brower, *A Desert Named Peace: The Violence of France's Empire in the Algerian Sahara, 1844–1902* (Columbia University Press, 2009), p. 23.

66. Appiah and Gates, *Encyclopedia of Africa*, p. 90.

67. Matthew Evangelista, *Gender, Nationalism, and War: Conflict on the Movie Screen* (Cambridge University Press, 2011), p. 28.

68. Mireille Rosello, "Tattoos or Earrings: Two Models of Historical Writing in Mehdi Lallaoui's *La colline aux oliviers*," in *Algeria and France, 1800–2000: Identity, Memory, Nostalgia*, edited by Patricia M. E. Lorcin (Syracuse University Press, 2006), p. 205.

69. Evangelista, *Gender, Nationalism, and War*, p. 30.

70. James Minahan, *Encyclopedia of the Stateless Nations: Ethnic and National Groups around the World*, vol. II D–K (Westport, Conn.: Greenwood Press, 2002), p. 866; Yves Beigbeder, *Judging War Crimes and Torture: French Justice and International Criminal Tribunals and Commission (1940–2005)* (Leiden: Martinus Nijhoff, 2006), p. 96.

71. Mehran Kamrava, *The Modern Middle East: A Political History since the First World War* (University of California Press, 2005), p. 102.

72. Thurston Clarke, *The Last Caravan* (New York: G. P. Putnam's Sons, 1978), pp. 22–23.

73. Susan J. Rasmussen, "Reflections on Myth and History: Tuareg Concepts of Truth, 'Lies,' and 'Children's Tales,'" *Oral Tradition* 13, no. 2 (1998): 273.

74. Douglas Porch, *The Conquest of the Sahara* (New York: Farrar, Straus & Giroux, 2005), p. 135.

75. Ibid.

76. David S. Woolman, *Rebels in the Rif: Abd el Krim and the Rif Rebellion* (Stanford University Press, 1968), p. 72.

77. Jose E. Alvarez, *The Betrothed of Death: The Spanish Foreign Legion during the Rif Rebellion, 1920–1927* (Westport, Conn.: Greenwood Press, 2001), p. 44.

78. Javier Espinosa, "Gas mostaza sobre el Rif," *El Mundo*, April 18, 2001.

79. Donald Bloxham and A. Dirk Moses, eds., *The Oxford Handbook of Genocide Studies* (Oxford University Press, 2010), p. xxiii.

80. Richard P. Hallion, *Strike from the Sky: The History of Battlefield Air Attack, 1910–1945* (University of Alabama Press, 1989), p. 68.

81. Martin Thomas, *The French Empire between the Wars: Imperialism, Politics, and Society* (Manchester University Press, 2005), p. 212.

82. Woolman, *Rebels in the Rif*, p. 196.

83. Michael Clodfelter, *Warfare and Armed Conflicts: A Statistical Reference to Casualties and Other Figures, 1500–2000* (Jefferson, N.C.: McFarland, 2002), pp. 397–98.

84. Peter Gowing, *Muslim Filipinos: Heritage and Horizon* (Quezon City: New Day, 1979), p. 30.

85. Ibid., p. 30.

86. Estelle Sylvia Pankhurst, *Ex-Italian Somaliland* (London: Watts, 1951), p. 64.

87. Ibid., p. 120.

88. Ali Abdullatif Ahmida, *The Making of Modern Libya: State Formation, Colonization, and Resistance* (State University of New York Press, 2009), p. 135.

89. Evans-Pritchard, *The Sanusi of Cyrenaica*, pp. 200–01.

90. Ibid., pp. 199, 201.

91. Ibid., p. 170.

92. Ibid., p. 172.

93. Ibid., p. 165.

94. Ahmida, *The Making of Modern Libya*, p. 107.

95. Evans-Pritchard, *The Sanusi of Cyrenaica*, p. 191.

96. Hurgronje, *The Acehnese*, p. ix.

97. Anthony Reid, "Colonial Transformation: A Bitter Legacy," in *Verandah of Violence: The Background to the Aceh Problem,* edited by Anthony Reid (National University of Singapore Press, 2006), pp. 97–99.

98. Anthony Reid, "Indonesia, Aceh, and the Modern Nation-State," in *The Politics of the Periphery in Indonesia: Social and Geographical Perspectives,* edited by Minako Sakai, Glenn Banks, and J. H. Walker (National University of Singapore Press, 2009), p. 94.

99. James T. Siegel, *Objects and Objections of Ethnography* (Fordham University Press, 2011), p. 80.

100. Anthony Reid, "Colonial Transformation," p. 102.

101. Tim Kell, *The Roots of Acehnese Rebellion, 1989–1992* (Singapore: Equinox, 1995), p. 25.

102. Victoria Clark, *Yemen: Dancing on the Heads of Snakes* (Yale University Press, 2010), p. 39.

103. John Baldry, "Al-Yaman and the Turkish Occupation 1849–1914," *Arabica* T 23 (June 1976): 177.

104. Clark, *Yemen: Dancing on the Heads of Snakes,* p. 42.

105. Baldry, "Al-Yaman and the Turkish Occupation 1949–1914," p. 169.

106. Ibid., p. 176.

107. Clark, *Yemen: Dancing on the Heads of Snakes,* p. 44.

108. Laitin and Samatar, *Somalia: Nation in Search of a State,* p. 34.

109. Akbar S. Ahmed, "Nomadism as Ideological Expression: The Case of the Gomal Nomads," *Newsletter of the Commission on Nomadic Peoples,* Number 9, September 1981.

110. Quoted in Louis Fischer, *The Story of Indonesia* (New York: Harper, 1959), p. 154. For a similar statement from a public speech of Sukarno, see Bernhard Dahm, *Sukarno and the Struggle for Indonesian Independence* (Cornell University Press, 1969), p. 200.

111. Elizabeth F. Drexler, *Aceh, Indonesia: Securing the Insecure State* (University of Pennsylvania, 2008), p. 55.

112. Wangari Muoria-sal and Henry Muoria, *Writing for Kenya: The Life and Works of Henry Muoria* (Leiden: Brill, 2009), p. 343.

113. Ibid., p. 345.

114. Thant Myint-U, *The River of Lost Footsteps: A Personal History of Burma* (New York: Farrar, Straus & Giroux, 2006), p. 254.

115. David I. Steinberg, *Burma/Myanmar: What Everyone Needs to Know* (Oxford University Press, 2009), p. 42.

116. Allan D. Cooper, *The Geography of Genocide* (Lanham, Md.: University Press of America, 2009), pp. 167–68.

117. "Bangladesh Sets Up War Crimes Court," Al Jazeera, March 25, 2010 (www.aljazeera.com/news/asia/2010/03/2010325151839747356.html).

118. Ayesha Siddiqa, *Military Inc.: Inside Pakistan's Military Economy* (London: Pluto Press, 2007).

119. Andrew Mango, "Atatürk and the Kurds," *Middle Eastern Studies* 35 (October 1999): 20.

120. Martin van Bruinessen, "Genocide in Kurdistan?: The Suppression of the Dersim Rebellion in Turkey (1937–38) and the Chemical War against the Iraqi Kurds (1988)," in *Genocide: Conceptual and Historical Dimensions,* edited by George J. Andreopoulos (University of Pennsylvania Press, 1994), p. 152.

121. Ibid., p. 151.

122. David McDowall, *A Modern History of the Kurds* (London: I. B. Tauris, 2004), p. 200.

123. Dana Adams Schmidt, *Journey among Brave Men* (New York: Little, Brown, 1964), p. 56.

124. McDowall, *A Modern History of the Kurds*, p. 199.

125. Van Bruinessen, "Genocide in Kurdistan?" pp. 146–47.

126. Ibrahim Sirkeci, *The Environment of Insecurity in Turkey and the Emigration of Turkish Kurds to Germany* (Lewiston, N.Y.: Edwin Mellon Press, 2006), p. 61.

127. McDowall, *A Modern History of the Kurds*, p. 405.

128. Ibid., p. 411.

129. Gokhan Bacik and Bezen Balamir Coskun, "The PKK Problem: Explaining Turkey's Failure to Develop a Political Solution," *Studies in Conflict and Terrorism* 34, no. 3 (2011): 254.

130. Ceren Belge, "State Building and the Limits of Legibility: Kinship Networks and Kurdish Resistance in Turkey," *International Journal of Middle East Studies* 43 (2011): 108.

131. McDowall, *A Modern History of the Kurds* (2010 edition), pp. 440–42.

132. "Over 50,000 Scored Zero on Turkey's University Entrance Exam," *Today's Zaman*, April 20, 2012.

133. "Turkey PM Erdogan Says Kurdish PPK Takes 500 Casualties," *BBC News*, September 17, 2012 (www.bbc.co.uk/news/world-europe-19624080).

134. "Al Jazeera World: The Smell of Gunpowder," Al Jazeera, October 11, 2012 (www.aljazeera.com/programmes/aljazeeraworld/2012/09/2012917151659292430.html).

135. Kerim Yildiz and Tanyel B. Taysi, *The Kurds in Iran: The Past, Present and Future* (London: Pluto Press, 2007), p. 35.

136. Lois Beck, *The Qashqa'i of Iran* (Yale University Press, 1986), p. 132.

137. Farideh Koohi-Kamali, *The Political Development of the Kurds in Iran: Pastoral Nationalism* (New York: Palgrave Macmillan, 2003), p. 42.

138. McDowall, *A Modern History of the Kurds*, p. 225.

139. Ibid., p. 251.

140. Ibid., p. 262.

141. Ibid., p. 272.

142. Ibid., p. 339.

143. Ibid., p. 349.

144. Ibid., pp. 339–40.

145. Ibid., p. 359.

146. Ibid., pp. 474–75.

147. J. Michael Kennedy, "Kurds Remain on the Sideline of Syria's Uprising," *New York Times*, April 17, 2012.

148. Hsain Ilahiane, *Historical Dictionary of the Berbers (Imazighen)* (Lanham, Md.: Scarecrow Press, 2006), p. 29.

149. Martin Stone, *The Agony of Algeria* (Columbia University Press, 1997), p. 64.

150. Robert Fisk, *The Great War for Civilization: The Conquest of the Middle East* (New York: Alfred A. Knopf, 2005), pp. 575, 582.

151. Bruce Maddy-Weitzman, *The Berber Identity Movement and the Challenge to North African States* (University of Texas Press, 2011), p. 186.

152. Winston Churchill, *The River War: An Account of the Reconquest of the Sudan* (Mineola, N.Y.: Dover, 2006), p. 79.

153. Gabriel Meyer, *War and Faith in Sudan* (Grand Rapids, Mich.: Wm. B. Eerdmans, 2005), p. 153.

154. Ibid., p. 89.

155. David Keen, *The Benefits of Famine: A Political Economy of Famine and Relief in Southwestern Sudan, 1983–1989* (Princeton University Press, 1994), p. 218.

156. Samuel Totten, "What Will It Take to Halt South Kordofan Atrocities," *Sudan Tribune*, June 27, 2011 (www.sudantribune.com/What-will-it-take-to-halt-South,39351).

157. Giles Fraser, "We Must Act Now to Stop the Genocide of Sudan's Nuba people," *The Guardian* (Manchester), June 6, 2012.

158. "Amnesty International Public Statement: Sudan's Civilians in Crisis: Indiscriminate Attacks and Arbitrary Arrests Pervade Southern Kordofan," December 11, 2012 (www.amnesty.org/ar/library/asset/AFR54/051/2012/en/d84e4390-2032-4def-b39e-b379cf247d08/afr540512012en.pdf).

159. Jean Sebastian Lecocq, *That Desert Is Our Country: Tuareg Rebellions and Competing Nationalisms in Contemporary Mali (1946–1996)* (Universiteit van Amsterdam, 2002), pp. 132–33.

160. Ibid., p. 162.

161. Samuel Decalo, *Historical Dictionary of Niger* (Lanham, Md.: Scarecrow Press, 1997), p. 130.

162. Clarke, *The Last Caravan*, p. 127.

163. Nadia Belalimat, "The *Ishumar* Guitar: Emergence, Circulation and Evolution from Diasporic Performances to the World Scene," in *Tuareg Society within a Globalized World: Saharan Life in Transition*, edited by Anja Fischer and Ines Kohl (London: I. B. Tauris, 2010), p. 163.

164. Jeremy Keenan, "Resisting Imperialism: Tuareg Threaten US, Chinese and Other Foreign Interests," in *Tuareg Society within a Globalized World*, edited by Fischer and Kohl, p. 269 n. 2.

165. "Niger, Africa's Second Largest Uranium Producer, Should See Great Growth," *International Mining*, September 16, 2009 (www.im-mining.com/2009/09/16/).

166. Cordula Meyer, "Tuareg Activist Takes on French Nuclear Company," *Der Spiegel*, April 2, 2010.

167. "NIGER: New Touareg Rebel Group Speaks Out," IRIN News, May 17, 2007 (www.irinnews.org/Report/72223/.

168. Kavkazskiy Uzel, "The Avars of Azerbaijan Ask the President of Dagestan to Protect Them from Azerbaijanization" (Kavkaz.memo.ru, June 18, 2008).

169. Linda J. Beck, *Brokering Democracy in Africa: The Rise of Clientelist Democracy in Senegal* (New York: Palgrave Macmillan, 2008), pp. 182–84.

170. Macartan Humphreys and Habaye Ag Mohamed, "Senegal and Mali," in *Understanding Civil War: Africa*, edited by Paul Collier and Nicholas Sambanis (Washington: World Bank, 2005), p. 250.

171. Nazaruddin Sjamsuddin, *The Republican Revolt: A Study of the Acehnese Rebellion* (Singapore: Institute of Southeast Asian Studies, 1985), pp. 125–26.

172. Edward Aspinall, "Place and Displacement in the Aceh Conflict," in *Conflict, Violence, and Displacement in Indonesia*, edited by Eva-Lotta Hedman (Cornell University Southeast Asia Program, 2008), p. 134.

173. Geoffrey Robinson, "Rawan Is As Rawan Does: The Origins of Disorder in New Order Aceh," *Indonesia* 66 (October 1998): 135.

174. Kell, *The Roots of Acehnese Rebellion, 1989–1992*, pp. 36–43.

175. "Declaration of Independence of Acheh Sumatra," Acheh-Sumatra National Liberation Front, December 4, 1976 (www.anslf.org).

176. Amnesty International, *Shock Therapy: Restoring Order to Aceh, 1989–1993* (New York, July 1993), pp. 17–18.

177. Robinson,"Rawan Is As Rawan Does," p. 143.

178. Michelle Ann Miller, *Rebellion and Reform in Indonesia: Jakarta's Security and Autonomy Policies in Aceh* (Abingdon, U.K.: Routledge, 2009), pp. 54–55.

179. "Aral Sea 'One of the Planet's Worst Environmental Disasters,'" *The Telegraph* (London), April 5, 2010.

180. "Growth in Tourism in South Sinai: Challenges Facing Tourism Development," South Sinai Environmental Action Plan, SEAM Programme (May 2004) (st-katherine.net/downloads/Challenges%20Facing%20Tourism.pdf).

181. Andrew McGregor, "Thirtieth Anniversary of Sinai's Liberation Marked by Libyan Arms, Bedouin Militancy and Growing Rift with Israel," *Terrorism Monitor* 10 (May 22, 2012).

182. "Egyptian Bedouins Claim Government Denying 75,000 Citizenship," *Daily News Egypt*, May 23, 2007.

183. Human Rights Watch, *Egypt: Mass Arrests and Torture in Sinai* (Washington, February 22, 2005), pp. 10, 13.

184. Christine Noelle, *State and Tribe in Nineteenth-Century Afghanistan: The Reign of Amir Dost Muhammad Khan (1826-1863)* (London: RoutledgeCurzon, 2004), p. 231.

185. Ibid., p. 20.

186. Ibid.

187. Ibid., p. 277.

188. Ibid., p. 211.

189. Ibid., p. 176.

190. James W. Spain, *The Pathan Borderland* (The Hague: Mouton, 1963), p. 135.

191. Hafizullah Emadi, *Repression, Resistance, and Women in Afghanistan* (Westport, Conn.: Praeger, 2002), p. 19.

192. Robert D. Kaplan, *Soldiers of God: With Islamic Warriors in Afghanistan and Pakistan* (New York: Random House, 2001), p. 115.

193. Bernd J. Fischer, *King Zog and the Struggle for Stability in Albania* (Columbia University Press, 1984), p. 41.

194. Bernd J. Fischer, "King Zog, Albania's Interwar Dictator," in *Balkan Strongmen: Dictators and Authoritarian Rulers of Southeast Europe,* edited by Bernd J. Fischer (Purdue University Press, 2007), p. 27.

195. Ibid., p. 30.

196. Owen Pearson, *Albania and King Zog: Independence, Republic and Monarchy, 1908–1939* (London: I. B. Tauris, 2004), p. 304.

197. Miranda Vickers, *The Albanians: A Modern History* (London: I. B. Taurus, 2006), p. 131.

198. Fischer, "King Zog, Albania's Interwar Dictator," pp. 35–36.

199. Ibid., p. 30.

200. Ibid., p. 30–32.

201. John R. Bradley, *Saudi Arabia Exposed: Inside a Kingdom in Crisis* (New York: Palgrave Macmillan, 2006), p. 74.

202. James M. Dorsey, "Ismaili Shiite Group Seeks an End to Saudi Religious Discrimination," *Wall Street Journal,* January 9, 2002; "The Ismailis of Najran: Second Class Saudi Citizens," *Human Rights Watch,* September 22, 2008 (www.hrw.org/reports/2008/09/22/ismailis-najran).

203. "Kuwait Grants Women Right to Vote," CNN, May 16, 2005 (http://articles.cnn.com/2005-05-16/world/).

204. Hussein, King of Jordan, *Uneasy Lies the Head: The Autobiography of His Majesty King Hussein I of the Hashemite Kingdom of Jordan* (New York: B. Geis Associates, 1962).

205. Gavin Maxwell, *Lords of the Atlas: The Rise and Fall of the House of Glaoua, 1893–1956* (London: Longmans, 1966), pp. 41–42.

206. John Shoup, "Are There Still Tribes in Morocco?" in *Nomadic Societies in the Middle East and North Africa: Entering the 21st Century,* edited by Dawn Chatty (Leiden: Brill, 2006), p. 138.

207. David Hart, *The Aith Waryaghar of the Moroccan Rif: An Ethnography and History* (New York: Werner-Gren Foundation for Anthropological Research, 1976), pp. 426–32.

208. Maddy-Weitzman, *The Berber Identity Movement and the Challenge to North African States*, p. 86.

209. James Sater, *Morocco: Challenges to Tradition and Modernity* (Abingdon, U.K.: Routledge, 2009), p. 27.

210. Samia Errazzouki, "Morocco's Rif: A History of Hidden Discontent," *Al Akhbar*, March 24, 2012 (English.al-akhbar.com/node/5590).

211. Terri Brint Joseph, "Poetry as a Strategy of Power: The Case of Riffian Berber Women," *Signs* 5 (Spring 1980): 420.

212. Maddy-Weitzman, *The Berber Identity Movement and the Challenge to North African States*, pp. 91–92.

213. Anne Lippert, "Emergence or Submergence of a Potential State: The Struggle in Western Sahara," *Africa Today* 24 (January–March 1977): 52.

214. Ibid., pp. 51–53.

215. Anne Lippert, "The Human Costs of War in Western Sahara," *Africa Today* 34 (3rd Quarter 1987): 53.

216. Michael Bhatia, "The Western Sahara under Polisario Control," *Review of African Political Economy* 28 (June 2001): 291.

217. Evans-Pritchard, *The Sanusi of Cyrenaica*, p. 47.

218. Herodotus, *The Histories*, translated by Aubrey de Selincourt (New York: Penguin, 2003), p. 306-307.

219. Justin Marozzi, "After Gaddafi: A New Libya Emerges," *Standpoint Magazine*, May 2011.

220. Jonathan Stock, "Gott entscheidet, was mit dir passiert," *Der Spiegel*, March 13, 2011.

221. "Arm Us to Save Us: Libyan Ex-prisoner Appeals," Agence France-Presse, March 13, 2011.

222. Mohammed Abbas, "Libya Clerics See Big Role for Islam after Gaddafi," Reuters, May 22, 2011.

223. Luis Martinez, *The Libyan Paradox* (Columbia University Press, 2007), p. 64.

224. Andrew Hammond, *Pop Culture Arab World!: Media, Arts, and Lifestyle* (Santa Barbara: ABC-CLIO, 2005), p. 32.

225. Peter Graff, "Ancient Language Renewed in Libyan Rebellion," *National Post*, July 11, 2011.

226. Borzou Daragahi, "Joint Fight with Arabs against Kadafi Spurs Berber Hopes of Equality in Libya," *Los Angeles Times*, July 16, 2011.

227. Julie Owono, "Unspoken History: The Last Genocide of the 20th Century," Al Jazeera, January 25, 2012 (www.aljazeera.com/indepth/opinion/2012/01/201211871746225899.html).

228. George Childs Kohn, *Dictionary of Wars* (New York: Facts on File, 2007), p. 100; E. S. D. Fomin and John W. Forje, *Central Africa: Crises, Reform and Reconstruction* (Dakar, Senegal: Council for the Development of Social Science Research in Africa, 2005), p. 35.

229. Mariame Maiga, *Gender, AIDS, and Food Security: Culture and Vulnerability in Rural Cote d'Ivoire* (Wageningen, Netherlands: Wageningen Academic, 2010), p. 27.

230. "'Mass Graves' Found in Guinea," *BBC News*, October 22, 2002 (http://news.bbc.co.uk/1/hi/world/africa/2349639.stm).

231. Amnesty International, "Guinea: 'They Ripped Off My Clothes with Their Knives and Left Me Completely Naked': Voice of Women and Girl Victims of Sexual Violence" (London, February 2010), p. 6 (www.amnesty.org/en/library/info/AFR29/002/2010).

232. "Guinea: The Story of Fatoumata Barry: The Forgotten Rape Victim of the September 2009 Stadium Massacre in Guinea," Make Every Woman Count, November 28, 2011 (www.makeeverywomancount.org/).

233. "Guinea: September 28 Massacre Was Premeditated," *Human Rights Watch*, October 27, 2009 (www.hrw.org/news/2009/10/27/guinea-september-28-massacre-was-premeditated).

234. "Guinea: The Story of Fatoumata Barry."

235. "Ethnicity in The Gambia: The Rise of the Jolas," Wikileaks, August 26, 2011 (http://wikileaks.org/cable/2007/11/07BANJUL589.html).

236. Assan Jallow, *Jammeh—The Nation Builder: A Testament of Jammeh's Achievements* (Buckinghamshire: AuthorHouse, 2011), p. 31.

237. "Gambia's Yahya Jammeh Threatens 'Lazy Workers,'" *BBC News*, January 19, 2012 (www.bbc.co.uk/news/world-africa-16636685).

238. Jallow, *Jammeh—The Nation Builder*, p. 40.

239. Ibid., p. 43.

240. Ebrima G. Sankareh, "As Alhaji Jahateh Fights for His Life; Samba Sowe Retells Ordeal with President Jammeh's Witch Hunters," *The Gambia Echo*, March 21, 2009.

241. "GAMBIA: Murky Voter Registration Mars Election Run-up," IRIN News, September 12, 2006 (www.irinnews.org/PrintReport.aspx?ReportId=61048).

242. "Gambia's Yahya Jammeh Ready for 'Billion-Year' Rule," *BBC News*, December 12, 2011 (www.bbc.co.uk/news/world-africa-16148458).

243. Paolo Tripodi, *The Colonial Legacy in Somalia: Rome and Mogadishu from Colonial Administration to Operation Restore Hope* (New York: St. Martin's Press, 1999), p. 100.

244. Helen Chapin Metz, ed., *Somalia: A Country Study* (Washington: Library of Congress, Federal Research Division, 1993), p. 50.

245. Mark Bradbury, *Becoming Somaliland* (London: Progressio, 2008), p. 60.

246. Metz, *Somalia: A Country Study*, p. 51.

247. Judith Gardner and Judy El Bushra, eds., *Somalia—The Untold Story: The War through the Eyes of Somali Women* (London: Pluto, 2004), p. 4.

248. Aidan Hartley, *The Zanzibar Chest: A Story of Life, Love, and Death in Foreign Lands* (New York: Atlantic Monthly Press, 2003), p. 169.

249. Michael R. Gordon, "Mission to Somalia; U.S. Is Sending Large Force as Warning to Somali Clans," *New York Times*, December 5, 1992; Peter Grier, "Logistics Challenges Await Troops in Somalia," *Christian Science Monitor*, December 7, 1992.

250. Dresch, *Tribes, Government, and History in Yemen*, p. 246.

251. Clark, *Yemen: Dancing on the Heads of Snakes*, p. 96.

252. Dresch, *Tribes, Government, and History in Yemen*, p. 261.

253. Shelagh Weir, *A Tribal Order: Politics and Law in the Mountains of Yemen* (University of Texas Press, 2007), p. 285.

254. Clark, *Yemen: Dancing on the Heads of Snakes*, p. 63.

255. Dresch, *Tribes, Government, and History in Yemen*, pp. 310–11.

256. Steven C. Caton, *Yemen Chronicle: An Anthropology of War and Mediation* (New York: Hill and Wang, 2005), p. 279.

257. "Tribes of Turkmenistan" (http://wikileaks.org/cable/2007/11/07ASHGABAT1284.html# [August 28, 2012]).

258. Christian Tyler, *Wild West China: The Taming of Xinjiang* (Rutgers University Press, 2004), p. 265.

259. Ibid., pp. 132–33.

260. Rob Johnson, *Oil, Islam and Conflict: Central Asia Since 1945* (London: Reaktion Books, 2007), p. 183.

261. J. Todd Reed and Diana Raschke, *The ETIM: China's Islamic Militants and the Global Terrorist Threat* (Santa Barbara, Calif.: Praeger, 2010), p. 27.

262. Tyler, *Wild West China,* p. 156.

263. Justin Jon Rudelson, *Oasis Identities: Uyghur Nationalism along China's Silk Road* (Columbia University Press, 1997), p. 79.

264. Tyler, *Wild West China,* pp. 213–14.

265. Diane Winston, ed., *The Oxford Handbook of Religion and the American News Media* (Oxford University Press, 2012), p. 483; "Xinjiang: China Jails 20 for Terrorism and Separatism," *BBC News,* August 2, 2012 (www.bbc.co.uk/news/world-asia-china-19099406).

266. Tyler, *Wild West China,* pp. 258–59.

267. "Death in Detention Draws Denigration," Radio Free Asia, June 4, 2012 (www.rfa.org/english/news/uyghur/death-06042012180843.html).

268. "Devastating Blows: Religious Repression of Uighurs in Xinjiang," *Human Rights Watch* 17 (April 2005): 59.

269. Tyler, *Wild West China,* p. 159.

270. Dru C. Gladney, "Response to Chinese Rule: Patterns of Cooperation and Opposition," in *Xinjiang: China's Muslim Borderland,* edited by S. Frederick Starr (New York: Central Asia-Caucasus Institute, 2004), p. 379.

271. "Protest Marks Xinjiang 'Massacre,'" Al Jazeera, February 6, 2007 (www.aljazeera.com/news/asia-pacific/2007/02/20085251383512763.html).

272. Tyler, *Wild West China,* p. 174.

273. Ibid., p. 187.

274. Ibid., p. 189.

275. Ibid., p. 192.

276. Atsuko Matsuoka and John Sorenson, *Ghosts and Shadows: Construction of Identity and Community in an African Diaspora* (University of Toronto Press, 2001), p. 41.

277. Mekuria Bulcha, *The Making of the Oromo Diaspora: A Historical Sociology of Forced Migration* (Minneapolis, Minn.: Kirk House, 2002), pp. 71–72.

278. Ibid., p. 73.

279. Mekuria Bulcha, *Flight and Integration: Causes of Mass Exodus from Ethiopia and Problems of Integration in the Sudan* (Motala, Sweden: Motala Grafiska, 1988), p. 40.

280. Ibid., p. 49.

281. Teshale Tibebu, *The Making of Modern Ethiopia: 1896–1974* (Lawrenceville, N.J.: Red Sea Press, 1995), p. 18.

282. Mohammed Hassen, "Conquest, Tyranny, and Ethnocide against the Oromo: A Historical Assessment of Human Rights Conditions in Ethiopia, ca. 1880s–2002," *Northeast African Studies* 9, no. 3 (2002): 21.

283. Asafa Jalata, *Oromia and Ethiopia: State Formation and Ethnonational Conflict, 1868–2004* (Trenton, N.J.: Red Sea Press, 2005), p. 176; Bulcha, *Flight and Integration,* p. 53.

284. Tirfe Mammo, *The Paradox of Africa's Poverty: The Role of Indigenous Knowledge, Traditional Practices and Local Institutions—The Case of Ethiopia* (Lawrenceville, N.J.: Red Sea Press, 1999), p. 99.

285. Jalata, *Oromia and Ethiopia,* p. 184.

286. Minority Rights Group, ed., *World Directory of Minorities* (Chicago: St. James Press, 1990), p. 256; Bonnie K. Holcomb and Sisai Ibssa, *The Invention of Ethiopia* (Trenton, N.J.: Red Sea Press, 1990), p. 397.

287. Robert D. Kaplan, *Surrender or Starve: Travels in Ethiopia, Sudan, Somalia, and Eritrea* (New York: Vintage, 2003), pp. 116, 129.

288. Minority Rights Group, *World Directory of Minorities,* p. 257.

289. Hassen, "Conquest, Tyranny, and Ethnocide against the Oromo," p. 25.

290. Kaplan, *Surrender or Starve*, pp. 6–7.

291. Mohammed Hassen, "The Development of Oromo Nationalism," in *Being and Becoming Oromo: Historical and Anthropological Enquiries*, edited by P. T. W. Baxter, Jan Hultin, and Alessandro Triulzi (Lawrenceville, N.J.: Red Sea Press, 1996), p. 78.

292. Hassen, "Conquest, Tyranny, and Ethnocide against the Oromo," p. 32.

293. Jalata, *Oromia and Ethiopia*, p. 238.

294. Asafa Jalata, *Fighting against the Injustice of the State and Globalization: Comparing the African American and Oromo Movements* (New York: Palgrave, 2001), p. 131.

295. Paolo Tablino, *The Gabra: Camel Nomads of Northern Kenya* (Nairobi: Paulines Publications Africa, 1999), p. 241.

296. Brian Otieno, "Kenya: Civil Servant Who Witnessed Garissa Massacre Speaks Out," *The Star* (Kenya), March 1, 2011.

297. S. Abdi Sheikh, *Blood on the Runway: The Wagalla Massacre of 1984* (Nairobi: Northern Publishing House, 2007), p. 66.

298. Abnasir Amin, "Kenya: Pain of Being a Kenyan Somali," *Daily Nation* (Kenya), November 3, 2011 (http://allafrica.com/stories/201111040033.html?viewall=1).

299. Rodolfo Stavenhagen, *Report of the Special Rapporteur on the Situation of Human Rights and Fundamental Freedoms of Indigenous People: Mission to Kenya* (New York: United Nations Human Rights Council, February 26, 2007), p. 16.

300. Martha Brill Olcott, *The Kazakhs* (Palo Alto, Calif.: Hoover Institution Press, 1995), pp. 184–85.

301. Karny, *Highlanders: A Journey to the Caucasus in Quest of Memory*, p. 226.

302. Amjad Jaimoukha, *Chechens: A Handbook* (Abingdon, U.K.: RoutledgeCurzon, 2005), p. 60.

303. Andrew Felkay, *Yeltsin's Russia and the West* (Westport, Conn.: Praeger, 2002), p. 46.

304. John Russell, *Chechnya: Russia's 'War on Terror'* (Abingdon, U.K.: Routledge, 2007), p. 71.

305. Vicken Cheterian, *War and Peace in the Caucasus: Ethnic Conflict and the New Geopolitics* (Columbia University Press, 2008), p. 353.

306. Arkady Babchenko, *One Soldier's War,* translated by Nick Allen (New York: Grove Press, 2007), pp. 145–46.

307. Andrew E. Kramer, "Chechnya's Capital Rises from the Ashes, Atop Hidden Horrors," *New York Times*, April 30, 2008.

308. James Hughes, *Chechnya: From Nationalism to Jihad* (University of Pennsylvania Press, 2007), p. 112.

309. Jillian Kestler-D'Amours, "Israel: No Place for Bedouin," Al Jazeera, June 29, 2011 (www.aljazeera.com/indepth/opinion/2011/06/20116238174269364.html).

310. Isma'el Abu-Sa'ad, "Forced Sedentarisation, Land Rights and Indigenous Resistance: The Palestinian Bedouin in the Negev," in *Catastrophe Remembered: Palestine, Israel and the Internal Refugees,* edited by Nur Masalha (London: Zed, 2005), p. 117.

311. Steven C. Dinero, *Settling for Less: The Planned Resettlement of Israel's Negev Bedouin* (New York: Berghahn, 2010), p. 3.

312. Kestler-D'Amours, "Israel: No Place for Bedouin."

313. "Israel Demolishes Bedouin Village for 39th Time," Ma'an News Agency, June 25, 2012 (www.maannews.net/eng/ViewDetails.aspx?ID=498678).

314. Harriet Sherwood, "Israel to Forcibly Remove Bedouin Communities in Settlements Push," *The Guardian* (Manchester), December 5, 2011.

315. Dalia Hatuqa, "Israel Expansion Threatens West Bank Bedouin," Al Jazeera, December 15, 2012.

316. *Clan Conflicts in the Palestinian Territory* (Oslo: Landinfo Country of Origin Information Centre, July 28, 2008), p. 10.

317. Nadav Shragai, "Jewish Presence in Hebron Is an Indisputable Historical Fact," *Israel Hayom*, November 4, 2011.

318. Ibid.

319. International Crisis Group, *Inside Gaza: The Challenge of Clans and Families*, Middle East Report 71 (December 20, 2007), p. 16.

320. Erin Cunningham, "Long the Glue of Gaza, Clans Say Hamas Is Undermining Tribal Justice," *Christian Science Monitor*, January 22, 2010.

321. International Crisis Group, *Inside Gaza*, p. 14.

322. Noel Malcolm, *Kosovo: A Short History* (New York University Press, 1998), p. 254.

323. Peter Gay, *The Cultivation of Hatred: The Bourgeois Experience, Victoria to Freud* (New York: W. W. Norton, 1993), p. 82.

324. Tim Judah, *Kosovo: War and Revenge* (Yale University Press, 2000), p. 22.

325. Malcolm, *Kosovo: A Short History*, p. 273.

326. Miranda Vickers, *Between Serb and Albanian: A History of Kosovo* (Columbia University Press, 1998), p. 143.

327. Roger D. Petersen, *Understanding Ethnic Violence: Fear, Hatred, and Resentment in Twentieth-Century Eastern Europe* (Cambridge University Press, 2002), p. 221 n. 32.

328. Judah, *Kosovo: War and Revenge*, p. 41.

329. Denisa Kostovicova, "Albanian Schooling in Kosovo 1992–1998: 'Liberty Imprisoned,'" in *Kosovo: The Politics of Delusion*, edited by Michael Waller, Kyril Drezov, and Bulent Gokay (London: Frank Cass, 2001), p. 13.

330. Nita Luci and Predrag Markovic, "Events and Sites of Difference: Marking Self and Other in Kosovo," in *Media Discourse and the Yugoslav Conflicts: Representations of Self and Other*, edited by Pal Kolsto (Surrey: Ashgate, 2009), p. 95.

331. Warren Zimmerman, *Origins of a Catastrophe: Yugoslavia and its Destroyers—America's Last Ambassador Tells What Happened and Why* (New York: Times Books, 1996), p. 60.

332. Ivo H. Daalder and Michael E. O'Hanlon, *Winning Ugly: NATO's War to Save Kosovo* (Brookings, 2000), p. 58.

333. Ibid., pp. 110–11.

334. Christopher Catherwood and Leslie Alan Horvitz, *Encyclopedia of War Crimes and Genocide* (New York: Facts on File, Inc., 2006), p. 270.

335. John Phillips, *Macedonia: Warlords and Rebels in the Balkans* (Yale University Press, 2004), p. 45.

336. Ibid., p. 87.

337. Ibid., p. 161.

338. Ibid., p. 114.

339. Gowing, *Muslim Filipinos: Heritage and Horizon*, p. 178.

340. E. San Juan Jr., *U.S. Imperialism and Revolution in the Philippines* (New York: Palgrave Macmillan, 2007), p. 101.

341. Ariel Macaspac Penetrante, "Negotiating Memories and Justice in the Philippines," in *The Slippery Slope to Genocide: Reducing Identity Conflicts and Preventing Mass Murder*, edited by I. William Zartman, Mark Anstey, and Paul Meerts (Oxford University Press, 2012), p. 87; Rudy B. Rodil, "Mindanao: A Historical Overview," in *Challenges to Human Security in Complex Situations: The Case of Conflict in the Southern Philippines*, edited by Merlie B. Mendoza and Victor M. Taylor (Kuala Lumpur: Asian Disaster Reduction and Response Network, 2010), p. 15.

342. Thomas M. Fraser Jr., *Fishermen of South Thailand: The Malay Villagers* (New York: Holt, Rinehart and Winston, 1966), p. 50.

343. Surin Pitsuwan, *Islam and Malay Nationalism: A Case Study of the Malay-Muslims of Southern Thailand* (Bangkok: Thammasat University, Thai Khadi Research Institute, 1985), p. 98.

344. Barbara Whittingham-Jones, "Patani—Malay State Outside Malaya," *The Straits Times* (Singapore), October 30, 1947.

345. Thanet Aphornsuvan, "Origins of Malay Muslims 'Separatism' in Southern Thailand," in *Thai South and Malay North: Ethnic Interactions on a Plural Peninsula,* edited by Patrick Jory and Michael J. Montesano (National University of Singapore Press, 2008), pp. 117–18.

346. "Thai Mosque Killings Criticised," *BBC News,* July 28, 2004 (http://news.bbc.co.uk/1/hi/world/asia-pacific/3932323.stm).

347. Duncan McCargo, *Tearing Apart the Land: Islam and Legitimacy in Southern Thailand* (Cornell University Press, 2008), p. 108.

348. Ibid., p. 159.

349. "Thai Separatists Fight for Independence," Al Jazeera, May 12, 2011 (www.aljazeera.com/video/asia/2011/05/2011512986527775.html).

350. Duncan McCargo, "Thaksin and the Resurgence of Violence in the Thai South," in *Rethinking Thailand's Southern Violence,* edited by Duncan McCargo (National University of Singapore Press, 2007), pp. 57–58.

351. Raymond Scupin, "Historical, Ethnographic, and Contemporary Analyses of the Muslims of Kampuchea and Vietnam," *Sojourn: Journal of Social Issues in Southeast Asia* 10 (October 1995): 315.

352. Ben Kiernan, *The Pol Pot Regime: Race, Power, and Genocide in Cambodia under the Khmer Rouge, 1975–1979* (Yale University Press, 2008), p. 286.

353. Scupin, "Historical, Ethnographic, and Contemporary Analyses," pp. 320–21.

354. Ibid., p. 322.

355. Kiernan, *The Pol Pot Regime,* p. 284.

356. "Cambodia and Islamism: Courting the Cham," *The Economist,* September 30, 2010; Philipp Bruckmayr, "The Cham Muslims of Cambodia: From Forgotten Minority to Focal Point of Islamic Internationalism," *American Journal of Islamic Social Sciences* 23 (January 2006): 8.

357. Kiernan, *The Pol Pot Regime,* p. 283.

358. Scupin, "Historical, Ethnographic, and Contemporary Analyses," pp. 322–23.

359. Moshe Yegar, *Between Integration and Secession: The Muslim Communities of the Southern Philippines, Southern Thailand, and Western Burma/Myanmar* (Lanham, Md.: Lexington Books, 2002), pp. 55–56.

360. Eileen Pittaway, "The Rohingya Refugees in Bangladesh: A Failure of the International Protection Regime," in *Protracted Displacement in Asia: No Place to Call Home,* edited by Howard Adelman (Hampshire: Ashgate, 2008), p. 87.

361. "Myanmar Envoy Brands Boat People 'Ugly as Ogres,'" Agence France-Presse, February 11, 2009.

362. Chris Lewa, *Unregistered Rohingya Refugees in Bangladesh: Crackdown, Forced Displacement, and Hunger* (Bangkok: Arakan Project, 2010), p. 2.

363. Joseph Allchin, "Between Dhaka and the Nasaka," *Himal Southasian,* July 2011.

364. For an excellent overview of the recent violence, see Ufuk Gokcen, "Rohingyas and the Democratization in Myanmar," *Huffington Post,* November 2, 2012 (www.huffingtonpost.com/amb-ufuk-gokcen/).

365. "UN Rejects Thein Sein's Potential Rohingya Plan," *Democratic Voice of Burma,* July 13, 2012 (www.dvb.no/news/).

366. Jonah Fisher, "Burmese Refugees Sold on by Thai Officials," *BBC News,* January 21, 2013.

367. "EU Chief Barroso Offers New Development Aid to Burma," *BBC News,* November 3, 2012 (www.bbc.co.uk/news/world-asia-20189448).

Chapter 5

1. *Inaugural Addresses of the Presidents of the United States* (Washington: U.S. Government Printing Office, 1969), p. 15.

2. Merrill D. Peterson, ed., *The Political Writings of Thomas Jefferson* (University of North Carolina Press, 1993), p. 50.

3. Walter Issacson, *Benjamin Franklin: An American Life* (New York: Simon & Schuster, 2003), p. 169.

4. Jon Meacham, *American Gospel: God, The Founding Fathers, and the Making of a Nation* (New York: Random House, 2006), p. 245.

5. Dana Adams Schmidt, *Journey among Brave Men* (New York: Little, Brown, 1964), p. 106.

6. Andrew Scott Cooper, *The Oil Kings: How the U.S., Iran, and Saudi Arabia Changed the Balance of Power in the Middle East* (New York: Simon & Schuster, 2011), p. 242.

7. Mahmood Mamdani, *Good Muslim, Bad Muslim: America, the Cold War, and the Roots of Terror* (New York: Three Leaves, 2005) p. 143.

8. Akbar Ahmed, *Journey into America: The Challenge of Islam* (Brookings, 2010).

9. Ken Dilanian, "Grieving Awlaki Family Protests Yemen Drone Strikes," *Los Angeles Times*, October 19, 2011.

10. Victoria Clark, *Yemen: Dancing on the Heads of Snakes* (Yale University Press, 2010), p. 243.

11. Ibid., p. 253.

12. Ibid., p. 244.

13. Robert F. Worth, "Ex-Jihadist Defies Yemen's Leader, and Easy Labels," *New York Times*, February 26, 2010.

14. Shukri Hussein, "Tariq Al-Fadhli Speaks on the Yemeni Protest Movement," National Yemen, February 26, 2011 (www.nationalyemen.com/2011/02/26/).

15. "Son of Last Sultan of Yemen Joins with His Children the Mujahideen of al-Qaeda," Kavkaz Center, April 21, 2012 (www.kavkazcenter.com).

16. Rania El Gamal, "Yemen Says 17 Soldiers Killed in Ambush," Reuters, December 10, 2012.

17. Barak A. Salmoni, Bryce Loidolt, and Madeleine Wells, *Regime and Periphery in Northern Yemen: The Huthi Phenomenon* (Santa Monica, Calif.: RAND, 2010), p. 8.

18. Michael Horton, "Back from the Grave: The Re-emergence of Houthi Rebel Leader Abdul Malik al-Houthi," *Jamestown Foundation Militant Leadership Monitor* 1, no. 3 (March 30, 2010); U.S, Department of State, "2008 Human Rights Report: Yemen" (Washington, February 25, 2009).

19. Benjamin Wiacek, "In Pictures: The Scars of North Yemen's Wars," Al Jazeera, July 2, 2012 (www.aljazeera.com/indepth/inpictures/2012/06/2012630195727807952.html); Salmoni, Loidolt, and Wells, *Regime and Periphery in Northern Yemen*, p. 2.

20. "Houthis: We Will Use Legitimate Ways if Drones Target Us," *Yemen Observer*, October 30, 2012 (www.yobserver.com/front-page/10022345.html).

21. "Houthi Leader Condemns US Drone Attack in Northern Yemen," *PressTV*, October 30, 2012 (www.presstv.ir/detail/2012/10/30/269595/yemeni-leader-condemns-us-drone-attack/).

22. Ibrahim Warde, *The Price of Fear: The Truth behind the Financial War on Terror* (University of California Press, 2007), p. 98.

23. Ibid., pp. 97, 102.

24. George W. Bush, "Remarks at the Financial Crimes Enforcement Network in Vienna, Virginia, November 7, 2001," *Public Papers of the Presidents of the United States:*

Administration of George W. Bush, 2001, Book 2 (Washington: GPO, April 16, 2004), pp. 1352–53.

25. National Commission on Terrorist Attacks upon the United States, "Al-Barakaat Case Study: The Somali Community and al-Barakaat" (Washington, 2004), pp. 82–83.

26. David Ignatius, "Ethiopia's Iraq," *Washington Post,* May 13, 2007.

27. Frank Nyakairu, "Somali Refugees Pour into Kenya by the Thousands," Reuters, June 4, 2009.

28. Jason Straziuso, "US: 29,000 Somali Children under 5 Dead in Famine," Associated Press, August 4, 2011.

29. Andrew McGregor, "Puntland's Shaykh Muhammad Atam: Clan Militia Leader or al-Qaeda Terrorist?" *Jamestown Foundation Militant Leadership Monitor* 1, no. 9 (September 29, 2010), p. 15.

30. Fredrick Nzwili, "Report: Kenyan Forces Abused Ethnic Somalis Near Border," *Christian Science Monitor,* May 4, 2012.

31. "Somalia Protests after Kenya Arrests MPs in Riot Swoop," *BBC News,* January 18, 2010 (http://news.bbc.co.uk/1/hi/world/africa/8465043.stm).

32. "Kenya: End Security Force Reprisals in North," Human Rights Watch, November 22, 2012.

33. Stepehn Astariko, "Garissa Chief Dies of Riot Wounds," *The Star* (Kenya), November 23, 2012.

34. Jason Straziuso, "After Attacks, Kenya Clamps Down on Refugee Freedoms in Move Aimed at Somali Community," Associated Press, December 14, 2012.

35. Armin Rosen, "The Zenawi Paradox: An Ethiopian Leader's Good and Terrible Legacy," *The Atlantic,* July 20, 2012.

36. William Davison, "Four People Die After Ethiopian Muslims Attack Police Station," Bloomberg, April 30, 2012 (www.bloomberg.com/news/2012-04-30/).

37. *"Waiting Here for Death": Forced Displacement and "Villagization" in Ethiopia's Gambella Region* (New York: Human Rights Watch, 2012), p. 2.

38. *Collective Punishment: War Crimes and Crimes against Humanity in the Ogaden Area of Ethiopia's Somali Region* (New York: Human Rights Watch, 2008), p. 122.

39. "Ethiopia 'Using Aid as Weapon of Oppression,'" *BBC News,* August 5, 2011 (http://news.bbc.co.uk/1/hi/programmes/newsnight/9556288.stm).

40. "U.S. Drone Initiated Strike on Kurds," United Press International, January 8, 2012 (www.upi.com/Top_News/World-News/2012/01/08/).

41. Mehmet Solmaz and Alyson Neel, "Bağış: What al-Qaeda Is to the West, the PKK Is to Turkey," *Today's Zaman* (Istanbul), October 23, 2011.

42. Adam Entous and Joe Parkinson, "Turkey's Attack on Civilians Tied to U.S. Military Drone," *Wall Street Journal,* May 16, 2012.

43. Ian O. Lesser, "Turkey: 'Recessed' Islamic Politics and Convergence with the West," in *The Muslim World after 9/11,* edited by Angel M. Rabasa (Santa Monica, Calif.: RAND, 2004), p. 194.

44. Martha Mendoza, "AP IMPACT: 35,000 Worldwide Convicted for Terror," Associated Press, September 3, 2011.

45. "Kurdish Mayor Aydin Budak Sentenced to 7,5 years in Turkish Prison," Kurd.net, December 24, 2010 (www.ekurd.net/mismas/articles/misc2010/12/turkey3087.htm).

46. Susanne Gusten, "Sensing a Siege, Kurds Hit Back in Turkey," *New York Times,* March 21, 2012.

47. Yigal Schleifer, "Turkey: Treating Minors as Terrorists Stirs Controversy," Eurasianet.org, June 1, 2009.

48. Ibid.

49. Mark Mazzetti, "The Drone Zone," *New York Times*, July 6, 2012.

50. Eduardo F. Ugarte, "The Alliance System of the Abu Sayyaf, 1993–2000," *Studies in Conflict and Terrorism* 31, no. 2 (2008): 139.

51. Victor M. Taylor, "Criminality: Focus on Kidnapping," in *Challenges to Human Security in Complex Situations: The Case of Conflict in the Southern Philippines*, edited by Merlie B. Mendoza and Victor M. Taylor (Kuala Lumpur: Asian Disaster Reduction and Response Network, 2010), p. 68.

52. Ugarte, "The Alliance System of the Abu Sayyaf, 1993–2000," p. 135.

53. Ibid., p. 131.

54. Ibid., p. 139.

55. "Commander Robot among 23 Killed in Prison Siege," *Sydney Morning Herald*, March 15, 2005.

56. Napoleon C. Reyes and Michael S. Vaughn, "Revisiting the *Bicutan Siege*: Police Use of Force in a Maximum Security Detention Center in the Philippines," *International Criminal Justice Review* 19 (March 2009): 26.

57. Pervez Musharraf, *In the Line of Fire: A Memoir* (New York: Simon & Schuster, 2006).

58. Declan Walsh, "WikiLeaks Cables: US and Pakistan Play Down Impact of 'Mischief,'" *The Guardian* (Manchester), December 1, 2010.

59. Pankaj Mishra, "Imran Khan Must Be Doing Something Right," *New York Times*, August 16, 2012.

60. Andy Worthington, "Who Are the Four Guantanamo Uighurs Sent to Bermuda?" *Huffington Post*, June 11, 2009.

61. Jonathan Kent, "'We'd Never Heard of al Qaeda' [Claim the Uighurs in Bermuda]," *Royal Gazette Bermuda*, June 13, 2009.

62. Worthington, "Who Are the Four Guantanamo Uighurs Sent to Bermuda?"

63. Ibid.

64. Justin Rood, "Report: U.S. Soldiers Did 'Dirty Work' for Chinese Interrogators," *ABC News*, May 20, 2008 (http://abcnews.go.com/Blotter/).

65. "Guantanamo Uighurs Placed in 'Nightmarish' Solitary: Lawyer," Agence France-Presse, January 26, 2007.

66. Peter Lee, "Uyghurs Sold Out in the US," *Asia Times Online*, May 28, 2009 (www.atimes.com/atimes/China/KE28Ad01.html).

67. Ibid.

68. Jeffrey Kaye, "Despite New Denials by Rumsfeld, Evidence Shows US Military Used Waterboarding-Style Torture," Truthout, August 2, 2011 (http://truth-out.org/news/item/2442).

69. Omar Nasiri, *Inside the Jihad: My Life with Al Qaeda, A Spy's Story* (New York: Basic Books, 2006), p. xiii.

70. Jane Mayer, *The Dark Side: The Inside Story of How the War on Terror Turned Into a War on American Ideals* (New York, Anchor, 2009), p. 106.

71. Ibid., p. 119.

72. Lisa Hajjar, "Suleiman: The CIA's Man in Cairo," Al Jazeera, February 7, 2011 (www.aljazeera.com/indepth/opinion/2011/02/201127114827382865.html).

73. Mayer, *The Dark Side*, p. 119.

74. Ibid., p. 135.

75. Ibid., pp. 135–36.

76. Ibid., p. 136.

77. Andy Worthington, "New Revelations about the Torture and Alleged Suicide of Ibn al-Shaykh al-Libi" (Pacific Palisades, Calif.: The Public Record, June 19, 2009).

78. Gary Gambill, "The Libyan Islamic Fighting Group (LIFG)," *Terrorism Monitor* 3 (May 5, 2005).

79. James M. Dorsey, "Libyan Islamists Stand to Gain with or without Qadhafi," *Deutsche Welle*, March 24, 2011.

80. Tim Dickinson, "U.S. Bombs Libya, Helps . . . Jihadists?!" *Rolling Stone,* March 21, 2012.

81. Anthony Shadid, "Diverse Character in City Qaddafi Calls Islamist," *New York Times*, March 7, 2011.

82. IntelCenter, *IntelCenter Words of Abu Yahya al-Libi,* Vol. 1 (Alexandria, Va.: Tempest, 2009), p. 7.

83. Nick Paton Walsh, "US Looks Away as New Ally Tortures Islamists," *The Guardian* (Manchester), May 25, 2003.

84. Don Van Natta Jr., "U.S. Recruits a Rough Ally to Be a Jailer," *New York Times*, May 1, 2005.

85. "Finland Must Further Investigate USA Rendition Flights," *Amnesty International News*, November 1, 2011 (www.amnesty.org/en/news/).

86. Joshua Kucera, "America's Uzbekistan Problem," *New York Times*, December 28, 2011.

87. U.S. State Department, *2010 Human Rights Report: Uzbekistan* (Washington, April 8, 2011), pp. 2, 4.

88. George W. Bush, "The President's Reply to the Remarks of the Newly Appointed Ambassador of the Republic of the Gambia Dodou Bammy Jagne upon the Occasion of the Presentation of His Letter of Credence," Office of the Gambian President, State House Online: Yahya A. J. J. Jammeh (www.statehouse.gm/bush-statement-credence.htm).

89. "MI5 Enabled UK Pair's 'Rendition,'" *BBC News*, March 28, 2006 (http://news.bbc.co.uk/1/hi/uk_politics/4851478.stm).

90. George B. Mickum, "MI5, Camp Delta, and the Story That Shames Britain," *The Independent* (London), March 16, 2006.

91. "Reprieve Reports of Growing Evidence of British Governmental Involvement in the Seizure and Rendition of Bisher Al-Rawi and Jamil El-Banna, British Residents 'Grabbed in The Gambia,' sent for torture in the 'Dark Prison' in Kabul, and then taken to Guantanamo Bay," *Reprieve*, April 29, 2006 (http://old.cageprisoners.com/articles.php?id=13655).

92. "MI5 Enabled UK Pair's 'Rendition,'" *BBC News*.

93. Rory Carroll, "Bush's Secret War," *The Guardian* (Manchester), August 20, 2003.

94. Ibid.

95. Jamie Dettmer, "Al-Qaeda's Links in the Balkans," *Insight*, July 22, 2002.

96. James Meek, "'They Beat Me from All Sides,'" *The Guardian* (Manchester), January 13, 2005.

97. "Khadr Should Go Back to Canada: UN Official," *CBC News*, October 27, 2010 (www.cbc.ca/news/world/story/2010/10/27/omar-khadr-united-nations-child-soldier.html).

98. "Witness: Four Days in Guantanamo," Al Jazeera, January 12, 2012 (www.aljazeera.com/programmes/witness/2012/01/20121121051543501.html).

99. Steven R. Weisman, "U.S. to Sell Military Gear to Algeria to Help It Fight Militants," *New York Times*, December 10, 2002.

100. Souad Mekhennet and others, "A Ragtag Insurgency Gains a Qaeda Lifeline," *New York Times*, July 1, 2008.

101. Salima Mellah and Jean-Baptiste Rivoire, "El Para, the Maghreb's Bin Laden," *Le Monde diplomatique*, February 2005.

102. "Al-Qaeda Claims Suicide Bombing in Algeria's East," Agence France-Presse, July 29, 2010.

103. Jeremy Keenan, "Resisting Imperialism: Tuareg Threaten US, Chinese and Other Foreign Interests," in *Tuareg Society within a Globalized World: Saharan Life in Transition*, edited by Anja Fischer and Ines Kohl (London: I. B. Tauris, 2010), p. 226.

104. Donna Cassata, "U.S. Military Helping Plan Mali Intervention," Associated Press, December 5, 2012.

105. U.S. Department of State, *Patterns of Global Terrorism 2002— Azerbaijan* (Washington, April 30, 2003).

106. U.S. Department of State, *Country Reports on Terrorism 2008—Azerbaijan* (Washington, April 30, 2009).

107. Yossef Bodansky, *Chechen Jihad: Al Qaeda's Training Ground and the Next Wave of Terror* (New York: HarperCollins, 2007), p. 362.

108. Simon Montlake, "Azerbaijan Says It Foils Attack on US Embassy," *Christian Science Monitor*, October 30, 2007.

109. Arzu Geybullayeva, "Is Azerbaijan Becoming a Hub of Radical Islam?" *Turkish Policy Quarterly* 6 (Fall 2007): 111; Shahla Sultanova, "Azerbaijan: Sunni Groups Viewed with Suspicion" (Washington: Institute For War & Peace Reporting, April 8, 2011).

110. Anar Valiyev, "Azerbaijan Increasingly Caught between Salafism and Iran," *Terrorism Monitor* 5 (October 24, 2007).

111. "Militants with Al Qaeda Links Jailed in Azerbaijan," Reuters, July 6, 2011.

112. "Azerbaijani Intelligence Service Detains 17 Members of Armed Group," Trend News Agency, April 6, 2012; Fuad Huseinzadeh, "Caucasian 'Robin Hoods' Threaten the Security of Azerbaijan," *Jamestown Foundation* (blog), April 13, 2012 (www.jamestown.org/blog/).

113. "Azerbaijan Says Armed Group in Western Town Trained by Al-Qa'idah," BBC Monitoring Newsfile, April 18, 2012; Huseinzadeh, "Caucasian 'Robin Hoods' Threaten the Security of Azerbaijan."

114. "Cambodia and Islamism: Courting the Cham," *The Economist*, September 30, 2010.

115. Ed Cropley, "Cambodia's Cham Muslims Latest Target in War on Terror," Reuters, June 29, 2003.

116. Agnes De Feo, "Le royaume bouddhique face au renouveau islamique," *Cahiers de l'Orient* 78, 2e trimestre (2005): 99–100.

117. Cropley, "Cambodia's Cham Muslims Latest Target in War on Terror."

118. Geoffrey Cain, "Cambodia's Muslims as Geopolitical Pawns," *Asia Times Online*, October 9, 2008.

119. Tom Fawthrop, "General Hok Lundy, Cambodia's Notorious and Brutal Police Chief, He Was Widely Feared," *The Guardian* (Manchester), November 12, 2008.

120. Cain, "Cambodia's Muslims as Geopolitical Pawns."

121. Elisabeth Bumiller, "In Cambodia, Panetta Reaffirms Ties with Authoritarian Government," *New York Times*, November 16, 2012.

122. "Emergency in Myanmar State Following Riots," Al Jazeera, June 11, 2012 (www.aljazeera.com/news/asia-pacific/2012/06/2012610144345611570.html).

123. "Report: Al-Qaida Active in Latin America's Triple Frontier," United Press International, April 4, 2011 (www.upi.com/Business_News/Security-Industry/2011/04/04/).

124. Colin Peacock, "Does New Zealand Face a Terror Threat?" *BBC News*, November 1, 2007 (http://news.bbc.co.uk/2/hi/world/asia-pacific/7062341.stm).

125. Christian Tyler, *Wild West China: The Taming of Xinjiang* (Rutgers University Press, 2004), p. 177.

126. People's Republic of China, "Terrorists Activities Perpetrated by "Eastern Turkistan" Organizations and Their Links with Osama Bin Laden and the Taliban," November 29, 2001 (www.fmprc.gov.cn/ce/ceee/eng/ztlm/fdkbzy/t112733.htm).

127. Richard McGregor, "Beijing Paper Links Xinjiang Separatists to bin Laden," *Financial Times*, January 22, 2002.

128. J. Todd Reed and Diana Raschke, *The ETIM: China's Islamic Militants and the Global Terrorist Threat* (Santa Barbara, Calif.: Praeger, 2010), p. 126.

129. Andrew McGregor, "Will Xinjiang's Turkistani Islamic Party Survive the Drone Missile Death of Its Leader?" *Terrorism Monitor* 8 (March 11, 2010).

130. Ritt Goldstein, "Freed from Guantanamo, a Uighur Clings to Asylum Dreams in Sweden," *Christian Science Monitor*, April 24, 2009.

131. Shaun Tandon, "US lawmakers Seek Review of Uighur 'Terror' Label," Agence France-Presse, June 16, 2009.

132. "Musharraf Backs China over Crackdown," CNN, December 22, 2001 (http://articles.cnn.com/2001-12-21/world/china.pakistan).

133. Kulbhushan Warikoo, "Ethnic-Religious Separatism in Xinjiang: Challenge to China's Security," in *Religion and Security in South and Central Asia,* edited by Kilbhushan Warikoo (New York: Routledge, 2011), p. 177.

134. McGregor, "Will Xinjiang's Turkistani Islamic Party Survive the Drone Missile Death of Its Leader?"

135. "People's Republic of China, China's Anti-Terrorism Legislation and Repression in the Xinjiang Uighur Autonomous Region," Amnesty International, March 2002.

136. Ibid.

137. Wu Chaofan, "Urumqi Riots Part of Plan to Help Al-Qaida," *China Daily*, July 16, 2009.

138. Justin McCurry, "10,000 Uighurs Disappeared during Unrest in China, Exiled Leader Claims," *The Guardian* (Manchester), July 29, 2009.

139. Kathrin Hille, "Xinjiang Widens Crackdown on Uighurs," *Financial Times*, July 19, 2009.

140. "China Expects Further Xinjiang Separatist Attacks," Associated Press, March 7, 2010.

141. Christopher Bodeen, "Beijing Report Says Chinese Muslims Are in Syria," Associated Press, October 29, 2012.

142. Simon Shuster, "How the War on Terrorism Did Russia a Favor," *TIME World*, September 19, 2011.

143. Kathy Lally, "Albright Confronts Russian Hosts over War in Chechnya," *Baltimore Sun*, February 1, 2000.

144. Caroline Wyatt, "Bush and Putin: Best of Friends," *BBC News*, June 16, 2001 (http://news.bbc.co.uk/1/hi/1392791.stm).

145. Robert Parsons, "Chechnya: Senior Commander Tells RFE/RL, 'No Alternative to Armed Struggle,'" Radio Free Europe, July 15, 2005 (www.rferl.org/content/article/1059958.html).

146. John B. Dunlop, *The Moscow Bombings of September 1999: Examinations of Russian Terrorist Attacks at the Onset of Vladimir Putin's Rule* (Stuttgart: Ibidem, 2012).

147. Emil Souleimanov, "The Republic of Dagestan: Epicenter of Islamist Insurgency in Russia's North Caucasus—Analysis" (Lisbon: Portuguese Institute of International Relations and Security, December 14, 2011).

148. Lucy Ash, "Dagestan—The Most Dangerous Place in Europe," *BBC News*, November 23, 2011 (www.bbc.co.uk/news/magazine-15824831).

149. Rahul Bedi, "Rumsfeld Says al-Qaeda in Kashmir," *Irish Times*, June 13, 2002.

150. Ved Prakash, *Terrorism in Northern India* (Delhi: Kalpaz, 2008), p. 279.

151. Imran Garda, "India Using Israel-Like Tactics to Suppress Kashmir Movement," *The Nation*, February 24, 2012.

152. Nusrat Ara, "Mass Rape Survivors Still Wait for Justice in Kashmir," Global Press Institute, March 7, 2012.

153. "Inside India's 'Red Corridor,'" Al Jazeera, October 20, 2011 (www.aljazeera.com/programmes/aljazeeracorrespondent/2011/10/2011101974422887318.html).

154. V. Geetha, ed., *Soul Force: Gandhi's Writings on Peace* (Chennai, India: Tara, 2004), p. 221.

155. Ibid., p. 159; Mahatma Gandhi, *India of My Dreams* (Delhi: Rajpal and Sons, 2009), p. 13.

156. Scott Wilson, "In Gaza, Lives Shaped by Drones," *Washington Post*, December 3, 2011.

157. "Precisely Wrong: Gaza Civilians Killed by Israeli Drone-Launched Missiles" (New York: Human Rights Watch), June 30, 2009, p. 3.

158. Israel Defense Forces, "IDF Targets Terrorists Involved in Attempted Terror Attack," December 27, 2011 (www.idf.il/english).

159. U.S. State Department, "Designation of Army of Islam," Press Release (Washington, May 19, 2011).

160. Sara Hussein, @sarahussein Twitter, November 16, 2012 (http://twitter.com/sara-hussein/status/269669324652961792); Sara Hussein, @sarahussein Twitter, November 19, 2012 (https://twitter.com/sarahussein/status/270784633380163584).

161. Ahmed Abu Hamda and Matthew Kalman, "Hunted by Drones, Dodging Rockets and Tank Shells: An Ordinary Family's Nightmare Trapped inside Gaza's Dead Zone," *Daily Mail* (UK), November 18, 2012.

CHAPTER 6

1. *Journal of the United States of America, Being the Second Session of the Second Congress, Begun and Held at the City of Philadelphia, November 5th, 1792, and in the Seventeenth Year of the Sovereignty of the Said United States* (Philadelphia: John Fenno, 1792), pp. 6–7.

2. Brett F. Woods, ed., *Thomas Jefferson: Thoughts on War and Revolution* (New York: Algora, 2009), p. 181.

3. Gordon S. Wood, *The Americanization of Benjamin Franklin* (New York: Penguin, 2004), p. 73.

4. David E. Wilkens, *The Navajo Political Experience* (Lanham, Md.: Rowman and Littlefield, 2003), p. 12.

5. Edmund S. Morgan, ed., *Not Your Usual Founding Father: Selected Readings from Benjamin Franklin* (Yale University Press, 2006), p. 52.

6. Ibid., p. 53.

7. Ibid.

8. Ibid.

9. Sir Evelyn Howell, *Mizh: A Monograph on Government's Relations with the Mahsud Tribe* (Oxford University Press, 1979), p. xii.

10. Bernard Lewis, *What Went Wrong?: The Clash between Islam and Modernity in the Middle East* (Oxford University Press, 2002).

11. C. Naseer Ahmad, "A Healthy Discussion on Islam between a Jewish and a Muslim Scholar," *Pakistan Link*, December 3, 2010.

12. Wajahat Ali and others, *Fear, Inc.: The Roots of the Islamophobia Network in America* (Washington: Center for American Progress, August 2012).

13. Muslim Public Affairs Council (MPAC), "Not Qualified: Exposing America's Top 25 Pseudo-Experts on Islam," September 2012 (mpac.org).

14. Frank J. Gaffney Jr., "GAFFNEY: Vote for Obama to Restrict Free Speech," *Washington Times*, November 5, 2012 (www.washingtontimes.com/news/2012/nov/5/).

15. Robert P. Jones, Daniel Cox, and Thomas Banchoff, *A Generation in Transition: Religion, Values, and Politics among College-Age Millennials* (Washington: Public Religion Research Institute and Georgetown University's Berkley Center for Religion, Peace and World Affairs, 2012).

16. Moni Basu, "Rising Anti-Islamic Sentiment in America Troubles Muslims," *CNN Belief* (blog), September 5, 2012 (http://religion.blogs.cnn.com/2012/09/05/).

17. Haris Tarin, "Michele Bachmann and Muslim Witch Hunts," CNN, July 30, 2012 (http://articles.cnn.com/2012-07-30/opinion/)

18. Council on American-Islamic Relations, "CAIR Asks GOP to Reject Anti-Islam Platform Plank," August 24, 2012 (www.cair.com/ArticleDetails.aspx?mid1=777&&ArticleID=26976&&name=n&&currPage=1).

19. Anti-Defamation League, "David Yerushalmi: A Driving Force behind Anti-Sharia Efforts in the U.S.," January 13, 2012 (www.adl.org/main_Interfaith/david_yerushalmi.htm).

20. MPAC, *Not Qualified*, p. 18.

21. American-Arab Anti-Discrimination Committee, "Urgent: Attacks on Places of Worship Increase: Alarming Rate of Attack Is Reason for Concern," ADC Urgent Release, August 15, 2012 (www.adc.org).

22. Richard Silverstein, "Santorum Calls for 'Long War' to 'Eradicate' Islam," *Tikun Olam*, January 9, 2012 (www.richardsilverstein.com/).

23. David Usborne, "Pentagon Instructor Urged Total War with Islam," *The Independent* (London), May 12, 2012.

24. "Transcript of President Bush's Address," CNN, September 21, 2001 (http://edition.cnn.com/2001/US/09/20/).

25. Thomas L. Friedman, "If It's a Muslim Problem, It Needs a Muslim Solution," *New York Times*, July 8, 2005.

26. Thomas L. Friedman, "The Losers Hang On," *New York Times*, July 25, 2009; Friedman, "If It's a Muslim Problem, It Needs a Muslim Solution."

27. Fareed Zakaria, "Build the Ground Zero Mosque," *Newsweek*, August 6, 2010.

28. Dilip Hiro, *Apocalyptic Realm: Jihadists in South Asia* (Yale University Press, 2012); Assaf Moghadam, *The Globalization of Martyrdom: Al Qaeda, Salafi Jihad, and the Diffusion of Suicide Attacks* (Johns Hopkins University Press, 2008); Omar Ashour, *The De-Radicalization of Jihadists: Transforming Armed Islamist Movements* (London: Routledge, 2009); Charles Allen, *God's Terrorists: The Wahhabi Cult and the Hidden Roots of Modern Jihad* (Cambridge, Mass.: Da Capo, 2006).

29. Jean-Pierre Filiu, *Apocalypse in Islam*, translated by M. B. DeBevoise (University of California Press, 2011).

30. Robert A. Pape, *Dying to Win: The Strategic Logic of Suicide Terrorism* (New York: Random House, 2005), p. 23.

31. Lawrence Wright, *The Looming Tower: Al-Qaeda and the Road to 9/11* (New York: Vintage Books, 2006).

32. Steve Coll, *Ghost Wars: The Secret History of the CIA, Afghanistan, and Bin Laden from the Soviet Invasion to September 10, 2001* (New York: Penguin, 2004).

33. Steve Coll, *The Bin Ladens: An Arabian Family in the American Century* (New York: Penguin, 2008), p. 140.

34. Stephen Schwartz, *The Two Faces of Islam: Saudi Fundamentalism and Its Role in Terrorism* (New York: Anchor Books, 2003), pp. 90–91.

35. Charles M. Sennott, "Before Oath to Jihad, Drifting and Boredom," *Boston Globe*, March 3, 2002.

36. K. Alan Kronstadt and Bruce Vaughn, *Terrorism in South Asia* (Washington: Congressional Research Service, March 8, 2004); Bertil Lintner, "Little-Known Muslim Communities and Concerns in Cambodia, Burma, and Northern Thailand," in Arnaud de Borchgrave, Thomas Sanderson, and David Gordon, eds., *Conflict, Community, and Criminality in Southeast Asia and Australia: Assessments from the Field* (Washington: Center for Strategic and International Studies, 2009), pp. 59–60; Bertil Lintner, "Bangladesh: Extremist Islamist Consolidation," *Faultlines* 14 (July 2003); Bertil Lintner, "Is Religious Extremism on the Rise in Bangladesh?" *Jane's Intelligence Review*, May 2002.

37. "Arakan Rohingya National Organization Contacts with al Qaeda and with Burmese Insurgent Groups on the Thai Border" (www.cablegatesearch.net/cable.php?id=02RANGOON1310).

38. Lintner, "Bangladesh: Extremist Islamist Consolidation."

39. Bertil Lintner, "Religious Extremism and Nationalism in Bangladesh," paper prepared for Religion and Security in South Asia—An International Workshop, August 19–22, 2002 (Honolulu: Asia Pacific Center for Security Studies, 2002), p. 7.

40. Bertil Lintner, "Bangladesh: A Cocoon of Terror," *Far Eastern Economic Review*, April 4, 2002.

41. Charles Allen, *God's Terrorists: The Wahhabi Cult and the Hidden Roots of Modern Jihad* (Cambridge, Mass.: Da Capo, 2006), pp. 20, 199–200.

42. Helen James, "The Assassination of Lord Mayo: The 'First' Jihad?" *International Journal of Asia-Pacific Studies* 5 (July 2009).

43. Geoff D. Porter, "AQIM's Objectives in North Africa" (West Point, N.Y.: Combating Terrorism Center at West Point, February 1, 2011).

44. Dana Priest and William M. Arkin, "A Hidden World, Growing beyond Control," *Washington Post*, July 19, 2010.

45. Touqir Hussain, personal communication, June 29, 2012.

46. Nathan Lean, *The Islamophobia Industry: How the Right Manufactures Fear of Muslims* (London: Pluto Press, 2012).

47. Phil Stewart, "Leon Panetta Says al Qaeda's Defeat 'Within Reach,'" Reuters, July 9, 2011.

48. "The Fight Against Al Qaeda: Today and Tomorrow," Speech delivered by Secretary of Defense Leon E. Panetta, Center for a New American Security, Washington, D.C., November 20, 2012 (www.defense.gov/Speeches/Speech.aspx?SpeechID=1737).

49. Matthias Gebauer, John Goetz, and Britta Sandberg, "The Forgotten Guantanamo: Prisoner Abuse Continues at Bagram Prison in Afghanistan," *Der Spiegel*, September 21, 2009; see also Naomi Wolf, "How the US Uses Sexual Humiliation as a Political Tool to Control the Masses," *The Guardian* (Manchester), April 5, 2012.

50. Akbar S. Ahmed, *Millennium and Charisma among Pathans: A Critical Essay in Social Anthropology* (London: Routledge, 1976).

51. David Sneath, *The Headless State: Aristocratic Orders, Kinship Society, and Misrepresentations of Nomadic Inner Asia* (Columbia University Press, 2007).

52. Tim Mak, "Stanley McChrystal: Understanding of Afghanistan 'Frighteningly Simplistic,'" *Politico*, October 7, 2011.

53. Michael E. Silverman, *Awakening Victory: How Iraqi Tribes and American Troops Reclaimed al Anbar Province and Defeated al Qaeda in Iraq* (Havertown, Pa.: Casemate Publishers, 2011).

54. Karen Parrish, "Special Operations Focuses on World's 'Unlit Spaces,'" American Forces Press Service, February 10, 2011.

55. "Powell: US Army Almost Broken," *The Guardian* (Manchester), December 18, 2006.

56. Ned Simons, "Lord Gilbert Suggests Dropping a Neutron Bomb on Pakistan-Afghanistan Border," *Huffington Post*, November 26, 2012 (www.huffingtonpost.co.uk/2012/11/26/lord-gilbert-neutron-bomb-n_2190607.html).

57. Michael Morfit, "Staying on the Road to Helsinki: Why the Aceh Agreement Was Possible in August 2005," paper prepared for the International Conference on Building Permanent Peace in Aceh: One Year after the Helsinki Accord, Jakarta, Indonesia, August 14, 2006.

58. John Phillips, *Macedonia: Warlords and Rebels in the Balkans* (Yale University Press, 2004), p. 129.

59. Report from Commissioner Sibi Division to Chief Secretary, Government of Baluchistan, June 26, 1986, Secret/Immediate/ No. 110-13-PA/SB.

60. D.O. letter from Alhaj Jam Mir Ghulam Qadir Khan, Chief Minister, Baluchistan, June 28, 1986, No. PS/CM/1986.

61. Circassian elders, interviewed by the author and his team in Washington, D.C., March 2012.

62. Hugh Macleod, "Little-Known Arab Group in Iran Faces Persecution/Ahwazis Call Occupation of Their Land a Plight Worse Than That of Palestinians," *San Francisco Chronicle*, November 5, 2006.

63. Ibid.

64. "Iran—New Government Fails to Address Dire Human Rights Situation," Amnesty International, February 16, 2006, p. 5.

65. "Iranian City Ranked World's Most Polluted," *Financial Times*, September 26, 2011.

66. Hugh Macleod, "Little-Known Arab Group in Iran Faces Persecution."

67. Najah Mohamed Ali, "Iran's Ethnic Minorities Tell Their Plight at United Nations," *Al Arabiya*, November 29, 2012 (http://english.alarabiya.net/articles/2012/11/29/252526.html).

68. Anthony Smith, *Machine Gun: The Story of the Men and the Weapon That Changed the Face of War* (New York: St. Martin's Press, 2002), p. 133.

69. Roger Runningen and Julianna Goldman, "Obama Wants Puerto Rico to Decide Statehood or Independence," Bloomberg, June 14, 2011 (www.bloomberg.com/news/2011-06-14/).

70. John F. Burns, "Basque Separatists Halt Campaign of Violence," *New York Times*, October 20, 2011.

71. His Imperial Highness Ermias Sahle Selassie, interview by the author, American University, Washington, D.C., February 2012.

72. Mukulika Banerjee, *The Pathan Unarmed: Opposition and Memory in the North West Frontier* (Suffolk: James Currey, 2000), pp. 149–50.

73. Ghulam Qadir Khan, "Cheegha" (unpublished manuscript available with author in Peshawar, 2011); Khan Idris, *Jirgas: The Pashtun Way of Conflict Resolution* (Richardson, Texas: Tribal Analysis, 2010); Alam Jan Mahsud, personal communications, 2011, 2012.

74. Sarah Bloomfield, executive director, and Arthur Berger, senior adviser for external affairs, the U.S. Holocaust Memorial Museum, interview by the author at American University, Washington, D.C., June 22, 2012.

75. "Disgust over 'Disturbing' Graffiti in City," *Cambridge News and Crier*, September 27, 2012.

76. "British Soccer Fans Again Face Anti-Semitic Chants," *JTA*, November 26, 2012 (www.jta.org/news/article/2012/11/26/3112826/british-soccer-fans-again-face-anti-semitic-chants).

77. "Spurs Attack: Italians Charged with Attempted Murder," *BBC News*, November 23, 2012 (www.bbc.co.uk/news/world-europe-20462617).

78. Samantha Power, *"A Problem from Hell": America and the Age of Genocide* (New York: Harper Perennial, 2002), p. 40.

79. Ibid., p. 43.

80. Ghulam Qadir Khan, personal communication, April 20, 2012.

81. Wakar Uddin, personal communication, March 2012.

Appendix

1. Akbar Ahmed, *Suspended Somewhere Between* (Washington: Busboys and Poets Press and PM Press, 2011), pp. 27, 29–30.

2. Ibid., pp. 29–30.

Acknowledgments

The following colleagues and friends lent their support and knowledge to this project: Amitav Acharya, Melody Fox Ahmed, Sikander Ahmed, Malik Siraj Akbar, Darrell Akins, Karen Armstrong, Mahmood Ayub, Khalid Aziz, Durriya Badani, Thomas Banchoff, Galit Baram, Zakaria Barsaqua, Jonathan Benthall, Arthur Berger, Sarah Bloomfield, Muin Boase, Roger Boase, Nazir Butt, Steven Caton, Meghnad Desai, Lesley Dixon, Rosa Rai Djalal, Abdullah Dogar, Robert Faherty, Akhtar Faruqui, Peter Friedrich, Natalie Fullenkamp, Jennifer Gibson, Ufuk Gokcen, James Goldgeier, Louis Goodman, Stephen Grand, Dennis Guertin, Amineh Ahmed Hoti, Touqir Hussain, Khan Idris, Martin Indyk, Ekmeleddin Ishanoglu, Jianping Jia, Neldy Jolo, Jeremy Keenan, Christopher Kelaher, Edward Kessler, Faiysal Ali Khan, Ghulam Qadir Khan, Naz Khan, David Kilcullen, Christopher Kolenda, Manjula Kumar, Tim Lenderking, Ioan M. Lewis, Julius Lipner, Clarence Lusane, Vicky Macintyre, Beverly Mack, Alam Jan Mahsud, Arif Mansuri, Shabbir Mansuri, Joseph Martin, Melissa McConnell, Shadi Mohktari, Mahdi Murad, Anthony Nathe, Jane O'Brien, Josef Olmert, Thomas Parsons, Randolph Persaud, Jafer Qureshi, Safi Qureshy, Umar Riaz, Lawrence Rosen, Polly Rossdale, Said Samatar, Ermias Sahle Haile Selassie, Jack Shenker, James Shera, Kekenus Sidik, Helen Skaer, James Smrikarov, Jon Snow, Marilyn Strathern, Steve Tankel, Andrew Tucker, Wakar Uddin, Benedict Ugoeze, Agri Verrija, John Voll, Janet Walker, Ian White, Lawrence Wilkerson, Rowan Williams, Dana Wojokh, Susan Woollen, Iyad Youghar, Moeed Yusuf, Sepehr Zanganeh, and Quansheng Zhao. In particular, my warm thanks to Professor Lawrence Rosen for his comments on and encouragement for the chapters of the book as they developed, and Dean James Goldgeier who, despite his many responsibilities as the new dean of the School of International Service at American University, consistently supported this project; their support and friendship meant more to me than they can imagine. I am grateful to the University of Cambridge Centre for Gender Studies in the idyllic town of Cambridge for inviting me as the Diane Middlebrook and Carl Djerassi Visiting Professor for the

Michaelmas term in 2012 and to Jesus College for appointing me a visiting fellow in the college. The unfailing courtesy and support I received from the Centre and Jesus College allowed me to finalize the book. I would also like to express my gratitude to the Center for Dialogue, Peace, and Action in Washington, D.C.

I am especially grateful to the team that worked on this project: Nafees Ahmed, Harrison Akins, Elise Alexander, Aja Anderson, Zoya Awan, Alex Christian, deRaismes Combes, James Davis, Pegi Dunsmore, Jonathan Hayden, Dylan Kaplan, Emily Manna, Frankie Martin, Laura Martin, Elayna Salak, Isa bin Salman, and Priyanka Srinivasa. Their enthusiasm was contagious. Dylan wrote to me from Calcutta to introduce himself and became a member of my team even before he joined American University, writing articles on the suffering of Muslim groups as a minority in the light of his own Jewish family's tragic experiences during the Holocaust. Similarly, Priyanka was a passionate advocate for the communities on the periphery of her native India and even resisted her family's plans to take her home for the summer in order to be able to work in our office. Nafees Ahmed was supportive of the project from its inception and stayed up several nights reading the entire manuscript diligently in order to make useful suggestions for its improvement. I am grateful to each and every one of them. I could not have written this book without their passion and commitment.

I do want to single out three members of the team for special thanks—Aja Anderson, Frankie Martin, and Harrison Akins. Aja worked on every aspect of the project with boundless enthusiasm. My debt to my senior research assistants, Frankie and Harrison, is immeasurable. Their notes, research material, capacity to make connections between our case studies, and participation in the discussions, all within the conceptual frame I had laid out and under my guidance, contributed significantly to the study. Their intellectual curiosity, support of the project, and good fellowship were unfailing. Not even the storm that battered Washington, D.C., in the summer of 2012 could slow them down; they worked right through it. When I came to Cambridge for the autumn term as visiting professor in late 2012, Harrison's arrival was not unlike the proverbial landing of the Marines, and he was of immense value to the project in its last, most critical, phase and the running of my office; his dealings with British lords, knights, masters, and fellows and assorted members of the Muslim community through common sense and natural courtesy would have made his folk back in the Great Smoky Mountains of East Tennessee proud.

Zeenat, my wife, has, as always, been fully involved in supporting this project with her typing, suggestions, and ideas. She provided magnificent logistic support in the completion of this project when we were in Cambridge. Our grandson, Alexander Akbar Ahmed, arrived shortly before this book was completed. He came freshly "trailing clouds of glory," and his presence at home was a sheer joy. Heir to so many rich cultural traditions, he faces an exciting future of extraordinary opportunities and challenges. It is our hope that in the spirit in which this book is written, Alexander uses his legacy to bring different peoples closer to each other and to work toward creating a more just, compassionate, and peaceful world. He has our prayers to accompany him on his journey. I would like to dedicate this book to him with love.

Akbar Ahmed
Washington, D.C.

Index

Personal names starting with al-, ag, ar, ash, el-, and ibn are alphabetized by the following part of the name.